Fundamentals of
Organizational Behaviour

SECOND
CANADIAN
EDITION

STEPHEN P. ROBBINS • NANCY LANGTON

San Diego State University   University of British Columbia

PEARSON

Prentice
Hall

Toronto

National Library of Canada Cataloguing in Publication

Robbins, Stephen P., 1943–
        Fundamentals of organizational behaviour / Stephen P. Robbins, Nancy
Langton.—2nd Canadian ed.

Includes index.
ISBN 0-13-122816-1

1. Organizational behavior—Textbooks.   I. Langton, Nancy. II. Title.

HD58.7.R613 2005   658.3   C2003-905782-8

0-13-122816-1

Vice President, Editorial Director: Michael J. Young
Acquisitions Editor: James Bosma
Marketing Director: Bill Todd
Developmental Editor: Su Mei Ku
Production Editor: Richard di Santo
Copy Editor: Cheryl Cohen
Proofreader: Sharon Kirsch
Production Coordinator: Deborah Starks
Page Layout: Hermia Chung
Permissions Manager: Susan Wallace-Cox
Permissions and Photo Research: Lisa Brant
Art Director: Mary Opper
Interior and Cover Design: Alex Li
Cover Image: © Sergio Baradat/The Stock Illustration Source

1 2 3 4 5   08 07 06 05 04

Printed and bound in the United States.

BRIEF CONTENTS

CONTENTS

PART 3
THE UNEASY SIDES OF INTERACTION 172

CHAPTER 6 Communication, Conflict, and
Negotiation 172

PART 4
SHARING THE ORGANIZATIONAL VISION 248

CHAPTER 8 Leadership 248

CHAPTER 9 Decision Making, Creativity, and Ethics . . 284

PREFACE

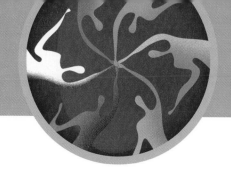

Welcome to the second edition of *Fundamentals of Organizational Behaviour*. This book has been developed specifically for the Canadian market, as there is no American equivalent. Thus, this is truly a made-in-Canada product.

Fundamentals of Organizational Behaviour, Second Canadian Edition, draws upon the many strengths of the third Canadian edition of *Organizational Behaviour: Concepts, Controversies, Applications* while also expressing its own vision and voice. Though it covers a reduced number of theories and concepts, it retains a strong mix of examples and applications, continuing to challenge students and instructors alike to consider all the ways in which understanding organizational behaviour is an important part of everyday life. It provides the context for understanding OB in the Canadian workplace and presents the many Canadian contributions to the field.

General Content and Approach

- *Writing style.* Clarity and readability are hallmarks of this text. The style is described by reviewers as "conversational," "interesting," "student-friendly," and "very clear and understandable." We have given even greater attention to considering the needs of ESL students in this edition.

- *Examples, examples, examples.* From our teaching experience, we know that students may not remember a concept, but they will remember an example. Moreover, a good example goes a long way in helping students to better understand a concept. You will find this book to be packed full of recent real-world examples drawn from a variety of organizations: business and not-for-profit, large and small, and local and international. We have also used photos as additional opportunities to provide examples by expanding the captions in order to give additional information.

- *Comprehensive and leading edge literature coverage.* This book follows in the path of *Organizational Behaviour*, Third Canadian Edition, in its comprehensive and up-to-date coverage of OB from both academic journals and business periodicals. It also includes the popular feature *OB on the Edge*, where we consider what's new and hot in organizational behaviour. *OB on the Edge* is unique to our Canadian editions, and unique to any organizational behaviour textbook on the market. The feature provides an opportunity to explore challenging issues and encourages students to read more about these hot topics. We cover two such topics in this edition: *Stress at Work* and *The Toxic Workplace*.

- *Technology.* A Companion Website dedicated to the book is provided at **www.pearsoned.ca/robbins**. The site includes an interactive study guide, links to the websites of many of the organizations mentioned in the text, search tools, and a special section for instructors that includes a syllabus builder and other tools for effective teaching.

- *Skill-building emphasis.* Each chapter's *OB at Work* section is full of exercises to help students make the connections between theories and real-world applications. Exercises at the end of each chapter reinforce critical thinking, behavioural analysis, and team building.

- *Relevance.* The text reminds both instructors and students alike that we have entered the 21st century and must contend with a new paradigm of work that may be considerably different from the past. The new paradigm is more globally focused and competitive, relies more heavily on part-time and contract jobs, and places a higher premium on entrepreneurial acumen, either within the traditional workplace structure, as an individual seeking out an alternative job, or as the creator of your own new business.

When the first Canadian edition of our textbook *Organizational Behaviour: Concepts, Controversies, Applications* appeared, it was the first text ever to emphasize that *OB is for everyone*, from the bottom-rung employee to the CEO, as well as anyone who has to interact with others to accomplish a task. We continue to emphasize this theme in *Fundamentals of Organizational Behaviour*. We remind readers of the material's relevance beyond a "9-to-5" job through each chapter's new feature *OB for You* which outlines how OB can be used by individuals in their daily lives. We continue the emphasis on *OB is for everyone* in the *From Concepts to Skills* ensemble at the end of each chapter.

HIGHLIGHTS OF THE SECOND CANADIAN EDITION

The goal of the second edition has been to create a textbook that is even more user-friendly and relevant than ever. The updated design, which helps to emphasize Canadian content and research, brings OB to life for students and instructors alike. The second edition includes new opening vignettes for every chapter, and new cases and exercises throughout.

The consideration of ethics is strongly woven throughout the text, rather than confined to just one chapter. To enhance discussion of ethical issues, we have introduced a new feature, *Focus on Ethics*, and we include an *Ethical Dilemma* exercise in every chapter. There is also a much stronger emphasis in this edition on diversity as a topic important to our knowledge and understanding of organizational behaviour.

Because OB is meant to be considered through a variety of lenses, through subtle design techniques, we encourage students to think about OB from the following perspectives:

OB in the Street: These examples identify applications beyond the workplace so that students can see how to use OB right now.

OB in the Workplace: These examples show the application of material to workplace issues.

Focus on Ethics: This new feature provides students more exposure to ethical considerations in the context of current business practices.

Focus on Diversity: This feature emphasizes how, in a multicultural environment such as ours, OB helps us know each other and get along better.

CHAPTER-BY-CHAPTER HIGHLIGHTS: WHAT'S NEW

The major emphasis for revisions to this edition has been to present an up-to-date research base and a broad array of examples. These changes make this text the strongest application of OB material on the market. Each chapter brings new examples, new research, and improved discussions of current issues. The key *changes* are listed below.

Chapter 1: What Is Organizational Behaviour? This chapter has been considerably revised and reorganized. Presenting an overview of the Canadian workplace as we move into the 21st century, this chapter considers the challenges of the workplace at the individual, group, and organizational levels. These include behaving ethically, being empowered, workforce diversity, productivity, and global competition. The chapter also introduces a more thorough discussion of OB as a field, and outlines why everyone, and not just managers, needs to know about it.

Chapter 2: Perception, Personality, and Emotions. This chapter contains more examples to show why understanding perception matters, and features a discussion that shows how personality affects perception. There is more depth to the discussion on perceptual errors. We have included additional examples to indicate how stereotyping negatively affects the workplace. We have also expanded the discussion of the important topic of emotional labour.

Chapter 3: Values, Attitudes, and Their Effects in the Workplace. This chapter continues to emphasize why we need a better understanding of the values of the many people we meet. In revising it, we have discussed the link between ethics and values. We have added a discussion of Milton Rokeach's terminal and instrumental values, as well as a discussion of The Global Leadership and Organizational Behavior Effectiveness (GLOBE) research program, which is the most recent work on cultural differences. We also present additional information about the multicultural mix in Canada, and have expanded our coverage of francophone and anglophone similarities and differences, and of what we can learn from Aboriginal values. We also consider the impact of the September 11 attacks on American values, and the impact this has on Canadian relations. There is a new discussion of Canada's Net Generation, who will be the next to enter the workplace. More attention is given to what attitudes are and how they are formed. There is also increased coverage of organizational commitment, looking at the types of commitment one can have, as well as how organizational commitment can be increased. The chapter includes an expanded discussion of organizational citizenship behaviour and examines its relationship to job satisfaction.

Chapter 4: Motivating Self and Others. This chapter has been significantly reorganized, and gives a more simple and coherent view of motivation theories than one finds in other textbooks. Clearer summary exhibits help to visually present differences among various motivation theories. Applied rewards are discussed after motivation theories are presented, showing their relationship to the theory. The chapter gives special consideration of the challenges of motivating unionized employees and public sector employees. End-of-chapter cases emphasize these topics further. We also look at motivating university and college athletes, and consider the role of incentives in the Enron scandal.

Chapter 5: Working in Teams. This chapter has been significantly rewritten. It starts with the characteristics of effective and ineffective teams. We also present a new, more focused discussion of how to create effective teams. We introduce the roles and responsibilities of team leaders, based on the work of Harvard professor Richard Hackman. We explore the dynamics of the virtual team—what it looks like and how it works—in greater depth. Given the multicultural nature of Canada, we have introduced more material on the effects of diversity on teams and indicate how to make diversity an advantage for teams.

Chapter 6: Communication, Conflict, and Negotiation. This chapter includes a new discussion of *proxemics*, and a longer discussion of nonverbal communication. We explore cultural differences in communication in greater depth by examining the impact of high- and low-context cultures. In response to the growing emphasis on email, the chapter looks at how to use this medium more effectively. We have also added a discussion of the difference between positions and interests in bargaining.

Chapter 7: Power and Politics. This chapter brings power and politics to life by considering how they apply to the Olympic ice skating controversy, and to the Enron scandal. The chapter offers an updated discussion of empowerment, and considers whether empowerment can be harmful to some people. It also looks at how empowerment is viewed in countries around the globe. We have also included a new discussion of types of political activities, as well as a discussion on making office politics work.

Chapter 8: Leadership. This chapter continues to explore leadership with a fresh eye. We have added a discussion of emotional intelligence as one of the traits of leaders, and rewritten the discussion of the path-goal model of leadership to make it clearer, and more applied. This chapter provides increased attention to charismatic leadership, considers the task of team leadership, and explores the moral foundation of leadership in much greater detail. We have also added a discussion on the differences in how male and female leaders are evaluated.

Chapter 9: Decision Making, Creativity, and Ethics. This chapter opens with a detailed discussion of the challenges in decision making. It gives fuller attention to bounded rationality and satisficing, and examines the role of intuition in decision making in greater detail. The chapter gives stronger emphasis on creativity and ethics. The new discussion of ethics also looks more specifically at ethical decision making. Finally, we define social responsibility and examine what it means to be a socially responsible organization.

Chapter 10: Organizational Culture and Change. This chapter has been considerably revised to offer a more clean and clear vision of what culture does and how it is transmitted. The chapter includes a new definition of culture as well as a discussion of the levels of culture. Strong cultures, such as those of Creo and WestJet, are included in the discussion. There is also a more detailed discussion of what happens to cultures when two organizations merge. The chapter looks at change, and gives more attention to why people are often so resistant to change.

PEDAGOGICAL FEATURES

The pedagogical features of *Fundamentals of Organizational Behaviour,* Second Canadian Edition, are designed to complement and reinforce the textual material. This book offers the most complete assortment of pedagogy available in any OB book on the market.

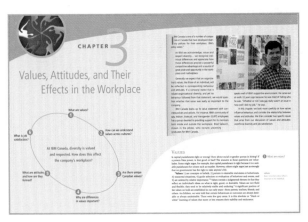

- The text is developed in a "story-line" format that emphasizes how the topics fit together. Each chapter opens with a concept map of key questions related to a main example that threads through the chapter. The opening vignette is shorter, and it is carried throughout the chapter to help students apply a story to the concepts they are learning. The questions from the concept map appear in the margin of the text, to indicate where they are addressed. The chapter ends with each of the opening questions repeated and answered, to summarize the contents of the chapter.

- Keyed examples, **OB in the Street, OB in the Workplace, Focus on Ethics,** and **Focus on Diversity** help students see the links between theoretical material and applications.

- Provided in the margins, **Weblinks** give students access to internet resources for companies and organizations discussed in the text, broadening their grasp of real-world issues. The Destinations button of the book's Companion Website provides hyperlinks and regular updating of the URLs for all weblinks (see **www.pearsoned.ca/robbins**).

- Each chapter concludes with **OB at Work**, a set of resources designed to help students apply the lessons of the chapter. Included in *OB at Work* are the following continuing and new features:

- **For Review** and **For Critical Thinking** provide thought provoking questions to review the chapter and consider ways to apply the material presented.

- **OB for You** outlines how OB can be used by individuals in their daily lives.

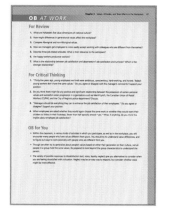

- **Point/CounterPoint** features promote debate on contentious OB issues. All have been shortened to present more focused arguments.

- **Learning About Yourself Exercises**, **Breakout Group Exercise** (NEW), **Working with Others**, and **Ethical Dilemma Exercises** are all now featured in every chapter. We have found great value in using application exercises in the classroom. The many new exercises included here are ones that we have found particularly stimulating in our own classrooms. Our students say that they both like these exercises *and* learn from them.

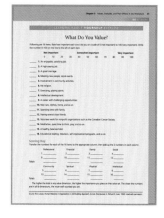
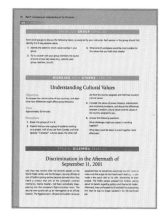

- **Case Incident** features deal with real-world scenarios and require students to exercise their decision-making skills. Each case will enable an instructor to quickly generate class discussion on a key theme within each chapter.

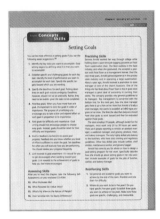

- **CBC Video Case Incident** presents a *CBC Venture* case tied to the material in each chapter. The segments were carefully selected by Victoria Digby of Fanshawe College, who also wrote the cases that appear in this text. The video cases provide instructors with audiovisual material to engage students' attention.

- **From Concepts to Skills** has been totally redesigned to provide a wider range of applications for the *Fundamentals* user. The section begins with a practical set of tips on topics such as "Reading Emotions," "Setting Goals," and "Solving Problems Creatively," which demonstrate real-world applications of OB theories. This is followed by the features **Assessing Skills** (NEW), **Practising Skills** (NEW), and **Reinforcing Skills** (NEW). *Assessing Skills* encourages students to assess their personalities, leadership skills, conflict-handling intentions, and a variety of other traits and skills on the CD-ROM that accompanies this book. Students can therefore link their personal behaviours and traits to material covered in the chapter. *Practising Skills* presents an additional case or group activity to apply the chapter's learning objectives. *Reinforcing Skills* asks students to talk about the material they have learned with others, or to apply it to their own personal experiences.

SUPPLEMENTS

We have created an outstanding supplements package for *Fundamentals of Organizational Behaviour*, Second Canadian Edition. The following materials are available:

Instructor's Resource Manual with CBC Video Guide (0-13-126688-8). Prepared by Nancy Langton, the *Instructor's Resource Manual* includes learning objectives, chapter outlines and synopses, annotated lecture outlines, teaching guides for in-text exercises, a summary and analysis of the *Point/CounterPoint* features, and answers to questions found under *For Review, For Critical Thinking, Case Incidents,* and *CBC Video Case Incidents.* There are additional cases, exercises, and teaching materials as well. This supplement can be downloaded from Pearson Education Canada's protected Instructor Central website, at **www.pearsoned.ca/instructor**.

Electronic Transparencies in PowerPoint (0-13-126687-X). Prepared by Nancy Langton, this package includes over 400 slides of content and exhibits from the text, prepared for electronic presentation in PowerPoint 7.0.

Pearson Education Canada Test Generator (0-13-126686-1). This test-generating and grading software allows instructors to assemble their own customized tests from the questions included in the Test Item File. Prepared by Victoria Digby of Fanshawe College, the Test Item File contains over 1500 items, including multiple choice, true/false, and discussion questions that relate not only to the body of the text but to *From Concepts to Skills, Point/Counterpoint,* and case materials. For each question, we have provided the correct answer, a page reference to the text, a difficulty rating (easy, moderate, or challenging), and a classification (factual or application).

CBC/Pearson Education Canada Video Library (0-13-126690-X). In an exclusive partnership, CBC and Pearson Education Canada have worked together to develop an exciting video package consisting of 10 segments from the prestigious series *Venture*. These were specially chosen by Victoria Digby of Fanshawe College. At an average of seven minutes in length, these segments show students issues of organizational behaviour as they affect real Canadian individuals and companies. Teaching notes are provided in the *Instructor's Resource Manual with CBC Video Guide.*

Companion Website with Online Study Guide (0-13-126685-3). Our exciting new Companion Website includes a comprehensive online study guide that presents students with numerous review exercises and research tools. Practice tests with true/false and multiple choice questions offer instant feedback to students. Destinations (hyperlinks to the text's weblinks) and search tools facilitate further research into key organizations and topics discussed in the text. A special section for instructors contains a syllabus builder and other materials. See **www.pearsoned.ca/robbins** and explore.

ACKNOWLEDGMENTS

My vision for this edition was a fundamentally different way of visually presenting material to students of organizational behaviour. A number of people deserve high praise for their help in realizing my dreams for this second edition. Su Mei Ku, who has been my developmental editor on several projects, again outdid her always excellent performance. Her wit, good humour, helpfulness, support, and organizational skills made revising this textbook immensely easier. Lesley Mann provided a wealth of research for this project, finding just the right articles and examples, and also providing terrific links between current events and organizational behaviour. Both Su Mei and Lesley also served as much valued sounding boards.

I received incredible support for this project from a variety of people at Pearson Education Canada. James Bosma, Acquisitions Editor, was simply terrific in encouraging a fresh look to this book, and did a great job as "project manager." James has taught me how important it is to have an understanding, knowledgeable and supportive AE onside. Andrew Winton, who has now gone on to other things, deserves special thanks for getting the stripped files in order for me, and working out the initial development ideas for this edition. Alex Li translated my thoughts about what this book should look like, creating an exciting design. I particularly appreciate his responsiveness to suggestions for changes. I appreciated working with Richard di Santo for the first time in his role as the Production Editor for this project. He was very responsive, and patiently and calmly handled that process. Stephen Broadbent was the Developmental Editor for the supplements for this project, and was quite helpful in tracking down files and exhibits for me. Deborah Starks, Production Coordinator, provided prompt and efficient help to the team in getting the files we needed. Steve O'Hearn, President of Higher Education, and Michael Young, Vice President and Editorial Director of Higher Education, are extremely supportive on the management side of Pearson Education Canada, and this kind of support makes it much easier for an author to get work done, and meet dreams and goals. Michael's support behind the scenes is particularly appreciated and valued. Lisa Brant was very helpful in doing the photo research, and made some incredible finds in her search for photos. There are a variety of others at Pearson Canada who had a hand in making sure the manuscript was transformed into this book, and that this book could then be delivered into your hands. To all of them I extend my thanks for jobs well done. The Pearson sales team is an exceptional group, and I know they will do everything possible to make this book successful. I continue to appreciate and value their support and interaction.

Cheryl Cohen served as copy editor for this project, and Sharon Kirsch served as the proofreader. Both showed wonderful attention to detail and helped to make the manuscript more simple and clear for the reader, while maintaining a good sense of humour, and patiently answering endless questions about the correct application of the *Chicago Manual of Style*. I enjoyed the opportunity to work with both of them again. Their keen eyes help to make the pages as clean as they are.

Victoria Digby of Fanshawe College selected and prepared all of the *CBC Video Case Incidents* for this edition. I am grateful for the excellent work that she has done on this task.

Finally, I want to acknowledge a number of people who provided personal support throughout the process of writing this book: the teaching staff of Commerce 292 and 329, our Introduction to Organizational Behaviour courses. We teach an intro course that we all really enjoy, and it is through the creative efforts of all of us that this is possible. Every summer we sit down and revisit the course, make considerable changes, and then try out our new ideas. The OB course is alive, dynamic, and open to change. This energy and enthusiasm gets fed into this textbook in a variety of ways. I am thrilled to work with such a dynamic group of instructors, who contribute considerably to the liveliness of our course, and provide countless insights into how we can make that course better every year. I have tried to capture that excitement in developing the material for this edition of the textbook. My undergraduate students also contribute greatly to each edition, both with their feedback and with the countless examples and ideas they supply.

More generally, my Organizational Behaviour and Human Resources Division colleagues at UBC brought various things to my attention, from newspaper articles to research reports, and engaged in various discussions with me about appropriate presentation of material and design issues. They also encouraged my writing efforts. I would like to thank them publicly for their support: Brian Bemmels, Peter Frost, Tom Knight, Sally Maitlis, Sandra Robinson, Martin Schulz, Marc-David Seidel, Dan Skarlicki, and Mark Thompson. Our divisional secretary, Irene Khoo, deserves special mention for helping to keep the project on track, doing some of the word processing, managing the courier packages and faxes, and always being attentive to detail. I could not ask for a better, more dedicated, or more cheerful assistant. She really helps keep things together.

Finally, I want to acknowledge the many reviewers of this textbook for their detailed and helpful comments: Gordon Barnard (Durham College), Lewis Callahan (Lethbridge College), Tony Dearness (Memorial University), Barbara Drakeland (Seneca College), Robert Fournier (Red Deer College), Beth Gilbert (University of New Brunswick), Sarah Holding (Malaspina College), David Inkster (Red Deer College), Nwab Iroaga (Seneca College), Nelson Lacroix (Niagara College), Beverly Linnell (SAIT), Helen MacDonald (Nova Scotia Community College), Garth Maguire (Okanagan University College), Jim Muraska (Cambrian College), and Eva Wetzel (University of Saskatchewan).

I dedicate this book to my father, Peter X. Langton. He was a man of many talents, and his understanding of organizational behaviour may have been greater than my own. To my family I give silent acknowledgment for everything else.

Nancy Langton
January 2004

ABOUT THE AUTHORS

STEPHEN P. ROBBINS

Stephen P. Robbins received his PhD from the University of Arizona and has taught at the University of Nebraska at Omaha, Concordia University in Montreal, the Unviersity of Baltimore, Southern Illinois University at Edwardsville, and San Diego State University. Dr. Robbins' research interests have focused on conflict, power, and politics in organizations, as well as the development of effective interpersonal skills. His articles on these and other topics have appeared in journals such as *Business Horizons,* the *California Management Review, Business and Economic Perspectives, International Management, Management Review, Canadian Personnel and Industrial Relations,* and *The Journal of Management Education.*

In recent years, Dr. Robbins has been spending most of his professional time writing textbooks. These include *Essentials of Organizational Behavior,* 7th ed. (Prentice Hall, 2003); *Training in InterPersonal Skills,* 3rd ed., with Phillip Hunsaker (Prentice Hall, 2003); *Management,* 7th ed., with Mary Coulter (Prentice Hall, 2002); *Human Resource Management,* 7th ed., with David DeCenzo (Wiley, 2002); *The Self-Assessment Library* 2.0 (Prentice Hall, 2002); *Fundamentals of Management,* 3rd ed., with David DeCenzo (Prentice Hall, 2001); *Business Today* (Harcourt, 2001); *Managing Today!* 2nd ed., (Prentice Hall, 2000); and *Organization Theory,* 3rd ed. (Prentice Hall, 1990).

In Dr. Robbins' "other life," he participates in masters' track competition. Since turning 50 in 1993, he has set numerous indoor and outdoor age-group world sprint records; won more than a dozen indoor and outdoor US championships at 60, 100, 200, and 400 metres; and captured gold medals at 100 and 200 metres and as the anchor on the US 4 × 100 relay in the Men's 55–59 age group at the 2001 World Championships in Brisbane, Australia.

NANCY LANGTON

Nancy Langton received her PhD from Stanford University. Since completing her graduate studies, Dr. Langton has taught at the University of Oklahoma and the University of British Columbia. Currently a member of the Organizational Behaviour and Human Resources division in the Sauder School of Business, University of British Columbia, and academic director of the Business Families Centre at UBC, she teaches at the undergraduate, MBA and PhD level and conducts executive programs on family business issues, time management, attracting and retaining employees, as well as women and management issues. Dr. Langton has received several major three-year research grants from the Social Sciences and Humanities Research Council of Canada, and her research interests have focused on human resource issues in the workplace, including pay equity, gender equity, and leadership and communication styles. She is currently conducting longitudinal research with entrepreneurs in the Greater Vancouver Region, trying to understand the relationship between their human resource practices and the success of their businesses. Her articles on these and other topics have appeared in such journals as *Administrative Science Quarterly, American Sociological Review, Sociological Quarterly, Journal of Management Education,* and *Gender, Work and Organizations.* She has won Best Paper commendations from both the Academy of Management and the Administrative Sciences Association of Canada, and in 2003 won the Best Women's Entrepreneurship Paper

Award given by the Center for Women's Business Research for work with Jennifer Cliff (University of Alberta) and Howard Aldrich (University of North Carolina). She has also published two textbooks on management.

Dr. Langton routinely wins high marks from her students for teaching. She has been nominated many times for the Commerce Undergraduate Society Awards, and has won several honourable mention plaques. In 1998 she won the University of British Columbia Faculty of Commerce's most prestigious award for teaching innovation, The Talking Stick. The award was given for Dr. Langton's redesign of the undergraduate organizational behaviour course as well as the many activities that were a spin-off of these efforts. In 2001 she was part of the UBC MBA Core design team that won the national Alan Blizzard award, which recognizes innovation in teaching.

In Dr. Langton's "other life," she teaches the artistry of quiltmaking, and one day hopes to win first prize at *Visions*, the juried show for quilts as works of art. When she is not designing quilts, she is either reading novels (often suggested by a favourite correspondent), or studying cookbooks for new ideas. All of her friends would say that she makes from scratch the best pizza in all of Vancouver.

A Great Way to Learn and Instruct Online

The Pearson Education Canada Companion Website is easy to navigate and is organized to correspond to the chapters in this textbook. Whether you are a student in the classroom or a distance learner you will discover helpful resources for in-depth study and research that empower you in your quest for greater knowledge and maximize your potential for success in the course.

Companion Website

[**www.pearsoned.ca/robbins**]

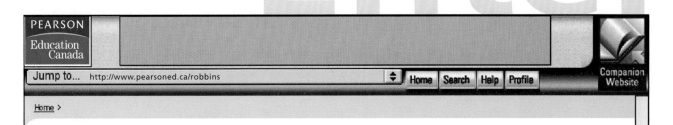

PEARSON
Education
Canada

Jump to...   http://www.pearsoned.ca/robbins   ⬍   Home   Search   Help   Profile

Companion
Website

Home >

Pearson Companion Website

Fundamentals of Organizational Behaviour, Second Canadian Edition, by Stephen P. Robbins and Nancy Langton

Student Resources

The modules in this section provide students with tools for learning course material. These modules include:

- Chapter Overviews
- Study Guide with Online Quizzes
- Web Destinations, and Websearch
- PowerPoint Presentations
- CBC Videos

Coaching comments and references to the textbook may be available to ensure that students take advantage of all available resources to enhance their learning experience.

Instructor Resources

The modules in this section provide instructors with additional teaching tools. Downloadable PowerPoint Presentations, Electronic Transparencies, and an Instructor's Manual are just some of the materials that may be available in this section. Where appropriate, this section will be password protected.

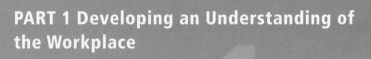

What Is Organizational Behaviour?

What is organizational
behaviour?

1

2 What challenges might we
encounter in today's workplace?

5

What are the
building blocks
to understanding
organizational
behaviour?

A young woman, unable to be a
pilot in the Canadian Forces,
becomes a logistics officer and later
works for RIM. What factors help
her smoothly change jobs?

4

Isn't organizational
behaviour common
sense? Or just like
psychology?

3 How does knowing about
organizational behaviour
make work and life more
understandable?

hen Angela Mondou first applied to the Canadian Forces, she was hoping to become a pilot.[1] Unfortunately, at that time, the military was not accepting women for this position. The recruiters encouraged her to pursue logistics because of her business degree from the University of Ottawa. Mondou ended up serving as a logistics officer with the Canadian peacekeeping force in Croatia. Her responsibilities included moving 1200 Canadian troops and their supplies into place. She finds her military experience invaluable in her present job as director for project implementation, business-integration services at Waterloo, Ontario-based Research in Motion (RIM) Limited, the company that manufactures the BlackBerry email pager.

Angela Mondou's experiences in the Canadian Forces and at RIM illustrate several of the concepts you will find as you study the field of organizational behaviour. She has held several jobs, including logistics officer and director of project implementation, and has gained a variety of technical skills to carry out those jobs. But she has also had to learn various skills that help her survive within organizations—including team-building, leadership, and political skills. Those skills can be used in nonprofit organizations as well. Let's take a look, then, at what organizational behaviour is.

DEFINING ORGANIZATIONAL BEHAVIOUR

Organizational behaviour (often abbreviated as OB) is a field of study that investigates how individuals, groups, and structure affect and are affected by behaviour within organizations. Behaviour refers to what people do in the organization, how they perform, and what their attitudes are. Because the organizations studied are often business organizations, OB is frequently applied to topics such as absenteeism, employment turnover, productivity, human performance, working in groups, and job satisfaction. For instance, studies might consider what factors lead to job satisfaction, and also examine the impact of an individual's job satisfaction on co-workers and the organization as a whole.

Much of organizational behaviour applies beyond the workplace, however. The study of OB can shed light on the interactions among family members, the voluntary group that comes together to do something about reviving the downtown area, the parents who sit on the board of their child's daycare centre, or even the members of a lunchtime pickup basketball team. Researchers in OB study individuals, groups, and the effects of structure on behaviour. The researchers use their findings to make organizations and groups work more effectively.

1 What is organizational behaviour?

organizational behaviour
A field of study that investigates how individuals, groups, and structure affect and are affected by behaviour within organizations.

What is organizational behaviour? It's a field of study that focuses on three levels of behaviour in organizations. One level is the individual, such as the Wal-Mart greeter handing out smiley balloons. Another level is the group, such as the three employees of Praxair, a distributor of bottled industrial gases, who meet to discuss their work. The third level is structure, which is depicted here by employees working in cubicles at Bloomberg, a financial media company.

OB AND TODAY'S CHALLENGES IN THE CANADIAN WORKPLACE

The workplace is changing, and so are the demands that it makes on employees. Many think of the Armed Forces as a command-and-control organization. However, one of the most important lessons Angela Mondou learned in the military was how to create teams of diverse individuals who could work together effectively. Mondou says it was "all about building an excellent team." She found that teamwork is important at Research in Motion too. One of RIM's goals is to appear on the product lists of such companies as AT&T Corp., Rogers AT&T Wireless, and Verizon Communications Inc. This means that Mondou and her RIM colleagues must work effectively with teams from these other companies. Let's consider other changes that are taking place in today's workplace.

2 What challenges might we encounter in today's workplace?

    The workplace that employees and managers face today differs greatly from the workplace of 20 or more years ago. The demand for physical labour is falling. At the same time decision-making skills, the ability to work in teams, and the flexibility to respond to a changing environment have become more important. Organizational behaviour examines individuals, groups, and entire organizations, each of which presents different challenges for today's workplaces. Exhibit 1–1 gives examples of the new challenges.

Exhibit 1-1

Challenges in the Canadian Workplace

Challenges at the Individual Level

Individuals enter the workplace with a variety of expectations and needs that arise out of their personalities and previous experiences. In the early chapters, therefore, we examine such topics as perception, personality, values, attitudes, and motivation.

Due to frequent downsizing in Canada, individuals are becoming more cynical about their employers. Thus, job satisfaction has become an important issue in today's organizations. This is particularly true after the horrific events of September 11, 2001, when individuals started questioning their work and personal values. Employees also face the trend toward an empowered workplace, where they are being asked to take on more responsibility than ever before. Perhaps the greatest challenge that individuals (and organizations) face is how to behave ethically, as the Enron scandal in the United States has shown. We discuss each of these developments in turn.

Job Satisfaction

Employees are increasingly demanding satisfying jobs. In a 2002 survey of 1100 Canadian and American employees, more than half reported negative feelings about their jobs. Many cited "boredom, overwork, concern about their future, and a lack of support and recognition from their bosses as key reasons for their unhappiness."[2] Money was only a problem if individuals perceived unfairness in pay. As Robert Gemmell, president and CEO of Toronto-based Citigroup Global Markets (Canada) Inc., noted: "Managing people has changed even over the past 10 years. Expectations for job satisfaction have grown. The main challenge is to ensure an environment to help meet expectations."[3]

Citigroup Global Markets (Canada) Inc.
www.citibank.com/citigroup/global/

As we discuss in Chapter 3, overall job satisfaction in the Canadian workplace has declined during the past decade. In 1991, 62 percent of employees reported they were highly satisfied with their jobs, compared to just 45 percent in 2001.[4] Individuals cite several factors that could be improved. For instance, 29 percent of employees responded that their jobs were not mentally challenging.[5] Moreover, sometimes job demands can seem downright irrational, as Steve Emery, who worked at a Vancouver Starbucks outlet, found. Emery did not appreciate Starbucks' Star Labor software, which created shift schedules that looked efficient on paper but caused erratic work schedules. For example, Emery objected to a shift that began at 5 a.m. and ended at 9:30 a.m. "You're supposed to come in at that hour for such a tiny shift? It was crazy," says Emery, who successfully brought a union to his workplace.[6]

Job dissatisfaction can lead to absenteeism and a turnover of staff, which cost organizations large amounts of money annually. We discuss this important topic in more detail in Chapter 3. We then consider issues of motivation in Chapter 4. This chapter's *Ethical Dilemma Exercise,* on page 24, looks at the extent to which organizations should be responsible for helping individuals achieve balance in their lives.

Starbucks Coffee Canada
www.starbucks.com

Empowerment

At the same time that managers are being held responsible for employee satisfaction and happiness, they are also being asked to share more of their power. If you read any popular business magazine nowadays, you will find that managers are referred to as "coaches," "advisers," "sponsors," or "facilitators," rather than "bosses."[7]

Employees' responsibilities are increasing too. In many organizations, employees have become "associates" or "teammates,"[8] and the roles of managers and workers have blurred. Decision making is being pushed down to the operating level, where workers are being given the freedom to make choices about schedules, procedures, and solving work-related problems.

empowerment
Giving employees responsibility for what they do.

What is happening is that managers are empowering employees. **Empowerment** means managers are putting employees in charge of what they do. In the process, managers are learning how to give up control, and employees are learning how to take responsibility for their work and make appropriate decisions. The roles for both managers and employees are changing, often without much guidance on how to perform these new roles.

How widespread are these changes in the workplace? While we have no specific Canadian data, a recent survey by the American Management Association of 1040 executives found that 46 percent of their companies were still using a hierarchical structure, but 31 percent defined their companies as empowered.[9] *OB in the Workplace* looks at how WestJet empowers its employees.

American Management Association
www.amanet.org

OB IN THE WORKPLACE

WestJet's Employees Work Together

What do empowered employees do? Calgary-based WestJet Airlines Ltd. employees are given lots of freedom to manage themselves.[10] Clive Beddoe, WestJet's president and CEO, was determined to create a company "where people wanted to manage themselves."

Employees are asked to be responsible for their tasks, rather than relying on supervisors to tell them what to do. That includes Beddoe. "I don't direct things," he says. "We set some standards and expectations, but [I] don't interfere in how our people do their jobs." Instead, employees are given guidelines for behaviour. For instance, flight attendants are directed to serve customers in a caring, positive, and cheerful manner. How do they carry that out? It's up to them. Employees also share tasks. When a plane lands, all employees on the flight, even those who are flying on their own time, are expected to prepare the plane for its next takeoff.

Obviously, WestJet can lower its costs by keeping the number of supervisors down. WestJet operates with about 60 employees per aircraft, while a typical full-service airline such as Air Canada needs more than 140. But allowing employees to manage themselves has a bigger benefit. Beddoe believes it encourages employees to take pride in what they do. "They are the ones making the decisions about what they're doing and how they're doing it," he says. 🧍

Throughout the text you will find reference to empowerment. We discuss it in terms of power in Chapter 7, and we discuss how leaders contribute to empowerment in Chapter 8.

Behaving Ethically

In an organizational world characterized by cutbacks, expectations of increasing worker productivity, and tough competition in the marketplace, it's not altogether surprising that many employees feel pressured to cut corners, break rules, and engage in other forms of questionable practices.

The recent Enron scandal illustrated how casually some people treat the subject of ethics. Enron executives creatively changed how they reported their profits and losses. When challenged, the company's chair, Kenneth Lay, chose to look the other way. The reputation of accounting firm Arthur Andersen was destroyed because it failed to challenge Enron's accounting practices.

Ethics start at the individual level. While the word refers to moral conduct, **ethics** is also the formal name for the study of moral values or principles that guide our behaviour and inform us whether actions are right or wrong. Ethics help us do the right thing.

Individuals as well as organizations can face ethical dilemmas. As we show in Chapter 9, the study of ethics does not come with black and white answers. Many factors need to be considered in determining the ethical thing to do. When individuals strive hard to create their own set of ethical values and when organizations encourage an ethical climate in the face of financial and other pressures, they will be more likely to do the right thing.

Throughout this book you will find references to ethical and unethical behaviour. The *Focus on Ethics* vignettes give thought-provoking illustrations of how various organizations deal with ethics.

Enron Corporation
www.enron.com

ethics
The study of moral values or principles that guide our behaviour and inform us whether actions are right or wrong.

Challenges at the Group Level

Few people work entirely alone, and some organizations make widespread use of teams. Therefore, most individuals interact with others during the workday. This can lead to a need for greater interpersonal skills. The workplace is also made up of people from a variety of backgrounds. Thus, learning how to work with people from different cultures has become more important.

Working With Others

Much of the success in any job involves developing good interpersonal or "people" skills. In fact, the Conference Board of Canada identified the skills that form the foundation for a high quality workforce in today's workplace as communication, thinking, learning, and working with others. Positive attitudes and behaviours and an ability to take responsibility for one's actions are also key skills, according to the Conference Board.[11]

Relic Entertainment Inc.
www.relic.com

Canadian Imperial Bank of Commerce (CIBC)
www.cibc.com

University recruiters consistently identify interpersonal skills as the most important quality an MBA graduate needs for job effectiveness.[12] Alex Garden, founder and CEO of Vancouver-based games development firm Relic Entertainment, was a genius, but what enabled him to run his successful business? The ability to communicate, according to chief operating officer Ron Moravek.[13] And John Hunkin, the chair and CEO of Canadian Imperial Bank of Commerce, has been hailed as a team builder. "He is a good listener, he is a good team builder and provides a consensus environment," says Wayne Fox, a CIBC executive who praises Hunkin's people skills.[14]

Interpersonal skills do not come easily to all people. A study of 191 top executives at six Fortune 500 companies sought to answer the question "Why do managers fail?" The single biggest reason for failure, according to these executives, is poor interpersonal skills.[15]

As these examples indicate, in Canada's increasingly competitive and demanding workplace, neither managers nor employees can succeed on their technical skills alone. They must also have good people skills. This book has been written to help you develop those people skills, whether as an employee, manager, or potential manager.

To learn more about the interpersonal skills needed in today's workplace, read *From Concepts to Skills* on pages 27–29.

Fortune 500
www.fortune.com/fortune/
fortune500

Working in Teams

Working in teams happens frequently in colleges and universities, and is a common experience in most workplaces. A Conference Board of Canada report found that over 80 percent of its 109 respondents used teams in the workplace.[16] This is similar to the United States, where 80 percent of Fortune 500 companies have half or more of their employees on teams. Among small US manufacturers, 68 percent use teams in their production areas.[17]

Effective teams need good leadership, a variety of resources, and a way to figure out how to solve problems. Team members need to build trust, be dedicated, and work well together. The study of organizational behaviour helps us understand not only how we can be more effective team members, but also how organizations can create more effective teams. This is developed in Chapter 5.

Workforce Diversity

The ability to adapt to many different people is one of the most important and broad-based challenges currently facing organizations. The term we use for describing this difference is workforce diversity. While globalization focuses on differences among people from different countries, workforce diversity addresses differences among people within the same country, particularly as seen in corporations.

workforce diversity
The variety of employees in organizations in terms of gender, race, ethnicity, disability, sexual preference, and age, as well as background characteristics such as education, income, and training.

Workforce diversity arises because organizations are becoming more heterogeneous, employing a greater variety of people in terms of their gender, race, and ethnicity. There is also more variety in their demographic characteristics, such as age, education, and socio-economic status. In addition to the more visible groups—women, First Nations peoples, Asian Canadians, African Canadians, Indo-Canadians—today's workplace also includes gays and lesbians, the elderly, and people with disabilities.

One of the challenges in Canadian workplaces is the mix of generations working side by side: the Elders (those over 60), Baby Boomers (born between the mid-1940s and mid-1960s), Generation X-ers (born between the mid-1960s and early 1980s), and the Net Generation (born between 1977 and 1997). Due to their very different life experiences, they bring different values and different expectations to the workplace. We discuss these issues in Chapter 3.

We used to assume that people in organizations who differed from the stereotypical employee would create no challenges for the organization. We now know that employees don't set aside their cultural values and lifestyle preferences when they come to work.

Organizations therefore try to accommodate diverse groups of people by addressing their different lifestyles, family needs, and work styles.[18] Because people differ in what motivates them and what styles of communication are more comfortable, we need to understand how culture shapes individuals, and learn to adapt our interaction style.

The *Focus on Diversity* features found throughout the text help to create awareness of the diversity issues that arise in organizations. Our first example looks at accommodations made to help Aboriginal cadets feel welcome at the RCMP training academy in Regina.

FOCUS ON **DIVERSITY**

Bringing Aboriginal Culture to the RCMP

How does a Heritage Room promote RCMP diversity? The sweet-smelling smoke of burning buffalo sage cleansed the air at opening ceremonies for the Aboriginal Heritage Room in the RCMP's Regina training academy. With cedar walls, Plains Indian artifacts, and reproductions of old photographs of Aboriginal Canadians, this is not a typical room in a police academy.[19]

The Heritage Room was set up in 2000 to help Aboriginal cadets engage in spiritual practices while they train. They can now practise ceremonies, meet with elders, and discuss their culture in the Heritage Room. Dustin Ward, a cadet from the Mi'kmaq reserve in New Brunswick, praised the opening of the room as "one more sign that the RCMP welcomes First Nations Mounties. It shows the children hope that they can come here some day and be an RCMP cadet."

The Heritage Room is the most recent in a series of RCMP programs to encourage diversity. In the late 1980s, the RCMP decided to allow Aboriginal Mounties to wear their hair in braids—if they wanted. Saskatchewan-born Aboriginal Pauline Busch, who helped get the Heritage Room opened, remembered that decision. "There's nothing that warms a child's heart and pride as seeing another Aboriginal person in the red serge, fully outlined with the braids."

Understanding how to work well with others is covered extensively in organizational behaviour. We examine communication in Chapter 6, conflict and negotiation in Chapter 8, and the effects of diversity on teams in Chapter 5.

Challenges at the Organizational Level

Canadian businesses face many challenges in the 21st century. Their ability to be as productive as US businesses is constantly questioned. The need to develop effective employees, and to manage human resource issues such as absenteeism and turnover, is critical. Meanwhile businesses face greater competition because of our global economy. Many companies have expanded their operations overseas, which means they have to learn how to manage people from different cultures. This chapter's *CBC Video Case Incident*, "The Challenges of Managing and Working at Nortel," highlights some of these issues.

Productivity

An organization or group is productive if it achieves its goals and does so by transferring inputs (labour and raw materials) to outputs (finished goods or services) at the lowest cost. **Productivity** implies a concern for both **effectiveness** (achieving goals) and **efficiency** (watching costs). Management expert Peter Drucker suggested that the difference between the two is: Efficiency is doing things right, while effectiveness is doing the right thing.[20]

A hospital, for example, is effective when it successfully meets the needs of its patients. It is efficient when it can do so at a low cost. If a hospital manages to achieve

CBC

"The Challenges of Managing and Working at Nortel"

productivity
A performance measure that includes effectiveness and efficiency.

effectiveness
Achievement of goals.

efficiency
The ratio of effective work output to the input required to produce the work.

Montreal-based Bombardier Inc., which manufactures a number of items including airplanes, rail cars, and snowmobiles, commands the respect of many business leaders—it finished first in a 2001 Ipsos-Reid/Ray & Berndtson poll of 300 Canadian CEOs. The company was ranked number one both for the way it manages people and for its long-term investment value.

higher output from its present staff—say, by reducing the average number of days a patient is confined to a bed, or by increasing the number of staff-patient contacts per day—we say that the hospital has gained productive efficiency. However, if the hospital simply cuts costs by reducing the number of patient days (efficiency), but the patients become sicker after they go home, and die, this is not particularly effective, assuming the goal of the hospital is to return patients to health.

As you study OB, you will begin to understand those factors that influence the effectiveness and efficiency of individuals, of groups, and of the overall organization. You may wonder whether organizations can both maximize profits and treat their employees well. For an answer to this question, take a look at this chapter's *Point/CounterPoint* on page 22.

Developing Effective Employees

One of the major challenges facing organizations in the 21st century is how to manage their human resources effectively. The issues include absenteeism, turnover, and organizational citizenship.

absenteeism
Failure to report to work.

Absenteeism   **Absenteeism** is the failure to report to work. It has been rising in recent years in Canada, with 7.6 percent of full-time employees absent for part of any given week in 2002, up from 5.5 percent in 1997.[21] At the job level, a one-day absence by a clerical worker can cost an employer several hundred dollars in reduced efficiency and increased supervisory workload. It's obviously difficult for an organization to operate smoothly and reach its goals if employees fail to go to work. Because absenteeism affects how organizations perform, OB is concerned with its impact on the organization.

turnover
Voluntary and involuntary permanent withdrawal from the organization.

Turnover   **Turnover** is the voluntary and involuntary permanent withdrawal from an organization. A high turnover rate leads to increased recruiting, selection, and training costs. All organizations, of course, have some turnover. In fact, if the "right" people are leaving the organization—those who are unproductive—turnover can be positive. But turnover often involves the loss of people the organization doesn't want to lose. For instance, one study covering 900 employees who had quit their jobs found that 92 percent earned performance ratings of "satisfactory" or better from their superiors.[22] So when turnover is excessive, or when it involves valuable performers, it can be a disruptive factor that lowers the organization's effectiveness. Because turnover affects how organizations perform, it is an OB concern.

Keeping turnover down and fighting the brain drain is a key concern of Canada's high-tech firms, many of which can't pay salaries comparable to their US competitors. Burnaby, BC-based Electronic Arts Canada Ltd. has an in-house laundry service, billiard tables, a basketball court, and comfortable lounges for its employees. These perks help keep the employees happy and productive. The employees here are playing in the gaming area off the café on the first floor of the company.

Organizational Citizenship We use the term **organizational citizenship behaviour (OCB)** to describe voluntary behaviour that is not part of an employee's formal job requirements, yet promotes the effective functioning of the organization.[23] In general, these acts are spontaneous, not suggested or ordered by someone else, and not something that is routinely expected and rewarded.

Successful organizations need employees who will perform beyond expectations and do more than their usual job duties. In today's dynamic workplace, where tasks are increasingly done in teams and where flexibility is critical, organizations need employees who will engage in "good citizenship" behaviours, such as making positive statements about their work group and the organization, helping others on their team, volunteering for extra job activities, avoiding unnecessary conflicts, showing care for organizational property, respecting the spirit as well as the letter of rules and regulations, and gracefully tolerating the occasional work-related impositions and nuisances.

Organizations want and need employees who will do those things that are not in any job description. The evidence indicates that organizations that have such employees outperform those that don't.[24] As a result, OB is concerned with organizational citizenship behaviour.

organizational citizenship behaviour (OCB)
Voluntary behaviour that is not part of an employee's formal job requirements, yet promotes the effective functioning of the organization.

Competition From the Global Environment

In recent years, Canadian businesses have faced tough competition from the United States, Europe, Japan, and even China, as well as from other companies within our borders. To survive, they have had to cut fat, increase productivity, and improve quality. A number of Canadian companies have found it necessary to merge in order to survive.

Employees, too, have new challenges, including the increased use of new technologies in their workplaces. This affects the number of jobs available and the number of skills required. For instance, production employees at companies such as *The Vancouver Sun*, Binney & Smith, and GM Canada now need to know how to operate computerized production equipment. This skill was not part of their job description 15 years ago.

These developments mean that the actual jobs workers perform, and even the managers to whom they report, are in a permanent state of change. To stay employable under these conditions, workers need to continually update their knowledge and skills so they can perform new job requirements.[25] Today's managers and employees have to learn to live with flexibility, spontaneity, uncertainty, and unpredictability.

One of the challenges facing Canadian businesses is the increasing globalization of the workplace. McDonald's Canada opened the first McDonald's restaurant in Moscow. The message? As multinational corporations develop operations around the world, as companies enter joint ventures with foreign partners, and as a growing number of individuals look for job opportunities across national borders, managers and employees must become capable of working with people from different cultures. Managing people well and understanding the interpersonal dynamics of the workplace are issues that affect all Canadian companies—not just those doing business in Canada.

Managing and Working in a Global Village

Twenty or 30 years ago, national borders protected most firms from foreign competitive pressures. National borders no longer hold competitors back. Trading blocs such as the North American Free Trade Agreement (NAFTA) and the European Union (EU) have greatly reduced tariffs and barriers to trade, and North America and Europe are no longer the only continents with highly skilled labour. The internet also helps companies increase their connections around the globe, through international sales and more opportunities to carry on business. Even small firms can bid on projects in different countries and compete with larger firms through the internet.

North American Free Trade Agreement (NAFTA)
www.nafta-sec-alena.org

The European Union (EU)
europa.eu.int

How Will Knowing OB Make a Difference?

We have already heard about Angela Mondou's need to understand teamwork. Another lesson the military taught her was that leadership skills are not necessarily innate, but can be learned: "The military takes people like me—a 21-year-old party animal—and turns them into officers."[26] Both companies and individuals can learn from this lesson. Companies should provide leadership training and individuals should "find a leadership model that works for them and follow it rigorously."[27] Mondou's time in the military also helped her develop her political skills. These are important skills that serve her well when she works with a diverse group of people. She knows that sharing information and keeping all parties informed through direct communication will decrease conflict among team members. What other aspects of organizational behaviour might be helpful for daily life or organizational life?

3 How does knowing about organizational behaviour make work and life more understandable?

When we talk about the impact of organizational behaviour in each chapter, we consider the impact on both the workplace and the individual (see our features *OB in the Workplace* and *OB in the Street*). So let's begin our discussion of OB's impact by looking broadly at how knowing about OB makes a difference in the workplace, before we look at how OB affects us individually.

For the Workplace

From a management point of view, understanding organizational behaviour can help you manage well. Still, you might wonder if managing well really makes a difference. Black Photo Corporation's president, Rod Smith, learned that not listening to employee demands can have undesirable consequences when he was confronted with a union drive at Black's. He notes the difficulties he has experienced in working with a union. "One of the things that you lose when you get unionized is that ability to be compassionate, because the rules are the rules, and they catch people in ways we prefer not to catch them."[28]

Black Photo Corporation
www.blackphoto.com

Aris Kaplanis, president and CEO of Toronto-based Teranet Inc., on the other hand, understands the importance of managing well. In the land information services industry, where turnover is typically 10 to 20 percent, Teranet's annual turnover rate is less than 1 percent. Kaplanis believes that his turnover is low because Teranet developed a corporate culture that is both humane and family-friendly. "My perspective is that the company has two assets—one is the customers, the other is our employees. Both of these assets have to be serviced."[29]

Teranet Inc.
www.teranet.ca

The evidence indicates that managing people well makes for better corporations overall. Exhibit 1–2 shows that many of the firms that made the KPMG–Ipsos-Reid top 10 list of "Most Respected Corporations for Human Resource Management" also scored high on financial performance, and investment value. Five of the companies placed in the top 10 on both financial measures, and 8 scored in the top 10 of at least one of the financial measures.

Report on Business magazine annually publishes a list of the 50 best companies to work for in Canada. The magazine's 2002 survey identified three main traits of best-loved companies: 1) they present a clear and consistent vision to employees, 2) they develop programs to keep employees focused on company goals, and 3) they listen to their employees and act on their suggestions.[30]

***Report on Business* magazine**
www.robmagazine.com

While the KPMG-Ipsos-Reid results showed that managing well added to the bottom line, the *ROB* study showed more directly the day-to-day return that managers receive from managing well. At *ROB's* best companies to work for, turnover is low and

Exhibit 1–2

Top 10 Most Respected Corporations for Human Resource Management (KPMG-Ipsos-Reid's 2002 Survey)

	Location	Industry	Rank on Financial Performance	Rank on Investment Value
1. RBC Financial Group	Toronto	Financial services	1	1
2. Dofasco Inc.	Hamilton, ON	Steelmaker	10	9
3. Magna International Inc.	Aurora, ON	Automotive	3	5
4. IBM Canada Ltd.	Markham, ON	Computers	n/a	n/a
5. BMO Financial Group	Montreal	Financial services	9	n/a
6. WestJet Airlines Ltd.	Calgary	Air transportation	n/a	n/a
7. BCE Inc.	Montreal	Telecommunications	7	4
8. Scotiabank Group	Toronto	Financial services	4	8
9. Bombardier Inc.	Montreal	Transportation	n/a	2
10. General Electric Canada Inc.	Mississauga, ON	Electronic controls/instruments	n/a	n/a

Source: Adapted from R. Bloom, "RBC Reclaims Top Spot in Survey," *The Globe and Mail*, January 20, 2003, pp. B1, B5.

employees want to stay with their firms, even when they are offered higher-paying jobs by other companies. Employees at the 50 best places to work don't mention money. Instead, they note that the company recognizes their performance in little ways that make the difference.

The message from each of these surveys: Managing people well pays off. It may also lead to greater **organizational commitment**. We use that term to refer to an employee's emotional attachment to the organization, resulting in identification and involvement with the organization.[31] This type of commitment is often called **affective commitment** and represents the attitude of managers and employees who go beyond expected behaviours to provide extra service, extra insight, or whatever else is needed to get the job done. There is some concern that organizational commitment carried to an extreme can have negative consequences, in that employees with strong organizational commitment may engage in unethical behaviour to protect the organization. But this should not be a reason to avoid encouraging commitment. One benefit of employee commitment is that it can help organizations achieve greater change. When Siemens Nixdorf Informationssysteme (SNI), the largest European supplier of information technology, needed to reduce its workforce from 52 000 to 35 000 in 1994, the CEO met with 11 000 employees to explain and ask for help in reducing costs. Employees showed a great deal of commitment to the organization, even in the event of downsizing, often working after hours to redesign the operations. Within a year, SNI was operating profitably, and employee satisfaction had almost doubled.

Finally, managing well may improve organizational citizenship, which we discussed earlier in the chapter.

For You as an Individual

You may be wondering how organizational behaviour will apply to you if you are planning to run your own business or work for a small nonprofit organization, rather than a large organization. Or you may be thinking to yourself, "I'm not planning on being a manager." We raise these questions below to help you see how organizational behaviour applies in a variety of situations.

What if I'm Not Going to Work in a Large Organization?

You may think that when we say "organization" we are referring to large manufacturing firms, to the exclusion of the variety of other forms of organization that exist. And you may even think that you won't be working in a large manufacturing firm, so OB has no relevance for you. But this would be short-sighted. An **organization** is simply a consciously coordinated social unit, composed of two or more people, that functions on a relatively continuous basis to achieve a common goal or set of goals. Thus, manufacturing and service firms are organizations, and so are schools, hospitals, churches, military units, retail stores, police departments, and local, provincial, and federal government agencies.

The examples in this text should help you get an idea of the large range of organizations that exist. Though you might not have considered this before, even the college or university you attend is as much a real organization as is Hudson's Bay Company or Air Canada or *The Globe and Mail*. The theories we cover in this book should be considered in light of the variety of organizations you may encounter. We try to point out instances where the theory may apply less (or especially) to a particular type of organization. For instance, some organizations are bureaucratic, while others are more open and loosely structured. The types of organizational culture that these organizations have, and how their leaders lead, would be quite different. Where we provide no caveat, however, you should expect that the discussions in this book apply across the broad spectrum of organizations.

---

organizational commitment
An employee's emotional attachment to the organization, resulting in identification and involvement with the organization.

affective commitment
The attitude of managers and employees who go beyond expected behaviours to provide extra service, extra insight, or whatever else is needed to get the job done.

Siemens Canada Limited
www.siemens.ca

organization
A consciously coordinated social unit, composed of two or more people, that functions on a relatively continuous basis to achieve a common goal or set of goals.

What if I Don't Want to Be a Manager?

Many of us carry around a simplistic view of work organizations, with the participants divided into set categories: owners, leaders and/or managers, and employees. These distinct roles probably most apply to large, publicly held organizations. Distinct organizational roles become more blurred when we discuss smaller, privately owned firms.

When we talk about leadership in organizations, we typically mean the person or persons responsible for setting the overall vision of the organization, although leadership can come from informal sources as well. While managers and leaders have seen their roles expand as a result of factors such as globalization and e-commerce, employees are also being asked to "move beyond their traditional role as inputs to the process of achieving organizational goals."[32] To some extent, then, the roles of managers and employees are becoming blurred in many organizations. Employees are being asked to share in some of the decision processes of managers, rather than simply follow orders. In particular, the Conference Board of Canada says that in high-performance organizations, "Employees are willing to be accountable for their own and the organization's success."[33] To be accountable means that employees "take charge of their own careers, decide what skills they need to acquire and determine where they wish to employ these skills."[34]

You may be thinking that you are not planning to work in an organization at all because you would prefer to be self-employed. While self-employed individuals often do not act as managers, they certainly interact with other individuals and organizations as part of their work. Thus, the study of organizational behaviour is equally important for the sole proprietor or entrepreneur as for those who work in large organizations. It gives all of us more insight into how to work with others, and how to prepare to become employees in the 21st-century workplace.

Conference Board of Canada
www.conferenceboard.ca

OB: MAKING SENSE OF BEHAVIOUR IN ORGANIZATIONS

We have thus far considered how OB can be applied in the workplace. In this next section we consider the discipline of OB, looking first at the fields of study that have contributed to OB. We then discuss the fact that OB is a scientific discipline, with careful research that is conducted to test and evaluate theories. Finally, we discuss the areas to which OB can be applied, giving you an overview of how this book is organized.

4 Isn't organizational behaviour common sense? Or just like psychology?

The Building Blocks of OB

Organizational behaviour is an applied behavioural science that is built upon contributions from a number of behavioural disciplines. The predominant areas are psychology, sociology, social psychology, anthropology, and political science.[35] As we will learn, psychology's contributions have been mainly at the individual or micro-level of analysis. The other four disciplines have contributed to our understanding of macro concepts, such as group processes and organization. Exhibit 1–3 presents an overview of the major contributions to the study of organizational behaviour.

The Rigour of OB

Whether you want to respond to the challenges of the Canadian workplace, manage well, or guarantee satisfying and rewarding employment for yourself, it pays to understand organizational behaviour. OB provides a systematic approach to the study of behaviour in organizations. Underlying this systematic approach is the belief that behaviour is not random. Thus research studies are conducted and are the basis for all of the claims made in this text. Researchers collect data in a variety of settings, to test hypotheses about the causes and consequences of behaviour. Researchers do not set out to prove

Exhibit 1-3

Toward an OB Discipline

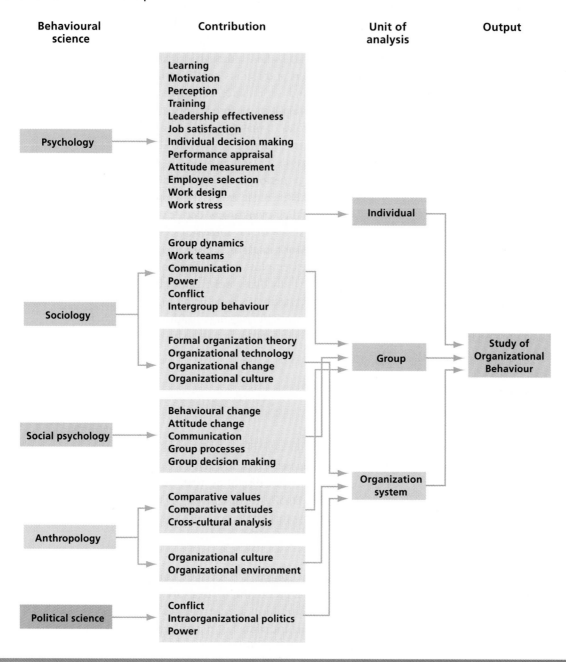

what they believe is true. Rather, they are charged with the responsibility of being objective in their collection and analysis of data.

OB Looks at Consistencies

Certainly there are differences among individuals. Placed in similar situations, people don't all act exactly alike. However, certain fundamental consistencies underlie the behaviour of all individuals. These can be identified and then modified to reflect individual differences.

The fundamental consistencies are very important because they allow predictability. When you get into your car, you make some definite and usually highly accurate predictions about how other people will behave. What may be less obvious is that there are rules (written and unwritten) in almost every setting. Thus, it can be argued that it's possible to predict behaviour (undoubtedly, not always with 100-percent accuracy) in supermarkets, classrooms, doctors' offices, elevators, and in most structured situations. For instance, do you turn around and face the doors when you get into an elevator? Almost everyone does. Is there a sign inside the elevator that tells you to do this? Probably not! Just as we make predictions about drivers, where there are definite rules of the road, we can make predictions about the behaviour of people in elevators, where there are few written rules. This example supports a major foundation of this text: Behaviour is generally predictable, and the *systematic study* of behaviour is a means to making reasonably accurate predictions.

OB Looks Beyond Common Sense

When we use the phrase **systematic study**, we mean looking at relationships, trying to attribute causes and effects, and basing our conclusions on scientific evidence—that is, on data gathered under controlled conditions, and measured and interpreted in a reasonably rigorous manner—rather than relying on common sense. A systematic approach does not necessarily mean that those things you have come to believe in an unsystematic way are incorrect. Some of the conclusions we make in this text, based on reasonably substantive research findings, will support what you always knew was true. You will also be exposed to research evidence that runs opposite to what you might have thought was common sense. In fact, one of the challenges to teaching a subject such as organizational behaviour is to overcome the notion, held by many, "that it's all common sense."[36]

systematic study
The examination of behaviour in order to draw conclusions, based on scientific evidence, about causes and effects in relationships.

If understanding behaviour were simply common sense, we would not observe many of the problems that take place in the workplace, because managers and employees would know how to behave. Unfortunately, as you will see from examples throughout the textbook, many individuals and managers exhibit less than desirable behaviour in the workplace. With a stronger grounding in the systematic analysis of organizational behaviour, you may be able to avoid some of these mistakes.

OB Has Few Absolutes

There are few, if any, simple and universal principles that explain organizational behaviour. In contrast, the physical sciences—chemistry, astronomy, and physics, for example—have laws that are consistent and apply in a wide range of situations. Such laws allow scientists to generalize about the pull of gravity or to confidently send astronauts into space to repair satellites. But, as one noted behavioural researcher concluded, "God gave all the easy problems to the physicists." Human beings are complex. Because we are not alike, our ability to make simple, accurate, and sweeping generalizations is limited. Two people often act differently in the same situation, and an individual's behaviour changes in different situations.

OB Takes a Contingency Approach

Just because people can behave differently at different times does not mean, of course, that we cannot offer reasonably accurate explanations of human behaviour or make valid predictions. It does mean, however, that OB concepts must reflect situational, or **contingency**, conditions. So, for example, OB scholars would avoid stating that effective leaders should always seek the ideas of their employees before making a decision. We may find that in some situations a participative style is clearly superior, but, in other situations, an autocratic decision style is more effective. In other words, the effectiveness of a particular leadership style depends on the situation in which it is used. The OB scholar would therefore try to describe the situations to which each style was suited.

contingency approach
Considers behaviour within the context in which it occurs.

To fit in with the contingency philosophy, *Point/CounterPoint* debates are provided in each chapter. These are included to reinforce the fact that, within the OB field, there is disagreement on many issues. When you see some of the more controversial issues addressed directly in the *Point/CounterPoint* format, you have an opportunity to explore different points of view, discover how diverse perspectives complement and oppose each other, and gain insight into some of the debates currently taking place within the OB field.

LEVELS OF ORGANIZATIONAL BEHAVIOUR

Angela Mondou outlined the personal changes she underwent as she became involved with the Canadian Forces. She mentioned that she had been a party animal, but learned how to become a leader. Clearly, she had to learn about herself, and what motivated her. She also had to learn how to work effectively in groups. When she moved from the Canadian Forces to RIM, she also had to learn how different organizations function. Even though she has been successful in both business and the military, Mondou has been looking for other places to apply her skills. She thinks she would like to work in a humanitarian organization, "making a difference to help people who are in a difficult way." For her, this means another type of organization that she will need to learn about. Mondou strikes us as a very committed employee, but what factors have shaped her commitment? What factors affect other issues such as productivity, absenteeism, turnover, job satisfaction, and organizational citizenship?

5 What are the building blocks to understanding organizational behaviour?

Exhibit 1–4 presents the three levels of analysis we consider in this textbook, and shows that as we move from the individual level to the organization systems level, we add systematically to our understanding of behaviour in organizations. The three basic levels are similar to building blocks: Each level is constructed on the previous level. Group concepts grow out of the foundation laid in the individual section. To arrive at organizational behaviour, we overlay structural constraints on the individual and the group.

Individual-Level Behaviour

People enter groups and organizations with certain characteristics that will influence their behaviour. The more obvious of these are personality characteristics, values, and

Exhibit 1–4

The Layers of OB

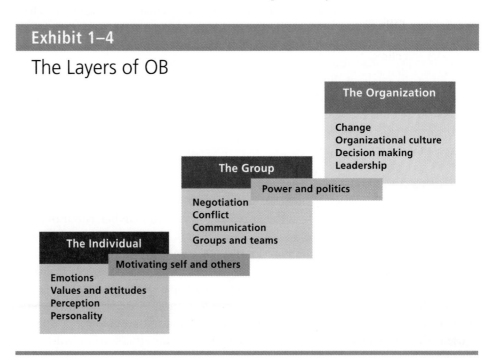

The Organization
Change
Organizational culture
Decision making
Leadership

The Group
Power and politics
Negotiation
Conflict
Communication
Groups and teams

The Individual
Motivating self and others
Emotions
Values and attitudes
Perception
Personality

attitudes. These characteristics are basically intact when an individual joins an organization, and for the most part, there is little that anyone in the organization can do to alter them. Yet they have a very real impact on behaviour. We therefore discuss each of these factors in Chapters 2 and 3.

Two other individual-level factors that have been shown to affect group and organizational behaviour are perception and motivation. Chapter 2 examines the role of perception in our interactions and understandings. Chapter 4 discusses the importance of rewards for motivating employees, and describes specific rewards that can be used in the workplace. You may find the discussion of motivation and rewards particularly interesting in light of the fact that while 67 percent of staffers at ROB's 50 best companies to work for find their pay appropriate for their jobs, only 42 percent say the same at companies not on the list.[37] The *Case Incident* on page 25 asks you to examine the impact of "putting people first" in managing an organization.

Group-Level Behaviour

The behaviour of people in groups is more than the sum total of all the individuals acting in their own way. People behave differently in groups than when they are alone. Therefore, the next step in the development of an understanding of OB is the study of group behaviour.

Chapter 5 lays the foundation for an understanding of the dynamics of group and team behaviour. The chapter discusses how individuals in groups are influenced by the patterns of behaviour they are expected to exhibit. Chapter 5 also helps us to understand how to design effective work teams. You may be interested in this chapter because in a 1997 Angus Reid survey, only 50 percent of employees reported having supportive colleagues.[38] Thus this chapter discusses ways that individuals could learn to work together more effectively and be more supportive of one another.

Ipsos-Reid Group
www.ipsos-reid.com/ca/

An important part of working together is communicating effectively. You may be interested to know that the same Angus Reid survey indicated companies do not communicate enough information to their employees.[39] We discuss the specific topic of communication, and how to do a better job at the individual, group, and organizational levels, in Chapter 6. We also examine conflict and negotiation in that chapter.

Chapter 7 explores some of the more complex issues of interaction, including power and politics. This chapter give you an opportunity to think about how communication processes sometimes become complicated because of office politicking. You will note in Exhibit 1–4 that power and politics create a bridge between the group and organizational levels of the organization. Groups and individuals engage in political behaviour, and this can affect organizational processes at the deepest levels.

Organization Systems-Level Behaviour

Organizational behaviour reaches its highest level of sophistication when we look at how organizational processes affect individual and group behaviour. Chapter 8 examines how we engage in supervision and leadership, including self-leadership. Chapter 9 considers how decisions are made in organizations. That chapter also considers how to increase creativity in organizations. Because decisions have an ethical component, we discuss both ethics and social responsibility in Chapter 9 as well. Finally, in Chapter 10, we examine how organizational culture sets the framework for how an organization carries out its goals. In that chapter we also discuss the cycle of organizational change and renewal, and ways to manage that change. As we have noted already, and as will become clear throughout the text, change is a key issue for organizations in the 21st century.

SUMMARY AND IMPLICATIONS

1 **What is organizational behaviour?** Organizational behaviour (OB) is a field of study that investigates the impact that individuals, groups, and structure have on behaviour within an organization. It uses that knowledge to make organizations work more effectively. Specifically, OB focuses on how to improve productivity, reduce both absenteeism and turnover, and increase employee job satisfaction. OB also helps us understand how people can work together more effectively in the workplace.

2 **What challenges might we encounter in today's workplace?** There are three levels of challenge: individual, group, and organizational. At the individual level, employees are becoming more cynical about their employers. Thus, job satisfaction has become an important issue in today's organizations. Employees are also confronted with the trend toward an empowered workplace. Perhaps the greatest challenge individuals (and organizations) face is how to behave ethically.

At the group level, individuals are increasingly expected to work in teams, which means that they need to do so more effectively. This leads to a greater need for more interpersonal skills. The workplace is now made up of people from many different backgrounds, requiring a greater ability to understand those different from ourselves.

At the organizational level, Canadian businesses face many challenges in the 21st century. Their ability to be as productive as US businesses is constantly questioned. The need to develop effective employees, and to manage human resource issues—such as absenteeism and turnover—is critical. Businesses also face greater competition because of our global economy.

3 **How does knowing about organizational behaviour make work and life more understandable?** From a management point of view, knowing organizational behaviour can help you manage well. Managing people well pays off. It may also lead to greater organizational commitment. From an individual point of view, knowing about OB helps each of us understand why the workplace functions in particular ways. It also helps you understand how to deal with others if you decide to start your own business.

4 **Isn't organizational behaviour common sense? Or just like psychology?** Organizational behaviour is built on contributions from a number of behavioural disciplines, including psychology, sociology, social psychology, anthropology, and political science. If understanding behaviour were simply common sense, we would see fewer problems in the workplace, because managers and employees would know how to behave.

5 **What are the building blocks to understanding organizational behaviour?** OB considers individuals, groups and the organization itself. Exhibit 1–4 presented the three levels of analysis we consider in this textbook, and shows that as we move from the individual level to the organization systems level, we add systematically to our understanding of behaviour in organizations.

OB AT WORK

For Review

1. Define organizational behaviour.

2. What is an organization? Is the family unit an organization? Explain.

3. "Behaviour is generally predictable, so there is no need to formally study OB." Do you agree or disagree with this statement? Why?

4. What are some of the challenges and opportunities that managers face as we move into the 21st century?

5. What are the three levels of analysis in our OB model? Are they related? If so, how?

6. Why is job satisfaction an important consideration for OB?

7. What are effectiveness and efficiency, and how are they related to organizational behaviour?

8. What does it mean to say OB takes a contingency approach in its analysis of behaviour?

For Critical Thinking

1. "The best way to view OB is through a contingency approach." Build an argument to support this statement.

2. "OB is for everyone." Build an argument to support this statement.

3. Why do you think the subject of OB might be criticized as being "only common sense," when we would rarely hear such a comment about a course in physics or statistics? Do you think this criticism of OB is fair?

4. On a scale of 1 to 10, measuring the sophistication of a scientific discipline in predicting phenomena, mathematical physics would probably be a 10. Where do you think OB would fall on the scale? Why?

OB for You

- As you journey through this course in organizational behaviour, bear in mind that the processes we describe are as relevant to you as an individual as they are to organizations, managers, and employees.

- When you work together with student teams, join a student organization, or volunteer time to a community group, your interactions with the other people in those groups is affected by your ability to get along with others and to help the group achieve its goals.

- Being aware of how your perceptions and personality affect your interactions with others helps you to be more careful in forming your initial impression of others.

- Knowing how to motivate others who are working with you and how to communicate effectively, negotiating and compromising where necessary, are all elements of getting along in a variety of situations that are not necessarily work-related.

 **POINT**

 **COUNTERPOINT**

Successful Organizations Put People First

Intel does it. So do Microsoft, Motorola, W.L. Gore & Associates, Southwest Airlines, Ben & Jerry's Homemade, Hewlett-Packard, Lincoln Electric, and Starbucks. What is it? These companies pursue "people-first" strategies.

There is an increasing amount of evidence that successful organizations put people first.[40] Why? Smart managers have come to learn that employees are the organization's only true competitive advantage. Competitors can match most organizations' products, processes, locations, distribution channels, and the like. It is far more difficult to copy a workforce made up of highly knowledgeable and motivated people. The characteristic that differentiates successful companies from their less successful counterparts in almost every industry is the quality of the people they are able to attract and keep.

What kinds of practices distinguish people-first organizations? We can list at least four: (1) They value cultural diversity. They actively seek a diverse workforce based on age, gender, and race. (2) They are family-friendly. They help employees balance work and personal responsibilities through such programs as flexible work schedules and on-site child-care facilities. (3) They invest in employee training. These organizations spend heavily to make sure employee skills levels are kept current. This ensures that employees can not only handle the latest technologies and processes for the organization but also that employees will be marketable to other employers. (4) People-first organizations empower their employees. They push authority and responsibility down to the lowest levels.

Organizations that put people first have a more dedicated and committed workforce. This, in turn, converts into higher employee productivity and satisfaction. These employees are willing to put forth the extra effort—to do whatever is necessary to see that their jobs are done properly and completely. People-first strategies also lead to organizations being able to recruit smarter, more conscientious, and more loyal employees.

Successful Companies Put Profits First

Putting "people first" is easy to say. And it's currently politically correct. What manager in his or her right mind is going to admit publicly that employees take a back seat to cost-cutting or profitability? It is important, however, not to confuse talk with action.

Putting people first is not necessarily consistent with long-term competitiveness. Managers recognize this fact and are increasingly acting on it. Today's organizations are more typically following a "labour-cost-minimization" strategy rather than a people-first strategy.

When you look beyond what managers say, you find most business firms place profits before people. To stay competitive in a global economy, they look for cost-cutting measures. They re-engineer processes and cut the size of their permanent workforce, sometimes by hiring temporary employees instead.

Organizations with problems typically look to staffing cuts first. Organizations without problems are regularly reviewing their staffing needs to identify redundancies and overstaffing. Their goal is to keep themselves "lean and mean." In today's competitive environment, few organizations have the luxury of providing workers with implied "permanent employment" or of offering anything more than minimal job security.

For almost all organizations today, employees are a variable cost. Staffing levels are kept to a minimum and employees are continually added or deleted as needed.

Interestingly, the labour-cost-minimization strategy appears to be spreading worldwide. It began in Canada and the United States in the early 1990s. Now it has become the model for companies in countries such as Japan, South Korea, and Thailand—places that historically protected their employees in good times and bad. Many firms in these countries have abandoned their permanent-employment, people-first policies. Why? Because such policies are inconsistent with aggressive, low-cost global competition.

The Competing Values Framework: Identifying Your Interpersonal Skills

Directions: From the list below, identify what you believe to be your strongest skills, and then identify those in which you think your performance is weak. You should identify about 4 strong skills and 4 weak skills.

1. Taking initiative
2. Goal setting
3. Delegating effectively
4. Personal productivity and motivation
5. Motivating others
6. Time and stress management
7. Planning
8. Organizing
9. Controlling
10. Receiving and organizing information
11. Evaluating routine information
12. Responding to routine information

13. Understanding yourself and others
14. Interpersonal communication
15. Developing subordinates
16. Team building
17. Participative decision making
18. Conflict management
19. Living with change
20. Creative thinking
21. Managing change
22. Building and maintaining a power base
23. Negotiating agreement and commitment
24. Negotiating and selling ideas

Scoring Key

These skills are taken from the "Competing Values Framework" discussed in *From Concepts to Skills*, and are shown in Exhibit 1–5. Below, you will see how the individual skills relate to various managerial roles. Using the skills you identified as strongest, identify which roles you feel especially prepared for right now. Then, using the skills you identified as weakest, identify areas in which you might want to gain more skill. You should also use this information to determine whether you are currently more internally or externally focused, or oriented more toward flexibility or control.

Director: 1, 2, 3   Mentor: 13, 14, 15
Producer: 4, 5, 6   Facilitator: 16, 17, 18
Coordinator: 7, 8, 9   Innovator: 19, 20, 21
Monitor: 10, 11, 12   Broker: 22, 23, 24

After reviewing how your strengths and weaknesses relate to the skills that today's managers and leaders need, as illustrated in Exhibit 1–6, you should consider whether you need to develop a broader range of skills.

Source: Created based on material from R.E. Quinn, S.R. Faerman, M.P. Thompson, and M.R. McGrath, *Becoming a Master Manager: A Competency Framework*, 1st ed. (New York: John Wiley and Sons, 1990), Chapter 1.

OB *AT WORK*

BREAKOUT **GROUP** EXERCISES

Form small groups to discuss the following topics, as assigned by your instructor:

1. Consider a group situation in which you have worked. To what extent did the group rely on the technical skills of the group members vs. their interpersonal skills? Which skills seemed most important in helping the group function well?

2. Identify some examples of "worst jobs." What conditions of these jobs made them unpleasant? To what extent were these conditions related to behaviours of individuals?

3. Develop a list of "organizational puzzles," i.e., behaviour you have observed in organizations that seemed to make little sense. As the term progresses, see if you can begin to explain these puzzles, using your knowledge of organizational behaviour.

WORKING WITH OTHERS EXERCISE

Interpersonal Skills in the Workplace

This exercise asks you to consider the skills outlined in the "Competing Values Framework" to develop an understanding of managerial expertise. Steps 1–4 can be completed in 15–20 minutes.

1. Using the skills listed in the *Learning About Yourself Exercise,* identify the 4 skills that you think all managers should have.

2. Identify the 4 skills that you think are least important for managers to have.

3. In groups of 5–7, reach a consensus on the most-needed and least-needed skills identified in Steps 1 and 2.

4. Using Exhibit 1–6, determine whether your "ideal" managers would have trouble managing in some dimensions of organizational demands.

5. Your instructor will lead a general discussion of your results.

ETHICAL DILEMMA EXERCISE

What Is the Right Balance Between Work and Personal Life?

When you think of work/life conflicts, you probably tend to think of people in lower levels of organizations. However, a recent survey of 179 CEOs revealed that many of them struggle with this issue. For instance, 31 percent said they have a high level of stress in their lives; 47 percent admitted that they would sacrifice some compensation for more personal time; and 16 percent considered changing jobs in the past 6 months to reduce stress or sacrifices made in their personal lives.

Most of these surveyed executives conceded that they had given up, and continue to give up, a lot to get to the top in their organizations. They are often tired from the extensive and exhausting travel their jobs demand, not to mention an average 60-hour workweek. Yet most feel the climb to the CEO position was worth whatever sacrifices they have had to make.

Jean Stone, while not representative of the group, indicates the price that some of these executives have had to pay. As CEO and president of Dukane Corp., an Illinois-based manufacturer of electronic communications equipment, Stone describes herself as highly achievement-oriented. She has an intense focus on her job and admits to having lost sight of her personal life. Recently divorced after a 10-year marriage, she acknowledges that "career and work pressures were a factor in that."

How much emphasis on work is *too much?* What is the right balance between work and personal life? How much would you be willing to give up to be CEO of a major company? And if you were a CEO, what ethical responsibilities, if any, do you think you have to help your employees balance their work/family obligations?

Source: Based on M.J. Critelli, "Striking a Balance," *Industry Week*, November 20, 2000, pp. 26–36.

CASE INCIDENT

Great Plains Software: Pursuing a People-First Strategy

Great Plains Software is a success story. It was begun in 1983, today employs 2,200 people and generates sales of $395 million, and was recently bought by Microsoft for $1.5 billion. Management attributes much of its success to the company's people-first strategy.

The company's CEO, Doug Burgum (now a Microsoft senior vice-president), says that Great Plains' growth and success can be attributed to three guiding principles. First, make the company such a great place to work that not only will employees want to stay, but people will be knocking down the door to get in. Second, give employees ownership at every level. Third, let people grow—as professionals and as individuals.

What does Great Plains do to bring about its people-first culture? Managers point to the company's structure, perks, and its commitment to helping employees develop their skills and leadership. Great Plains has a flat organization structure with a minimal degree of hierarchy. Work is done mostly in teams, and there are no traditional status rewards such as executive parking spaces or corner-office suites. Perks include stock options for everyone, casual dress standards, an on-site child-care centre, and daily extracurricular classes in everything from aerobics to personal finance. But management is most proud of its commitment to the development of its people. The company offers a long list of training and educational opportunities to its employees. These are run on site and are designed to help employees build their skill level. Great Plains' premier training program is called "Leadership Is Everywhere." It's designed to ensure that the company will have people who can assume new leadership roles in a continuously changing environment. The company reinforces class training by placing its workers in departmental teams. At the helm of these teams are "team leaders," whose job is to help foster their charges' ideas and projects. They are also expected to provide one-on-one job coaching and career planning advice. Nearly all Great Plains employees are given the opportunity to become team leaders.

Burgum has more than higher revenues to support his belief that his people-first strategy works. The strategy has also succeeded in keeping employees contented. Turnover, for instance, is only 5 percent a year—far below the information technology average of 18 to 25 percent.

Questions

1. Putting people first has worked for Great Plains. If it's so effective, why do you think every firm has not adopted these practices?

2. Do you think a people-first approach is better for certain businesses or industries than others? If so, what might they be? Why?

3. What downside, if any, do you see in working at a company like Great Plains?

4. What downside, if any, do you see in managing at a company like Great Plains?

5. Some critics have argued that "People-first policies don't lead to high profits. High profits allow people-first policies." Do you agree? Explain your position.

Source: Based on S. Boehle, "From Humble Roots," *Training*, October 2000, pp. 106–13.

CBC ⬤ VIDEO CASE INCIDENT

The Challenges of Managing and Working at Nortel

Since 2001, Nortel Networks of Brampton, Ontario, once considered a world class company, has cut more than 60 000 jobs worldwide—two-thirds of its peak work-force—in an aggressive attempt to retain earnings, weather the tech-stock crisis, and regain control over high operating costs.

Historically, Nortel has had strong and stable roots in Canada, attracting worldwide attention with innovative products and impressive equipment standards. Throughout the 1990s, Nortel became a significant network and communications provider by being part of the tech boom that helped build the internet backbone. In 2000, it was no surprise to hear investment counsellors advising their clients to have Nortel as part of their investment portfolios.

More recently, life at Nortel has had its ups and downs. In July 2000, company stock hit an all-time high of $124.50 per share, only to fall to single digit levels within months. As profits fell drastically, investors lost faith not only in Nortel, but in the entire tech industry. In October 2002, Nortel stock hit an all-time low of 67 cents per share.

Layoffs, restructuring, and new directions have become a way of life at Nortel as the organization continues to battle the challenging process of regaining investor trust while securing new business deals in a highly competitive world.

Today, under the leadership of CEO Frank Dunn, Nortel continues to fight for the prestigious position of being one of Canada's largest technology companies. Thanks to new multi-million dollar deals with France Telecom and Sprint Communications US, stock prices have climbed to a 16-month high of $6.50.

Questions

1. What downside, if any, do you see in working at a company like Nortel?

2. What downside, if any, do you see in managing at a company like Nortel?

3. If successful organizations put people first, then should more firms reconsider laying off employees and just take greater care to hire highly qualified people to begin with?

Source: Based on "Nortel," *CBC Venture*, June 9, 2002, VA2033, 830; Nortel Networks website, "Company History," www.nortelnetworks.com; G. Norris, "Shares Rise 8% After Deal," *National Post*, September 16, 2003, p. C1.

From **Concepts**
To **Skills**

Developing Interpersonal Skills

We note in the chapter that having a broad range of interpersonal skills to draw on makes us more effective organizational participants. So what kinds of interpersonal skills does an individual need in today's workplace? Robert Quinn, Kim Cameron, and their colleagues have developed a model known as the "Competing Values Framework" that can help us identify some of the most useful skills.[41] They note that the range of issues organizations face can be divided along two dimensions: an internal-external and a flexibility-control focus. This is illustrated in Exhibit 1–5. The internal-external dimension refers to the extent that organizations focus on one of two directions: either inwardly, toward employee needs and concerns and/or production processes and internal systems; or outwardly, toward such factors as the marketplace, government regulations, and the changing social, environmental, and technological conditions of the future. The flexibility-control dimension refers to the competing demands of organizations to stay focused on doing what has been done in the past vs. being more flexible in orientation and outlook.

Because organizations face the competing demands shown in Exhibit 1–5, it becomes obvious that managers and employees need a variety of skills to help them function within the various quadrants at different points. For instance, the skills needed to operate an efficient assembly-line process are not the same as those needed to scan the environment or to create opportunities in anticipation of changes in the environment. Quinn and his colleagues use the term *master manager* to indicate that successful managers learn and apply skills that will help them manage across the range of organizational demands; at some times moving toward flexibility, at others moving toward control, sometimes being more internally focused, sometimes being more externally driven.[42]

As organizations increasingly cut their layers, reducing the number of managers while also relying more on the use of teams in the workplace, the skills of the master manager apply as well to the employee. In other words, considering the "Competing Values Framework," we can see that both managers and individual employees need to learn new skills and new ways of interpreting their organizational contexts. Continuing to use traditional skills and practices that worked in the past is not an

Exhibit 1–5

Competing Values Framework

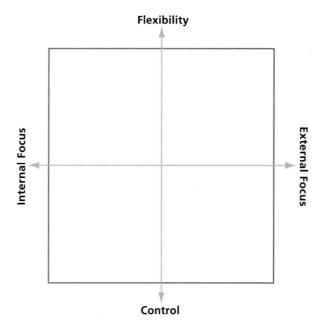

Source: Adapted from K. Cameron and R.E. Quinn, *Diagnosing and Changing Organizational Culture: Based on the Competing Values Framework*, 1st ed. (Reading, MA: Addison Wesley Longman Inc., 1999).

Exhibit 1–6

Skills for Mastery in the New Workplace

Source: R.E. Quinn, *Beyond Rational Management* (San Francisco: Jossey-Bass Inc., 1988), p. 86.

skills of innovators and brokers. On the control side, organizations need to set clear goals about productivity expectations, and they have to develop and implement systems to carry out the production process. To be effective on the production side, employees need to have the skills of monitors, coordinators, directors, and producers. The *Working With Others Exercise* will help you better understand how closely your views on the ideal skills of managers and leaders match the skills needed to be successful in the broad range of activities that managers and leaders encounter.

At this point, you may wonder whether it is possible for people to learn all of the skills necessary to become a master manager. More important, you may wonder

option. The growth in self-employment also indicates a need to develop more interpersonal skills, particularly for anyone who goes on to build a business that involves hiring and managing employees.

Exhibit 1–6 outlines the many skills required of today's manager. It gives you an indication of the complex roles that managers and employees fill in the changing workplace. The skills are organized in terms of four major roles: maintaining flexibility, maintaining control, maintaining an external focus, and maintaining an internal focus. The *Learning About Yourself Exercise* will help you identify your own strengths and weaknesses in these skill areas so that you can have a better sense of how close you are to becoming a successful manager. For instance, on the flexibility side, organizations want to inspire their employees toward high-performance behaviour. Such behaviour includes looking ahead to the future and imagining possible new directions for the organization. To do these things, employees need to think and act like mentors and facilitators. It is also important to have the

whether we can change our individual style, say from more controlling to more flexible. Here's what Peggy Witte, who used to be chair, president, and CEO of the now-defunct Royal Oak Mines, said about how her managerial style changed from controlling to more flexible over time: "I started out being very dictatorial. Everybody in head office reported to me. I had to learn to trust other executives so we could work out problems together."[43] So, while it is probably true that each of us has a preferred style of operating, it is also the case that we can develop new skills if that is something we choose to do.

Assessing Skills

After reading this chapter, take the following self-assessments on your enclosed CD-ROM:

23. Am I likely to become an entrepreneur?

45. How motivated am I to manage?

46. Am I well-suited for a career as a global manager?

Practising Skills

As the father of two young children, Marshall Rogers thought that serving on the board of Marysville Daycare would be a good way to stay in touch with those who cared for his children during the day. But he never dreamed that he would become involved in union-management negotiations with daycare-centre workers.

Late one Sunday evening, in his ninth month as president of the daycare centre, Rogers received a phone call from Grace Ng, a union representative of the Provincial Government Employees' Union (PGEU). Ng informed Rogers that the daycare workers would be unionized the following week. Rogers was stunned to hear this news. Early the next morning, he had to present his new marketing plan to senior management at Techtronix Industries, where he was vice-president of marketing. Somehow he made it through the meeting, wondering why he hadn't been aware of the employees' unhappiness, and how this action would affect his children.

Following his presentation, Rogers received documentation from the Labour Relations Board indicating that the daycare employees had been working to unionize themselves for more than a year. Rogers immediately contacted Xavier Breslin, the board's vice-president, and together they determined that no one on the board had been aware that the daycare workers were unhappy, let alone prepared to join a union.

Hoping that there was some sort of misunderstanding, Rogers called Emma Reynaud, the Marysville supervisor. Reynaud attended most board meetings, but had never mentioned the union-organizing drive. Yet Reynaud now told Rogers that she had actively encouraged the other daycare workers to consider joining the PGEU because the board had not been interested in the employees' concerns, had not increased their wages sufficiently over the past two years, and had not maintained communication channels between the board and the employees.

All of the board members had full-time jobs elsewhere, and many were upper- and middle-level managers in their own companies. They were used to dealing with unhappy employees in their own workplaces, although none had experienced a union-organizing drive. Like Rogers, they had chosen to serve on the board of Marysville to stay informed about the day-to-day events

of the centre. They had not really thought of themselves as the centre's employer, although, as board members, they represented all the parents of children enrolled at Marysville. Their main tasks on the daycare-centre board had been setting fees for the children and wages for the daycare employees. The board members usually saw the staff members several times a week, when they picked up their children, yet the unhappiness represented by the union-organizing drive was surprising to all of them. When they met at an emergency board meeting that evening, they tried to evaluate what had gone wrong at Marysville.

Questions

1. If you were either a board member or a parent, how would you know that the employees taking care of your children were unhappy with their jobs?

2. What might you do if you learned about their unhappiness?

3. What might Rogers have done differently as president of the board?

4. In what ways does this case illustrate that knowledge of organizational behaviour can be applied beyond your own workplace?

Source: Nancy Langton and Joy Begley ©1999. (The events described are based on an actual situation, although the participants, as well as the centre, have been disguised.)

Reinforcing Skills

1. Talk to several managers you know and ask them what skills they think are most important in today's workplace. Ask them to specifically consider the use of teams in their workplace, and what skills their team members most need to have but are least likely to have. How might you use this information to develop greater interpersonal skills?

2. Talk to several managers you know and ask them what skills they have found to be most important in doing their jobs. Why did they find these skills most important? What advice would they give a would-be manager about skills worth developing?

CHAPTER 2

Perception, Personality, and Emotions

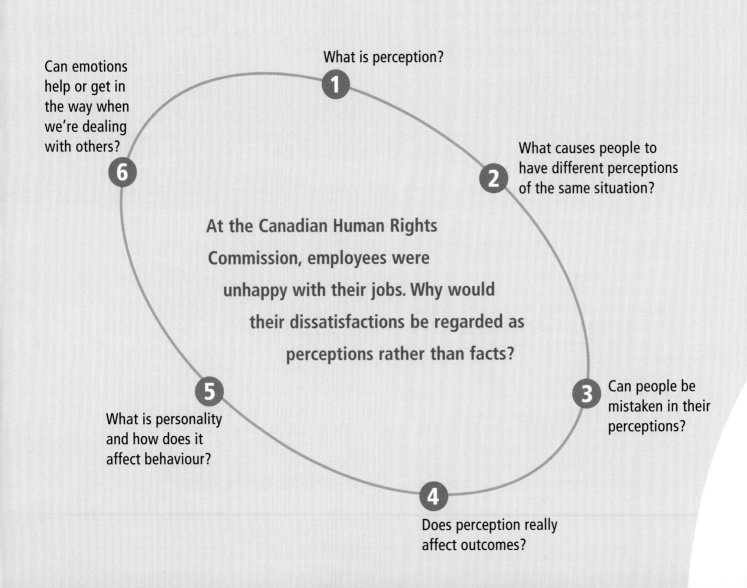

What is perception?

1

Can emotions help or get in the way when we're dealing with others?

6

What causes people to have different perceptions of the same situation?

2

At the Canadian Human Rights Commission, employees were unhappy with their jobs. Why would their dissatisfactions be regarded as perceptions rather than facts?

Can people be mistaken in their perceptions?

3

What is personality and how does it affect behaviour?

5

Does perception really affect outcomes?

4

Many employees at the Canadian Human Rights Commission (CHRC) cheered in May 2001 when a commissioned report revealed widespread dissatisfaction in their workplace.[1] Ordinarily an exposé of on-the-job problems is not something to cheer about, but the CHRC workers were grateful their concerns were finally being made public.

Much to the employees' dismay, however, senior managers at CHRC suggested that the workplace problems were only a matter of employee "perception," not objective reality. Michelle Falardeau-Ramsay, who was chief commissioner at the time, even said, "It's a report that is based on perceptions and perceptions can become facts at one point."[2] The employees were left to wonder whether they and their managers were actually part of the same workplace.

All of our behaviour is somewhat shaped by our perceptions, personalities, emotions, and experiences. In this chapter, we consider the role that perception plays in affecting the way we see the world and the people around us. We also consider how personality characteristics affect our attitudes toward people and situations. We then consider how emotions shape many of our work-related behaviours.

PERCEPTION DEFINED

Perception is the process by which individuals select, organize, and interpret their sensory impressions in order to give meaning to their environment.

However, what we perceive can be substantially different from objective reality. We often disagree about what is real. As we have seen, employees and senior management at the Canadian Human Rights Commission had very different views of their workplace conditions. Michelle Falardeau-Ramsay, the chief commissioner, even said it was all a matter of "perception."

Why is perception important in the study of organizational behaviour? Simply because people's behaviour is based on their perception of what reality is, not on reality itself. *The world as it is perceived is the world that is behaviourally important.* Paul Godfrey, the CEO of Toronto-based Sun Media Corp., notes that "a lot of things in life are perception." He claims that as chair of Metropolitan Toronto for 11 years, he had little real power, but people believed he could get things done, and so he did.[3]

1 What is perception?

perception
The process by which individuals select, organize, and interpret their sensory impressions in order to give meaning to their environment.

Sun Media Corporation
www.sunmedia.ca

City of Toronto
www.city.toronto.on.ca

FACTORS INFLUENCING PERCEPTION

Comments by employees and managers illustrate different perceptions of the environment at the Canadian Human Rights Commission. For example, one unnamed employee said that chief commissioner Falardeau-Ramsay was an absentee manager who lacked important job skills. "When she does conduct a meeting she will occupy the time describing entertainment details of the latest trip she has taken at taxpayers' expense. She's out of touch."[4]

Meanwhile, in responding to negative employee comments, Falardeau-Ramsay told reporters she felt complaints were directed against other senior managers, not her. "I was so overwhelmed, [the report] was so surprising that I didn't even think in those terms," she said.[5] Falardeau-Ramsay and her employees clearly had different perceptions of the same situation. What factors might have influenced these different perceptions?

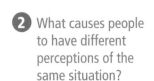

2 What causes people to have different perceptions of the same situation?

Canadian Human Rights Commission (CHRC)
www.chrc-ccdp.ca

How do we explain that individuals may look at the same thing, yet perceive it differently? A number of factors help shape and sometimes distort perception. These factors can be found in the *perceiver*, in the object or *target* being perceived, or in the context of the *situation* in which the perception is made. Exhibit 2–1 summarizes the factors influencing perception. This chapter's *Working With Others Exercise* on page 63 will help you understand how your perceptions affect your evaluation of others.

The Perceiver

When an individual ("the perceiver") looks at something ("the target") and tries to interpret what he or she sees, that interpretation is heavily influenced by the perceiver's personal characteristics. Have you ever bought a new car and then suddenly noticed a large number of cars like yours on the road? It's unlikely that everyone else has suddenly bought the same model. Rather, your own purchase has influenced your perception so

Exhibit 2–1
Factors That Influence Perception

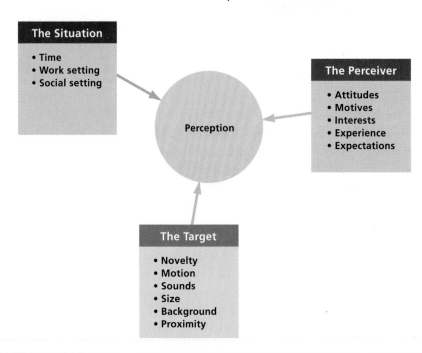

that you are now more likely to notice the other cars. This is an example of how factors related to the perceiver influence what he or she perceives.

A variety of factors affect our perception. Our attitudes and motives, interests, and past experiences all shape the way we perceive an event. When Chief Commissioner Michelle Falardeau-Ramsay suggested that employees' complaints about the CHRC were simply a matter of their perception, she was thinking about her own interests and motives in the situation. As head of the agency, she did not want to believe that she was responsible for any of the problems the employees reported.

Consider, too, how we often interpret others' behaviours based on our own characteristics. People who take an optimistic approach to life act as if others will be just as upbeat, while those who are devious suspect others are equally devious.

Expectations can also distort our perceptions—we see what we expect to see. For example, if you expect police officers to be authoritarian, young people to have no ambitions, human resources directors to like people, or politicians to be unethical, you may perceive individuals from these categories in this way, regardless of their actual traits.

Finally, perceptions are likely to vary cross-culturally. Thus, something that you do in a friendly way may be viewed as too aggressive, or too informal, by someone from another country.

The Target

A target's characteristics can affect what is perceived. Loud people are more likely to be noticed in a group than are quiet ones. So, too, are extremely attractive or unattractive individuals. Motion, sound, size, and other attributes of a target shape the way we see it.

Because targets are not looked at in isolation, the relationship of a target to its background influences perception. Objects that are close to each other will tend to be perceived together rather than separately. Events that are close in time may also be seen as related, even if they are not. Employees in a particular department are seen as a group. If two people in a four-member department suddenly resign, we tend to assume that their departures were related when, in fact, they may be totally unrelated. Timing may also imply dependence when, for example, a new sales manager is assigned to a territory and, soon after, sales in that territory skyrocket. The assignment of the new sales manager and the increase in sales may not be related—the increase may be due to the introduction of a new product line or to one of many other reasons—but people would tend to see the two occurrences as being related.

Persons, objects, or events that are similar to each other also tend to be grouped together. The greater the similarity, the greater the probability that we will tend to perceive them as a common group. People who are female, or Black, or members of any other clearly distinguishable group will tend to be perceived as similar not only in physical terms but in other unrelated characteristics as well.

The Situation

The context in which we see objects or events is important. Elements in the surrounding environment influence our perceptions. You are more likely to notice your employees goofing off if your manager from head office happens to be in town. Your employees may be acting as they always do, but it is the situation that affects your perception. The time at which an object or event is seen can influence attention, as can location, light, heat, or any number of situational factors. *OB in the Street* looks at how, in light of the events of September 11, 2001, a situation led one airline passenger to think that he was facing terrorists, when in fact, he was being viewed as a terrorist. As you will see, truth is often in the eye of the perceiver.

OB IN THE STREET

Terrorist or Security Officer?

How do you tell the difference between a terrorist and an air marshal? Richard Bizzaro is still wondering about the answer to this question. Bizzaro flew to Salt Lake City, Utah, during the 2002 Winter Olympics. Twenty-five minutes before his flight was to land, he decided to visit the washroom. For some reason, he had not heard the warning that passengers were not to leave their seats for the last 30 minutes of the flight.

When he came out of the washroom, Bizzaro was confronted by a flight attendant. Plainclothes federal air marshals saw the interaction between Bizzaro and the flight attendant, and they also thought they saw Bizzaro signal to another passenger. Worried that he could be trying to use the plane as a weapon, targeted at an Olympic site, the marshals took control of the passenger cabin. They ordered everyone to put their hands on top of their heads and look straight ahead. All the passengers complied, except Bizzaro, who kept looking behind him, as if trying to make contact with another passenger.

Given heightened airline security concerns, what passenger in his or her right mind would defy air marshals? It all comes down to perception. Bizzaro claimed he never heard the announcement about remaining seated for the last 30 minutes of the flight. As to why he didn't listen to the air marshals, Bizzaro explained, "When the young men claiming to be sky marshals directed everyone in the plane to place their hands on their heads, I did not initially believe them. They were dressed in street clothes and one of them wore a ball cap backwards. They did not give the appearance that they were law enforcement officers and I did not pay them the proper respect. I believed I was witnessing a hijacking of our airplane."[6] Bizzaro claimed he was looking around the plane to get others to help him rescue it from the "terrorist" air marshals. Unfortunately for Bizzaro, the ultimate judge of whether his perceptions were reasonable will be the one who decides whether he is guilty of disrupting the flight.

People's expectations about what employees working for a full-service web development agency should look like often leave them startled when they meet Jason Billingsley (left) and Justin Tilson (foreground), two of the founders of Vancouver-based Ekkon Technologies. Both men are in wheelchairs after a skiing accident for Billingsley and a mountain bike accident for Tilson. "It's an eye-opener sometimes," says Billingsley. "You've been talking on the phone for two or three weeks before you meet someone and they have no clue, and they kind of walk in and you see a little 'oh.'"

PERCEPTUAL ERRORS

In their workplace assessment report of the Canadian Human Rights Commission, consultants Watson Wyatt Worldwide identified numerous problems reported by employees. The employees suggested that three top managers should be replaced. They also claimed that female employees were discriminated against. The problems were considered so severe that some people outside the commission thought it should be closed. Chief commissioner Falardeau-Ramsay disagreed. She said the findings were "unpleasant" and "painful," but suggested that those calling for the commission's closure had read the report in a "simplistic and irresponsible manner." These differences in response might suggest that the employees, Falardeau-Ramsay, or her critics were engaged in making perceptual errors. What might have caused this to happen?

It's difficult to perceive and interpret what others do. As a result, we develop shortcuts to make this task more manageable. These shortcuts are often very helpful—they allow us to make accurate perceptions quickly and provide valid information for making predictions. However, they are not foolproof. They can and do get us into trouble. Below we cover a variety of the errors that distort the perception process.

3 Can people be mistaken in their perceptions?

Attribution Theory

Attribution theory has been proposed to help explain the ways in which we judge people differently, depending on what meaning we attribute to a given behaviour.[7] Basically, the theory suggests that when we observe an individual's behaviour, we try to determine whether the individual is responsible for the behaviour (the cause is internal), or whether something outside the individual caused the behaviour (the cause is external). Whether we realize it or not, we use attribution theory whenever we try to come up with explanations for why people behaved the way they did.

attribution theory
When individuals observe behaviour, they try to determine whether it is internally or externally caused.

In trying to understand another person's behaviour, then, we consider whether the behaviour was internally or externally caused. *Internally* caused behaviour is believed to be under the personal control of the individual, so that the person chooses to engage in that behaviour. *Externally* caused behaviour is believed to result from outside causes; that is, the person does not have control over his or her actions, but is forced into the behaviour by the situation. For example, while waiting for one of your team members who is late for a meeting, you could imagine either an internal or an external reason for the lateness. An internal reason might be that the team member must have partied into the wee hours of the morning and then overslept. An external attribution might be that there was a major automobile accident that tied up traffic.

Rules for Determining Attribution
In trying to determine whether behaviour is internally or externally caused, we rely on three rules about the behaviour: 1) distinctiveness, 2) consensus, and 3) consistency. Exhibit 2–2 summarizes the main elements in attribution theory.

Distinctiveness Distinctiveness refers to whether an individual acts the same way in other situations. What we want to know is whether the individual's behaviour is unusual. If it is, the observer is likely to give the behaviour an external attribution. If this action is not unusual, it will probably be judged as internally caused.

Consensus Consensus considers how an individual behaves compared to his or her peers. If everyone who is faced with a similar situation responds in the same way, we can say the behaviour shows consensus. When consensus is high, an external attribution is given to an individual's behaviour. But if an individual's behaviour is different from everyone else's, you would conclude the cause for that individual's behaviour was internal.

Exhibit 2–2

Attribution Theory

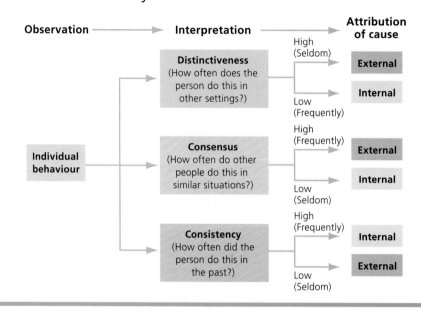

fundamental attribution error
The tendency to underestimate the influence of external factors and overestimate the influence of internal factors when making judgments about the behaviour of others.

self-serving bias
The tendency for individuals to attribute their own successes to internal factors while putting the blame for failures on external factors.

Consistency   Finally, an observer looks for *consistency* in a person's actions. Is this the same way the person has been acting over time? Being 10 minutes late for work is not perceived in the same way for the employee for whom lateness is unusual (she hasn't been late for several months) as it is for the employee for whom it is routine (he is regularly late two or three times a week). The more consistent the behaviour, the more likely the observer is to attribute it to internal causes.

How Attributions Get Distorted

One of the more interesting findings from attribution theory is that there are errors or biases that distort attributions. For instance, there is substantial evidence that when we judge the behaviour of other people, we tend to put more emphasis on internal or personal factors and less emphasis on external factors.[8] This is called the **fundamental attribution error** and can explain why a sales manager is prone to attribute the poor performance of his or her sales agents to laziness rather than to the innovative product line introduced by a competitor.

We use **self-serving bias** when we judge ourselves, however. This means that when we are successful, we are more likely to believe it was because of internal factors, such as ability or effort. When we fail, however, we blame external factors, such as luck.

Attribution theory was developed largely in the United States on the basis of experiments with Americans, but there is no particular reason to believe it would not apply in Canada. However, evidence from Japan[9] and Korea[10] suggests we should be careful

Many day traders credited the gains they made in high-tech stocks between 1996 and early 2000 to their personal skills. But they blamed external sources for the losses they incurred when the prices of high-tech stocks took a nosedive.

in making attribution theory predictions in non-Western countries or in those with strong collectivist traditions, such as Spain, Portugal, and some Eastern European countries.

Selective Perception

Because it is impossible for us to absorb everything we see, we engage in **selective perception**. Any characteristic that makes a person, object, or event stand out will increase the probability that we see it. This tendency explains why, as we noted earlier, you are more likely to notice cars like your own. A classic example shows how selective perception works.

Dearborn and Simon performed a perceptual study in which 23 business executives read a comprehensive case describing the organization and activities of a steel company.[11] Six of the 23 executives were in sales, five in production, four in accounting, and eight in miscellaneous areas. Each manager was asked to write down the most important problem he or she found in the case. Eighty-three percent of the sales executives rated sales important; only 29 percent of the others did so. This, along with other results of the study, led the researchers to conclude that the participants perceived aspects of a situation that were specifically related to their own jobs. People see things that are consistent with their own interests. This explains why Falardeau-Ramsay thought that complaints about CHRC managers were directed against other senior managers and not at her.

How does selectivity work as a shortcut in judging other people? Since we cannot absorb all that we observe, we take in bits and pieces. Those bits and pieces are not chosen randomly, but are selectively chosen according to our interests, background, experience, and attitudes. Selective perception allows us to "speed-read" others, but we may draw an inaccurate picture. Because we see what we want to see, we can make unwarranted conclusions about an ambiguous situation. Suppose there is a rumour going around the office that your company's sales are down and that large layoffs may be coming soon. If a senior executive from head office makes a routine visit around this time, it might be interpreted as management's first step in identifying which people to lay off. In reality, such an action might be the furthest thing from the senior executive's mind.

> **selective perception**
> People selectively interpret what they see based on their interests, background, experience, and attitudes.

Halo Effect

When we draw a general impression about an individual on the basis of a single characteristic, such as intelligence, sociability, or appearance, a **halo effect** is operating. This often happens when students evaluate their instructor. Students may give more weight to a single trait, such as enthusiasm, and allow their entire evaluation to be affected by how they judge the instructor on that one trait. Thus, an instructor may be quiet, assured, knowledgeable, and highly qualified, but if his or her presentation style lacks enthusiasm, those students would probably give the instructor a low rating.

The reality of the halo effect was confirmed in a classic study. Subjects were given a list of traits and asked to evaluate the person to whom those traits applied.[12] When traits such as intelligent, skillful, practical, industrious, determined, and warm were used, the person was judged to be wise, humorous, popular, and imaginative. When cold was substituted for warm, a completely different set of perceptions was obtained, though otherwise the list was identical. Clearly, the subjects were allowing a single trait to influence their overall impression of the person being judged.

The halo effect does not operate at random. Research suggests that it is likely to be most extreme when the traits to be perceived are ambiguous in behavioural terms, when the traits have moral overtones, and when the perceiver is judging traits with which he or she has had limited experience.[13]

> **halo effect**
> Drawing a general impression about an individual based on a single characteristic.

Contrast Effects

There is an old saying among entertainers who perform in variety shows: Never follow an act that has children or animals in it.

contrast effects
Our reaction to one person is often influenced by other people we have recently encountered.

This example demonstrates how **contrast effects** can distort perceptions. We don't evaluate a person in isolation. Our reaction to one person is often influenced by other people we have recently encountered.

Consider what happens when a manager interviews job candidates from a pool of applicants. The evaluation of a candidate can be affected by his or her place in the interview schedule. The candidate is likely to receive a better evaluation if interviewed after a mediocre applicant, and a worse evaluation if interviewed after a strong applicant.

Projection

It is easy to judge others if we assume that they are similar to us. For instance, if you want challenge and responsibility in your job, you assume that others want the same. Or, you are honest and trustworthy, so you take it for granted that other people are equally honest and trustworthy. This tendency for people to attribute their own characteristics to other people—which is called **projection**—can distort perceptions.

projection
Attributing your own characteristics to other people.

People who engage in projection tend to perceive others according to what they themselves are like rather than perceiving others as they really are. Because they always judge people as being similar to themselves, when they observe someone who is actually like them their perceptions are naturally correct. But when they observe others who are not like them, their perceptions are not so accurate. When managers engage in projection, they compromise their ability to respond to individual differences. They tend to see people as more alike than they really are.

Stereotyping

When we judge someone on the basis of our perception of the group to which he or she belongs, we are using the shortcut called **stereotyping**. According to a popular literary anecdote, F. Scott Fitzgerald engaged in stereotyping when he told Ernest Hemingway, "the rich are very different from you and me," implying that the wealthy have values and behaviour unlike regular people. Hemingway's reply, "Yes, they have more money,"

stereotyping
Judging someone on the basis of your perception of the group to which that person belongs.

Stereotyping cost a contractor in Ontario the opportunity to build the facility for Fern Hill School, a private school in Oakville, Ontario. Instead of speaking to co-owners Wendy Derrick (on left) and Joanne McLean, the contractor kept pitching his bid to their male architect. He did not even give the owners an opportunity to speak during the meeting. The job went to another builder.

indicated that he refused to generalize characteristics of people on the basis of their wealth.

Generalization, of course, is not without advantages. It helps us simplify a complex world, and it permits us to maintain consistency. It is easier to deal with an unmanageable number of stimuli if we use stereotypes. As an example, assume you are a sales manager looking to fill a sales position in your territory. You want to hire someone who is ambitious and hard-working and who can deal well with adversity. You have had good success in the past by hiring individuals who played university sports. So you focus your search by looking for candidates who played university athletics. In so doing, you have cut down considerably on your search time. Furthermore, to the extent that athletes are ambitious, hard-working, and able to deal with adversity, the use of this stereotype can improve your decision making. The problem, of course, is when we inaccurately stereotype.[14] All university athletes are *not necessarily* ambitious, hard-working, or good at dealing with adversity, just as all accountants are *not necessarily* quiet and introspective. Moreover, when we stereotype like this, we run the risk of overlooking highly qualified people who do not meet our stereotypes. Recent research that examined how Hollywood studio executives and producers judge the creative potential of relatively unknown screenwriters makes this clear.[15] When the screenwriters did not meet the stereotype of creative individuals in their presentation or appearance, they were judged as not creative (and often not taken seriously) without consideration of the content of their idea. The researchers noted that this could result in hiring uncreative individuals simply because they fit the creative stereotype, and failing to hire truly creative individuals who did not fit the stereotype.

In organizations, we frequently hear comments that represent stereotypes based on gender, age, race, ethnicity, and even weight:[16] "Women won't relocate for a promotion"; "men aren't interested in child care"; "older workers are more reliable"; "Asian immigrants are hard-working and conscientious"; "overweight people lack self-discipline." From a perceptual standpoint, if people expect to see these stereotypes, that is what they will perceive, whether or not the stereotypes are accurate.

Obviously, one of the problems of stereotypes is that they are widespread, despite the fact that they may not contain a shred of truth or that they may be irrelevant. Perhaps they are widespread only because many people are making the same inaccurate perception based on a false premise about a group.

WHY DO PERCEPTION AND JUDGMENT MATTER?

The employees at the Canadian Human Rights Commission felt that chief commissioner Falardeau-Ramsay was not up to her role. They cited as evidence that she spent meeting time describing entertainment details of the latest trip she had taken at taxpayers' expense. This, and other perceptions of bad management, had led to high turnover at the commission and low morale. About 63 percent of the employees had left in the previous two years and 37 percent of those still working at the time of the survey were looking for another job. Falardeau-Ramsay was unaware of employee unhappiness. She said she had regularly met with employees and had never heard complaints of "managers openly showing favouritism, promoting men over women, and nurturing 'an anti-union culture.'"[17] Thus her perception led her to the judgment that there was nothing she needed to fix at the CHRC. It had not occurred to her that perhaps employees would be reluctant to share bad news with her. Perceptions and judgments by both Falardeau-Ramsay and her employees led to actions that were harmful to the organization.

People in organizations are always judging each other. For instance, to get a job, a person typically goes through an employment interview. Interviewers make perceptual judgments during the interview, which then affect whether the individual is hired.

4 Does perception really affect outcomes?

Studies show that if negative information is exposed early in the interview, it tends to be more heavily weighted than if that same information comes out later.[18] When multiple interviewers are present, agreement among interviewers is often poor; that is, different interviewers see different things in the same candidate and thus arrive at different conclusions about the applicant. If the employment interview is an important input into the hiring decision—and it usually is—you should recognize that perceptual factors influence who is hired and, eventually, the quality of an organization's labour force.

An employee's performance appraisal is another process that depends very much on the perceptual process.[19] An employee's future is closely tied to his or her appraisal—promotions, pay raises, and continuation of employment are among the most obvious outcomes. The performance appraisal represents an evaluation of an employee's work. Although the appraisal can be objective (e.g., a salesperson is appraised on how many dollars of sales he or she generates in a given territory), many jobs are evaluated in subjective terms. Subjective measures are easier to implement, they provide managers with more freedom to do as they like, and many jobs do not readily lend themselves to objective measures. Subjective measures are, by definition, judgmental. The evaluator forms a general impression of an employee's work. To the degree that managers use subjective measures in appraising employees or choosing whom to promote, what the evaluator perceives to be good or bad employee characteristics or behaviours will significantly influence the outcome of the appraisal. One recent study found that managers in both Hong Kong and the United States were more likely to promote individuals who were more similar to themselves.[20]

Managers are not the only people making judgments at work. When a new person joins a work team, he or she is immediately "sized up" by the other team members. McMaster University Professor Kathleen Martin found that even small things can make a difference in how a team member is viewed. In her study, students read descriptions of individuals and were then asked to evaluate 12 personality characteristics of "Tom" or "Mary."[21] Some of these descriptions included information about whether "Tom" or "Mary" exercised. Students evaluated non-exercisers more negatively on every personality and physical characteristic than those described as exercisers. In fact, those described as non-exercisers were rated more negatively than those for whom no information about exercise was provided. Martin noted, "When Mary and Tom were described as exercisers, they were considered to be harder workers, more confident, braver, smarter, neater, happier, and more sociable than the non-exerciser."

As you can see, perception plays a large role in the way that day-to-day activities are carried out in an organization. Personality, which we review below, is another major factor affecting how people relate in the workplace.

McMaster University
www.mcmaster.ca

PERSONALITY

5 What is personality and how does it affect behaviour?

When we talk of personality, we don't mean that a person has charm, a positive attitude toward life, a smiling face, or is a finalist for "Happiest and Friendliest" in this year's Best Student Contest. When psychologists talk of personality, they mean a dynamic concept describing the growth and development of a person's whole psychological system. Rather than looking at parts of the person, personality looks at the whole person.

Gordon Allport produced the most frequently used definition of personality more than 60 years ago. He said personality is "the dynamic organization within the individual of those psychophysical systems that determine his unique adjustments to his environment."[22] For our purposes, you should think of **personality** as the stable patterns of behaviour and consistent internal states that determine how an individual reacts to and interacts with others. It is most often described in terms of measurable traits that a person exhibits. For an interesting look at how personality can affect business dealings,

personality
The stable patterns of behaviour and consistent internal states that determine how an individual reacts and interacts with others.

you might want to read this chapter's *Point/CounterPoint* discussion on page 54. The discussion centres on how flexible and inflexible personality is.

Personality Determinants

An early argument in personality research centred on whether an individual's personality was the result of heredity or of environment. Was the personality predetermined at birth, or was it the result of the individual's interaction with his or her environment? Clearly, there is no simple answer. Personality appears to be a result of both influences. In addition, today we recognize a third factor—the situation. Thus, an adult's personality is now generally considered to be made up of both hereditary and environmental factors, moderated by situational conditions.

Heredity

Heredity refers to those factors that were determined at conception. Physical stature, facial attractiveness, gender, temperament, muscle composition and reflexes, energy level, and biological rhythms are characteristics that are generally considered to be either completely or largely influenced by who your parents were: that is, by their biological, physiological, and inherent psychological makeup. The heredity approach argues that the ultimate explanation of an individual's personality is genetic.

If personality characteristics were *completely* dictated by heredity, they would be fixed at birth and no amount of experience could alter them. If you were tense and irritable as a child, for example, that would be the result of your genes, and it would not be possible for you to change those characteristics. But personality characteristics are not completely dictated by heredity.

Environment

Among the factors that exert pressures on our personality formation are the culture in which we are raised; our early conditioning; the norms among our family, friends, and social groups; and other influences that we experience. The environment we are exposed to plays a substantial role in shaping our personalities.

Culture establishes the norms, attitudes, and values that are passed along from one generation to the next and create consistencies over time. However, an ideology that is

Early training and the culture in which we are raised are important environmental factors that shape our personalities. Other influences are family norms and memberships in social groups.

intensely fostered in one culture may have only a moderate influence in another. For instance, North Americans have had the themes of industriousness, success, competition, independence, and the Protestant work ethic constantly drilled into them through books, the school system, family, and friends. North Americans, as a result, tend to be ambitious and aggressive compared with individuals raised in cultures that have emphasized getting along with others, cooperation, and the priority of family over work and career.

If we carefully consider the arguments favouring either heredity or environment as the main determinant of personality, we are forced to conclude that both are important. Heredity sets the parameters, or outer limits, but an individual's full potential will be determined by how well he or she adjusts to the demands and requirements of the environment.

Situation

A third factor, the situation, influences the effects of heredity and environment on personality. An individual's personality, although generally stable and consistent, may be more effective in some situations than others. More specifically, the different demands of different situations call forth different aspects of an individual's personality. We should not, therefore, look at personality patterns in isolation.[23]

Personality Traits

The early work in the structure of personality revolved around attempts to identify and label enduring characteristics that describe an individual's behaviour. Popular characteristics include shy, aggressive, submissive, lazy, ambitious, loyal, and timid. Those characteristics, when they are exhibited in a large number of situations, are called **personality traits**.[24] The more consistent the characteristic and the more often it occurs in different situations, the more important that trait is in describing the individual.

To give an idea of the range of personality traits studied, one researcher identified 16 personality factors that he called the source, or primary, traits.[25] These 16 traits have been found to be generally steady and constant sources of behaviour. These traits can help predict an individual's behaviour in specific situations by weighing them for their situational relevance. They are shown in Exhibit 2–3.

Our personality traits, by the way, are evaluated differently by different people. This is partly a function of perception, which we discussed earlier in the chapter. In Exhibit 2–4, you will note that Lucy tells Linus a few things about his personality.

The Big Five Model

The most widely accepted model of personality is the five-factor model of personality—more typically called the "Big Five."[26] An impressive body of research supports the notion that five basic personality dimensions underlie all others and include most of the significant variations in human personality. The Big Five are:

- *Extroversion*. This dimension captures a person's comfort level with relationships. Extroverts (high in **extroversion**) tend to be gregarious, assertive, and sociable. Introverts tend to be reserved, timid, and quiet.

- *Agreeableness*. This dimension refers to how readily an individual will defer to others. Highly agreeable people are cooperative, warm, and trusting. People who score low on **agreeableness** are cold, disagreeable, and antagonistic.

- *Conscientiousness*. This dimension is a measure of reliability. A highly **conscientious** person is responsible, organized, dependable, and persistent. Those who score low on this dimension are easily distracted, disorganized, and unreliable.

personality traits
Enduring characteristics that describe an individual's behaviour.

extroversion
A personality dimension; someone who is high in extroversion is sociable, talkative, and assertive.

agreeableness
A personality dimension; highly agreeable people are good-natured, cooperative, and trusting.

conscientiousness
A personality dimension; a highly conscientious person is responsible, dependable, persistent, and achievement-oriented.

Exhibit 2–3

Sixteen Primary Personality Traits

1.	Reserved	vs.	Outgoing
2.	Less intelligent	vs.	More intelligent
3.	Affected by feelings	vs.	Emotionally stable
4.	Submissive	vs.	Dominant
5.	Serious	vs.	Happy-go-lucky
6.	Expedient	vs.	Conscientious
7.	Timid	vs.	Venturesome
8.	Tough-minded	vs.	Sensitive
9.	Trusting	vs.	Suspicious
10.	Practical	vs.	Imaginative
11.	Forthright	vs.	Shrewd
12.	Self-assured	vs.	Apprehensive
13.	Conservative	vs.	Experimenting
14.	Group-dependent	vs.	Self-sufficient
15.	Uncontrolled	vs.	Controlled
16.	Relaxed	vs.	Tense

Source: R.B. Catell, "Personality Pinned Down," *Psychology Today*, July 1973, pp. 40–46.

- *Emotional stability*. This dimension taps a person's ability to withstand stress. People with positive **emotional stability** tend to be characterized as calm, self-confident, and secure. Those with high negative scores tend to be nervous, anxious, depressed, and insecure.

- *Openness to experience*. The final dimension addresses our range of interests and fascination with novelty. Extremely open people are creative, curious, and artistic. Those at the other end of the **openness to experience** category are more conventional and find comfort in the familiar.

In addition to providing a unifying personality framework, research on the Big Five has found important relationships between these personality dimensions and job performance.[27] A broad spectrum of occupations was examined: professionals (including engineers, architects, accountants, and lawyers), as well as police officers, managers, salespeople, and semi-skilled and skilled employees. Job performance was defined in terms of performance ratings, training proficiency (performance during training programs), and information such as salary level.

emotional stability
A personality dimension that characterizes someone as calm, enthusiastic, and secure (positive), vs. tense, nervous, depressed, and insecure (negative).

openness to experience
A personality dimension that characterizes someone in terms of imaginativeness, artistic sensitivity, and intellectualism.

Exhibit 2–4

Source: *Peanuts* reprinted with permission of United Features Syndicate, Inc.

Exhibit 2–5

Research Results: How Big Five Personality Factors Affect Individual Job and Team Performance

Big Five Personality Factor	Relationship to Job Performance	Relationship to Team Performance
Extroversion	• Positively related to job performance in occupations requiring social interaction • Positively related to training proficiency for all occupations	• Positively related to team performance • Positively related to degree of participation within team
Agreeableness	• Positively related to job performance in service jobs	• Most studies found no link between agreeableness and performance or productivity in team • Some found a negative link between person's likeability and team performance
Conscientiousness	• Positively related to job performance for all occupational groups • May be better than ability in predicting job performance	
Emotional Stability	• A minimal threshold amount may be necessary for adequate performance; greater degrees not related to job performance • Positively related to performance in service jobs • May be better than ability in predicting job performance across all occupational groups	
Openness to Experience	• Positively related to training proficiency	

Source: Adapted from S.L. Kichuk and W.H. Wiesner, "Work Teams: Selecting Members for Optimal Performance," *Canadian Psychology*, 39(1–2), 1999, pp. 24–26.

All of the Big Five factors have been found to have at least some relationship to performance in some situations.[28] Exhibit 2–5 summarizes the main research findings on the relationship of the Big Five personality factors to both individual job performance and team performance.[29] Research finds a strong relationship between some of the Big Five factors and motivation. Lower emotional stability is associated with lower motivation, while conscientiousness appears to be positively related to motivation.[30] Finally, evidence finds a relatively strong and consistent relationship between conscientiousness and organizational citizenship behaviour (OCB).[31] This, however, seems to be the only personality dimension that predicts organizational citizenship behaviour.

Major Personality Attributes Influencing OB

In this section, we will evaluate specific personality attributes that have been found to be powerful predictors of behaviour in organizations. The first is related to locus of control—how much power over your destiny you think you have. The others are machiavellianism, self-esteem, self-monitoring, propensity for risk-taking, and Type A personality. If you want to know more about your own personal characteristics, this chapter's

Learning About Yourself Exercises on pages 55–62 present you with a variety of personality measures to explore. This chapter's *CBC Video Case Incident*, "NovaScotian Crystal," gives you the opportunity to see how personality affects decision making.

CBC ◉
"NovaScotian Crystal"

Locus of Control

Some people believe that they are in control of their own destiny. Other people see themselves as pawns of fate, believing that what happens to them in their lives is due to luck or chance. The first type, those who believe that they control their destinies, have been labelled **internals**, whereas the latter, who see their lives as being controlled by outside forces, have been called **externals**.[32] A person's perception of the source of his or her fate is termed **locus of control**.

A large amount of research has compared internals with externals. Internals report greater well-being, and this finding appears to be universal.[33] Research has consistently shown that individuals who rate high in externality are less satisfied with their jobs, have higher absenteeism rates, are more alienated from the work setting, and are less involved in their jobs than are internals.[34]

Why are externals more dissatisfied? The answer is probably because they perceive themselves as having little control over those organizational outcomes that are important to them. Internals, facing the same situation, attribute organizational outcomes to their own actions. If the situation is unattractive, they believe that they have no one else to blame but themselves. Also, the dissatisfied internal is more likely to quit a dissatisfying job.

The impact of locus of control on absenteeism is an interesting one. Internals believe that health is substantially under their own control through proper habits, so they take more responsibility for their health and have better health habits. Consequently, their incidences of sickness and, hence, of absenteeism, are lower.[35]

We should not expect any clear relationship between locus of control and turnover, because there are opposing forces at work. One researcher has observed: "On the one hand, internals tend to take action and thus might be expected to quit jobs more readily. On the other hand, they tend to be more successful on the job and more satisfied, factors associated with less individual turnover."[36]

The overall evidence indicates that internals generally perform better at their jobs, but that conclusion should be moderated to reflect differences in jobs. Internals search more actively for information before making a decision, are more motivated to achieve, and make a greater attempt to control their environment. Externals, however, are more compliant and willing to follow directions. Therefore, internals do well on sophisticated tasks—including most managerial and professional jobs—that require complex information processing and learning. In addition, internals are more suited to jobs that require initiative and independence of action. In contrast, externals should do well on jobs that are well structured and routine, and in which success depends heavily on complying with the direction of others. If you are interested in determining your locus of control, you might want to complete *Learning About Yourself Exercise #1* on page 55.

Machiavellianism

The personality characteristic of **machiavellianism** (Mach) is named after Niccolò Machiavelli, who wrote in the 16th century on how to gain and use power. An individual high in machiavellianism is highly practical, maintains emotional distance, and believes that ends can justify means. "If it works, use it" is consistent with a high-Mach perspective.

A considerable amount of research has been directed toward relating high- and low-Mach personalities to certain behavioural outcomes.[37] High Machs manipulate more, win more, are persuaded less, and persuade others more than do low Machs.[38] Yet these high-Mach outcomes are moderated by situational factors. It has been found that high

internals
Individuals who believe that they control what happens to them.

externals
Individuals who believe that what happens to them is controlled by outside forces, such as luck or chance.

locus of control
The degree to which people believe they are in control of their own fate.

machiavellianism
Degree to which an individual is practical, maintains emotional distance, and believes that ends can justify means.

Niccolò Machiavelli
www.encyclopedia.com/html/
M/Machiave.asp

Machs flourish (1) when they interact face to face with others rather than indirectly; (2) when the situation has a minimum number of rules and regulations, thus allowing latitude for improvisation; and (3) when emotional involvement with details irrelevant to winning distracts low Machs.[39]

Should we conclude that high Machs make good employees? That answer depends on the type of job and whether you consider ethical implications in evaluating performance. In jobs that require bargaining skills (such as labour negotiation) or that offer substantial rewards for winning (as in commissioned sales), high Machs will be productive. But if the ends can't justify the means, if there are absolute standards of behaviour, or if the three situational factors noted in the preceding paragraph are not in evidence, our ability to predict a high Mach's performance will be severely curtailed. If you are interested in determining your level of machiavellianism, you might want to complete *Learning About Yourself Exercise #2* on page 56.

Self-Esteem

self-esteem

Individuals' degree of liking or disliking of themselves.

People differ in the degree to which they like or dislike themselves. This trait is called **self-esteem**.[40] The research on self-esteem (SE) offers interesting insights into organizational behaviour. For example, self-esteem is directly related to expectations for success. High SEs believe that they have the ability to succeed at work. Individuals with high self-esteem will take more risks in job selection and are more likely to choose unconventional jobs than are people with low self-esteem.

The most generalizable finding on self-esteem is that low SEs are more easily influenced by external factors than are high SEs. Low SEs are dependent on the receipt of positive evaluations from others. As a result, they are more likely than high SEs to seek approval from others and more prone to conform to the beliefs and behaviours of those they respect. In managerial positions, low SEs tend to be concerned with pleasing others and, therefore, are less likely to take unpopular stands than are high SEs.

Not surprisingly, self-esteem has also been found to be related to job satisfaction. A number of studies confirm that high SEs are more satisfied with their jobs than are low SEs. If you are interested in determining your self-esteem score, you might want to complete *Learning About Yourself Exercise #3* on page 57.

Self-Monitoring

self-monitoring

A personality trait that measures an individual's ability to adjust his or her behaviour to external situational factors.

A personality trait that has recently received increased attention in the organizational literature is called **self-monitoring**.[41] It refers to an individual's ability to adjust his or her behaviour to external situational factors.

Individuals high in self-monitoring show considerable ability to adjust their behaviour to external situational factors. They are highly sensitive to external cues and can behave differently in different situations. High self-monitors are capable of presenting striking contradictions between their public and their private selves. Low self-monitors can't disguise themselves in the same way. They tend to display their true dispositions and attitudes in every situation; hence, there is high behavioural consistency between who they are and what they do.

The research on self-monitoring is in its infancy, so predictions must be guarded. However, initial evidence suggests that high self-monitors tend to pay closer attention to the behaviour of others and are more capable of conforming than are low self-monitors.[42] In addition, high self-monitoring managers tend to be more mobile in their careers and receive more promotions (both internal and cross-organizational).[43] We might also hypothesize that high self-monitors will be more successful in managerial positions in which individuals are required to play multiple, and even contradicting, roles. The high self-monitor is capable of putting on different "faces" for different audiences. To determine whether you are a high or low self-monitor, you might want to complete *Learning About Yourself Exercise #4* on page 58.

Risk-Taking

People differ in their willingness to take chances. Matthew Barrett, the former CEO and chair of Bank of Montreal, and Frank Stronach, the subject of this chapter's *Case Incident*, are good examples of high risk-takers. The tendency to assume or avoid risk has been shown to have an impact on how long it takes managers to make a decision and how much information they require before making their choice. For instance, 79 managers worked on simulated exercises that required them to make hiring decisions.[44] High **risk-taking** managers made more rapid decisions and used less information in making their choices than did the low risk-taking managers. Interestingly, the decision accuracy was the same for both groups.

While it is generally correct to conclude that managers in organizations are risk-aversive,[45] there are still individual differences on this dimension.[46] As a result, it makes sense to recognize these differences and even to consider matching risk-taking tendencies with specific job demands. For instance, high risk-taking might lead to higher performance for a stock trader in a brokerage firm because that type of job demands rapid decision making. On the other hand, a willingness to take risks would not be suitable for an accountant who performs auditing activities. If you are interested in determining where you stand on risk-taking, you might want to complete *Learning About Yourself Exercise #5* on pages 59–60.

Richard Branson's tendency to take risks aligns with his job demands as an entrepreneur. Branson, founder and chairman of London-based Virgin Group, starts risky ventures that compete against industry giants. His Virgin Atlantic airline, for example, has taken market share from British Airways and has earned a reputation as one of the financially healthiest airlines in the world. Branson's risk-taking personality extends to his leisure activities of speedboat racing, skydiving, and ballooning.

Type A and Type B Personalities

Do you know any people who are excessively competitive and always seem to be pushed for time? If you do, it's a good bet that those people have a Type A personality. An individual with a **Type A personality** is "aggressively involved in a chronic, incessant struggle to achieve more and more in less and less time, and, if required to do so, against the opposing efforts of other things or other persons."[47] In the North American culture, such characteristics tend to be highly prized and positively associated with ambition and the successful acquisition of material goods.

Type As

- are always moving, walking, and eating rapidly;

- feel impatient with the rate at which most events take place;

- strive to think or do two or more things at once;

- cannot cope with leisure time;

- are obsessed with numbers, measuring their success in terms of how many or how much of everything they acquire.

In contrast to the Type A personality is the Type B, who is exactly the opposite. Type Bs are "rarely harried by the desire to obtain a wildly increasing number of things or participate in an endless growing series of events in an ever-decreasing amount of time."[48]

Type Bs

- never suffer from a sense of time urgency with its accompanying impatience;

- feel no need to display or discuss either their achievements or accomplishments unless such exposure is demanded by the situation;

risk-taking
Refers to a person's willingness to take chances or risks.

Type A personality
A personality with aggressive involvement in a chronic, non-stop struggle to achieve more and more in less and less time and, if necessary, against the opposing efforts of other things or other people.

- play for fun and relaxation, rather than to exhibit their superiority at any cost;

- can relax without guilt.

Type As are often impatient, hurried, competitive, and hostile, but these traits tend to emerge most often when a Type A individual experiences stress or challenge.[49] Type As are fast workers because they emphasize quantity over quality. In managerial positions, Type As demonstrate their competitiveness by working long hours and, not infrequently, making poor decisions because they make them too fast. Stressed Type As are also rarely creative. Because of their concern with quantity and speed, they rely on past experiences when faced with problems. They will not allocate the time that is necessary to develop unique solutions to new problems. They seldom vary in their responses to specific challenges in their environment, and so their behaviour is easier to predict than that of Type Bs.

Are Type As or Type Bs more successful in organizations? Despite the hard work of Type As, Type Bs are the ones who appear to make it to the top. Great salespeople are usually Type As; senior executives are usually Type Bs. Why? The answer lies in the tendency of Type As to trade off quality of effort for quantity. Promotions in corporate and professional organizations "usually go to those who are wise rather than to those who are merely hasty, to those who are tactful rather than to those who are hostile, and to those who are creative rather than to those who are merely agile in competitive strife."[50]

Recent research has looked at the effect of job complexity on the cardiovascular health of both Type A and Type B individuals to see whether Type As always suffered negative health consequences.[51] Type B individuals did not suffer negative health consequences from jobs with psychological complexity. Type A workers who faced high job complexity had higher death rates from heart-related disorders than Type As who faced lower job complexity. These findings suggest that, health-wise, Type B workers suffer less when handling more complex jobs than do Type As. It also suggests that Type As who face lower job complexity do not encounter the same health risks as Type As who face higher job complexity.

If you are interested in determining whether you have a Type A or Type B personality, you might want to complete *Learning About Yourself Exercise #6* on page 61.

Personality and National Culture

There are certainly no common personality types for a given country. You can, for instance, find high and low risk-takers in almost any culture. Yet a country's culture should influence the dominant personality characteristics of its population. Let's build this case by looking at one personality attribute—locus of control.

There is evidence that cultures differ in terms of people's relationship to their environment.[52] In some cultures, such as those in North America, people believe that they can dominate their environment. People in other societies, such as Middle Eastern countries, believe that life is essentially preordained. Notice the close parallel to internal and external locus of control. We should expect a larger proportion of internals in the Canadian and American workforces than in the Saudi Arabian or Iranian workforces.

One caveat regarding personality tests is that they may be subject to cultural bias when used on samples of people other than those for whom the tests were designed. For instance, on common American personality tests, British people are characterized as "less dominant, achievement-orientated or flexible than Americans, but more self-controlled."[53] An example of a bias that can appear in such tests is that only 10 percent of British men answer "true" to the statement "I very much like hunting," while 70 percent of American men agree.[54] When these tests are used to select managers, they may result in the selection of individuals who are not as suitable in the British workplace as they would be in the American workplace.

EMOTIONS

Given the obvious role that emotions play in our everyday life, it might surprise you to learn that, until very recently, the topic of emotions was given little or no attention within the field of OB. When emotions were considered, the discussion focused on strong negative emotions—especially anger—that interfered with an employee's ability to do his or her job effectively. Emotions were rarely viewed as being constructive or able to stimulate performance-enhancing behaviours.

Certainly some emotions, particularly when exhibited at the wrong time, can reduce employee performance. But this does not change the reality that employees bring an emotional component with them to work every day, and that no study of OB could be comprehensive without considering the role of emotions in workplace behaviour.

What Are Emotions?

Emotions are intense feelings that are directed at someone or something.[55] Emotions are different from **moods**, which are feelings that tend to be less intense than emotions and that lack a contextual stimulus.[56]

Emotions are reactions to an object, not a trait. They are object-specific. You show your emotions when you are "happy about something, angry at someone, afraid of something."[57] Moods, on the other hand, are not directed at an object. Emotions can turn into moods when you lose focus on the contextual object. So when a colleague criticizes you for the way you spoke to a client, you might become angry at him. That is, you show emotion (anger) toward a specific object (your colleague). But later in the day, you might find yourself just generally dispirited. You cannot attribute this feeling to any single event; you are just not your normal, upbeat self. This **affect** state describes a mood.

Research has identified six universal emotions: anger, fear, sadness, happiness, disgust, and surprise.[58] One factor that has strongly shaped what is and isn't listed in this basic set is the manner in which the emotions were identified. Researchers tended to look for universally identified facial expressions and then convert them into categories (see the facial expressions in *From Concepts to Skills* on page 66). Emotions that could not be identified readily by others through facial expressions, or that were considered a subset of one of the basic six, were not selected.

Exhibit 2–6 illustrates that the six emotions can be conceptualized as existing along a continuum.[59] The closer any two emotions are to each other on this continuum, the more people are likely to confuse them. For instance, happiness and surprise are frequently mistaken for each other, while happiness and disgust are rarely confused. Be aware that cultural factors can also influence interpretations of facial expressions.

Choosing Emotions: Emotional Labour

Sometimes individuals are required to manage their emotions. For instance, you may be very angry with a co-worker or manager, but you may choose to suppress that anger in the interest of keeping the peace and/or your job. You may also decide not to kiss a co-worker in a moment of overwhelming exuberance, to make sure that your intentions are not misinterpreted.

Emotional labour refers to the requirement to express particular emotions at work (for instance, enthusiasm or loyalty) to maximize organizational productivity.[60] All employees expend physical and mental labour when they do their jobs. But most jobs also require emotional labour. This term was first coined by Professor Arlie Hochschild of the University of California at Berkeley and refers to the demand organizations make on their employees to display "appropriate" emotions during interpersonal transactions.[61]

The concept of emotional labour originally developed in relation to service jobs. Flight attendants, for instance, are expected to be cheerful, funeral counsellors sad, and

---

6 Can emotions help or get in the way when we're dealing with others?

emotions
Intense feelings that are directed at someone or something.

moods
Feelings that tend to be less intense than emotions and that lack a contextual stimulus.

affect
A broad range of feelings that people experience.

emotional labour
When an employee expresses organizationally desired emotions during interpersonal interactions.

University of California, Berkeley
www.berkeley.edu

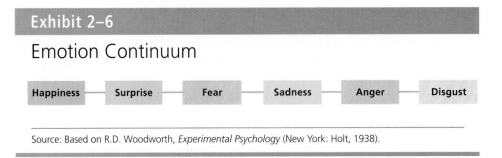

Exhibit 2–6

Emotion Continuum

| Happiness | — | Surprise | — | Fear | — | Sadness | — | Anger | — | Disgust |

Source: Based on R.D. Woodworth, *Experimental Psychology* (New York: Holt, 1938).

doctors emotionally neutral. Studies of emotional labour have explored how smiling flight attendants, cheerful grocery clerks, gossipy hairdressers, and nasty bill collectors are expected to control their emotional expression to improve productivity, customer satisfaction, efficiency, and even profitability.[62] But today, the concept of emotional labour seems relevant to almost every job. You are expected, for example, to be courteous and not hostile in interactions with co-workers. And leaders are expected to draw on emotional labour to "charge the troops." Almost every great speech, for instance, contains a strong emotional component that stirs feelings in others.

As these studies show, however, managing emotions can take a toll when there is a discrepancy between the outward behaviour the person is required to display as part of his or her job and the inward feelings that the person has.[63] Therefore, while emotional labour can have positive implications within the workplace, it can also have negative personal consequences when a person consistently hides real emotions behind a work "face."[64] Flight attendants use the phrase "go robot" to describe how they separate their private feelings from their public behaviour.[65] Other researchers have discussed both the individual effects of emotional labour, such as distancing, burnout, and phoniness,[66] and the organizational effects, such as suppressed disagreements, reduced upward information flow, and loss of "voice."[67] A Vancouver Safeway employee described her company's requirement to smile at all shoppers: "My personal opinion is, they're expecting us not to be human. I just can't walk around with a smile on my face all day."[68]

Canada Safeway Limited
www.safeway.com

Emotional labour creates dilemmas for employees when their job requires them to exhibit emotions that are inconsistent with their actual feelings. Not surprisingly, this is a frequent occurrence. There are people you have to work with to whom you find it very difficult to be friendly. Maybe you consider their personality abrasive. Maybe you know they have said negative things about you behind your back. Regardless, your job requires you to interact with these people on a regular basis. So you are forced to pretend to be friendly.

Why Should We Care About Emotions in the Workplace?

There are a number of reasons to be concerned about understanding emotions in the workplace.[69] People who know their own emotions and are good at reading others' emotions may be more effective in their jobs. That, in essence, is the theme underlying recent research on *emotional intelligence* (EI).[70] Maria Gonzalez, vice-president of strategic initiatives and corporate planning at Bank of Montreal, believes EI is so important that she suggests, "MBA schools will become obsolete if they don't imbed elements of EI in their programs, as that's what makes people successful in the workplace."[71]

Emotional Intelligence

emotional intelligence
An assortment of noncognitive skills, capabilities, and competencies that influence a person's ability to succeed in coping with environmental demands and pressures.

Emotional intelligence refers to an assortment of noncognitive skills, capabilities, and competencies that influence a person's ability to succeed in coping with environmental demands and pressures. It's composed of five dimensions:

- *Self-awareness*. Being aware of what you are feeling. It is exhibited by self-confidence, realistic self-assessment, and a self-deprecating sense of humour.

- *Self-management*. The ability to manage your own emotions and impulses. It is exhibited by trustworthiness and integrity, comfort with ambiguity, and openness to change.

- *Self-motivation*. The ability to persist in the face of setbacks and failures. It is exhibited by a strong drive to achieve, optimism, and high organizational commitment.

- *Empathy*. The ability to sense how others are feeling. It is exhibited by expertise in building and retaining talent, cross-cultural sensitivity, and service to clients and customers.

- *Social skills*. The ability to handle the emotions of others. It is exhibited by persuasiveness, and expertise in building and leading groups and teams.

Emotional labour is an important component of effective job performance at the Happy Beauty Salon in Long Island, New York. Owner Happy Nomikos, shown here serving customers strawberries and grapes, requires that her nail technicians and hairstylists build customer loyalty by being courteous and cheerful. In interacting with her employees and customers, Nomikos says, "I have to keep everyone happy." She hugs loyal customers, jokes with her staff, and offers customers pizza and cake in celebration of employees' birthdays.

Several studies suggest EI may play an important role in job performance.[72] For instance, one study looked at the characteristics of Bell Lab engineers who were rated as stars by their peers. The scientists concluded that stars were better at relating to others. That is, it was EI, not academic IQ, that characterized high performers. A second study of US Air Force recruiters generated similar findings. Top-performing recruiters exhibited high levels of EI. Using these findings, the US Air Force revamped its selection criteria. A follow-up investigation found that hires who had high EI scores were 2.6 times more successful than those who did not. A recent poll of human resource managers asked: How important is it for your workers to demonstrate EI to move up the corporate ladder? Forty percent replied "Very Important." Another 16 percent said "Moderately Important."

The implications from the initial evidence on EI is that employers should consider it as a factor in selection, especially in jobs that demand a high degree of social interaction. Tony Comper, the CEO of Bank of Montreal, certainly agrees with the importance of understanding emotional intelligence. He cites Daniel Goleman's *Working With Emotional Intelligence* [73] as one of his three favourite recent books on leadership.[74] This chapter's *From Concepts to Skills* gives you some insight into reading the emotions of others. To find out about your own EI, complete *Learning About Yourself Exercise* #7 on pages 61–62.

US Air Force
www.af.mil

BMO Financial Group
www.bmo.com

Negative Workplace Emotions

Negative emotions can lead to a number of deviant workplace behaviours. Anyone who has spent much time in an organization realizes that people often engage in voluntary actions that violate established norms and threaten the organization, its members, or both. These actions are called **employee deviance**.[75] They fall into categories such as production (e.g., leaving early, intentionally working slowly); property (e.g., stealing, sabotage); political (e.g., gossiping, blaming co-workers); and personal aggression (e.g., sexual harassment, verbal abuse).[76]

Many of these deviant behaviours can be traced to negative emotions. For instance, envy is an emotion that occurs when you resent someone for having something that

employee deviance
Voluntary actions that violate established norms and that threaten the organization, its members, or both.

you don't have but strongly desire.[77] It can lead to malicious deviant behaviours. Envy, for example, has been found to be associated with hostility, "backstabbing," and other forms of political behaviour, as well as with negatively distorting others' successes and positively distorting one's own accomplishments.[78]

SUMMARY AND IMPLICATIONS

1 **What is perception?** Perception is the process by which individuals select, organize, interpret and give meaning to the environment. Individuals often behave based not on the way their external environment actually is but, rather, on what they see or believe it to be. It is a person's perception of a situation that becomes the basis for his or her behaviour.

2 **What causes people to have different perceptions of the same situation?** A number of factors operate to shape and sometimes distort perception. These factors can be present in the *perceiver*, in the object or *target* being perceived, or in the context of the *situation* in which the perception is made. For the perceiver, attitudes and motives, interests, and past experiences all shape the way the person perceives an event. A target's characteristics can affect what is perceived. Motion, sound, size, and other attributes of a target shape the way we see it. Because of nearness in space or time, we often put together objects or events that are unrelated. For instance, employees in a particular department are seen as a group. The context in which we see objects or events also affects how they are perceived.

3 **Can people be mistaken in their perceptions?** Perceiving and interpreting what others do is difficult. As a result, we develop shortcuts to make this task more manageable. These shortcuts are often valuable—they allow us to make accurate perceptions quickly and provide valid data for making predictions. However, they are not foolproof. They can and do get us into trouble.

4 **Does perception really affect outcomes?** The evidence suggests that what individuals perceive about their work situation influences their productivity more than the situation does. Whether a job is actually interesting or challenging is irrelevant. Whether a manager actually helps employees to structure their work more efficiently and effectively is far less important than how employees perceive the manager's efforts. Similarly, issues such as fair pay, the validity of performance appraisals, and the adequacy of working conditions are not judged "objectively." Rather, individuals interpret conditions surrounding their jobs based on how they *perceive* their jobs.

5 **What is personality and how does it affect behaviour?** Personality is the stable patterns of behaviour and consistent internal states that determine how an individual reacts to and interacts with others. Personality characteristics give us a framework for predicting behaviour. Personality affects how people react to others, and the types of jobs that they may desire. For example, individuals who are shy, introverted, and uncomfortable in social situations would probably make poor salespeople. Individuals who are submissive and conforming might not be effective as advertising "idea" people.

6 **Can emotions help or get in the way when we're dealing with others?** Emotions are a natural part of an individual's makeup. Positive emotions can be motivating for everyone in the workplace. Negative emotions may make it difficult to get along with others.

OB AT WORK

For Review

1. Define perception.

2. What is attribution theory? What are its implications for explaining organizational behaviour?

3. How are our perceptions of our own actions different from our perceptions of the actions of others?

4. What is stereotyping? Give an example of how stereotyping can create perceptual distortion.

5. Give some positive results of using shortcuts when judging others.

6. What behavioural predictions might you make if you knew that an employee had a) an external locus of control? b) a low-Mach score? c) low self-esteem? d) a Type A personality?

7. What are the personality dimensions of the Big Five model?

8. What is emotional labour and why is it important to understanding OB?

9. What is emotional intelligence and why is it important?

For Critical Thinking

1. How might the differences in experience of students and instructors affect their perceptions of students' written work and class comments?

2. An employee does an unsatisfactory job on an assigned project. Explain the attribution process that this person's manager will use to form judgments about this employee's job performance.

3. One day your boss comes in and he is nervous, edgy, and argumentative. The next day he is calm and relaxed. Does this behaviour suggest that personality traits are not consistent from day to day?

4. What, if anything, can managers do to manage emotions?

5. Give some examples of situations where expressing emotions openly might improve job performance.

OB for You

- The discussion of perception might get you thinking about how you view the world. When we perceive someone as a troublemaker, for instance, this may be only a perception, and not a real characteristic of the other person. It is always good to question your perceptions, just to be sure that you are not reading something into a situation that is not there.

- One important thing to consider when looking for a job is whether your personality will fit the organization to which you are applying. For instance, it may be a highly structured organization. If you, by nature, are much less formal, this may not be a good fit for you.

- When working in groups, you may have sometimes noticed that personalities get in the way. You may want to see if you can figure out ways to get personality differences working in favour of group goals.

- Emotions need not always be suppressed when working with others. While emotions can sometimes hinder performance, positive emotions can motivate you and those around you.

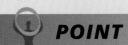

POINT

COUNTERPOINT

Traits Are Powerful Predictors of Behaviour

The essence of trait approaches in OB is that employees possess stable personality characteristics that significantly influence their attitudes toward, and behavioural reactions to, organizational settings. People with particular traits tend to be relatively consistent in their attitudes and behaviour over time and across situations.[79]

Of course, trait theorists recognize that all traits are not equally powerful. They tend to put traits into one of three categories. *Cardinal traits* are those so strong and generalized that they influence every act a person performs. *Primary traits* are generally consistent influences on behaviour, but they may not show up in all situations. Finally, *secondary traits* are attributes that do not form a vital part of the personality, but come into play only in particular situations. For the most part, trait theories have focused on the power of primary traits to predict employee behaviour.

Trait theorists do a fairly good job of meeting the average person's common-sense beliefs. Think of friends, relatives, and acquaintances you have known for a number of years. Do they have traits that have remained essentially stable over time? Most of us would answer that question in the affirmative. If cousin Anne was shy and nervous when we last saw her 10 years ago, we would be surprised to find her outgoing and relaxed now.

Managers seem to have a strong belief in the power of traits to predict behaviour. If managers believed that situations determined behaviour, they would hire people almost at random and put great effort into structuring situations properly. But the employee selection process in most organizations places a great deal of emphasis on how applicants perform in interviews and on tests. Assume you're interviewing job candidates and ask yourself: What kind of person am I looking for? If you answer with terms such as *conscientious, hard-working, persistent, confident,* and *dependable,* you are a trait theorist!

Traits Reflect the Surrounding Situation

Few people would dispute that there are some stable individual attributes that affect reactions to the workplace. But trait theorists go beyond that generality and argue that individual behaviour consistencies are widespread and account for much of the difference in behaviour among people.[80]

There are two important problems with using traits to explain a large proportion of behaviour in organizations. First, organizational settings are strong situations that have a large impact on employee behaviour. Second, individuals are highly adaptive and personality traits change in response to organizational situations.

It has been well known for some time that the effects of traits are likely to be strongest in relatively weak situations, and weakest in relatively strong situations. Organizational settings tend to be strong situations because they have rules and other formal regulations that define acceptable behaviour and punish deviant behaviour; and they have informal norms that dictate appropriate behaviours. These formal and informal constraints minimize the effects of personality traits.

By arguing that employees possess stable traits that lead to cross-situational consistencies in behaviours, trait theorists are implying that individuals don't really adapt to different situations. But there is a growing body of evidence that an individual's traits are changed by the organizations in which an individual participates. If the individual's personality changes as a result of exposure to organizational settings, in what sense can that individual be said to have traits that persistently and consistently affect his or her reactions to those very settings? Moreover, people typically belong to multiple organizations, which often include very different kinds of members. They adapt to those different situations. Instead of being the prisoners of a rigid and stable personality framework, as trait theorists propose, people regularly adjust their behaviour to reflect the requirements of various situations.

LEARNING ABOUT **YOURSELF** EXERCISE #1

Assess Your Locus of Control

Instructions: Read the following statements and indicate whether you agree more with choice A or choice B.

A

1. Making a lot of money is largely a matter of getting the right breaks.

2. I have noticed that there is a direct connection between how hard I study and the grades I get.

3. The number of divorces indicates that more and more people are not trying to make their marriages work.

4. It is silly to think that you can really change another person's basic attitudes.

5. Getting promoted is really a matter of being a little luckier than the next person.

6. If you know how to deal with people, they are really quite easily led.

7. The grades I make are the result of my own efforts; luck has little or nothing to do with it.

8. People like me can change the course of world affairs if we make ourselves heard.

9. A great deal that happens to me is probably a matter of chance.

10. Getting along with people is a skill that must be practised.

B

1. Promotions are earned through hard work and persistence.

2. Many times, the reactions of teachers seem haphazard to me.

3. Marriage is largely a gamble.

4. When I am right, I can convince others.

5. In our society, a person's future earning power depends on his or her ability.

6. I have little influence over the way other people behave.

7. Sometimes I feel that I have little to do with the grades I get.

8. It is only wishful thinking to believe that one can readily influence what happens in our society.

9. I am in control of my destiny.

10. It is almost impossible to figure out how to please some people.

Scoring Key

Give yourself 1 point for each of the following selections: 1B, 2A, 3A, 4B, 5B, 6A, 7A, 8A, 9B, and 10A.

Scores can be interpreted as follows:

8–10	=	High internal locus of control
6–7	=	Moderate internal locus of control
5	=	Mixed
3–4	=	Moderate external locus of control
1–2	=	High external locus of control

Source: Adapted from J.B. Rotter, "External Control and Internal Control," *Psychology Today*, June 1971, p. 42. Copyright 1971 by the American Psychological Association. Adapted with permission.

LEARNING ABOUT **YOURSELF** EXERCISE #2

How Machiavellian Are You?

Instructions: For each statement, circle the number that most closely resembles your attitude.

Statement	Disagree			Agree	
	A Lot	A Little	Neutral	A Little	A Lot
1. The best way to handle people is to tell them what they want to hear.	1	2	3	4	5
2. When you ask someone to do something for you, it is best to give the real reason for wanting it rather than giving reasons that might carry more weight.	1	2	3	4	5
3. Anyone who completely trusts anyone else is asking for trouble.	1	2	3	4	5
4. It is hard to get ahead without cutting corners here and there.	1	2	3	4	5
5. It is safest to assume that all people have a vicious streak, and it will come out when they are given a chance.	1	2	3	4	5
6. One should take action only when it is morally right.	1	2	3	4	5
7. Most people are basically good and kind.	1	2	3	4	5
8. There is no excuse for lying to someone else.	1	2	3	4	5
9. Most people more easily forget the death of their father than the loss of their property.	1	2	3	4	5
10. Generally speaking, people won't work hard unless they're forced to do so.	1	2	3	4	5

Scoring Key

To obtain your Mach score, add the number you have checked on questions 1, 3, 4, 5, 9, and 10. For the other 4 questions, reverse the numbers you have checked: 5 becomes 1, 4 is 2, 2 is 4, and 1 is 5. Total your 10 numbers to find your score. The higher your score, the more machiavellian you are. Among a random sample of American adults, the national average was 25.

Source: R. Christie and F.L. Geis, *Studies in Machiavellianism* (New York: Academic Press, 1970). Reprinted by permission.

LEARNING ABOUT **YOURSELF** EXERCISE #3

How's Your Self-Esteem?

Instructions: Answer each of the following questions honestly. Next to each question write a 1, 2, 3, 4, or 5 depending on which answer best describes you.

1	=	Very often
2	=	Fairly often
3	=	Sometimes
4	=	Once in a great while
5	=	Practically never

_____ **1.** How often do you have the feeling that there is nothing that you can do well?

_____ **2.** When you talk in front of a class or group of people your own age, how often do you feel worried or afraid?

_____ **3.** How often do you feel that you have handled yourself well at social gatherings?

_____ **4.** How often do you have the feeling that you can do everything well?

_____ **5.** How often are you comfortable when starting a conversation with people you don't know?

_____ **6.** How often do you feel self-conscious?

_____ **7.** How often do you feel that you are a successful person?

_____ **8.** How often are you troubled with shyness?

_____ **9.** How often do you feel inferior to most people you know?

_____ **10.** How often do you feel that you are a worthless individual?

_____ **11.** How often do you feel confident that your success in your future job or career is assured?

_____ **12.** How often do you feel sure of yourself when among strangers?

_____ **13.** How often do you feel confident that some day people will look up to you and respect you?

_____ **14.** In general, how often do you feel confident about your abilities?

_____ **15.** How often do you worry about how well you get along with other people?

_____ **16.** How often do you feel that you dislike yourself?

_____ **17.** How often do you feel so discouraged with yourself that you wonder whether anything is worthwhile?

_____ **18.** How often do you worry about whether other people like to be with you?

_____ **19.** When you talk in front of a class or a group of people of your own age, how often are you pleased with your performance?

_____ **20.** How often do you feel sure of yourself when you speak in a class discussion?

Scoring Key

Add up your score for the following 10 items: 1, 2, 6, 8, 9, 10, 15, 16, 17, and 18. For the other 10 items, reverse your scoring (that is, a 5 becomes a 1; a 4 becomes a 2, etc.). The higher your score, the higher your self-esteem.

Source: Developed by A.H. Eagly and adapted from J.R. Robinson and P.R. Shaver, *Measures of Social Psychological Attitudes* (Ann Arbor, MI: Institute of Social Research, 1973), pp. 79–80. With permission.

LEARNING ABOUT **YOURSELF** EXERCISE #4

Are You a High Self-Monitor?

Instructions: Indicate the degree to which you think the following statements are true or false by circling the appropriate number. For example, if a statement is always true, circle the 5 next to that statement.

0 = Certainly, always false
1 = Generally false
2 = Somewhat false, but with exceptions
3 = Somewhat true, but with exceptions
4 = Generally true
5 = Certainly, always true

1. In social situations, I have the ability to alter my behaviour if I feel that something else is called for.　　0　1　2　3　4　5

2. I am often able to read people's true emotions correctly through their eyes.　　0　1　2　3　4　5

3. I have the ability to control the way I come across to people, depending on the impression I wish to give them.　　0　1　2　3　4　5

4. In conversations, I am sensitive to even the slightest change in the facial expression of the person I'm conversing with.　　0　1　2　3　4　5

5. My powers of intuition are quite good when it comes to understanding others' emotions and motives.　　0　1　2　3　4　5

6. I can usually tell when others consider a joke in bad taste, even though they may laugh convincingly.　　0　1　2　3　4　5

7. When I feel that the image I am portraying isn't working, I can readily change it to something that does.　　0　1　2　3　4　5

8. I can usually tell when I've said something inappropriate by reading the listener's eyes.　　0　1　2　3　4　5

9. I have trouble changing my behaviour to suit different people and different situations.　　0　1　2　3　4　5

10. I have found that I can adjust my behaviour to meet the requirements of any situation I find myself in.　　0　1　2　3　4　5

11. If someone is lying to me, I usually know it at once from that person's manner of expression.　　0　1　2　3　4　5

12. Even when it might be to my advantage, I have difficulty putting up a good front.　　0　1　2　3　4　5

13. Once I know what the situation calls for, it's easy for me to regulate my actions accordingly.　　0　1　2　3　4　5

Scoring Key

To obtain your score, add up the numbers circled, except reverse scores for questions 9 and 12. On those, a circled 5 becomes a 0, 4 becomes 1, and so forth. High self-monitors are defined as those with scores of 53 or higher.

Are You a Risk-Taker?

Instructions: For each of the following situations, you will be asked to indicate the minimum odds of success you would demand before recommending that one alternative be chosen over another. Try to place yourself in the position of the adviser to the central person in each of the situations.

1. Mr. B, a 45-year-old accountant, has recently been informed by his physician that he has developed a severe heart ailment. The disease will be sufficiently serious to force Mr. B to change many of his strongest life habits—reducing his workload, drastically changing his diet, giving up favourite leisure-time pursuits. The physician suggests that a delicate medical operation could be attempted. If successful, the operation would completely relieve the heart condition. But its success cannot be assured, and, in fact, the operation might prove fatal.

   Imagine that you are advising Mr. B. Listed below are several probabilities or odds that the operation will prove successful. Check the lowest probability that you would consider acceptable for the operation to be performed.

   _____ Place a check mark here if you think that Mr. B should not have the operation, no matter what the probabilities.

   _____ The chances are 9 in 10 that the operation will be a success.

   _____ The chances are 7 in 10 that the operation will be a success.

   _____ The chances are 5 in 10 that the operation will be a success.

   _____ The chances are 3 in 10 that the operation will be a success.

   _____ The chances are 1 in 10 that the operation will be a success.

2. Mr. D is the captain of University X's varsity football team. University X is playing its traditional rival, University Y, in the final game of the season. The game is in its final seconds, and Mr. D's team, University X, is behind in the score. University X has time to make one more play. Mr. D, the captain, must decide on a strategy. Would it be best to try a play that would be almost certain to work and try to settle for a tie score? Or, on the other hand, should he try a more complicated and risky play that would bring victory if it succeeded or defeat if it failed? Imagine that you are advising Mr. D. Listed below are several probabilities or odds that the risky play will work. Check the lowest probability that you would consider acceptable for the risky play to be attempted.

   _____ Place a check mark here if you think that Mr. D should not attempt the risky play, no matter what the probabilities.

   _____ The chances are 9 in 10 that the risky play will work.

   _____ The chances are 7 in 10 that the risky play will work.

   _____ The chances are 5 in 10 that the risky play will work.

   _____ The chances are 3 in 10 that the risky play will work.

   _____ The chances are 1 in 10 that the risky play will work.

3. Ms. K is a successful businesswoman who has taken part in a number of civic activities of considerable value to the community. Ms. K has been approached by the leaders of her political party as a possible candidate in the next provincial election. Ms. K's party is a minority party in the constituency, though the party has won occasional elections in the past. Ms. K would like to hold political office, but to do so would involve a serious financial sacrifice, since the party does not have enough campaign funds. She would also have to endure the attacks of her political opponents in a hot campaign.

   Imagine that you are advising Ms. K. Listed below are several probabilities or odds of Ms. K's winning the election in her constituency. Check the lowest probability that you would consider acceptable to make it worthwhile for Ms. K to run for political office.

   _____ Place a check mark here if you think that Ms. K should not run for political office, whatever the probabilities.

   _____ The chances are 9 in 10 that Ms. K will win the election.

LEARNING ABOUT **YOURSELF** EXERCISE #5 (continued)

_____ The chances are 7 in 10 that Ms. K will win the election.

_____ The chances are 5 in 10 that Ms. K will win the election.

_____ The chances are 3 in 10 that Ms. K will win the election.

_____ The chances are 1 in 10 that Ms. K will win the election.

4. Ms. L, a 30-year-old research physicist, has been given a five-year appointment by a major university laboratory. As she considers the next five years, she realizes that she might work on a difficult long-term problem. If a solution to the problem could be found, it would resolve basic scientific issues in the field and bring high scientific honours. If no solution were found, however, Ms. L would have little to show for her five years in the laboratory, and it would be hard for her to get a good job afterward. On the other hand, she could, as most of her professional associates are doing, work on a series of short-term problems for which solutions would be easier to find. Those solutions, though, would be of lesser scientific importance.

Imagine that you are advising Ms. L. Listed below are several probabilities or odds that a solution will be found to the difficult long-term problem that Ms. L has in mind. Check the lowest probability that you would consider acceptable to make it worthwhile for Ms. L to work on the more difficult long-term problem.

_____ Place a check mark here if you think Ms. L should not choose the long-term, difficult problem, no matter what the probabilities.

_____ The chances are 9 in 10 that Ms. L will solve the long-term problem.

_____ The chances are 7 in 10 that Ms. L will solve the long-term problem.

_____ The chances are 5 in 10 that Ms. L will solve the long-term problem.

_____ The chances are 3 in 10 that Ms. L will solve the long-term problem.

_____ The chances are 1 in 10 that Ms. L will solve the long-term problem.

Scoring Key

These situations were based on a longer questionnaire. Your results are an indication of your general orientation toward risk rather than a precise measure. To calculate your risk-taking score, add up the chances you were willing to take and divide by 4. For any of the situations in which you would not take the risk, regardless of the probabilities, give yourself a 10. The lower your number, the more risk-taking you are.

Source: Adapted from N. Kogan and M.A. Wallach, *Risk Taking: A Study in Cognition and Personality* (New York: Holt, Rinehart and Winston, 1964), pp. 256–261.

Are You a Type A?

Instructions: Circle the number on the scale below that best characterizes your behaviour for each trait.

1. Casual about appointments	1	2	3	4	5	6	7	8	Never late
2. Not competitive	1	2	3	4	5	6	7	8	Very competitive
3. Never feel rushed	1	2	3	4	5	6	7	8	Always feel rushed
4. Take things one at a time	1	2	3	4	5	6	7	8	Try to do many things at once
5. Slow doing things	1	2	3	4	5	6	7	8	Fast (eating, walking, etc.)
6. Express feelings	1	2	3	4	5	6	7	8	"Sit on" feelings
7. Many interests	1	2	3	4	5	6	7	8	Few interests outside work

Scoring Key

Total your score on the 7 questions. Now multiply the total by 3. A total of 120 or more indicates that you are a hard-core Type A. Scores below 90 indicate that you are a hard-core Type B. The following gives you more specifics:

Points	Personality Type
120 or more	A1
106–119	A
100–105	A2
90–99	B1
Less than 90	B

Source: Adapted from R.W. Bortner, "Short Rating Scale as a Potential Measure of Pattern A Behavior," *Journal of Chronic Diseases*, June 1969, pp. 87–91. With permission.

What's Your EI at Work?

Evaluating the following 25 statements will allow you to rate your social skills and self-awareness, the components of emotional intelligence (EI). EI, the social equivalent of IQ, is complex, in no small part because it depends on some pretty slippery variables—including your innate compatibility, or lack thereof, with the people who happen to be your co-workers. But if you want to get a rough idea of how your EI stacks up, this quiz will help.

As honestly as you can, estimate how you rate in the eyes of peers, bosses, and subordinates on each of the following traits, on a scale of 1–4, with 4 representing strong agreement, and 1 representing strong disagreement.

_____ I usually stay composed, positive, and unflappable even in trying moments.

_____ I can think clearly and stay focused on the task at hand under pressure.

_____ I am able to admit my own mistakes.

LEARNING ABOUT **YOURSELF** EXERCISE #7 (continued)

_____ I usually or always meet commitments and keep promises.

_____ I hold myself accountable for meeting my goals.

_____ I'm organized and careful in my work.

_____ I regularly seek out fresh ideas from a wide variety of sources.

_____ I'm good at generating new ideas.

_____ I can smoothly handle multiple demands and changing priorities.

_____ I'm results-oriented, with a strong drive to meet my objectives.

_____ I like to set challenging goals and take calculated risks to reach them.

_____ I'm always trying to learn how to improve my performance, including asking advice from people younger than I am.

_____ I readily make sacrifices to meet an important organizational goal.

_____ The company's mission is something I understand and can identify with.

_____ The values of my team—or of our division or department, or the company—influence my decisions and clarify the choices I make.

_____ I actively seek out opportunities to further the overall goals of the organization and enlist others to help me.

_____ I pursue goals beyond what's required or expected of me in my current job.

_____ Obstacles and setbacks may delay me a little, but they don't stop me.

_____ Cutting through red tape and bending outdated rules are sometimes necessary.

_____ I seek fresh perspectives, even if that means trying something totally new.

_____ My impulses or distressing emotions don't often get the best of me at work.

_____ I can change tactics quickly when circumstances change.

_____ Pursuing new information is my best bet for cutting down on uncertainty and finding ways to do things better.

_____ I usually don't attribute setbacks to a personal flaw (mine or someone else's).

_____ I operate from an expectation of success rather than a fear of failure.

Scoring Key

A score below 70 indicates very low EI. EI is not unimprovable. Says Daniel Goleman, author of *Working With Emotional Intelligence*, "Emotional intelligence can be learned, and in fact we are each building it, in varying degrees, throughout life. It's sometimes called maturity. EQ is nothing more or less than a collection of tools that we can sharpen to help ensure our own survival."

Source: A. Fisher, "Success Secret: A High Emotional IQ," *Fortune*, October 26, 1998, p. 298. Reprinted with permission of Time Warner Inc.

BREAKOUT **GROUP** EXERCISES

Form small groups to discuss the following topics, as assigned by your instructor:

1. Think back to your perception of this course and your instructor on the first day of class. What factors might have affected your perceptions of what the rest of the term would be like?

2. Describe a situation where your perception turned out to be wrong. What perceptual errors did you make that might have caused this to happen?

3. Compare your scores on the *Learning About Yourself Exercises* at the end of the chapter. What conclusions could you draw about your group based on these scores?

WORKING WITH **OTHERS** EXERCISE

Evaluating Your Stereotypes

1. Your instructor will choose 4 volunteers willing to reveal an interesting true-life background fact about themselves. Examples of such background facts are:
   - I can perform various dances, such as polka, rumba, bossa nova, and waltz.
   - I am the youngest of four children, and I attended a Catholic high school.
   - Neither of my parents attended school beyond Grade 8.
   - My mother is a homemaker and my father is an author.

2. The instructor will put the 4 facts on the board without revealing to which person each belongs, and the 4 students will remain in the front of the room for the first part of the group discussion below.

3. Students in the class should silently decide which person belongs to which fact.

4. Students should break into groups of about 5 or 6 and try to reach consensus about which person belongs to which fact. Meanwhile, the 4 students can serve as observers to group discussions, listening in on rationales for how students decide to link the facts with the individuals.

5. After 15 minutes of group discussion, several groups will be asked to present their consensus to the class, with justifications.

6. The classroom discussion will focus on perceptions, assumptions, and stereotyping that led to the decisions made.

7. At the end of the discussion, the instructor will reveal which student belongs to each fact.

ETHICAL **DILEMMA** EXERCISE

Managing Emotions at Work

Our understanding of emotions at work has increased rapidly in the past decade. We are now at the point where we are capable (or close to it) of managing the emotions of employees. For instance, companies that want to create open and friendly workplaces are using the selection process to "select out" job applicants who aren't outgoing and enthusiastic, and are providing training to teach employees how to smile and appear cheerful. Some organizations are going further in trying to create "emotionally humanistic" work environments not only by shaping the emotions that employees evoke in their daily contacts with customers but also by selecting employee applicants with high emotional intelligence; controlling the emotional atmosphere of teams and work groups; and using similar emotion-management practices.

Groucho Marx once joked that "the secret of success in show business is honesty and sincerity. Once you learn how to fake that, you've got it made." In many service organizations today, Groucho's remark is being applied. For instance, telephone-sales staff in a number of insurance companies are trained to invoke positive feelings from customers—to make it easy for them to say "yes." Employees are taught to avoid words with negative connotations and replace them with upbeat and confidence-building words such as "certainly," "rest assured," "immediate," and "great." Moreover, employees are taught to convey these "scripts" in a way that seems natural and spontaneous. To ensure that these "authentic" positive feelings are consistently evoked, the phone calls of these salespeople are often monitored.

Organizations such as McDonald's, Disney, and Starbucks select and program employees to be upbeat and friendly. They allow employees no choices. Moreover, these organizations export their emotional expectations to wherever they locate in the world. When the hamburgers or lattes come to town, the typical grimace of the Moscovite or shyness of the Finnish employee is subject to a similar genre of smile-training.

Is asking people to feign specific job-related emotions unethical if it conflicts with their basic personality? Is exporting standardized emotional "rule books" to other cultures unethical? What do you think?

Source: This dilemma is based on S. Fineman, "Managing Emotions at Work: Some Political Reflections," paper presented at a symposium at the Academy of Management Conference, Washington, DC, August 2001.

CASE INCIDENT

Frank Stronach, Risk-Taker and Fair Enterprise Creator

When people describe the personality of Frank Stronach, chair of Aurora, Ontario-based Magna International Inc., they typically use such words as "smart aleck," "obnoxious," "canny," "crazy," and "arrogant." Stronach provides an excellent illustration of how an individual's personality shapes his or her behaviour.

Frank Stronach was born in Weiz, Austria, in 1932, the son of a Communist factory worker. He moved to Canada at the age of 22, with $200 in his pocket, plus his expertise as a tool-and-die maker. Within 2 years he had scraped together enough money to start Multimatic Investments Ltd., a small automotive tool-and-die shop, in the east end of Toronto. In the 47 years since, he has built that shop into today's Magna—an auto-parts giant that employs 49 000 workers and has annual sales in excess of $17 billion. In 2001, he was paid $55 million for his role as chair of Magna.

Stronach personifies the driven executive in terms of his various business acquisitions over the years. He has also taken a number of risks, some of which have resulted in huge failure. In 1990, for example, Magna reported a loss of $224.2 million, incredible by almost any standard. But Stronach turned the company around, got back to its roots, and between 1990 and 1994 share prices rose from $2.25 to $66.88. In October 1997, prices had risen to their highest yet, $101.50. However, Stronach made a number of forays into other business ventures, and by late 1999, despite rising sales and a boom in the North American auto

industry, shares were trading at $61.50. Stronach stepped down as CEO in 2001 (while maintaining the role of chair), and his daughter Belinda has replaced him as CEO. But that doesn't mean Frank Stronach is taking it easy. His new business venture is Magna Entertainment Corp. (MEC), with interests in media, sports gaming, and online betting.

Stronach believes in "fair enterprise," including a universal charter of rights, and a fairer distribution of wealth. He criticizes socialist systems ("they stifle individualism"), totalitarianism ("benefits the few"), and even free enterprise ("from time to time self-destroying"). This may seem like a paradox from someone who earns more than $50 million as chair of Magna. However, as Hugh Segal, former chief of staff to Brian Mulroney and contender for leadership of the Progressive Conservative Party in 1998, explains, "If Frank were the kind of person for whom conventional orthodoxy mattered, he'd probably still be running a one-man machine shop on Dupont [in Toronto]," where he first started out in the mid-1950s.

Stronach created Magna's corporate philosophy to foster a "strong sense of ownership and entrepreneurial energy" among his employees. Ten percent of pre-tax profit is allocated to employees in the form of cash and share purchase plans, thus giving all employees a share in the profits of the company. Stronach insists that managers' salaries are to be pegged "below industry standards." At the same time, plant managers are given considerable autonomy over buying, selling, and hiring. Magna also tries to keep up with employee attitudes: Plant managers are required to meet with all their workers at least once a month, and employees return a comprehensive survey once a year.

Questions

1. To what extent would you say that Frank Stronach's personality is reflected in his corporate policy?

2. What might the study of perceptions reveal about how different people might view Stronach's personality?

3. What kind of people might be unhappy working for Frank Stronach?

4. What are the pros and cons of being a manager who works under such a strong personality?

Sources: "CEO Pay Soars as Profits Fall, Globe and Mail Survey Indicates," *Canadian Press Newswire*, April 23, 2002; B. Simon, "Work Ethic and the Magna Carta," *The Financial Post Daily*, March 20, 1997, p. 14; "Magna in Overdrive: No Canadian Has Profited From Contracting out as Much as Stronach," *Maclean's*, September 30, 1996, pp. 50–54; "Car and Striver (Will the World's Leading Auto-Parts Supplier Become the Globe's Newest Automaker?)," *Canadian Business*, September 1996, pp 92–94; "Magna-Mania: Resurrecting His on-the-Brink Auto Parts Empire Didn't Satisfy Frank Stronach Who Plans Growth and Monuments With Equal Flair," *The Financial Post*, August 12/14, 1995, pp. 12–13; D. Steinhart, "Magna Moving Into Sports Gaming: Stock on Long Slide: Auto-Parts Giant Takes 17% Drop in Third-Quarter Profit," *Financial Post (National Post)*, November 9, 1999, p. C3; D. Steinhart, "Market Remains Leery of Magna," *Financial Post (National Post)*, November 5, 1999, pp. D1, D3; and D. Olive, "Some Canadian CEOs Did Better Than Their US Counterparts," *Financial Post (National Post)*, June 14, 1999, p. C6.

CBC   VIDEO CASE INCIDENT

NovaScotian Crystal

In the late 1990s, Denis Ryan, ex-singer, entertainer, and financial services entrepreneur, had an impulsive idea to establish a Canadian glassworks company in Halifax, Nova Scotia. Armed with little more than intrigue, some artisans from Ireland, and a lot of guts, Ryan tried for several years to make his company, NovaScotian Crystal, work. Finally, facing possible financial ruin, Ryan hired Rod McColough, a "numbers guy," to take the job of president. Ryan assumed the roles of chairman, figurehead and cheerleader for the project.

Throughout the summer of 2001, major discussions of financial position, investor loans, and possible closure could be heard around the Halifax waterfront plant. McColough was organized, detail oriented, and cost conscious as he worked out production glitches in an attempt to turn the company around. Yet, throughout the daily challenges that McColough had to face, Ryan could always be found somewhere in the background, offering him a moment of peace by inviting him for a cup of tea, offering inspiration, encouraging new attempts, and bringing levity to otherwise discouraging situations.

Problems continued as McColough tried new strategies and redefined plans, but nothing seemed to be working. Despite the setbacks over the next 18 months, Ryan never lost sight of his dream to bring the all but lost artistic tradition of mouth-blown hand-cut crystal to Canada. Not giving up, McColough and the other executives continued to stay focused on the numbers while looking for new markets. Finally, after years of operating on the edge of bankruptcy, NovaScotian Crystal began to turn a profit in late 2001.

Today, the company has expanded its product lines, launched a series of successful catalogues through online sales, and is shipping its fine product all around the world.

Questions

1. How would you describe Denis Ryan's personality?

2. To what extent would you say that personality plays a role in how Denis Ryan runs NovaScotian Crystal?

3. Study the behaviours of Denis Ryan and Rod McColough. Compare and contrast these two businessmen by making a list of specific behaviours that each exhibit in their respective managerial roles.

4. If what we know is based on what we perceive, then is it possible that what we know to be true can be incorrect? Relate your answer back to the perception that Denis Ryan had back in the late 1990s of there being a need for old-fashioned glassware craftsmanship in Canada.

Source: "NovaScotian Crystal," *CBC Venture*, April, 2002, VA2020F, 822; NovaScotian Crystal website, "About Us," www.novascotiancrystal.com.

From **Concepts** to **Skills**

Reading Emotions

Understanding another person's felt emotions is very difficult. But we can learn to read others' displayed emotions.[81] We do this by focusing on verbal, nonverbal, and paralanguage cues.

The easiest way to find out what someone is feeling is to ask. Saying something as simple as "Are you OK? What's the problem?" can often provide you with the information to assess an individual's emotional state. But relying on a verbal response has two drawbacks. First, almost all of us conceal our emotions to some extent for privacy and to reflect social expectations. So we might be unwilling to share our true feelings. Second, even if we want to verbally convey our feelings, we may be unable to do so. As we noted earlier, some people have difficulty understanding their own emotions and, hence, are unable to express them verbally. So, at best, verbal responses provide only partial information.

You are talking with a co-worker. Does the fact that his back is rigid, his teeth are clenched, and his facial muscles tight tell you something about his emotional state? It probably should. Facial expressions, gestures, body movements, and physical distance are nonverbal cues that can provide additional insights into what a person is feeling. The facial expressions shown in Exhibit 2–7, for instance, are a window into a person's feelings. Notice the difference in facial features: the height of the cheeks, the raising or lowering of the brow, the turn of the mouth, the positioning of the lips, and the configuration of muscles around the eyes. Even something as subtle as the distance someone chooses to position him- or herself from you can convey how much intimacy, aggressiveness, repugnance, or withdrawal that person feels.

When you speak with someone, you may notice a sharp change in the tone of her voice and the speed at

Exhibit 2-7

Facial Expressions Convey Emotions

Each picture portrays a different emotion. Try to identify them before looking at the answers.

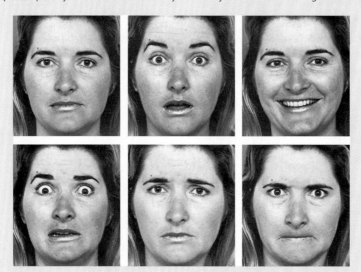

Top, left to right: neutral, surprise, happiness. Bottom: fear, sadness, anger.

Source: S.E. Taylor, L.A. Peplan, and D.O. Sears, *Social Psychology*, 9th ed. (Upper Saddle River, NJ: Prentice Hall, 1997), p. 98; photographs by Paul Eikman, Ph.D. Used with permission.

which she speaks. You are tapping into the third source of information on a person's emotions—paralanguage. This is communication that goes beyond the specific spoken words. It includes pitch, amplitude, rate, and voice quality of speech. Paralanguage reminds us that people convey their feelings not only in what they say, but also in how they say it.

Assessing Skills

After you've read this chapter, take the following Self-Assessments on your enclosed CD-ROM.

1. What's My Basic Personality?

2. What's My MBTI Personality Type?

3. What's My Locus of Control?

6. Am I a Type A?

20. What's My Emotional Intelligence Score?

Practising Skills

Part A. Form groups of two. Each person is to spend a couple of minutes thinking of a time in the past when she or he was emotional about something. Examples might include being upset with a parent, sibling, or friend; being excited or disappointed about an academic or athletic achievement; being angry with someone over an insult or slight; being disgusted by something someone has said or done; or being happy because of something good that happened.

Part B. Now you will conduct two role plays. Each will be an interview. In the first, one person will play the interviewer and the other will play the job applicant. The job is for a summer management internship with a large retail chain. Each role play will last no longer than 10 minutes. The interviewer is to conduct a normal job interview, except you are to continually rethink the emotional episode you envisioned in Part A. Try hard to convey this emotion while, at the same time, being professional in interviewing the job applicant.

Part C. Now reverse positions for the second role play. The interviewer becomes the job applicant and vice versa. The new interviewer will conduct a normal job interview, except that he or she will continually rethink the emotional episode chosen in Part A.

Part D. Spend 10 minutes analyzing the interview, with specific attention focused on these questions: What emotion(s) do you think the other person was conveying? What cues did you pick up? How accurate were you in reading those cues?

Reinforcing Skills

1. Rent a video of an emotionally laden film such as *Death of a Salesman* or *12 Angry Men*. Carefully watch the actors for clues to the emotions they are exhibiting. Try to determine the various emotions projected and explain how you arrived at your conclusion.

2. Spend a day specifically looking for emotional cues in the people with whom you interact. Did this improve communication?

CHAPTER 3

Values, Attitudes, and Their Effects in the Workplace

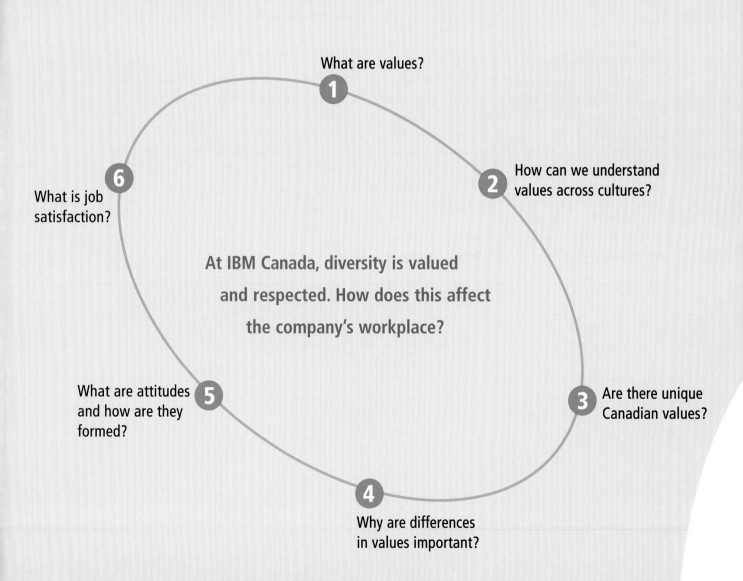

What are values?

1

How can we understand
values across cultures?

2

Are there unique
Canadian values?

3

Why are differences
in values important?

4

What are attitudes
and how are they
formed?

5

What is job
satisfaction?

6

**At IBM Canada, diversity is valued
and respected. How does this affect
the company's workplace?**

IBM Canada is one of a number of companies in Canada that have developed diversity policies for their workplace. IBM's policy states:[1]

> At IBM we acknowledge, value and respect diversity.... we recognize individual differences and appreciate how these differences provide a powerful competitive advantage and a source of great pride and opportunity in the workplace and marketplace.

Generally we expect that an organization's values, like those of an individual, will be reflected in corresponding behaviour and attitudes. If a company stated that it valued organizational diversity, and yet no behaviour followed from that statement, we would question whether that value was really so important to the company.

IBM Canada backs up its value statement with concrete policies and actions. For instance, IBM's community of gay, lesbian, bisexual, and transgender (GLBT) employees has a group devoted to providing support for its members both inside and outside the workplace. Brad Salavich, shown in the photo, who recruits university graduates for IBM Canada,

speaks well of IBM's supportive environment. He came out at work 10 years ago because he was tired of hiding who he was. "Whether or not I was gay really wasn't an issue in how well I did my job," he says.

In this chapter, we look more carefully at how values influence behaviour, and consider the relationship between values and attitudes. We then consider two specific issues that arise from our discussion of values and attitudes: workforce diversity and job satisfaction.

VALUES

Is capital punishment right or wrong? How about racial or gender quotas in hiring? If a person likes power, is that good or bad? The answers to these questions are value-laden. Some might argue, for example, that capital punishment is right because it is a suitable punishment for crimes such as murder. However, others might argue just as strongly that no government has the right to take anyone's life.

"**Values** 1) are concepts or beliefs, 2) pertain to desirable end-states or behaviours, 3) transcend situations, 4) guide selection or evaluation of behaviour and events, and 5) are ordered by relative importance."[2] Values contain a judgmental element in that they reflect an individual's ideas on what is right, good, or desirable. Values are not fluid and flexible; they tend to be relatively stable and enduring.[3] A significant portion of the values we hold are established in our early years—from parents, teachers, friends, and others. As children, we were told that certain behaviours or outcomes are always desirable or always undesirable. There were few grey areas. It is this absolute or "black or white" learning of values that more or less ensures their stability and endurance.

1 What are values?

values
Basic convictions about what is important to the individual.

What kinds of values do people have? Milton Rokeach classified the values that people hold into two sets, with each set containing 18 individual value items.[4] One set, called **terminal values**, refers to desirable end-states of existence. These are the goals that individuals would like to achieve during their lifetime, such as a comfortable life, or happiness. The other set, called **instrumental values**, refers to preferable modes of behaviour, or ways of achieving the terminal values, such as being courageous or helpful. Exhibit 3-1 gives common examples for each of these sets.

The issue of values is strongly linked to the issue of ethics, which is developed in Chapter 9. *The Canadian Oxford Dictionary* defines ethics as 1) the science of morals in human conduct; and 2) moral principles; rules of conduct. Thus ethical values are related to moral judgments about right and wrong.

However, there are few universal values or consistent ethical principles. Differences in values can thus lead to people engaging in behaviours that might be found unethical in some countries and yet be standard operating procedure in others. For instance, bribery is not an accepted way to do business in North America, but it is more common in Nigeria, Bolivia, Russia, and Mexico. Canadian managers are faced with decisions about how to operate when doing business in those countries.

Not all values (self-respect, for instance) have an ethical content. Some values, though, may lead to ethical conflicts. For instance, Jeff Skilling, a former CEO of Enron, "wanted the biggest profits on the shortest timetable."[5] This may have led employees to take shortcuts and engage in various reporting activities that violated generally accepted accounting practices.

Exhibit 3–1

Terminal and Instrumental Values in Rokeach Value Survey

Terminal Values	Instrumental Values
A comfortable life (a prosperous life)	Ambitious (hard-working, aspiring)
An exciting life (a stimulating, active life)	Broad-minded (open-minded)
A sense of accomplishment (lasting contribution)	Capable (competent, effective)
A world at peace (free of war and conflict)	Cheerful (lighthearted, joyful)
A world of beauty (beauty of nature and the arts)	Clean (neat, tidy)
Equality (brotherhood, equal opportunity for all)	Courageous (standing up for your beliefs)
Family security (taking care of loved ones)	Forgiving (willing to pardon others)
Freedom (independence, free choice)	Helpful (working for the welfare of others)
Happiness (contentedness)	Honest (sincere, truthful)
Inner harmony (freedom from inner conflict)	Imaginative (daring, creative)
Mature love (sexual and spiritual intimacy)	Independent (self-reliant, self-sufficient)
National security (protection from attack)	Intellectual (intelligent, reflective)
Pleasure (an enjoyable, leisurely life)	Logical (consistent, rational)
Salvation (saved, eternal life)	Loving (affectionate, tender)
Self-respect (self-esteem)	Obedient (dutiful, respectful)
Social recognition (respect, admiration)	Polite (courteous, well-mannered)
True friendship (close companionship)	Responsible (dependable, reliable)
Wisdom (a mature understanding of life)	Self-controlled (restrained, self-disciplined)

Source: M. Rokeach, *The Nature of Human Values* (New York: Free Press, 1973).

Importance of Values

Values are important to the study of organizational behaviour because they lay the foundation for understanding attitudes and motivation, and because they influence our perceptions. Individuals enter an organization with preconceived notions of what "ought" and what "ought not" to be. Of course, these notions are not value-free. On the contrary, they contain interpretations of right and wrong. Furthermore, they imply that certain behaviours or outcomes are preferred over others. As a result, values cloud objectivity and rationality. This chapter's *CBC Video Case Incident*, "Corporate Culture Meets G.A.P. Adventures," shows how people react when their employer changes the values that guide the company.

Values usually influence attitudes and behaviour.[6] If, for example, you put a high value on a healthy lifestyle and find out that your manager is a smoker, your attitude toward your boss may be more negative than if he or she were a nonsmoker. When you notice smokers taking breaks from their jobs, your work performance (behaviour) may start to decline, because you start to wonder why they take more breaks than you do. Would your attitudes and behaviour be different if your values were the same as the smokers' with respect to the importance (or lack thereof) of leading a healthy lifestyle? Most likely. In this chapter's *Learning About Yourself Exercise* on page 89, you are given the opportunity to examine some of the things that you value.

CBC ⬤

"Corporate Culture Meets G.A.P. Adventures"

A FRAMEWORK FOR ASSESSING CULTURAL VALUES

② How can we understand values across cultures?

Do values vary by culture? One of the most widely referenced approaches for analyzing variations among cultures has come from Geert Hofstede.[7] He surveyed more than 116 000 IBM employees in 40 countries about their work-related values. He found that managers and employees vary on five value dimensions of national culture.

Hofstede's value dimensions include:

- *Power distance.* The degree to which people in a country accept that power in institutions and organizations is distributed unequally. **Power distance** ranges from relatively equal (low power distance) to extremely unequal (high power distance).

- *Individualism vs. collectivism.* **Individualism** is the degree to which people in a country prefer to act as individuals rather than as members of groups. **Collectivism** is the equivalent of low individualism and refers to a tight social framework in which people expect others in their group to look after and protect them.

- *Quantity of life vs. quality of life.* **Quantity of life** is the degree to which values such as assertiveness, competition, and the acquisition of money and material goods prevail. **Quality of life** is the degree to which people value relationships, and show sensitivity and concern for the welfare of others.[8]

- *Uncertainty avoidance.* The degree to which people in a country prefer structured over unstructured situations. In countries that score high on **uncertainty avoidance**, people have an increased level of anxiety, which manifests itself in greater nervousness, stress, and aggressiveness.

- *Long-term vs. short-term orientation.* People in cultures with **long-term orientations** look to the future and value thrift and persistence. A **short-term orientation** values the past and present, and emphasizes respect for tradition and fulfilling social obligations.

power distance
The extent to which a society accepts that power in institutions and organizations is distributed unequally.

individualism
The degree to which people in a country prefer to act as individuals rather than as members of groups.

collectivism
A tight social framework in which people expect others in their groups to look after and protect them.

quantity of life
The extent to which societal values such as assertiveness and materialism prevail.

quality of life
An emphasis on relationships and concern for others.

uncertainty avoidance
The extent to which a society feels threatened by uncertain and ambiguous situations, and tries to avoid them.

long-term orientation
The extent to which a society emphasizes the future, thrift, and persistence.

short-term orientation
Emphasis on the past and present, respect for tradition, and fulfilling social obligation.

Exhibit 3–2 provides a summary of how a number of countries rate on Hofstede's five dimensions. Not surprisingly, most Asian countries are more collectivist than individualistic. On the other hand, the United States ranked highest on individualism among all countries surveyed.

Hofstede's findings are based on research that is nearly three decades old, and has been subject to some criticism, which he rejects.[9] In addition, he has recently updated his research, and included studies from a variety of disciplines that correlate with his own work.[10] For the most part, the basic implications of his original research still hold.

The Global Leadership and Organizational Behavior Effectiveness research program (GLOBE)
www.haskayne.ucalgary.ca/GLOBE/Public/

The Global Leadership and Organizational Behavior Effectiveness (GLOBE) research program is an ongoing cross-cultural investigation of leadership and national culture that has been used to evaluate Hofstede's cultural dimensions.[11] Using data from 825 organizations in 62 countries, the GLOBE team identified nine dimensions where national cultures differ. Comparing these results with Hofstede's suggests that the GLOBE study has extended Hofstede's work rather than replaced it. The GLOBE study confirms that Hofstede's five dimensions are still valid. However, it has added more dimensions and provides us with an updated measure of where countries rate on each dimension. We can expect future cross-cultural studies of human behaviour and organizational practice to increasingly use the GLOBE dimensions to assess differences between countries.

Do Values Change Over Time?

It's important that you treat the ratings in Exhibit 3–2 as general guidelines that need to be modified over time to reflect that the world has changed since Hofstede conducted his study. Some examples: Communism has fallen in Eastern Europe; Hong Kong is run by the Chinese rather than the British; Germany has become unified; and there has

Exhibit 3–2

Examples of National Cultural Values

Country	Power Distance	Individualism*	Quantity of Life**	Uncertainty Avoidance	Long-term Orientation***
Canada	Moderate	High	High	Moderate	Low
China	High	Low	Moderate	Moderate	High
France	High	High	Moderate	High	Low
Germany****	Low	High	High	Moderate	Moderate
Hong Kong	High	Low	High	Low	High
Indonesia	High	Low	Moderate	Low	Low
Japan	Moderate	Moderate	High	Moderate	Moderate
Mexico	High	Low	High	High	NA
Netherlands	Low	High	Low	Moderate	Moderate
Russia	High	Moderate	Low	High	Low
United States	Low	High	High	Low	Low
West Africa	High	Low	Moderate	Moderate	Low

*A low score is synonymous with collectivism. **A low score is synonymous with high quality of life.
***A low score is synonymous with a short-term orientation. ****Includes only former West Germany.

Source: Adapted from G. Hofstede, "Cultural Constraints in Management Theories," *Academy of Management Executive*, February 1993, p. 91; G. Hofstede, "The Cultural Relativity of Organizational Practices and Theories," *Journal of International Business Studies*, 14, 1983, pp. 75–89. Mexico's scores were abstracted from G.K. Stephens and C.R. Greer, "Doing Business in Mexico: Understanding Cultural Differences," *Organizational Dynamics, Special Report*, 1998, pp. 43–59.

been a dramatic increase in the proportion of women in the labour force and in management positions in countries such as Canada and the United States. A recent follow-up to Hofstede's study confirmed many of the original findings but also found that transformational changes have made their way into various cultural values.[12] For instance, Mexico has moved in 30 years from an emphasis on collectivism to individualism. This is consistent with Mexico's economic development and the growth of capitalistic values. Similarly, in the United States, values have shifted away from emphasizing quantity of life and more toward quality, which undoubtedly reflects the influence of women and younger people on the workforce. This can be seen in the emphasis on more flexible work schedules and the emphasis of these groups on work-family balance. Our point here is that even though cultural values are generally stable and enduring, we should remember that Hofstede's classifications might, in some cases, need to be modified to include transformational changes within countries.

Below we examine some specific value issues across a variety of cultures, both within Canada and with some of Canada's trading partners: the parties of the North American Free Trade Agreement (NAFTA), and some of the Asian and Pacific Rim countries. In trying to understand the impact of cultural values on Canadian society, you should consider how multicultural Canada has become in recent years. For instance, in 1996, 41 percent of Metropolitan Toronto's population, 35 percent of Vancouver's, and 18 percent of Montreal's were made up of immigrants.[13] The 2001 census found that 17 percent of Canada's population over age five spoke neither of the country's two official languages as their first language. In Vancouver and Toronto, this rate was 38 percent and 41 percent respectively, so considerably more than one-third of the population of those two cities does not speak either English or French as a first language.[14]

In the discussion of values below, bear in mind that we present broad generalizations, and you should certainly avoid stereotyping individuals on the basis of these generalizations. There are individual differences in values, even among cultural groups. For instance, not every baby boomer thinks alike, and neither does every member of the Net Generation. Thus, the important point about the values discussion is that you should try to understand how others might view things differently from you, even when they are exposed to the same situation.

CANADIAN SOCIAL VALUES

When IBM Canada made the decision to value diversity in its workplace, it was reflecting a dominant value of Canada as a multicultural country. This is very different from the United States, which considers itself a melting pot with respect to different cultures. Are there other social values that make Canada unique?

In his recent books *Sex in the Snow* and *Fire and Ice*, pollster Michael Adams identifies the social values of today's Canadians.[15] He found that within three broad age groups of adult Canadians—those over 55 ("the elders"), baby boomers (born between the mid-1940s and mid-1960s), and Generation X (born between the mid-1960s and early 1980s)—there are at least 12 quite distinct "value tribes." We present some of his findings below. For further information and an opportunity to see where you might be classified in terms of your social values, visit the Environics website.

The Elders

These individuals are characterized as "playing by the rules," and their core values are belief in order, authority, discipline, the Judeo-Christian moral code, and the Golden Rule (do unto others as you would have others do unto you). About 80 percent of the elders resemble this description of traditional values, although some individuals are a stronger match than others.

3 Are there unique Canadian values?

Environics Research Group
www.environics.net

The Boomers

Boomers are often lumped together as a somewhat spoiled, hedonistic, rebellious group, but in fact there are four categories of boomers: autonomous rebels (25 percent), anxious communitarians (20 percent), connected enthusiasts (14 percent), and disengaged Darwinists (41 percent). So, compared with the elders, the boomers are a bit more fragmented in their views. Yet all but the disengaged Darwinists reflect, to some extent, the stereotypes of this generation: rejection of authority, scepticism regarding the motives of big business and government, a strong concern for the environment, and a strong desire for equality in the workplace and society. Of course, the disengaged Darwinists—the largest single group—do not fit this description as well. The Darwinists are characterized as being angry, intimidated by change, and anxious about their professional and financial futures.

Generation X

While this group is quite fragmented in its values, the research showed that the common values are experience-seeking, adaptability, and concern with personal image among peers. Despite these common values, Generation Xers can be divided into five tribes. *Thrill-seeking materialists* (25 percent) desire money and material possessions, as well as recognition, respect, and admiration. *Aimless dependants* (27 percent) seek financial independence, security, and stability. *Social hedonists* (15 percent) are experience-seeking, committed to their own pleasure, and seek immediate gratification. *New Aquarians* (13 percent) are experience-seeking, and also egalitarian and ecologically minded. Finally, *autonomous post-materialists* (20 percent) seek personal autonomy and self-fulfillment, and are concerned about human rights.

The Ne(x)t Generation

Since Adams' book *Sex in the Snow* appeared, another generation has been identified. The so-called Net (or Next) Generation,[16] or the Millennials[17]—born between 1977 and 1997—are "creators, not recipients. And they are curious, contrarian, flexible, collaborative and high in self-esteem."[18] People in this generation are also identified as team players and optimists with a desire for order.[19]

Vancouver-based Mainframe Entertainment, the company behind *Reboot* and *Beasties,* understands the values of its Generation X employees: experience, recognition, respect, and admiration. Mainframe's animators get leadership opportunities, including the opportunity to direct shows, which they would not get at higher-paying studios in Los Angeles. Mainframe has one of the lowest turnover rates in the animation business because of its emphasis on giving its young employees the opportunity to acquire new skills.

Beyond the differences in the four generational groups, it is safe to say that, overall, the values of Canadians have changed a lot in the past 10 years. Air Canada recently studied the core values of Canadians as part of an effort to develop its brand strategy.[20] The results show that Canadians have become more confident and less nationalistic. They are also human, caring, and humble, but seek respect. Finally, the Air Canada results indicate that while there is a strong social conscience among Canadians, the emphasis on the individual rather than the collective is currently stronger than in the past.

Applying Canadian Values in the Workplace

While the boomers currently dominate the workplace (in 2001 they made up 47 percent of the workforce), their years of being in charge are limited. Ten years from now, half of them will be at least 55 and 18 percent will be over 60.[21] Thus, an awareness of people's value structures helps us to understand better how to manage and relate to others in the workplace. Within any organization you are likely to find people from different generations working together. Senior management is often led by the elders, who have spent much of their careers working in hierarchical organizations. As boomers move into head offices, the "play-by-the-rules," "boss-knows-best" elders are being replaced by boomers who have a more egalitarian view of the workplace. They dislike the command-and-control rules that were part of their parents' lives. Meanwhile, the Generation Xers in the workplace are comfortable in adapting, but also want more experiences. They are not in awe of authority. Most important, they are not interested in copying the workaholic behaviour of their boomer parents. Those in the Net Generation will have their own significant impact on the workplace. They have mastered a communication and information system that many of their parents have yet to understand. Managing the expectations of each of these very different groups is not an easy task. It requires managers to be flexible, observant, and willing to adjust more to the individual needs of these different employees.

Organizations can mould their workplace by hiring people with similar values and/or aligning individuals' jobs and values. For instance, Toronto-based investment banking firm Griffiths McBurney & Partners Inc. hires people who are aggressive and risk-taking, because that is the kind of firm the partners have created. "Everyone starts the year with zero salary, zero draw, and no guarantees," and compensation is based on revenues.[22] Studies have shown that when individual values align with organizational values, the results are positive. Individuals who have an accurate understanding of the job requirements and the organization's values adjust better to their jobs, and have greater levels of satisfaction and organizational commitment.[23] Shared values between the employee and the organization also lead to more positive work attitudes,[24] lower turnover,[25] and greater productivity.[26]

Griffiths, McBurney & Partners Inc. (GMP)
www.gmponline.com

Some workplaces try to change employee values through education or "propagandistic interventions."[27] Later in the chapter, for instance, we discuss how workplaces have tried to introduce the value of cultural diversity. Interestingly enough, however, there is little research showing that values can be changed successfully.[28] Values tend to be relatively stable, and thus more interventions are aimed at changing attitudes.

Below we identify a number of value differences cross-culturally. Be aware that these are generalizations, and do not cover all possibilities of cultural differences. Moreover, just as all baby boomers are not alike, it would be a mistake to assume that everyone coming from the same cultural background behaves similarly. These overviews are simply meant to encourage you to think about differences among people, as well as similarities.

Francophone and Anglophone Values

One of the larger issues that has confronted Canada in recent years is the question of Quebec separatism and anglophone-francophone differences. Thus, it may be of interest

Asked to define the fundamentals that give National Bank Financial its edge, senior vice-president and company director John Wells believes Montreal-based National Bank Financial's edge comes from company management that is largely francophone. He argues that French-speaking Canadians treat their employees well, and will try to find *any* means of reducing expenses rather than lay off staff, in sharp contrast to the cost-cutting mechanisms of either English-speaking Canadian or American firms.

to managers and employees in Canadian firms to be aware of some of the potential cultural differences when managing in various environments. A number of studies show that anglophones and francophones have distinctive value priorities. Francophones have been found to be more collectivist, or group-oriented, with a greater need for achievement, while anglophones were found to be more individualist, or I-centred.[29] Francophones have also been shown to be more concerned about interpersonal aspects of the workplace than about task competence.[30] Anglophones have been shown to take more risks.[31] Other studies have found that anglophone managers tended to value autonomy and intrinsic job values, such as achievement, and thus were more achievement-oriented, while francophone managers tended to value affiliation and extrinsic job values, such as technical supervision.[32]

A study conducted at the University of Ottawa and Laval University suggests that some of the differences reported in previous research may be decreasing.[33] For instance, that study reported that there were no significant differences in individualism and collectivism. While this is only one study, and thus needs further confirmation, the researchers suggest that some of the differences found in previous studies were linked to characteristics that had nothing to do with whether a person was francophone or anglophone. Specifically, once the socio-economic status of the individuals is controlled, there are no differences due to linguistic background.

Despite evidence that anglophone and francophone values are becoming more similar on some dimensions, there is evidence of some differences in lifestyle values. A recent Canadian Institute for Health Information report noted that Quebecers experience more stress than other Canadians.[34] The study also found that Quebecers smoke more, have the highest workplace absenteeism rate, and are less physically active than the rest of the country. Another study found that francophones and anglophones have different values regarding cultural activities. Francophones are more likely to attend symphonic, classical, or choral music performances than anglophones. English-speaking Canadians are more likely to read newspapers, magazines, and books than French-speaking Canadians.[35]

Even though they have some cultural and lifestyle value differences, francophone and anglophone managers today have been exposed to similar types of organizational theories during their post-secondary school training, which might also influence their outlooks as managers. Thus we would not expect to find large differences in the way that firms in francophone Canada are managed, compared with those in the rest of Canada. Throughout the textbook you will see a number of examples of Quebec-based businesses that support this conclusion.

Canadian Aboriginal Values

Entrepreneurial activity among Canada's Aboriginal people has been growing, as has the number of partnerships and alliances between Aboriginal and non-Aboriginal businesses. There are now more than 20 000 Aboriginal-owned businesses in Canada. Half of these are on reserves, and two-thirds of the total are located west of Ontario. While Aboriginal businesses represent only 1 percent of all Canadian businesses, their growth rate has been huge: increasing by 170 percent between 1981 and 1996.

With this strong increase in both the number of Aboriginal businesses and the number of partnerships and alliances between Aboriginal and non-Aboriginal businesses, it

Prime Minister Jean Chrétien helped celebrate the opening of the Saskatoon head office of First Nations Bank of Canada. The bank's opening ceremonies, as well as its operating procedures, emphasize a strong attachment to Aboriginal values.

is important to examine whether and how each culture manages differently.[36] "Aboriginal values are usually perceived (by non-Aboriginals) as an impediment to economic development and organizational effectiveness."[37] Such values include reluctance to compete, a time orientation different from the Western one, and an emphasis on consensus decision making.[38] Aboriginals do not necessarily agree that these values are business impediments, however.

Specifically, while Canadian businesses and government have historically assumed that "non-Native people must teach Native people how to run their own organizations," the First Nations of Canada are not convinced.[39] They believe that traditional culture, values, and languages do not have to be compromised to build a self-sustaining economy. Moreover, they believe that their cultural values may actually be a positive force in conducting business.[40]

In recent years there have been some difficulties for Canadian businesses facing Native land claims. In order to address these difficulties, two anthropologists from the University of Alberta, Cliff Hickey and David Natcher, worked with the Red River Cree Nation in northern Alberta to develop a new model for forestry operations to work with First Nations peoples.[41] The anthropologists sought to balance the community's traditional lifestyle with the economic concerns of forestry operations. Exhibit 3–3 outlines several of their recommended ground rules, which they say could be used in oil and gas developments as well. Johnson Sewepegaham, chief of the Little Red River Cree, said they will use these recommendations for working out difficulties with treaty lands for which Vernon, BC-based Tolko Industries Ltd. and High Level, Alberta-based Footner Forest Products Ltd. jointly hold forest tenure.

To use Hofstede's framework to understand Aboriginal and non-Aboriginal cultures, we can rely on the research of Lindsay Redpath of Athabasca University.[42] Aboriginal cultures are more collectivist in orientation than non-Aboriginal cultures in either Canada or the United States. Aboriginal organizations are much more likely to reflect and advance the goals of the community. There is also a greater sense of family within the workplace, with greater affiliation and loyalty. Power distance in Aboriginal cultures is smaller than in non-Aboriginal cultures of Canada and the United States, and

University of Alberta
www.ualberta.ca

Little Red River Cree Nation
lrrcn.ab.ca

Tolko Industries Ltd.
www.tolko.com

Exhibit 3–3

Ground Rules for Developing Aboriginal and Business Partnerships

- Modify management operations to reduce negative impact to wildlife species
- Modify operations to ensure community access to lands and resources
- Protect all those areas identified by community members as having biological, cultural, and historical significance
- Recognize and protect Aboriginal and treaty rights to hunting, fishing, and trapping and gathering activities
- Increase forest-based economic opportunities for community members
- Increase the involvement of community members in decision making

Source: Adapted from D.C. Natcher and C.G. Hickey, "Putting the Community Back Into Community-Based Resource Management: A Criteria and Indicators Approach to Sustainability," *Human Organization*, 61, no. 4, 2002, pp. 350–363.

Alcan Inc.
www.alcan.ca

Athabasca University
www.athabascau.ca

First Nations Bank of Canada
www.tdcanadatrust.com/fnbank/

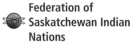

Federation of Saskatchewan Indian Nations
www.fsin.com

there is an emphasis on consensual decision making. Aboriginal cultures are lower on uncertainty avoidance than non-Aboriginal cultures in either Canada or the United States. Aboriginal organizations and cultures tend to have fewer rules and regulations. Each of these differences suggests that organizations created by Aboriginals will differ from non-Aboriginal businesses, and both research and anecdotal evidence support this view.[43] For instance, Richard Prokopanko, director of corporate affairs for Montreal-based Alcan Inc., said that shifting from handling issues in a generally legalistic, contract-oriented manner to valuing more dialogue and collaboration helps ease some of the tension that had built up over 48 years between Alcan and First Nations people.[44]

Certainly the opening ceremony for the First Nations Bank of Canada's head office branch in Saskatoon in September 1997 was different from many openings of Western businesses. The ceremony was accompanied by the burning of sweetgrass. "This is a blessing," Blaine Favel, then chief of the Federation of Saskatchewan Indian Nations, said to a large outdoor gathering. "We are celebrating a great accomplishment by our people."[45]

Saskatoon-based Adam's Active Auto Wrecking is owned by Sandra Bighead, a member of the Beardy's and Okemasis First Nation. Her philosophy about running her business exhibits the family-value orientation that is more likely to be found in Aboriginal businesses. She believes in taking care of her staff: "For me, success is gaining personal satisfaction, self-confidence, and self-worth from the work I do," she said. "Part of that satisfaction comes from knowing that a lot of people and their families are depending on me."[46]

Canadian Values and the Values of NAFTA Partners

United States

Pollster Michael Adams, in his recent book *Fire and Ice*, finds that there is a growing dissimilarity between Canadian and American values. The two groups differed on 41 of 56 trends that Adams examined. For 24 trends, the gap actually widened between 1992 and 2000, suggesting that Canadians' social values are growing more distinct from Americans'.[47]

Adams finds that compared with Canadians, "Americans have a greater faith in the family, the state (that is, 'America'), religion, and the market."[48] Americans are also more comfortable with big business, probably because to them it means American big business, whereas in Canada big business means a foreign-owned, often American, business. The American business environment is characterized by intense competition, whereas Canada has historically had a more protectionist attitude in the market, as well as public sector monopolies and private sector oligopolies. While these "antimarket" forces are changing slowly, Canadian businesses are still adapting to the open markets that globalization has brought.

If we can talk about a national "personality," Canadians have always been portrayed as more shy and deferential than Americans, as well as less violent and more courteous. In Canada, there is more emphasis on being polite and following the rules. Canadians are more pragmatic and less ideological. They value peace, order, and equality, whereas Americans value individuality and freedom.[49] Adams suggests the September 11 attacks have had an impact on the American personality. He finds Americans are more accepting of patriarchy and hierarchy these days, and he concludes that it is "the supposedly bold, individualistic Americans who are the nodding conformists, and the supposedly shy, deferential and law-abiding Canadians who are most likely to assert their personal autonomy and political agency."[50]

Americans are thought to be more comfortable with the unknown, taking risks, and pushing the boundaries of creativity than Canadians. As one columnist notes, "ever since the late '50s, when singer Paul Anka couldn't record *Diana* in Canada but made it a hit in the U.S., there has been a perception that it is harder to take risks in Canada, the nation of life insurers."[51] Canadians also seem uncomfortable celebrating success and even try to play it down. And Canada's broad social safety net makes it easier to fail in Canada than in the United States.

These differences in values and national personalities suggest that Canadian and American workplaces will likely look and operate somewhat differently. Canadians may be more suited to the teams that many organizations are creating and more willing to work together than to be individual stars. They may follow the directives of their managers more, even as new organizational models suggest that both employees and managers need to take more responsibility to learn and share information. An awareness of these values will help you understand some of the differences you might observe in Canadian and American businesses.

Mexico

The Free Trade Agreement of the Americas (FTAA) calls for a free-trade zone across the Western hemisphere by 2005. The treaty would remove trade barriers across the Americas from the Arctic Circle to Cape Horn. Thus, Canadian managers may want to consider the issue of business etiquette when dealing with individuals from Latin America. Penny Caceres, director of Seneca College's Spanish Institute, says: "Canadians tend to be very direct. They want to get right into business. It's the reverse in Latin America, where you have to build relationships before they decide if they want to do business with you. You can ruin the chances of getting a deal if you don't do that."[52]

Mexico has a higher power distance than either Canada or the United States.[53] However, while the Mexican managerial style is characterized as autocratic and paternalistic, managers do not rely exclusively on these traits. Mexican workers defer more to their managers, but they are less likely than Canadians or Americans to tolerate abrasiveness and insensitivity by their managers.

Mexico in general is characterized by a greater degree of uncertainty avoidance than either Canada or the United States. However, it would appear that Mexican managers are greater risk-takers than their counterparts in other North American countries. Because of the higher power distance and an autocratic style, managers in Mexico may feel freer to take risks than managers in Canada and the United States. Both Canada and the United States are much more individualistic than Mexico. In part, this is reflected in the greater reliance on personal networks and relationships in Mexico. Mexican employees

The Free Trade Agreement of the Americas (FTAA)
www.ftaa-alca.org

Seneca College of Language and Culture
www.senecac.on.ca

are also much more agreeable to teamwork, perhaps because of their greater need for affiliation. Mexico, Canada, and the United States score similarly high on quantity-of-life values.

All of these differences in values suggest that Mexican workplaces will look and operate differently from Canadian and American workplaces. Mexicans may be the most suited to teams, and are much less likely to try to stand out individually. They are likely to defer to their managers more, but they also expect more respect from their managers. An awareness of these values will help you understand some of the differences you might observe in workplaces across North America.

East and Southeast Asian Values

Simon Fraser University
www.sfu.ca

Professor Rosalie Tung of Simon Fraser University and her student Irene Yeung examined the importance of *guanxi* (personal connections with the appropriate authorities or individuals) for a sample of North American, European, and Hong Kong firms doing business with companies in mainland China.[54] They suggest that their findings will also be relevant in understanding how to develop relationships with firms from Japan, South Korea, and Hong Kong.

"*Guanxi* refers to the establishment of a connection between two independent individuals to enable a bilateral flow of personal or social transactions. Both parties must derive benefits from the transaction to ensure the continuation of such a relationship."[55] *Guanxi* relations are based on reciprocation, unlike Western networked relationships, which may be characterized more by self-interest. *Guanxi* relationships are meant to be long-term and enduring, in contrast with the immediate gains sometimes expected in Western relationships. *Guanxi* also relies less on institutional law, and more on personal power and authority, than do Western relationships. And finally, *guanxi* relations are governed more by the notion of shame (i.e., external pressures on performance), while Western relations often rely on guilt (i.e., internal pressures on performance) to maintain agreements. *Guanxi* is seen as extremely important for business success in China—more than such factors as right location, price or strategy, or product differentiation and quality. For Western firms wanting to do business with Asian firms, an understanding of *guanxi* and an effort to build relationships are important strategic advantages.

Our discussion about differences in cross-cultural values should suggest to you that understanding other cultures matters. When Canadian firms develop operations overseas or in the United States, the need to understand other cultures becomes important for employees transferred to foreign locations.

Dell Computer learned that Chinese work values differ from US work values when it opened a computer factory in Xiamen, China. Chinese workers hold the concept of a job for life. They expect to drink tea and read the papers on the job—and still keep their jobs. Dell China executives had to train employees so they understood that their jobs depended on their performance. To instill workers with a sense of ownership, managers gave employees stock options and explained to them how their increased productivity would result in higher pay.

IMPLICATIONS OF CULTURAL DIFFERENCES FOR OB

While Canadian researchers have contributed to the body of knowledge we call *organizational behaviour*, much of the theory we use in Canada has been developed by Americans using American subjects within domestic contexts.[56] What this means is that 1) not all OB theories and concepts are universally applicable to managing people around the world, especially in countries where work values are considerably different from those in either the United States or Canada; and 2) you should take into consideration cultural values when trying to understand the behaviour of people of different backgrounds within a country, as well as when you try to understand people in different countries.

Researchers have noted that when managers introduce common workplace practices into non-North American countries, they are sometimes not as effective as in Canada and the United States. A recent theory—cultural self-presentation theory—suggests that employee responses to these interventions are affected by the individual's interpretation of the dominant social values. For instance, the introduction of pay for performance, which rewards individual behaviour, is less likely to be welcomed by employees in a more collectivist culture, where the group is more important than any individual. This theory may also be relevant for comparing Aboriginal firms with non-Aboriginal firms in Canada, or for considering how to motivate and reward individuals from different cultural backgrounds who work in Canadian organizations.

4 Why are differences in values important?

Values and Workforce Diversity

Many organizations have attempted to incorporate workforce diversity initiatives into their workplaces. For example, IBM Canada's explicit statement about employment diversity, presented in the chapter opening, is representative of the types of statements that organizations often include in their annual reports and employee information packets. These statements signal corporate values to both employees and other people who might do business with the company. Some corporations choose to signal the value of diversity because they think it is an important strategic goal. IBM Canada recognizes that the purchasing power of the gay, lesbian, bisexual, and transgendered community is substantial.

IBM Canada Ltd.
www.ibm.com/ca/en/

When companies design and then publicize statements about the importance of diversity, they are basically producing value statements. The hope, of course, is that the statements will then change the attitudes of the members of the organization. But as noted above, values themselves do not often change. So the introduction of a company value statement about diversity (or anything else) is not likely, in and of itself, to change the values of organization members. The *Case Incident* on page 91 asks you to consider whether particular values should be shut out from the workplace.

Women wearing the *hajib*, the traditional head cover of Muslim women, face discrimination in getting a job in Canada. A recent study found that visibly Muslim women were either told there were no jobs available or not given a chance to apply for a job almost 40 percent of the time that they asked an employer whether a job was available.

ATTITUDES

One of the reasons why IBM has been proactive in developing a diversity policy is that it aims to change the attitudes of employees who appear to be slow in working with people different from themselves. Susan Turner, IBM Canada Ltd.'s director of Diversity and Workplace Programs, explains that these policies help to attract and retain very good employees who might otherwise feel excluded from the company. "Making a proactive effort to accommodate and foster all employees means everyone within the company's culture wins." Thus, IBM realizes the link between values and attitudes. So how do attitudes get formed, and can they really be changed?

5 What are attitudes and how are they formed?

attitudes
Fairly stable feelings about objects, people, or events.

Attitudes are fairly stable positive or negative feelings about objects, people, or events. When I say "I like my job," I am expressing my attitude to work. Attitudes are thus judgment responses to situations.

Attitudes are not the same as values, because values are convictions about what is important, but the two are interrelated. In organizations, attitudes are important because they affect job behaviour. Workers may believe, for example, that supervisors, auditors, managers, and time-and-motion engineers are all conspiring to make employees work harder for the same or less money. This may then result in a negative attitude toward management after a request to stay late for help on a special project. It makes sense to try to understand how employees form attitudes, the relationship of attitudes to actual job behaviour, and how attitudes might be changed. In *From Concepts to Skills* on pages 92–93, we discuss whether it is possible to change someone's attitude, and how that might happen in the workplace. *Focus on Diversity* looks at how attitudes toward who can make proper sushi attitudes affect who gets hired to be a sushi maker.

FOCUS ON **DIVERSITY**

Nontraditional Sushi Makers

What determines a good sushi maker? For many sushi restaurants in Japan and in North America, a sushi chef "should" be male. It's what's expected, and it's what's observed. Yoko Ogawa, 30, a female sushi chef at Yamaguchi in Midtown Manhattan, explains the problem women face: "They say that women cannot make sushi because their hands are too warm and that will ruin the fish."

Hiromi Suzuki, whose father is the chef and owner of Mie in the East Village of New York, shared some of her father's stories about women sushi makers: "Women can't make sushi because they wear perfume and makeup, and the smell of the perfume and makeup will ruin the food." Others believe that women can't become sushi chefs because the area behind the counter is sacred.

These attitudes have made it difficult for women to become sushi makers in Japan and North America, although that is starting to change. When Toshi Sugiura started the California Sushi Academy in Venice, California, in 1998, he expected that his students would be Asian immigrants. Instead, most of the students were American. This required him to change his vision: "Sushi is becoming a worldwide food. Why can't black people and white people make sushi?"

All of these examples suggest that who gets hired into any position can be affected by attitudes about what the "right" person should look like. ⫯

Types of Attitudes

A person can have thousands of attitudes, but OB focuses our attention on a limited number of job-related attitudes. These attitudes tap positive or negative evaluations that employees hold about aspects of their work environment. Most of the research in OB has been concerned with three attitudes: job involvement, organizational commitment, and job satisfaction.[57] In this chapter's *Working With Others Exercise* on page 90, you have the opportunity to examine the attitudes that you and others hold toward the Canadian workplace.

Job Involvement

While there isn't complete agreement over what the term **job involvement** means, a workable definition does exist: Job involvement measures the degree to which a person identifies psychologically with his or her job, and considers his or her perceived performance level important to self-worth.[58] Employees with a high level of job involvement identify strongly with, and really care about, the kind of work they do.

High levels of job involvement have been found to be related to fewer absences and lower resignation rates.[59] However, it seems to predict turnover more consistently than absenteeism.[60]

job involvement
The degree to which a person identifies with his or her job, actively participates in it, and considers his or her performance important to self-worth.

Organizational Commitment

Organizational commitment is defined as a state in which an employee identifies with a particular organization and its goals, and wishes to maintain membership in the organization.[61] So, high *job involvement* means identifying with one's specific job, while high *organizational commitment* means identifying with one's employing organization.

As with job involvement, the research evidence demonstrates that individuals with low organizational commitment are more likely to be absent or quit their jobs.[62] The idea of organizational commitment has changed in recent years. Twenty years ago, employees and employers had an unwritten loyalty contract, with employees typically remaining with a single organization for most of their career. Canadian business consultant Barbara Moses notes that "40-somethings still value loyalty: they think people should be prepared to make sacrifices, to earn their way. The 20-somethings are saying, 'No, I want to be paid for my work; I have no belief in the goodness of organizations, so I'm going to be here as long as my work is meaningful.'"[63] This suggests that *organizational* commitment is probably less important as a job-related attitude than it once was. In its place we might expect something akin to *occupational* commitment to become a more relevant variable because it better reflects today's fluid workforce.[64]

organizational commitment
The degree to which an employee identifies with a particular organization and its goals, and wishes to maintain membership in the organization.

Organizational Citizenship Behaviour When individuals have high organizational commitment, they are likely to engage in more organizational citizenship behaviour (OCB). We mentioned in Chapter 1 that organizations are looking for OCB in their employees. OCB is employee behaviour that goes above and beyond the call of duty, is not explicitly rewarded, is voluntary, and contributes to organizational effectiveness. Examples of such behaviour include helping one's colleagues with their workloads, taking only limited breaks, and alerting others to work-related problems.[65] More recently OCB has been associated with the following workplace behaviours: "altruism, conscientiousness, loyalty, civic virtue, voice, functional participation, sportsmanship, courtesy, and advocacy participation."[66]

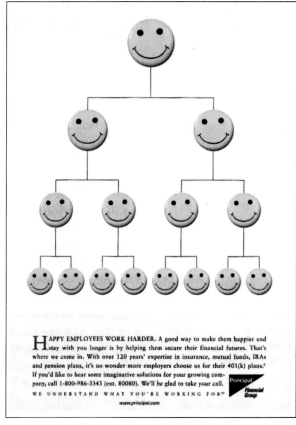

This Principal Financial Group ad accepts the widespread belief that happy workers are more productive workers.

and loyalty—constructive behaviours that allow individuals to tolerate unpleasant situations or to revive satisfactory working conditions. It helps us to understand situations, such as those sometimes found among unionized workers, where low job satisfaction is coupled with low turnover.[81] Union members often express dissatisfaction through the grievance procedure or through formal contract negotiations. These voice mechanisms allow the union members to continue in their jobs while convincing themselves that they are acting to improve the situation.

SUMMARY AND IMPLICATIONS

1 What are values? Values represent basic convictions about what is important, right, and good to the individual. Although they do not have a direct impact on behaviour, values strongly influence a person's attitudes. So knowledge of an individual's values can provide insight into his or her attitudes.

2 How can we understand values across cultures? Geert Hofstede found that managers and employees vary on five value dimensions of national culture. These are power distance; individualism vs. collectivism; quantity of life vs. quality of life; uncertainty avoidance; and long-term vs. short-term orientation.

3 Are there unique Canadian values? In his recent books, pollster Michael Adams identified the social values of today's Canadians. He found that within three broad age groups of adult Canadians—those over 55 ("the elders"), baby boomers (born between the mid-1940s and mid-1960s), and Generation X (born between the mid-1960s and early 1980s)—there are at least 12 quite distinct "value tribes." Canada also differs from the United States and its other trading partners in a variety of ways. The Ne(x)t generation also has distinct values.

4 Why are differences in values important? An employee's performance and satisfaction are likely to be higher if his or her values fit well with those of the organization. For instance, the person who places high importance on imagination, independence, and freedom is likely to be poorly matched with an organization that seeks conformity from its employees. Managers are more likely to appreciate, evaluate positively, and allocate rewards to employees who fit in, and employees are more likely to be satisfied if they perceive that they do fit. This argues for management to strive to find new employees who not only have the ability, experience, and motivation to perform, but also have a value system that is compatible with the organization's.

5 What are attitudes and how are they formed? Attitudes are positive or negative feelings concerning objects, people, or events. When I say "I like my job," I am expressing my attitude to work. Attitudes are thus responses to situations. A person can have thousands of attitudes, but OB focuses our attention on a limited number of job-related attitudes. These job-related attitudes tap positive or negative evaluations that employees hold about aspects of their work environment. Most of the research in OB has been concerned with three attitudes: job involvement, organizational commitment, and job satisfaction.

6 What is job satisfaction? The term job satisfaction refers to an individual's general attitude toward his or her job. A person with a high level of job satisfaction holds positive attitudes toward the job, while a person who is dissatisfied with his or her job holds negative attitudes toward the job. When people speak of employee attitudes, more often than not they mean job satisfaction. In fact, the two are frequently used interchangeably.

OB *AT WORK*

For Review

1. What are Hofstede's five value dimensions of national culture?

2. How might differences in generational values affect the workplace?

3. Compare Aboriginal and non-Aboriginal values.

4. How can managers get employees to more readily accept working with colleagues who are different from themselves?

5. Describe three job-related attitudes. What is their relevance to the workplace?

6. Are happy workers productive workers?

7. What is the relationship between job satisfaction and absenteeism? Job satisfaction and turnover? Which is the stronger relationship?

For Critical Thinking

1. "Thirty-five years ago, young employees we hired were ambitious, conscientious, hard-working, and honest. Today's young workers don't have the same values." Do you agree or disagree with this manager's comments? Support your position.

2. Do you think there might be any positive and significant relationship between the possession of certain personal values and successful career progression in organizations such as Merrill Lynch, the Canadian Union of Postal Workers (CUPW), and the City of Regina's police department? Discuss.

3. "Managers should do everything they can to enhance the job satisfaction of their employees." Do you agree or disagree? Support your position.

4. When employees are asked whether they would again choose the same work or whether they would want their children to follow in their footsteps, fewer than half typically answer "yes." What, if anything, do you think this implies about employee job satisfaction?

OB for You

- Within the classroom, in various kinds of activities in which you participate, as well as in the workplace, you will encounter many people who have values different from yours. You should try to understand value differences, and to figure out ways to work positively with people who are different from you.

- Though we often try to generalize about people's values based on either their generation or their culture, not all people in a group hold the same values. Be prepared to look beyond the group characteristics to understand the person.

- The variety of possible responses to dissatisfaction (exit, voice, loyalty, neglect) give you alternatives to consider when you are feeling dissatisfied with a situation. Neglect may be an easy way to respond, but consider whether voice might be more effective.

OB *AT WORK*

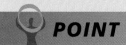

POINT

Managers Create Job Satisfaction

A review of the evidence has identified four factors conducive to high levels of employee job satisfaction: mentally challenging work, equitable rewards, supportive working conditions, and supportive colleagues.[82] Importantly, each of these factors is controllable by management.

Mentally challenging work. People prefer jobs that give them opportunities to use their skills and abilities and offer a variety of tasks, freedom, and feedback on how well they are doing. These characteristics make work mentally challenging.

Equitable rewards. Employees want pay systems and promotion policies that they perceive as being just, unambiguous, and in line with their expectations. When pay is seen as fair based on job demands, individual skill level, and community pay standards, satisfaction is likely to result. Similarly, employees seek fair promotion policies and practices. Promotions provide opportunities for personal growth, more responsibilities, and increased social status. Individuals who perceive that promotion decisions are made in a fair and just manner, therefore, are likely to experience satisfaction from their jobs.

Supportive working conditions. Employees want work environments that support personal comfort and good job performance. Studies demonstrate that employees prefer physical surroundings that are not dangerous or uncomfortable. Most employees also prefer working relatively close to home, in clean and relatively modern facilities, and with adequate tools and equipment.

Supportive colleagues. People get more out of work than merely money or tangible achievements. For most employees, work also fills the need for social interaction. Not surprisingly, therefore, having friendly and supportive co-workers leads to increased job satisfaction. The behaviour of an employee's manager is also a major determinant of satisfaction. Studies generally find that employee satisfaction increases when the immediate supervisor is understanding and friendly, offers praise for good performance, listens to employees' opinions, and shows a personal interest in them.

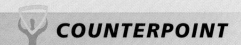

COUNTERPOINT

Satisfaction Is Individually Determined

The notion that managers and organizations can control the level of employee job satisfaction is inherently attractive. It fits nicely with the view that managers directly influence organizational processes and outcomes. Unfortunately there is a growing body of evidence challenging the notion that managers control the factors that influence employee job satisfaction. The most recent findings indicate that employee job satisfaction is largely genetically determined.[83]

Whether people are happy or not is essentially determined by their gene structure. You either have happy genes or you don't. Approximately 80 percent of people's differences in happiness, or subjective well-being, has been found to be attributable to their different genes.

Analysis of satisfaction data for a selected sample of individuals over a 50-year period found that individual results were consistently stable over time, even when these people changed employers and occupations. This and other research suggests that an individual's disposition toward life—positive or negative—is established by his or her genetic makeup, holds over time, and carries over into his or her disposition toward work.

Given these findings, there is probably little that most managers can do to influence employee satisfaction. In spite of the fact that managers and organizations go to extensive lengths to try to improve employee job satisfaction through actions such as manipulating job characteristics, working conditions, and rewards, these actions are likely to have little effect. The only place where managers will have significant influence is through their control of the selection process. If managers want satisfied workers, they need to make sure their selection process screens out the negative, maladjusted, troublemaking fault-finders who derive little satisfaction in anything job-related. This is probably best achieved through personality testing, in-depth interviewing, and careful checking of applicants' previous work records.

LEARNING ABOUT **YOURSELF** EXERCISE

What Do You Value?

Following are 16 items. Rate how important each one is to you on a scale of 0 (not important) to 100 (very important). Write the number 0–100 on the line to the left of each item.

Not important				**Somewhat important**				**Very important**		
0	10	20	30	40	50	60	70	80	90	100

_____ **1.** An enjoyable, satisfying job.

_____ **2.** A high-paying job.

_____ **3.** A good marriage.

_____ **4.** Meeting new people; social events.

_____ **5.** Involvement in community activities.

_____ **6.** My religion.

_____ **7.** Exercising, playing sports.

_____ **8.** Intellectual development.

_____ **9.** A career with challenging opportunities.

_____ **10.** Nice cars, clothes, home, and so on.

_____ **11.** Spending time with family.

_____ **12.** Having several close friends.

_____ **13.** Volunteer work for nonprofit organizations such as the Canadian Cancer Society.

_____ **14.** Meditation, quiet time to think, pray, and so on.

_____ **15.** A healthy, balanced diet.

_____ **16.** Educational reading, television, self-improvement programs, and so on.

Scoring Key

Transfer the numbers for each of the 16 items to the appropriate column; then add up the 2 numbers in each column.

	Professional	Financial	Family	Social
	1._____	2._____	3._____	4._____
	9._____	10._____	11._____	12._____
Totals	_____	_____	_____	_____

	Community	Spiritual	Physical	Intellectual
	5._____	6._____	7._____	8._____
	13._____	14._____	15._____	16._____
Totals	_____	_____	_____	_____

The higher the total in any value dimension, the higher the importance you place on that value set. The closer the numbers are in all 8 dimensions, the more well rounded you are.

Source: R.N. Lussier, *Human Relations in Organizations: A Skill Building Approach*, 2nd ed. (Homewood, IL: Richard D. Irwin, 1993). Used with permission.

OB *AT WORK*

BREAKOUT **GROUP** EXERCISE

Form small groups to discuss the following topics, as assigned by your instructor. Each person in the group should first identify 3 to 5 key personal values.

1. Identify the extent to which values overlap in your group.

2. Try to uncover with your group members the source of some of your key values (e.g., parents, peer group, teachers, church).

3. What kind of workplace would be most suitable for the values that you hold most closely?

WORKING WITH **OTHERS** EXERCISE

Understanding Cultural Values

Objective
To compare the cultural values of two countries, and determine how differences might affect group behaviour.

Time
Approximately 30 minutes.

Procedure

1. Break into groups of 5 or 6.

2. Pretend that you are a group of students working on a project. Half of you are from Canada, and hold typically "Canadian" cultural values; the other half are from the country assigned, and hold that country's cultural values.

3. Consider the values of power distance, individualism, and uncertainty avoidance, and discuss the differences between Canadian cultural values and the values of the country assigned to you.

4. Answer the following questions:

   What challenges might you expect in working together?

   What steps could be taken to work together more effectively?

ETHICAL **DILEMMA** EXERCISE

Discrimination in the Aftermath of September 11, 2001

Less than two months after the terrorist attacks on the World Trade Center and the Pentagon, security officials at one of FedEx's sorting centres became alarmed when they heard a rumour that one of the company's contract mechanics, Osama Sweilan, had been periodically disappearing into the company's flight-simulator room. The security men quickly set up an interrogation at an off-site location. The Egyptian-born, 35-year-old Sweilan nervously explained how he sometimes would slip into the room to make sure that a pipe he had fixed wasn't leaking. He also made a few quick calls to his wife. Sometimes he even prayed. The FedEx people pressed him further, asking about his beliefs regarding politics and Osama bin Laden. Afterward, they confiscated his ID and told his outsourcing firm that he was no longer wanted in his 16-month-old job.

Organizations have a responsibility to know who is working for them. But how far does that responsibility allow management to go? Although it's illegal for employers to discriminate, how should managers have responded to the heightened wariness that many employees and customers felt toward anyone from the Arab world after the terrorist attack? What can managers do if one or more of their employees are discriminating against an Arab Canadian co-worker?

Source: This dilemma is based on M. Conlin, "Taking Precautions—Or Harassing Workers?" *Business Week*, December 3, 2001, p. 84.

CASE INCIDENT

You Can't Do That

Paul Fromm is a high school teacher employed in one of the most ethnically diverse school districts in Canada. He is an excellent teacher, and receives high ratings from his students.

During weekends and summer holidays, when he is not working, he takes part in conferences held by white supremacists and anti-Semitic groups. For instance, he attended a conference at which swastikas were waving and individuals gave Nazi salutes. Fromm also attended a celebration of Adolf Hitler's birthday.

Though it is known that Fromm attends these conferences, he has never expressed racist views in the classroom or discriminated against any student. "I am here to teach English, not to make a political statement. This is my job, that's what I do. And I do it very well," he says.

The school board and some of the teachers are upset with Fromm's behaviour. They feel that what he does, even though it's outside of work time, is not consistent with the school board's values of encouraging multicultural diversity.

Questions

1. What, if anything, should the school board do in this instance?

2. Should Fromm consider not going to further conferences of this sort?

Source: Reconstructed, based on H. Sokoloff, "Firing of Teacher Upheld for His Opinions on Race," *National Post*, March 13, 2002, pp. A1, A11.

CBC VIDEO CASE INCIDENT

Corporate Culture Meets G.A.P. Adventures

In 2002, Bruce Poon Tip, president and CEO of G.A.P. Adventures won the regional Canadian Entrepreneur of the Year Award at the Metro Toronto Convention Centre. Anyone surfing this adventure travel website would be impressed with the prestige of the many awards honouring Poon Tip and G.A.P. Adventures over the past several years. The organization is just a little over a dozen years old, and Poon Tip is barely 40 years old. The awards highlight the hard work, dedication, and sacrifices made since undergoing a major corporate change in the late 1990s.

When Poon Tip started the company, it was a two-person egalitarian operation with a "family-like" atmosphere. Today,

it has grown into a worldwide 80-employee corporation with three North American and 17 international offices. The company has total annual sales exceeding $16 million. In order to grow to its current size, G.A.P. Adventures underwent a number of changes. The drastic corporate culture change took several years to implement with the help of Dave Bowen, vice-president of marketing who was recruited away from one of G.A.P. Adventures' top US competitors. Bowen ("Corporate Dave") was brought in by Poon Tip to help G.A.P. expand, diversify, and generally shake up the informal systems and procedures.

Corporate Dave's keen eye helped identify inefficiencies

in current processes, the need for corporate discipline and the necessity for formal structures. The corporate attitude of Bowen was in direct contrast to the easygoing laid-back approach Poon Tip had created. The impact of the change in attitudes around the workplace quickly caused two key employees to quit G.A.P.

Currently, G.A.P. Adventures is reaping the benefits of its corporate renewal program. A new division, Real Traveller, opened its doors to compete against G.A.P. An IT Reservation System Division and G.A.P. Adventure TV are in the works, and G.A.P. is recruiting more corporate types to head up vital managerial positions within the organization.

Questions

1. How have the values at G.A.P. Adventures changed since Dave Bowen's arrival?

2. To what extent might differences in values affect how individuals interact with one another?

3. Should managers try to change the values of employees whose values differ from management?

Source: Based on "Corporate Culture Meets G.A.P. Adventures," *CBC Venture*, June 23, 2002, 833; G.A.P. Adventures: World Wide Adventure Travel and Eco Tour website, www.gap.ca.

From **Concepts** to **Skills**

Changing Attitudes

Can you change unfavourable employee attitudes? Sometimes! It depends on who you are, the strength of the employee's attitude, the magnitude of the change, and the technique you choose to try to change the attitude.

People are most likely to respond to changes suggested by someone who is liked, credible, and convincing. If people like you, they are more apt to identify and adopt your message. Credibility implies trust, expertise, and objectivity. So you are more likely to change someone's attitude if that person views you as believable, knowledgeable about what you're saying, and unbiased in your presentation. Finally, successful attitude change is enhanced when you present your arguments clearly and persuasively.

It's easier to change a person's attitude if he or she is not strongly committed to it. Conversely, the stronger the belief in the attitude, the harder it is to change it. Also, attitudes that have been expressed publicly are more difficult to change because doing so requires admitting having made a mistake.

It's also easier to change attitudes when the change required is not very significant. To get a person to accept a new attitude that varies greatly from his or her current position requires more effort. It may also threaten other deeply held attitudes and create increased dissonance.

All attitude-change techniques are not equally effective across situations. Oral persuasion techniques are most effective when you use a positive, tactful tone; present strong evidence to support your position; tailor your argument to the listener; use logic; and support your evidence by appealing to the person's fears, frustrations, and other emotions. But people are more likely to embrace change when they can experience it. The use of training sessions where employees share and personalize experiences, and practise new behaviours, can be powerful stimulants for change. Consistent with self-perception theory, changes in behaviour can lead to changes in attitudes.

Assessing Skills

After you have read this chapter, take the following Self-Assessments on your enclosed CD-ROM.

9. What Do I Value?

10. How Involved Am I in My Job?

11. How Satisfied Am I With My Job?

12. What's My Attitude Toward Achievement?

35. How Satisfied Am I With My Job?

43. How Committed Am I to My Organization?

Practising Skills

Form into groups of two. Person A is to choose any topic that he or she feels strongly about and state his or her position on the topic in 30 words or less. Person B's task will be to try to change Person A's attitude on this topic. Person B will have 10 minutes to make his or her case. When the time is up, the roles are reversed. Person B picks the topic and Person A has 10 minutes to try to change Person B's attitude.

Potential topics (you can choose *either* side of a topic) include: politics, the economy, world events, social practices, or specific management issues, such as that organizations should require all employees to undergo regular drug testing; there is no such thing as organizational loyalty any more; the customer is always right; and layoffs are an indication of management failures.

Questions

1. Were you successful at changing the other person's attitude? Why or why not?

2. Was the other person successful at changing your attitude? Why or why not?

3. What conclusions can you draw about changing the attitudes of yourself and others?

Reinforcing Skills

1. Try to convince a friend or relative to go with you to see a movie or play that you know the subject doesn't want to see.

2. Try to convince a friend or relative to try a different brand of toothpaste.

OB | ON THE EDGE

Stress at Work

Celebrated clothing designer and entrepreneur Linda Lundström, founder of Toronto-based Linda Lundström Inc., knew she was under too much stress the day she started crying uncontrollably after she couldn't find a parking spot near her doctor's office.[1] "It was the proverbial last straw," she says about the parking incident. At the time, she was dealing with success, recognition, a growing business, and two small children. She had started to develop physical symptoms: skin rashes, intestinal disorders, neuralgia, and insomnia. That day, she walked into her doctor's office chanting over and over again, "I can't do it any more."

Calgary school bus driver Marvin Franks had a much more negative response to stress.[2] Franks was arrested in March 2002 when a scared student on his bus phoned 911 from her cellphone after smelling alcohol on his breath and finding his driving erratic. When police stopped Franks, his blood alcohol level was three times the legal limit. Franks' excuse? "If you had these kids on your bus, you'd drink too." He admitted that he was unable to control the children, but said that he smelled of alcohol only because he had a hangover, and had drunk only two beers before starting his route.

Are We Overstressed?

Stress appears to be a major factor in the lives of many Canadians. A survey conducted by POLLARA found that Canadians experience a great deal of stress, with those from Quebec topping the list.[3] The survey also found that women were more stressed than men. The inset *Stress Across the Country* reports the findings.

Among employees, stress is also a fact of life. A 2001 survey done by Ipsos-Reid of 1500 Canadians with employer-sponsored health care plans found that 62 percent reported experiencing "a great deal of stress on the job." Workplace stress was bad enough to cause 34 percent of those surveyed to say that it had made them physically ill.[4] In a 2000 Statistics Canada survey, one-third of employees blamed long hours or overwork for their stress, while 15 percent blamed "poor interpersonal relations" and 13 percent blamed risk of accident or injury.[5] Front-line employees are not the only members of the organization who experience stress, however. In another recent study, conducted by researchers Darren Larose and Bernadette Schell at Ontario's Laurentian University, 88 percent of the executives surveyed indicated elevated levels of stress and/or unhealthy personality traits.[6] They also had higher levels of predisposition to serious illnesses such as cancer and heart disease.

Perhaps one of the biggest problems for employees is that they are increasingly asked to donate labour to their employers, according to Professor Linda Duxbury, of Carleton University's Sprott School of Business, and Professor Chris Higgins, of the Richard Ivey School of Business at the University of Western Ontario. Their survey of 31 571 Canadians found that in the previous month half of them had worked an extra 2.5 days of unpaid overtime, and more than half had donated 3.5 days of working at home to catch up.[7] Canadians are frequently reporting that they want more balance in their work and family lives.[8]

The Most Stressful Jobs

How do jobs rate in terms of stress? The inset *The Most Stressful Jobs* shows how selected occupations ranked in an evaluation of 250 jobs. Among the criteria used in the rankings were overtime, quotas, deadlines, competitiveness, physical demands, environmental conditions, hazards encountered, initiative required, stamina required, win-lose situations, and working in the public eye.

Stress is not something that can be ignored in the workplace. A 2001 study conducted in 15 developed countries found that individuals who report that they are stressed in their jobs are 25 percent more likely to quit and 25 percent more likely to miss days of work.[9] Canadian, French, and Swedish employees reported the highest stress levels. In Canada, 41 percent of employees noted that they "often" or "always" experience stress at work, while only 31 percent of employees in Denmark and Switzerland reported stress levels this high. "In the wake of years of fiscal downsizing, workers across all sectors are working harder and longer than ever while trying to balance family responsibilities," said Scott Morris, former head of the Vancouver-based consulting firm Priority Management Systems Inc.[10]

Professor Daniel Ondrack, of the University of Toronto's Joseph L. Rotman School of Management, notes that "one of the major reasons for absenteeism is the logistical problems workers face in just getting to work, including transporting children to school and finding daycare. Single parents, especially female, have to juggle all the daycare and family responsibilities, and that makes it extremely difficult for people to keep up with work demands."[11]

What Is Stress?

Stress is usually defined in terms of a situation that creates excessive psychological or physiological demands on a person. Thus the situation, often referred to as the stressor, and the response *together* create the stress that an individual experiences. This distinction is important because what is stressful to one person may be enjoyable or at least viewed neutrally by another. Although almost anyone might feel stress if followed by a stranger in a dark alley, not everyone feels stressed when given the opportunity for public speaking.

Stress Across the Country, 2001/2002

Region	% with no life stresses	% with quite a lot of stress
Alberta	9.8	26.0
Atlantic Canada	14.6	18.7
British Columbia	12.0	23.6
Ontario	10.7	25.7
The Prairies	8.7	24.5
Quebec	18.0	30.0

Source: Compliled using data from http://www.statcan.ca/english/freepub/82-221-XIE/00503/tables/html/2336.htm

Dr. Hans Selye, a Montreal-based researcher, pioneered the study of stress and its effects. His model, the general adaptation syndrome (GAS), suggests that stress occurs in three stages: alarm, resistance, and exhaustion.[12] The alarm stage occurs when the body tries to meet the initial challenge of the stressor. The brain reacts by sending a message to the rest of the body's systems, causing such symptoms as increased respiration, raised blood pressure, dilated pupils, and tensed muscles.

The resistance stage occurs if the stressor continues. At this stage, a person feels such symptoms as fatigue, anxiety, and tension due to the body's attempt to fight the stressor. The exhaustion stage occurs from prolonged and continual exposure to the same stressor. The important thing to remember about how GAS works is that it puts heavy demands on the body. The more that GAS is activated and the longer that it goes on, the more wear and tear your body experiences. Individuals who frequently go through alarm, resistance, and exhaustion cycles are more likely to be susceptible to fatigue, disease, aging, and other negative physical and psychological consequences.

Stress is not necessarily bad in and of itself. It is typically discussed in a negative context, but it also has a positive value. Consider, for example, athletes or stage performers who use stress positively to rise to the occasion and perform at or near their maximum potential. On the other hand, students who put off studying for exams until the last moment and then develop the flu are not able to use their stress to perform at a maximum level.

Causes of Stress

A variety of sources of stress have been identified, including "work overload; role conflict; ineffective, hostile and incompetent bosses; lack of personal fit with a job; lack of recognition; lack of a clear job description or chain of command; fear, uncertainty, and doubt about career progress; and prejudice based on age, gender, ethnicity or religion."[13] In their research on stress, Professors Duxbury and Higgins found that more than 50 percent of employees feel they will not advance unless they put in long hours, and that turning down extra work is unacceptable.[14] They also found that although only 10 percent of employees worked 50 or more hours a week in 1991, 25 percent were working those hours in 2001.[15]

A variety of changes in the workplace have resulted in additional causes of stress. We identify some of these key changes below:[16]

- **Competition and Change.** With globalization has come increasing pressure to compete and innovate, which has led to an increase in re-engineering and restructuring. Alicja Muszynski, a sociology professor at the University of Waterloo, notes that "As corporations, including universities, have been asked to tighten their belts, there are fewer jobs and people that are left have to take on more responsibility."[17] Meanwhile, she adds, "people are afraid to take on less in the workplace, or to complain, because they're afraid they're going to get downsized."

- **Technological Change.** Employees are often expected to learn new technologies without

The Most Stressful Jobs

How do jobs rate in terms of stress? The following shows how selected occupations ranked in an evaluation of 250 jobs. Criteria used in the rankings included overtime, quotas, deadlines, competitiveness, physical demands, environmental conditions, hazards encountered, initiative required, stamina required, win-lose situations, and working in the public eye.

Rank Score	Stress Score	Rank Score	Stress Score
1. US president	176.6	47. Auto salesperson	56.3
2. Firefighter	110.9	50. College professor	54.2
3. Senior executive	108.6	60. School principal	51.7
6. Surgeon	99.5	103. Market research analyst	42.1
10. Air traffic controller	83.1	104. Personnel recruiter	41.8
12. Public relations executive	78.5	113. Hospital administrator	39.6
16. Advertising account executive	74.6	119. Economist	38.7
17. Real estate agent	73.1	122. Mechanical engineer	38.3
20. Stockbroker	71.7	124. Chiropractor	37.9
22. Pilot	68.7	132. Technical writer	36.5
25. Architect	66.9	149. Retail salesperson	34.9
31. Lawyer	64.3	173. Accountant	31.1
33. General physician	64.0	193. Purchasing agent	28.9
35. Insurance agent	63.3	229. Broadcast technician	24.2
42. Advertising salesperson	59.9	245. Actuary	20.2

Source: Reprinted by permission of *The Wall Street Journal*, © 1996 Dow Jones & Company, Inc. All rights reserved worldwide.

being given adequate training. Or they are not consulted when new technology is introduced. In addition, employees at all levels are flooded with information because of technological changes. As well, employees are frequently asked to be "on" for their jobs more hours each day: Pagers, voice mail, faxes, email, the internet, and intranets make it possible to stay in touch with the workplace 24 hours a day. Research by Professor Christina Cavanagh of the Richard Ivey School of Business at the University of Western Ontario, shows that email is an increasing cause of stress. Individuals receive an average of 80 or 90 emails daily, and devote an hour more each day to handling it than they did two years ago. The frustration is not just with quantity or time. When Cavanagh asked 10 middle managers to keep track of their emails, she discovered that nearly half of the messages were "junk or notes with little relevance."[18]

- **Increasingly Diverse Workforce.** "If diversity is not managed effectively it may lead to interpersonal stress, competition among different groups for attention and resources, and decreased interaction because of the perceived need for political correctness in speech, interaction, and recognition." In diverse groups, individuals experience differences in beliefs and values, differences in role expectations, and differences in perceptions about fairness in procedures.

- **Downsizing.** With downsizing seemingly a routine procedure in many companies, even the threat of layoffs can be stressful. Moreover, after downsizing,

firms often increase the workloads of those remaining, leading to more stress.

- **Employee Empowerment and Teamwork.** Both empowerment and teamwork require greater decision-making responsibility and interaction skills from employees. Although this alone is stressful, it is particularly stressful for individuals who "have little or no interest in empowerment or teamwork structures and processes. Many people do not function well in a group setting, and they and their work may suffer if forced into a team environment."

- **Work/Home Conflict**. Trying to balance work life and family life is difficult at the best of times, but more employees are finding that their jobs are demanding longer hours, either formally or informally. This makes it difficult to manage the nonwork parts of life. Families with children where both parents work, or where parents are raising children alone, often have the added stress of managing child-care arrangements.

About one in eight workers was responsible for providing some form of care for aging parents in 1997, and one survey found that one in three were doing so in 2002.[19] Being a caregiver is an additional stress both at home and at work. Studies indicate that those who have difficulties finding effective child care or eldercare have lower work performance and increased absenteeism, decreased satisfaction, and lower physical and psychological well-being.[20]

A fact that tends to be overlooked when stressors are reviewed individually is that stress is an additive phenomenon.[21] Stress builds up. Each new and persistent stressor adds to

an individual's stress level. A single stressor may seem relatively unimportant in and of itself, but if it is added to an already high level of stress, it can be "the straw that breaks the camel's back." You may recall that the final straw for Linda Lundström was not being able to find a parking space.

Consequences of Stress

Stress manifests itself in a number of ways. For instance, an individual who is experiencing a high level of stress may develop high blood pressure, ulcers, irritability, difficulty in making routine decisions, loss of appetite, accident proneness, and the like. These symptoms can be placed under three general categories: physiological, psychological, and behavioural symptoms.[22]

- **Physiological Symptoms.** Most of the research on stress suggests that it can create changes in metabolism, increase heart and breathing rates, increase blood pressure, cause headaches, and induce heart attacks. An interesting aspect of illness in today's workplace is the considerable change in how stress shows up. In the past, older workers were the ones claiming sick leave, workers' compensation, and short- and long-term disability—most often in cases of catastrophic illness such as heart attacks, cancer, and major back surgeries. These days, however, it's not unusual for long-term disability programs to be filled with employees in their 20s, 30s, and 40s. Employees are claiming illnesses that are either psychiatric (such as depression) or more difficult to diagnose (such as chronic fatigue syndrome or fibromyalgia, a musculoskeletal discomfort). The increase in disability claims may be the result of downsizing taking its toll on the psyches of those in the workforce.[23]

- **Psychological Symptoms.** Job dissatisfaction is "the simplest and most obvious psychological effect" of stress.[24] However, stress also manifests itself in other psychological states—for instance, tension, anxiety, irritability, boredom, and procrastination.

  The evidence indicates that when people are placed in jobs that make multiple and conflicting demands or in which there is a lack of clarity as to the person's duties, authority, and responsibilities, both stress and dissatisfaction increase.[25] Similarly, the less control that people have over the pace of their work, the greater the stress and dissatisfaction. More research is needed to clarify the relationship, but the evidence suggests that jobs providing a low level of variety, significance, autonomy, feedback, and identity create stress and reduce satisfaction and involvement in the job.[26]

- **Behavioural Symptoms.** Behaviourally related stress symptoms include changes in productivity, absence, and turnover, as well as changes in eating habits, increased smoking or consumption of alcohol, rapid speech, fidgeting, and sleep disorders. More recently stress has been linked to aggression and violence in the workplace.

Why Do Individuals Differ in Their Experience of Stress?

Some people thrive on stressful situations, while others are overwhelmed by them. What is it that differentiates people in terms of their ability to handle stress? What individual difference variables moderate the relationship between *potential* stressors and *experienced* stress? At least five variables—perception, job experience, social support, belief in locus of control, and hostility—have been found to be relevant moderators.

- **Perception.** Individuals react in response to their *perception* of reality rather than to reality itself. Perception, therefore, will moderate the relationship between a potential stress condition and an employee's reaction to it. One person's fear of losing a job because the company is laying off staff may be perceived by another as an opportunity to receive a large severance allowance and start a small business. Similarly, what one employee perceives as a challenging job may be viewed as threatening and demanding by others.[27] So the stress potential in environmental, organizational, and individual factors does not lie in objective conditions. Rather, it lies in an employee's interpretation of those factors.

- **Job Experience.** Experience is said to be a great teacher. It can also be a great stress reducer. Think back to your first date or your first few days in college or university. For most of us, the uncertainty and newness of those situations created stress. But as we gained experience, that stress disappeared or at least significantly decreased. The same phenomenon seems to apply to work situations. That is, experience on the job tends to be negatively related to work stress. Two explanations have been offered.[28] First, people who experience more stress on the job when they are first hired may be more likely to quit. Therefore, people who remain with the organization longer are those with more stress-resistant traits or those who are more resistant to the stress characteristics of their organization. Second, people eventually develop coping mechanisms to deal with stress. Because this takes time, senior members of the organization are more likely to be fully adapted and should experience less stress.

- **Social Support.** There is increasing evidence that social support—that is, collegial relationships with co-workers or supervisors—can buffer the impact of stress.[29] The logic underlying this moderating variable is that social support helps to ease the negative effects of even high-strain jobs.

  For individuals whose work associates are unhelpful or even actively hostile, social support may be found outside the job. Involvement with family, friends, and community can provide the support—especially for those with a high social need—that is missing at work, and this can make job stressors more tolerable.

- **Belief in Locus of Control.** The personality trait locus of control determines the extent to which individuals believe they have control over the things that happen in their lives. Those with an internal locus of control believe they control their own destiny. Those with an external locus believe their lives are controlled by outside forces. Evidence indicates that internals perceive their jobs to be less stressful than do externals.[30]

When internals and externals confront a similar stressful situation, the internals are likely to believe that they can have a significant effect on the results. They therefore act to take control of events. Externals are more likely to experience stress because they frequently act helpless, often by being passive and defensive, while feeling helpless.

- **Hostility.** Some people's personality includes a high degree of hostility and anger. These people are chronically suspicious and mistrustful of others. Recent evidence indicates that such *hostility* significantly increases a person's stress and risk for heart disease.[31] More specifically, people who are quick to anger, maintain a persistently hostile outlook, and project a cynical mistrust of others are more likely to experience stress in situations.

How Do We Manage Stress?

Both the individual and the organization can take steps to help the individual manage stress. Below we discuss ways that individuals can manage stress, and then we examine programs that organizations are using to help employees manage stress.

Individual Approaches

An employee can take personal responsibility for reducing his or her stress level. Individual strategies that have proven effective include time management techniques, physical exercise, relaxation training, and a close social support network.

- **Time Management.** Many people manage their time poorly. The things we have to accomplish in any given day or week are not necessarily beyond completion

if we manage our time properly. The well-organized employee, like the well-organized student, can often accomplish twice as much as the person who is poorly organized. So understanding and using basic *time management* principles can help individuals cope better with tensions created by job demands.[32] A few of the more well-known time management principles are: 1) making daily lists of activities to be accomplished; 2) prioritizing activities by importance and urgency; 3) scheduling activities according to the priorities set; and 4) knowing your daily cycle and handling the most demanding parts of your job during the high part of your cycle when you are most alert and productive.[33]

- **Physical Activity.** Noncompetitive physical exercise, such as aerobics, walking, jogging, swimming, and riding a bicycle, has long been recommended by physicians as a way to deal with excessive stress levels. These forms of *physical exercise* increase heart capacity, lower at-rest heart rate, provide a mental diversion from work pressures, and offer a means to "let off steam."[34]

- **Relaxation Techniques.** Individuals can teach themselves to reduce tension through *relaxation techniques* such as meditation, hypnosis, and biofeedback. The objective is to reach a state of deep relaxation, where you feel physically relaxed, somewhat detached from the immediate environment, and detached from body sensations.[35] Fifteen or 20 minutes a day of deep relaxation releases tension and provides a person with a pronounced sense of peacefulness. Importantly, significant changes in heart rate,

blood pressure, and other physiological factors result from achieving the deep relaxation condition.

- **Building Social Supports.** Having friends, family, or colleagues to talk to provides an outlet when stress levels become excessive. Expanding your *social support network*, therefore, can be a means for tension reduction. It provides you with someone to listen to your problems and to offer a more objective perspective

FactBox[36]

- One in three Canadians between the ages of 25 and 44 claims to be a workaholic.
- 38% of people in management report being workaholics.
- 85% of married women who are employed full-time and have at least one child at home, and 75% of similarly situated men, say that weekdays are too short to accomplish what needs to get done.
- The financial cost to companies because employees are trying to balance work and family obligations is estimated to be at least $2.7 billion a year.
- 25% of white-collar workers and 40% of blue-collar workers had a stress-related absence in 1998. The cost of this to companies was $12 billion.
- 1/3 of Canadians don't take all of their vacation days, saving their employers $8 billion a year.
- When Canadians do go on holiday, 36% of them take work, and check their office voice mail and email.

on the situation. Research also demonstrates that social support moderates the stress-burnout relationship.[37] That is, high support reduces the likelihood that heavy work stress will result in job burnout.

The inset *Tips for Reducing Stress* offers additional ideas for reducing stress.

Organizational Approaches

Employees who work at Toronto-based BCS Communications Ltd., a publishing, advertising and public relations agency, receive biweekly shiatsu massages, paid for by the company. The company spends about $700 a month for the massages, equivalent to the amount it used to spend providing coffee to the employees. "It's in my company's best interest to have my employees be healthy," says Caroline Tapp-

Tips for Reducing Stress

- At least two or three times a week, spend time with supportive friends or family.

- Ask for support when you are under pressure. This is a sign of health, not weakness.

- If you have spiritual or religious beliefs, increase or maintain your involvement.

- Use a variety of methods to reduce stress. Consider exercise, nutrition, hobbies, positive thinking, and relaxation techniques such as meditation or yoga.

Source: J. Lee, "How to Fight That Debilitating Stress in Your Workplace," *The Vancouver Sun*, April 5, 1999, p. C3. Reprinted with permission.

McDougall, the BCS group publisher.[38]

Vancouver-based QLT Inc. has an in-house gym and offers aerobics and stretch classes and Friday-morning shiatsu massage treatments to its employees. QLT's cafeteria has healthy food choices, and Weight Watchers products. Robyn Crisanti, a QLT spokesperson, explains the company's investment in wellness: "Corporate wellness is good for employees and there is a lot of research that shows healthy employees take fewer sick days and are more productive."[39] The programs also make it easier for QLT to attract talented employees.

Most firms that have introduced wellness programs have found significant benefits. Health Canada reports that businesses get back $3.39 for each corporate dollar they invest in wellness initiatives. For individuals with three to five risk factors (such as high cholesterol, being overweight, or smoking) the return was $2.04 for each dollar spent.[40] The savings come about because there is less turnover, greater productivity, and reduced medical claims.[41] About 64 percent of Canadian companies surveyed by Health Canada in 1999 offered some sort of wellness initiative, including programs such as stop-smoking, stress courses, and back-pain management; 17.5 percent of companies offered on-site wellness programs.[42]

So what else can organizations do to reduce employee stress? In general, strategies to reduce stress include improved processes for choosing employees, placement of employees in appropriate jobs, realistic goal setting, designing jobs with employee needs and skills in mind, increased employee involvement, improved organizational communication, and establishment of corporate wellness programs.

Certain jobs are more stressful than others, but individuals also differ in their response to stress situations. We know, for example, that individuals with little experience or an external locus of control tend to be more prone to stress. Selection and placement decisions should take these facts into consideration. Although management should not restrict hiring to only experienced individuals with an internal locus of control, such individuals may adapt better to high-stress jobs and perform those jobs more effectively.

Research shows that individuals perform better when they have specific and challenging goals and receive feedback on how well they are progressing toward them. The use of goals can reduce stress as well as provide motivation. Specific goals that are perceived as attainable clarify performance expectations. Additionally, goal feedback reduces uncertainties as to actual job performance. The result is less employee frustration, role ambiguity, and stress.

Creating jobs that give employees more responsibility, more meaningful work, more autonomy, and increased feedback can reduce stress because these factors give the employee greater control over work activities and lessen dependence on others. Of course, not all employees want jobs with increased responsibility. The right job for employees with a low need for growth might be less responsibility and increased specialization. If individuals prefer structure and routine, more structured jobs should also reduce uncertainties and stress levels.

One idea that has received considerable recent attention is allowing employees to take short naps during the workday.[43] Nap time, apparently, isn't just for preschool kids any more! An increasing number of companies are finding that allowing employees to catch 10 to 30 minutes of sleep in the afternoon increases productivity and makes them less prone to errors.

Increasing formal organizational communication with employees reduces uncertainty by lessening role ambiguity and role conflict. Given the importance that perceptions play in moderating the stress-response relationship, management can also use effective communications as a means to shape employee perceptions. Remember that what employees categorize as demands, threats, or opportunities are merely interpretations, and those interpretations can be affected by the symbols and actions communicated by management.

Our final suggestion is to offer organizationally supported wellness

Reducing Stress in the Workplace

- Avoid electronic monitoring of staff. Personal supervision generates considerably less stress.

- Allow workers time to recharge after periods of intense or demanding work.

- Important information that significantly affects employees is best transmitted face to face.

- Encourage positive social interactions between staff to promote problem-solving around work issues and increase emotional support.

- Staff need to balance privacy and social interaction at work. Extremes can generate stress.

Source: J. Lee, "How to Fight That Debilitating Stress in Your Workplace," *The Vancouver Sun*, April 5, 1999, p. C3. Reprinted with permission.

FACE**OFF**

When organizations provide on-site daycare facilities, they are filling a needed role in parents' lives, and making it easier for parents to attend to their job demands rather than worry about child-care arrangements.

When employees expect organizations to provide child care, they are shifting their responsibilities to their employers, rather than keeping their family needs and concerns private. Moreover, it's unfair to give child-care benefits when not all employees have children.

programs, such as those provided by QLT and BCS Communications. These programs focus on the employee's total physical and mental condition.[44] For example, they typically provide workshops to help people quit smoking, control alcohol use, lose weight, eat better, and develop a regular exercise program. The assumption underlying most wellness programs is that employees need to take personal responsibility for their physical and mental health. The organization is merely a vehicle to make this happen. The inset *Reducing Stress in the Workplace* offers additional ideas.

Research Exercises

1. Look for data on stress levels in other countries. How do these data compare with the Canadian data presented above? Are the sources of stress the same in different countries? What might you conclude about how stress affects people in different cultures?

2. Find out what three Canadian organizations in three different industries have done to help employees manage stress. Are there common themes in these programs? Did you find any unusual programs? To what extent are these programs tailored to the needs of the employees in those industries?

Your Perspective

1. Think of all of the technological changes that have happened in the workplace in recent years, including email, faxes, and intranets. What are the positive benefits of this change? What are the downsides? As an employee facing the demand to "stay connected" to your workplace, how would you try to maintain a balance in your life?

2. How much responsibility should individuals take for managing their own stress? To what extent should organizations become involved in the personal lives of their employees when trying to help them manage stress? What are the pros and cons for whether employees or organizations take responsibility for managing stress?

Want to Know More?

If you are wondering how stressed you are, go to www.heartandstroke.ca and click on "Assess Your Risk." The site also offers tips on how to relax and manage stress.

CHAPTER 4

Motivating Self and Others

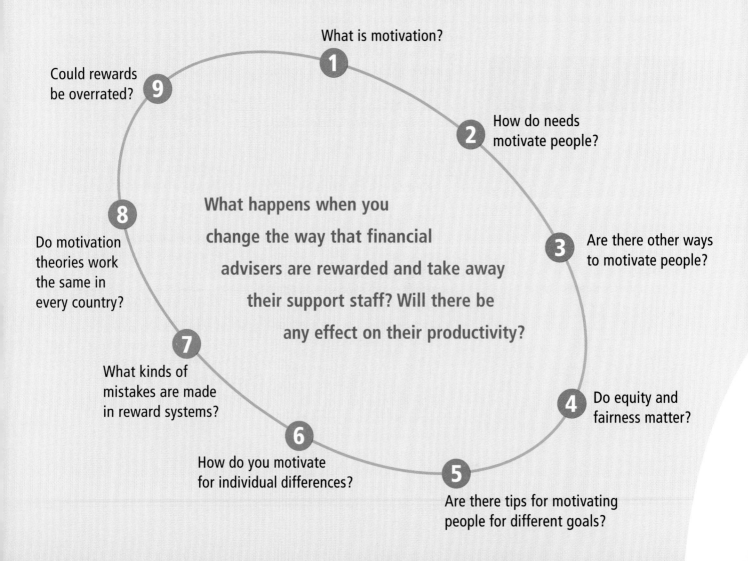

What is motivation?

1

Could rewards
be overrated?

9

How do needs
motivate people?

2

8

Do motivation
theories work
the same in
every country?

What happens when you
change the way that financial
advisers are rewarded and take away
their support staff? Will there be
any effect on their productivity?

Are there other ways
to motivate people?

3

7

What kinds of
mistakes are made
in reward systems?

Do equity and
fairness matter?

4

6

How do you motivate
for individual differences?

5

Are there tips for motivating
people for different goals?

A year after being hired, 12 employees of Toronto-based Charles Schwab Canada started expressing discontent about their pay structure loudly and publicly.[1] They wrote a letter to the co-CEO of the US parent corporation on Valentine's Day 2000, outlining their concerns. One of their major complaints was that their CEO, Paul Bates, changed their bonus plan three times during the year, making it impossible for the employees to know how they would be rewarded. The employees' letter concluded that Schwab Canada was not fair, responsive, or empathetic to its employees. The San Francisco head office sent a group of managers to investigate the complaints, but did not remove Bates, whom employees blamed for their unhappiness.

The behaviour of the employees at Schwab—high turnover and feelings of anger—illustrates the problems that can develop if employees feel they are not being rewarded fairly for their performance. This chapter examines the subject of motivation and rewards in some detail.

Defining Motivation

We define **motivation** as the processes that account for an individual's intensity, direction, and persistence of effort toward reaching a goal.[2]

The three key elements in our definition are intensity, direction, and persistence. *Intensity* is concerned with how hard a person tries. This is what most of us focus on when we talk about motivation. However, high intensity is unlikely to positively affect job performance unless the effort is channelled in a *direction* that is useful. Finally, the effort requires *persistence*. This is a measure of how long a person can maintain his or her effort. Motivated individuals stay with a task long enough to achieve their goal.

Many people incorrectly view motivation as a personal trait—that is, some have it and others don't. Along these lines, Douglas McGregor proposed two distinct views of human beings. **Theory X**, which is basically negative, suggests that employees dislike work, will try to avoid it, and must be coerced, controlled, or threatened with punishment to achieve goals. **Theory Y**, which is basically positive, suggests that employees will use self-direction and self-control if they are committed to the goals.[3]

1 What is motivation?

motivation
The processes that account for an individual's intensity, direction, and persistence of effort toward reaching a goal.

Theory X
The assumption that employees dislike work, are lazy, dislike responsibility, and must be coerced to perform.

Theory Y
The assumption that employees like work, are creative, seek responsibility, and can use self-direction.

Our knowledge of motivation tells us that neither of these theories fully accounts for employee behaviour. What we know is that motivation is the result of the interaction of the individual and the situation. Certainly, individuals differ in their basic motivational drive. But the same employee who is quickly bored when pulling the lever on a drill press may enthusiastically pull a slot machine lever in Casino Windsor for hours. You may read a thriller at one sitting, yet find it difficult to concentrate on a textbook for more than 20 minutes. It's not necessarily you—it's the situation. So as we analyze the concept of motivation, keep in mind that the level of motivation varies both between individuals and within individuals at different times. What motivates people will also vary for both the individual and the situation.

Motivation theorists talk about *intrinsic motivators* and *extrinsic motivators*. **Extrinsic motivators** come from outside the person and include such things as pay, bonuses, and other tangible rewards. **Intrinsic motivators** come from a person's internal desire to do something, motivated by such things as interest, challenge, and personal satisfaction. Individuals are intrinsically motivated when they genuinely care about their work, look for better ways to do it, and are energized and fulfilled by doing it well.[4] The rewards the individual gets from intrinsic motivation come from the work itself, rather than from external factors such as increases in pay or compliments from the boss.

Are individuals mainly intrinsically or extrinsically motivated? Theory X suggests that people are almost exclusively driven by extrinsic motivators. However, Theory Y suggests that people are more intrinsically motivated. Intrinsic and extrinsic motivation may reflect the situation, however, rather than individual personalities.

For example, suppose your mother has asked you to take her to a meeting an hour away and then drop off your twin brother somewhere else. You may be willing to drive her, without any thought of compensation, because it will make you feel nice to do something for her. That is intrinsic motivation. But if you have a love-hate relationship with your brother, you may insist that he buy you lunch for helping out. Lunch would then be an extrinsic motivator—something that came from outside yourself and motivated you to do the task. If you think money is a powerful motivator, you may be surprised to read an opposing viewpoint in this chapter's *Point/CounterPoint* on page 133.

extrinsic motivators
Motivation that comes from outside the person, such as pay, bonuses, and other tangible rewards.

intrinsic motivators
A person's internal desire to do something, due to such things as interest, challenge, and personal satisfaction.

NEEDS THEORIES OF MOTIVATION

2 How do needs motivate people?

The main theories of motivation fall into one of two categories: needs theories and process theories. *Needs theories* describe the types of needs that must be met in order to motivate individuals. *Process theories* help us understand the actual ways by which we and others can be motivated. There are a variety of needs theories, including Maslow's hierarchy of needs, Herzberg's two-factor theory (sometimes also called motivation-hygiene theory), Alderfer's ERG theory, and McClelland's theory of needs. We briefly review the first two of these to illustrate the basic properties of needs theories.

Maslow's Hierarchy of Needs

Abraham Maslow
www.ship.edu/~cgboeree/
maslow.html

It's probably safe to say that the most well-known theory of motivation is Abraham Maslow's hierarchy of needs.[5] He hypothesized that within every human being there exists a hierarchy of five needs:

- *Physiological.* Includes hunger, thirst, shelter, sex, and other bodily needs.

- *Safety.* Includes security and protection from physical and emotional harm.

- *Social.* Includes affection, belongingness, acceptance, and friendship.

- *Esteem.* Includes internal esteem factors such as self-respect, autonomy, and achievement; and external esteem factors such as status, recognition, and attention.

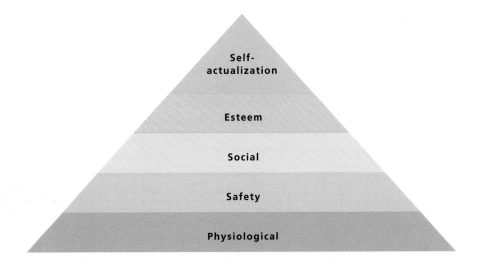

Exhibit 4–1

Maslow's Hierarchy of Needs

- *Self-actualization.* Includes growth, achieving one's potential, and self-fulfillment. This is the drive to become what one is capable of becoming.

As each of these needs becomes substantially satisfied, the next need becomes more important to fulfill. In terms of Exhibit 4–1, the individual moves up the steps of the needs hierarchy. From the perspective of motivation, the theory would say that while no need is ever fully satisfied, a substantially satisfied need no longer motivates. So if you want to motivate someone, according to Maslow, you need to understand what level of the hierarchy that person is currently on and focus on satisfying the needs at or above that level.

Maslow's needs theory continues to receive wide recognition some 50 years after he proposed it, particularly among practising managers. The theory is intuitive and easy to understand. Unfortunately, research does not generally validate the theory. Maslow himself provided no empirical evidence for his theory. Several studies that examined the theory found little support for the prediction that needs form the hierarchy proposed by Maslow, that unsatisfied needs motivate, or that a satisfied need moves a person to seek satisfaction at a new need level.[6]

Motivation-Hygiene Theory

The motivation-hygiene theory was proposed by psychologist Frederick Herzberg.[7] Herzberg investigated the question "What do people want from their jobs?" in an effort to determine what might lead to a person's success or failure at work.

Frederick Herzberg
www.lib.uwo.ca/business/herzberg.html

He found that intrinsic factors—such as achievement, recognition, the work itself, responsibility, advancement, and growth—seem to be related to job satisfaction. Herzberg also found that there were characteristics that led to job dissatisfaction. The factors that caused dissatisfaction were extrinsic—such as company policy and administration, supervision, interpersonal relations, and working conditions.

Herzberg's research led him to conclude that the opposite of satisfaction is not dissatisfaction, as was traditionally believed. Removing dissatisfying characteristics from a job does not necessarily make the job satisfying. As illustrated in Exhibit 4–2, Herzberg proposes a dual continuum: the opposite of "Satisfaction" is "No Satisfaction," and the opposite of "Dissatisfaction" is "No Dissatisfaction."

Exhibit 4–2

Exhibit 4–2

Contrasting Views of Satisfaction and Dissatisfaction

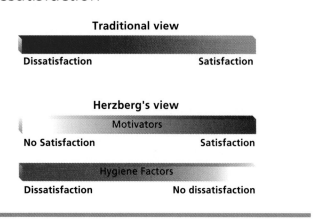

Herzberg explained that the factors leading to job satisfaction were *motivators* that are separate and distinct from the *hygiene* factors that lead to job dissatisfaction. Thus managers who try to get rid of factors that create job dissatisfaction can bring about peace, but not necessarily motivation. *Hygiene* factors include company policy and administration, supervision, interpersonal relations, working conditions, and salary. When these factors are adequate, people will not be dissatisfied; however, neither will they be satisfied. Motivating factors include achievement, recognition, the work itself, responsibility, and growth. These are the characteristics that people find intrinsically rewarding or motivating. In this chapter's *Working With Others Exercise* on pages 135–136 you can discover what motivates both you and others in the workplace.

Herzberg's theory has received some criticism.[8] However, it has been widely read and few managers are unfamiliar with his recommendations. Over the past 40 years the popularity of jobs that allow employees greater responsibility in planning and controlling their work can probably be largely attributed to Herzberg's findings and recommendations.

Summarizing Needs Theories

All needs theories of motivation, including Maslow's hierarchy of needs, Herzberg's two-factor theory (sometimes also called motivation-hygiene theory), Alderfer's ERG theory, and McClelland's theory of needs, propose a similar idea: Individuals have needs that, when unsatisfied, will result in motivation. For instance, if you have a need to be praised, you may work harder at your task in order to receive recognition from your manager or other co-workers. Similarly, if you need money and you are asked to do something, within reason, that offers money as a reward, you will be motivated to complete the task in order to earn the money. Where needs theories differ is in the types of needs they consider, and whether they propose a hierarchy of needs (where some needs have to be satisfied before others) or simply a list of needs. Exhibit 4–3 illustrates the relationship of four needs theories to each other. While the theories use different names for the needs, and also have different numbers of needs, we can see that

Exhibit 4–3

Relationship of Various Needs Theories

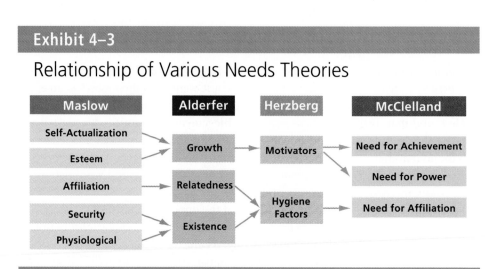

they are consistent in the types of needs addressed. Exhibit 4–4 also indicates the contribution and empirical support for each theory. This chapter's *CBC Video Case Incident*, "Under 21 and Self-Employed," encourages you to think about needs and job choices.

"Under 21 and Self-Employed"

Needs Theories in the Workplace

What can we conclude from the needs theories? We can safely say that individuals have needs and that they can be highly motivated to achieve those needs. The types of needs, and their importance, vary by individual, and probably vary over time for the same individual as well. When rewarding individuals, one should consider their specific needs. Some employees may be struggling to make ends meet, while others are looking for more opportunities to reach self-actualization. Individual needs also change over time, depending on one's stage in life. Obviously, in a workplace it would be difficult to design a reward structure that could completely take into account the specific needs of each employee. At Burnaby, BC-based Telus, employees earn points through a variety of job-related activities. They then choose gifts from a catalogue that lists rewards and their point values. To get an idea of the factors that might motivate you in the workplace, turn to this chapter's *Learning About Yourself Exercise* on page 134.

Telus Communications Inc.
www.telus.com

Exhibit 4–4

Summarizing the Various Needs Theories

Theory	Maslow	Herzberg	Alderfer	McClelland
Is there a hierarchy of needs?	Argues that lower-order needs must be satisfied before one progresses to higher-order needs.	Hygiene factors must be met if person is not to be dissatisfied. This will not lead to satisfaction, however. Motivators lead to satisfaction.	More than one need can be important at the same time. If a higher-order need is not being met, the desire to satisfy a lower-level need increases.	People vary in the types of needs they have. Their motivation and how well they perform in a work situation are related to whether they have a need for achievement, affiliation, or power.
What is the theory's impact/ contribution?	Enjoys wide recognition among practising managers. Most managers are familiar with it.	The popularity of giving workers greater responsibility for planning and controlling their work can be attributed to his findings. Shows that more than one need may operate at the same time.	Seen as a more valid version of the needs hierarchy. Tells us that achievers will be motivated by jobs that offer personal responsibility, feedback, and moderate risks.	Tells us that high need achievers do not necessarily make good managers, since high achievers are more interested in how they do personally.
What empirical support/ criticisms exist?	Research does not generally validate the theory. In particular, there is little support for the hierarchical nature of needs. Criticized for how data were collected and interpreted.	Not really a *theory* of motivation: Assumes a link between satisfaction and productivity that was not measured or demonstrated.	Ignores situational variables.	Mixed empirical support, but theory is consistent with our knowledge of individual differences among people. Good empirical support, particularly on needs achievement.

PROCESS THEORIES OF MOTIVATION

> One of the complaints of the employees of Toronto-based Charles Schwab Canada was that they had been promised leading-edge technology and a corporate environment that emphasized the quality of service given to clients. This represented a big change, they hoped, from competing investment firms such as Merrill Lynch. However, they soon discovered drawbacks in that technology. It was hard to see their clients' portfolios, making it difficult to provide quality service. Then, because the reward structure kept changing, employees couldn't tell which of their efforts would be valued and rewarded. Why would these factors make Schwab's employees feel less motivated?

3 Are there other ways to motivate people?

While needs theories identify the different needs that could be used to motivate individuals, process theories focus on the broader picture of how someone can set about motivating another individual. Process theories include *expectancy theory* and *goal-setting theory* (and its application, *management by objectives*). Focusing greater attention on these process theories might help you understand how to motivate yourself or someone else.

Expectancy Theory

expectancy theory
The strength of a tendency to act in a certain way depends on the strength of an expectation that the act will be followed by a given outcome and on the attractiveness of that outcome to the individual.

Currently, one of the most widely accepted explanations of motivation is Victor Vroom's **expectancy theory**.[9]

From a practical perspective, expectancy theory says that an employee will be motivated to exert a high level of effort when he or she believes:

- that effort will lead to a good performance;
- that a good performance will lead to organizational rewards, such as a bonus, a salary increase, or a promotion;
- that the rewards will satisfy the employee's personal goals.

The theory, therefore, focuses on the three relationships illustrated in Exhibit 4–5. This exhibit also provides an example of how you might apply the theory.

Effort-Performance Relationship

expectancy
The belief that effort leads to performance.

The effort-performance relationship is commonly called **expectancy**. It refers to the individual's perception of how probable it is that exerting a given amount of effort will

Exhibit 4–5

How Does Expectancy Theory Work?

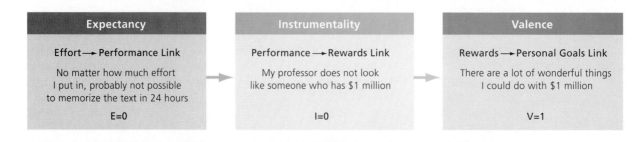

My professor offers to give me $1 million if I memorize the textbook by tomorrow morning.

Expectancy	Instrumentality	Valence
Effort → Performance Link	Performance → Rewards Link	Rewards → Personal Goals Link
No matter how much effort I put in, probably not possible to memorize the text in 24 hours	My professor does not look like someone who has $1 million	There are a lot of wonderful things I could do with $1 million
E=0	I=0	V=1

Conclusion: Though I value the reward, I will not be motivated to do this task.

lead to good performance. For example, employees are sometimes asked to perform tasks for which they do not have suitable skills or training. When that is the case, they will be less motivated to try hard, because they already believe that they will not be able to accomplish what they are being asked to do.

The Schwab Canada employees were frustrated because instead of being able to help their clients, they were slowed down by Schwab's technology and swamped with paperwork demands. Thus, these employees were not likely to feel that their effort would lead to good performance.

Performance-Reward Relationship

The performance-reward relationship is commonly called **instrumentality**. It refers to the individual's perception of whether performing at a particular level will lead to the attainment of a desired outcome. In particular, will the performance be acknowledged by those who have the power to allocate rewards?

In a study by the Angus Reid Group, only 44 percent of employees said the workplace recognizes employees who excel at their job.[10] Thus, one possible source of low motivation is the employee's belief that no matter how hard he or she works, the performance will not be recognized. Certainly Schwab Canada's CEO made it difficult for employees to believe they would be rewarded when he kept changing how rewards would be assessed.

Rewards–Personal Goals Relationship

The rewards–personal goals relationship is commonly called **valence**. It refers to the degree to which organizational rewards satisfy an individual's personal goals or needs and the attractiveness of those potential rewards for the individual. Unfortunately, many managers are limited in the rewards they can distribute, which makes it difficult to personalize rewards.

Moreover, some managers incorrectly assume that all employees want the same thing. They overlook the motivational effects of differentiating rewards. In either case, employee motivation may be lower because the specific need the employee has is not being met through the reward structure.

Vancouver-based Radical Entertainment, creator of such digital entertainment as *The Hulk* and *Simpsons Road Rage*, makes sure it meets the needs of its employees, because it doesn't want to lose them to the United States.[11] The company employs a "Radical fun guru" whose job is to make the workplace so much fun no one wants to leave. The company provides free food all day, including catered lunches a few times a week, and there is a log cabin on site, fitted out with big screens, DVDs, and gaming equipment, where employees can take time out to recharge during their long workdays. Radical Entertainment offers these benefits to meet the needs of its young employees, who find greater motivation from being part of a cool workplace than having a bigger pension plan.

Expectancy Theory in the Workplace

Does expectancy theory work? Although it has its critics,[12] most of the research evidence supports the theory.[13]

Exhibit 4–6 shows how managers can increase the motivation of employees, using insights from expectancy theory. Managers can increase the effort-to-performance expectancy, the performance-to-reward expectancy, or use rewards that are valued by

Golfers such as Prince Edward Island's Lorie Kane illustrate the effectiveness of the expectancy theory of motivation, where rewards are tied to effort and outcome. Players on the LPGA tour are paid strictly according to their performance, unlike members of professional team sports. Kane's first LPGA tour victory came in 2000, at the Michelob Light Classic. It ended a string of nine runner-up finishes. She had two more victories in 2000 and won the 2001 LPGA Takefuji Classic. As Kane has put more effort into her play, she has been increasing her earnings each year.

instrumentality
The belief that performance is related to rewards.

valence
The value or importance an individual places on a reward.

Radical Entertainment Inc.
www.radical.ca

Exhibit 4–6

Steps to Increasing Motivation, Using Expectancy Theory

Improving Expectancy	**Improving Instrumentality**	**Improving Valence**
Improve the ability of the individual to perform	Increase the individual's belief that performance will lead to reward	Make sure that the reward is meaningful to the individual
• Make sure employees have skills for the task • Provide training • Assign reasonable tasks and goals	• Observe and recognize performance • Deliver rewards as promised • Indicate to employees how previous good performance led to greater rewards	• Ask employees what rewards they value • Give rewards that are valued

employees. To further appreciate how expectancy theory might apply in the workplace, see this chapter's *Case Incident* on page 138 for an example of what happens when expected rewards are withdrawn.

Goal-Setting Theory

goal-setting theory
The theory that specific and difficult goals lead to higher performance.

"Just do your best. That's all anyone can ask for." You've probably heard that before. But what does "do your best" mean? Do we ever know if we've achieved that vague goal? Might you have done better in your high school English class if your parents had said, "You should strive for 75 percent or higher on all your work in English" instead of "do your best"? The research on **goal-setting theory** addresses these issues, and as you will see, the findings are impressive in terms of the effects of goal specificity, challenge, and feedback on performance.

In the late 1960s, Edwin Locke proposed that intentions to work toward a goal are a major source of work motivation.[14] That is, goals tell an employee what needs to be done and how much effort will need to be expended.[15] The evidence strongly supports the value of goals. More to the point, we can say that specific goals increase performance; that difficult goals, when accepted, result in higher performance than do easy goals; and that feedback leads to higher performance than does nonfeedback.[16]

Goal-setting theory is not inconsistent with expectancy theory. The goals can be considered the effort-performance link—in other words, the goals determine what must be done. Feedback can be considered the performance-reward relationship, where the individual's efforts are recognized. While goal setting does not explicitly address rewards or the value of the rewards, the implication is that the achievement of the goals will result in intrinsic satisfaction (and may of course be linked to external rewards). We discuss how to set effective goals in *From Concepts to Skills* on page 139.

Management by Objectives

management by objectives (MBO)
A program that encompasses specific goals, participatively set, for an explicit time period, with feedback on goal progress.

As a manager, how do you make goal setting operational? The best answer to that question is: Implement a management by objectives (MBO) program. **Management by objectives (MBO)** emphasizes jointly or participatively set goals that are tangible, verifiable, and measurable.

MBO programs share four common ingredients: goal specificity, participative decision making, an explicit time period, and performance feedback.[17]

Goal Specificity

The objectives in MBO should be concise statements of specific accomplishments by the individual. It's not adequate, for example, to merely state a desire to cut costs, improve service, or increase quality. Such desires must be converted into tangible objectives that can be measured and evaluated. To cut departmental costs *by 7 percent*, to improve service by ensuring that all telephone orders are processed *within 24 hours of receipt*, or to increase quality by keeping returns to *less than 1 percent of sales* are examples of specific objectives.

Participative Decision Making

Unlike in goal setting, the objectives in MBO are not simply set by the manager and then assigned to employees. Instead, the manager and employee jointly choose the goals and agree on how they will be measured.

The evidence is mixed regarding the superiority of participative over assigned goals.[18] Sometimes, participatively set goals brought superior performance, while in other cases, individuals performed best when assigned goals by their manager. But a major advantage of participation may be in increasing acceptance of the goal itself as a desirable one to work toward.[19] As we noted, resistance is greater when goals are difficult. If people participate in goal setting, they are more likely to accept even a difficult goal than if their boss arbitrarily assigns it.[20]

Explicit Time Period

Under MBO, each objective has a specific time period in which it is to be completed—typically three months, six months, or a year. So managers and employees have specific objectives and a stipulated time period in which to accomplish them.

Performance Feedback

The final ingredient in an MBO program is feedback on performance. MBO tries to give continuous feedback on progress toward goals. Ideally, this is done by giving ongoing feedback to individuals so they can monitor and correct their own actions. This is supplemented by periodic managerial evaluations, when progress is reviewed and further feedback can be provided.

MBO in Practice

You will find management by objectives programs in many business, health care, educational, government, and nonprofit organizations.[21] But MBO's popularity should not be taken to mean that such programs always work. There are a number of documented cases where MBO has been put into place but failed to meet management expectations.[22] A close look at these cases, however, indicates that the problems seldom lie with the basic MBO components. Rather, the culprits tend to be factors such as unrealistic expectations, lack of flexibility when the situation or the environment changes, lack of top-management commitment, and an inability or unwillingness by management to allocate rewards based on goal accomplishment. Many of these problems can be resolved with realistic implementations of goal-setting theory.

Goal Setting and MBO in a Global Context

Goal-setting theory and MBO programs are well adapted to countries such as Canada and the United States because the key components fit in reasonably well with North American cultures. These theories assume that employees will be somewhat independent (not too high a score on power distance), that managers and employees will seek challenging goals (low in uncertainty avoidance), and that performance is considered important by both (high in quantity of life). But don't expect goal setting and MBO to necessarily lead to higher employee performance in countries such as Portugal or Chile, where the opposite conditions exist.

RESPONSES TO THE REWARD SYSTEM

> The Schwab employees wrote to head office in San Francisco because they perceived that they were treated unfairly by their CEO, Paul Bates. Many of the analysts Bates hired as he was growing Schwab quit within three years, and the remaining ones were hoping changes would be made. Was it unusual for the Schwab employees to be so concerned about fairness?

4 Do equity and fairness matter?

To a large extent, motivation theories are about rewards. The theories suggest that individuals have needs, and will exert effort to have those needs met. The needs theories specifically identify those needs. Goal-setting and expectancy theories portray processes by which individuals act and then receive desirable rewards (intrinsic or extrinsic) for their behaviour.

Two other process theories ask us to consider the issue of fairness in rewards. *Equity theory* suggests that individuals not only respond to rewards, but also evaluate and interpret them, which further complicates the motivation process. *Fair process* goes one step further, suggesting that employees are sensitive to a variety of fairness issues in the workplace that extend beyond the reward system but also affect employee motivation. Thus it was not unusual for the Schwab employees to be concerned about fairness.

Equity Theory

equity theory

Individuals compare their job inputs and outcomes with those of others and then respond so as to eliminate any inequities.

Equity theory suggests that employees compare their job inputs (i.e., effort, experience, education, competence) and outcomes (i.e., salary levels, raises, recognition) with those of others. We perceive what we get from a job situation (outcomes) in relation to what we put into it (inputs), and then we compare our outcome-input ratio with the outcome-input ratio of relevant others. This is shown in Exhibit 4–7. If we perceive our ratio to be equal to that of the relevant others with whom we compare ourselves, a state of equity is said to exist. We perceive our situation as fair—that justice prevails. When we see the ratio as unequal, we experience this as inequity.

Imagine that you wrote a case analysis for your marketing professor and spent 18 hours researching and writing it up. Your classmate spent 6 hours doing her analysis. Each of you received a mark of 75 percent. It is likely that you would perceive this as unfair, as you worked considerably harder (i.e., exerted more effort) than your classmate. J. Stacy Adams has proposed that those experiencing inequity are motivated to do something to correct it.[23] Thus, you might be inclined to spend considerably less time on your next assignment for your accounting professor.

What Happens When We Feel Treated Inequitably?

Based on equity theory, when employees perceive an inequity, they can be predicted to make one of six choices:[24]

- *Change their inputs* (e.g., don't exert as much effort).

- *Change their outcomes* (e.g., individuals paid on a piece-rate basis can increase their pay by producing a higher quantity of units of lower quality).

- *Adjust perceptions of self* (e.g., "I used to think I worked at a moderate pace but now I realize that I work a lot more slowly than everyone else").

- *Adjust perceptions of others* (e.g., "Mike's job isn't as desirable as I previously thought it was").

- *Choose a different relevant other* (e.g., "I may not make as much as my brother-in-law, but I'm doing a lot better than my Dad did when he was my age").

- *Leave the field* (e.g., quit the job).

Bear in mind that being treated equitably is not the same as being treated equally. Equity theory tells us that people who perform better should observe that they are rewarded better than those who do not perform as well. Thus poor performers should also observe that they receive lesser rewards than those who perform at a higher level. Paying equally would mean that everyone is paid the same, regardless of performance.

Research Findings

Equity theory has generally been supported, with a few minor qualifications.[25] First, inequities created by overpayment do not seem to have a significant impact on behaviour in most work situations. Apparently, people have a great deal more tolerance of overpayment inequities than of underpayment inequities, or are better able to rationalize them. Second, not all people are equity sensitive. For example, some employees simply do not worry about how their rewards compare with those of others. Predictions from equity theory are unlikely to be very accurate with these individuals.

Equity Theory in the Workplace

It is important to note that while most research on equity theory has focused on pay, employees seem to look for equity in the distribution of other organizational rewards. For instance, it's been shown that the use of high-status job titles, as well as large and lavishly furnished offices, may function as desirable outcomes for some employees in their equity equation.[26]

Equity theory demonstrates that, for most employees, motivation is influenced significantly by relative rewards, as well as by absolute rewards. However, some key issues are still

Because of the financial crisis in Russia, many firms do not have money to pay their employees. Instead of receiving a salary, employees get paid in goods the factories produce. Velta Company, a bicycle maker in Russia, gives workers one bicycle a month instead of a paycheque. Workers then have to sell their bike for cash or barter it for food. Some workers deal with the inequity of not getting a salary by using a different referent. "We are luckier than people over at the chemical plant," says one Velta employee. "At least our factory gives us something we can sell."

Exhibit 4–7

Equity Theory

Ratio of Output to Input	Person 1's Perception
Person 1 / Person 2	Inequity, underrewarded
Person 1 / Person 2	Equity
Person 1 / Person 2	Inequity, overrewarded

unclear.[27] For instance, how do employees handle conflicting equity signals, such as when unions point to other employee groups who are substantially *better off*, while management argues how much things have *improved*? How do employees define inputs and outcomes? How do they combine and weigh their inputs and outcomes to arrive at totals? Despite these problems, equity theory continues to offer some important insights into employee motivation.

Fair Process and Treatment

Recent research has been directed at redefining what is meant by equity or fairness.[28] Historically, equity theory focused on **distributive justice**, or the perceived fairness of the *amount* and *allocation* of rewards among individuals. But people also care about **procedural justice**—the perceived fairness of the *process* used to determine the distribution of rewards. (This includes having a voice in a decision and finding accuracy in decision making.) And they care, too, about **interactional justice**—the quality of the *interpersonal treatment* received from a manager. (Being treated sensitively and being provided an explanation for decisions are examples.)

The evidence indicates that distributive justice has a greater influence on employee satisfaction than procedural justice, while procedural and interactional justice tend to affect an employee's organizational commitment, trust in his or her manager, and intention to quit.[29] Researchers have found that when managers and employees believed that the company's processes were fair, they were more likely to show a high level of trust and commitment to the organization. Employees engaged in negative behaviour when they felt the process was unfair.[30]

For example, employees at Volkswagen's plant in Puebla, Mexico, staged a lengthy walkout *after* being offered a 20-percent raise. The reason? Their union leaders had agreed to work-rule concessions without consulting them. The employees, even though happy about the raise, did not believe that the process leading to the change in the work rules was fair. This behaviour is consistent with economist Alan Blinder's findings that "Changing the way workers are *treated* may boost productivity more than changing the way they are *paid*."[31]

To increase employees' perception of procedural justice, managers should consider openly sharing information on how allocation decisions are made and follow consistent and unbiased procedures. With increased procedural and interactional fairness, employees are likely to view their managers and the organization as positive, even if they are dissatisfied with pay, promotions, and other personal outcomes. Professor Daniel Skarlicki at the Sauder School of Business at the University of British Columbia has found that it is when unfavourable outcomes are combined with unfair procedures or poor interpersonal treatment that resentment and retaliation (e.g., theft, bad-mouthing, sabotage) are most likely.[32] This explains why Schwab Canada's investment advisers quit their jobs: They did not think they were being treated fairly, and found the CEO's behaviour antagonistic.

Motivating for Specific Organizational Goals

In the late 1990s, Charles Schwab Canada sought to be the leading brokerage house in Canada. To do so, it needed to improve the quality of service given to clients. The company introduced leading-edge technology and a corporate environment that emphasized the quality of service given to clients. Investment advisers were told that their bonuses would be conditional on the quality of service given. This should have led to increased customer service. Why did it fail in the case of Charles Schwab Canada?

---

distributive justice
Perceived fairness of the amount and allocation of rewards among individuals.

procedural justice
The perceived fairness of the process used to determine the distribution of rewards.

interactional justice
The quality of the interpersonal treatment received from another.

Volkswagen Canada Inc.
www.vw.com/ca/

Sauder School of Business
www.sauder.ubc.ca

Thus far we have discussed the general framework for motivating individuals, using process theories as our guide. Let's now turn to specific practices in organizations, to see how organizations link their goals and individual performance to rewards. Below we examine two specific practices that organizations use (employee recognition and variable-pay programs) to show how organizations motivate individuals to achieve organizational goals. We then follow with a brief discussion of how to motivate for some additional organizational goals.

5 Are there tips for motivating people for different goals?

Employee Recognition: Motivating to Show People Matter

Expectancy theory tells us that a key component of motivation is the link between performance and reward—that is, having one's behaviour recognized. In today's highly competitive global economy, most organizations are under severe cost pressures. That makes recognition programs particularly attractive. Recognizing an employee's superior performance often costs little or no money.

Employee recognition programs can take numerous forms. *The Globe and Mail* gives the Stephen Godfrey Prize for Newsroom Citizenship. Other ways of recognizing performance include sending personal notes or emails for good performance, putting employees on prestigious committees, sending them for training, and giving someone an assistant for a day to help clear backlogs.

Employee recognition may reduce turnover in organizations, particularly that of good employees. When executives were asked the reasons why employees left for jobs with other companies, 34 percent said it was due to lack of recognition and praise, compared with 29 percent who mentioned low compensation, 13 percent who mentioned limited authority, and 8 percent who cited personality problems.[33]

Variable Pay Programs: Motivating for Improved Productivity

When organizations want to improve productivity, they can consider a variety of incentive schemes. Some of these are individually based, some are team based, and some

At Toronto-based Snap Promotions Inc., rewards are given spontaneously, for extraordinary effort. CEO Warren Kotler (kneeling at right, with employees Leilani Nolan and Mez Lalji) shows his deep appreciation for his entire team by giving them tickets to shows and concerts, buying them lunch, and even sending a masseuse to someone's home. Kotler recently organized a "Steak & Beans" contest, dividing the company into two teams that received points for meetings set, quotes generated, and sales achieved. At the end of the period, the losing team ate beans at the Toronto Morton's of Chicago (a well-known upscale restaurant) while watching the winners feast on steak.

reward all members of the organization for working together toward productivity goals. The rewards used are all forms of **variable-pay programs**. What differentiates these forms of compensation from more traditional programs is that they do not pay a person only for time on the job or seniority. Instead, a portion of an employee's pay is based on some individual and/or organizational measure of performance. Unlike more traditional base-pay programs, with variable pay there is no guarantee that just because you made $60 000 last year, you will make the same amount this year. Instead, earnings fluctuate up and down annually, based on performance.[34]

The number of employees affected by variable-pay plans has been rising in Canada. A 2002 survey of 191 firms by Hewitt Associates found that 76 percent of them have variable-pay plans in place, compared with 43 percent in 1994.[35] These programs are more common among nonunionized workers, although more than 30 percent of unionized companies had such plans in 2002.[36] Prem Benimadhu, of the Conference Board of Canada, notes, "Canadian unions have been very allergic to variable compensation."[37] Under variable-pay programs, individuals are not guaranteed specific annual wages, making their work experience riskier. Union members, and others as well, may worry about not being able to predict wages ahead of time. Union members are also concerned that factors out of their control might affect whether bonuses are awarded, and that rewards could be set by political processes rather than objective factors so that bonuses failed to affect performance at all.

At Markham, Ontario-based Pillsbury Canada Limited, employees are eligible for a "Value Incentive Plan," which rewards performance at three levels: corporate, team, and individual.[38] If the corporate financial target is met or exceeded, a percentage-of-pay bonus results. Employees can earn additional percentage-of-pay bonuses if teams meet their own cost reduction goals and quality and profit improvement are above the corporate plan. Finally, employees can earn an equivalent percentage-of-pay bonus if they meet two or three key individual objectives.

Variable-based pay can be applied at individual, team, and company-wide levels, making it possible to link rewards to the appropriate level of performance. Below, we briefly describe some examples of incentives at these different levels of the organization.

Individual-Based Incentives

Piece-Rate Wages   Piece-rate wages are one of the earliest forms of individual performance pay. They have long been popular as a means for compensating production workers. In **piece-rate pay plans**, workers are paid a fixed sum for each unit of production completed. When an employee gets no base salary and is paid only for what he or she produces, this is a pure piece-rate plan. People who work at baseball parks selling peanuts and soft drinks frequently are paid this way. They might get to keep 25 cents for every bag of peanuts they sell. If they sell 200 bags during a game, they make $50. If they sell only 40 bags, their take is a mere $10. Commissions based on sales represent another form of individual-based incentives.

Many organizations use a modified piece-rate plan, where employees earn a base hourly wage plus a piece-rate differential. So a legal typist might be paid an hourly wage plus a certain rate per typed page. Such modified plans provide a basic security net, while still offering a productivity incentive.

Bonuses   Bonuses are becoming an increasingly popular form of individual incentive in Canada.[39] They are used in such companies as Toronto-based Molson Inc., Toronto-based Hydro One Inc., and the Bank of Montreal.

Bonus systems are more common in the United States than in Canada, both in terms of the proportion of employees covered and the size of the rewards.[40] This is because Canada has a more unionized economy, a relative lack of competition, and a large public sector. Until recently the only bonus for federal civil servants was $800 for those in

Even though the cost of the gun registry grew from $2 million to over $1 billion and an internal Justice Department investigation reported problems with the usability of the data, 96 percent of civil servants at the Department of Justice received bonuses for their performance in 2002. This calls into question whether the federal government actually uses a pay-for-performance system when giving out rewards to employees.

bilingual jobs. More recently the federal and provincial governments have been introducing bonuses for public sector workers. For instance, the Alberta government, which already had performance bonuses for senior administrators and for colleges and universities, introduced them for public school teachers and administrators in March 1999.[41] And in August 1999, federal executives were introduced to a new bonus plan, with their performance evaluated against business plans and corporate priorities of their departments. Their pay also depends on their "leadership qualities, ethics, values and how they treat their staff."[42] The reason that bonuses failed to improve service at Charles Schwab Canada was that the CEO kept changing the way that bonuses would be given out, thus confusing the employees. In addition, the technology was making it more difficult to service the customers properly.

Group-Based Incentives

Gainsharing   The variable-pay program that has received the most attention in recent years is undoubtedly **gainsharing**.[43] This is a formula-based group incentive plan. Improvements in group productivity—from one period to another—determine the total amount of money that is to be allocated. The division of productivity savings can be divided between the company and employees in any number of ways, but 50–50 is fairly typical.

Gainsharing differs from profit-sharing, discussed below. Gainsharing focuses on productivity gains rather than profits, and so it rewards specific behaviours that are less influenced by external factors. Employees in a gainsharing plan can receive incentive awards even when the organization is not profitable. Gainsharing was initially popular only in large unionized manufacturing companies,[44] such as Molson and Hydro-Québec. This has changed in recent years, with smaller companies, such as Delta, BC-based Avcorp Industries, and governments, such as Ontario's Town of Ajax and City of Kingston, also introducing gainsharing.

Organizational-Based Incentives

Profit-Sharing Plans   **Profit-sharing plans** are organization-wide programs that distribute compensation based on some established formula designed around a company's

gainsharing
An incentive plan where improvements in group productivity determine the total amount of money that is allocated.

profit-sharing plans
Organization-wide programs that distribute compensation based on some established formula designed around a company's profitability.

Ikea Canada Limited Partnership
www.ikea.ca

profitability. These can be direct cash outlays or stock options given to employees. Though senior executives are most likely to be rewarded through profit-sharing plans, employees at any level can be recipients. For instance, Ikea divided every penny rung up in its 152 stores on October 8, 1999, among its 44 000 staffers in 28 countries. This amounted to $2500 for each employee.[45]

One point to note about profit-sharing programs is that they focus on past financial results. They don't necessarily focus employees on the future. They also tend to ignore factors such as customer service and employee development, which may not be seen as having a direct link to profits. Moreover, industries that have a somewhat cyclical nature, such as the financial services industry, would offer few or no rewards during economic slumps. From an expectancy theory perspective, employees would be less motivated during these times because they would know that the likelihood of receiving significant bonuses was low. This is consistent with expectancy theory, which argues that for employees to be motivated, performance must be directly linked to rewards.

Stock Options and ESOPs Some companies try to encourage employees to adopt the values of top management by making them owners of their firms. This is done either through granting stock options, or through **employee stock ownership plans (ESOPs)**.[46] ESOPs are company-established benefit plans in which employees acquire stock as part of their benefits.

employee stock ownership plans (ESOPs)
Company-established benefit plans in which employees acquire stock as part of their benefits.

Canadian companies lag far behind the United States in the use of ESOPs because Canada's tax environment is less conducive. More recently, both the dot-com meltdown and the high-tech meltdown have made employees more reluctant to accept stock options instead of cash. Lisa Slipp, head of executive compensation at Toronto-based consulting firm Mercer Human Resources Consulting LLC, notes that "people are recognizing the reality of stock options, that they are attractive in an up market and less so in a down market."[47]

Mercer Human Resource Consulting LLC
www.mercerhr.com

Research Findings on ESOPs The research on ESOPs indicates that they increase employee satisfaction.[48] But their impact on performance is less clear. For instance, one study compared 45 ESOPs against 238 conventional companies.[49] The ESOPs outperformed the conventional firms in terms of both employment and sales growth. But other studies have shown disappointing results.[50] More importantly, stock ownership plans can sometimes focus employees on trying to increase short-term stock prices,

Pay-for-performance means that if you don't perform as well, you don't get paid as much. This principle seems to be applied more to employees than CEOs. In 2002, more than half of the CEOs of Canada's largest companies had increased compensation, while stock prices and profits sank. Gerry Schwartz, chairman, president, and CEO of Toronto-based Onex Corp., was a notable exception. In 2001, he received $17.2 million in salary and bonuses alone. In 2002 he received just $1 million in salary and no bonus. This reflected the fact that Onex stock fell 26 percent between 2000 and 2002.

while not worrying about the impact of their behaviour on the long-term effectiveness of the organization.

ESOPs have the potential to increase employee job satisfaction and work motivation. But for this potential to be realized, employees need to psychologically experience ownership.[51] That is, in addition to merely having a financial stake in the company, employees need to be kept regularly informed on the status of the business and also have the opportunity to exercise influence over the business.

Linking Productivity-Related Incentives to Motivation Theories

Variable pay is probably most compatible with expectancy theory predictions. Specifically, under these plans, individuals should perceive a strong relationship between their performance and the rewards they receive, and thus be more motivated. They should also be more productive.

However, the evidence is mixed, at best. One study of 400 manufacturing firms found that those companies with wage incentive plans achieved 43- to 64-percent greater productivity than those without such plans.[52] Other studies generally support that organizations with profit-sharing plans or gain-sharing plans have higher levels of profitability and productivity than those without.[53] But there are studies that question effectiveness of pay-for-performance approaches, suggesting they can lead to less group cohesiveness in the workplace.[54] Some researchers note that much of the evidence supporting pay-for-performance "is based on anecdotal testimonials and one-time company cases, rather than on methodologically more rigorous empirical studies."[55] The most recent study in Canada, however, looked at both unionized and nonunionized workplaces, and found that variable pay plans result in "increased productivity, a safer work environment, a better understanding of the business by employees, and little risk of employees losing base pay," according to Prem Benimadhu, an analyst with the Conference Board of Canada.[56]

Using pay for performance can be difficult for some managers. They worry about what should constitute performance and how it should be measured. There is also some belief by management and employees alike that wages should keep pace with inflation. Other barriers include salary scales keyed to what the competition is paying; traditional compensation systems that rely heavily on specific pay grades and relatively narrow pay ranges; and performance appraisal practices that produce inflated evaluations and expectations of full rewards.

Of course, from the employees' perspective, the major concern is a potential drop in earnings. Pay for performance means employees must share in the risks as well as the rewards of their employer's business. They are not guaranteed the same salary year in and year out under this system. The recent Conference Board of Canada study may ease some fears about this particular concern. There was no evidence that pay for performance led to a reduction in salary in unionized settings. Instead, it "is used as an 'add-on' to the employees' base salary."[57]

What About Teamwork?

Incentive pay, especially when it is awarded to individuals, can have negative effects in terms of group cohesiveness and productivity, and in some cases may not offer significant benefits to a company.[58] For example, Montreal-based National Bank of Canada offered a $5 employee bonus for every time employees referred clients for loans, mutual funds, or other bank products. But the bonus so upset workers that the plan was abandoned after just three months.[59] Tellers complained that the bonus caused colleagues to compete against one another. Meanwhile, the bank could not determine whether the referrals actually generated new business.

National Bank of Canada
www.nbc.ca

Organized labour is, in general, cool to the idea of pay for performance. Andrew Jackson, who was senior economist for the Canadian Labour Congress in Ottawa,

Canadian Labour Congress
www.clc-ctc.ca

explains that "it hurts co-operation in the workplace. It can lead to competition between workers, speeding up the pace of work. It's a bad thing if it creates a stressful work environment where older workers can't keep up."[60] Pay for performance can also be problematic if work is speeded up to unfair levels, so that employees injure themselves. Still, not all unions oppose pay for performance, and the benefits and drawbacks of incentive plans must be carefully considered before introduction.

If an organization wants a group of individuals to function as a "team" (which will be defined in Chapter 5), emphasis needs to be placed on team-based rewards, rather than individual rewards. We will discuss the nature of team-based rewards in Chapter 5.

Motivating for Other Types of Performance

In recent years, organizations have been paying for performances on bases other than strict productivity. Compensation experts Patricia Zingheim and Jay Schuster note the following activities that merit additional compensation:[61]

- *Commissions beyond sales.* Commissions might be determined by customer satisfaction and/or sales team outcomes, such as meeting revenue or profit targets.

- *Leadership effectiveness.* This form of reward may include employee satisfaction, or measures of how the manager handles his or her employees.

- *New goals.* Rewards go to all employees who contribute to specific organizational goals, such as customer satisfaction, cycle time, or quality measures.

- *Knowledge workers in teams.* Pay is linked to the performance of knowledge workers and/or professional employees who work on teams.

- *Competency and/or skills.* This rewards abstract knowledge or competencies, such as knowledge of technology, the international business context, customer service, or social skills.

Exhibit 4–8 compares the strengths and weaknesses of variable pay, team-based pay, and skill-based pay, and team rewards.

Exhibit 4–8

Comparing Various Pay Programs

Approach	Strengths	Weaknesses
Variable pay	• Motivates for performance. • Cost-effective. • Makes a clear link between organizational goals and individual rewards.	• Individuals do not always have control over factors that affect productivity. • Earnings vary from year to year. • Can cause unhealthy competition among employees.
Team-based pay	• Encourages individuals to work together effectively. • Promotes goal of team-based work.	• Difficult to evaluate team performance sometimes. • Equity problems could arise if all members paid equally.
Skill-based pay	• Increases the skill levels of employees. • Increases the flexibility of the workforce. • Can reduce the number of employees needed.	• Employers may end up paying for unneeded skills. • Employees may not be able to learn some skills, and thus feel demotivated.

While rewarding individuals for something other than performance may make sense in some instances, not everyone agrees that these rewards are fair. *OB in the Street* examines the question of athletic scholarships given just for athletic skills, rather than academic merit.

OB IN THE STREET

Scholarships for Jocks: Skills or Smarts?

Should university athletes be awarded money just for their athletic abilities? Jack Drover, athletic director at Mount Allison University in Sackville, New Brunswick, thinks not.[62] He objects to student-athlete awards that are often offered because of what coaches and teams need, not what the individual student needs.

Many university presidents react negatively to schools using financial rewards to recruit athletes. Some high school athletes can get full-tuition scholarships to university, even though they have not achieved high marks in school. While not every university finds this problematic, others feel awarding scholarships that don't recognize academic achievement or financial need is "an affront to the values of higher education."

Schools across the country interpret the rules for scholarships differently, which may affect the quality of school's teams. Universities in Ontario (which rarely give scholarships to first-year students) have had particular difficulty competing with schools across the country. Since 1994 only the University of Ottawa football team has won the Vanier Cup, and U Ottawa is one of the few Ontario schools that give many athletic scholarships. Some members of Canadian Interuniversity Sport (CIS) suggest that a level playing field, with no scholarships granted to first-year athletes except in cases of financial need and academic merit, would be fairer to all teams. CIS president Marg MacGregor, however, argues that "We're asking a lot of our students when we say compete every weekend and practise all the time without any support."

MOTIVATING SPECIFIC GROUPS

When we discussed needs theories, we pointed out that there are differences in individuals' needs. Thus one might expect that different groups of people have differing needs as well. Below we discuss how to motivate particular types of employees.

6 How do you motivate for individual differences?

Motivating Professionals

In contrast to a generation ago, the typical employee today is more likely to be a highly trained professional with a college or university degree than a blue-collar factory worker. These professionals receive a great deal of intrinsic satisfaction from their work. They tend to be well paid. So what, if any, special concerns should you be aware of when trying to motivate a team of engineers at Nortel Networks Corp., a product designer at Research in Motion, or a group of accountants at Deloitte & Touche LLP?

Carol Stephenson, dean of the Richard Ivey School of Business, describes the challenge that managing professionals presents. "Knowledge workers like to be autonomous. They are more concerned with content of work rather than their place on the organization chart. If you manage by command and control, people will leave."[63]

What motivates professionals? Money and promotions typically are low on their priority list. Why? Because they tend to be paid well and enjoy what they do. In contrast, job challenge tends to rank high. They like to tackle problems and find solutions. Their chief reward in their job is the work itself. Professionals also value support. They want

Richard Ivey School of Business
www.ivey.uwo.ca

Exhibit 4–9

Guidelines for Motivating Professionals

- Provide them with ongoing challenging projects.

- Give them autonomy to follow their interests and allow them to structure their work in ways that they find productive.

- Reward them with educational opportunities—training, workshops, conferences—that allow them to keep current in their field.

- Reward them with recognition, and ask questions and engage in other actions that demonstrate to them that you are sincerely interested in what they are doing.

others to think what they're working on is important. Although this may be true for all employees, professionals tend to be more focused on their work as their central life interest, while nonprofessionals typically have other interests outside of work that can compensate for needs not met on the job. Professionals also place a high level of importance on having skill-development opportunities. Exhibit 4–9 provides guidelines for motivating professionals.

Motivating Contingent Workers

One of the more comprehensive changes taking place in organizations is the addition of temporary or contingent employees. As downsizing has eliminated millions of "permanent" jobs, an increasing number of new openings are for nonpermanent workers. The number of Canadians relying on temporary jobs grew by 24 percent—from 799 000 to 2.7 million—between 1989 and 1998.[64] These include part-timers, on-call workers, short-term hires, temps, day labourers, independent contractors, and leased workers.

Because these contingent employees lack the security and stability that permanent employees have, they don't always identify with the organization or display the commitment of other employees. Temporary workers typically lack pension plans and have few or no extended health care benefits such as dental care, prescription plans, or vision care.[65]

There is no simple solution for motivating temporary employees. For those who prefer the freedom of a temporary status that permits them to attend school, care for their children, or have the flexibility to travel or pursue other interests, the lack of stability may not be an issue. For instance, in 1998, 68 percent of youths worked part-time because they were going to school, while 20 percent of adult women worked part-time to allow them the time to take care of children. However, about 23 percent of youths, 30 percent of adult women, and 44 percent of adult men working part-time would have preferred to work full-time.[66] The motivational challenge in dealing with these employees lies in the fact that their temporary status is involuntary.

What will motivate involuntarily temporary employees? An obvious answer is the opportunity for permanent status. In those cases where permanent employees are selected from the pool of temporaries, temporaries will often work hard in hopes of becoming permanent. A less obvious answer is the opportunity for training. The ability of a temporary employee to find a new job is largely dependent on his or her skills. If the employee sees that the job he or she is doing can help develop saleable skills, motivation is increased.

From an equity standpoint, there are repercussions from mixing permanent and temporary workers where pay differentials are significant.[67] When temps work alongside permanent employees who earn more, and get benefits too, for doing the same job, the performance of temps is likely to suffer. Separating such employees or converting all employees to a variable-pay or skill-based pay plan might help to lessen this problem.

Motivating Low-Skilled Service Workers

For a variety of reasons, many young people are struggling to begin a career. Unemployment among 15- to 24-year-olds is around 14.2 percent across Canada, about twice the national average rate of unemployment. Service-sector jobs, which were once regarded as either a temporary after-school job or a stepping stone to a career, have become permanent positions for many young people. Pay levels are often little above minimum wage.

Here, then, is one of the most challenging motivation problems in industries such as retailing and fast food: How do you motivate individuals who are making very low wages and who have little opportunity to significantly increase their pay in either their current jobs or through promotions?

Starbucks' outlets in Vancouver discovered what can happen when managers fail to pay attention to the concerns of these workers.[68] In the summer of 1996, the company introduced an unpopular computerized scheduling system. Then management rolled back a 50-cent increase to the starting wage, to match the new BC provincial minimum of $7 an hour. Finally, management cut "T-shirt Fridays," the only day each week when staff could wear Starbucks T-shirts rather than the regulation dress shirts. For Steve Emery, a then–26-year-old employee of the coffee giant, that was the last straw. "The taboo on T-shirts triggered us," he says. By 2002, there were 11 unionized Starbucks outlets in Vancouver, with a total of 140 employees.

Many employees working in low-skilled service jobs feel that they do not get the respect they deserve from their employers. In response to similar employee concerns, Taco Bell has tried to make some of its service jobs more interesting and challenging, but with limited results.[69] It has experimented with incentive pay and stock options for cashiers and cooks. These employees also have been given broader responsibility for inventory, scheduling, and hiring. But over four years, this experiment reduced annual turnover only from 223 percent to 160 percent.

What choices are left? Unless pay and benefits are significantly increased, high dissatisfaction is probably inevitable in these jobs. This can be somewhat offset by recruiting

Taco Bell Canada
www.tacobell.com

McDonald's sends their employees to Hamburger University to train them to give good service. Employees working in fast food stores are often part-time, and they view their jobs as temporary. McDonald's uses the experience at Hamburger U and other training opportunities to help employees feel part of the organization and more committed to their work.

more widely, making these jobs more appealing, and raising pay levels. Trying to understand the needs of such employees might help motivate them better. Nontraditional approaches might also be useful.

Motivating in a Unionized Environment

The workplace environment is considerably more unionized in Canada than in the United States, and so we should consider that context when looking at motivation theories and practices. For example, earlier in the chapter we noted that Canadian unions have not been very receptive to pay-for-performance plans. The concern is that differential pay to employees doing similar work can hurt cooperation and lead to competition in the workplace.

Unionized employees are typically paid on the basis of job categories, with very little range within a category, and by seniority. Does this mean that it is impossible to motivate unionized employees? While the ability of managers to hand out rewards of any sort may be limited, that does not prevent managers from creating environments that are conducive to a better work environment. Showing appreciation in less tangible ways, providing opportunities for training and advancement, and listening to employees' concerns all help create a more positive environment.

Motivating Public Sector Employees

There are special challenges in applying motivation theories to public sector workers (those who work for local, provincial, or federal governments). Because the work carried out is often of a service nature, it is hard to measure productivity in the same way manufacturing or retail firms do. Therefore, it becomes more difficult to make a meaningful link between rewards and productivity.

Several researchers have suggested that goal-setting theory can be used to improve performance in public sector organizations.[70] More recently, another researcher found that goal difficulty and goal specificity, as well as the belief that the goal could be achieved, significantly improved motivation of public sector employees.[71] Because many public sector workers are also unionized, the challenges faced in motivating unionized employees also apply to government employees.

BEWARE THE SIGNALS THAT REWARDS SEND

Charles Schwab Canada's employees were told that the quality of service given to clients was the most important aspect of their job. Bonuses were set up to help reinforce this idea. However, it soon became clear to the investment advisers that there was something seriously flawed with the bonus system. CEO Paul Bates said that the pay scheme did not encourage advisers to pressure investors toward greater trading activity that they might not want. In private, however, employees felt they were constantly being pushed "to produce revenue, and quickly," rather than worry about client needs. Schwab Canada employees were also upset with their general working conditions. Because there were not enough support staff, advisers spent many hours filling out paperwork, even though this was not a rewarded activity. What happens when employees are told to do one thing, but rewarded for another?

7 What kinds of mistakes are made in reward systems?

In 1998, Vancouver's bus drivers claimed, on average, 18.6 sick days. Victoria's bus drivers averaged only 16.6 sick days.[72] Are Vancouver's driver's more likely to catch cold than Victoria's? Not likely! Rather, differences in the way that sick days are paid may account for the differences. Victoria's drivers get paid in full for 6 sick days, no matter how the days are taken. But once they take their second "sick time," Vancouver's drivers are paid only if they are off more than 3 days for their illness, so it makes sense for them to stay home sick longer.

Perhaps more often than we would like, organizations engage in what has been called "the folly of rewarding A, while hoping for B."[73] Organizations do this when they hope that employees will engage in one type of behaviour yet they reward for another type. Managers of Vancouver's bus drivers had hoped that by increasing the number of days a driver had to be out sick to get paid, bus drivers would take fewer days off. Instead, managers might have considered giving bonuses for perfect attendance. Hoping for the behaviour you are not rewarding is unlikely to make it happen to any great extent. In fact, as expectancy theory suggests, individuals will generally perform in ways to raise the probability of receiving the rewards offered.

Exhibit 4–10 provides further examples of common management reward follies. Three themes seem to account for some of the biggest obstacles to ending this folly:[74]

- First, individuals are unable to break out of old ways of thinking about reward and recognition practices. This is demonstrated in such practices as management emphasizing quantifiable behaviours, to the exclusion of nonquantifiable behaviours; management being reluctant to change the existing performance system; and employees having an entitlement mentality (i.e., they don't support changing the reward system because they are comfortable with the current behaviours that are rewarded).

- Second, organizations often do not look at the big picture of their performance system. Thus, rewards are allocated at subunit levels, with the result that units often compete against each other.

- Third, both management and shareholders often focus on short-term results, rather than rewarding employees for longer-range planning.

Organizations would do well to ensure that they do not send the wrong message when offering rewards. When organizations outline an organizational objective of "team performance," for example, but reward each employee according to individual productivity, does this send a message that teams are valued? Or when a retailer tells commissioned employees that they are responsible for monitoring and replacing stock as

---

Exhibit 4–10

Management Reward Follies

We hope for ...	But we reward ...
Teamwork and collaboration	The best team members
Innovative thinking and risk-taking	Proven methods and not making mistakes
Development of people skills	Technical achievements and accomplishments
Employee involvement and empowerment	Tight control over operations and resources
High achievement	Another year's effort
Long-term growth; environmental responsibility	Quarterly earnings
Commitment to total quality	Shipping on schedule, even with defects
Candour; surfacing bad news early	Reporting good news, whether it's true or not; agreeing with the manager, whether or not (s)he's right

Source: Constructed from S. Kerr, "On the Folly of Rewarding A, While Hoping for B," *Academy of Management Executive*, 9, no. 1, 1995, pp. 7–14; "More on the Folly," *Academy of Management Executive*, 9, no. 1, 1995, pp. 15–16.

necessary, are employees more likely to concentrate on making sales or stocking the floor? Employees motivated by the promise of rewards will do those things that earn them the rewards they value.

CAVEAT EMPTOR: MOTIVATION THEORIES ARE CULTURE-BOUND

8 Do motivation theories work the same in every country?

Reward strategies that have been used successfully in Canada and the United States do not always work successfully in other cultures. Take, for instance, a study comparing sales reps at a large electronics company in the United States with one in Japan. The study found that while Rolex watches, expensive dinners, and fancy vacations were valued rewards for star performers in the United States, taking the whole sales team bowling was more appreciated in Japan. The study's authors found that "being a member of a successful team with shared goals and values, rather than financial rewards, is what drives Japanese sales representatives to succeed."[75]

Why do our motivation theories perform less well when we look at their use in countries beyond Canada and the United States? Most current motivation theories were developed in the United States and so take US cultural norms for granted.[76] That may account for why Canada and the United States rely more heavily on extrinsic motivating factors than some other countries.[77] Japanese and German firms rarely make use of individual work incentives.[78]

Many of the social-psychological theories of motivation rely heavily on the idea of motivating the individual through individual rewards. Thus they emphasize, particularly in an organizational context, the meaning of "pay" and give little attention to the informal rewards that come from group norms and prestige from peers.[79] Exhibit 4–11 gives a quick summary of the differences observed by a number of other studies.

Motivation theories also assume that needs are similar across society. For instance, Maslow's needs hierarchy argues that people start at the physiological level and then move progressively up the hierarchy in this order: physiological, safety, social, esteem, and self-actualization. This hierarchy, if it applies at all, aligns well with American

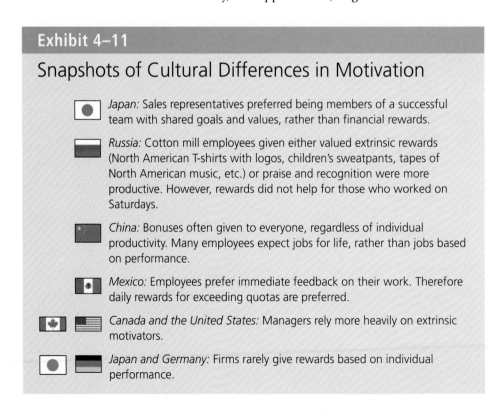

Exhibit 4–11

Snapshots of Cultural Differences in Motivation

Japan: Sales representatives preferred being members of a successful team with shared goals and values, rather than financial rewards.

Russia: Cotton mill employees given either valued extrinsic rewards (North American T-shirts with logos, children's sweatpants, tapes of North American music, etc.) or praise and recognition were more productive. However, rewards did not help for those who worked on Saturdays.

China: Bonuses often given to everyone, regardless of individual productivity. Many employees expect jobs for life, rather than jobs based on performance.

Mexico: Employees prefer immediate feedback on their work. Therefore daily rewards for exceeding quotas are preferred.

Canada and the United States: Managers rely more heavily on extrinsic motivators.

Japan and Germany: Firms rarely give rewards based on individual performance.

culture and reasonably well with Canadian culture. However, in countries such as Japan, Greece, and Mexico, where uncertainty avoidance characteristics are strong, security needs would be at the top of the needs hierarchy. Countries that score high on quality-of-life characteristics—Denmark, Sweden, Norway, the Netherlands, and Finland—would have social needs on top.[80] We would predict, for instance, that group work will motivate employees more when the country's culture scores high on the quality-of-life criterion.

Equity theory has gained a relatively strong Canadian and US following. That is no surprise, since North American reward systems assume that workers are highly sensitive to equity in the granting of rewards, and expect pay to be tied closely to performance. However, recent evidence suggests that in collectivist cultures, especially in the former socialist countries of Central and Eastern Europe, employees expect rewards to reflect their individual needs as well as their performance.[81] Moreover, consistent with a legacy of Communism and centrally planned economies, employees showed an entitlement attitude—they expected outcomes to be *greater* than their inputs.[82] These findings suggest that Canadian- and US-style pay practices may need modification, especially in Russia and former Communist countries, in order to be perceived as fair by employees.

The international findings support the need to examine the internal norms of a country in developing an incentive system, rather than simply importing one that works well in Canada and the United States.

MOTIVATION IN PRACTICE: PERHAPS REWARDS ARE OVERRATED

Schwab Canada's employees complained about changes in their bonus plans, which made it difficult for them to know how they would be rewarded. But they also complained about lack of support staff to handle paperwork that they did not feel was part of their jobs. They were unhappy with technology that made it difficult to easily advise clients. The employees' complaints may have finally made an impact on head office. In early 2002, parent company Charles Schwab put its Canadian division up for sale, preferring to exit the Canadian market. They didn't even notify CEO Paul Bates until two weeks before the sale. The division had not performed as well as expected. Scotiabank bought the brokerage, to enhance its ScotiaMcLeod investment line. Would a better working environment have had a more positive impact on the employees and the Canadian division?

All of the theories we have covered suggest that rewards can be used to motivate employees by offering ways to meet their needs in exchange for performance consistent with organizational goals. However, several researchers suggest that the introduction of extrinsic rewards, such as pay, for work effort that had been intrinsically rewarding previously will tend to decrease the overall level of motivation.[83]

This proposal—which has come to be called **cognitive evaluation theory**—has been extensively researched, and a large number of studies have been supportive.[84] Alfie Kohn, often cited for his work on rewards, argues that people are actually punished by rewards, doing inferior work when they are enticed by money, grades, or other incentives. His extensive review of incentive studies concluded that "rewards usually improve performance only at extremely simple—indeed, mindless—tasks, and even then they improve only quantitative performance."[85]

9 Could rewards be overrated?

cognitive evaluation theory
Allocating extrinsic rewards for behaviour that had been previously intrinsically rewarded tends to decrease the overall level of motivation.

Extrinsic vs. Intrinsic Rewards

Historically, motivation theorists have generally assumed that intrinsic motivators are independent of extrinsic motivators. That is, the stimulation of one would not affect the other. But cognitive evaluation theory suggests otherwise. It argues that when organizations use extrinsic rewards as payoffs for superior performance, the intrinsic rewards—which are derived from individuals doing what they like—are reduced.

In other words, when extrinsic rewards are given to someone for performing an interesting task, it causes intrinsic interest in the task itself to decline. For instance, while a taxi driver expects to be paid for taking your best friend to the airport, you do not expect your friend to pay you if you volunteer to drive her to the airport. In fact, the offer of pay might diminish your pleasure in doing a favour for your friend.

Why would this happen? The popular explanation is that individuals experience a loss of control over their behaviour when it is being rewarded by external sources. This causes the previous intrinsic motivation to diminish. Extrinsic rewards can produce a shift—from an internal to an external explanation—in an individual's perception of why he or she works on a task. If you read a novel a week because your contemporary literature instructor requires you to, you can attribute your reading behaviour to an external source. If you stop reading novels the moment the course ends, this is more evidence that your behaviour was due to an external source. However, if you find yourself continuing to read a novel a week when the course ends, your natural inclination is to say, "I must enjoy reading novels because I'm still reading one a week!"

The Research Findings

Although further research is needed to clarify some of the current ambiguity, the evidence does lead us to conclude that the interdependence of extrinsic and intrinsic rewards is a real phenomenon.[86] A large body of research shows that large external rewards can undermine the positive performance of employees.[87] When employees work for a large reward, they will explain their behaviour through that reward—"I did it for the money." However, in the absence of large rewards, employees are more likely to reflect on the interesting nature of the work, or the positive benefits of being an organizational member, to explain their behaviour. When organizations give employees intrinsically interesting work, they will often work longer and harder than one might predict from the actual external rewards.

In studies dating back to the 1940s, employees have always ranked factors such as being shown appreciation for work done, feeling "in" on things, and having interesting work as being more important to them than their salaries.[88] Of course, organizations cannot simply ignore financial rewards. When people feel they are being treated unfairly in the workplace, pay often becomes a focal point of their concerns. If tasks are dull or unpleasant, extrinsic rewards will probably increase intrinsic motivation.[89] Even when a job is inherently interesting, there still exists a powerful norm for extrinsic payment.[90] But creating fun, challenging, and empowered workplaces may do more for motivation and performance than focusing simply on the compensation system.

Can We Just Eliminate Rewards?

We opened this chapter describing how Schwab Canada's investment advisers became angry because their reward plans kept changing. We conclude this chapter by raising a thought-provoking discussion about the possibility of eliminating rewards and concentrating more on the design of the workplace, to make the work experience itself more motivating. You may recall that one of the complaints of the Schwab employees was that they had to spend too much time doing paperwork. They also took jobs at Schwab because they expected to work more closely with clients. It may be that had the Schwab environment been more supportive of advisers getting work done and spending time with clients, the employees would have focused less on the reward structure itself.

Alfie Kohn, in his book *Punished by Rewards,* argues that "the desire to do something, much less to do it well, simply cannot be imposed; in this sense, it is a mistake to talk

Alfie Kohn
www.alfiekohn.org

about motivating other people. All we can do is set up certain conditions that will maximize the probability of their developing an interest in what they are doing and remove the conditions that function as constraints."[91]

Creating a Motivating Environment

Based on his research and consulting experience, Kohn proposes ways that organizations can create a motivating environment in their workplace:

Abolish Incentives. Pay people generously and fairly, make sure they don't feel exploited, and then make sure that pay is not on their minds. Individuals will then be more able to focus on the goals of the organization, rather than having paycheques as their main goal.

Re-Evaluate Evaluation. Rather than making performance appraisals look and feel like a punitive effort—who gets raises, who gets promoted, who is told he or she is performing poorly—the performance evaluation system might be structured more like a two-way conversation to trade ideas and questions, done continuously, not as a competition. And the discussion of performance should not be tied to compensation. "Providing feedback that employees can use to do a better job ought never to be confused or combined with controlling them by offering (or withholding) rewards."[92]

Create the Conditions for Authentic Motivation. A noted economist recently summarized the evidence about pay-for-productivity as follows: "Changing the way workers are treated may boost productivity more than changing the way they are paid."[93] There is some consensus about what these conditions might be: Help employees rather than put them under surveillance; listen to their concerns and think about problems from their viewpoint; and provide plenty of informational feedback so they know what they have done right and what they need to improve.[94]

Support Collaboration. People are more likely to perform better in well-functioning groups where they can get feedback and learn from each other.[95] Therefore, it is important to provide the necessary supports to create well-functioning teams.

Pay Attention to Content. People are generally the most motivated when their jobs give them an opportunity to learn new skills, provide variety in the tasks that are performed, and enable them to demonstrate competence. Some of this can be fostered by carefully matching people to their jobs and giving them the opportunity to try new jobs. It is also possible to increase the meaningfulness of many jobs.

But what about jobs that don't seem inherently interesting? One psychologist suggested that in cases where the jobs are fundamentally unappealing, the manager might acknowledge frankly that the task is not fun, give a meaningful rationale for why it must be done, and then give people as much choice as possible in how the task is completed.[96] One sociologist studying a group of garbage collectors in San Francisco discovered that they were quite satisfied with their work.[97] Their satisfaction came from the way the work and the company were organized: Relationships among the crew were important, the tasks and routes were varied to provide interest, and the company was set up as a cooperative, so that each worker owned a share of the company, and thus felt "pride of ownership."

Provide Choice. "We are most likely to become enthusiastic about what we are doing—and all else being equal, to do it well—when we are free to make decisions about the way we carry out a task."[98] Extrinsic rewards (and punishments too) actually remove choice, because they focus us on rewards, rather than on tasks or goals. A variety of research suggests that burnout, dissatisfaction, absenteeism, stress, and coronary heart disease are related to situations where individuals did not have enough control over their work situations.[99] By choice we do not mean lack of management, but rather, involving people in the decisions that are to be made. A number of case studies indicate that participative management, when it includes full participation by everyone, is successful.[100]

These steps represent an alternative to simply providing more and different kinds of incentives to try to induce people to work more effectively. They suggest that providing the proper environment may be more important than the reward structure.

Final Thoughts on the Use of Extrinsic Rewards

Not all employees value money as their main rewards. Some value interesting work or recognition more than money.[101] And our discussion above suggests that extrinsic rewards can lose their motivational abilities over time. One consultant suggested a variety of reasons why rewards fail to motivate, including that rewards often don't really show appreciation for a job well done; rewards can sometime reinforce the wrong behaviours; and there may be delays between performance and rewards. In addition, layoffs, across-the-board raises and cuts, and excessive executive compensation create a lot of cynicism about rewards.[102]

Many organizations would find it difficult to simply get rid of rewards, however, and create more supportive environments that encourage performance. Doing so would require managers who were willing to give up control and instead take on the job of coaching. It would require employees who truly believed that their participation and input mattered, and that might require breaking down some of the suspicion that employees feel when managers give them directives rather than seek collaborative input. Nevertheless, these steps, when put in place, can lead to quite a different workplace than what we often see. Moreover, these issues suggest that sometimes it is not the type or amount of rewards that makes a difference as much as whether the work itself is intrinsically interesting.

Summary and Implications

1 **What is motivation?** Motivation is the process that accounts for an individual's intensity, direction, and persistence of effort toward reaching a goal. *Intensity* is concerned with how hard a person tries. This is the element most of us focus on when we talk about motivation. However, high intensity is unlikely to lead to good job performance unless the effort is channelled in a useful *direction*. Finally, the effort requires *persistence*.

2 **How do needs motivate people?** All needs theories of motivation, including Maslow's hierarchy of needs, Herzberg's two-factor theory (sometimes also called motivation-hygiene theory), Alderfer's ERG theory, and McClelland's theory of needs, propose a similar idea: Individuals have needs that, when unsatisfied, will result in motivation. Needs theories suggest that motivation will be high to the degree that the rewards individuals receive for high performance satisfy their dominant needs.

3 **Are there other ways to motivate people?** Process theories focus on the broader picture of how someone can set about motivating another individual. Process theories include expectancy theory and goal-setting theory (and its application, management by objectives). Expectancy theory says that an employee will be motivated to exert a high level of effort when he or she believes 1) that effort will lead to good performance; 2) that good performance will lead to organizational rewards, such as a bonus, salary increase, or promotion; and 3) that the rewards will satisfy the employee's personal goals.

Goal-setting theory suggests that intentions to work toward a goal are a major source of work motivation. That is, goals tell an employee what needs to be done and how much effort will need to be expended. Specific goals increase performance; difficult goals, when accepted, result in higher performance than do easy goals; and feedback leads to higher performance than does nonfeedback.

4 **Do equity and fairness matter?** Individuals look for fairness in the reward system. Rewards should be perceived by employees as related to the inputs they bring to the job. At a simplistic level, this means that experience, skills, abilities, effort, and other obvious inputs should explain differences in performance and, hence, pay, job assignments, and other obvious rewards.

5 **Are there tips for motivating people for different goals?** When organizations want to reward individuals for specific high performance, they often turn to employee recognition programs. Recognizing an employee's superior performance often costs little or no money.

When organizations want to improve productivity, they often use variable-pay programs. With these programs a portion of an employee's pay is based on some individual and/or organizational measure of performance.

6 **How do you motivate for individual differences?** Employees have different needs and a given reward does not motivate all individuals similarly. Managers should spend the time necessary to understand what is important to each employee and then align goals, level of involvement, and rewards with individual needs.

7 **What kinds of mistakes are made in reward systems?** Individuals are responsive to the signals sent out by organizations, and if they determine that some activities are not valued, they may not engage in them, even when the firm expects employees to do so. Rewards should be linked to the type of performance expected. It is important that employees perceive a clear linkage between rewards and performance. If individuals perceive this relationship to be low, the results will be low performance, a decrease in job satisfaction, and an increase in turnover and absenteeism.

8 **Do motivation theories work the same in every country?** Motivation theories do not always perform as well when they are used in countries beyond Canada and the United States. These two countries rely more heavily on extrinsic motivating factors than some other countries, and also use more individual-based rewards. By contrast, Japanese and German firms rarely make use of individual work incentives. These countries rely more heavily on group processes providing motivation to employees.

9 **Could rewards be overrated?** In the right context, individuals often motivate themselves intrinsically and can achieve quite high levels of performance doing so. We also know that giving rewards for things that were previously done for intrinsic motivation will decrease motivation.

For Review

1. What are the implications of Theories X and Y for motivation practices?

2. Identify the variables in expectancy theory.

3. Relate goal-setting theory to the MBO process. How are they similar? Different?

4. What are the pluses and minuses of variable-pay programs from an employee's viewpoint? From management's viewpoint?

5. What is an ESOP? How might it positively influence employee motivation?

6. What motivates professional employees?

7. What motivates contingent employees?

8. Explain cognitive evaluation theory. How applicable is it to management practice?

9. What can firms do to create more motivating environments for their employees?

For Critical Thinking

1. Identify three activities you really enjoy. Next, identify three activities you really dislike. Using the expectancy model, analyze why some activities stimulate your effort while others don't.

2. Identify five different criteria by which organizations can compensate employees. Based on your knowledge and experience, is performance the criterion most used in practice? Discuss.

3. "Recognition may be motivational for the moment but it doesn't have any staying power. Why? Because they don't take recognition at Safeway or the Bay!" Do you agree or disagree? Discuss.

4. "Performance cannot be measured, so any effort to link pay with performance is a fantasy. Differences in performance are often caused by the system, which means the organization ends up rewarding the circumstances. It's the same thing as rewarding the weather forecaster for a pleasant day." Do you agree or disagree with this statement? Support your position.

5. Your text argues for recognizing individual differences. It also suggests paying attention to members of diverse groups. Does this view contradict the principles of equity theory? Discuss.

OB for You

- To motivate yourself to finish a particularly long and dry chapter in a text, plan a snack break. Or buy yourself a new CD once that major accounting assignment is finished.

- The people you interact with appreciate recognition, which might include brief notes on nice cards to mention a job well done. Or a basket of flowers. Sometimes just sending a pleasant, thankful email is enough to make a person feel valued. All of these things are easy enough to do, and appreciated greatly by the recipient.

- You may be unhappy with the way a professor teaches. Consider giving positive, helpful feedback, and also participating more in class. This would convey interest in the course, which would be motivating to most instructors.

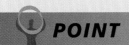

POINT

Money Motivates!

The importance of money as a motivator has been consistently downgraded by most behavioural scientists. They prefer to point out the value of challenging jobs; goals; participation in decision making; feedback; cohesive work teams; and other nonmonetary factors as stimulants to employee motivation. We argue otherwise here—that money is the crucial incentive to work motivation. As a medium of exchange, it is the vehicle by which employees can purchase the numerous need-satisfying things they desire. Money also performs the function of a scorecard, by which employees assess the value that the organization places on their services and by which employees can compare their value to others.[103]

Money's value as a medium of exchange is obvious. People may not work only for money, but remove the money and how many people would come to work? A recent study of nearly 2500 employees found that while these people disagreed over what their primary motivator was, they unanimously ranked money in second spot.[104] This study reaffirms that for the vast majority of the workforce, a regular paycheque is absolutely necessary in order to meet basic physiological and safety needs.

The best case for money as a motivator is presented by Professor Ed Locke, of the RH Smith School of Business at the University of Maryland, who reviewed a number of studies.[105] Locke looked at four methods of motivating employee performance: money, goal setting, participation in decision making, and redesigning jobs to give employees more challenge and responsibility. He found that the average improvement from money was 30 percent; goal setting increased performance 16 percent; participation improved performance by less than 1 percent; and job redesign positively impacted performance by an average of 17 percent. Moreover, every study Locke reviewed that used money as a method of motivation resulted in some improvement in employee performance. Such evidence demonstrates that money may not be the only motivator, but it's difficult to argue that it does not motivate!

COUNTERPOINT

Money Doesn't Motivate Most Employees Today!

Money can motivate some people under some conditions, so the issue isn't really whether money can motivate. The answer to that is: "It can!" The more relevant question is this: Does money motivate most employees in the workforce today to higher performance? The answer to this question, we will argue, is "no."[106]

For money to motivate an individual's performance, certain conditions must be met. First, money must be important to the individual. Second, money must be perceived by the individual as being a direct reward for performance. Third, the marginal amount of money offered for the performance must be perceived by the individual as being significant. Finally, management must have the discretion to reward high performers with more money. Let's take a look at each of these conditions.

Money is not important to all employees. High achievers, for instance, are intrinsically motivated. Money should have little impact on these people. Similarly, money is relevant to those individuals with strong lower-order needs; but for most of the workforce, lower-order needs are substantially satisfied.

Money would motivate if employees perceived a strong linkage between performance and rewards in organizations. Unfortunately, pay increases are far more often determined by levels of skills and experience, community pay standards, the national cost-of-living index, and the organization's current and future financial prospects than by each employee's level of performance.

For money to motivate, the marginal difference in pay increases between a high performer and an average performer must be significant. In practice, it rarely is. How much motivation is there in knowing that if you work really hard you will end up with $20 a week more than someone who is doing just enough to get by? For a large number of people, not much! Research indicates that merit raises must be at least 7 percent of base pay for employees to perceive them as motivating. Unfortunately, recent surveys find nonmanagerial employees averaging merit increases of only 4.9 percent.[107]

In most organizations, managers have a very small area of discretion within which they can reward their higher-performing employees. So money might be theoretically capable of motivating employees to higher levels of performance, but most managers are not given enough flexibility to do much about it.

LEARNING ABOUT **YOURSELF** EXERCISE

What Motivates You?

Circle the number that most closely agrees with how you feel. Consider your answers in the context of your current job or a past work experience.

	Strongly Disagree				Strongly Agree
1. I try very hard to improve on my past performance at work.	1	2	3	4	5
2. I enjoy competition and winning.	1	2	3	4	5
3. I often find myself talking to those around me about nonwork matters.	1	2	3	4	5
4. I enjoy a difficult challenge.	1	2	3	4	5
5. I enjoy being in charge.	1	2	3	4	5
6. I want to be liked by others.	1	2	3	4	5
7. I want to know how I am progressing as I complete tasks.	1	2	3	4	5
8. I confront people who do things I disagree with.	1	2	3	4	5
9. I tend to build close relationships with co-workers.	1	2	3	4	5
10. I enjoy setting and achieving realistic goals.	1	2	3	4	5
11. I enjoy influencing other people to get my way.	1	2	3	4	5
12. I enjoy belonging to groups and organizations.	1	2	3	4	5
13. I enjoy the satisfaction of completing a difficult task.	1	2	3	4	5
14. I often work to gain more control over the events around me.	1	2	3	4	5
15. I enjoy working with others more than working alone.	1	2	3	4	5

Scoring Key

To determine your dominant needs—and what motivates you—place the number 1 through 5 that represents your score for each statement next to the number for that statement.

Achievement	Power	Affiliation
1. _____	2. _____	3. _____
4. _____	5. _____	6. _____
7. _____	8. _____	9. _____
10. _____	11. _____	12. _____
13. _____	14. _____	15. _____
Totals: _____	_____	_____

Add up the total of each column. The sum of the numbers in each column will be between 5 and 25 points. The column with the highest score tells you your dominant need.

Source: Based on R. Steers and D. Braunstein, "A Behaviorally Based Measure of Manifest Needs in Work Settings," *Journal of Vocational Behavior*, October 1976, p. 254; and R.N. Lussier, *Human Relations in Organizations: A Skill Building Approach* (Homewood, IL: Richard D. Irwin, 1990), p. 120.

BREAKOUT **GROUP** EXERCISES

Form small groups to discuss the following topics, as assigned by your instructor:

1. One of the members of your team continually arrives late for meetings and does not turn drafts of assignments in on time. Choose one of the available theories and indicate how the theory explains the member's current behaviour and how the theory could be used to motivate the group member to perform more responsibly.

2. You are unhappy with the performance of one of your instructors and would like to encourage the instructor to present more lively classes. Choose one of the available theories and indicate how the theory explains the instructor's current behaviour. How could you as a student use the theory to motivate the instructor to present more lively classes?

3. Harvard University recently changed its grading policy to recommend to instructors that the average course mark should be a B. This was the result of a study showing that more than 50 percent of students were receiving an A or A– for coursework. Harvard students are often referred to as "the best and the brightest," and they pay $27 000 (US) for their education, so they expect high grades. Discuss the impact of this change in policy on the motivation of Harvard students to study harder.

WORKING WITH **OTHERS** EXERCISE

Rewards for Workforce Diversity

Purpose
To learn about the different needs of a diverse workforce.

Time
Approximately 40 minutes.

Directions
Divide the class into groups of approximately 6 students. Each group is assigned 1 of the following people and is to determine the best benefits package for that person.

- Lise is 28 years old. She is a divorced mother of 3 children, aged 3, 5, and 7. She is the department head. She earns $37 000 a year on her job and receives another $3600 a year in child support from her ex-husband.

- Ethel is a 72-year-old widow. She works 25 hours a week to supplement her $8000 annual pension. Including her hourly wage of $7.50, she earns $17 750 a year.

- John is a 34-year-old Black male born in Trinidad who is now a Canadian resident. He is married and the father of two small children. John attends college at night and is within a year of earning his bachelor's degree. His salary is $24 000 a year. His wife is an attorney and earns approximately $54 000 a year.

- Sanjay is a 26-year-old physically impaired Indo-Canadian male. He is single and has a master's degree in education. Sanjay is paralyzed and confined to a wheelchair as a result of a car accident. He earns $29 000 a year.

- Wei Mei is a single 22-year-old immigrant. Born and raised in China, she came to Canada only three months ago. Wei Mei's English needs considerable improvement. She earns $18 000 a year.

- Mike is a 16-year-old white male in his 2nd year of high school. He works 15 hours a week after school and during vacations. He earns $6.25 an hour, or approximately $4875 a year.

Background
Our 6 participants work for a company that has recently installed a flexible benefits program. Instead of the traditional "one benefit package fits all," the company is allocating an additional 25 percent of each employee's annual pay to be used for discretionary benefits. Those benefits and their annual cost are listed below.

Benefit	Yearly Cost
Extended medical care (for services such as private hospital room, eyeglasses, and dental care that are not provided by the Medical Services Plan) for employee:	
Plan A (No deductible and pays 90%)	$3000
Plan B ($200 deductible and pays 80%)	$2000
Plan C ($1000 deductible and pays 70%)	$ 500
Extended medical care for dependants (same deductibles and percentages as above):	
Plan A	$2000
Plan B	$1500
Plan C	$ 500
Supplementary dental plan	$ 500
Life insurance:	
Plan A ($25 000 coverage)	$ 500
Plan B ($50 000 coverage)	$1000
Plan C ($100 000 coverage)	$2000
Plan D ($250 000 coverage)	$3000
Mental health plan	$ 500
Prepaid legal assistance	$ 300
Vacation	2% of annual pay for each week, up to 6 weeks a year
Pension at retirement equal to approximately 50% of final annual earnings	$1500
Four-day workweek during the three summer months	4% of annual pay (available only to full-time employees)
Daycare services (after company contribution)	$2000 for all of an employee's children, regardless of number
Company-provided transportation to and from work	$ 750
University tuition reimbursement	$1000
Language class tuition reimbursement	$ 500

The Task

1. Each group has 15 minutes to develop a flexible benefits package that consumes 25 percent (and no more!) of its character's pay.

2. After completing Step 1, each group appoints a spokesperson who describes to the entire class the benefits package the group has arrived at for its character.

3. The entire class then discusses the results. How did the needs, concerns, and problems of each participant influence the group's decision? What do the results suggest for trying to motivate a diverse workforce?

Source: Exercise developed by Steve Robbins, with special thanks to Professor Penny Wright (San Diego State University) for her suggestions during the development of this exercise. Exercise modified by Nancy Langton.

ETHICAL **DILEMMA** EXERCISE

Are Canadian CEOs Paid Too Much?

Critics have described the astronomical pay packages given to Canadian and American CEOs as "rampant greed." Consider the data in Exhibit 4–12.

In 2001, the compensation of CEOs of 100 of the largest companies on the Toronto Stock Exchange increased by 54 percent. At the same time, corporate profits showed the biggest decline in years, and the TSX 100-stock index fell 16 percent on the year.[108] In 2000, the CEOs of large publicly traded Canadian companies earned on average 21 times as much as their typical hourly employee.[109]

How do you explain such large pay packages to CEOs? Some say this represents a classic economic response to a situation in which the demand is great for high quality top-executive talent, and the supply is low. Other arguments in favour of paying executives $1 million a year or more are the need to compensate people for the tremendous responsibilities and stress that go with such jobs; the motivating potential that 7- and 8-figure annual incomes provide to senior executives and those who might aspire to be; and the influence of senior executives on the company's bottom line. (For example, research findings cited on page 263 of Chapter 8 attribute a 15- to 25-percent variation in profitability to the leadership quality of CEOs.)

Critics of executive pay practices in Canada and the United States argue that CEOs choose board members whom they can count on to support ever-increasing pay for top management. If board members fail to "play along," they risk losing their positions, their fees, and the prestige and power inherent in board membership.

In addition, it is not clear that executive compensation is tied to firm performance. For instance, KPMG LLP found in one survey that for 40 percent of the respondents, there was no correlation between the size of the bonus and how poorly or well the company fared.

Is high compensation of chief executives a problem? If so, does the blame for the problem lie with CEOs or with the shareholders and boards that knowingly allow the practice? Are Canadian and American CEOs greedy? Are these CEOs acting unethically? Should their pay reflect more closely some multiple of their employees' wages? What do you think?

Exhibit 4–12

2002 Compensation of Canada's Five Best-Paid CEOs

CEO and Company	2002 Total Compensation ($000's)	Rank on share return past 3 years (out of 150)
1. Jozef Straus JDS Uniphase Corp.	229 122	148
2. Eugene Melnyk Biovail Corp.	122 481	28
3. Gerald Schwartz Onex Corp.	49 266	46
4. Peter C. Godsoe Scotiabank	20 365	40
5. Firoz A. Rasul Ballard Power Systems Inc.	19 354	137

Source: "CEO Scorecard 2002," *National Post Business*, November 2002, p. 86.

CASE INCIDENT

Wage Reduction Proposal

The following proposal was made to employees of Montreal-based Quebecor's Vidéotron cable division in February 2002:

> *Employees are asked to increase the number of hours worked per week to 40 from 35, while receiving the same pay as working the shorter work week. In addition, they are asked to accept less paid holiday time.*

Quebecor spokesman Luc Lavoie justified the request made to the employees by saying: "They have the richest work contract in the country, including eight weeks of holiday and high absenteeism."

The company made it clear that if this proposal was not accepted, it would sell its cable television and internet installation and repair operations to Brossard, Quebec-based Entourage Technology Solutions.

The employees, members of Canadian Union of Public Employees (CUPE) local 2815, were reluctant to agree to these conditions. If they accepted, 300 to 400 employees were likely to be laid off, and the company could still consider outsourcing the work later.

Questions

1. Analyze this proposal in terms of motivation concepts.
2. How would you respond if you received this proposal?

Source: "Quebecor Plays Hardball With Defiant Union: Videotron 'Ready to Listen': Aims to Sell Cable Installation Operations," *Financial Post (National Post)*, March 5, 2002, p. FP6, and S. Silcoff, "Quebecor and Union in Showdown over Costs," *Financial Post (National Post)*, February 28, 2002, p. FP3.

 VIDEO CASE INCIDENT

Under 21 and Self-Employed

Meet the new entrepreneurs of Canada: they are young, motivated, and wanting to make a better world. In 2002, there was a 25 percent increase over the previous year of business start-ups by people between the ages of 15 and 24. This new breed of entrepreneurs is comparing the risks of starting a new business against those found climbing the traditional corporate ladder. But that's not all. Once established, these young people want to give back to their communities.

Meet Evan Clifford, the 21-year-old owner of Parallel, a contemporary retail store located on trendy Queen Street West in Toronto. Halfway through grade 13, Clifford decided to leave school and pursue something that interested him—designing his own line of casual clothing. His hard work paid off quickly, as Clifford landed some major corporate contracts early on. Although running the store kept Clifford busy, he still found time to consider how he could help others. For Christmas 2002, Clifford joined forces with a local rap artist to introduce a new clothing line with proceeds going to help street kids. As a way to celebrate the holidays and bring people together, Clifford decided to distribute phone cards to street kids who could not afford cards themselves in the hope that they would get in contact with someone they cared about.

In early 2002, Alexandra Hickey left her comfortable, stable government job to become a personal chef. Hickey, who has a chef-training diploma, wanted a job that would inspire her, not bore her. Hickey now enjoys owning her own business and feels fulfilled in her new role as chef and owner. She doesn't own a car and cycles to her clients when necessary. She feels that giving up the convenience and comfort of driving a car is a small price to pay for cleaner air.

Now more than ever in Canada, young business owners like Clifford and Hickey are discarding traditional processes, going their own way and trying new pathways towards success. As one expert commented, "what we are seeing here is capitalism with a conscience."

Questions

1. What motivates Evan Clifford? What does he value?
2. What motivated Alexandra Hickey to quit her stable government job?
3. What can firms do to create more motivating environments that will appeal to talented young employees?

Source: "Under 21," *CBC Venture*, December 1, 2002, VA2039H, 856; Young Entrepreneurs Association of Canada, www.yea.ca; Advancing Canadian Entrepreneurship (A.C.E.), www.acecanada.ca.

From **Concepts**
to **Skills**

Setting Goals

You can be more effective at setting goals if you use the following seven suggestions.[110]

1. *Identify the key tasks you want to accomplish.* Goal setting begins by defining what it is that you want to accomplish.

2. *Establish specific and challenging goals for each key task.* Identify the level of performance you want to accomplish for each task. Specify the specific targets toward which you are working.

3. *Specify the deadlines for each goal.* Putting deadlines on each goal reduces ambiguity. Deadlines, however, should not be set arbitrarily. Rather, they need to be realistic given the tasks to be completed.

4. *Prioritize goals.* When you have more than one goal, it's important to rank the goals in order of importance. The purpose of prioritizing is to encourage you to take action and expend effort on each goal in proportion to its importance.

5. *Rate goals for difficulty and importance.* Goal setting should not encourage people to choose easy goals. Instead, goals should be rated for their difficulty and importance.

6. *Build in feedback mechanisms to assess goal progress.* Feedback lets you know whether your level of effort is sufficient to attain the goal. Set deadlines for when you will evaluate how you are performing. You should review your progress frequently.

7. *Link rewards to goal attainment.* It's natural for you to get discouraged when working toward your goals. Link rewards to the achievement of goals to help you feel more encouraged.

Assessing Skills

After you've read this chapter, take the following Self-Assessments on your enclosed CD-ROM.

13. What Motivates Me?

14. What Rewards Do I Value Most?

15. What's My View on the Nature of People?

16. How Sensitive Am I to Equity Differences?

Practising Skills

Tammie Arnold worked her way through college while holding down a part-time job bagging groceries at Food Town supermarket chain. She liked working in the food industry, and when she graduated, she accepted a position with Food Town as a management trainee. Over the next three years, Arnold gained experience in the grocery store industry and in operating a large supermarket. About a year ago, Arnold received a promotion to store manager at one of the chain's locations. One of the things she has liked about Food Town is that it gives store managers a great deal of autonomy in running their stores. The company provides very general guidelines to its managers. Top management is concerned with the bottom line; for the most part, how the store manager gets there is up to him or her. Now that Arnold is finally a store manager, she wants to establish an MBO-type program in her store. She likes the idea that everyone should have clear goals to work toward and then be evaluated against those goals.

The store employs 70 people, although except for the managers, most work only 20 to 30 hours per week. There are 6 people reporting to Arnold: an assistant manager; a weekend manager; and grocery, produce, meat, and bakery managers. The only highly skilled jobs belong to the butchers, who have strict training and regulatory guidelines. Other less skilled jobs include cashier, shelf stocker, maintenance worker, and grocery bagger.

Arnold has come to you for advice on how to design a goal-setting program for her store. Specifically describe how she should go about setting goals in her new position. Include examples of goals for the jobs of butcher, cashier, and bakery manager.

Reinforcing Skills

1. Set personal and academic goals you want to achieve by the end of this term. Prioritize and rate them for difficulty.

2. Where do you want to be in five years? Do you have specific five-year goals? Establish three goals you want to achieve in five years. Make sure these goals are specific, challenging, and measurable.

CHAPTER 5

Working in Teams

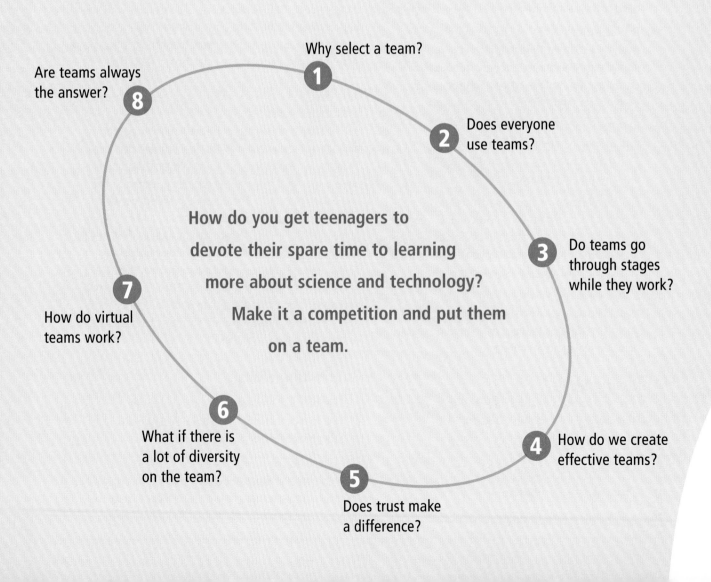

Why select a team?

1

Are teams always the answer?

8

Does everyone use teams?

2

Do teams go through stages while they work?

3

How do you get teenagers to devote their spare time to learning more about science and technology? Make it a competition and put them on a team.

7

How do virtual teams work?

What if there is a lot of diversity on the team?

6

5

4

How do we create effective teams?

Does trust make a difference?

The students at Glenforest Secondary School in Mississauga, Ontario, took part in the ninth annual Canada FIRST Robotic Competition in spring 2002. They had eight weeks to design and build a remotely operated robot that would compete with other robots built by secondary school teams across the country. The students wanted to do a better job than they had the previous year. The team's previous robot moved well, but it could not meet the challenge of firing balls at pie plates. The students knew a little about teamwork, and they had support and encouragement from teachers, engineering mentors, and corporate sponsors. What factors contributed to the students building a better robot in 2002?

For teams to excel a number of conditions need to be met. Effective teams need wise leadership, a variety of resources, and a way to solve problems. Team members need to be dedicated, and they need to build trust. In this chapter we examine when it's best to have a team, how to create effective teams, and how to deal with diversity on teams.

TEAMS VS. GROUPS: WHAT'S THE DIFFERENCE?

Groups and teams are not the same thing.[1] A **work group** is a group that interacts mainly to share information and make decisions that will help individual members perform within their area of responsibility. Work groups are not expected to engage in collective work that requires joint effort. So their performance is merely the sum of each group member's individual contribution. There is no positive synergy that would create an overall level of performance that is greater than the sum of the inputs.

A **team** is "a small number of people with complementary skills who are committed to a common purpose, performance goals, and approach for which they hold themselves mutually accountable."[2] Groups become teams when they meet the following conditions:[3]

- Team members share leadership.

- The individuals and the team as a whole share accountability for the work of the team.

 Why select a team?

work group
A group that interacts mainly to share information and to make decisions to help each member perform within his or her area of responsibility.

team
A group whose individual efforts result in a performance that is greater than the sum of those individual inputs.

- The team develops its own purpose or mission.

- The team works on problem-solving continuously, rather than just at scheduled meeting times.

- The effectiveness of the team is measured in terms of *team* outcomes and goals, not *individual* outcomes and goals.

This chapter's *Point/CounterPoint* on page 164 discusses whether sports teams are a good model for helping to understand how teams function in the workplace.

WHY HAVE TEAMS BECOME SO POPULAR?

When Glenforest Secondary teachers decided that students should enter the Canada FIRST competition, they could have asked the smartest kids in the science class to build their own robots. This is not what the teachers and students chose to do, however. Instead they created a team. Was this a reasonable way for Glenforest to proceed?

 **2** Does everyone use teams?

Glenforest Secondary School
www.peel.edu.on.ca/glenforest/

Canada FIRST Robotic
www.adsb.on.ca/KOR/ducttape/canadafirst.html

Pick up almost any business newspaper or magazine today and you will read how teams have become an essential part of the way business is done in companies such as Zellers, Xerox, Sears Canada, General Electric, AT&T, Hewlett-Packard, Motorola, Apple Computer, DaimlerChrysler AG, 3M Co., Australian Airlines, Johnson & Johnson, and London Life. A Conference Board of Canada report found that more than 80 percent of its 109 respondents used teams in the workplace.[4] This is similar to the United States, where 80 percent of Fortune 500 companies have half or more of their employees on teams. And 68 percent of small US manufacturers are using teams in their production areas.[5] Thus it's not surprising that Glenforest Secondary also selected a team to build a robot.

The extensive use of teams creates the *potential* for an organization to generate greater outputs with no increase in inputs. Notice, however, we said "potential." Creating a team does not lead magically to this positive synergy. Merely calling a group a *team* will not automatically increase its performance. As we show later in this chapter, successful, or high-performing, teams have certain common characteristics. If management

Many employees are asked to work in teams in order to accomplish their tasks. In a self-managed work team, such as the one from Xerox shown here, members make decisions about how to manage and schedule production, and also monitor the quality of their output.

hopes to gain increases in organizational performance through the use of teams, it must ensure that its teams possess these characteristics.

UNDERSTANDING THE STAGES IN TEAMS

Consider when the Glenforest Secondary students first started working together to build the robot. If they were anything like most ordinary teams, they all might not have known each other, or trusted each other. They might not have known who should be the leader or how to form the plans for what they had to do. Besides building a successful robot, they had to raise $16 000 to take part in the contest. They also had several deadlines to meet. To build a successful team that would achieve their goals, the students would have had to go through several stages. So what are the stages through which teams go?

While we make a distinction between groups and teams, some of the processes they go through are similar. Thus, in trying to understand how teams move from the "get-acquainted stage" to the "performing" stage, we look at two models that were developed to explain group processes. The models apply as readily to teams. Below, we review the better-known five-stage model of group development, and then the more recently discovered punctuated-equilibrium model.

The Five-Stage Model

From the mid-1960s, it was believed that groups passed through a standard sequence of five stages.[6] As shown in Exhibit 5–1, these five stages have been labelled *forming, storming, norming, performing,* and *adjourning.* Although we now know that not all groups pass through these stages in a linear fashion, the stages can still help in addressing your anxieties about working in groups.

3 Do teams go through stages while they work?

- *Stage I: Forming.* Think about the first time you met with a new group that had been put together to accomplish a task. Do you remember how some people seemed silent and others felt confused about the task you were to accomplish? Those feelings arise during the first stage of group development, know as **forming**. Forming is characterized by a great deal of uncertainty about the group's purpose, structure, and leadership. Members are "testing the waters" to determine what types of behaviour are acceptable. This stage is complete when members have begun to think of themselves as part of a group.

forming
The first stage in group development, characterized by much uncertainty.

- *Stage II: Storming.* Do you remember how some people in your group just didn't seem to get along, and sometimes power struggles even emerged? These reactions are typical of the **storming** stage, which is one of intragroup conflict. Members accept the existence of the group, but resist the constraints that the

storming
The second stage in group development, characterized by intragroup conflict.

Exhibit 5–1

Stages of Group Development

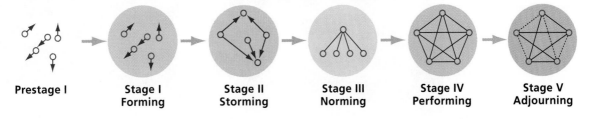

| Prestage I | Stage I Forming | Stage II Storming | Stage III Norming | Stage IV Performing | Stage V Adjourning |

group imposes on individuality. Furthermore, there is conflict over who will control the group. When this stage is complete, a relatively clear hierarchy of leadership will emerge within the group.

Some groups never really emerge from the storming stage, or they move back and forth through storming and the other stages. A group that remains forever planted in the storming stage may have less ability to complete the task because of all the interpersonal problems.

- *Stage III: Norming.* Many groups resolve the interpersonal conflict and reach the third stage, in which close relationships develop and the group demonstrates cohesiveness. There is now a strong sense of group identity and camaraderie. The group develops **norms**, acceptable standards of behaviour that are shared by the group's members. All groups have established norms that tell members what they ought and ought not to do under certain circumstances. When agreed to and accepted by the group, norms act as a means of influencing the behaviour of group members with a minimum of external controls. This **norming** stage is complete when the group structure solidifies, and the group has assimilated a common set of expectations about what defines correct member behaviour.

- *Stage IV: Performing.* Next, and you may have noticed this in some of your own group interactions, some groups just seem to come together well and start to do their work. This fourth stage, when significant task progress is being made, is called **performing**. The structure at this point is fully functional and accepted. Group energy has moved from getting to know and understand each other to performing the task at hand. In our opening vignette, when Glenforest Secondary raced its robot in the annual competition, it was performing.

- *Stage V: Adjourning.* For permanent work groups, performing is the last stage in their development. However, for temporary committees, teams, task forces, and similar groups that have a limited task to perform, there is an **adjourning** stage. This is when the group prepares to disband. High task performance is no longer the group's top priority. Instead, attention is directed toward wrapping up activities. Group members' responses vary at this stage. Some members are upbeat, basking in the group's accomplishments. Others may be depressed over the loss of camaraderie and friendships gained during the work group's life.

norms
Acceptable standards of behaviour within a group that are shared by the group's members.

norming
The third stage in group development, characterized by close relationships and cohesiveness.

performing
The fourth stage in group development, when the group is fully functional.

adjourning
The final stage in group development for temporary groups, characterized by concern with wrapping up activities rather than task performance.

As part of her training to become an astronaut, Julie Payette, who flew aboard the space shuttle Discovery in 1999, worked with other NASA astronauts to become a team player. Members of shuttle crews have to work harmoniously with other crew members to achieve the mission's goals. By stressing that the mission's success depends on teamwork, NASA teaches astronauts how to compromise and make decisions that benefit the entire team.

Putting the Five-Stage Model Into Perspective

Many interpreters of the five-stage model have assumed that a group becomes more effective as it progresses through the first four stages. While that is usually true, what makes a group effective is more complex than this model acknowledges. Under some conditions, high levels of conflict lead to high group performance, as long as the conflict is directed toward the task and not toward group members. So we might expect to find situations where groups in Stage II outperform those in Stages III or IV. Similarly, groups do not always proceed clearly from one stage to the next. Sometimes, in fact, several stages go on simultaneously, as when groups are storming and performing at the same time. Groups even occasionally regress to previous stages. Therefore, even the strongest proponents of this model do not assume that all groups follow the five-stage process precisely or that Stage IV is always the most preferable.

Another problem with the five-stage model is that it ignores organizational context.[7] For instance, a study of a cockpit crew in an airliner found that, within 10 minutes, three strangers assigned to fly together for the first time had become a high-performing group. What allowed for this speedy group development was the strong organizational context surrounding the tasks of the cockpit crew. This context provided the rules, task definitions, information, and resources needed for the group to perform. They didn't need to develop plans, assign roles, determine and allocate resources, resolve conflicts, and set norms the way the five-stage model predicts. Within the workplace, some group behaviour takes place within a strong organizational context, and the five-stage development model might have limited applicability for those groups. However, there are a variety of situations in the workplace where groups are assigned to tasks, and the individuals do not know each other. They must therefore work out interpersonal differences at the same time that they work through the assigned tasks.

The Punctuated-Equilibrium Model

Studies of more than a dozen field and laboratory task-force groups confirmed that not all groups develop in a universal sequence of stages.[8] In particular, temporary groups with deadlines have their own unique sequencing of action (or inaction): 1) The first meeting sets the group's direction; 2) the first phase of group activity is one of inertia; 3) a transition takes place at the end of the first phase, which occurs exactly when the group has used up half its allotted time; 4) the transition initiates major changes; 5) a second phase of inertia follows the transition; and 6) the group's last meeting is characterized by markedly accelerated activity. This pattern is called the *punctuated-equilibrium model* and is shown in Exhibit 5–2.[9] It is important for you to understand these shifts in group behaviour. If you are ever in a group that is not working well, knowing about the shifts could help you think of ways to make the group move to a more productive phase.

Phase 1

As a group member and possibly a group leader, you need to recognize that the first meeting sets the group's direction. This is where the framework of behavioural patterns and assumptions through which the group will approach its project gets set. These lasting patterns can appear as early as the first few seconds of the group's life.

Once set, the group's direction becomes accepted and is unlikely to be re-examined throughout the first half of the group's life. This is a period of inertia—that is, the group tends to stand still or become locked into a fixed course of action. Even if it gains new insights that challenge initial patterns and assumptions, the group is incapable of acting on these new insights in Phase 1. You may recognize that in some groups, during the early period of trying to get things accomplished, no one really did his or her assigned tasks. You may also recognize this phase as one where everyone carries out the tasks, but

Exhibit 5–2

The Punctuated-Equilibrium Model

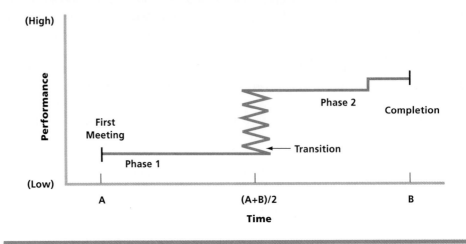

not in a very coordinated fashion. Thus, the team is performing at a relatively low state. This does not necessarily mean that it is doing nothing at all, however.

Phase 2

At some point, the group moves out of the inertia stage and recognizes that work needs to get completed. One of the more interesting discoveries made in these studies was that each group experienced its transition at the same point in its calendar—precisely halfway between its first meeting and its official deadline. The similarity occurred despite the fact that some groups spent as little as an hour on their project while others spent six months. It was as if the groups universally experienced a mid-life crisis at this point. The midpoint appears to work like an alarm clock, heightening members' awareness that their time is limited and that they need to "get moving." When you work on your next group project, you might want to examine when your group starts to "get moving."

This transition ends Phase 1 and is characterized by a concentrated burst of changes, dropping of old patterns, and adoption of new perspectives. The transition sets a revised direction for Phase 2, which is a new equilibrium or period of inertia. In this phase, the group executes plans created during the transition period. The group's last meeting is characterized by a final burst of activity to finish its work. There have been a number of studies that support the basic premise of punctuated equilibrium, though not all of them found that the transition in the team occurred exactly at the midpoint.[10]

Applying the Punctuated-Equilibrium Model

Let's use this model to describe some of your experiences with student teams created for doing group term projects. At the first meeting, a basic timetable is established. Members size up one another. They agree they have nine weeks to do their project. The instructor's requirements are discussed and debated. From that point, the group meets regularly to carry out its activities. About four or five weeks into the project, however, problems are confronted. Criticism begins to be taken seriously. Discussion becomes more open. The group reassesses where it has been and aggressively moves to make necessary changes. If the right changes are made, the next four or five weeks find the group developing a first-rate project. The group's last meeting, which will probably occur just before the project is due, lasts longer than the others. In it, all final issues are discussed and details resolved.

In summary, the punctuated-equilibrium model characterizes groups as exhibiting long periods of inertia interspersed with brief revolutionary changes triggered primarily by their members' awareness of time and deadlines. Several researchers have suggested that the five-stages model and punctuated equilibrium are at odds with each other.[11] However, it makes more sense to view the models as complementary: The five-stage model considers the interpersonal process of the group, while punctuated equilibrium considers the time challenges that the group faces.[12] To use the terminology of the five-stage group development model, the group begins by combining the *forming* and *norming* stages, then goes through a period of *low performing*, followed by *storming*, then a period of *high performing*, and, finally, *adjourning*. Keep in mind that this model is more suitable for understanding temporary task groups that are working under a tight deadline.

CREATING EFFECTIVE TEAMS

Beatrice Sze, Glenforest Secondary School's robotics team co-captain, gave her teammates a sense of responsibility and ownership over their work. For example, when a team member came to her with questions about what to do next, she would say encouragingly, "Use your brain. You can figure this out. You know how to do this."

The students at Glenforest Secondary School also had to be resourceful. One team member's parents provided the family basement for a team gathering place. That enabled the students to get extra parts from the family's snowblower and dehumidifier. Sometimes they worked so late into the evening that they had sleepovers on the basement floor, huddled in sleeping bags. They also got a mentor—a computer and electrical engineer with Bell Mobility—who tried to guide the students in the right direction without telling them what to do. What other considerations might have helped Glenforest's robotics team be more effective?

The Glenforest students had some of the characteristics of an effective team, but how can we judge whether a team that we are on is really effective? Exhibit 5–3 provides a checklist for knowing when you have an effective team.

4 How do we create effective teams?

Bell Mobility
www.bell.ca

Characteristics of Ineffective Teams

Before we consider how to create more effective teams, you may want to consider the characteristics of ineffective teams. There are several key indicators you can use to help identify whether a team is working effectively, or whether it needs to make some changes in behaviour:[13]

- *Not sharing issues and concerns.* When team members refuse to share information, it usually signals a problem with the way the team is functioning. Silence, avoidance, and meetings behind closed doors where not all members are included are some of the signals that information sharing is a problem.

- *Overdependence on the leader.* Members of the team should be able to make decisions and carry out actions even if the leader is not present. When the leader is relied upon to carry out all group actions, this suggests that team members are not carrying out their responsibilities.

- *Failure to carry out decisions.* Teams should put their decisions into action as soon as possible. A lack of action after decision making suggests that team members may view the needs of the team as having low priority, or they may not be committed to the decisions that were made.

- *Hidden conflict.* It is okay for team members to disagree, and to work through disagreements so that members have an understanding of each other. When

Exhibit 5–3

Characteristics of an Effective Team

1.	**Clear purpose**	The vision, mission, goal, or task of the team has been defined and is now accepted by everyone. There is an action plan.
2.	**Informality**	The climate tends to be informal, comfortable, and relaxed. There are no obvious tensions or signs of boredom.
3.	**Participation**	There is much discussion, and everyone is encouraged to participate.
4.	**Listening**	The members use effective listening techniques such as questioning, paraphrasing, and summarizing to get out ideas.
5.	**Civilized disagreement**	There is disagreement, but the team is comfortable with this and shows no signs of avoiding, smoothing over, or suppressing conflict.
6.	**Consensus decisions**	For important decisions, the goal is substantial but not necessarily unanimous agreement through open discussion of everyone's ideas, avoidance of formal voting, or easy compromises.
7.	**Open communication**	Team members feel free to express their feelings on the tasks as well as on the group's operation. There are few hidden agendas. Communication takes place outside of meetings.
8.	**Clear rules and work assignments**	There are clear expectations about the roles played by each team member. When action is taken, clear assignments are made, accepted, and carried out. Work is distributed among team members.
9.	**Shared leadership**	While the team has a formal leader, leadership functions shift from time to time depending on the circumstances, the needs of the group, and the skills of the members. The formal leader models the appropriate behaviour and helps establish positive norms.
10.	**External relations**	The team spends time developing key outside relationships, mobilizing resources, and building credibility with important players in other parts of the organization.
11.	**Style diversity**	The team has a broad spectrum of team-player types including members who emphasize attention to task, goal setting, focus on process, and questions about how the team is functioning.
12.	**Self-assessment**	Periodically, the team stops to examine how well it is functioning and what may be interfering with its effectiveness.

Source: G.M. Parker, *Team Players and Teamwork: The New Competitive Business Strategy* (San Francisco: Jossey-Bass, 1990), Table 2, p. 33. Copyright 1990 by Jossey-Bass Inc, Publishers. Reprinted by permission of John Wiley and Sons, Inc.

team members do not reveal that they have a difference of opinion, but this causes tension, then the team will be less productive, and individual members will be less satisfied.

- *Not resolving conflict.* A lot of infighting, put-downs, and attempts to hurt other members suggests that the team has very serious problems.

- *Subgroups.* When teams break up into smaller groups, and these smaller groups put their needs ahead of the team as a whole, the team will have difficulty functioning effectively.

You may want to evaluate your own team experiences against this checklist to give you some idea of how well your team is functioning, or what issues are causing problems for your team.

Components of Effective Teams

So how can we create more effective teams? There is no shortage of efforts to identify factors related to team effectiveness.[14] However, recent studies have taken what was once a "veritable laundry list of characteristics"[15] and organized them into a relatively focused model.[16] Exhibit 5–4 summarizes what we currently know about what makes teams effective, assuming a situation demands a team. Keep in mind two caveats before you proceed:

- First, teams differ in form and structure. Since the model we present tries to generalize across all varieties of teams, you need to be careful not to rigidly apply the model's predictions to all teams.[17] The model should be used as a guide, not as strict rules.

- Second, the model assumes that it's already been determined that teamwork would be better than individual work. Creating "effective" teams in situations where individuals can do the job better is like solving the wrong problem perfectly.

The key components of effective teams fit into four general categories:

- work design;
- the team's composition;
- the context within which the team works;
- team process variables (those things that go on in the team that influence how effective the team is).

When measuring effectiveness, one might consider objective measures of the team's productivity; managers' ratings of the team's performance; and measures of team satisfaction based on adding up member satisfaction.

Work Design

Effective teams need to work together and take collective responsibility to complete significant tasks. They must be more than a "team-in-name-only."[18] The work-design category includes variables such as freedom and autonomy, the opportunity to use different skills and talents, the ability to complete a whole and identifiable task or product,

Exhibit 5–4

A Model of Team Effectiveness

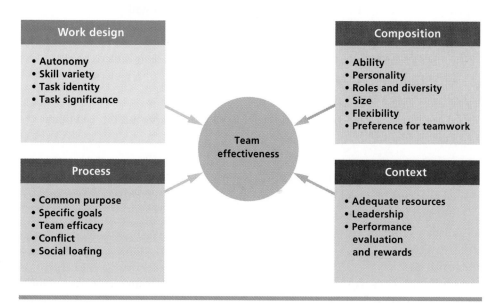

Separated work stations, such as these at a Hong Kong toy factory, reduce work group interactions.

and the participation in a task or project that has a substantial impact on others. The evidence indicates that these factors enhance member motivation and increase team effectiveness.[19] These work design characteristics motivate teams because they increase members' sense of responsibility and ownership over the work, and because they make the work more interesting to perform.[20]

Team Composition

Managers need to understand the individual strengths that each person can bring to a team, select members with their strengths in mind, and allocate work assignments that fit with members' preferred styles. By matching individual preferences with team role demands, managers increase the likelihood that the team members will work well together. This chapter's *CBC Video Case Incident*, "Earthbuddies," demonstrates how putting together a good team can lead to a very successful company.

"Earthbuddies"

Abilities

To perform effectively, a team requires three different types of skills.

1. It needs people with *technical expertise*.

2. It needs people with the *problem-solving* and *decision-making skills* to be able to identify problems, generate alternatives, evaluate those alternatives, and make competent choices.

3. It needs people with good listening, feedback, conflict resolution, and other *interpersonal skills*.[21]

No team can achieve its performance potential without developing all three types of skills. The right mix is crucial. Too much of one at the expense of others will result in lower team performance. But teams don't need to have all the complementary skills in place at the beginning. It's not uncommon for one or more members to take responsibility to learn skills that are lacking in the team, thus allowing the team to reach its full potential.

Personality

Teams have different needs, and people should be selected for a team on the basis of their personalities and preferences, as well as the team's needs for diversity and filling of roles. We demonstrated in Chapter 2 that personality has a significant influence on individual employee behaviour. This can also be extended to team behaviour. For instance, teams that rate higher in mean levels of extroversion, agreeableness, conscientiousness, and emotional stability tend to receive higher managerial ratings for team performance.[22]

Roles

Shakespeare said, "All the world's a stage, and all the men and women merely players." Using the same metaphor, all group members are actors, each playing a **role**. By this term, we mean a set of expected behaviour patterns attributed to someone occupying a given position in a social unit. The understanding of role behaviour would be dramatically simplified if each of us chose one role and "played it out" regularly and consistently. Unfortunately, we are required to play a number of diverse roles, both on and off our jobs. As we will see, one of the tasks in understanding behaviour is grasping the role that a person is currently playing.

Watching a veteran employee on the housekeeping staff helped Lisa Jackson (left) learn her role as a housekeeper at a Marriott hotel. In addition to teaching on-the-job skills such as the proper way to make a bed, Jackson's apprenticeship training included observing how employees should react in stressful situations.

Task-Oriented and Maintenance Roles Within almost any team, two sets of role relationships need to be considered: task-oriented roles and maintenance roles. The **task-oriented roles** are performed by team members to ensure that the tasks of the team are accomplished. The **maintenance roles** are carried out to ensure that team members maintain good relations. Exhibit 5–5 identifies a number of task-oriented and maintenance roles that you might find in a team.

Effective teams keep some balance between task orientation and maintenance of relations. Beatrice Sze was an encourager—helping team members achieve their best. She knew that she had to help keep the stress level of teammates down, while encouraging them to do their best. Other students likely played other roles on the team that helped keep the group together and get the tasks accomplished. The *Working With Others Exercise* on page 166 gives you the opportunity to see how these roles actually apply in a group interaction. *From Concepts to Skills* on page 169 gives guidelines for conducting a team meeting. These will help in many instances to keep discussions on track.

Individual Roles Occasionally within teams, you will see people take on **individual roles** that are not productive for keeping the team on task. When this happens, the individual is demonstrating more concern for himself or herself than the team as a whole. At the summer 2003 Commonwealth Games, Canadian sprinter Nick Macrozonaris was determined to put himself above the rest of his 4x100-metre teammates. Though his precise statement is disputed, Macrozonaris admits to demanding that he be allowed to run one of the straight portions of the relay, rather than the curved ones. "I'm not willing to go out there and shoot myself in the foot and look like a jackass. I cannot run the curve," claimed Macrozonaris. The team's coach, Glenroy Gilbert, decided against Macrozonaris participating at all, given his lack of team spirit. Team Canada's head coach supported Gilbert's decision: "We're here to make team decisions. There will not be individual camps, lobbies, or negotiations."[23] When organizations use teams, it is important that they emphasize to all members that they act as part of those teams.

role
A set of expected behaviour patterns attributed to someone occupying a given position in a social unit.

task-oriented roles
Task-oriented roles are performed by team members to ensure that the tasks of the team are accomplished.

maintenance roles
Maintenance roles are carried out to ensure that team members maintain good relations.

individual roles
Roles performed by group members that are not productive for keeping the group on task.

Exhibit 5–5

Roles Required for Effective Team Functioning

	Function	Description	Example
Roles that build task accomplishment	*Initiating*	Stating the goal or problem, making proposals about how to work on it, setting time limits.	"Let's set up an agenda for discussing each of the problems we have to consider."
	Seeking Information and Opinions	Asking group members for specific factual information related to the task or problem, or for their opinions about it.	"What do you think would be the best approach to this, Jack?"
	Providing Information and Opinions	Sharing information or opinions related to the task or problems.	"I worked on a similar problem last year and found...."
	Clarifying	Helping one another understand ideas and suggestions that come up in the group.	"What you mean, Sue, is that we could...?"
	Elaborating	Building on one another's ideas and suggestions.	"Building on Don's idea, I think we could...."
	Summarizing	Reviewing the points covered by the group and the different ideas stated so that decisions can be based on full information.	Appointing a recorder to take notes on a blackboard.
	Consensus Testing	Periodic testing about whether the group is nearing a decision or needs to continue discussion.	"Is the group ready to decide about this?"
Roles that build and maintain a team	*Harmonizing*	Mediating conflict among other members, reconciling disagreements, relieving tensions.	"Don, I don't think you and Sue really see the question that differently."
	Compromising	Admitting error at times of group conflict.	"Well, I'd be willing to change if you provided some help on...."
	Gatekeeping	Making sure all members have a chance to express their ideas and feelings and preventing members from being interrupted.	"Sue, we haven't heard from you on this issue."
	Encouraging	Helping a group member make his or her point. Establishing a climate of acceptance in the group.	"I think what you started to say is important, Jack. Please continue."

Source: "Team Processes," in D. Ancona, T. Kochan, M. Scully, J. Van Maanen, and D.E. Westney, *Managing for the Future* (Cincinnati, OH: South-Western College Publishing, 1996), p. 9.

Size

Does the size of a team affect the team's overall behaviour? The answer to this question is a definite "yes," but the effect depends on what dependent variables you consider.[24]

The evidence indicates that smaller teams are faster at completing tasks than larger ones. However, if the team is engaged in problem-solving, large teams consistently get better marks than their smaller counterparts.

Translating these results into specific numbers is a bit more hazardous, but we can offer some guidelines. Large teams—with a dozen or more members—are good for gaining diverse input. So if the goal of the team is fact-finding, larger groups should be more effective. On the other hand, smaller groups are better at doing something productive with that input. Teams of about seven members, therefore, tend to be more effective for taking action.

Member Flexibility

Teams made up of flexible individuals have members who can complete each other's tasks. This is an obvious plus to a team because it greatly improves its adaptability and makes it less reliant on any single member.[25] So selecting members who themselves value flexibility, then cross-training them to be able to do each other's jobs, should lead to higher team performance over time.

Member Preferences

Not every employee is a team player. Given the option, many employees would avoid team participation. When people who would prefer to work alone are required to team up, there is a direct threat to the team's morale.[26] This suggests that, when selecting team members, individual preferences be considered as well as abilities, personalities, and skills. High-performing teams are likely to be composed of people who prefer working as part of a group.

Context

The three contextual factors that appear to be most significantly related to team performance are the presence of adequate resources, effective leadership, and a performance evaluation and reward system that reflects team contributions. Hamilton, Ontario-based Dofasco is a clear example of getting the context right for team performance. Dofasco started using teams in the early 1990s, by putting almost 7000 employees through team-building exercises. Today, multidisciplinary teams are given improvement goals; teams assume the responsibility for developing plans to reach the goals. The teams are self-managed to a large extent. "The supervisor became less of an ass-kicker and more of a resource person," explained former CEO John Mayberry.[27] Pay is partly tied to how well Dofasco does each year, which helps to motivate employees to work with their teams, rather than as individuals.

Resources

All work teams rely on resources outside the team to sustain them. And a scarcity of resources directly reduces the ability of a team to perform its job effectively. Teams must receive the necessary support from management and the larger organization if they are going to succeed in achieving their goals. One of the reasons for the Glenforest team's failure in 2001 was that they didn't have the kind of coaching they needed to build a great robot. For the 2002 competition, they found a mentor, and also created a team workshop at one of the team member's homes.

Leadership and Structure

Leadership plays a crucial role in the development and success of teams. Professor Richard Hackman of Harvard University, the leading expert on teams, suggests that the role of team leader involves:[28]

- creating a real team rather than a team in name only;

- setting a clear and meaningful direction for the team's work;

- making sure that the team structure will support working effectively;

- ensuring that the team operates within a supportive organizational context;

- providing expert coaching.

There are some practical problems that must be resolved when a team first starts working together. Team members must agree on who is to do what, and ensure that all members share the workload equally. The team also needs to decide how schedules will be set, what skills need to be developed, how the team will resolve conflicts, and how the team will make and modify decisions. Agreeing on the specifics of work and how they fit together to integrate individual skills requires team leadership and structure. This, incidentally, can be provided directly by management or by the team members themselves. In the case of the Glenforest students, the team was led by two student co-captains. The adult advisers did not try to tell the students what to do.

On traditionally managed teams, we find that two factors seem to be important in influencing team performance: the leader's *expectations* and his or her *mood.* Leaders who expect good things from their team are more likely to get them. For instance, military platoons under leaders who held high expectations performed significantly better in training than platoons whose leaders did not set expectations.[29] Studies have also found that leaders who exhibit positive moods get better team performance and lower turnover.[30]

Leadership, of course, is not always needed. For instance, the evidence indicates that self-managed work teams often perform better than teams with formally appointed leaders.[31] And leaders can obstruct high performance when they interfere with self-managed teams.[32]

Performance Evaluation and Rewards

How do you get team members to be both individually and jointly accountable? The traditional individually oriented evaluation must be modified to reflect team performance.[33] At Imperial Oil, team members provide feedback to each other in three critical areas: *team results, team functioning/effectiveness,* and *personal effectiveness.*

Imperial Oil Limited
www.imperialoil.ca

This type of appraisal reminds members of their responsibilities to the team. Teams should not rely solely on the formal performance appraisal process, however. To manage the team process more effectively, members should present work in progress to get feedback from other members and/or outsiders on quality and completeness of work. Sitting down together informally and reviewing both individual and team behaviour helps keep the team on track.

Teams also need to make sure that rewards recognize team work, rather than individual effort. A Conference Board of Canada study of teams in the workplace found that the most commonly used incentive to acknowledge teamwork was recognition, including "small financial rewards, plaques, ceremonies, publicity in company newspapers, and celebrations of success at company gatherings," used by well over half of the companies surveyed.[34] Other forms of team reward include team cash bonus plans (used by 25 percent of the surveyed companies) and gainsharing (used by 17 percent of the companies).[35]

Process

Process variables make up the final component of team effectiveness. These include member commitment to a common purpose; establishment of specific team goals; team efficacy; a managed level of conflict; and a system of accountability.

A Common Purpose

Effective teams have a common and meaningful purpose that provides direction, momentum, and commitment for members.[36] This purpose is a vision. It's broader than specific goals.

Members of successful teams put a tremendous amount of time and effort into discussing, shaping, and agreeing upon a purpose that belongs to them both collectively and individually. This common purpose, when accepted by the team, becomes the equivalent of what celestial navigation is to a ship captain—it provides direction and guidance under any and all conditions.

Specific Goals

Successful teams translate their common purpose into specific, measurable, and realistic performance goals. Just as we demonstrated in Chapter 4 how goals lead individuals to higher performance, goals also energize teams. These specific goals make clear communication easier. They also help teams maintain their focus on achieving results.

Consistent with the research on individual goals, team goals should be challenging. Difficult goals have been found to raise team performance for targeted criteria. So, for instance, goals for quantity tend to raise quantity, goals for speed tend to raise speed, goals for accuracy raise accuracy, and so on.[37]

Along with goals, teams should be encouraged to develop milestones—tangible steps toward completion of the project. This allows teams to focus on their goal and evaluate progress toward the goal. The milestones should be important enough and easy enough to reach that teams can celebrate some of their accomplishments along the way.

A recent study of 23 National Basketball Association (NBA) teams found that "shared experience"—tenure on the team and time on court—tended to improve turnover and boost win-loss performance significantly. Why do you think teams that stay together longer tend to play better?

Team Efficacy

Effective teams have confidence in themselves. They believe they can succeed. We call this *team efficacy*.[38]

Success breeds success. Teams that have been successful raise their beliefs about future success which, in turn, motivates them to work harder. One of the factors that helps teams build their efficacy is cohesiveness—the degree to which members are attracted to each other and are motivated to stay on the team.[39] Though teams differ in their cohesiveness, it is important because it has been found to be related to the team's productivity.[40]

How can management increase team efficacy? Two possibilities are to help the team achieve small successes and to provide skills training. Small successes build team confidence. As a team develops an increasingly stronger performance record, it also increases the collective belief that future efforts will lead to success. Managers should also consider providing training to improve members' technical and interpersonal skills. The greater the abilities of team members, the greater the likelihood that the team will develop confidence and the capability to deliver on that confidence.

Conflict Levels

Conflict on a team isn't necessarily bad. Though relationship conflicts—those based on interpersonal incompatibilities, tension, and animosity toward others—are almost always dysfunctional, teams that are completely void of conflict are likely to become apathetic and stagnant. We elaborate on this in Chapter 6.

Some types of conflict can actually improve team effectiveness.[41] On teams performing nonroutine activities, disagreements among members about task content (called task conflicts) are often beneficial because they lessen the likelihood of groupthink. Task conflicts stimulate discussion, promote critical assessment of problems and options, and can lead to better team decisions. So effective teams will be characterized by an appropriate level of conflict.

Social Loafing and Accountability

One of the most important findings related to the size of a team has been labelled **social loafing**. This is the tendency for individuals to spend less effort when working collectively than when working individually.[42] It directly challenges the logic that the productivity of the team as a whole should at least equal the sum of the productivity of each individual in that team.

What causes this social loafing effect? It may be due to a belief that others in the team are not carrying their fair share. If you view others as lazy or inept, you can re-establish equity by reducing your effort. Another explanation is the dispersion of responsibility. Because the results of the team cannot be attributed to any single person, the relationship between an individual's input and the team's output is clouded. In such situations, individuals may be tempted to become "free riders" and coast on the team's efforts. In other words, efficiency will drop when individuals believe that their contribution cannot be measured.

Successful teams make members individually and jointly accountable for the team's purpose, goals, and approach.[43] They clearly define what members are individually responsible for and what they are jointly responsible for.

social loafing
The tendency for individuals to spend less effort when working collectively than when working individually.

DEVELOPING TRUST

5 Does trust make a difference?

High-performance teams are characterized by high mutual trust among members. That is, members believe in the integrity, character, and ability of each other. But as you know from personal relationships, trust is fragile. It takes a long time to build, can be easily destroyed, and is hard to regain.[44] Also, since trust begets trust and distrust begets

At Montreal-based PEAK Financial Group, CEO Robert Frances (left) lets his teams do their own hiring. Everyone who might work with the potential hire, including subordinates, is invited to sit in on the interview. "If a team is to work properly as a team, then they should have a say in who the other team members are," says Frances. His philosophy is that if those involved don't think they will get along at the start, it's better to know this before they are hired. At right, we see some of PEAK's client services employees getting ready for the RRSP season.

distrust, maintaining trust requires careful attention by leaders and team members. As trust is one issue in accountability, you may want to look at the *Learning About Yourself Exercise* on page 165 to gain a sense of whether others would view you as trustworthy.

Trust is a positive expectation (or belief) that another will not—through words, actions, or decisions—act opportunistically.[45] Trust involves making oneself vulnerable as when, for example, we disclose intimate information or rely on another's promises.[46] By its very nature, trust provides the opportunity for us to be disappointed or taken advantage of.[47] So when I trust someone, I expect that they will not take advantage of me.

trust
A positive expectation that another will not act opportunistically.

What are the key dimensions that underlie the concept of trust? Recent evidence has identified five: *integrity, competence, consistency, loyalty,* and *openness.*[48] These are illustrated in Exhibit 5–6 and listed below in their order of importance in determining one's trustworthiness.

- *Integrity.* Honesty and truthfulness. Of all five dimensions, this one seems to be most critical when someone assesses another's trustworthiness. "Without a perception of the other's 'moral character' and 'basic honesty,' other dimensions of trust [are] meaningless."[49]

- *Competence.* Technical and interpersonal knowledge and skills. Does the person know what he or she is talking about? You're unlikely to listen to or depend on someone whose abilities you don't respect. You need to believe that people have the skills and abilities to carry out what they say they will do.

- *Consistency.* Reliability, predictability, and good judgment in handling situations. "Inconsistencies between words and action decrease trust."[50] Individuals quickly notice if one does not practise what one preaches.[51]

- *Loyalty.* Willingness to protect and save face for another person. Trust requires that you can depend on someone not to act opportunistically.

- *Openness.* Willingness to share ideas and information freely. Can you rely on the person to give you the full truth?

Exhibit 5–6

Dimensions of Trust

TEAMS AND WORKFORCE DIVERSITY

(6) What if there is a lot of diversity on the team?

group diversity
The heterogeneity of individual characteristics within a group.

Group diversity is defined by the heterogeneity of individual characteristics within a group.[52] These differences include not only functional characteristics (i.e., jobs, positions, or work experiences) but also demographic or cultural characteristics (e.g., age, race, sex, and citizenship). Some recent studies have also examined heterogeneity of values on performance, and suggested that this may have a greater impact than functional, demographic, or cultural differences.[53]

Managing diversity on teams is a balancing act (see Exhibit 5–7). On the one hand, a number of researchers have suggested that diversity brings a greater number of ideas, perspectives, knowledge, and skills to the group, which can be used to perform at a higher level.[54] On the other hand, researchers have suggested that diversity can lead people to recall stereotypes and therefore bring bias into their evaluation of people who are different than them.[55] Diversity can thus make it more difficult to unify the team and reach agreements. We consider some of the evidence to help us resolve these opposing views.

In a study examining the effectiveness of teams of strangers and teams of friends on bargaining, researchers found that teams of strangers gained greater profit than teams of friends when teams reported to a supervisor.[56] However, teams of friends were more cohesive than teams of strangers. One potentially negative finding of this research is that teams of friends were more concerned about maintaining their relationship than were teams of strangers. In the workplace, the importance of maintaining relationships could lead to lower productivity.

Overall, studies suggest that the strongest case for diversity on work teams can be made when these teams are engaged in problem-solving and decision-making tasks.[57] Heterogeneous teams may have qualities that lead to creative or unique solutions.[58] The lack of a common perspective also means diverse teams usually spend more time discussing issues, which decreases the possibility that a weak alternative will be chosen. Although diverse groups have more difficulty working together and solving problems, this goes away with time as the members come to know each other.

Recent research suggests that if team members share a common belief that diversity will positively affect their performance, this sets the foundation for the team to manage the diversity in a positive way. Specifically, if team members set out early on trying to learn about each other in order to understand and use their differences, this will have a positive effect on the team.[59] Laurie Milton, at the Haskayne School of Business at the University of Calgary, and several co-authors, found that even 10 minutes spent sharing

Haskayne School of Business, University of Calgary
www.haskayne.ucalgary.ca

Exhibit 5–7

Advantages and Disadvantages of Diversity

Advantages	Disadvantages
Multiple perspectives	Ambiguity
Greater openness to new ideas	Complexity
Multiple interpretations	Confusion
Increased creativity	Miscommunication
Increased flexibility	Difficulty in reaching a single agreement
Increased problem-solving skills	Difficulty in agreeing on specific actions

Source: Adapted from *International Dimensions of Organizational Behavior*, 4th ed., by N.J. Adler. Copyright © 2002 (p. 109). By permission of South-Western College Publishing, a division of International Thomson Publishing, Inc., Cincinnati, OH 45227.

personal information when a group first started working together lowered subsequent group conflict and improved creative performance.[60] When groups didn't share personal information at the beginning of their work, they were less likely to do so later.

The research findings taken as a whole suggest that diversity can bring increased benefits to the team, but for this to happen, teams must have some commonality in values, and they need to be willing to share information about themselves early on. We can thus expect that the value-added component of diverse teams increases as members become more familiar with each other and the team becomes more cohesive.

TEAMS FOR THE 21ST CENTURY: VIRTUAL TEAMS

When we think of teams, we often picture face-to-face interactions. **Virtual teams**, however, use computer technology to tie together physically separated members in order to achieve a common goal.[61] They allow people to collaborate online—using communication links such as wide-area networks, videoconferencing, or email—whether they are only a room away or continents apart. With greater availability of technology and increasing globalization, virtual teams become not only possible, but necessary. To the extent that work is knowledge-based rather than production-oriented, virtual teams are also more possible.

Virtual teams can do all the things that other teams do—share information, make decisions, complete tasks. And they can include members from the same organization or link an organization's members with employees from other organizations (i.e., suppliers and joint partners). They can convene for a few days to solve a problem, a few months to complete a project, or exist permanently.[62] Often they can be more efficient at tasks as well, because of the ease of sharing information through email and voice mail. Virtual teams also make it possible for people who face geographical and time-zone restrictions to work together.

Virtual teams can suffer from the absence of *paraverbal* and *nonverbal* cues and limited social contact. In face-to-face conversation, people use paraverbal (tone of voice, inflection, voice volume) and nonverbal (eye movement, facial expression, hand gestures, and other body language) cues to provide increased meaning. Virtual teams often suffer from less social rapport and less direct interaction among members. They are unable to duplicate the normal give and take of face-to-face discussion.

7 How do virtual teams work?

virtual teams
Teams that use computer technology to tie together physically dispersed members in order to achieve a common goal.

Sheila Goldgrab coaches virtual teams from the comfort of her home in Toronto. She can do that coaching via teleconference, videoconference, or email. She gets hired as a consultant to help virtual teams work together more smoothly. As one recipient of her coaching said, "Sheila was the rudder of the planning group. While we were going at high speed in different directions, she ensured there was a link among the group that kept us focused on the task at hand."

Virtual Teams and Trust

There has been some concern that because virtual teams lack face-to-face interaction, it may be more difficult to build trust among individuals. However, a recent study examining how virtual teams work on projects indicates that virtual teams can develop close interaction and trust; these qualities simply evolve differently than in face-to-face groups.[63] In face-to-face groups, trust comes from direct interaction, over time. In virtual teams, trust is either established at the outset or it generally does not develop. The researchers found that initial electronic messages set the tone for how interactions occurred throughout the entire project. In one team, for instance, when the appointed leader sent an introductory message that had a distrustful tone, the team suffered low morale and poor performance throughout the duration of the project. The researchers suggest that virtual teams should start with an electronic "courtship," where members provide some personal information. Then the teams should assign clear roles to members, helping members to identify with each other. Finally, the researchers noted that teams that had the best attitude (eagerness, enthusiasm, and intense action orientation in messages) did considerably better than teams that had one or more pessimists among them. The article by S.L. Jarvenpaa et al. about team struggle, cited in endnote 63 for this chapter, provides more detail on this subject. You might find the team experience reported there interesting.

Some additional tips for improving the way that virtual teams function include making sure that the team addresses feelings of isolation that members might have, making sure that team members have a mix of interpersonal and technical skills, and paying careful attention to assessing performance and providing recognition and feedback.[64]

BEWARE! TEAMS AREN'T ALWAYS THE ANSWER

When the Glenforest Secondary students got together to build a robot, it made sense for them to form a team. No student had all the knowledge and skills required to complete the task, as we saw in the opening vignette. But does every task need a team?

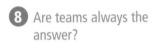 **8** Are teams always the answer?

The evidence suggests that teams typically outperform individuals when the tasks being done require multiple skills, judgment, and experience.[65] Teams might not be suitable for every situation, however. Teamwork takes more time and often more resources than individual work. Teams, for instance, have increased communication demands, conflicts to be managed, and meetings to be run. So the benefits of using teams have to exceed the costs. And that is not always the case. In the excitement to enjoy the benefits of teams, some managers have introduced them into situations where the work is better done by individuals. So before you rush to implement teams, you should carefully assess whether the work requires or will benefit from a collective effort.

How do you know if the work of your group would be better done in teams? It's been suggested that three tests be applied to see if a team fits the situation:[66]

- *Can the work be done better by more than one person?* Simple tasks that don't require diverse input are probably better left to individuals.

- *Does the work create a common purpose or set of goals for the people in the group that is more than the aggregate of individual goals?* For instance, the service departments of many new-car dealers have introduced teams that link customer service personnel, mechanics, parts specialists, and sales representatives. Such teams can better manage collective responsibility for ensuring that customer needs are properly met.

- *Are the members of the group interdependent?* Teams make sense where there is interdependence between tasks; where the success of the whole depends on the success of each one *and* the success of each one depends on the success of the others. Soccer, for instance, is an obvious *team* sport because of the interdependence of the players. Swim teams, by contrast, are not really teams, but groups of individuals whose total performance is merely the sum of the individual performances.

Others have outlined the conditions under which organizations would find teams more useful: "when work processes cut across functional lines; when speed is important (and complex relationships are involved); when the organization mirrors a complex, differentiated, and rapidly changing market environment; when innovation and learning have priority; and when the tasks that have to be done require online integration of highly interdependent performers."[67]

SUMMARY AND IMPLICATIONS

1 Why select a team? A team generates positive synergy through coordinated effort. The combined individual efforts result in a level of performance that is greater than the sum of those individual inputs.

2 Does everyone use teams? Teams have become an essential part of the way business is being done these days. A Conference Board of Canada report found that more than 80 percent of its 109 respondents used teams in the workplace. This is similar to the United States, where 80 percent of Fortune 500 companies have half or more of their employees on teams. And 68 percent of small US manufacturers are using teams in their production areas.

3 Do teams go through stages while they work? Two different models discuss how teams develop. The first, the five-stage model, considers how teams go through forming, storming, norming, performing, and adjourning. Through these stages they learn how to settle conflicts and develop norms, which enable them to perform. The second model is the punctuated-equilibrium model, which indicates how teams use their time. Teams show two great periods of activity, one midway through the project, after which they perform at a higher level than previously. The second peak in performance takes place right as the project comes due.

4 How do we create effective teams? For teams to be effective, careful consideration must be given to planning tasks, assigning members, choosing the appropriate size, and providing resources. Teams will be more effective if members have freedom and opportunity to do their tasks, as well as a belief that the task will have a substantial impact on others. Effective teams are neither too large nor too small—typically they range in size from 5 to 12 people. They have members who fill role demands, are flexible, and who prefer to be part of a group. Finally, effective teams have members committed to a common purpose and specific team goals.

5 Does trust make a difference? High-performance teams are characterized by high mutual trust among members. That is, members believe in the integrity, character, and ability of each other. The key dimensions that underlie the concept of trust are: integrity, competence, consistency, loyalty, and openness.[68]

6 What if there is a lot of diversity on the team? Diversity typically provides fresh views on issues, but it also makes it more difficult to unify the team and reach agreements. Diverse teams bring multiple perspectives to the discussion, thus increasing the likelihood that these teams will identify creative or unique solutions and decreasing the possibility that a weak alternative will be chosen.

Expect the value-added component of diverse teams to increase as members become more familiar with each other and the team becomes more cohesive.

7 **How do virtual teams work?** Virtual teams can do many of the same things as face-to-face teams, but they do encounter difficulties, especially when it comes to building trust. Members of virtual teams should provide some personal information early on, and then assign clear roles to members to help build understanding of each other. Virtual teams with positive attitudes do better than those who have pessimistic members.

8 **Are teams always the answer?** Teams are not necessarily appropriate in every situation. How do you know if the work of your group would be better done in teams? It's been suggested that three tests be applied to see if a team fits the situation: 1) simple tasks that don't require diverse input are probably better left to individuals; 2) tasks that require multiple inputs are best left to teams; and 3) teams make sense where there is interdependence between tasks— where the success of the whole depends on the success of each one *and* the success of each one depends on the success of the others.

OB *AT WORK*

For Review

1. How can teams increase employee motivation?

2. Describe the five-stage group development model.

3. What is the punctuated-equilibrium model?

4. What are the characteristics of an effective team?

5. What are the characteristics of an ineffective team?

6. What is the difference between trust-oriented roles and maintenance roles?

7. How can a team minimize social loafing?

8. What are the five dimensions that underlie the concept of trust?

9. Contrast the pros and cons of having diverse teams.

10. What conditions favour creating a team, rather than letting an individual perform a given task?

For Critical Thinking

1. How could you use the punctuated-equilibrium model to better understand group behaviour?

2. Have you experienced social loafing as a team member? What did you do to prevent this problem?

3. Would you prefer to work alone or as part of a team? Why? How do you think your answer compares with that of others in your class?

4. What effect, if any, do you expect that workforce diversity has on a team's performance and satisfaction?

OB for You

- You will be asked to work on teams and groups both during your post-secondary years and later on in life, so understanding how teams work is an important skill to have.

- Think about the roles that you play on teams. Teams need task-oriented people to get the job done, but they also need maintenance-oriented people who help with keeping people working together and feeling committed to the team.

- Help your team set specific, measurable, realistic goals, as this leads to more successful outcomes.

OB *AT WORK*

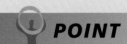

POINT

COUNTERPOINT

Sports Teams Are Good Models for Workplace Teams

Studies from football, soccer, basketball, hockey, and baseball have found a number of elements in successful sports teams that can be applied to successful work teams.[69]

Successful teams integrate cooperation and competition. Effective team coaches get athletes to help one another but also push one another to perform at their best. Sports teams with the best win-loss record had coaches who promoted a strong spirit of cooperation and a high level of healthy competition among their players.

Successful teams score early wins. Early successes build teammates' faith in themselves and their capacity as a team. For instance, research on hockey teams of relatively equal ability found that 72 percent of the time the team that was ahead at the end of the first period went on to win the game. So managers should provide teams with early tasks that are simple and provide "easy wins."

Successful teams avoid losing streaks. Losing can become a self-fulfilling prophecy. A couple of failures can lead to a downward spiral if a team becomes demoralized and believes it is helpless to end its losing streak. Managers need to instill confidence in team members that they can turn things around when they encounter setbacks.

Practice makes perfect. Successful sports teams execute on game day but learn from their mistakes in practice. A wise manager carves out time and space in which work teams can experiment and learn.

Successful teams use half-time breaks. The best coaches in basketball and football use halftime during a game to reassess what is working and what isn't. Managers of work teams should similarly build in assessments at about the halfway point in a team project to evaluate what improvements can be made.

Winning teams have a stable membership. Studies of professional basketball teams have found that the more stable a team's membership, the more likely the team is to win. The more time teammates have together, the more able they are to anticipate one another's moves and the clearer they are about one another's roles.

Successful teams debrief after failures and successes. The best sports teams study the game video. Similarly, work teams need to take time to routinely reflect on both their successes and failures and to learn from them.

Sports Teams Are Not the Model for All Teams

There are flaws in using sports as a model for developing effective work teams. Here are just four caveats.[70]

All sport teams aren't alike. In baseball, for instance, there is little interaction among teammates. Rarely are more than two or three players directly involved in a play. The performance of the team is largely the sum of the performance of its individual players. In contrast, basketball has much more interdependence among players. Usually all players are involved in every play, team members have to be able to switch from offence to defence at a moment's notice, and there is continuous movement by all, not just the player with the ball. The performance of the team is more than the sum of its individual players. So when using sports teams as a model for work teams, you have to make sure you are making the correct comparison.

Work teams are more varied and complex. In an athletic league, the design of the task, the design of the team, and the team's context vary relatively little from team to team. But these factors can vary tremendously between work teams. As a result, coaching plays a much more significant part in a team's performance on the sports field than in the workplace. Performance of work teams is more a function of getting the team's structural and design variables right. So, unlike in sports, managers of work teams should focus less on coaching and more on getting the team set up for success.

A lot of employees can't relate to sports metaphors. Not everyone on work teams is conversant in sports. Women, for instance, often are not as interested in sports as men and aren't as savvy about sports terminology. And team members from different cultures may not know the sports metaphors you are using. Most Americans, for instance, are unfamiliar with the rules and terminology of Australian football.

Work team outcomes aren't easily defined in terms of wins and losses. Sports teams usually measure success in terms of wins and losses. Such measures of success are rarely as clear for work teams. Managers who try to define success in wins and losses tend to infer that the workplace is ethically no more complex than the playing field, which is rarely true.

Do Others See Me as Trustworthy?

To get some insight into how others may view your trustworthiness, complete this questionnaire. First, however, identify the person that will be evaluating you (i.e., a colleague, friend, manager, team leader).

Use the following scale to score each question:

Strongly Disagree 1 2 3 4 5 6 7 8 9 10 **Strongly Agree**

Score

1. I can be expected to play fair. _____

2. You can confide in me and know I will keep what's told to me in confidence. _____

3. I can be counted on to tell the truth. _____

4. I would never intentionally misrepresent my point of view to others. _____

5. If I promise to do a favour, I can be counted on to carry out that promise. _____

6. If I have an appointment with someone, I can be counted on to show up promptly. _____

7. If I'm lent money, I can be counted on to pay it back as soon as possible. _____

Source: Based on C. Johnson-George and W.C. Swap, "Measurement of Specific Interpersonal Trust: Construction and Validation of a Scale to Assess Trust in a Specific Other," *Journal of Personality and Social Psychology*, December 1982, pp. 1306–1317.

Scoring Key

Add up your total score for the 7 statements. The following provides general guidelines for interpreting your score.

57–70 points = You're seen as highly trustworthy

21–56 points = You're seen as moderately trustworthy

7–20 points = You're rated low on this characteristic

Form small groups to discuss the following topics, as assigned by your instructor:

1. One of the members of your team continually arrives late for meetings and does not turn drafts of assignments in on time. In general this group member is engaging in social loafing. What can the members of your group do to reduce social loafing?

2. Consider a team with which you've worked. Using the information in Exhibit 5–5, consider whether there were more task-oriented or maintenance-oriented roles in the group. What impact did this have on the group's performance?

3. Identify 4 or 5 norms that a team could put into place near the beginning of its life to help it function better over time.

WORKING WITH OTHERS EXERCISE

The Paper Tower Exercise

Step 1

Each group will receive 20 index cards, 12 paper clips, and 2 marking pens. Groups have 10 minutes to plan a paper tower that will be judged on the basis of 3 criteria: height, stability, and beauty. No physical work (building) is allowed during this planning period.

Step 2

Each group has 15 minutes for the actual construction of the paper tower.

Step 3

Each tower will be identified by a number assigned by your instructor. Each student is to individually examine all the paper towers. Your group is then to come to a consensus as to which tower is the winner (5 minutes). A spokesperson from your group should report its decision and the criteria the group used in reaching it.

Step 4

In your small groups, discuss the following questions (your instructor may choose to have you discuss only a subset of these questions):

a. What percentage of the plan did each member of your group contribute on average?

b. Did your group have a leader? Why or why not?

c. How did the group generally respond to the ideas that were expressed during the planning period?

d. To what extent did your group follow the five-step group development model?

e. List specific behaviours exhibited during the planning and building sessions that you felt were helpful to the group. Explain why you found them to be helpful.

f. List specific behaviours exhibited during the planning and building sessions that you felt were dysfunctional to the group. Explain why you found them dysfunctional.

Source: This exercise is based on "The Paper Tower Exercise: Experiencing Leadership and Group Dynamics" by Phillip L. Hunsaker and Johanna S. Hunsaker, unpublished manuscript. A brief description is included in "Exchange," *Organizational Behavior Teaching Journal*, 4, no. 2, 1979, p. 49. Reprinted by permission of the authors. The materials list was suggested by Sally Maitlis, Sauder School of Business, UBC.

ETHICAL DILEMMA EXERCISE

Can Teams Prevent Corruption?

Enron's performance review committee rated every employee in the company on a scale of 1 to 5, with 1 symbolizing excellent performance. An employee who received a 5 was usually gone within six months. Former CEO Jeff Skilling's division replaced 15 percent of its workforce every year. One manager said Skilling found this a point of personal pride: "Jeff viewed this like turning over the inventory in a grocery store." Because employees worried about their jobs, teamwork simply didn't exist in the company. Though company protocol sometimes demanded that Enron higher-ups help with a project, they did not always do this. Instead, they constantly searched for the most lucrative projects available.

1. Why would Enron's performance rating system make it more difficult for individuals to work as team members?

2. Would a more team-like environment have prevented the Enron scandal from occurring?

3. How could teams be set up to prevent a company from experiencing an Enron-type scandal?

Source: Based on M. Swartz, *Texas Monthly*, November 2001.

A Virtual Team at T.A. Stearns

T.A. Stearns is a national tax accounting firm whose main business is tax preparation services for individuals. Stearns' superior reputation is based on the high quality of its advice and the excellence of its service. Key to the achievement of its reputation are the state-of-the-art computer databases and analysis tools that its people use when counselling clients. These programs were developed by highly trained individuals.

The programs are highly technical, in terms of both the code in which they are written and the tax laws they cover. Perfecting them requires high levels of programming skill as well as the ability to understand the law. New laws and interpretations of existing laws have to be integrated quickly and flawlessly into the existing regulations and analysis tools.

The creation of these programs is carried out in a virtual environment by four programmers in the greater Vancouver area. The four work at home and are connected to each other and to the company by email, telephone, and conference software. Formal on-site meetings among all of the programmers take place only a few times a year, although the workers sometimes meet informally at other times. The four members of the team are Tom Andrews, Cy Crane, Marge Dector, and Megan Harris.

These four people exchange email messages many times every day. In fact, it's not unusual for them to step away from guests or family to log on and check in with the others. Often their emails are amusing as well as work-related. Sometimes, for instance, when they were facing a deadline and one of Marge's kids was home sick, they helped each other with the work. Tom has occasionally invited the others to visit his farm; and Marge and Cy have gotten their families together several times for dinner. About once a month the whole team gets together for lunch.

All four of these Stearns employees are on salary, which, consistent with company custom, is negotiated separately and secretly with management. Although each is required to check in regularly during every workday, they were told when they were hired that they could work wherever they wanted. Clearly, flexibility is one of the pluses of these jobs. When the four get together, they often joke about the managers and workers who are tied to the office, referring to them as "face timers" and to themselves as "free agents."

When the programmers are asked to make a major program change, they often develop programming tools called macros to help them do their work more efficiently. These macros greatly enhance the speed at which a change can be written into the programs. Cy, in particular, really enjoys hacking around with macros. On one recent project, for instance, he became obsessed with the prospect of creating a shortcut that could save him a huge amount of time. One week after turning in his code and his release notes to the company, Cy bragged to Tom that he had created a new macro that had saved him eight hours of work that week.

Tom was skeptical of the shortcut, but after trying it out, he found that it actually saved him many hours too.

Stearns has a suggestion program that rewards employees for innovations that save the company money. The program gives an employee 5 percent of the savings generated by his or her innovation over three months. The company also has a profit-sharing plan. Tom and Cy felt that the small amount of money that would be generated by a company reward would not offset the free time that they gained using their new macro. They wanted the time for leisure or consulting work. They also feared their group might suffer if management learned about the innovation. It would allow three people to do the work of four, which could lead to one of them being let go. So they didn't share their innovative macro with management.

Although Tom and Cy wouldn't share the innovation with management, they were concerned that they were entering their busy season and knew everyone on the team would be stressed by the heavy workload. They decided to distribute the macro to the other members of their team and swore them to secrecy.

Over lunch one day, the team set itself a level of production that it felt would not arouse management's suspicion. Several months passed and the four used some of their extra time to push the quality of their work even higher. But they also now had more time to pursue their own personal interests.

Dave Regan, the in-house manager of the work group, picked up on the innovation several weeks after it was first implemented. He had wondered why production time had gone down a bit, while quality had shot up, and he got his first inkling of an answer when he saw an email from Marge to Cy thanking him for saving her so much time with his "brilliant mind." Not wanting to embarrass his employees, the manager hinted to Tom that he wanted to know what was happening, but he got nowhere. He did not tell his own manager about his suspicions, reasoning that since both quality and productivity were up he did not really need to pursue the matter further.

Dave very recently learned that Cy has boasted about his trick to a member of another virtual work group in the company. Suddenly, the situation seemed to have gotten out of control. Dave decided to take Cy to lunch. During the meal, Dave asked Cy to explain what was happening. Cy told him about the innovation, but he insisted the group's actions had been justified to protect itself.

Dave knew that his own boss would soon hear of the situation and that he would be looking for answers—from him.

Questions

1. Is this group a team?

2. What role have norms played in how this team acted?

3. Has anyone in this case acted unethically?

4. What should Dave do now?

Source: Adapted from "The Virtual Environment Work Team," a case prepared by R. Andre, professor, Northeastern University. With permission.

 VIDEO CASE INCIDENT

Earthbuddies

On December 11, 1998, Anton Rabie, Ronnen Harary, and Ben Varadi found themselves on the cover of Canadian Business Magazine. In the article, they were referred to as "Marketing Maniacs"... examples of the young and enthusiastic entrepreneurs in today's marketplace.

Fresh out of business school in 1993 and based in Toronto, the partnership between Rabie, Harary, and Varadi quickly flourished with the initial success of their product release: Earth Buddy, a small novelty head that sprouted grass hair when set in water. Thanks to successful negotiations with retail giants such as K-Mart, Canadian Tire and Zellers, sales grew steadily for the first few years. In 1995, the partnership changed the company name to Spin Master Toys Inc. After only four years of operating, Spin Master reported $10 million in sales in 1998.

Over the years, the friends have had their share of disagreements, triumphs, and failures. Together, they have recruited talented outsiders to join their executive committee, researched and successfully launched innovative toy products from Asia, and nurtured the company to where it is today. Although a private company, Spin Master Toys Inc. reported $103 million in sales in 2000.

Today, the executive team at Spin Master has grown to 12 members. Rabie is the president, Harary is the CEO, and Varadi is the executive vice-president. In 2002, the firm introduced a variety of new products, including the Air Hogs Helicopter, Air Hogs Radio Control, and Air Hogs Quick Charge. In addition, the company re-branded itself by changing the corporate logo and name. In 2004, Rabie, Harary, and Varadi will be able to reflect upon the growth of their fledgling business as it celebrates its 10th year anniversary, and what it truly means to work together as a team.

Questions

1. Describe the partnership norms at Spin Master Toys Inc.

2. Describe the roles displayed by the firm's executive team members: Anton Rabie, Ronnen Harary, and Ben Varadi.

3. Using the model of group development, analyze the changes on the executive team. Be sure to address how the team's decision-making process was affected by the introduction of Michelle (Harary's sister) and Austin (Michelle's husband) to the team.

Source: Based on "Earthbuddies," *CBC Venture*, July 21, 2002, VA2035H & I, 837; Spin Master Toys Inc. website, "Company History," www.spinmaster.com; S. Steinberg and J. Chidley, "Fun for the Money," *Canadian Business Magazine*, December 11, 1998, pp. 44–52.

From **Concepts** to **Skills**

Conducting a Team Meeting

Meetings have a reputation for inefficiency. For instance, noted Canadian-born economist John Kenneth Galbraith has said, "Meetings are indispensable when you don't want to do anything."

When you are responsible for conducting a meeting, what can you do to make it more efficient and effective? Follow these 12 steps:[71]

1. *Prepare a meeting agenda*. An agenda defines what you hope to accomplish at the meeting. It should state: the meeting's purpose; who will be in attendance; what, if any, preparation is required of each participant; a detailed list of items to be covered; the specific time and location of the meeting; and a specific finishing time.

2. *Distribute the agenda in advance*. Participants should have the agenda far enough in advance that they can adequately prepare for the meeting.

3. *Consult with participants before the meeting*. An unprepared participant cannot contribute to his or her full potential. It is your responsibility to ensure that members are prepared, so check with them ahead of time.

4. *Get participants to go over the agenda*. The first thing to do at the meeting is to have participants review the agenda, make any changes, and then approve the final agenda.

5. *Establish specific time limits*. Meetings should begin on time and have a specific time for completion. It is your responsibility to specify these times and to hold to them.

6. *Maintain focused discussion*. It is your responsibility to give direction to the discussion; to keep it focused on the issues; and to minimize interruptions, disruptions, and irrelevant comments.

7. *Encourage and support participation of all members*. To maximize the effectiveness of problem-oriented meetings, each participant must be encouraged to contribute. Quiet or reserved personalities need to be drawn out so their ideas can be heard.

8. *Maintain a balanced style*. The effective group leader pushes when necessary and is passive when need be.

9. *Encourage the clash of ideas*. You need to encourage different points of view, critical thinking, and constructive disagreement.

10. *Discourage the clash of personalities*. An effective meeting is characterized by the critical assessment of ideas, not attacks on people. When running a meeting, you must quickly intercede to stop personal attacks or other forms of verbal insult.

11. *Be an effective listener*. You need to listen with intensity, empathy, and objectivity, and do whatever is necessary to get the full intended meaning from each participant's comments.

12. *Bring proper closure*. You should close a meeting by summarizing the group's accomplishments; clarifying what actions, if any, need to follow the meeting; and allocating follow-up assignments. If any decisions are made, you also need to determine who will be responsible for communicating and implementing them.

Assessing Skills

After you have read this chapter, take the following Self-Assessment on your enclosed CD-ROM.

30. How Good Am I at Building and Leading a Team?

Practising Skills

Jameel Saumur is the leader of a five-member project team that has been assigned the task of moving his engineering firm into the booming area of high-speed inter-city rail construction. Saumur and his team members have been researching the field, identifying specific business opportunities, negotiating alliances with equipment vendors, and evaluating high-speed rail experts and consultants from around the world. Throughout the process, Tonya Eckler, a highly qualified and respected engineer, has challenged a number of things Saumur said during team meetings and in the workplace. For example, at a meeting two weeks ago, Saumur presented the team with a list of 10 possible high-speed rail projects and started evaluating the company's ability to compete for them. Eckler contradicted virtually all Saumur's comments, questioned his statistics, and was quite pessimistic about the possibility of getting contracts on these projects. After this latest display of displeasure, two other group members, Bryan Worth and Maggie Ames, are complaining that Eckler's actions are damaging the team's effectiveness. Eckler was originally assigned to the team for her unique expertise and insight.

If you had to advise this team, what suggestions would you make to get the team on the right track to achieve its fullest potential?

Reinforcing Skills

1. Interview three managers at different organizations. Ask them about their experiences in managing teams. Have each describe teams that they thought were effective and why they succeeded. Have each also describe teams that they thought were ineffective and the reasons that might have caused this.

2. Contrast a team you were on where members trusted each other with another team where members lacked trust in each other. How did these conditions develop? What were the consequences in terms of interaction patterns and performance?

CHAPTER 6

Communication, Conflict, and Negotiation

How does communication occur?

1

What is negotiation and how does it help?

8

Are there barriers to communication?

2

How can communication be encouraged?

3

What do you do when a group of former employees think they have been treated unfairly and current employees are thinking about joining a union? Will communication and negotiation help reduce tensions?

How does a situation turn into conflict?

7

What are the sources of conflict?

6

What are the current issues in communication?

4

What is conflict?

5

In late 1997, mill employees of Hamilton, Ontario-based Dofasco Inc. were unhappy with the company.[1] The number of jobs had fallen from 10 300 to 7000 in the previous five years. Former employees had started a group called SHAFT (So How Many Are Fired Tomorrow) to press grievances against the company for what they claimed was unfair dismissal. In fall 1996, the Canadian Auto Workers and the United Steelworkers were approached by employees with requests to form a union at Dofasco.

John Mayberry, then CEO, showed little respect for his employees. From his early days as a manager, he was not popular: He was disliked "for his habit of springing surprise inspections, and there were rumours that he had threatened to fire employees he thought were malingering." Mayberry, who took over as CEO in 1993, said the employees were used to being taken care of by the Sherman family, who founded the company in 1912. Mayberry said he had to "change the culture to an earning culture from an entitlement culture, where the only job security we can offer is through earning it through performance."

The culture at Dofasco in the early 1990s did not support open communication, as there was a great

deal of conflict between Mayberry and his employees. Mayberry tended to use one-way communication: He would talk and employees were to listen. His concern that employees had been treated too kindly by the previous management meant that he was not open to negotiating resolutions to the challenges the company faced. In this chapter we explore the foundations of communication and then consider the effects of communication on conflict and negotiation. As you will see later in the chapter, Mayberry did learn to work with his employees more effectively.

THE COMMUNICATION PROCESS

Research indicates that poor communication is probably the most frequently cited source of interpersonal conflict.[2] Individuals spend nearly 70 percent of their waking hours communicating—writing, reading, speaking, listening—which means that they have many opportunities in which to engage in poor communication. A WorkCanada survey of 2039 Canadians in six industrial and service categories explored the state of communication in Canadian businesses.[3] The survey found that 61 percent of senior executives believed they did a good job of communicating with employees. However, those who worked below the senior executives failed to share this feeling—only 33 percent of the managers and department heads believed that senior executives were effective communicators. The report of good communication was even lower for those in nonmanagerial positions: Only 22 percent of hourly workers, 27 percent of clerical employees, and 22 percent of professional staff reported that senior executives did a good job of communicating with them. Moreover, a recent study found that Canadians reported less favourable perceptions about their companies' communications than did Americans.[4]

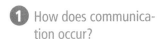

1 How does communication occur?

Exhibit 6–1

The Communication Process Model

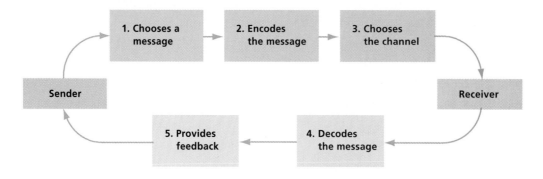

communication
sender → 1. Chooses a message → 2. Encodes the message → 3. Chooses the channel → Receiver → 4. Decodes the message → 5. Provides feedback → Sender

communication
The transference and understanding of meaning.

Despite these communication problems, no group can exist without **communication**: the transference of meaning among its members. Communication can be thought of as a process, or flow, as shown in Exhibit 6–1. The model indicates that both the sender and the receiver are part of the communication process, with the sender establishing a message, encoding the message, and choosing the channel to send it, and the receiver decoding the message and providing feedback to the sender. Communication problems occur when something disrupts the flow during encoding, channel selection, decoding, or feedback.

Encoding and Decoding

encoding
Converting a communication message to symbolic form.

decoding
Retranslating a sender's communication message.

Four factors have been described that affect message **encoding** by the sender and **decoding** by the receiver: skill, attitudes, knowledge, and the social-cultural system.

The Canadian Alliance learned in its early days that it's easy to communicate unintended messages. The party's first choice of name, Canadian Conservative Reform Alliance Party, caused quite a stir for its acronym (CCRAP). People across the country wondered what the new party was trying to communicate about its objectives.

For example, our success in communicating to you depends on our writing skills and your reading skills. Communicative success also includes speaking, listening, and reasoning skills. As we discussed in Chapter 3, our interactions with others are affected by our attitudes, values, and beliefs. Thus, the attitudes of the sender and receiver toward each other will affect how the message is transmitted. Clearly, the amount of knowledge the source and receiver hold about a subject will affect the clarity of the message that is transferred. Finally, our position in the social-cultural system in which we exist affects our ability to successfully engage in communication. Messages sent and received by people in equal positions are sometimes interpreted differently than messages sent and received by people in very different positions.

The Message

The **message** is the actual physical product from the source encoding. "When we speak, the speech is the message. When we write, the writing is the message. When we paint, the picture is the message. When we gesture, the movements of our arms, the expressions on our face are the message."[5] Our message is affected by the code, or group of symbols, that we use to transfer meaning, the content of the message itself, and the decisions that we make in selecting and arranging both codes and content. The poor choice of symbols, and confusion in the content of the message, can cause problems. McDonald's recently settled a lawsuit over its choice of words, as this *Focus on Ethics* reveals.

message
What is communicated.

FOCUS ON **ETHICS**

Vegetarian or Not Vegetarian?

Does "no beef" really mean what it implies? In March 2002, Oak Brook, Illinois-based McDonald's Corporation agreed to pay $19 million (CDN) to settle lawsuits from vegetarians who suggested the company had deceived them about how it produced french fries.[6] Under the agreement, McDonald's had to pay $10 million to charities that support vegetarianism. The company was also ordered to publicly apologize and learn about vegetarian dietary issues.

McDonald's communication practices were questioned in the lawsuit. In 1990, the company had announced that its restaurants would no longer use beef fat to cook french fries. Instead, only pure vegetable oil would be used. What the company didn't say was that it would continue to add beef tallow to the fries as a flavouring agent.

When vegetarians discovered that they had been unwittingly eating beef-flavoured fries, they were upset. McDonald's claimed that it never said the french fries were vegetarian. The company did apologize for any confusion its announcement caused, however.

Messages can also get "lost in translation" when two parties formalize their understanding through contracts. Contracts are meant to be written in legal terms, for lawyers, but these may not always capture the underlying meaning of the parties' understandings. Collective agreements written between management and unions sometimes suffer from this problem as well. When union leaders point to the collective agreement for every interaction in the workplace, they are relying on the encoding of their negotiations, but this may not permit some of the flexibility that was intended in some cases.

The Channel

The **channel** is the medium through which the message travels. It is selected by the source, who must determine which channel is formal and which one is informal. Formal channels are established by organizations to transmit messages about the job-related activities of members. They traditionally follow the authority network within the organization. Other forms of messages, such as personal or social messages, follow the informal channels in the organization. Examples of channels include formal memos, voice mail, email, and meetings. Choosing a poor channel, or one with a high noise level, can lead to distorted communication.

channel
The medium through which a communication message travels.

communication apprehension
Undue tension and anxiety about
oral communication, written
communication, or both.

Why do people choose one channel of communication over another—for instance, a phone call instead of a face-to-face talk? One answer might be anxiety. An estimated 5 to 20 percent of the population suffer from debilitating **communication apprehension** or anxiety.[7] We all know people who dread speaking in front of a group, but some people may find it extremely difficult to talk with others face to face or become extremely anxious when they have to use the telephone.

As a result, they may rely on memos, letters, or email to convey messages when a phone call would not only be faster but also more appropriate.

But what about the 80 to 95 percent of the population who do not suffer from this problem? Is there any general insight we might be able to provide regarding choice of communication channel? The answer is a qualified "yes." A model of media richness has been developed to explain channel selection among managers.[8]

Recent research has found that channels differ in their capacity to convey information. Some are rich in that they have the ability to 1) handle multiple cues at the same time, 2) allow rapid feedback, and 3) be very personal. Others are lean in that they score low on these three factors. As Exhibit 6–2 illustrates, face-to-face talk scores highest in terms of **channel richness** because it provides for the maximum amount of information to be transmitted during a communication episode. That is, it offers multiple information cues (words, postures, facial expressions, gestures, intonations), immediate feedback (both verbal and nonverbal), and the personal touch of "being there." Impersonal written media such as bulletins and general reports rate lowest in richness.

channel richness
The amount of information that
can be transmitted during a communication episode.

The choice of one channel over another depends on whether the message is routine or nonroutine. Routine messages tend to be straightforward and have a minimum of ambiguity. Nonroutine messages are likely to be complicated and have the potential for misunderstanding. Managers can communicate routine messages efficiently through channels that are lower in richness. However, they can communicate nonroutine messages effectively only by selecting rich channels. Evidence indicates that high-performing managers tend to be more media-sensitive than low-performing managers.[9] In other words, they are better able to match appropriate media richness with the ambiguity involved in the communication.

Exhibit 6–2

Information Richness of Communication Channels

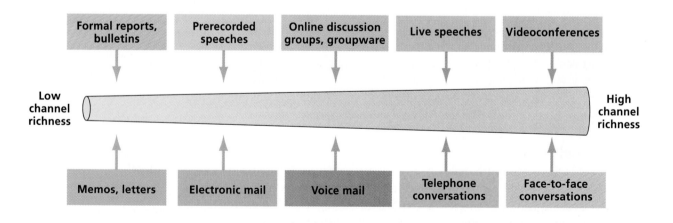

Source: Based on R.H. Lengel and R.L. Daft, "The Selection of Communication Media as an Executive Skill," *Academy of Management Executive,* August 1988, pp. 225–232; and R.L. Daft and R.H. Lengel, "Organizational Information Requirements, Media Richness, and Structural Design," *Managerial Science,* May 1996, pp. 554–572. Reproduced from R.L. Daft and R.A. Noe, *Organizational Behavior* (Fort Worth, TX: Harcourt, 2001), p. 311.

A 1999 study at Boston University revealed that managers found it easier to deliver bad news (layoffs, promotion denials, and negative feedback) via email, and that the messages were delivered more accurately this way. This does not mean that sending negative information through email is always recommended. One of the co-authors of the study noted that "offering negative comments face-to-face is often taken as a sign that the news is important and the deliverer cares about the recipient."[10] The *Case Incident* on page 204 asks you to evaluate one manager's use of email to tell his employees to work harder.

The Feedback Loop

The final link in the communication process is a **feedback loop**. Feedback lets us know whether understanding has been achieved. If the feedback loop is to succeed in preventing miscommunication, the receiver needs to give feedback and the sender needs to check for it.

feedback loop
The final link in the communication process; puts the message back into the system as a check against misunderstandings.

filtering
A sender's manipulation of information so that it will be seen more favourably by the receiver.

BARRIERS TO EFFECTIVE COMMUNICATION

Dofasco's CEO, John Mayberry, initially had difficulty communicating with his employees. He didn't really respect them, because he felt they represented an entitlement culture ("good day's work, a day's pay, nice retirement package").[11] Thus, he used selective perception when evaluating their concerns. Because he carried out surprise inspections, employees worried they would be fired for any little problem. This caused them to be defensive. What are other ways that communication can be negatively affected?

A number of factors have been identified as barriers to communication. Below we review some of the more well-known ones.

2 Are there barriers to communication?

Filtering

Filtering occurs when a sender manipulates information so that the receiver will view it more favourably. For example, when a manager tells a senior executive what the manager thinks the executive wants to hear, the manager is filtering information. Does this happen much in organizations? Sure! As information is passed up to senior executives, employees must condense and summarize it so that those on top don't become overloaded with information. The personal interests and perceptions of what is important by those doing the summarizing will result in filtering.

The major determinant of filtering is the number of levels in an organization's structure. The more vertical levels in an organization's hierarchy, the more opportunities there are for filtering. The *Ethical Dilemma Exercise* on page 204 asks you to consider whether lying is ever a reasonable strategy.

Selective Perception

Receivers in the communication process selectively see and hear based on their needs, motivations, experience, background, and other personal characteristics. Receivers also project their interests and expectations into communications as they decode them. For example, the employment interviewer who believes that young people are more interested in spending time on leisure and social activities than working extra hours to further

Companies use the technique of 360-degree feedback to ensure that individuals get feedback from co-workers and subordinates. As senior vice-president with Scotiabank Group, Claude Norfolk found that sometimes feedback hurts. "I was really surprised, for example, to find out that I needed to work on my listening skills, because I thought I was a pretty good listener." Turns out his wife agreed with Norfolk's colleagues. Still, he found value in the exercise. Feedback almost always brings with it valuable insights, which we can use for greater understanding.

their careers is likely to apply that stereotype to all young job applicants. As we discussed in Chapter 2, we do not see reality; rather, we interpret what we see and call it "reality."

When Enron's former CEO, Jeff Skilling, was interviewed as information about Enron's accounting problems was just starting to emerge in November 2001, he refused to acknowledge that anything wrong had gone on at the company. To him, Enron represented "a totally different way of thinking about business—we got it."[12] His implication was that it was everyone else who was using selective perception in failing to recognize Enron's greatness. As the scandal continued to unfold, it was likely Skilling who suffered from selective perception.

Defensiveness

When people feel that they are being threatened, they tend to react in ways that reduce their ability to achieve mutual understanding. That is, they become defensive—engaging in behaviours such as verbally attacking others, making sarcastic remarks, being overly judgmental, and questioning others' motives. So when individuals interpret another's message as threatening, they often respond in ways that hinder effective communication. *OB in the Workplace* shows how defensiveness between the new head of FPI and the company's employees led to the breakdown of a merger deal.

OB IN THE WORKPLACE

FPI Proposed Merger Fails

Why does defensiveness harm communication? John Risley, CEO of Halifax-based Clearwater Fine Foods, aimed to create a seafood giant by merging his company with St. John's, Newfoundland-based Fishery Products International Ltd. (FPI).[13] He may wish that he had studied the communication process a bit more carefully before he spoke in public, however.

At first Risley was successful in his goal, when in May 2001 he engineered a takeover of the FPI board. Immediately, he promised Newfoundlanders that they would lose no jobs. This was a relief to the fishery workers, who had seen jobs tumble by two-thirds in the past decades.

However, by January 2002 union representatives were told that up to 580 jobs would be lost from three rural Newfoundland plants. This announcement angered workers and politicians alike. Risley defensively argued that the culture of Newfoundland was the real problem: "This is a culture in which people think there's value in the number of jobs that become eligible for unemployment insurance," he said.

Allan Moulton, a union leader and employee at FPI's Marystown plant for 30 years, spoke up at a public hearing on the FPI-Clearwater merger: "We're not the only seasonal workers in Canada and it's unfortunate Newfoundland really got pegged with this," he added. "We worked long hours in this industry and every single worker worked hard to save Fishery Products International, and we were successful and we want to get back to doing that."

The merger was called off, and plans to modernize FPI's plants were also scrapped. The provincial government is exploring ways to keep FPI running effectively.

More considerate communication by Risley might have led to fewer problems, and less defensiveness. This might have allowed his planned merger to go through.

Language

Words mean different things to different people. "The meanings of words are not in the words; they are in us."[14] Age, education, and cultural background are three of the more obvious variables that influence the language a person uses and the definitions he or she gives to words. For instance, when Alanis Morissette sang "Isn't It Ironic?" middle-aged English professors complained that she completely misunderstood the meaning of "irony"—but the millions who bought her CD understood what she meant.

In an organization, employees usually come from diverse backgrounds and, therefore, have different patterns of speech. Additionally, the grouping of employees into departments creates specialists who develop their own jargon or technical language. In large organizations, members are also often widely dispersed geographically—even operating in different countries—and individuals in each locale will use terms and phrases that are unique to their area. The existence of vertical levels can also cause language problems. The language of senior executives, for instance, can be mystifying to operative employees who are unfamiliar with management jargon.

The point is that even with a common language, such as English, our usage of that language is far from uniform. Senders tend to assume that the words and terms they use mean the same to the receiver as they do to them. This, of course, is often incorrect, thus creating communication difficulties. The multicultural environment of many of today's workplaces makes communication issues even more complex. Many of us interact, or will interact, with colleagues for whom English is a second language. This means that even more opportunities arise for confusion about meaning. It is therefore important to be aware that your understanding of the particular meaning of a word or phrase may not be shared similarly. For more about effective listening skills, refer to *From Concepts to Skills* on pages 206–207.

Selective perception worked against C. Richard Cowan (in photo), founder and president of Power Lift, a distributor of forklift trucks. After a year in business, Cowan bought a competitor, where most employees had worked at least 15 years. Perceiving their new boss as young and inexperienced, 40 of the 200 employees quit their jobs, which caused rumours that Power Lift had financial problems. Cowan blamed the situation on poor communication, admitting that he should have met with his new employees to reassure them of the importance of their roles at Power Lift and of the firm's financial soundness. Now Cowan has made communication his top priority, talking personally with each employee to learn about his or her concerns.

CREATING EFFECTIVE MECHANISMS FOR COMMUNICATION

John Mayberry may have started off on the wrong foot when he took over as Dofasco CEO in 1993. But things turned around considerably over the next two years. By late 2001, no employees had been laid off during the entire year and the employees were looking forward to a lavish company Christmas party. How does change like this happen? Mayberry said that he had to get people "working together and communicating," and he created a flatter organizational structure to do this. Communication has clearly helped the company survive, and even thrive in a troubled economic period. "Five years ago, we'd still be arguing about whether or not we had a problem—let alone how to go about fixing it," Mayberry said.[15] Employees at Dofasco are more confident these days that management will keep them informed of what's happening with the company, which makes them more likely to work together to solve company problems. So what can managers do to make communication more effective?

3 How can communication be encouraged?

mechanisms
Practices designed to reinforce your message and enable people to carry it out.

Jim Collins: *Built to Last*
www.harpercollins.com/
catalog/guide_xml.asp?
isbn=0887307396

Graniterock Company
www.graniterock.com

Stanford Graduate School of Business
www.gsb.stanford.edu

4 What are the current issues in communication?

How many of us have been told, "If you have any problems, just let us know." Or a professor might have said to you, "Class participation is important in this course, so please speak up in class." In both of these instances, the person giving the message may genuinely want information or participation, but often the listener is not inspired to act on that request. For instance, the request for feedback about problems does not really inform the listener about how to advise the speaker of the problems. And the request for more class participation does not necessarily convey how to participate.

Jim Collins, co-author of the bestselling management book *Built to Last*,[16] notes the importance of creating effective **mechanisms**, "the practices that bring what you stand for to life and stimulate change."[17] Mechanisms can be used to support the messages that managers and organizations are trying to convey. For instance, Collins cites the example of Graniterock Co., which wanted to signal to customers its commitment to quality and customer service. To make this clear to customers, each Graniterock invoice contains the following guarantee: "If you're not satisfied with something, don't pay us for it. Simply scratch out the related line item and send your cheque for the remaining balance." By doing this, Graniterock is not simply claiming a strategy of good customer service, but is putting in place a mechanism so that if a customer is dissatisfied, he or she knows what to do. And the company clearly receives the message that there is a problem when a line item is crossed off the invoice by the customer and less money is received than expected.

When Collins was a professor at the Stanford Graduate School of Business, he wanted to ensure that students who had an important insight to share with the class had the opportunity to be heard. He also knew, however, that with 66 students in his class, some very important insights might go unnoticed. So he created a mechanism to guarantee students that when they had something really important to say, they would have the opportunity to speak up. At the beginning of the term he gave each student a sheet of bright red paper and said, "This is your red flag. You get to raise it only one time in a quarter, but when you do—no matter what's going on—the world will stop for you. So when you have your best contribution to make, your key insight or challenge or story, that's your red-flag point. You're the only screen. Raise the flag, and the floor is yours."

In the workplace, Collins notes that most executives try to solve problems with initiatives and memos, rather than by creating mechanisms that signal how people are to act. He suggests that an executive facing the problem of getting people to share their important ideas might have come into Collins' classroom and addressed the students by saying, "It's come to my attention that people may not be getting their comments in. I really want to emphasize again that if you have something important to say, make sure you get heard." However, this would not have conveyed what students could do to ensure that they were heard. Organizations and managers can improve communication by providing mechanisms to employees, customers, and clients so that they know the specific action they are to take.

CURRENT ISSUES IN COMMUNICATION

How important is nonverbal communication? Why do men and women often have difficulty communicating with each other? How can individuals improve their cross-cultural communications? And how is electronics changing the way people communicate with each other in organizations? We address each of these issues below.

Nonverbal Communication

Anyone who has ever paid a visit to a singles bar or a nightclub is aware that communication need not be verbal in order to convey a message. A glance, a stare, a smile, a frown, a provocative body movement—they all convey meaning. This example illustrates that no discussion of communication would be complete without a discussion of

nonverbal communication. This includes body movements, facial expressions, and the physical distance between the sender and receiver.

The academic study of body motions has been labelled **kinesics**. It refers to gestures, facial configurations, and other movements of the body. Because it is a relatively new field, there is not complete agreement on findings. Still, body movement is an important segment of the study of communication.

It has been argued that every body movement has a meaning and that no movement is accidental.[18] Through body language, we can say "Help me, I'm confused," or "Leave me alone, I'm really angry." And rarely do we send our messages consciously. We act out our state of being with nonverbal body language, even if we are not aware of doing so. We lift one eyebrow for disbelief. We rub our noses for puzzlement. We clasp our arms to isolate ourselves or to protect ourselves. We shrug our shoulders for indifference, wink one eye for intimacy, tap our fingers for impatience, slap our forehead for forgetfulness.[19] While we may disagree on the specific meaning of these movements, body language adds to and often complicates verbal communication. For instance, if you read the transcript of a meeting, you do not grasp the impact of what was said in the same way you would if you had been there or had seen the meeting on video. Why? There is no record of nonverbal communication. The *intonations*, or emphasis, given to words or phrases is missing.

The *facial expression* of a person also conveys meaning. A snarling face says something different from a smile. Facial expressions, along with intonations, can show arrogance, aggressiveness, fear, shyness, and other characteristics that would never be communicated if you read a transcript of the meeting.

Studies indicate that those who maintain *eye contact* while speaking are viewed with more credibility than those whose eye contact wanders. People who make eye contact are also deemed more competent than those who do not.

The way individuals space themselves in terms of *physical distance*, commonly called **proxemics**, also has meaning. What is considered proper spacing is largely dependent on cultural norms. For instance, studies have shown that those from "contact" cultures (e.g., Arabs, Latin Americans, southern Europeans) are more comfortable with body closeness and touch than those from "noncontact" cultures (e.g., Asians, North Americans, northern Europeans).[20] These differences can lead to confusion. If someone stands closer to you than expected according to your cultural norms, you may interpret the action as an expression of aggressiveness or sexual interest. However, if the person stands farther away than you expect, you might think he or she is displeased with you or uninterested. Someone whose cultural norms differ from yours might be very surprised by your interpretation.

Environmental factors such as seating arrangements or the conditions of the room can also send intended or unintended messages. A person whose desk faces the doorway demonstrates command of his or her physical space, while perhaps also conveying that one should not come too close.

It is important for the receiver to be alert to these nonverbal aspects of communication. You should look for nonverbal cues as well as listen to the literal meaning of a sender's words. You should particularly be aware of contradictions between the messages. The manager may say that she is free to talk to you about that raise you have been seeking, but you may see nonverbal signals (such as looking at her watch) that suggest that this is not the time to discuss the subject. It is not uncommon for people to express one emotion verbally and another nonverbally. These contradictions often suggest that "actions speak louder (and more accurately) than words."

We should monitor body language with some care. While it is often thought that individuals who cross their arms in front of their chest are showing resistance to a message, they might also do this if they are feeling cold, regardless of their reaction to a message.

nonverbal communication
Messages conveyed through body movements, facial expressions, and the physical distance between the sender and receiver.

kinesics
The study of body motions, such as gestures, facial configurations, and other movements of the body.

proxemics
The study of physical space in interpersonal relationships.

Communication Barriers Between Women and Men

Deborah Tannen
www.georgetown.edu/
faculty/tannend/

Research by Deborah Tannen provides us with important insights into differences in the conversation styles of men and women.[21] In particular, Tannen has been able to explain why gender often creates oral communication barriers. Her research does not suggest that *all* men or *all* women behave the same way in their communication, but she illustrates some important generalizations.

The essence of Tannen's research is that men use talk to emphasize status, while women use it to create connection. According to Tannen, women speak and hear a language of connection and intimacy, while men speak and hear a language of status and independence. So, for many men, conversations are primarily a way to preserve independence and maintain status in a hierarchical social order. For many women, however, conversations are negotiations for closeness in which people try to seek and give confirmation and support. The following examples will illustrate Tannen's thesis.

Men often complain that women talk on and on about their problems. Women criticize men for not listening. What is happening is that when men hear a problem, they often assert their desire for independence and control by offering solutions. Many women, on the other hand, view telling a problem as a means to promote closeness. The women present the problem to gain support and connection, not to get the male's advice. Mutual understanding, as sought by women, is symmetrical. But giving advice is asymmetrical—it sets up the (male) advice giver as more knowledgeable, more reasonable, and more in control. This contributes to distancing men and women in their efforts to communicate.

Men often criticize women for seeming to apologize all the time. Men tend to see the phrase "I'm sorry" as a weakness because they interpret the phrase to mean the woman is accepting blame. However, women typically use "I'm sorry" to express empathy: "I know you must feel bad about this. I probably would too in the same position."

While Tannen has received wide acknowledgment of her work, some suggest that it is anecdotal and/or based on faulty research. Goldsmith and Fulfs argue that men and women have more similarities than differences as communicators, although they acknowledge that when communication difficulties do appear, it is appealing to attribute them to gender.[22] Despite this, Nancy Langton, your Vancouver-based author, has noted, based on evidence from role plays, that men and women make requests for raises differently, and men are more likely to state that men were more effective at mak-

Michele Wong (right) supports Tannen's thesis that women speak and hear a language of connection and intimacy. Wong, president and CEO of software firm Synergex, fosters open communication. She shares the company's monthly financial statements with employees and holds biweekly open forums where employees can inform, thank, and question one another. She sponsors learning-at-lunch programs where employees share what they do with workers from other departments. Wong also publishes a newsletter on the company's intranet that keeps employees informed about Synergex products and people.

ing requests, while women are more likely to indicate that it was women who handled the interaction more favourably.[23]

Cross-Cultural Communication

Effective communication is difficult under the best of conditions. Cross-cultural factors clearly create the potential for increased communication problems.

Cultural Barriers

One author has identified four specific problems related to language difficulties in cross-cultural communications.[24] First, there are *barriers caused by semantics*. As we have noted previously, words mean different things to different people. This is particularly true for people from different national cultures. Some words, for instance, do not translate between cultures. For instance, the new capitalists in Russia may have difficulty communicating with their Canadian or British counterparts because English terms such as *efficiency, free market,* and *regulation* cannot be directly translated into Russian.

Second, there are *barriers caused by word connotations*. Words imply different things in different languages. The Japanese word *hai* translates as "yes," but its connotation may be "yes, I am listening," rather than "yes, I agree." Western executives may be hampered in their negotiations if they do not understand this connotation.

Third are *barriers caused by tone differences*. In some cultures language is formal, and in others it's informal. In some cultures, the tone changes depending on the context: People speak differently at home, in social situations, and at work. Using a personal, informal style in a situation where a more formal style is expected can be embarrassing and offensive.

Fourth, there are *barriers caused by differences in perceptions*. People who speak different languages actually view the world in different ways. The Inuit perceive snow differently because they have many words for it. Thais perceive "no" differently than Canadians because the former have no such word in their vocabulary.

Overcoming the Difficulties

When communicating with people from a different culture, what can you do to reduce misperceptions, misinterpretations, and misevaluations? Following these four rules can be helpful:[25]

- *Assume differences until similarity is proven.* Most of us assume that others are more similar to us than they actually are. But people from different countries often are very different from us. So you are far less likely to make an error if you assume others are different from you rather than assuming similarity until difference is proven.

- *Emphasize description rather than interpretation or evaluation.* Interpreting or evaluating what someone has said or done, in contrast with describing, is based more on the observer's culture and background than on the observed situation. As a result, delay judgment until you have had sufficient time to observe and interpret the situation from the differing viewpoints of all the cultures involved.

- *Be empathetic.* Before sending a message, put yourself in the recipient's shoes. What are his or her values, experiences, and frames of reference? What do you know about his or her education, upbringing, and background that can give you added insight? Try to see the other person as he or she really is.

- *Treat your interpretations as a working hypothesis.* Once you have developed an explanation for a new situation or think you empathize with someone from a foreign culture, treat your interpretation as a hypothesis that needs further

Ottawa-based Donna Cona made history when it designed and installed the computer network for the government of the new Nunavut territory. Two-thirds of the firm's software engineers are Aboriginal. Peter Baril, Nunavut's director of informatics operations, notes: "Donna Cona's quiet and knowledgeable approach was perhaps the most important skill brought to our project. No other style could have worked in this predominantly Aboriginal environment."

testing rather than as a certainty. Carefully assess the feedback provided by recipients to see if it confirms your hypothesis. For important decisions or communiqués, you can also check with other foreign and home-country colleagues to ensure that your interpretations are on target.

Electronic Communications

Since the early 1980s, we have been subjected to an onslaught of new electronic technologies that are largely reshaping the way we communicate in organizations.[26] These include pagers, fax machines, videoconferencing, electronic meetings, email, cellphones, voice messaging, and palm-sized personal communicators.

Electronic communications mean that you no longer have to be at your workstation or desk to be "available." You can be reached even when you are in a meeting, on lunch break, visiting a customer's office across town, watching a movie in a crowded theatre, or playing golf on a Saturday morning. The line between an employee's work and non-work life is no longer distinct. In the electronic age, all employees can theoretically be on call 24 hours a day.

Changes to Communication

Organizational boundaries become less relevant as a result of electronic communications. Why? Because networked computers allow employees to jump vertical levels within the organization, work full-time at home or someplace other than "the office," and hold ongoing communications with people in other organizations.

While electronic communications have revolutionized the ability to both access other people and reach them almost instantaneously, this has come with some costs. Email has added considerably to the number of hours worked each week, according to a recent study by Christina Cavanagh, professor of management communications at Western's Richard Ivey School of Business. Between 2000 and 2002, business professionals and executives said they were working six more hours a week, responding to email.[27] Email does not provide either the verbal or nonverbal nuances that a face-to-face meeting does. There has been some attempt to remedy this by using "emoticons" (e.g., the smiley face :-)) to indicate a friendly tone, and abbreviations (e.g., IMHO, "in my humble opinion") to indicate that a person is respectfully trying to convey his or her own viewpoint. There is also the standard warning not to write emails in ALL CAPS, as doing so is an indication that one is shouting. Exhibit 6-3 illustrates some of the conventional symbols used in email.

Videoconferences and electronic meetings have similar drawbacks to email. It's been noted that meetings have historically served two distinct purposes: fulfilling a need for group affiliation and serving as a forum for completing work tasks.[28] Videoconferences and electronic meetings do a good job at supporting tasks but do not address affiliation needs. For people with a high need for social contact, a heavy reliance on electronic communications is likely to lead to lower job satisfaction.

Considerations for Writing and Sending Email

Despite many advantages to email, it is important to realize that it is virtually indestructible once it gets backed up on your company's server. And its very speed and accessibility often lend themselves to miscommunication and misdirected messages. With these issues in mind, consider the following tips for writing and sending email, offered by Professor Christina Cavanagh of the Richard Ivey School of Business:[29]

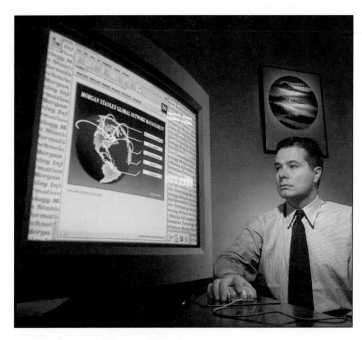

Investment bank Morgan Stanley uses the company's intranet to distribute data and information to employees at its 37 offices around the world. For example, the global network allows traders in Japan to receive up-to-the-minute information on securities transactions from colleagues in New York. Morgan Stanley has also connected its "hoot-and-holler" worldwide voice-messaging system to its intranet, allowing salespeople to receive messages from their workstation speakers on the trading floor.

- Don't send emails without a subject line.

- Be careful in your use of emoticons and acronyms for business communication.

- Write your message clearly, and briefly.

- Copy emails to others only if they really need the information.

- Sleep on angry emails before sending to be sure you are sending the right message.

Employees should also be aware that email is not necessarily private, and companies often take the position that they have the right to scrutinize your email. Some wonder, however, whether reading employee email is ethical. *Focus on Ethics* illustrates some of the difficulties of assuming your email is private.

Exhibit 6–3

Emoticons: Showing Emotions in Email

Electronic mail need not be emotion-free. Over the years, email users have developed a set of symbols *(emoticons)* for expressing emotions. For instance, the use of all caps (as in THIS PROJECT NEEDS YOUR IMMEDIATE ATTENTION!) is the email equivalent of shouting. The following highlights some emoticons:

:)	Smile	:-e	Disappointed
<g>	Grin	:-@	Scream
:(	Frown	:-0	Yell
;)	Wink	:-D	Shock or surprise
:-[	Really sad face	:'(	Crying

Your Email Can Get You Fired

Should your email be safe from your manager's eyes? The Canadian Auto Workers (CAW) union expressed outrage in early 1998 when it discovered that Montreal-based Canadian National Railway Co. (CN) was reading employees' email messages.[30] "Our people feel violated. You're given an e-mail address and you have a password, and it's yours. It's personal," is the view of Abe Rosner, a national CAW representative. CN, however, disagrees: "E-mail is to be used for CN business-approved activities only. Flowing from this is that any communication exchanged on the system is viewed as company property," explains Mark Hallman, a CN spokesperson.

While most employees do not think managers should listen to their subordinates' voice mail messages or read their emails, some managers do not agree. More than 20 percent of managers surveyed recently said that they monitored their employees' voice mail, email, and/or computer files. The managers argue that the company owns the systems used to produce this material, and therefore, they should have access to the information.

Fred Jones (not his real name) was fired from a Canadian company for forwarding dirty jokes to his clients.[31] Until this incident, Jones had been a high-performing employee who sold network computers for his company. Jones thought that he was sending the jokes only to clients who liked them, and assumed someone would tell him if they didn't want to receive the jokes. Instead, a client complained to the company about receiving the dirty jokes. After an investigation, the company fired Jones. Jones is still puzzled about being fired. He views his email as private, and sees sending the jokes as similar to telling jokes at the water cooler.

Jones was not aware that under current law, employee information, including email, is not necessarily private. Most federal employees, provincial public sector employees, and employees working for federally regulated industries are covered by the federal Privacy and Access to Information Acts, in place since 1983. Many private sector employees are not covered by privacy legislation, however. ⚕

HOW COMMUNICATION BREAKDOWN LEADS TO CONFLICT

We noted earlier that Dofasco Inc.'s mill employees were quite unhappy with the company after jobs had fallen from 10 300 to 7000 between 1992 and 1997. In addition to former employees starting a group called SHAFT (So How Many Are Fired Tomorrow) to press grievances against the company, some employees were looking to the Canadian Auto Workers and the United Steelworkers to help them form a union at Dofasco. Employees were kept out of the loop, felt they were not respected, and looked to alternative arrangements to get their voices heard by management. The communication breakdown led to a major conflict between the employees and the company's CEO. What can be done about conflict to make sure it doesn't get out of control?

5 What is conflict?

Conflict can be a serious problem in *any* organization. It might not lead to co-CEOs going after each other in court, as happened when brothers Wallace and Harrison McCain battled over command of McCain Foods Ltd., the New Brunswick-based french-fry empire they had built together. Still, it can certainly hurt an organization's performance and lead to the loss of good employees.

Conflict Defined

Several common themes underlie most definitions of conflict.[32] Conflict must be perceived by the parties to it. If no one is aware of a conflict, it is generally agreed that no conflict exists. Conflict also involves opposition or incompatibility, and some form of interaction between the parties.[33] These factors set the conditions that determine the beginning point of the conflict process. We can define **conflict**, then, as a process that begins when one party perceives that another party has negatively affected, or is about to negatively affect, something that the first party cares about.[34]

This definition is deliberately broad. It describes that point in any ongoing activity when an interaction "crosses over" to become conflict. It includes the wide range of conflicts that people experience in groups and organizations—incompatibility of goals, differences over interpretations of facts, disagreements based on behavioural expectations, and the like. Finally, our definition is flexible enough to cover the full range of conflict levels—from subtle forms of disagreement to overt and violent acts.

Conflict has positive sides and negative sides, which we will discuss further when we cover functional and dysfunctional conflict. For more on this debate, refer to the *Point/CounterPoint* discussion on page 201.

For 37 years, Wallace McCain and his older brother, Harrison (shown here), shared command of McCain Foods Ltd., the New Brunswick-based french-fry empire they had built together. In August 1993, however, that partnership came to an end, much to the surprise of the public.

SOURCES OF CONFLICT

In the mid-1990s, one of the problems facing Dofasco employees was that there were too many layers of management. Another was that employees didn't really know what was expected of them, or how bad the situation at Dofasco really was. In 2000, Mayberry informed his employees that the company had to cut production costs by $100 million over the next year to stay in the black. Besides poor communication, are there are other conditions that lead to conflict?

As we have seen, communication can be a source of conflict through semantic difficulties, misunderstandings, and "noise" in the communication channels. But, of course, poor communication is certainly not the source of all conflicts. For simplicity's sake, the conditions that lead to conflict have been condensed into three general categories. The two categories other than communication are structure and personal variables.[35]

6 What are the sources of conflict?

conflict
A process that begins when one party perceives that another party has negatively affected, or is about to negatively affect, something that the first party cares about.

Structure

The term *structure* in this context includes variables such as group size, degree of specialization in the tasks assigned to group members, jurisdictional clarity, member-goal compatibility, leadership styles, reward systems, and the degree of dependence between groups.

A review of the conditions that can lead to conflict suggests that:

- *Size, specialization,* and *composition* of the group act as forces to stimulate conflict. The larger the group and the more specialized its activities, the greater the likelihood of conflict. The potential for conflict tends to be greatest where group members are younger and where turnover is high.

- The *greater the ambiguity* in outlining where responsibility for actions lies, the greater the potential for conflict to emerge. Such jurisdictional ambiguities increase intergroup fighting for control of resources and territory.

- Too much *reliance on participation* may also stimulate conflict. Research tends to confirm that participation and conflict are highly correlated, apparently because participation encourages the promotion of differences.

- *Reward systems* create conflict when one member's gain is at another's expense.

- The *diversity of goals* among groups is a major source of conflict. When groups within an organization seek diverse ends, some of which are inherently at odds—such as sales and credit at the discount-furniture retailer—there are greater opportunities for conflict. If one group is dependent on another group, rather than the two being mutually independent, or if interdependence allows one group to gain at another's expense, opposing forces are stimulated.

Focus on Diversity illustrates how the goal of getting all exams marked on time conflicted with the religious needs of some students at York University. Rather than dealing with the differences, the university chose to treat everyone equally.

FOCUS ON **DIVERSITY**

Exam-Taking Students Faced With Sabbath Dilemma

Should students be accommodated, or should they have to ask for accommodation? Sabbath-observant Jewish students at York University had a choice to make during the final exam period of spring 2002.[36] They could ask for special arrangements, or take their exam on the Sabbath, something they would not ordinarily expect to do.

The University of Toronto, McGill University, and York University, which all have significant Jewish faculty and student populations, had not previously scheduled exams on Saturdays. Administrators at York University decided that it could no longer follow this practice, and scheduled final exams for two Saturdays.

York's student population had been growing faster than could be accommodated with existing space, which was one reason for scheduling on Saturdays, according to Deborah Hobson, York's former vice-president of enrollment and student services. More professors were also giving exams rather than term papers to prevent the use of internet-purchased papers.

Hobson noted that no special accommodation had been made for Christian or Muslim students regarding exam scheduling. "In scheduling exams on the Jewish Sabbath, it was felt that all religions would be treated fairly," Hobson said.

The Sabbath does present limitations on exam writing that most other religions do not, but Hobson felt that providing alternative arrangements requested by students would pose little difficulty.

Prof. Martin Lockshin, director of York's Centre for Jewish Studies, worried that Jewish students may not want to ask for special accommodations. Some students fear that asking professors for make-up exams not only burdens professors, but may also harm the student. It means extra work for professors, and the concern is that students' marks might be affected.

Some faculty members also wondered whether "the way to demonstrate tolerance to...various multicultural communities is by not giving religious accommodation to anyone."

Personal Variables

Have you ever met people that you immediately dislike? You disagree with most of their opinions. The sound of their voice, their smirk when they smile, and their personality annoy you. We have all met people like that. When you have to work with such individuals, there is often the potential for conflict.

Our last category of potential sources of conflict is *personal variables*. As indicated, they include the individual value systems that each person has, and the personality characteristics that account for individual idiosyncrasies and differences.

The evidence indicates that certain personality types—for example, individuals who are highly authoritarian and dogmatic, and who demonstrate low self-esteem—lead to potential conflict. Most important, and probably the most overlooked variable in the study of social conflict, is differing value systems. Value differences are the best explanation of such diverse issues as prejudice, disagreements over one's contribution to the group and the rewards one deserves, and assessments of whether this particular book is any good. That John dislikes Indo-Canadians and Dana believes John's position indicates his ignorance, that an employee thinks he is worth $60 000 a year but his manager believes him to be worth $55 000, and that Ann thinks this book is interesting while Jennifer views it as garbage are all value judgments. And differences in value systems are important sources of potential conflict. This chapter's *CBC Video Case Incident*, "Buggy Wars," shows how personal variables can lead to major conflict.

"Buggy Wars"

FROM POTENTIAL TO ACTUAL CONFLICT

Though the situation at Dofasco seemed grim during the mid-1990s, there was a remarkable turnaround in the fortune of the company by the late 1990s, which has continued. CEO John Mayberry organized people into a flatter organizational structure and got them to work together to solve problems. Management learned to work effectively with the employees. The employees worked together in their various teams and came up with a plan that exceeded Mayberry's target. All of this helped diffuse the conflict that had challenged employee-management relations at the start of Mayberry's tenure as CEO. Today, employees at Dofasco are more confident that management will keep them informed of what is happening with the company. This makes them more likely to work together to solve company problems. When Mayberry stepped down as CEO in May 2003, Dofasco was considered one of the most "outstanding steel companies in the world." The company had just had 10 profitable years in a row, including the best performance among North American integrated steelmakers in 2001. So what can be done to make sure that conflict turns out positively rather than negatively?

Even if conditions arise that may lead to conflict, conflict does not necessarily have to occur. For instance, you may notice something about someone's behaviour that bothers you, but you may also choose to ignore that behaviour, thus avoiding the conflict. The way a conflict is defined goes a long way toward establishing the sort of outcomes that might settle it. If I define our budget disagreement as a "zero-sum situation," for example, an increase in your budget means a decrease in mine, I will be far less willing to compromise than if I frame the conflict as a "potential win-win situation" (i.e., the dollars in the budget pool might be increased so that both of us could get the added resources we want). So the definition of a conflict is important, for it typically delineates the set of possible settlements. In a potential conflict situation, one progresses through stages, from perceiving and evaluating the situation, to forming intentions, engaging in behaviour, and achieving an outcome. The process is diagrammed in Exhibit 6–4.

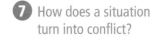

7 How does a situation turn into conflict?

Intentions

Intentions intervene between people's perceptions and emotions and their overt behaviour. These intentions are decisions to act in a given way.[37] For instance, if I feel that someone has slighted me, I may intend to confront that person the next time I see

intentions

Decisions to act in a given way in a situation.

Exhibit 6–4

How Conflict Builds

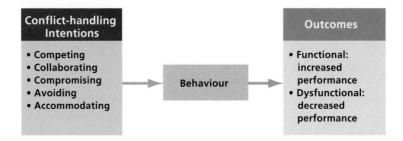

behaviour
Statements, actions, and reactions by an individual.

him or her. Why are intentions important? Many conflicts escalate because one party attributes the wrong intentions to the other party. One person may be simply trying to clarify his or her position, while the other may view the exchange as a serious threat. There is also typically a great deal of slippage between intentions and **behaviour**, so that individuals' statements, actions, and reactions do not always accurately reflect their intentions.

Exhibit 6–5 represents one author's effort to identify the primary conflict-handling intentions. Using two dimensions—*cooperativeness* (the degree to which one party tries to satisfy the other party's concerns) and *assertiveness* (the degree to which one party tries to satisfy his or her own concerns)—five conflict-handling intentions can be identified: *competing* (assertive and uncooperative), *collaborating* (assertive and cooperative), *avoiding* (unassertive and uncooperative), *accommodating* (unassertive and cooperative), and *compromising* (mid-range on both assertiveness and cooperativeness).[38] Exhibit 6–6 describes these behaviours and gives examples of each. *OB in the Street* looks at how compromise, a solution favoured by many students, can lead to unexpected outcomes.

Exhibit 6–5

Dimensions of Conflict-Handling Intentions

Source: K.W. Thomas, "Conflict and Negotiation Processes in Organizations," in M.D. Dunnette and L.M. Hough (eds.), *Handbook of Industrial and Organizational Psychology,* 2nd ed., vol. 3 (Palo Alto, CA: Consulting Psychologists Press, 1992), p. 668. With permission.

Exhibit 6–6

Understanding Conflict-Handling Intentions

Description	Examples	When Best Used
Competing When one person seeks to satisfy his or her own interests, regardless of the impact on the other parties to the conflict, he or she is competing.	Intending to achieve your goal at the sacrifice of the other's goal; attempting to convince another that your conclusion is correct and his or hers is mistaken; and trying to make someone else accept blame for a problem.	When quick, decisive action is vital (in emergencies); on important issues, where unpopular actions need implementing (in cost-cutting, enforcing unpopular rules, discipline); on issues vital to the organization's welfare when you know you're right; and against people who take advantage of noncompetitive behaviour.
Collaborating When the intention of the parties is to solve the problem by clarifying differences rather than by accommodating various points of view, they are collaborating for mutually beneficial outcome.	Attempting to find a win-win solution that allows both parties' goals to be completely achieved; seeking a conclusion that incorporates the valid insights of both parties.	To find an integrative solution when both sets of concerns are too important to be compromised; when your objective is to learn; to merge insights from people with different perspectives; to gain commitment by incorporating concerns into a consensus; and to work through feelings that have interfered with a relationship.
Avoiding A person may recognize that a conflict exists and want to withdraw from it or suppress it.	Trying to just ignore a conflict; avoiding others with whom you disagree.	When an issue is trivial, or more important issues are pressing; when you perceive no chance of satisfying your concerns; when potential disruption outweighs the benefits of resolution; to let people cool down and regain perspective; when gathering information supersedes immediate decision; when others can resolve the conflict more effectively; and when issues seem tangential or symptomatic of other issues.
Accommodating One party seeks to appease an opponent by placing the opponent's interests above his or her own.	Willingness to sacrifice your goal so the other party's goal can be attained; supporting someone else's opinion despite your reservations about it; forgiving someone for an infraction and allowing subsequent ones.	When you find you're wrong and to allow a better position to be heard; to learn, and to show your reasonableness; when issues are more important to others than yourself, and to satisfy others and maintain cooperation; to build social credits for later issues; to minimize loss when you are outmatched and losing; when harmony and stability are especially important; and to allow others to develop by learning from mistakes.
Compromising When each party to the conflict seeks to give up something, sharing occurs, resulting in a compromised outcome. In compromising, there is no clear winner or loser, and each party intends to give up something.	Willingness to accept a raise of $1.50 an hour rather than the $2 desired and the $1 initially offered by the employer; acknowledging partial agreement with a specific viewpoint; taking partial blame for an infraction.	When goals are important but not worth the effort of potential disruption of more assertive approaches; when opponents with equal power are committed to mutually exclusive goals; to achieve temporary settlements to complex issues; to arrive at expedient solutions under time pressure; and as a backup when collaboration or competition is unsuccessful.

Source: K.W. Thomas, "Toward Multidimensional Values in Teaching: The Example of Conflict Behaviors," *Academy of Management Review*, July 1977, p. 487.

OB IN THE STREET

One Wall Centre Goes Two-Toned

Is compromise necessarily the best way to go? When developer Peter Wall hired architect Peter Busby to design One Wall Centre in downtown Vancouver, the two planned a massive glass skyscraper.[39] City council reviewed the plans and approved the design, even granting a building height considerably higher than those in the surrounding neighbourhood.

The plans made the building look translucent, but as the tower went up, the glass looked black and impenetrable. Complaints started coming in to City Hall. The architect said that Wall had changed his mind about the colour of the glass once construction started. Wall claimed, however, that the city had approved the glass sample in use. Unfortunately, no one could find the glass samples. A planned lawsuit by the city was stopped for lack of evidence. So the two sides reached a compromise: The 48-storey building would have its lower levels in blackened glass, and the top 17 floors in lighter glass, rather than tearing down the building and starting over. Neither the city nor the developer is completely happy with the solution, and meanwhile, residents of Vancouver will have the two-toned building towering over them for many years to come. ⬛

Intentions provide general guidelines for parties in a conflict situation. They define each party's purpose. Yet people's intentions are not fixed and can alter in reaction to changes in the situation or behaviour of the other party. However, research indicates that people have an underlying disposition to handle conflicts in certain ways:[40] When confronting a conflict situation, some people want to win it all at any cost, some want to find an optimum solution, some want to run away, others want to be obliging, and still others want to "split the difference." This chapter's *Learning About Yourself Exercise* on page 202 gives you the opportunity to discover your own conflict-handling style.

Behaviours

Conflict behaviours (statements, actions, and reactions made by the conflicting parties) are usually overt attempts to carry out each party's intentions. However, overt behaviours sometimes deviate from original intentions.[41]

At some point conflict can result in interaction between the two parties. For example, you make a demand on me, I respond by arguing, you threaten me, I threaten you back, and so on. Exhibit 6–7 provides a way of visualizing conflict behaviour. All conflicts exist somewhere along this continuum. At the lower part of the continuum, we have conflicts characterized by subtle, indirect, and highly controlled forms of tension. An illustration might be a student questioning in class a point the instructor has just made. Conflict intensities escalate as they move upward along the continuum, until they become highly destructive. Strikes and lockouts, riots, and wars clearly fall in this upper range.

Outcomes

The action-reaction interplay between the conflicting parties results in consequences. As Exhibit 6-8 demonstrates, these outcomes may be functional in that the conflict results in an improvement in the group's performance, or dysfunctional in that it hinders group performance. We see that there is an optimal level of conflict that results in the highest productivity.

One should not label all conflict as either good or bad. Rather, conflicts that support the goals of the group and improve its performance are **functional**, or constructive,

functional conflict
Conflict that supports the goals of the group and improves its performance.

Exhibit 6–7

Conflict Intensity Continuum

Source: Based on S.P. Robbins, *Managing Organizational Conflict: A Nontraditional Approach* (Upper Saddle River, NJ: Prentice Hall, 1974), pp. 93–97; and F. Glasl, "The Process of Conflict Escalation and the Roles of Third Parties," in G.B.J. Bomers and R. Peterson (eds.), *Conflict Management and Industrial Relations* (Boston: Kluwer-Nijhoff, 1982), pp. 119–140.

forms of conflict. Conflicts that hinder group performance are **dysfunctional**, or destructive, forms of conflict. The conflict between CEO John Mayberry and his employees at Dofasco eventually turned around, and the company has been quite profitable in the past 10 years.

Of course, it is one thing to argue that conflict can be valuable for the group, and another to be able to tell whether a conflict is functional or dysfunctional.[42] The boundary between functional and dysfunctional is neither clear nor precise. No one level of conflict can be regarded as acceptable or unacceptable under all conditions. The type and level of conflict that creates healthy and positive involvement toward one group's goals today may, in another group or in the same group at another time, be highly dysfunctional. The one criterion that differentiates functional from dysfunctional conflict is group performance. If performance is negatively affected, the conflict is definitely

dysfunctional conflict
Conflict that hinders group performance.

Exhibit 6–8

Conflict and Unit Performance

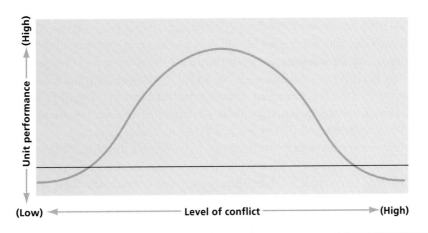

dysfunctional. You might want to review the *Case Incident* on page 204 to help you determine situations where conflict needs to be reduced or increased.

Functional Outcomes

We often think of conflict only in negative terms, but a lack of conflict can be just as problematic as too much conflict. For instance, many of the problems that faced both Eaton's and IBM Canada as they entered the 1990s can be traced to a lack of functional conflict. They hired and promoted individuals who were loyal to the organization to the point of never questioning company actions. Managers for the most part resisted change—they preferred looking back to past successes rather than forward to new challenges. Moreover, both firms kept their senior executives sheltered at headquarters, protected from hearing anything they might not want to hear, and a world away from the changes that were dramatically altering the retailing and computer industries. Eaton's, for instance, ignored such signs of trouble as losses endured by its in-store drug sections in competition with Shoppers Drug Mart, as well as the drain on profits of its small-town stores.[43] Eaton's did not survive, while IBM Canada managed to turn its fortunes around.

Dean Tjosvold, of Simon Fraser University, suggests three desired outcomes for conflict:[44]

- *Agreement*. Equitable and fair agreements are the best outcome. If agreement means that one party feels exploited or defeated, this will likely lead to further conflict later.

- *Stronger relationships*. When conflict is resolved positively, this can lead to better relationships and greater trusts. If the parties trust each other, they are more likely to keep the agreements they make.

- *Learning*. Handling conflict successfully teaches one how to do it better next time. It gives an opportunity to practise the skills one has learned for handling conflict.

Dysfunctional Outcomes

The destructive consequences of conflict on a group's or organization's performance are generally well known. Basically, uncontrolled opposition breeds discontent, which acts to dissolve common ties and eventually leads to the destruction of the group. And, of course, there is a substantial body of literature to document how conflict—the dysfunctional variety—can reduce group effectiveness.[45] Among the more undesirable consequences are slowdowns in communication, reductions in group cohesiveness, and subordination of group goals to the dominant issue of infighting between members. At the extreme, conflict can bring group functioning to a halt and threaten the group's survival.

Canada Post is a classic example of a company that experiences dysfunctional conflict from time to time. Canada experienced a 15-day postal strike just before the Christmas 1997 holiday season because of a labour conflict at the Crown corporation. As Alphonso Gagliano, the former federal public works minister, commented after the strike ended, "Labour-management relations are not the way you and I would like them to be. There is a historical mistrust here," he added. "Management is the enemy. Worker is the enemy."[46] This does not mean that once conflict between two groups starts, there is no chance for peace. In February 2000, Canada Post and the Canadian Union of Postal Workers signed their first negotiated agreement since 1995.[47]

This discussion returns us to the issue of what conflict is functional and what is dysfunctional. Research on conflict has yet to clearly identify those situations where conflict is more likely to be constructive than destructive. However, there is growing evidence that the source of the conflict is a significant factor determining functionality.[48] **Cognitive conflict**, which is task-oriented and occurs because of differences in perspectives and judgments, can often result in identifying potential solutions to problems. Thus it would

cognitive conflict

Conflict related to differences in perspectives and judgments.

be regarded as functional conflict. **Affective conflict**, which is emotional and aimed at a person rather than an issue, tends to be dysfunctional conflict. One study of 53 teams found that cognitive conflict, because it generates more alternatives, led to better decisions, more acceptance of the decisions, and ownership of the decisions. Teams experiencing affective conflict, where members had personality incompatibilities and disputes, had poorer decisions and lower levels of acceptance of the decisions.[49] Because conflict can involve our emotions in a variety of ways, it can also lead to stress. You may want to refer to the *OB on the Edge* on pages 94–101 to get some ideas of how to manage the stress that might arise from conflicts you experience.

affective conflict
Emotional conflict aimed at a person rather than an issue.

RESOLVING CONFLICT: NEGOTIATION

It is not unusual, when management-employee relations completely break down, that employees start to consider joining a labour union. If the employees are successful in their bid for unionization, then it is the labour union that negotiates with management over wage and working conditions. Earlier, we noted that Dofasco's employees did consider joining either the Canadian Auto Workers or the United Steelworkers, although they have not yet done that. Instead, CEO John Mayberry learned how to effectively negotiate with his employees, creating a supportive environment for all. He did this by creating a performance culture, where employee bonuses and pay are tied to how well the company does. He also encouraged employees to learn from other companies, and sent them around the world to see what other companies do. Employees were organized in teams and it was the teams that made plans, assigned accountability and schedules, and provided feedback to members. In other words, Mayberry created a "win-win" situation. What other steps can be taken to ensure effective negotiations among parties?

When parties are potentially in conflict, they may choose to negotiate a resolution. Negotiation occurs in the interactions of almost everyone in groups and organizations: Labour bargains with management; managers negotiate with employees, peers, and senior management; salespeople negotiate with customers; purchasing agents negotiate with suppliers; employees agree to answer a colleague's phone for a few minutes in exchange for some past or future benefit. In today's team-based organizations, negotiation skills become critical so that teams can work together effectively.

8 What is negotiation and how does it help?

negotiation
A process in which two or more parties try to agree on the exchange rate for goods or services they are trading.

We define **negotiation** as a process in which two or more parties try to agree on the exchange rate for goods or services they are trading.[50] Note that we use the terms *negotiation* and *bargaining* interchangeably. Within a negotiation, one should be aware that individuals have *issues, positions,* and *interests*. Issues are items that are specifically placed on the bargaining table for discussion. Positions are the individual's stand on the issue. For instance, salary may be an issue for discussion. The salary you hope to receive is your position. Finally, interests are the underlying concerns that are affected by the negotiation resolution. For instance, the reason that you might want a six-figure salary is that you are trying to buy a house in Vancouver, and that is your only hope of being able to make mortgage payments. Negotiators who recognize the underlying interests of themselves and the other party may

US-Russian arms reduction negotiations have moved from distributive to integrative. Slowly but surely, as relations between the two superpowers improved over the years, negotiators became more open and candid, trusting, and sensitive to each other's needs.

have more flexibility in achieving a resolution. For instance, in the example just given, an employer who offers you a mortgage at a lower rate than the bank does, or who provides you with an interest-free loan that can be used against the mortgage, may be able to address your underlying interests without actually meeting your salary position. You may be satisfied with this alternative, if you understand what your interest is. Interest-based bargaining enabled Vancouver-based NorskeCanada Ltd. to sign a mutually beneficial five-year contract with the Communications, Energy and Paperworkers Union of Canada in fall 2002, after just nine days of negotiations.[51] While the union and NorskeCanada had experienced bitter conflict in previous negotiations, in this particular situation both sides agreed to focus more on the interests of the parties, rather than on demands and concessions. Both sides were pleased with the outcome.

Bargaining Strategies

There are two general approaches to negotiation—*distributive bargaining* and *integrative bargaining*.[52] These are compared in Exhibit 6–9.

Distributive Bargaining

distributive bargaining
Negotiation that seeks to divide up a fixed amount of resources; a win-lose situation.

The negotiating strategy known as **distributive bargaining** operates under zero-sum (win-lose) conditions. That is, any gain I make is at your expense, and vice versa. Probably the most widely cited example of distributive bargaining is in labour-management negotiations over wages. Typically, management comes to the bargaining table determined to keep its labour costs as low as possible. Since every cent more that labour negotiates increases management's costs, each party bargains aggressively and treats the other as an opponent who must be defeated.

When engaged in distributive bargaining, a party focuses on trying to get the opponent to agree to a specific target point, or to get as close to it as possible. Examples of such tactics are persuading your opponent of the impossibility of reaching his or her target point and the advisability of accepting a settlement near yours; arguing that your target is fair, while your opponent's isn't; and trying to get your opponent to feel emotionally generous toward you and thus accept an outcome close to your target point.

Integrative Bargaining

integrative bargaining
Negotiation that seeks one or more settlements that can create a win-win solution.

In contrast to distributive bargaining, **integrative bargaining** operates under the assumption that there exists one or more settlements that can create a *win-win* solution. In terms of intraorganizational behaviour, all things being equal, integrative bargaining is preferable to distributive bargaining. Why? Because the former builds long-term

---

Exhibit 6–9

Distributive vs. Integrative Bargaining

Bargaining Characteristic	Distributive Bargaining	Integrative Bargaining
Available resources	Fixed amount of resources to be divided	Variable amount of resources to be divided
Primary motivations	I win, you lose	I win, you win
Primary interests	Opposed to each other	Convergent or congruent with each other
Focus of relationships	Short-term	Long-term

Source: Based on R.J. Lewicki and J.A. Litterer, *Negotiation* (Homewood, IL: Irwin, 1985), p. 280.

relationships and facilitates working together in the future. It bonds negotiators and allows each to leave the bargaining table feeling that he or she has achieved a victory. For instance, in union-management negotiations, both sides might sit down to figure out other ways to reduce costs within an organization, so that it is possible to have greater wage increases. Distributive bargaining, on the other hand, leaves one party a loser. It tends to build animosities and deepen divisions when people must work together on an ongoing basis.

How to Negotiate

In any negotiation, each party assesses its goals, considers the other party's goals and interests, and develops a strategy. In determining goals, parties are well advised to consider their "target and resistance" points, as well as their "best alternative to a negotiated agreement" (**BATNA**).[53] Exhibit 6–10 illustrates this notion. Parties A and B represent two negotiators. Each has a *target point,* which defines what he or she would like to achieve. Each also has a *resistance point,* which marks the lowest outcome that is acceptable—the point below which each would break off negotiations rather than accept a less favourable settlement. The area between these two points makes up each negotiator's aspiration range. As long as there is some overlap between A's and B's aspiration ranges, there exists a settlement range where each one's aspirations can be met.

One's BATNA represents the alternative that will be faced if negotiations fail. For instance, suppose you are interested in buying *either* a Ford Contour or a Daewoo Leganza. You are already comfortable with the price that the dealer has offered for the Contour, so you know that if the negotiations don't go well with the Leganza salesperson, you will buy the Contour. Thus your BATNA, when speaking to the Leganza dealer, is the Ford Contour. On the other hand, suppose your heart is set on the Contour, your own car has broken down, and you need a car to go on holiday in two days. Your BATNA is no car, which may encourage you to negotiate less forcefully with the Ford salesperson. To understand more about participating in negotiations, turn to the *Working With Others Exercise* on pages 203–204.

To improve your negotiating skills, you might consider the following:[54]

- *Begin with a positive overture.* Studies on negotiation show that concessions tend to be reciprocated and lead to agreements. As a result, begin bargaining with a positive overture—perhaps a small concession—and then reciprocate your opponent's concessions.

- *Address problems, not personalities.* Concentrate on the negotiation issues, not on the personal characteristics of your opponent. When negotiations get tough, avoid the tendency to attack your opponent. It's your opponent's ideas or position that you disagree with, not him or her personally. Separate the people from the problem, and do not personalize differences.

BATNA
The best alternative to a negotiated agreement; the lowest acceptable value to an individual for a negotiated agreement.

BATNA
www.batna.com

Exhibit 6–10

Staking out the Bargaining Zone

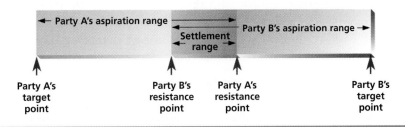

- *Pay little attention to initial offers.* Treat an initial offer as merely a point of departure. Everyone has to have an initial position. These initial offers tend to be extreme and idealistic. Treat them as such.

- *Emphasize win-win solutions.* Inexperienced negotiators often assume that their gain must come at the expense of the other party. But assuming a zero-sum game means missed opportunities for trade-offs that could benefit both sides. If conditions are supportive, look for an integrative solution. Frame options in terms of your opponent's interests and look for solutions that can allow your opponent, as well as yourself, to declare a victory.

- *Create an open and trusting climate.* Skilled negotiators are better listeners, ask more questions, focus their arguments more directly, are less defensive, and have learned to avoid words and phrases that can irritate an opponent (e.g. "generous offer," "fair price," "reasonable arrangement"). In other words, they are better at creating the open and trusting climate necessary for reaching an integrative settlement.

SUMMARY AND IMPLICATIONS

1 **How does communication occur?** Findings in the chapter suggest that the goal of perfect communication is unattainable. Yet there is evidence that demonstrates a positive relationship between effective communication (which includes factors such as perceived trust, perceived accuracy, desire for interaction, top-management receptiveness, and upward information requirements) and employee productivity.[55] Choosing the correct channel, being an effective listener, and using feedback well make for more effective communication.

2 **Are there barriers to communication?** Human beings will always be subject to errors in communication. What is said may not be what is heard. Whatever the sender's expectations, the decoded message in the mind of the receiver represents his or her reality. And this "reality" will determine the individual's reactions, including performance, motivation, and degree of satisfaction in the workplace.

3 **How can communication be encouraged?** Jim Collins, co-author of the best-selling management book *Built to Last,* notes the importance of creating effective mechanisms, "the practices that bring what you stand for to life and stimulate change." When you want someone to communicate, you need to show them how to do so.

4 **What are the current issues in communication?** The big topics in communication are nonverbal communication, gender differences in communication, cross-cultural differences in communication, and electronic communication. As we saw in the chapter, nonverbal cues help provide a clearer picture of communication. Men and women have some differences in their style, with men more likely to use communication to emphasize status, while women use it to create connection. We noted that there are a variety of barriers when communicating with someone from a different culture, and that it's best to be empathetic when communicating with others. Finally, we noted that email has become far more prevalent, is causing more stress, and can be misused, so that it is not always the most effective mechanism of communication.

5 **What is conflict?** Conflict occurs when one person perceives that another person's actions will have a negative effect. Many people automatically assume that all conflict is bad. However, conflict can be either constructive or destructive to the functioning of a group or unit. An optimal level of conflict encourages communication, prevents stagnation, stimulates creativity, allows tensions to be released, and initiates the seeds for change, yet not so much as to be disruptive or deter coordination of activities.

6 **What are the sources of conflict?** For simplicity's sake, the conditions that lead to conflict have been condensed into three general categories. These include communication, structure, and personal variables. The size and composition of the group can affect conflict, and also the ambiguity of roles. Personal values and personality can also lead to conflict.

7 **How does a situation turn into conflict?** Conflict starts with someone's intentions. If intentions are misinterpreted, this can lead to an escalation of conflict. From intentions, individuals choose behaviours that reflect their intentions. Those behaviours generally determine whether conflict will be functional or dysfunctional.

8 **What is negotiation and how does it help?** Negotiation is a process in which parties try to agree on the exchange rate for goods or services they are trading. Negotiation is an ongoing activity in groups and organizations. Distributive bargaining can resolve disputes, but it often negatively affects the satisfaction of one or more of the negotiators because it focuses on the short term and because it is confrontational. Integrative bargaining, in contrast, tends to provide outcomes that satisfy all parties and that build lasting relationships.

OB AT WORK

For Review

1. Describe the communication process and identify its key components. Give an example of how this process operates with both oral and written messages.

2. Contrast encoding and decoding.

3. What is nonverbal communication? Does it aid or hinder verbal communication?

4. List three specific problems related to language difficulties in cross-cultural communication.

5. What are the managerial implications from the research contrasting male and female communication and negotiation styles?

6. What is the difference between functional and dysfunctional conflict? What determines functionality?

7. What defines the settlement range in distributive bargaining?

8. Why isn't integrative bargaining more widely used in organizations?

9. How can you improve your negotiating effectiveness?

For Critical Thinking

1. "Ineffective communication is the fault of the sender." Do you agree or disagree? Discuss.

2. Using the concept of channel richness, give examples of messages best conveyed by email, by face-to-face communication, and on the company bulletin board.

3. Why do you think so many people are poor listeners?

4. Assume one of your co-workers had to negotiate a contract with someone from China. What problems might he or she face? If the co-worker asked for advice, what suggestions would you make to help facilitate a settlement?

5. From your own experience, describe a situation you were involved in where the conflict was dysfunctional. Describe another example, from your experience, where the conflict was functional. Would the other parties agree with your assessment of what is functional or dysfunctional?

OB for You

- If you are having difficulty communicating with someone, you might consider that both you and the other person are contributing something to that breakdown. This tends to be true even if you are inclined to believe that the other person is the party more responsible for the breakdown.

- Often either selective perception or defensiveness gets in the way of communication. As you work in your groups on student projects, you may want to observe communication flows more critically to help you understand ways that communication can be improved and dysfunctional conflict avoided.

- Avoiding conflict does not necessarily have a positive outcome.

 **POINT**

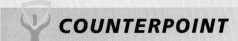 **COUNTERPOINT**

Conflict Is Good for an Organization

We have made considerable progress in the last 25 years toward overcoming the negative stereotype given to conflict. Most behavioural scientists and an increasing number of practising managers now accept that the goal of effective management is not to eliminate conflict. Rather, it is to create the right intensity of conflict so as to reap its functional benefits.

Let's briefly review how stimulating conflict can provide benefits to the organization.[56]

- *Conflict is a means by which to bring about radical change.* It's an effective device by which management can drastically change the existing power structure, current interaction patterns, and entrenched attitudes.

- *Conflict facilitates group cohesiveness.* While conflict increases hostility between groups, external threats tend to cause a group to pull together as a unit. Intergroup conflicts raise the extent to which members identify with their own group and increase feelings of solidarity, while, at the same time, internal differences and irritations dissolve.

- *Conflict improves group and organizational effectiveness.* The stimulation of conflict sparks the search for new means and goals and clears the way for innovation. The successful resolution of a conflict leads to greater effectiveness, to more trust and openness, to greater attraction of members for each other, and to depersonalization of future conflicts. In fact, it has been found that as the number of minor disagreements increases, the number of major clashes decreases.

- *Conflict brings about a slightly higher, more constructive level of tension.* This improves the chances of solving the conflicts in a way satisfactory to all parties concerned. When the level of tension is very low, the parties are not sufficiently motivated to do something about a conflict.

These points are clearly not comprehensive. As noted in the chapter, conflict provides a number of benefits to an organization. However, groups or organizations with no conflict are likely to suffer from apathy, stagnation, groupthink, and other debilitating diseases. In fact, more organizations probably fail because they have too little conflict rather than too much.

All Conflicts Are Dysfunctional!

It may be true that conflict is an inherent part of any group or organization. It may not be possible to eliminate it completely. However, just because conflicts exist is no reason to worship them. All conflicts are dysfunctional, and it is one of management's major responsibilities to keep conflict intensity as low as humanly possible. A few points will support this case.

- *The negative consequences from conflict can be devastating.* The list of negatives associated with conflict is awesome. Obvious negatives include increased turnover, decreased employee satisfaction, labour grievances and strikes, sabotage, physical aggression, and inefficiencies between work units.

- *Effective managers build teamwork.* A good manager builds a coordinated team. Conflict works against such an objective. A successful work group is like a successful sports team: Each member knows his or her role and supports his or her teammates. When a team works well, the whole becomes greater than the sum of the parts. Management creates teamwork by minimizing internal conflicts and facilitating internal coordination.

- *Competition is good for an organization, but not conflict.* Competition and conflict should not be confused with each other. Conflict is behaviour directed against another party, whereas competition is behaviour aimed at obtaining a goal without interference from another party. Competition is healthy; it's the source of organizational vitality. Conflict, on the other hand, is destructive.

- *Managers who accept and stimulate conflict don't survive in organizations.* The whole argument on the value of conflict may be open to question as long as most senior executives in organizations view conflict traditionally. In the traditional view, any conflict will be seen as bad. Since the evaluation of a manager's performance is made by higher-level executives, those managers who do not succeed in eliminating conflicts are likely to be appraised negatively. This, in turn, will reduce opportunities for advancement. Any manager who aspires to move up in such an environment will be wise to follow the traditional view and eliminate any outward signs of conflict. Failure to follow this advice might result in the premature departure of the manager.

OB *AT WORK*

What Is Your Primary Conflict-Handling Intention?

Indicate how often you rely on each of the following tactics by circling the number that you feel is most appropriate.

		Rarely				Always
1.	I argue my case with my co-workers to show the merits of my position.	1	2	3	4	5
2.	I negotiate with my co-workers so that a compromise can be reached.	1	2	3	4	5
3.	I try to satisfy the expectations of my co-workers.	1	2	3	4	5
4.	I try to investigate an issue with my co-workers to find a solution acceptable to us.	1	2	3	4	5
5.	I am firm in pursuing my side of the issue.	1	2	3	4	5
6.	I attempt to avoid being put on the spot and try to keep my conflict with my co-workers to myself.	1	2	3	4	5
7.	I hold on to my solution to a problem.	1	2	3	4	5
8.	I use give-and-take so that a compromise can be made.	1	2	3	4	5
9.	I exchange accurate information with my co-workers to solve a problem together.	1	2	3	4	5
10.	I avoid open discussion of my differences with my co-workers.	1	2	3	4	5
11.	I accommodate the wishes of my co-workers.	1	2	3	4	5
12.	I try to bring all our concerns out in the open so that the issues can be resolved in the best possible way.	1	2	3	4	5
13.	I propose a middle ground for breaking deadlocks.	1	2	3	4	5
14.	I go along with the suggestions of my co-workers.	1	2	3	4	5
15.	I try to keep my disagreements with my co-workers to myself in order to avoid hard feelings.	1	2	3	4	5

Scoring Key

To determine your primary conflict-handling intention, place the number 1 through 5 that represents your score for each statement next to the number for that statement. Then total up the columns.

Competing	Collaborating	Avoiding	Accommodating	Compromising
1. _____	4. _____	6. _____	3. _____	2. _____
5. _____	9. _____	10. _____	11. _____	8. _____
7. _____	12. _____	15. _____	14. _____	13. _____
Totals _____	_____	_____	_____	_____

Your primary conflict-handling intention is the category with the highest total. Your fall-back intention is the category with the second-highest total.

Source: This is an abbreviated version of a 35-item instrument described in M.A. Rahim, "A Measure of Styles of Handling Interpersonal Conflict," *Academy of Management Journal*, June 1983, pp. 368–376.

SMALL BREAKOUT **GROUP** EXERCISES

Form small groups to discuss the following topics, as assigned by your instructor:

1. Describe a situation in which you ignored someone. What impact did it have on that person's subsequent communication behaviours?

2. What differences have you observed in the ways that men and women communicate?

3. You and two other students carpool to school every day. The driver has recently taken to playing a new radio station quite loudly. You do not like the music, or the loudness. Using one of the conflict-handling intentions outlined in Exhibit 6–6, indicate how you might go about resolving this conflict. Identify a number of BATNAs (best alternatives to a negotiated agreement) available to you, and then decide whether you should continue carpooling.

WORKING WITH **OTHERS** EXERCISE

A Negotiation Role Play

This role play is designed to help you develop your negotiating skills. The class is to break into pairs. One person will play the role of Terry, the department supervisor. The other person will play Dale, Terry's boss.

The Situation

Terry and Dale work for Bauer. Terry supervises a research laboratory. Dale is the manager of research and development. Terry and Dale are former skaters who have worked for Bauer for more than 6 years. Dale has been Terry's boss for 2 years.

One of Terry's employees has greatly impressed Terry. This employee is Lisa Roland. Lisa was hired 11 months ago. She is 24 years old and holds a master's degree in mechanical engineering. Her entry-level salary was $52 500 a year. She was told by Terry that, in accordance with corporation policy, she would receive an initial performance evaluation at 6 months and a comprehensive review after 1 year. Based on her performance record, Lisa was told she could expect a salary adjustment at the time of the 1-year evaluation.

Terry's evaluation of Lisa after 6 months was very positive. Terry commented on the long hours Lisa was working, her cooperative spirit, the fact that others in the lab enjoyed working with her, and her immediate positive impact on the project she had been assigned. Now that Lisa's 1st anniversary is coming up, Terry has again reviewed Lisa's performance. Terry thinks Lisa may be the best new person the R&D group has ever hired. After only a year, Terry has ranked Lisa third highest in a department of 11.

Salaries in the department vary greatly. Terry, for instance, has a basic salary of $93 800, plus eligibility for a bonus that might add another $7000 to $11 000 a year.

The salary range of the 11 department members is $42 500 to $79 000. The lowest salary is a recent hire with a bachelor's degree in physics. The two people that Terry has rated above Lisa earn base salaries of $73 800 and $78 900. They are both 27 years old and have been at Bauer for 3 and 4 years, respectively. The median salary in Terry's department is $65 300.

Terry's Role

You want to give Lisa a big raise. While she's young, she has proven to be an excellent addition to the department. You don't want to lose her. More important, she knows in general what other people in the department are earning and she thinks she is underpaid. The company typically gives 1-year raises of 5 percent, although 10 percent is not unusual and 20 to 30 percent increases have been approved on occasion. You would like to get Terry as large an increase as Dale will approve.

Dale's Role

All your supervisors typically try to squeeze you for as much money as they can for their people. You understand this because you did the same thing when you were a supervisor, but your boss wants to keep a lid on costs. He wants you to keep raises for recent hires generally in the range of 5 to 8 percent. In fact, he has sent a memo to all managers and supervisors stating this objective. However, your boss is also very concerned with equity and paying people what they are worth. You feel assured that he will support any salary recommendation you make, as long as it can be justified. Your goal, consistent with cost reduction, is to keep salary increases as low as possible.

The Negotiation

Terry has a meeting scheduled with Dale to discuss Lisa's performance review and salary adjustment. Take a couple of minutes to think through the facts in this exercise and to prepare a strategy. Then you have up to 15 minutes to conduct your negotiation. When your negotiation is complete, the class will compare the various strategies used and pair outcomes.

ETHICAL **DILEMMA** EXERCISE

Is It Wrong to Tell a Lie?

When we were children, our parents told us, "It's wrong to tell a lie." Yet we all have told lies at one time or another. If most of us agree that telling lies is wrong, how do we justify continuing to do it? The answer is: Most of us differentiate between "real lies" and "little white lies"—the latter being an acceptable, even necessary, part of social interaction.

A recent survey of 10 000 people 18 to 50 years old provides some insights into people's attitudes toward lying. Eighty percent described honesty as important but nearly one-quarter said that they would lie to an employer "if necessary." More than 15 percent admitted to lying on a résumé or job application. And more than 45 percent said they would happily tell you a "little white lie."

Since lying is so closely intertwined with interpersonal communication, let's look at an issue many managers confront: Does a sound purpose justify intentionally distorting information? Consider the following situation:

An employee who works for you asks you about a rumour she's heard that your department and all its employees will be transferred from New York City to Dallas. You know the rumour is true, but you would rather not let the information out just yet. You're fearful it could hurt departmental morale and lead to premature resignations. What do you say to your employee? Do you lie, evade the question, distort your answer, or tell the truth?

In a larger context, where do you draw the line between the truth and lying? And if you're in a managerial position, how does your answer to the previous question fit with your desire to be trusted by those who work for you? How might lying affect your ability to be an effective negotiator?

Source: Cited in "Who's Lying Now?" *Training*, October 2000, p. 34.

CASE INCIDENT

Emailing "Lazy" Employees

Imagine receiving the following email from your CEO:

We are getting less than 40 hours of work from a large number of our EMPLOYEES. The parking lot is sparsely used at 8 a.m., likewise at 5 p.m. As managers, you either do not know what your EMPLOYEES are doing or you do not CARE. In either case, you have a problem and you will fix it or I will replace you.

NEVER in my career have I allowed a team which worked for me to think they had a 40-hour job. I have allowed YOU to create a culture which is permitting this. NO LONGER.

The note (paraphrased) continues: "Hell will freeze over before any more employee benefits are given out. I will be watching the parking lot and expect it to be substantially full at 7:30 a.m. and 6:30 p.m. on weekdays and half full on Saturdays. You have two weeks. Tick, tock."

Questions

1. Is email the best way to convey such a message?
2. What problems might arise if people outside the organization saw this email?
3. What suggestions, if any, would you make to the CEO to help improve communication effectiveness?
4. What conflict-handling style is this CEO using? What might be a more effective style? Why?

Source: Based on E. Wong, "Stinging Office E-Mail Lights 'Firestorm,'" *The Globe and Mail*, April 9, 2001, p. M1; P.D. Broughton, "Boss's Angry Email Sends Shares Plunging," *Daily Telegraph of London*, April 6, 2001; D. Stafford, "Shattering the Illusion of Respect," *The Kansas City Star*, March 29, 2001, p. C1.

CBC ⬤ VIDEO CASE INCIDENT

Buggy Wars

In 1993, Bob Bell and his good friend and neighbour Michael Sharpe, were living on Oxford Street in Guelph, Ontario. Bell, an engineer by trade, began designing a new trailer buggy for bicycles in his garage. Soon afterward, he shared his new idea with Sharpe, a computer software manager with a sales background. Over several months, the two entrepreneurs met at their respective homes and shared ideas about this new invention. Bell's role was being the "R & D guy," while Sharpe focused on identifying marketing opportunities.

Before long, Bell and Sharpe had a serious disagreement that deteriorated their friendship. Bell's lawyer served Sharpe with legal papers, suing for theft of intellectual property. All of the other Oxford Street neighbours were dismayed. It was difficult for them to understand how such a deep friendship could have come to such a disappointing end.

Bell, who was calculating and cautious in his behaviour, started his own business to build the "Wike." At the same time, just down the street, Sharpe started his own company called Greenways, Inc.—building his own version of the bicycle trailer that he called the "Wonderwagon." They developed different business philosophies and strategies for nearly identical products. Bell preferred to start small, local, and confident, while Sharpe mortgaged his home, hired people to work at a local factory, and began to mass market his product.

By the autumn of 1996, each businessman was experiencing some success with his own brand of bicycle trailer. However, when Bell won the patent infringement case against Sharpe, Bell's product became the winner of the bike buggy war. Today, ten years after its introduction and protected by legal patent rights, Bell's line of Wike bicycle trailers has expanded across Canada and the United States with great success. As for Sharpe, he decided to switch careers to...the fitness industry.

Questions

1. Identify the source(s) of conflict between Bob Bell and Michael Sharpe.

2. Which of the five conflict resolution techniques does each man prefer in handling his conflict?

Source: Based on "Buggy Wars," *CBC Venture*, August 18, 2002, 2037B, 841; Pi Manufacturing & WIKE website, "History," www.wicycle.com.

From **Concepts**
to **Skills**

Effective Listening

Too many people take listening skills for granted.[57] They confuse hearing with listening.

What's the difference? Hearing is merely picking up sound vibrations. Listening is making sense out of what we hear. That is, listening requires paying attention, interpreting, and remembering sound stimuli.

The average person normally speaks at a rate of 125 to 200 words per minute. However, the average listener can comprehend up to 400 words per minute. This leaves a lot of time for idle mind-wandering while listening. For most people, it also means they've acquired a number of bad listening habits to fill in the "idle time."

The following eight behaviours are associated with effective listening skills. If you want to improve your listening skills, look to these behaviours as guides:

1. *Make eye contact.* How do you feel when somebody doesn't look at you when you are speaking? If you are like most people, you are likely to interpret this behaviour as aloofness or lack of interest. We may listen with our ears, but others tend to judge whether we are really listening by looking at our eyes.

2. *Exhibit affirmative head nods and appropriate facial expressions.* The effective listener shows interest in what is being said. How? Through nonverbal signals. Affirmative head nods and appropriate facial expressions, when added to good eye contact, convey to the speaker that you're listening.

3. *Avoid distracting actions or gestures.* The other side of showing interest is avoiding actions that suggest your mind is somewhere else. When listening, don't look at your watch, shuffle papers, play with your pencil, or engage in similar distractions. They make the speaker feel you're bored or uninterested. Maybe more important, they indicate that you aren't fully attentive and may be missing part of the message that the speaker wants to convey.

4. *Ask questions.* The critical listener analyzes what he or she hears and asks questions. This behaviour provides clarification, ensures understanding, and assures the speaker that you are listening.

5. *Paraphrase.* Paraphrasing means restating what the speaker has said in your own words. The effective listener uses phrases such as "What I hear you saying is..." or "Do you mean...?" Why rephrase what has already been said? Two reasons! First, it's an excellent control device to check on whether you are listening carefully. You can't paraphrase accurately if your mind is wandering or if you are thinking about what you are going to say next. Second, it's a control for accuracy. By rephrasing what the speaker has said in your own words and feeding it back to the speaker, you verify the accuracy of your understanding.

6. *Avoid interrupting the speaker.* Let the speaker complete his or her thought before you try to respond. Don't try to second-guess where the speaker's thoughts are going. When the speaker is finished, you will know!

7. *Don't overtalk.* Most of us would rather voice our own ideas than listen to what someone else says. Too many of us listen only because it's the price we have to pay to get people to let us talk. While talking may be more fun and silence may be uncomfortable, you can't talk and listen at the same time. The good listener recognizes this fact and doesn't overtalk.

8. *Make smooth transitions between the roles of speaker and listener.* When you are a student sitting in a lecture hall, you find it relatively easy to get into an effective listening frame of mind. Why? Because communication is essentially one-way: The teacher talks and you listen. But the teacher-student dyad is not typical. In most work situations, you are continually shifting back and forth between the roles of speaker and listener. The effective listener, therefore, makes transitions smoothly from speaker to listener and back to speaker. From a listening perspective, this means concentrating on what a speaker has to say and practising not thinking about what you are going to say as soon as you get an opportunity.

▶

Assessing Skills

After you have read this chapter, take the following Self-Assessments on your enclosed CD-ROM.

24. What's My Face-to-Face Communication Style?

25. How Good Are My Listening Skills?

26. How Good Am I at Giving Feedback?

34. What's My Preferred Conflict-Handling Style?

Practising Skills

Break into groups of two. This exercise is a debate. Person A can choose any contemporary issue. Some examples: business ethics, value of unions, stiffer college grading policies, gun control, money as a motivator. Person B then selects a position on this issue. Person A must automatically take the counter-position. The debate is to proceed for 8 to 10 minutes, with only one catch. Before each speaks, he or she must first summarize, in his or her own words and without notes, what the other has said. If the summary doesn't satisfy the speaker, it must be corrected until it does.

Reinforcing Skills

1. In another class—preferably one with a lecture format—practise active listening. Ask questions, paraphrase, exhibit affirming nonverbal behaviours. Then ask yourself: Was this harder for me than a normal lecture? Did it affect my note taking? Did I ask more questions? Did it improve my understanding of the lecture's content? What was the instructor's response?

2. Spend an entire day fighting your urge to talk. Listen as carefully as you can to everyone you talk to and respond as appropriately as possible to understand, not to make your own point. What, if anything, did you learn from this exercise?

3. The next time you purchase a relatively expensive item (e.g., automobile, apartment lease, appliance, jewellery), negotiate a better price and gain some concessions such as an extended warranty, smaller down payment, maintenance services, or the like.

CHAPTER 7

Power and Politics

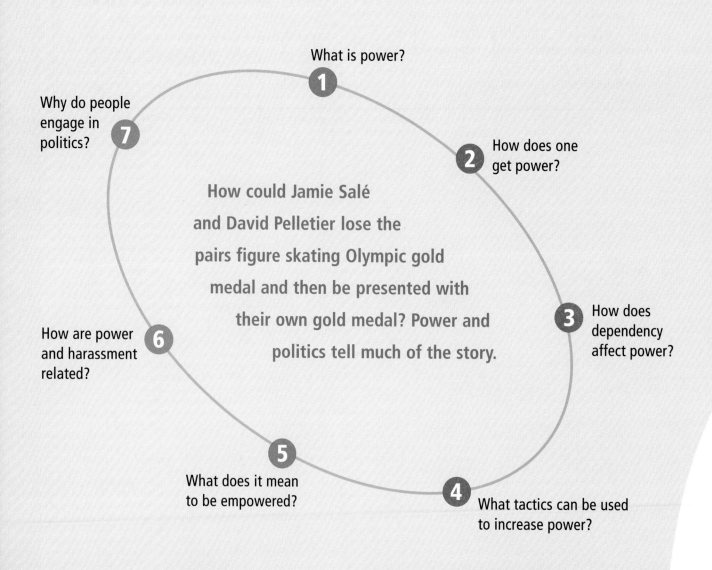

What is power?

1

Why do people engage in politics?

7

How does one get power?

2

How could Jamie Salé and David Pelletier lose the pairs figure skating Olympic gold medal and then be presented with their own gold medal? Power and politics tell much of the story.

How does dependency affect power?

3

How are power and harassment related?

6

What does it mean to be empowered?

5

What tactics can be used to increase power?

4

Any Canadian, and many Americans, watching the pairs figure skating competition in the 2002 Winter Olympics seemed sure they had watched a gold-medal performance when Jamie Salé and David Pelletier gave their final bow.[1] Moments later, however, fans looked on in horror as the gold medal was awarded to Russian skaters Yelena Berezhnaya and Anton Sikharulidze. North Americans were shocked: What they remembered was a flawed performance by the Russians, with Sikharulidze shaky on a double axel and Berezhnaya stiff in some of her landings, and a perfect performance by the Canadian duo.

Figure skating has long been considered a political rather than an artistic event, where the Soviet Union influenced its allies to support Russian skaters, while Western judges tended to side with US skaters. Thus it was not surprising that charges of politics and abuse of power surfaced quickly.

A major theme throughout this chapter is that power and politics are a natural process in any group or organization. Although you might have heard the saying "Power corrupts, and absolute power corrupts absolutely," power is not always bad. Understanding how to use power and politics effectively makes organizational life more manageable, because it can help you gain the support you need to do your job effectively.

A DEFINITION OF POWER

Power refers to a capacity that A has to influence the behaviour of B, so that B acts in accordance with A's wishes.[2] This definition implies that there is a *potential* for power if someone is dependent on another. But one can have power and not impose it.

Probably the most important aspect of power is that it is a function of **dependency**. The more that B depends on A, the more A has power in the relationship. Dependence, in turn, is based on the alternatives that B perceives and the importance that B places on the alternative(s) that A controls. A person can have power over you only if he or she controls something you desire. If you are attending college or university on funds totally provided by your parents, you probably recognize the power that your parents hold over you. You are dependent on them for financial support. But once you are out of school, have a job, and are making a good income, your parents' power is reduced significantly. Who among us, though, has not known or heard of the rich relative who is able to control a large number of family members merely through the implicit or explicit threat of "writing them out of the will"?

1 What is power?

power
A capacity that A has to influence the behaviour of B, so that B acts in accordance with A's wishes.

dependency
B's relationship to A when A possesses something that B requires.

Within larger organizations, the information technology (IT) group often has considerable power, because everyone, right up to the CEO, is dependent on this group keeping computers and networks running. Since few people have the technical expertise to do so, IT personnel end up being viewed as irreplaceable. This gives them a lot of power within the organization.

Power should not be considered a bad thing, however. "Power, if used appropriately, should actually be a positive influence in your organization," says Professor Patricia Bradshaw, of the Schulich School of Business at York University. "Having more power doesn't necessarily turn you into a Machiavellian monster. It can help your team and your organization achieve its goals and increase its potential."[3]

Is Leadership Different From Power?

A careful comparison of our description of *power* with our description of *leadership* in Chapter 8 reveals that the two concepts are closely intertwined. Leaders use power as a means of reaching goals.

What differences are there between the two terms? One main difference relates to goal acceptance. Power does not require that individuals accept the goals of the person in power. If the individuals are dependent on the person, however, they have to go along with the goals. Leadership, on the other hand, requires that those being led agree to some extent with the leader's goals.

BASES OF POWER

As the figure skating controversy swirled, International Skating Union president Ottavio Cinquanta tried to contain the uproar by announcing three days after the event that "We cannot change the result of the competition." He was sending out a signal to the Americans, who had taken to the airwaves to protest the results of the competition, that lobbying could not turn judges' scores around, or change ISU procedures. Forty-eight hours later, however, he changed his mind and announced that the results would be changed, and Salé and Pelletier would receive gold medals. How could Cinquanta be forced to change his decision so quickly?

2 How does one get power?

Where does power come from? What is it that gives an individual or a group influence over others? The answer to these questions is a five-category classification scheme identified by French and Raven.[4] They proposed that there were five bases or sources of power: coercive, reward, legitimate, expert, and referent (see Exhibit 7–1).

Coercive Power

coercive power
Power that is based on fear.

The **coercive power** base is defined by French and Raven as being dependent on fear. One reacts to this power out of fear of the negative results that might occur if one failed to comply. It rests on the application, or the threat of the application, of physical sanctions such as the infliction of pain, the generation of frustration through restriction of movement, or the controlling by force of basic physiological or safety needs. When Jacques Rogge, the International Olympic Committee president, threatened to ban judged sports from the Olympics because of the skating scandal, he was using a form of coercion. He was trying to intimidate the ISU, making them fear that if the controversy was not ended quickly, figure skaters would no longer compete in the Olympics.

Of all the bases of power available, the power to hurt others is possibly the most often used, most often condemned, and most difficult to control. The state relies on its military and legal resources to intimidate nations, or even its own citizens. Businesses rely upon the control of economic resources. Schools and universities rely on their rights to deny students formal education. Religious institutions threaten individuals with dire consequences in the afterlife if they do not conduct themselves properly in this

International Olympic Committee (IOC)
www.olympic.org

International Skating Union (ISU)
www.isu.org

Exhibit 7–1

Measuring Bases of Power

Does a person have one or more of the five bases of power? Affirmative responses to the following statements can answer this question:

- The person can make things difficult for people, and you want to avoid getting him or her angry. [*Coercive power*]

- The person is able to give special benefits or rewards to people, and you find it advantageous to trade favours with him or her. [*Reward power*]

- The person has the right, considering his or her position and your job responsibilities, to expect you to comply with legitimate requests. [*Legitimate power*]

- The person has the experience and knowledge to earn your respect, and you defer to his or her judgment in some matters. [*Expert power*]

- You like the person and enjoy doing things for him or her. [*Referent power*]

Source: G. Yukl and C.M. Falbe, "Importance of Different Power Sources in Downward and Lateral Relations," *Journal of Applied Psychology*, June 1991, p. 417. With permission.

life. At the personal level, individuals use coercive power through a reliance on physical strength, words, or the ability to grant or withhold emotional support from others. These bases provide the individual with the means to physically harm, bully, humiliate, or deny love to others.[5]

At the organizational level, A has coercive power over B if A can dismiss, suspend, or demote B, assuming that B values his or her job. Similarly, if A can assign B work activities that B finds unpleasant or treat B in a manner that B finds embarrassing, A possesses coercive power over B.

Reward Power

The opposite of coercive power is **reward power**. People comply with the wishes or directives of another because doing so produces positive benefits; therefore, one who can distribute rewards that others view as valuable will have power over those others. These rewards can be anything that another person values. In an organizational context, we think of money, favourable performance appraisals, promotions, interesting work assignments, friendly colleagues, important information, and preferred work shifts or sales territories.[6]

Coercive power and reward power are actually opposites of each other. If you can remove something of positive value from another or inflict something of negative value on him or her, you have coercive power over that person. If you can give someone something of positive value or remove something of negative value, you have reward power over that person. As with coercive power, you do not have to be a manager to be able to exert influence through rewards. Rewards such as friendliness, acceptance, and praise are available to everyone in an organization. To the degree that an individual seeks such rewards, your ability to give or withhold them gives you power over that individual.

reward power
Power that brings compliance based on the ability to distribute rewards that others view as valuable.

Microsoft chair Bill Gates' power comes from a variety of sources. He has *legitimate* power within Microsoft because he co-founded the company and was until recently its CEO. His *expert* power is recognized throughout the world. It is based on his software development expertise and his reputation for building a first-rate company. Gates also has *referent* power, because many people look up to him and admire his incredible accomplishments. The US government, however, was not persuaded by his referent power and used its *coercive* power to try to break up what it views as Gates' monopolistic hold on the computer world.

Legitimate Power

legitimate power
The power a person receives as a result of his or her position in the formal hierarchy of an organization.

In formal groups and organizations, probably the most frequent access to one or more of the power bases is one's structural position. This is called **legitimate power**. It represents the power a person receives as a result of his or her position in the formal hierarchy of an organization.

Positions of authority include coercive and reward powers. Legitimate power, however, is broader than the power to coerce and reward. Specifically, it includes acceptance by members of an organization of the authority of a position. When school principals, bank presidents, or army captains speak (assuming that their directives are viewed to be within the authority of their positions), teachers, tellers, and lieutenants listen and usually comply. You will note in Exhibit 7–2 that one of the men in the meeting identifies himself as the rule maker, which means that he has legitimate power. Because Jacques Rogge was president of the International Olympic Committee, he was one of the few individuals who had legitimate power to try to bring resolution to the skating controversy.

Expert Power

expert power
Influence based on special skills or knowledge.

Expert power is influence wielded as a result of expertise (i.e., special skills or knowledge). Expertise has become one of the most powerful sources of influence as the world has become more technologically oriented. As jobs become more specialized, we become increasingly dependent on experts to achieve goals. So, while it is generally acknowledged that physicians have expertise and hence expert power—most of us follow the advice that our doctor gives us—you should also recognize that computer specialists, tax accountants, economists, industrial psychologists, and other specialists are able to wield power as a result of their expertise. Young people may find they have increased power in the workplace these days because of their technical knowledge and expertise that their baby-boomer managers may not have.

Exhibit 7–2

"I was just going to say 'Well, I don't make the rules.' But, of course, I do make the rules."

Referent Power

The last category of influence that French and Raven identified was **referent power**. Its base is identification with a person who has desirable resources or personal traits. If I admire you and identify with you, you can exercise power over me because I want to please you.

referent power
Influence based on possession by an individual of desirable resources or personal traits.

Referent power develops out of admiration of another and a desire to be like that person. In a sense, then, it is a lot like charisma. If you admire someone to the point of modelling your behaviour and attitudes after him or her, that person possesses referent power over you. Referent power explains why celebrities are paid millions of dollars to endorse products in commercials. Marketing research shows that people such as Jaime Salé and David Pelletier can influence your choice of toothpaste or your choice of computer printers. And advertisers such as Toronto-based Roots Canada Ltd. have developed advertising themes around popular Canadians, such as "bad boy" Olympic gold-medallist and snowboarder Ross Rebagliati, to convince people to buy specific products[7]—with the stars sometimes providing their own music, as in Canadian jazz diva Diana Krall's TV commercials for Chrysler. Similarly, Nike has used sports celebrities such as Toronto Raptors star centre Vince Carter to promote its products. With a little practice, you and I could probably deliver as smooth a sales pitch as these celebrities, but the buying public does not identify with you and me. In organizations, if you are articulate, domineering, physically imposing, or charismatic, you hold personal characteristics that may be used to get others to do what you want.

Evaluating the Bases of Power

A review of the research on the effectiveness of these forms of power finds that they differ in their ability to improve a person's performance.[8] Exhibit 7–3 summarizes some of this research. Coercive power tends to result in negative performance responses from individuals, decreases satisfaction, increases mistrust, and creates fear. Legitimate power does not have a negative effect, but it also does not generally stimulate employees to improve their attitudes or performance, and it does not generally result in increased commitment. In other words, legitimate power does not inspire individuals to act beyond the basic level.

Exhibit 7–3

Continuum of Responses to Power

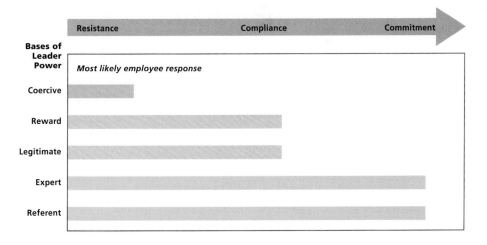

Source: R.M. Steers and J.S. Black, *Organizational Behavior*, 5th edition (New York: HarperCollins, 1994).

Roots hired Ross Rebagliati as a spokesperson after his controversial gold-medal performance in the 1998 Winter Olympics. The Toronto-based company was relying on Rebagliati's *referent* power with teens and 20-somethings to increase sales.

Sears Canada Inc.
www.sears.ca

Reward power may improve performance in a variety of situations if the rewards fit in with what the individuals want as rewards. Reward power can also lead to unethical behaviour, however. For instance, former Sears Roebuck chair Edward A. Brennan introduced a compensation program aimed at encouraging increased sales. Two years later, Sears' Auto Centers in California were accused of overcharging customers an average of $235 (US) for unnecessary repairs that resulted from unreasonably high quotas, commission-based compensation, and attractive incentives for top sellers.[9] Even if reward power does not always lead to unethical behaviour, you may remember from the discussion in Chapter 4 that extrinsic rewards can lead to demotivated behaviour when they replace intrinsic rewards. Ironically, the least effective power bases—coercive, legitimate, and reward—are the ones most likely to be used by managers, perhaps because they are the easiest to implement.

By contrast, effective leaders use referent and/or expert power.[10] These forms of power are not derived from the person's position. Referent and expert powers are thus "personal" forms of influence and are achieved through interpersonal interactions and relationships with employees. When people identify with someone because of referent or expert power, their respect and admiration make them more likely to copy the performance of that individual.

Expert power relies on trust that all relevant information is given out honestly and completely. Of course, since knowledge is power, the more that information is shared, the less expert power a person has. Thus, some individuals try to protect their power by withholding information.[11] This tactic can result in poor quality performance by those who need the information.[12] The *Working With Others Exercise* on pages 236–237 gives you the opportunity to explore the effectiveness of different power bases in changing someone's behaviour.

DEPENDENCY: THE KEY TO POWER

As the 2002 Olympics figure skating furor unfolded, some claimed that French judge Marie-Reine Le Gougne was pressured by the French skating federation to vote for the Russians, in exchange for which the Russian judge would vote for the French skaters in the Olympic ice dancing competition. In August 2002, a Russian mobster was arrested for possible bribery charges in the case, suggesting that external pressures were applied to higher-ups in the skating organizations, who then pressured judges to fix votes. "Though it doesn't excuse them for not judging honestly, it suggests that individuals highly ranked within their federations are indeed setting the tone for their [the judges'] behaviour," noted US dance judge Sharon Rogers.[13] The French judge was dependent on her superiors to keep her judging job, something she valued very much. Meanwhile, a dependence on bribes from the Russian mobster made higher-ups pressure their judges. What other factors might result in one party having greater power over another?

In this section, we show how an understanding of dependency is central to furthering your understanding of power.

3 How does dependency affect power?

The General Dependency Postulate

Let's begin with a general postulate: *The greater B's dependency on A, the greater the power A has over B.* When you possess anything that others require but that you alone control, you make them dependent upon you and, therefore, you gain power over them.[14] Dependency, then, is inversely proportional to the alternative sources of supply. If something is plentiful, possession of it will not increase your power. If everyone is intelligent, intelligence gives no special advantage. Similarly, in the circles of the superrich, money does not result in power. But, as the old saying goes, "In the land of the blind, the one-eyed man is king!" If you can create a monopoly by controlling information, prestige, or anything that others crave, they become dependent on you. Conversely, the more that you can expand your options, the less power you place in the hands of others. This explains, for example, why most organizations develop multiple suppliers rather than give their business to only one. It also explains why so many of us aspire to financial independence. Financial independence reduces the power that others can have over us.

What Creates Dependency?

Dependency is increased when the resource you control is important, scarce, and cannot be substituted.[15]

Importance

If nobody wants what you have, there is no dependency. To create dependency, the thing(s) you control must be perceived as being important. In some organizations, people who control the budget have a great deal of importance. In other organizations, those who possess the knowledge to keep technology working smoothly would be viewed as important. What is important is situational. It varies among organizations and undoubtedly also varies over time within any given organization. When individuals or organizations are regarded as important, however, unethical behaviour may result, as the *Focus on Ethics* suggests.

FOCUS ON **ETHICS**

Enron Requests Action from PaineWebber

Did Enron use its power to cause a UBS PaineWebber employee to be fired? In August 2001, months before the Enron scandal broke, executives of the company pressured UBS PaineWebber (now UBS Financial Services Inc.) to discipline one of its brokers.[16] The broker, Chung Wu, had advised Enron employees to sell their stock options. Within hours of the complaint, the broker was fired.

When the Enron executive in charge of the stock option program learned that Wu had warned employees that the company's "financial situation is deteriorating," he notified PaineWebber immediately via email. His message stated: "Please handle this situation. This is extremely disturbing to me."

PaineWebber went even further than firing Wu, however. It also sent his clients a report that Enron was "likely heading higher than lower from here on out."

PaineWebber has since suggested that Wu acted unethically because his email messages to Enron clients were unauthorized, and because he did not tell them that PaineWebber's research analyst rated Enron a "strong buy."

One might question PaineWebber's behaviour, however. When Wu sent the email messages, the stock was worth $36. Only a few months later, it was worthless. PaineWebber managed Enron's stock option program and handled large personal accounts for many of Enron's executives. It also did investment banking for Enron. Thus it did not want to risk losing Enron's business by suggesting the stock was in trouble. 🕴

Scarcity

As noted previously, if something is plentiful, possession of it will not increase your power. A resource must be perceived as being scarce to create dependency.

This can help to explain how low-ranking members in an organization gain power if they have important knowledge not available to high-ranking members. Possession of a scarce resource—in this case, important knowledge—makes the high-ranking member dependent on the low-ranking member. This also helps to make sense out of behaviours of low-ranking members that otherwise might seem illogical, such as destroying the procedure manuals that describe how a job is done, refusing to train people in their jobs or even to show others exactly what they do, creating specialized language and terminology that inhibit others from understanding their jobs, or operating in secrecy so an activity will appear more complex and difficult than it really is. The use of knowledge and the power it brings will become increasingly important in organizations of the

The location of power varies among organizations. At Walt Disney Co., enormous power is held by high-tech scientists in the research and development group of Disney Imagineering, a division started by Walt Disney in 1952 to create Disneyland. Today, the company is relying on Bran Ferren (upper left), who heads the R&D unit, and his highly skilled and creative staffers to develop cyberland fantasies such as virtual-reality theme parks, websites for kids, and smart TV sets that learn viewers' programming preferences and automatically record programs they forget to watch.

21st century. One of the major tasks of organizations is to figure out ways to handle the volume of information that is available. Individuals who acquire excellent information-handling abilities will have more power in their organizations.

Nonsubstitutability

The more that a resource has no workable substitutes, the more power that control over that resource provides. At Apple Computer, for example, most observers, as well as the board, believed that no one other than Steve Jobs could turn the company around when they returned him to the role of CEO in 1997. When a union goes on strike, and management is not permitted to replace the striking employees, the union has considerable control over the organization's ability to carry out its tasks.

POWER TACTICS

In looking at the Olympics skating controversy, we can find a number of instances where the various people involved in the controversy used power tactics to get their way. There is some evidence that the French and Russian judges formed a coalition to ensure that the French ice dancers would get a gold medal in a later event. The Russian mobster used bargaining, trading bribes for votes. International Olympic Committee president Jacques Rogge used assertiveness to convince Ottavio Cinquanta, the president of the International Skating Union (ISU), that in fact there would be two gold medals. He also threatened the ISU with sanctions, including banning judged sports from the Olympics, if they did not award the second medal. So how and why do power tactics work?

How do individuals translate their power bases into specific actions? What tactics can they use to try to influence people to act in ways that the power holder wants? Recent research indicates that there are common **power tactics** power holders use to get what they want.[17]

One particular study identified seven tactical dimensions, or strategies, that managers and employees use to increase their power:[18]

- *Reason.* Using facts and data to make a logical or rational presentation of ideas.

- *Friendliness.* Using flattery, creating goodwill, acting humble, and being friendly before making a request.

- *Coalition.* Getting the support of other people in the organization to back up the request.

- *Bargaining.* Using negotiation through the exchange of benefits or favours.

- *Assertiveness.* Using a direct and forceful approach, such as demanding compliance with requests, repeating reminders, ordering individuals to do what is asked, and pointing out that rules require compliance.

- *Higher authority.* Gaining the support of higher levels in the organization to back up requests.

- *Sanctions.* Using organizationally derived rewards and punishments, such as preventing or promising a salary increase, threatening to give an unsatisfactory performance evaluation, or withholding a promotion.

You may want to review the opening vignette to see whether you can identify examples of most of these power tactics used by participants in the ice skating controversy.

Researchers found that employees do not rely on the seven tactics equally. However, as shown in Exhibit 7–4, the most popular strategy was the use of reason, regardless of whether the influence was directed upward or downward. The researchers also uncov-

4 What tactics can be used to increase power?

power tactics
Ways in which individuals translate power bases into specific actions.

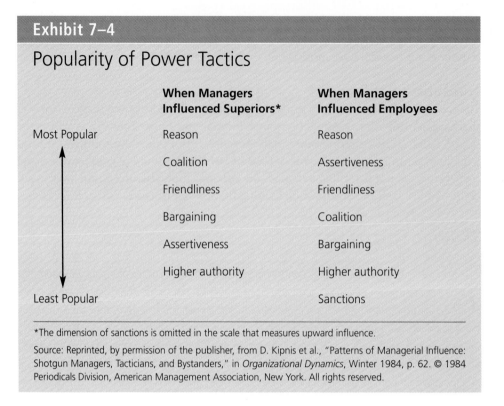

Exhibit 7–4

Popularity of Power Tactics

	When Managers Influenced Superiors*	When Managers Influenced Employees
Most Popular	Reason	Reason
	Coalition	Assertiveness
	Friendliness	Friendliness
	Bargaining	Coalition
	Assertiveness	Bargaining
	Higher authority	Higher authority
Least Popular		Sanctions

*The dimension of sanctions is omitted in the scale that measures upward influence.

Source: Reprinted, by permission of the publisher, from D. Kipnis et al., "Patterns of Managerial Influence: Shotgun Managers, Tacticians, and Bystanders," in *Organizational Dynamics*, Winter 1984, p. 62. © 1984 Periodicals Division, American Management Association, New York. All rights reserved.

ered four contingency variables that affect the selection of a power tactic: the manager's relative power, the manager's objectives for wanting to influence, the manager's expectation of the target person's willingness to comply, and the organization's culture.

A manager's relative power affects the selection of tactics in two ways. First, managers who control resources that are valued by others or who are perceived to be in positions of dominance use a greater variety of tactics than do those with less power. Second, managers with power use assertiveness with greater frequency than do those with less power. Initially, we can expect that most managers will try to use simple requests and reason. Assertiveness is a backup strategy, used when the target of influence refuses or appears reluctant to comply with the request. Resistance leads to managers using more directive strategies. Typically, they shift from using simple requests to insisting that their demands be met. The manager with relatively little power is more likely to stop trying to influence others when he or she encounters resistance because he or she perceives the costs associated with assertiveness as unacceptable.

Managers vary their power tactics in relation to their objectives. When managers seek benefits from a more senior manager, they tend to rely on kind words and the promotion of pleasant relationships—that is, they use friendliness. In comparison, managers trying to persuade top management to accept new ideas usually rely on reason. This matching of tactics to objectives also holds true for downward influence. For example, managers use reason to sell ideas to employees and friendliness to obtain favours.

Managers' expectations of success guide their choice of tactics. When past experience indicates a high probability of success, managers use simple requests to gain compliance. Where success is less predictable, managers are more tempted to use assertiveness and sanctions to achieve their objectives.

Finally, the organization itself will influence which subset of power tactics managers view as acceptable for use. For example, some organizations are warm, relaxed, and supportive, while others are formal and conservative. This will have a significant bearing on defining which tactics are considered appropriate. Some organizations encourage the use of friendliness, some encourage reason, and still others rely on sanctions and assertiveness.

EMPOWERMENT: GIVING POWER TO EMPLOYEES

Thus far our discussion has implied that—to some extent, at least—power is most likely to reside in the hands of managers, to be used as part of their interaction with employees. However, in today's workplace, there is a movement toward sharing more power with employees by putting them in teams and also by making them responsible for some of the decisions regarding their jobs. With the flattening of organizations, so that there are fewer middle managers, employees also end up with more responsibilities. Organizational specialists refer to this increasing responsibility as *empowerment*. We briefly mention in Chapter 8 that one of the current trends in leadership is empowering workers. Between 1995 and 1999 alone, nearly 30 000 articles about empowerment appeared in the print media.[19]

5 What does it mean to be empowered?

Definition of Empowerment

The definition of **empowerment** that we use here refers to the freedom and the ability of employees to make decisions and commitments.[20] Unfortunately, neither managers nor researchers can agree on the definition of empowerment. Quinn and Spreitzer, in their work with a *Fortune* 50 manufacturing company, found that executives were split about 50–50 in their definition.[21] One group of executives "believed that empowerment was about delegating decision making within a set of clear boundaries." Empowerment would start at the top, specific goals and tasks would be assigned, responsibility would be delegated, and people would be held accountable for their results. The other group believed that empowerment was "a process of risk taking and personal growth." This type of empowerment starts at the bottom, with considering the employees' needs, showing them what empowered behaviour looks like, building teams, encouraging risk-taking, and demonstrating trust in employees' ability to perform.

empowerment
The freedom and the ability of employees to make decisions and commitments.

Much of the press on empowerment has been positive, with both executives and employees applauding the ability of front-line workers to make and execute important decisions.[22] However, not all reports are favourable. One management expert noted that much of the talk about empowerment is simply lip service,[23] with organizations telling employees that they have decision-making responsibility, but not giving them the authority to carry out their decisions. In order for an employee to be fully empowered, he or she needs access to the information required to make decisions; rewards for acting in appropriate, responsible ways; and authority to make the necessary decisions. Empowerment means that the employees understand how their jobs fit into the organization and that they are able to make decisions regarding job action in light of the organization's purpose and mission.

The concept of empowerment has caused much cynicism in many workplaces. Employees are told that they are empowered, and yet they do not feel that they have the authority to act, or they feel that their managers still micromanage their performance. Some managers are reluctant to empower their employees, because this means sharing or even relinquishing their own power. Other managers worry that empowered workers may decide to work on goals and jobs that are not as closely aligned

Empowered employees, whether they work individually or in teams like this one at Carbon Give, need the tools and training to take responsibility for their work. Teams at Carbon Give have a great deal of freedom to make decisions, while their managers act as advisers and coaches.

to the organizational goals. Some managers, of course, do not fully understand how to go about empowering their employees.

In other cases, employees do not want to be empowered, and it can even make them ill. A study carried out by Professor Jia Lin Xie, of University of Toronto's Joseph L. Rotman School of Management, and colleagues found that when people are put in charge at work, but don't have the confidence to handle their responsibilities, they can become ill.[24] Specifically, people who blame themselves when things go wrong are more likely to suffer colds and infections if they have high levels of control at work. This finding by Professor Xie and her colleagues was somewhat unexpected, as some have hypothesized that greater control at work would lead to less stress. The study showed, instead, that it depended on personality and job factors. Those who had control, but did not blame themselves when things went wrong, suffered less stress, even if the job was demanding. The study's findings suggest the importance of choosing carefully when empowering employees.

When employees are empowered, it means that they are expected to act, at least in a small way, as owners of the company, rather than just as employees. Ownership is not necessary in the financial sense, but in terms of identifying with the goals and mission of the organization. For employees to be empowered, however, and to have an ownership mentality, four conditions need to be met, according to Professor Dan Ondrack at the Rotman School of Management: 1) There must be a clear definition of the values and mission of the company; 2) the company must help employees gain the relevant skills; 3) employees need to be supported in their decision making and not criticized when they try to do something extraordinary; and 4) workers need to be recognized for their efforts.[25] Exhibit 7–5 outlines what two researchers discovered in studying the characteristics of empowered workers.

Does empowerment work? Researchers have shown that at both the individual level[26] and the team level,[27] empowerment leads to greater productivity. Vancouver-based Dominion Information Services Inc., which publishes *Superpages* directories in British Columbia, Alberta, Ontario, and Quebec, cut customer complaints by 40 percent in three years by empowering its employees. The company also reduced the time it takes to deal with complaints from 27 days down to 48 hours. Not ready to rest on this accomplishment, however, it aims for same-day complaint resolution. Dominion reports that its employee-empowerment efforts also led to revenues growing by 40 percent over six years and an annual employee turnover that became the lowest in the business at 5.27 percent.[28]

Four US researchers investigated whether empowerment works similarly in different countries.[29] Their findings showed that employees in India gave their supervisors low ratings when empowerment was high, while employees in the United States, Mexico, and Poland rated their supervisors favourably when empowerment was high. In both the United States and Mexico, empowerment had no effect on satisfaction with co-workers. However, satisfaction with co-workers was higher when employees were empowered in Poland. In India, empowerment led to lowered satisfaction with co-workers.

Similar findings in a study comparing empowerment in the United States, Brazil, and Argentina suggest that in hierarchical societies, empowerment may need to be introduced with care.[30] Employees in those

Joseph L. Rotman School of Management, University of Toronto
www.rotman.utoronto.ca

Dominion Information Services Inc.
www.dominioninfo.com

Workers at Redwood Plastics in Langley, BC, have been cross-trained so that they know the jobs that other employees do. This training is part of Redwood Plastics' aim to empower its workers and reach 100-percent on-time delivery.

> **Exhibit 7–5**
>
> ## Characteristics of Empowered People
>
> Robert E. Quinn and Gretchen M. Spreitzer, in their research on the characteristics of empowered people (through both in-depth interviews and survey analysis), found four characteristics that most empowered people have in common:
>
> - Empowered people have a sense of *self-determination* (this means that they are free to choose how to do their work; they are not micromanaged).
>
> - Empowered people have a sense of *meaning* (they feel that their work is important to them; they care about what they are doing).
>
> - Empowered people have a sense of *competence* (this means that they are confident about their ability to do their work well; they know they can perform).
>
> - Empowered people have a sense of *impact* (this means that people believe they can have influence on their work unit; others listen to their ideas).
>
> Source: R.E. Quinn and G.M. Spreitzer, "The Road to Empowerment: Seven Questions Every Leader Should Consider," *Organizational Dynamics*, Autumn 1997, p. 41.

countries may be more used to working in teams, but they also expect their manager to be the person with all the answers.

Our discussion of empowerment suggests that several problems can occur when organizations decide they want to empower employees. First, some managers do not want empowered employees, because this can take away some of their own power base. Second, some employees have little or no interest in being empowered, and therefore resist any attempts to be empowered. And finally, empowerment is not something that works well in every workplace throughout the world.

THE ABUSE OF POWER: HARASSMENT IN THE WORKPLACE

People who engage in harassment in the workplace are typically abusing their power position. Some categories of harassment have long been illegal in Canada, including those based on race, religion, and national origin, as well as sexual harassment. Unfortunately, some types of harassment that occur in the workplace are not deemed illegal, even if they create problems for employees and managers. We focus here on sexual harassment because it is currently the most publicized form of harassment. Yet many of us are also aware, anecdotally, of managers who harass employees, demanding excessive work performance or overtime without pay. And some of the recent stories of workplace violence have reportedly been the result of an employee feeling intimidated at work.

6 How are power and harassment related?

Sexual Harassment

The issue of sexual harassment has received increasing attention by corporations and the media because of the growing ranks of female employees, especially in nontraditional work environments, and because of a number of high-profile cases. For example, the Canadian Armed Forces were subject to intense media scrutiny in 1998 for alleged cover-ups of sexual harassment. A recent survey by York University found that 48 percent of working women in Canada reported they had experienced some form of "gender harassment" in the year before they were surveyed. Barbara Orser, a research affiliate with the Conference Board of Canada, notes that "sexual harassment is more likely to occur in workplace environments that tolerate bullying, intimidation, yelling, innu-

sexual harassment
Unwelcome behaviour of a sexual nature in the workplace that negatively affects the work environment or leads to adverse job-related consequences for the employee.

Supreme Court of Canada
www.scc-csc.gc.ca

endo and other forms of discourteous behaviour."[31] These behaviours indicate one person trying to use power over another.

The Supreme Court of Canada defines **sexual harassment** as unwelcome behaviour of a sexual nature in the workplace that negatively affects the work environment or leads to adverse job-related consequences for the employee. Despite the legal framework for defining sexual harassment, there continues to be disagreement as to what *specifically* constitutes sexual harassment. Sexual harassment includes unwanted physical touching, recurring requests for dates when it is made clear the person isn't interested, and coercive threats that a person will lose her or his job if she or he refuses a sexual proposition. The problems of interpreting sexual harassment often surface around some of its more subtle forms—unwanted looks or comments, off-colour jokes, sexual artifacts such as nude calendars in the workplace, sexual innuendo, or misinterpretations of where the line between "being friendly" ends and "harassment" begins. The *Case Incident* on page 238 illustrates how these problems can make people feel uncomfortable in the workplace. Most studies confirm that the concept of power is central to understanding sexual harassment.[32] This seems to be true whether the harassment comes from a manager, a co-worker, or even an employee.

The manager-employee relationship best characterizes an unequal power relationship, where position power gives the manager the capacity to reward and coerce. Managers give employees their assignments, evaluate their performance, make recommendations for salary adjustments and promotions, and even decide whether employees keep their jobs. These decisions give a manager power. Since employees want favourable performance reviews, salary increases, and the like, it's clear that managers control the resources that most employees consider important and scarce. It's also worth noting that individuals who occupy high-status roles (such as management positions) sometimes believe that sexually harassing employees is merely an extension of their right to make demands on lower-status individuals. Because of power inequities, sexual harassment by one's manager typically creates the greatest difficulty for the person being harassed. If there are no witnesses, it is the manager's word against the employee's word. Are there others whom this manager has harassed, and if so, will they come forward? Because of the manager's control over resources, many of those who are harassed are afraid of speaking out for fear of retaliation by the manager.

Although co-workers do not have position power, they can have influence and use it to sexually harass peers. In fact, although co-workers appear to engage in somewhat less severe forms of harassment than do managers, co-workers are the most frequent perpetrators of sexual harassment in organizations. How do co-workers exercise power? Most often it's by providing or withholding information, cooperation, and support. For example, the effective performance of most jobs requires interaction and support from co-workers. This is especially true nowadays as work is assigned to teams. By threatening to withhold or delay providing information that is necessary for the successful achievement of your work goals, co-workers can exert power over you.

One of the places where there has been a dramatic increase in the number of sexual harassment complaints is at university campuses across Canada, according to Paddy Stamp, sexual harassment officer at the University of Toronto.[33] However, agreement on what constitutes sexual harassment, and how it should be investigated, is no clearer for universities than for industry.

While nonconsensual sex between professors and students is rape and subject to criminal charges, it is harder to evaluate apparently consensual relationships that occur outside the classroom. There is some argument over whether truly consensual sex is ever possible between students and professors. In an effort to underscore the power discrepancy and potential for abuse of it by professors, Yale University recently decided that there could be no sexual relations between students and professors. Most universities have been unwilling to take such a strong stance. However, this issue is certainly one of concern, because the power distance between professors and students is considerable.

In concluding this discussion, we would like to point out that sexual harassment is about power. It's about an individual controlling or threatening another individual. It's wrong. Moreover, it's illegal. You can understand how sexual harassment surfaces in organizations if you analyze it in power terms. We should also point out that sexual harassment is not something done only by men, to women. There have been several cases of males reporting harassment by male managers.[34] While there have been no media reports of women sexually harassing either men or women in Canada, under the framework of the law, it is certainly feasible.

POLITICS: POWER IN ACTION

As the Olympic skating controversy unfolded, both Jacques Rogge, the president of the International Olympic Committee, and Ottavio Cinquanta, the president of the International Skating Union (ISU), paid a lot of attention to what the media said about the event. The event had happened in the United States, and Americans made it clear that they were dismayed when the Canadians lost. As a result, the controversy was discussed on a variety of talk shows and news programs, and in newspapers. This was a way of keeping the controversy alive, and trying to persuade the Olympics head that the decision needed to be changed. Rogge arguably was affected by the pressure, fearing that the negative publicity surrounding the skating controversy was harming the rest of the Olympics. Thus, when he pressured the ISU to reconsider the judges' decision and award an unprecedented second gold medal, it may have had less to do with making the "right" decision, and more to do with making a political decision. So why is politics so prevalent?

Organizational behaviour researchers have learned a lot in recent years about how people gain and use power in organizations. Part of using power in organizations is engaging in organizational politics to influence others to help you achieve your personal objectives. Lobbying others to get them to vote with you on a particular decision is engaging in organizational politics.

7 Why do people engage in politics?

When people get together in groups, power will be exerted. People want to carve out a niche from which to exert influence, to earn rewards, and to advance their careers.[35] When employees in organizations convert their power into action, we describe them as being engaged in politics. Those with good political skills have the ability to use their bases of power effectively.[36] Political skills are not confined to adults, of course. When your Vancouver author's six-year-old nephew wanted Game Boy Color knowing full well his parents did not approve, he waged a careful, deliberate campaign to wear them down, explaining how he would use the toy only at assigned times, etc. His politicking paid off: Within six weeks he succeeded in getting the toy.

Defining Politics

There has been no shortage of definitions for organizational politics. One clever definition of politics comes from Tom Jakobek, Toronto's former budget chief, who said, "In politics, you may have to go from A to C to D to E to F to G and then to B."[37]

For our purposes, we will define **political behaviour** in organizations as those activities that influence, or try to influence, the distribution of advantages and disadvantages within the organization.[38]

This definition encompasses key elements from what most people mean when they talk about organizational politics. Political behaviour is *outside* one's specified job requirements. The behaviour requires some attempt to use one's *power* bases. Our definition also encompasses efforts to influence the goals, criteria, or processes used

political behaviour
Activities that are not required as part of one's formal role in the organization, but that influence, or attempt to influence, the distribution of advantages and disadvantages within the organization.

for decision making when we state that politics is concerned with "the distribution of advantages and disadvantages within the organization." Our definition is broad enough to include such varied political behaviours as whistle-blowing, spreading rumours, withholding key information from decision makers, leaking confidential information about organizational activities to the media, exchanging favours with others in the organization for mutual benefit, and lobbying on behalf of or against a particular individual or decision alternative. Exhibit 7–6 provides a quick measure to help you assess how political your workplace is.

Now that you have learned a bit about political behaviour, you may want to assess your own political behaviour in our *Learning About Yourself Exercise* on page 235.

Political behaviour is not confined to just individual hopes and goals. Politics might also be used to achieve organizational goals. For instance, if a CEO wanted to change the way employees were paid, say from salaries to commissions, this might not be a popular

---

Exhibit 7–6

A Quick Measure of How Political Your Workplace Is

How political is your workplace? Answer the 12 questions using the following scale:

SD = Strongly disagree
D = Disagree
U = Uncertain
A = Agree
SA = Strongly agree

1. Managers often use the selection system to hire only people who can help them in their future. _____

2. The rules and policies concerning promotion and pay are fair; it is how managers carry out the policies that is unfair and self-serving. _____

3. The performance ratings people receive from their managers reflect more of the managers' "own agenda" than the actual performance of the employee. _____

4. Although a lot of what my manager does around here appears to be directed at helping employees, it is actually intended to protect my manager. _____

5. There are cliques or "in-groups" that hinder effectiveness around here. _____

6. My co-workers help themselves, not others. _____

7. I have seen people deliberately distort information requested by others for purposes of personal gain, either by withholding it or by selectively reporting it. _____

8. If co-workers offer to lend some assistance, it is because they expect to get something out of it. _____

9. Favouritism rather than merit determines who gets ahead around here. _____

10. You can usually get what you want around here if you know the right person to ask. _____

11. Overall, the rules and policies concerning promotion and pay are specific and well-defined. _____

12. Pay and promotion policies are generally clearly communicated in this organization. _____

This questionnaire taps the three main dimensions that have been found to be related to perceptions of politics: manager behaviour; co-worker behaviour; and organizational policies and practices. To calculate your score for items 1–10, give yourself 1 point for Strongly disagree; 2 points for Disagree; and so forth (through 5 points for Strongly agree). For items 11 and 12, reverse the score (that is, 1 point for Strongly agree, etc.). Sum up the total: the higher the total score, the greater degree of perceived organizational politics.

Source: G.R. Ferris, D.D. Frink, D.P.S. Bhawuk, J. Zhou, and D.C. Gilmore, "Reactions of Diverse Groups to Politics in the Workplace," *Journal of Management*, 22, no. 1, 1996, pp. 32–33.

choice to employees. While it might make good organizational sense to make this change (perhaps the CEO believes this will increase productivity), simply imposing the change through the use of power ("Go along with this or you're fired!") might not be very popular. Instead, the CEO may try to pitch the reasons for the change to sympathetic managers and employees, trying to get them to understand the necessity for the change. The CEO could even promise rewards for helping convince other employees of the necessity of this change.

The Reality of Politics

Why, you may wonder, must politics exist? Isn't it possible for an organization to be politics-free? It's *possible*, but most unlikely. Organizations are made up of individuals and groups with different values, goals, and interests.[39] This sets up the potential for conflict over resources. The allocation of departmental budgets, space, project responsibilities, and bonuses are the kind of resource issues about which organizational members will disagree.

Resources in organizations are also limited, which often turns potential conflict into real conflict. If resources were abundant, then all the various constituencies within the organization could satisfy their goals. Because they are limited, not everyone's interests can be provided for. Moreover, whether true or not, gains by one individual or group are often *perceived* as being at the expense of others within the organization. These forces create a competition among members for the organization's limited resources. Peter Godsoe, CEO of Toronto-based Scotiabank, demonstrated an awareness of how to get the most resources for whatever unit he headed, while enhancing his own career, as this *OB in the Workplace* shows.

Scotiabank Group
www.scotiabank.com

OB IN THE WORKPLACE

Godsoe Acquires Resources to Rise to the Top

How do you ensure your way to the top? Peter Godsoe was determined to become CEO of Scotiabank. In his quest for this job, he learned how to "outlast and outwit other hopefuls."[40] When he was put in charge of the bank's lending in the United States and Latin America, he made the operation his own by giving it a new name, the Western Hemisphere International Regional Office (WHIRO). While heading WHIRO, he reported to Scott McDonald, who was regarded as a potential successor to then CEO Ced Ritchie. In order to raise his profile, Godsoe built "a loyal following by making WHIRO the hot shop," thus making himself look better than McDonald. Godsoe developed cartoons, WHIRO hero awards, a crest, jackets, and a Latin motto that translated: "If you don't have a hernia, you're not pulling your weight," all with the aim of strengthening his unit's culture and making it more prominent within the bank. After his time at WHIRO, Godsoe had the remarkable knack for getting himself appointed the head of every organizational division created. Eventually, McDonald ended up leaving the bank, while Godsoe replaced Ritchie (but not before he threatened to leave for another job offer).

Maybe the most important factor behind politics within organizations is the realization that most of the "facts" that are used to allocate the limited resources are open to interpretation. What, for instance, is good performance? What is an *adequate* improvement? What constitutes an *unsatisfactory* job? It is in this large and ambiguous middle ground of organizational life—where the facts *don't* speak for themselves—that politics flourish.

Finally, because most decisions must be made in a climate of ambiguity—where facts are rarely fully objective and thus are open to interpretation—people within organizations will use whatever influence they can to taint the facts to support their goals and interests. That, of course, creates the activities we call *politicking*. For more about how one engages in politicking, see *From Concepts to Skills* on pages 240–241.

Therefore, to answer the earlier question of whether it is possible for an organization to be politics-free, we can say "yes"—but only if all members of that organization hold the same goals and interests, organizational resources are not scarce, and performance outcomes are completely clear and objective. However, that does not describe the organizational world that most of us live in! The debate about the importance of politics continues in this chapter's *Point/CounterPoint* on page 234.

Factors Contributing to Political Behaviour

Not all groups or organizations are equally political. In some organizations, for instance, politicking is overt and rampant, while in others, politics plays a small role in influencing outcomes. Why is there this variation? Recent research and observation have identified a number of factors that appear to encourage political behaviour. Some are individual characteristics, derived from the unique qualities of the people the organization employs; others are a result of the organization's culture or internal environment. Exhibit 7–7 illustrates how both individual and organizational factors can increase political behaviour and provide favourable outcomes (increased rewards and averted punishments) for both individuals and groups in the organization. This chapter's *CBC Video Case Incident*, "The Breakdown in Corporate Trust," asks you to consider the role that politics plays in unethical behaviour.

"The Breakdown in Corporate Trust"

Individual Factors

At the individual level, researchers have identified certain personality traits, needs, and other factors that are likely to be related to political behaviour. In terms of traits,

Exhibit 7–7

Factors Influencing Political Behaviour

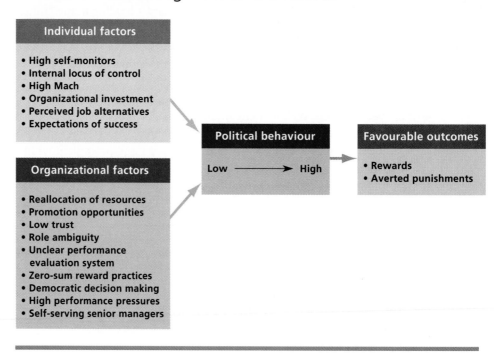

we find that employees who are high self-monitors, who possess an internal locus of control, and who have a high need for power are more likely to engage in political behaviour.[41]

The high self-monitor is more sensitive to social cues, exhibits higher levels of social conformity, and is more likely to be skilled in political behaviour than the low self-monitor. Individuals with an internal locus of control, because they believe they can control their environment, are more prone to take a proactive stance and try to manipulate situations in their favour. You may remember our discussion of machiavellianism in Chapter 2. Not surprisingly, the Machiavellian personality—which is characterized by the will to manipulate and the desire for power—is comfortable using politics as a means to further his or her self-interest. As can be seen in the television show *Survivor*, the participants with Machiavellian tendencies lead the way in self-serving politicking and in plotting the demise of their opponents. You may want to review your Machiavellian score in the *Learning About Yourself Exercise* in Chapter 2 on page 56.

Additionally, an individual's perceived alternatives, expectations of success, and investment in the organization will influence the degree to which he or she will pursue illegitimate means of political action.[42] The more that a person has invested in the organization in terms of expectations of increased future benefits, the more a person has to lose if forced out and the less likely he or she is to use illegitimate means. The more alternative job opportunities an individual has—due to a favourable job market or the possession of scarce skills or knowledge, a prominent reputation, or influential contacts outside the organization—the more likely he or she is to risk illegitimate political actions. Finally, if an individual has a low expectation of success in using illegitimate means, it is unlikely that he or she will try to do so. Those who have high expectations of success in the use of illegitimate means are most likely to be either experienced and powerful individuals with polished political skills or inexperienced and naive employees who misjudge their chances.

Organizational Factors

Political activity is probably linked more to the organization's characteristics than to individuals' traits. Why? Many organizations have a large number of employees with the individual characteristics we listed, yet the extent of political behaviour varies widely.

Although we acknowledge the role that individual differences can play in fostering politicking, the evidence more strongly supports that certain situations and cultures promote politics. More specifically, when an organization's resources are declining, when the existing pattern of resource allocation is changing, and when there is opportunity for promotions, politics is more likely to surface.[43] In addition, cultures characterized by low trust, role ambiguity, unclear performance evaluation systems, democratic decision making, high pressures for performance, a zero-sum (or win-lose) approach to reward allocation, and self-serving senior managers will create breeding grounds for politicking.[44]

When organizations downsize to improve efficiency, resources need to be reduced. Threatened with the loss of resources, people may engage in political actions to safeguard what they have. Any changes, especially those that imply significant reallocation of resources within the organization, are likely to stimulate conflict and increase politicking.

Promotion decisions have consistently been found to be one of the most political arenas in organizations. The opportunity for promotion or advancement encourages people to compete for a limited resource and to try to positively influence the decision outcome.

The less trust there is within the organization, the higher the level of political behaviour and the more likely that the political behaviour will be of the illegitimate kind. High trust should suppress the level of political behaviour in general and inhibit illegitimate actions in particular.

Performance evaluation is far from a perfected science. The more that organizations use subjective criteria in the appraisal, emphasize a single outcome measure, or allow significant time to pass between the time of an action and its appraisal, the greater the likelihood that an employee can get away with politicking. Subjective performance criteria create ambiguity. The use of subjective criteria in figure skating judging may have led to the 2002 Olympic controversy. The International Skating Union has since proposed new judging criteria that are more objectively defined. The new system would also make it difficult for judges to influence each other, since it would be impossible to determine whether a particular judge voted for one's candidate.

The more that an organization's culture emphasizes the zero-sum or win-lose approach to reward allocations, the more employees will be motivated to engage in politicking. The zero-sum approach treats the reward "pie" as fixed, so that any gain one person or group achieves has to come at the expense of another person or group. If I win, you must lose! If $10 000 in annual raises is to be distributed among five employees, then any employee who receives more than $2000 takes money away from one or more of the others. Such a practice encourages making others look bad and increasing the visibility of what you do.

In the past 25 years, there has been a general move in North America and among most developed nations toward making organizations less autocratic. Managers in these organizations are being asked to behave more democratically. They are told that they should allow employees to advise them on decisions and that they should rely more on group input into the decision process. Such moves toward democracy, however, are not necessarily embraced by all individual managers. Many managers sought their positions in order to have legitimate power so as to be able to make unilateral decisions. They fought hard and often paid high personal costs to achieve their influential positions. Sharing their power with others runs directly against their desires. The result is that managers, especially those who began their careers in the 1960s and 1970s, may use the required committees, conferences, and group meetings in a superficial way, as arenas for manoeuvring and manipulating.

The more pressure that employees feel to perform well, the more likely they are to engage in politicking. When people are held strictly accountable for outcomes, this puts great pressure on them to "look good." If a person perceives that his or her entire career is riding on next quarter's sales figures or next month's plant productivity report, there is motivation to do whatever is necessary to ensure that the numbers come out favourably.

President and CEO Aris Kaplanis of Toronto-based high-tech firm Teranet Inc. (shown here at far right with his senior management group) discourages negative office politics by his employees. The company employs the Golden Rule, "Do unto others as you would have others do unto you." He tells his employees, "If you're here to play a game, you're in the wrong business."

Finally, when employees see the people on top engaging in political behaviour, especially when they do so successfully and are rewarded for it, a climate is created that supports politicking. Politicking by top management, in a sense, gives permission to those lower in the organization to play politics by implying that such behaviour is acceptable.

Types of Political Activity

People who work in organizations take part in various political activities. These include attacking or blaming others, controlling information, forming coalitions, networking, creating obligations, and managing impressions.[45] By blaming others, individuals can makes themselves look better, and also possibly harm the credibility of others. We have already identified information as a source of power, but it is also a political tool. People can be left off mailing lists, or not invited to meetings. Thus, not everyone has access to the necessary information. We discussed coalition formation earlier in the chapter.

Networking is a way of building up contacts through social relationships. Networks help individuals gain access to valuable information, and also make it easier for individuals to get help on projects and assignments.

Another way of engaging in political activity can be through the use of favours. When someone does you a favour, often you feel obligated to return a favour at a later time. Thus, the person has created an obligation for you, and you will feel some pressure to respond favourably when you are approached by that person later. Though later cleared, Glen Clark, the former premier of British Columbia, was driven from office over the allegation that he traded favours with a neighbour who was trying to get a casino licence. The neighbour did renovations on Clark's East Vancouver home. Clark claimed repeatedly that he did not view the work done on his house as having any link to helping his neighbour get a casino licence. The neighbour, however, may have felt that the premier had an obligation to help him after providing free labour for his home improvements.

The final type of political activity that we describe is impression management, which we cover in a bit more detail.

Impression Management

We know that people and organizations have an ongoing interest in how others perceive and evaluate them. For example, North Americans spend billions of dollars on diets, health-club memberships, cosmetics, and plastic surgery—all intended to make them more attractive to others.[46] Organizations spend billions convincing people that they are more socially conscious, more ethical, and more concerned with quality than their competitors. You should return to the opening vignette to see if you can identify possible impression management behaviours by the participants in the Olympics story.

Being perceived positively by others should have benefits for people in organizations. It might, for instance, help them initially to get the jobs they want in an organization and, once hired, to get favourable evaluations, superior salary increases, and more rapid promotions. In a political context, it might help sway the distribution of advantages in their favour. For instance, during the figure skating controversy, Jaime Salé and David Pelletier were seen on many different television shows and news conferences, always giving the impression that they were not lobbying for a gold medal after the fact, and presenting an image of clean-cut, soft-spoken individuals. This led to even more sympathy for their plight.

This process by which individuals try to control the impression others form of them is called **impression management** (IM).[47] Impression management is more likely to be used by high self-monitors than low self-monitors.[48] Low self-monitors tend to present images of themselves that are consistent with their personalities, regardless of the beneficial or detrimental effects for them. In contrast, high self-monitors are skilled at reading situations and moulding their appearances and behaviour to fit each situation.

impression management
The process by which individuals try to control the impression others form of them.

Research by Professor Marc-David Seidel at the Sauder School of Business at UBC and his colleagues suggests that impression management is engaged in more frequently by those who spent at least some time telecommuting. These employees felt the need to keep their supervisor more informed about their activities, because they were physically absent.[49]

Given that you want to control the impression others form of you, what techniques could you use? Exhibit 7–8 summarizes some of the more popular IM techniques and provides an example of each.

Keep in mind that IM does not imply that the impressions people convey are necessarily false (although, of course, they sometimes are).[50] Excuses and acclamations, for instance, may be offered with sincerity. Referring to the examples used in Exhibit 7–8, you can *actually* believe that ads contribute little to sales in your region or that you are the key to the tripling of your division's sales. But misrepresentation can have a high cost. If the image claimed is false, you may be discredited.[51] If you "cry wolf"

Exhibit 7–8

Impression Management (IM) Techniques

Conformity

Agreeing with someone else's opinion in order to gain his or her approval.

Example: A manager tells his boss, "You're absolutely right on your reorganization plan for the western regional office. I couldn't agree with you more."

Excuses

Explanations of a predicament-creating event with the aim of minimizing the apparent severity of the predicament.

Example: Sales manager to boss, "We failed to get the ad in the paper on time, but no one responds to those ads anyway."

Apologies

Admitting responsibility for an undesirable event and simultaneously trying to get a pardon for the action.

Example: Employee to boss, "I'm sorry I made a mistake on the report. Please forgive me."

Acclamations

Explanation of favourable events to maximize the desirable implications for oneself.

Example: A salesperson informs a peer, "The sales in our division have nearly tripled since I was hired."

Flattery

Complimenting others on their virtues in an effort to make oneself appear perceptive and likeable.

Example: New sales trainee to peer, "You handled that client's complaint so tactfully! I could never have handled that as well as you did."

Favours

Doing something nice for someone to gain that person's approval.

Example: Salesperson to prospective client, "I've got two tickets to the theatre tonight that I can't use. Take them. Consider it a thank you for taking the time to talk with me."

Association

Enhancing or protecting one's image by managing information about people and things with which one is associated.

Example: A job applicant says to an interviewer, "What a coincidence. Your boss and I were roommates in university."

Sources: Based on B.R. Schlenker, *Impression Management* (Monterey, CA: Brooks/Cole, 1980); W.L. Gardner and M.J. Martinko, "Impression Management in Organizations," *Journal of Management*, June 1988, p. 332; and R.B. Cialdini, "Indirect Tactics of Image Management: Beyond Basking," in R.A. Giacalone and P. Rosenfeld (eds.), *Impression Management in the Organization* (Hillsdale, NJ: Lawrence Erlbaum Associates, 1989), pp. 45–71.

once too often, no one is likely to believe you when the wolf really comes. The impression manager must be cautious not to be perceived as insincere or manipulative.[52]

A number of studies have examined the effectiveness of IM techniques in a variety of work situations. Studies show that IM behaviour is associated positively with job-interview success.[53] For instance, one study found that recent university graduates who used more self-promotion tactics got higher evaluations by interviewers and more follow-up job-site visits, even after adjusting for grade point average, gender, and job type.[54]

Other studies have found that those using IM techniques received better performance evaluations from their managers,[55] were liked more by their managers,[56] and were criticized less.[57] IM effects seem to work more strongly when the measures of performance are subjective, however, than when they can be measured more objectively.[58] For instance, those using IM techniques were rated more highly for interpersonal effectiveness, but they could be evaluated more negatively on their business competence.[59] Overall, the findings of these studies suggest that there is some advantage to engaging in IM, as long as the person delivers on the objective measures of performance as well. And for those who intend to become leaders, engaging in impression management techniques makes it more likely that you will be chosen.[60]

Making Office Politics Work

One thing to be aware of is that extreme office politics can have a negative effect on employees. Researchers have found that organizational politics is associated with less organizational commitment,[61] lower job satisfaction,[62] and decreased job performance.[63] Individuals who experience greater organizational politics are more likely to report higher levels of job anxiety[64] and they are more likely to consider leaving the organization.[65]

Is there an effective way to engage in office politics that is less likely to be disruptive or negative? We discussed different negotiation strategies in Chapter 6, including a *win-lose* strategy, which means that if I win, you lose, and a *win-win* strategy, which means creating situations where both of us can win. *Fast Company*, an online business magazine, identifies several rules that may help you to improve the climate of the organization as you negotiate your way through the office politics maze:[66]

Fast Company Magazine
www.fastcompany.com

- *Nobody wins unless everybody wins.* The most successful proposals look for ways to acknowledge, if not include, the interests of others. This requires building support for your ideas across the organization. "Real political skill isn't about campaign tactics," says Lou DiNatale, a veteran political consultant at the University of Massachusetts. "It's about pulling people toward your ideas and then pushing those ideas through to other people." When ideas are packaged to look as if they are best for the organization as a whole and will help others, it is harder for others to counteract your proposal.

- *Don't just ask for opinions—change them.* It is helpful to find out what people think and then, if necessary, set out to change their opinions so that they can see what you want to do. It is also important to seek out the opinions of those you don't know well, or who are less likely to agree with you. Gathering together people who always support you is often not enough to build an effective coalition.

- *Everyone expects to be paid back.* In organizations, as in life, we develop personal relationships with those around us. And it is those personal relationships that affect much of the behaviour in organizations. By building good relationships with colleagues, supporting them in their endeavours, and showing appreciation for what they accomplish, you are building a foundation of support for your own ideas.

- *Success can create opposition.* As part of the office politics, success can be viewed as a "win-lose" strategy, which we identified above. Some people may feel that your success comes at their expense. So, for instance, your higher profile may mean that a project of theirs will be received less favourably. You have to be prepared to deal with this opposition.

SUMMARY AND IMPLICATIONS

1 **What is power?** Power refers to a capacity that A has to influence the behaviour of B, so that B acts in accordance with A's wishes.

2 **How does one get power?** There are five bases or sources of power: coercive, reward, legitimate, expert, and referent. These forms of power differ in their ability to improve a person's performance. *Coercive power* tends to result in negative performance responses from individuals, decreases satisfaction, increases mistrust, and creates fear. *Legitimate power* does not have a negative effect, but does not generally stimulate employees to improve their attitudes or performance, and it does not generally result in increased commitment. *Reward power* may improve performance, but it can also lead to unethical behaviour. Ironically, the least effective power bases—coercive, legitimate, and reward—are the ones most likely to be used by managers, perhaps because they are the easiest to implement. By contrast, effective leaders use *referent* and/or *expert power*. These forms of power are not derived from the person's position.

3 **How does dependency affect power?** To maximize your power, you will want to increase others' dependence on you. You can, for instance, increase your power in relation to your employer by developing knowledge or a skill that he or she needs and for which there is no ready substitute. However, power is a two-way street. You will not be alone in trying to build your power bases. Others, particularly employees and peers, will be seeking to make you dependent on them. The result is a continual battle. While you try to maximize others' dependence on you, you will be trying to minimize your dependence on others. And, of course, others you work with will be trying to do the same.

4 **What tactics can be used to increase power?** One particular study identified seven tactical dimensions, or strategies, that managers and employees use to increase their power: *reason, friendliness, coalitions, bargaining, assertiveness, higher authority,* and *sanctions.*[67]

5 **What does it mean to be empowered?** Empowerment refers to the freedom and the ability of employees to make decisions and commitments. There is a lot of positive press on empowerment, but much of the talk of empowerment does not result in employees being empowered. Some managers have difficulties letting employees have more power.

6 **How are power and harassment related?** People who engage in harassment in the workplace are typically abusing their power position. Harassment can come in many forms, from gross abuse of power toward anyone of lower rank, to abuse of individuals because of some personal characteristics, such as age, ethnicity, or gender.

7 **Why do people engage in politics?** Part of using power in organizations is engaging in organizational politics to influence others to help you achieve your personal objectives. Whenever people get together in groups, power will be exerted. People want to carve out a niche from which to exert influence, so that they can achieve their goals. When people in organizations convert their power into action, we describe them as being engaged in politics.

OB *AT WORK*

For Review

1. What is power? How do you get it?

2. Contrast power tactics with power bases. What are some of the key contingency variables that determine which tactic a power holder is likely to use?

3. Which of the five power bases lie with the individual? Which are derived from the organization?

4. State the general dependency postulate. What does it mean?

5. What creates dependency? Give an applied example.

6. How are power and politics related?

7. Define political behaviour. Why is politics a fact of life in organizations?

8. What factors contribute to political activity?

9. Define sexual harassment. Who is most likely to harass an employee: a manager, a co-worker, or a subordinate?

For Critical Thinking

1. Based on the information presented in this chapter, if you were a recent university graduate entering a new job, what would you do to maximize your power and accelerate your career progress?

2. "Politics isn't inherently bad. It is merely a way to get things accomplished within organizations." Do you agree or disagree? Defend your position.

3. You are a sales representative for an international software company. After four excellent years, sales in your territory are off 30 percent this year. Describe three impression management techniques you might use to convince your manager that your sales record is better than one could hope under the circumstances.

4. "Sexual harassment should not be tolerated at the workplace." "Workplace romances are a natural occurrence in organizations." Are both of these statements true? Can they be reconciled?

5. Which impression management techniques have you used? What ethical implications, if any, are there in using impression management?

OB for You

- There are a variety of ways to increase your power in an organization. As an example, you could acquire more knowledge about a situation and then use that information to negotiate a bonus with your employer. Even if you don't get the bonus, the knowledge may help you in other ways.

- To increase your power, consider how dependent others are on you. Dependency is affected by your importance, substitutability, and scarcity options. If you have needed skills that no one else has, you will have more power.

- Politics is a skill for individuals to develop. Remembering to take time to join in an office birthday celebration for someone is part of developing the skill of working with others effectively.

POINT

COUNTERPOINT

It's a Political Jungle out There!

It would be nice if all organizations or formal groups within organizations could be described as supportive, harmonious, objective, trusting, collaborative, or cooperative. A nonpolitical perspective can lead one to believe that employees will always behave in ways consistent with the interests of the organization, and that competence and high performance will always be rewarded. In contrast, a political view can explain much of what may seem to be irrational behaviour in organizations. It can help to explain, for instance, why employees withhold information, restrict output, try to "build empires," publicize their successes, hide their failures, distort performance figures to make themselves look better, and engage in similar activities that appear to be at odds with the organization's desire for effectiveness and efficiency.

For those who want tangible evidence that "it's a political jungle out there" in the real world, let's look at two studies. The first analyzed what it takes to get promoted fast in organizations. The second addressed the performance-appraisal process.

Fred Luthans and his associates[68] studied more than 450 managers. They found that these managers engaged in four managerial activities: *traditional management* (decision making, planning, and controlling), *communication* (exchanging routine information and processing paperwork), *human resource management* (motivating, disciplining, managing conflict, staffing, and training), and *networking* (socializing, politicking, and interacting with outsiders). Those managers who were promoted fastest spent 48 percent of their time networking. The average managers spent most of their efforts on traditional management and communication activities, and only 19 percent of their time networking. We suggest that this provides strong evidence of the importance that social and political skills play in getting ahead in organizations.

Longenecker and his associates held in-depth interviews with 60 upper-level executives to find out what went into performance ratings.[69] They found that executives frankly admitted to deliberately manipulating formal appraisals for political purposes. Accuracy was not a primary concern of these executives. Rather, they manipulated the appraisal results in an intentional and systematic manner to get the outcomes they wanted.

Corporate Politics: What You See Is What You Get!

Organizational behaviour currently appears to be undergoing a period of fascination with workplace politics. Is organizational politics inevitable? Maybe not. The existence of politics may be a perceptual interpretation.[70]

A recent study suggests that politics is more myth and interpretation than reality.[71] In this study of 180 experienced managers, 92 men and 88 women completed questionnaires. They analyzed a series of decisions and indicated the degree to which they thought the decisions were influenced by politics. They also completed a measure that assessed political inevitability. This included items such as "Politics is a normal part of any decision making process," and "Politics can have as many helpful outcomes for the organizations as harmful ones." Additionally, the questionnaire asked respondents their beliefs about power and control in the world at large. Finally, respondents provided data on their income, job responsibilities, and years of managerial experience.

The study found that beliefs about politics affected how respondents perceived organizational events. Those managers who held strong beliefs in the inevitability of politics tended to see their own organization and the decision situations in the questionnaire in highly political terms. Managers who viewed the world as posing difficult and complex problems and as being ruled by luck also tended to perceive events as highly politicized. That is, they perceived organizations as part of a disorderly and unpredictable world where politics is inevitable.

Interestingly, not all managers viewed organizations as political jungles. It was typically the inexperienced managers, with lower incomes and more limited responsibilities, who held this view. The researchers concluded that because junior managers often lack clear understandings of how organizations really work, they tend to interpret events as irrational. It's through their attempts to make sense of their situations that these junior managers may come to make political attributions.

So if there is a corporate political jungle, it appears to be mostly in the eyes of the young and inexperienced. More experienced and higher-ranking managers are more likely to see the corporate political jungle as a myth.

How Political Are You?

To determine your political tendencies, please review the following statements. Check the answer that best represents your behaviour or belief, even if that particular behaviour or belief is not present all the time.

	True	False
1. You should make others feel important through an open appreciation of their ideas and work.	_____	_____
2. Because people tend to judge you when they first meet you, always try to make a good first impression.	_____	_____
3. Try to let others do most of the talking, be sympathetic to their problems, and resist telling people that they are totally wrong.	_____	_____
4. Praise the good traits of the people you meet and always give people an opportunity to save face if they are wrong or make a mistake.	_____	_____
5. Spreading false rumours, planting misleading information, and backstabbing are necessary, if somewhat unpleasant, methods to deal with your enemies.	_____	_____
6. Sometimes it is necessary to make promises that you know you will not or cannot keep.	_____	_____
7. It is important to get along with everybody, even with those who are generally recognized as windbags, abrasive, or constant complainers.	_____	_____
8. It is vital to do favours for others so that you can call in these IOUs at times when they will do you the most good.	_____	_____
9. Be willing to compromise, particularly on issues that are minor to you but major to others.	_____	_____
10. On controversial issues, it is important to delay or avoid your involvement if possible.	_____	_____

Scoring Key

According to the author of this instrument, a complete organizational politician will answer "true" to all 10 questions. Organizational politicians with fundamental ethical standards will answer "false" to questions 5 and 6, which deal with deliberate lies and uncharitable behaviour. Individuals who regard manipulation, incomplete disclosure, and self-serving behaviour as unacceptable will answer "false" to all or almost all of the questions.

Source: J.F. Byrnes, "The Political Behavior Inventory." With permission.

BREAKOUT **GROUP** EXERCISES

Form small groups to discuss the following topics, as assigned by your instructor:

1. Describe an incident where you tried to use political behaviour in order to get something you wanted. What tactics did you use?

2. In thinking about the incident described above, were your tactics effective? Why?

3. Describe an incident where you saw someone engaging in politics. What was your reaction to observing the political behaviour? Under what circumstances do you think political behaviour is appropriate?

WORKING WITH **OTHERS** EXERCISE

Understanding Power Bases

Step 1: Your instructor will divide the class into groups of about 5 or 6 (making sure there are at least 5 groups). Each group will be assigned 1 of the following bases of power: (1) coercive, (2) reward, (3) legitimate, (4) expert, and (5) referent. Refer to your text for discussion of these terms.

Step 2: Each group is to develop a role play that highlights the use of the power assigned. The role play should be developed using the following scenario:

You are the leader of a group that is trying to develop a website for a new client. One of your group members, who was assigned the task of researching and analyzing the websites of your client's competition, has twice failed to bring the analysis to scheduled meetings, even though the member knew the assignment was due. Consequently, your group is falling behind in getting the website developed. As leader of the group, you have decided to speak with this team member, and to use your specific brand of power to influence the individual's behaviour.

Step 3: Each group should select 1 person to play the group leader, and another to play the member who has not done the assignment. You have 10 minutes to prepare an influence plan.

Step 4: Each group will conduct its role play. In the event of multiple groups assigned the same power base, 1 of the groups may be asked to volunteer. While you are watching the other groups' role plays, try to put yourself in the place of the person being influenced, to see whether that type of influence would cause you to change your behaviour.

Immediately after each role play, while the next one is being set up, you should pretend that you were the person being influenced, and then record your reaction using the questionnaire below. To do this, take out a sheet of paper and tear it into 5 pieces. At the top of each piece of paper write the type of influence that was used. Then write the letters *A, B, C,* and *D* in a column, and indicate which number on the scale reflects the influence attempt.

Reaction to Influence Questionnaire

For each role play, think of yourself on the receiving end of the influence attempt described, and record your own reaction.

Type of power used _____

A. As a result of the influence attempt, I will...

definitely not comply	1	2	3	4	5	**definitely comply**

B. Any change that does come about will be...

temporary	1	2	3	4	5	**long-lasting**

C. My own personal reaction is...

resistant   1   2   3   4   5   **acceptant**

D. As a result of this influence attempt, my relationship with my group leader will probably be...

worse   1   2   3   4   5   **better**

Step 5: For each influence type, 1 member of each group will take the pieces of paper from group members and calculate the average group score for each of the 4 questions. For efficiency, this should be done while the role plays are being conducted.

Step 6: Your instructor will collect the summaries from each group, and then lead a discussion based on these results.

Step 7: Discussion.

1. Which kind of influence is most likely to immediately result in the desired behaviour?

2. Which will have the most long-lasting effects?

3. What effect will using a particular base of power have on the ongoing relationship?

4. Which form of power will others find most acceptable? Least acceptable? Why?

5. Are there some situations where a particular type of influence strategy might be more effective than others?

This exercise was inspired by one found in Judith R. Gordon, *Organizational Behavior*, 2nd ed. (Englewood Cliffs, NJ: Prentice Hall, 1992), pp. 499–502.

ETHICAL **DILEMMA** EXERCISE

Your manager has just asked you to complete a major project by the end of the week. Given your other commitments for the week, you are not sure you can get the job done. You know that all managers will be turning in performance appraisals of their subordinates in 10 days. You are worried how you will be evaluated if you do not do the assignment.

You also have to turn in evaluations of your subordinates next week. One of your subordinates has just finished a major assignment, and is counting on taking the next few days off, after working seven days a week for three weeks. Should you ask the subordinate to do your manager's project for you? Evaluate your decision with respect to the various bases of power you have available to you.

CASE INCIDENT

Damned if You Do; Damned if You Don't

Fran Gilson has spent 15 years with the Thompson Grocery Company, starting out as a part-time cashier and rising up through the ranks of the grocery store chain.* Today, at 34, she is a regional manager, overseeing seven stores and earning nearly $110 000 a year. About five weeks ago, she was contacted by an executive-search firm inquiring about her interest in the position of vice-president and regional manager for a national drugstore chain. The position would mean responsibility for more than 100 stores in five provinces. After two meetings with top executives at the drugstore chain, she was notified two days ago that she was one of two finalists for the job.

The only person at Thompson who knows this news is Fran's good friend and colleague, Ken Hamilton. Ken is director of finance for the grocery chain. "It's a dream job, with a lot more responsibility," Fran told Ken. "The pay is almost double what I earn here and I'd be their only female vice-president. The job would allow me to be a more visible role model for young women and give me a bigger voice in opening up doors for women and ethnic minorities in retailing management."

Since Fran wanted to keep the fact that she was looking at another job secret, she asked Ken, whom she trusted completely, to be one of her references. He promised to write a great recommendation for her. Fran made it very clear to the recruiter that Ken was the only person at Thompson who knew she was considering another job. She knew that if anyone heard she was talking to another company, it might seriously jeopardize her chances for promotion. It's against this backdrop that this morning's incident became more than just a question of sexual harassment. It became a full-blown ethical and political dilemma for Fran.

Jennifer Chung has been a financial analyst in Ken's department for five months. Fran met Jennifer through Ken and her impression of Jennifer is quite positive. In many ways, Jennifer strikes Fran as a lot like she was 10 years ago. This morning, Jennifer came into Fran's office. It was immediately evident that something was wrong. Jennifer was very nervous and uncomfortable, which was most unlike her. Jennifer said that about a month after she joined Thompson, Ken began making off-colour comments to her when they were alone. And from there the behaviour escalated further. Ken would leer at her, put his arm over her shoulder when they were reviewing reports, even pat her bum. Every time one of these incidents happened, Jennifer would ask him to stop and not do it again, but her requests fell on deaf ears. Yesterday, Ken reminded Jennifer that her six-month probationary review was coming up. "He told me that if I didn't sleep with him that I couldn't expect a very favourable evaluation."

Jennifer said that she had come to Fran because she didn't know what to do or to whom to turn. "I came to you, Fran, because you're a friend of Ken's and the highest-ranking woman here. Will you help me?" Fran had never heard anything like this about Ken before, but neither did she have any reason to suspect that Jennifer was lying.

Questions

1. Analyze Fran's situation in a purely legal sense.

2. Analyze Fran's dilemma in political terms.

3. Analyze Fran's situation in an ethical sense. What is the ethically right thing for her to do? Is that also the politically right thing to do?

4. If you were Fran, what would you do? Why?

---

*The identity of this organization and the people described are disguised for obvious reasons.

CBC 🔵 VIDEO CASE INCIDENT

The Breakdown in Corporate Trust

North American investors have become wary in the 21st century—with good reason. Within the space of a few years, a significant number of business leaders have been disgraced for misusing their power. One of the most spectacular cases involved the collapse of Enron Corp. Its president, Kenneth Lay, stepped down due to securities hearings and FBI investigations into billions of dollars in inflated profits. However, a number of other cases have involved criminal investigations, questions about ethical management principles, and threats of jail terms for what business leaders knew about or allowed to happen in their organizations.

Corel Corporation executives pleaded guilty to insider trading, for example. Nortel Networks ousted its CFO for improper stock trades. US regulators launched an investigation into Bernard Ebbers, former CEO of MCI/WorldCom, in a $12-billion corporate bankruptcy. Former Livent Inc. vice-chair Garth Drabinsky was suspended indefinitely amid allegations of "serious" accounting irregularities.

Investors become alarmed at any suggestion that an organization in which they hold stock is under investigation for accounting irregularities. "When executives break the law," says Linda Thorne, professor of accounting ethics at York University, "they effectively steal from shareholders." Thorne says that people in positions of trust who break the law should have to pay for what they have done.

What has happened to these fallen executives is a matter of learned behaviour, according to Howard Schilit, author and professor at the Wharton School of Business, University of Pennsylvania. High-powered corporate executives are rewarded handsomely for their efforts to turn a profit. Schilit claims that if we want to stop such accounting irregularities, attention must shift to how these individuals are motivated, the unrelenting expectation for high corporate performance, and the generous pay allotted for what they accomplish.

Questions

1. Was political behaviour present in the controversies surrounding Enron, Nortel, Corel, and Worldcom?

2. What sort of individual and corporate factors contribute to some people engaging in politics at the office more than others?

3. In your opinion, is it possible for an individual to climb the corporate ladder and not engage in power politics at the office?

Source: Based on "Public Trust," CBC Venture, June 30, 2002, VA2038A, 834; Worldcom Stock Fraud website, www.worldcomstockfraud.com; H. Schilit, *Financial Shenanigans*, 2nd ed. (New York: McGraw Hill, 2002).

From **Concepts**
to **Skills**

Politicking

Forget, for a moment, the ethics of politicking and any negative impressions you may have of people who engage in organizational politics.[72] If you wanted to be more politically adept in your organization, what could you do? The following eight suggestions are likely to improve your political effectiveness.

1. *Frame arguments in terms of organizational goals.* Effective politicking requires camouflaging your self-interest. No matter that your objective is self-serving; all the arguments you marshal in support of it must be framed in terms of the benefits that the organization will gain. People whose actions appear to blatantly further their own interests at the expense of the organization's are almost universally denounced, are likely to lose influence, and often suffer the ultimate penalty of being expelled from the organization.

2. *Develop the right image.* If you know your organization's culture, you understand what the organization wants and values from its employees—in terms of dress; associates to cultivate, and those to avoid; whether to appear risk-taking or risk-aversive; the preferred leadership style; the importance placed on getting along well with others; and so forth. Then you are equipped to project the appropriate image. Because the assessment of your performance is not a fully objective process, both style and substance must be addressed.

3. *Gain control of organizational resources.* The control of organizational resources that are scarce and important is a source of power. Knowledge and expertise are particularly effective resources to control. They make you more valuable to the organization and, therefore, more likely to gain security, advancement, and a receptive audience for your ideas.

4. *Make yourself appear indispensable.* Because we are dealing with appearances rather than objective facts, you can enhance your power by appearing to be indispensable. That is, you don't have to really be indispensable as long as key people in the organization believe that you are. If the organization's prime decision makers believe there is no ready substitute for what you are giving the organization, they are likely to go to great lengths to ensure that your desires are satisfied.

5. *Be visible.* Because performance evaluation has a substantial subjective component, it's important that your manager and those in power in the organization be made aware of your contribution. If you are fortunate enough to have a job that brings your accomplishments to the attention of others, it may not be necessary to take direct measures to increase your visibility. But your job may require you to handle activities that are low in visibility, or your specific contribution may be indistinguishable because you are part of a team endeavour. In such cases—without appearing to be tooting your own horn or creating the image of a braggart—you'll want to call attention to yourself by highlighting your successes in routine reports, having satisfied customers relay their appreciation to senior executives in your organization, being seen at social functions, being active in your professional associations, developing powerful allies who speak positively about your accomplishments, and similar tactics. Of course, the skilled politician actively and successfully lobbies to get those projects that will increase his or her visibility.

6. *Develop powerful allies.* It helps to have powerful people in your camp. Cultivate contacts with potentially influential people above you, at your own level, and in the lower ranks. They can provide you with important information that may not be available through normal channels. There will be times, too, when decisions will be made in favour of those with the greatest support. Having powerful allies can provide you with a coalition of support if and when you need it.

7. *Avoid "tainted" members.* In almost every organization, there are fringe members whose status is questionable. Their performance and/or loyalty is ▶

suspect. Keep your distance from such individuals. Given the reality that effectiveness has a large subjective component, your own effectiveness might be called into question if you are perceived as being too closely associated with tainted members.

8. *Support your manager*. Your immediate future is in the hands of your current manager. Since he or she evaluates your performance, you will typically want to do whatever is necessary to have your manager on your side. You should make every effort to help your manager succeed, make her look good, support her if she is under siege, and spend the time to find out what criteria she will be using to assess your effectiveness. Do not undermine your manager, and do not speak negatively of her to others.

Assessing Skills

After you have read this chapter, take the following Self-Assessments on your enclosed CD-ROM.

31. How Power-Oriented Am I?

32. What's My Preferred Type of Power?

33. How Well Do I Manage Impressions?

41. How Politically-Oriented Am I?

Practising Skills

You used to be the star marketing manager for Hilton Electronics Corporation. But for the past year, you have been outpaced again and again by Sean, a new manager in the design department who has been accomplishing everything expected of him and more. Meanwhile your best efforts to do your job well have been sabotaged and undercut by Maria—your and Sean's manager. For example, before last year's international consumer electronics show, Maria moved $30 000 from your budget to Sean's. Despite your best efforts, your marketing team could not complete all the marketing materials normally developed to showcase all of your organization's new products at this important industry show. And Maria has chipped away at your staff and budget ever since. Although you have been able to meet most of your goals with less staff and budget, Maria has continued to slice away resources from your group. Just last week, she eliminated two positions in your team of eight marketing specialists to make room for a new designer and some extra equipment for Sean. Maria is clearly taking away your resources while giving Sean whatever he wants and more. You think it's time to do something or soon you will not have any team or resources left. What do you need to do to make sure your division has the resources to survive and grow?

Reinforcing Skills

1. Keep a one-week journal of your behaviour describing incidents when you tried to influence others around you. Assess each incident by asking: Were you successful at these attempts to influence them? Why or why not? What could you have done differently?

2. Outline a specific action plan, based on concepts in this module, that would improve your career progression in the organization in which you currently work or an organization in which you think you would like to be employed.

The Toxic Workplace

It's not unusual to find the following employee behaviours in today's workplace:

> Answering the phone with a "yeah," neglecting to say thank you or please, using voice mail to screen calls, leaving a half cup of coffee behind to avoid having to brew the next pot, standing uninvited but impatiently over the desk of someone engaged in a telephone conversation, dropping trash on the floor and leaving it for the maintenance crew to clean up, and talking loudly on the phone about personal matters.[1]

Some employers or managers fit the following descriptions:

> In the months since [the new owner of the pharmacy] has been in charge [he] has made it clear that he is at liberty to fire employees at will... change their positions, decrease their bonus percentages, and refuse time-off and vacation choices. Furthermore, he has established an authoritarian work structure characterized by distrust, cut-backs on many items deemed essential to work comfort, disrespect, rigidity and poor-to-no-communication.[2]

> He walked all over people. He made fun of them; he intimidated them. He criticized work for no reason, and he changed his plans daily.[3]

What's Happening in Our Workplaces?

Workplaces today are receiving highly critical reviews, being called everything from "uncivil" to "toxic."

Lynne Anderson and Christine Pearson, two management professors from St. Joseph's University and the University of North Carolina respectively, note that "Historians may view the dawn of the twenty-first century as a time of thoughtless acts and rudeness: we tailgate, even in the slow lane; we dial wrong numbers and then slam the receiver on the innocent respondent; we break appointments with nonchalance."[4] The workplace has often been seen as one of the places where civility still ruled, with co-workers treating each other with a mixture of formality and friendliness, distance and politeness. However, with downsizing, re-engineering, budget cuts, pressures for increased productivity, autocratic work environments, and the use of part-time employees, there has been an increase in "uncivil and aggressive workplace behaviours."[5]

What does civility in the workplace mean? A simple definition of workplace civility is behaviour "involving politeness and regard for others in the workplace, within workplace norms for respect."[6] Workplace incivility then "involves acting with disregard for others in the workplace, in violation of workplace norms for respect."[7] Of course, different workplaces will have different norms for what determines mutual respect. For instance, in most restaurants, if the staff were rude to you when you were there for dinner, you would be annoyed, and perhaps even complain to the manager. However, at the Elbow Room Cafe in downtown Vancouver, if customers complain they are in a hurry, manager Patrick

Savoie might well say: "If you're in a hurry, you should have gone to McDonald's."[8] Such a comeback is acceptable to the diners at the Elbow Room Cafe, because rudeness is its trademark.

Most work environments are not expected to be characterized by such rudeness. However, this has been changing in recent years. Robert Warren, a University of Manitoba marketing professor, notes that "simple courtesy has gone by the board."[9]

There is documented evidence of the rise of violence and threats of violence at work,[10] but little research has been done on less extreme forms of negative interaction, such as rudeness, thoughtlessness, and negative gestures.[11] However, several studies have found that there is persistent negative behaviour in the workplace that is not of a violent nature.[12] For instance, a survey of 603 Toronto nurses found that 33 percent had experienced verbal abuse during the five previous days of work.[13]

Another recent study found that 78 percent of employees interviewed think that workplace incivility has increased in the past 10 years.[14] The researchers found that men are mostly to blame for this change: "Although men and women are targets of disrespect and rudeness in equal numbers...men instigate the rudeness 70 percent of the time."[15]

Rude behaviour is not confined to men, however. Professor André Roberge at Laval University suggests that some of the rudeness is generational. He finds that "young clerks often lack both knowledge and civility. Employers are having to train young people in simple manners because that is not being done at home."[16] Professor Warren backs this up: "One of the biggest complaints I hear from businesses when I go to talk about graduates is the lack of interpersonal skills."[17]

Workplace Violence

Recently, researchers have suggested that incivility may be the beginning of more negative behaviours in the workplace, including aggression and violence.[18]

Pierre Lebrun chose a deadly way to exhibit the anger he had stored up from his workplace.[19] He took a hunting rifle to Ottawa-Carleton–based OC Transpo and killed four public transit co-workers on April 6, 1999, before turning the gun on himself. Lebrun felt that he had been the target of harassment by his co-workers for years because of his stuttering. If this sounds like an unusual response for an irate employee, consider the circumstances at OC Transpo. "Quite apart from what's alleged or otherwise with Mr. Lebrun's situation, we know [OC Transpo's] had a very unhappy work environment for a long time," Al Loney, former chair of Ottawa-Carleton's transit commission, noted. A consultant's report produced the year before the shooting found a workplace with "rock-bottom morale and poor management." It was not uncommon for fights to break out in the unit where the four men were killed.

Workplace violence, according to the International Labour Organization (ILO), includes

any incident in which a person is abused, threatened or assaulted in circumstances relating to [his or her] work. These behaviours would originate from customers or co-workers at any level of the organization. This definition would include all forms of harassment, bullying, intimidation, physical threats, assaults, robbery and other intrusive behaviour.[20]

No Canadian statistics on anger at work are available.[21] However, studies show that anger pervades the

US workplace. While 25 percent of Americans reported being "generally at least somewhat angry at work," 49 percent say that they felt "at least 'a little angry' at work."[22] A 2000 Gallup poll conducted in the United States found that 25 percent of the working adults surveyed felt like screaming or shouting because of job stress, 14 percent had considered hitting a co-worker, and 10 percent worry about colleagues becoming violent. This worry is not unfounded. Twenty employees are murdered each week in the United States.[23]

Canadian workplaces are not murder free, however. In 2001, 60 murders occurred at work, 10 percent of all murders for the year.[24] Most of these workplace incidents were carried out by male spouses and partners of female employees. Surprisingly, Canada scores higher than the United States on workplace violence. In a recent ILO study involving 130 000 workers

in 32 countries, Argentina was ranked the most violent. Romania was second, France third, and Canada fourth. The United States placed ninth.[26]

Sixty-four percent of union representatives who were surveyed recently reported an increase in workplace aggression, based on their review of incident reports, grievance files, and other solid evidence.[27] The ILO, in a separate 1998 study, found that, per capita, the rate of assault at work for Canadian women is four times that of American women.[28] To understand the seriousness of this situation, consider that one quarter of Nova Scotia teachers surveyed reported that they faced physical violence at work during the 2001–02 school year.[29]

What Causes Incivility (and Worse) in the Workplace?

If employers and employees are acting with less civility toward each other, what is causing this to happen?

Managers and employees often have different views of the employee's role in the organization. Jeffrey Pfeffer, a professor of OB at Stanford's Graduate School of Business, notes that many companies do not really value their employees: "Most managers, if they're being honest with themselves, will admit it: When they look at their people, they see costs, they see salaries, they see benefits, they see overhead. Very few companies look at their people and see assets."[30]

Most employees, however, like to think that they are assets to their organization. The realization that they are simply costs and not valued members of an organization can cause frustration for employees.

In addition, "employers' excessive demands and top-down style of management are contributing to the rise of 'work rage,'" claims Gerry Smith, of Toronto-based Warren Shepell Consultants.[31] He is the author of the recently released *Work Rage*.[32] He cites demands coming from a variety of sources: "overtime, downsizing, rapid technological changes, company restructuring and difficulty balancing the demands of job and home."[33] Smith worries about the consequences of these demands: "If you push people too hard, set unrealistic expectations and cut back their benefits, they're going to strike back."[34]

Smith's work supports the findings of a recent study that reported the most common cause of anger is the actions of supervisors or managers.[35] Other common causes of anger identified by the researchers include lack of productivity by co-workers and others; tight deadlines; heavy workload; interaction with the public; and bad treatment.

The Pyschological Contract

Some researchers have looked at this frustration in terms of a breakdown of the psychological contract formed between employees and employers. Employers and employees begin to develop psychological contracts as they are first introduced to each other in the hiring process.[36] These continue over time as the employer and the employee come to understand each other's expectations about the amounts and quality of work to be performed and the types of rewards to be given. For instance, when an employee is continually asked to work late and/or be available at all hours through pagers and email, the employee may assume that doing so will result in greater rewards or faster promotion down the line. The employer may have had no such intention, and may even be thinking that the employee should be grateful simply to have a job. Later, when the employee does not get expected (though never promised) rewards, he or she is disappointed.

Sandra Robinson, an OB professor at the University of British Columbia, and her colleagues have found that when a psychological contract is violated (perceptually or actually), the relationship between the employee and the employer is damaged. This can result in the loss of trust.[37] The breakdown in trust can cause employees to be less ready to accept decisions or obey rules.[38] The erosion of the trust can also lead employees to take revenge on the employer. So they don't carry out their end of a task. Or they refuse to pass on messages. They engage in any number of subtle and not-so-subtle behaviours that affect the way work gets done—or prevents work from getting done.

The Toxic Organization

Jeffrey Pfeffer of Stanford suggests that companies have become "toxic places to work."[39] He notes that companies, particularly in Silicon Valley, ask their employees to sign contracts on the first day of work indicating the employee's understanding that the company has the right to fire at will and for any reason. Some employers also ask their employees to choose between having a life and having a career. Pfeffer relates a joke people used to tell about Microsoft: "We offer flexible time—you can work any 18 hours you want."[40] This kind of attitude can be toxic to employees, though this does not imply that Microsoft is a toxic employer.

What does it mean to be a toxic organization? UBC Professor Peter Frost notes that there will always be pain in organizations, but that sometimes it becomes so intense or pro-

longed that conditions within the organization begin to break down. In other words, the situation becomes toxic. This is not dissimilar to what the liver or kidneys do when toxins become too intense in a human body.[41]

What causes organizations to be toxic? Like Pfeffer, UBC's Peter Frost and Sandra Robinson (both at the Sauder School of Business) identify a number of factors. Downsizing and organizational change are two main factors, particularly in recent years. Sometimes organizations experience unexpected events—such as the sudden death of a key manager, an unwise move by senior management, strong competition from a start-up company—that lead to toxicity. Other organizations are toxic throughout their system due to policies and practices that create distress. Such factors as unreasonable stretch goals or performance targets, or unrelenting internal competition, can create toxicity. There are also toxic managers

Do You Have a Toxic Manager?

Below are some of the toxic behaviours of managers and the workplace cultures that allow these behaviours to thrive.

Managerial Toxic Behaviour	**Workplace Culture That Fosters This Behaviour**
Actor Behaviour. These managers act out anger rather than discuss problems. They slam doors, sulk, and make it clear they are angry, but refuse to talk about it.	*Macho Culture.* People don't discuss problems. The emphasis is to "take it like a man."
Fragmentor Behaviour. These managers see no connection between what they do and the outcome, and take no responsibility for their behaviour.	*Specialist Culture.* Employees who are technically gifted or great in their fields don't have to consider how their behaviour or work impacts anyone.
Me-First Behaviour. These managers make decisions based on their own convenience.	*Elitist Culture.* Promotes and rewards not according to work but to who your buddies are.
Mixed-Messenger Behaviour. These managers present themselves one way, but their behaviour doesn't match what they say.	*Office-Politics Culture.* Promotes and rewards based on flattery and positioning.
Wooden-Stick Behaviour. These managers are extremely rigid and controlling.	*Change-Resistant Culture.* Upper management struggles to maintain the status quo regardless of the outcome.
Escape-Artist Behaviour. These managers don't deal with reality, often lying, or at the extreme, escaping through drugs or alcohol.	*Workaholic Culture.* Forces employees to spend more time at the office than necessary.

Source: L. McClure, *Risky Business* (Binghamton, NY: Haworth Press, 1996).

How Toxin Handlers Alleviate Organizational Pain

- They listen empathically
- They suggest solutions
- They work behind the scenes to prevent pain
- They carry the confidences of others
- They reframe difficult messages

Source: P. Frost and S. Robinson, "The Toxic Handler: Organizational Hero—and Casualty," *Harvard Business Review*, July–August 1999, p. 101 (Reprint 99406).

who lead through insensitivity, vindictiveness, and failure to take responsibility, or they are control freaks or are unethical. The inset *Do You Have a Toxic Manager?* lists some types of toxic managers and the cultures that inspire their behaviour.

What Are the Effects of Incivility and Toxicity in the Workplace?

In general, researchers have found that the effects of workplace anger are sometimes subtle: a hostile work environment and the tendency to do only enough work to get by.[42]

Those who feel chronic anger in the workplace are more likely to report "feelings of betrayal by the organization, decreased feelings of loyalty, a decreased sense that respondent values and the organization's values are similar, a decreased sense that the employer treated the respondent with dignity and respect, and a decreased sense that employers had fulfilled promises made to respondents."[43] So do these feelings make a difference? Apparently so. Researchers have found that those who felt angry with their employers were less likely to put forth their best effort, more likely to be competitive toward other employees, and less likely to suggest "a quicker and better

way to do their job."[44] All of these actions tend to decrease the productivity possible in the workplace.

It is not just those who work for an organization who are affected by incivility and toxicity. Poor service, from indifference to rudeness to outright hostility, characterizes many transactions in Canadian businesses. "Across the country, better business bureaus, provincial government consumer-help agencies and media ombudsmen report a lengthening litany of complaints about contractors, car dealers, repair shops, moving companies, airlines and department stores."[45] This suggests that customers and clients may well be feeling the impact of internal workplace dynamics.

The Toxin Handler

Employees of toxic organizations suffer pain from their experiences in a toxic environment. In some organizations, mechanisms, often informal,

are set up to deal with the results of toxicity.

Frost and Robinson identified a special role that some employees play in trying to relieve the toxicity within an organization: the toxin handler. This person tries to mitigate the pain by softening the blow of downsizing, or change, or the behaviour of the toxic leader. Essentially the toxin handler helps others around him or her deal with the strains of the organization, by counselling, advising, shielding employees from the wrath of angry managers, reinterpreting the managers' messages to make them less harsh, etc.

So who takes on this role? Certainly no organization to date has a line on its organizational chart for "the toxin handler." Often the role emerges as part of an individual's position in an organization, for instance, a manager in the human resources department. In many cases, however, handlers are pulled into the role "bit by bit—by their colleagues, who turn to them because they are trustworthy, calm, kind and nonjudgmental."[46]

Frost and Robinson, in profiling these individuals, suggest that toxin handlers are predisposed to say yes, have a high tolerance for pain, a surplus of empathy, and when they notice people in pain, they have a need to make the situation right. But these are not individuals who thrive simply on dealing with the emotional needs of others. Quoting one of the managers in their study, Frost

FACEOFF

Manners are an over-romanticized concept. The big issue isn't that employees need to be concerned about their manners. Rather employers should be paying better wages.

The Golden Rule, "Do unto others as you would have others do unto you," should still have a role in today's workplace. Being nice pays off.

and Robinson cite the full range of activities of most toxin handlers: "These people are usually relentless in their drive to accomplish organizational targets and rarely lose focus on business issues. Managing emotional pain is one of their means."[47]

The inset *How Toxin Handlers Alleviate Organizational Pain* identifies the many tasks that toxin handlers take on in an organization. Frost and Robinson suggest that these tasks will probably need to be handled forever, and they recommend that organizations take steps to actively support people performing this role.

Research Exercises

1. Look for data on violence and anger in the workplace in other countries. How do these data compare with the Canadian and American data presented here? What might you conclude about how violence and anger in the workplace are expressed in different cultures?

2. Identify 3 Canadian organizations that are trying to foster better and/or less toxic environments for their employees. What kind of effect is this having on the organizations' bottom lines?

Your Perspective

1. Is it reasonable to suggest, as some researchers have, that young people today have not learned to be civil to others, or do not place a high priority on doing so? Do you see this as one of the causes of incivility in the workplace?

2. What should be done about managers who create toxicity in the workplace while being rewarded because they achieve bottom-line results? Should bottom-line results justify their behaviour?

Want to Know More?

If you would like to read more on this topic, see Peter Frost, *Toxic Emotions at Work* (Cambridge, MA: Harvard Business School Press, 2003); P. Frost and S. Robinson, "The Toxic Handler: Organizational Hero—and Casualty," *Harvard Business Review*, July–August 1999, pp. 96–106 (Reprint 99406); and A.M. Webber, "Danger: Toxic Company," *Fast Company*, November 1998, pp. 152–157. You can find the latter article at http://www.fastcompany.com/online/19/toxic.html. It contains an interview with Jeffrey Pfeffer, professor of organizational behaviour at Stanford University, who discusses examples of toxic organizations.

CHAPTER 8

Leadership

What is the difference
between a manager
and a leader?

1

What are some
of the hot topics
in leadership?

6

Are there specific traits,
behaviours, and situations
that affect how one leads?

2

What questions arise
when a very successful father is
replaced by his daughter to head
Canada's largest independent auto
parts manufacturer? Belinda
Stronach heard them all.

What is
self-leadership?

5

3 How does a
leader lead
with vision?

4

Can a person be an
informal leader?

When Belinda Stronach took over as CEO of Aurora, Ontario-based Magna International in February 2001, she was stepping into the shoes of her father, Frank Stronach, who had started the company more than 45 years before.[1] While it is not uncommon for shareholders to question the ability of a new CEO, in Belinda's case many wondered if she was appointed simply because she was her father's daughter. She reacted to her critics by acknowledging that "I have to go that extra step in terms of proving myself." Belinda Stronach did not come to power at an optimal time: The auto industry was in a slump, and she was better known as a socialite than as an auto parts executive. She had little training or background in design, engineering, or assembly, all viewed as key characteristics for someone taking on such an important role.

As the transition from Frank to Belinda Stronach shows, most believe that leaders do make a difference. In this chapter, we examine the various studies on leadership to determine what makes an effective leader. We first consider the traits, behaviours, and situations that affect one's ability to lead, and then we consider visionary leadership. We then look at how leadership is being spread throughout the organization, with more demands for everyone to take on leadership responsibilities. Then we consider how you might lead yourself, through self-management. As we

will see, leading is no longer just for supervisors and CEOs. Thus, learning about leadership helps you relate better to different leadership styles and enables you to take on the role of leader if necessary. Finally, we consider such contemporary issues as the moral dimension of leadership. We begin this exploration by looking at the differences between managers and leaders.

ARE MANAGERS AND LEADERS THE SAME?

Leadership and management are two terms that are often confused. What is the difference between them?

1 What is the difference between a manager and a leader?

John Kotter of the Harvard Business School argues that "managers promote stability while leaders press for change and only organizations that embrace both sides of the contradiction can survive in turbulent times."[2]

Professor Rabindra Kanungo at McGill University sees a growing consensus emerging "among management scholars that the concept of 'leadership' must be distinguished from the concept of 'supervision/management.'"[3] Exhibit 8–1 illustrates Kanungo's distinctions between management and leadership. Leaders provide vision and strategy; managers implement that vision and strategy, coordinate and staff the organization, and handle day-to-day problems.

In developing our discussion of leadership below, we focus on two major tasks of those who lead in organizations: managing those around them to get the day-to-day tasks done (leadership as supervision) and inspiring others to do the extraordinary (leadership as vision).

Exhibit 8–1

Distinguishing Leadership From Managership

Managership	Leadership
1. Engages in day-to-day caretaker activities: Maintains and allocates resources	Formulates long-term objectives for reforming the system: Plans strategy and tactics
2. Exhibits supervisory behaviour: Acts to make others maintain standard job behaviour	Exhibits leading behaviour: Acts to bring about change in others congruent with long-term objectives
3. Administers subsystems within organizations	Innovates for the entire organization
4. Asks how and when to engage in standard practice	Asks what and why to change standard practice
5. Acts within established culture of the organization	Creates vision and meaning for the organization
6. Uses transactional influence: Induces compliance in manifest behaviour using rewards, sanctions, and formal authority	Uses transformational influence: Induces change in values, attitudes, and behaviour using personal examples and expertise
7. Relies on control strategies to get things done by subordinates	Uses empowering strategies to make followers internalize values
8. Status Quo supporter and stabilizer	Status Quo challenger and change creator

Source: R.N. Kanungo, "Leadership in Organizations: Looking Ahead to the 21st Century," *Canadian Psychology*, 39, no. 1–2, 1998, p. 77.

LEADERSHIP AS SUPERVISION

When Belinda Stronach took over as CEO of Magna International, she was doing so as a leader, not as a supervisor. Her job is to set the vision of the organization. Still, some of the questions raised and comments made as she took over reflected concerns over what it takes to be in charge. She was compared to her father, and many noted that she was not as charismatic as him, but that she was also more people-oriented than him. The way that she came to power was different too: Her father had started Magna, and some questioned whether she was appointed CEO simply because she was his daughter. She has less operating experience than her father, as her previous work experience was largely confined to handling human resource issues at Magna, and engaging in philanthropic activities. These are very different situations than being at the top of a major automotive parts company. Will these differences in style between Frank and Belinda Stronach have an impact on the company's fortunes?

2 Are there specific traits, behaviours, and situations that affect how one leads?

Belinda Stronach and Frank Stronach

www.magnaint.com/magnaweb. nsf/webpages/news&media/

In this section we discuss theories of leadership that were developed before about 1980. These theories focused on the supervisory nature of leadership—that is, how leaders managed the day-to-day functioning of employees. The theories took different approaches in understanding how best to lead in a supervisory capacity, and three general themes emerged: 1) Is there a particular set of traits that all leaders have, making them different from nonleaders? 2) Are there particular behaviours that make for better leaders? 3) How much impact does the situation have on leaders? When you think about these theories, remember that, although they have been considered "theories of leadership," they rely on an older understanding of what "leadership" means, and they do not convey Kanungo's distinction between leadership and supervision. As you read through these theories you may also want to consider how they apply to the leadership of Mogens Smed, the subject of the *Case Incident* on pages 278–279.

Trait Theory: Are Leaders Different From Others?

Have you ever wondered whether there is some fundamental personality difference that makes some people "born leaders"? The dominant research on leadership up until the 1940s was the trait approach, where researchers looked to find universal personality traits that leaders were more likely to have than nonleaders.[4] Trait theory was also revisited for a time in the late 1980s.[5] Trait theory emerged in the hope that if it were possible to identify the traits of leaders, it would be easier to select people to fill leadership roles.

The media have long been believers in **trait theories of leadership**. They identify people such as Nelson Mandela, Richard Branson of Virgin, and Steve Jobs of Apple as leaders, and then describe them in terms such as *charismatic, enthusiastic, decisive*, and *courageous*. The media are not alone. The search for personality, social, physical, or intellectual attributes that would describe leaders and differentiate them from nonleaders goes back to research done by psychologists in the 1930s.

Until recently, research efforts at isolating leadership traits resulted in a number of dead ends.[6] The bulk of the studies considered one of three categories of traits: "physical traits, such as physique, height, and appearance; abilities, such as intelligence and fluency of speech; and personality characteristics, such as conservatism, introversion-extroversion, and self-confidence."[7] It is still the case that researchers have not found a set of traits that would always differentiate leaders from followers and effective from ineffective leaders. However, six traits have been identified that are consistently associated with leadership: 1) ambition and energy, 2) the desire to lead, 3) honesty and integrity, 4) self-confidence, 5) intelligence, and 6) job-relevant knowledge.[8] Recent research also provides strong evidence that people who are high self-monitors—that is, are highly flexible in adjusting their behaviour in different situations—are much more likely to emerge as leaders in groups than low self-monitors.[9] Overall, the cumulative findings from more than half a century of research lead us to conclude that some traits increase the likelihood of success as a leader, but none of the traits guarantees success.[10] Exhibit 8–2 shows the findings of a recent survey of 200 CEOs, and what they cited as the most

trait theories of leadership
Theories that sought personality, social, physical, or intellectual traits that differentiated leaders from nonleaders.

Nelson Mandela
www.anc.org.za/people/
mandela.html

Richard Branson, Virgin Group
www.virgin.com/aboutus/
autobiography/

Steve Jobs, Apple Computer
www.apple.com/pr/bios/
jobs.html

Exhibit 8–2

What CEOs Identify as Key Leadership Qualities

Quality	CEOs Rating It Most Important (%)
Communication Skills	52
Ability to Motivate People	47
Honesty	34
Ability to Listen	25
Team-Building Expertise	24
Analytical Skills	19
Aggressiveness in Business	10

Source: Survey conducted by American Express for the National Quality Institute. Reported in R. Nutt, "Survey Finds Leadership Key," *The Vancouver Sun*, June 1, 2000, p. D6.

important leadership qualities. Both Frank and Belinda Stronach score high on many of the traits needed to be a leader.

Emotional Intelligence and Leadership

Daniel Goleman
www.eiconsortium.org/
members/goleman.htm

While trait theories in general have failed to identify what makes good leaders, recent studies indicate that emotional intelligence (EI) is a better predictor than IQ, expertise, or any other single factor of who will emerge as a leader.[11] Daniel Goleman has written a number of books and articles in this area, and his latest book, *Primal Leadership*,[12] continues to argue that effective leadership needs people who are aware and in control of their emotions. He and his co-authors suggest that employees benefit most from leaders who show positive emotion and enthusiasm, and that fear and repression are harmful in the workplace. "Leaders who freely vent their anger, catastrophize or otherwise let their distressing emotions run amok can't also lead the group into a positive register, where the best work gets done," the authors say.

The work on EI suggests that leaders need more than the basic traits of intelligence and job-relevant knowledge.[13] It's the possession of the five components of emotional intelligence—self-awareness, self-management, self-motivation, empathy, and social skills—that allows an individual to become a star performer. Without EI, a person can have outstanding training, a highly analytical mind, a long-term vision, and an endless supply of terrific ideas, but still not make a great leader. This is especially true as individuals move up in an organization. The evidence indicates that the higher the rank of a person considered to be a star performer, the more that EI capabilities surface as the reason for his or her effectiveness. Specifically, when star performers were compared with average ones in senior management positions, nearly 90 percent of the difference in their effectiveness was the result of EI factors rather than basic intelligence.

EI has been shown to be positively related to job performance at all levels. But it appears to be especially relevant in jobs that demand a high degree of social interaction. And, of course, that is what leadership is all about. Great leaders demonstrate their EI by exhibiting all five of its key components.

The recent evidence makes a strong case for concluding that EI is an essential element in leadership effectiveness. As such, it should probably be added to our earlier list of traits associated with leadership.

Behavioural Theories: Do Leaders Behave in Particular Ways?

Limited success in the study of traits led researchers to look at the behaviours that specific leaders exhibit. They wondered if there was something unique in the way that effective leaders behave. Trait theory, had it been successful, would have provided a basis for selecting the "right" people to assume formal positions in groups and organizations requiring leadership. In contrast, behavioural theories tried to identify critical behavioural determinants of leadership, in the hope that we could train people to be leaders.

behavioural theories of leadership
Theories proposing that specific behaviours differentiate leaders from nonleaders.

The three most well-known **behavioural theories of leadership** are the Ohio State University studies that started in the late 1940s, the University of Michigan studies conducted at about the same time, and Blake and Mouton's Leadership Grid, which reflects the behavioural definitions of both the Ohio and Michigan studies. All three approaches consider two main dimensions by which managers can be characterized: attention to production and attention to people.

initiating structure
The extent to which a leader is likely to define and structure his or her role and those of employees in the search for goal attainment.

The Ohio State Studies

In the Ohio State studies, these two dimensions are known as *initiating structure* and *consideration*.[14] **Initiating structure** refers to the extent to which a leader is likely to define and structure his or her role and those of employees in the search for goal attainment, and includes behaviour that tries to organize work, work relationships, and goals. **Consideration** is described as the extent to which a person is likely to have job relationships that are characterized by mutual trust, respect for employees' ideas, and regard for their feelings. He or she shows concern for followers' comfort, well-being, status, and satisfaction.

The Michigan Studies

The Michigan group also developed two dimensions of leadership behaviour that they labelled *employee-oriented* and *production-oriented*.[15] **Employee-oriented leaders** were described as emphasizing interpersonal relations. They took a personal interest in the needs of their subordinates and accepted individual differences among members. The **production-oriented leaders**, in contrast, tended to emphasize the technical or task aspects of the job. Their main concern was in accomplishing their group's tasks, and the group members were a means to that end.

The Leadership Grid

A graphic portrayal of a two-dimensional view of leadership style was developed by Blake and Mouton.[16] They proposed a "Managerial Grid" (now called a **Leadership Grid**)[17] based on the styles of "concern for people" and "concern for production," which essentially represent the Ohio State dimensions of consideration and initiating structure, or the Michigan dimensions of employee orientation and production orientation.

The grid, shown in Exhibit 8–3, has 9 possible positions along each axis, creating 81 different positions in which the leader's style may fall. The grid shows the main factors in a leader's thinking with respect to how to get results from employees.

Empirical Findings for Behavioural Theories

Each of the three behavioural approaches received some empirical support for the idea that being people-oriented was an important behaviour of leaders, although there were also exceptions in each case. In the Ohio studies, leaders who were production-oriented (i.e., high on initiating structure) experienced greater rates of grievances, absenteeism, and turnover, and lower levels of job satisfaction from employees performing routine tasks. In the Michigan studies, employee-oriented leaders were associated with higher group productivity and higher job satisfaction. Production-oriented leaders tended to be associated with low group productivity and lower job satisfaction.

The results based on the findings of Blake and Mouton are consistent with those of the Ohio and Michigan studies. Managers were found to perform best under a 9,9 (team management style), as contrasted, for example, with a 9,1 (authority-obedience) or 1,9 (country club) style.[18] However, there is little substantive evidence to support the conclusion that a 9,9 style is most effective in all situations.[19]

While the results of the behavioural studies have been somewhat mixed,[20] a careful evaluation of the situations that leaders face provides insights into when leaders should be production-oriented, and when they should be people-oriented.[21]

- When subordinates experience a lot of pressure because of deadlines or unclear tasks, leaders who are people-oriented will increase satisfaction and performance.

- When the task is interesting or satisfying, there is less need for people orientation.

- When it is clear how to perform the task, and what the goals are, people orientation will lead to greater satisfaction, while task orientation will lead to dissatisfaction.

- When people do not know what to do, or individuals do not have the knowledge or skills to do the job, production orientation is much more important than people orientation.

---

consideration
The extent to which a leader is likely to have job relationships characterized by mutual trust, respect for employees' ideas, and regard for their feelings.

employee-oriented leader
A leader who emphasizes interpersonal relations.

production-oriented leader
A leader who emphasizes technical or task aspects of the job.

Leadership Grid
A 9-by-9 matrix outlining 81 different leadership styles based on one's task orientation and people orientation.

Exhibit 8–3

The Leadership Grid

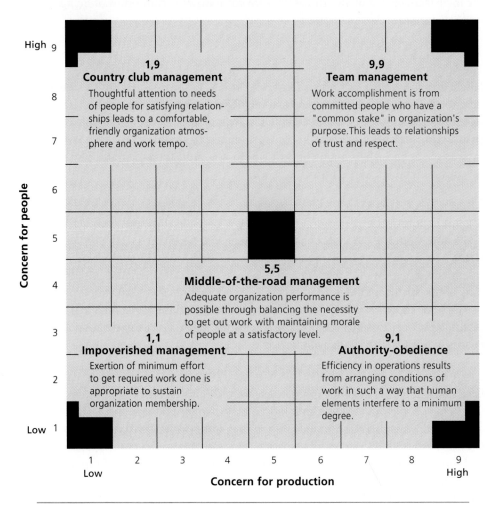

Source: Reprinted by permission of *Harvard Business Review*: An exhibit from "Breakthrough in Organization Development" by R.R. Blake, J.S. Mouton, L.B. Barnes, and L.E. Greiner (November–December 1964). Copyright © 1964 by the President and Fellows of Harvard College; all rights reserved.

Contingency Theories: Considering the Situation

It became increasingly clear to those who were studying the leadership phenomenon that predicting leadership success was more complex than simply isolating a few traits or preferable behaviours. Starting in the 1960s, leadership theories began to examine the situational factors that affect the leader's ability to act. To understand the role of situation, consider changes that occurred at Eaton's before it finally failed. For the first 127 years of Eaton's existence, members of the Eaton family provided the leadership. However, by the late 1980s the leadership style that had kept Eaton's so successful for much of the century no longer worked. Even a change in leadership in 1997 did nothing to halt the fall of a once-great Canadian institution. In other words, the situation for Eaton's had changed, with consumers less interested in what Eaton's had to sell, and the once-successful leadership no longer worked. Unfortunately, the behavioural approaches do not recognize the impact that situations have on one's ability to lead. As we recall from the description of Frank and Belinda Stronach, the style that Frank would have used to lead when he started his company would have been different than what was needed by the time Belinda took over 45 years later.

Chronology of Eaton's chain

www.cbc.ca/news/features/ eatons_timeline.html

The relationship between leadership style and effectiveness suggests that that there is no one right style, but that style depends upon the condition the leader faces.

There has been no shortage of studies trying to isolate critical situational factors that affect leadership effectiveness. The volume is illustrated by the number of moderating variables that researchers have identified in their discussions of **situational, or contingency, theories**. These variables include the degree of structure in the task being performed, the quality of leader-member relations, the leader's position power, group norms, information availability, employee acceptance of leader's decisions, employee maturity, and the clarity of the employees' role.[22]

We consider four situational theories below: the Fiedler contingency model, Hersey and Blanchard's situational theory, the path-goal theory, and substitutes for leadership. This chapter's *CBC Video Case Incident*, "Who's Got the Power?" illustrates how Jean Monty's fortunes changed with the situation at Montreal-based BCE, Inc.

Fiedler Contingency Model

The first comprehensive contingency model for leadership was developed by Fred Fiedler.[23] The **Fiedler contingency model** proposes that effective group performance depends on the proper match between the leader's style and the degree to which the situation gives control to the leader.

Fiedler created the *least preferred co-worker (LPC) questionnaire* to determine whether individuals were mainly interested in good personal relations with co-workers, and thus *relationship-oriented*, or mainly interested in productivity, and thus *task-oriented*. Fiedler assumed that an individual's leadership style is fixed. Therefore, if a situation requires a task-oriented leader and the person in that leadership position is relationship-oriented, either the situation has to be modified or the leader must be removed and replaced for optimum effectiveness to be achieved.

Fiedler identified three contingency dimensions that together define the situation a leader faces:

- *Leader-member relations*. The degree of confidence, trust, and respect members have in their leader.

- *Task structure*. The degree to which the job assignments are procedurized (i.e., structured or unstructured).

- *Position power*. The degree of influence a leader has over power variables such as hiring, firing, discipline, promotions, and salary increases.

Fiedler stated that the better the leader-member relations, the more highly structured the job, and the stronger the position power, the more control the leader has. He suggested that task-oriented leaders perform best in situations of high and low control, while relationship-oriented leaders perform best in moderate control situations.[24] In a high-control situation, a leader can "get away" with task orientation, because the relationships are good, and followers are easily influenced.[25] In a low-control situation (which is characterized by poor relations, ill-defined task, and low influence), task orientation may be the only thing that makes it possible to get something done. In moderate-control situations, being relationship-oriented may smooth the way to getting things done.

Hersey and Blanchard's Situational Theory

Paul Hersey and Ken Blanchard have developed a leadership model that has gained a strong following among management development specialists.[26] This model, called **situational leadership theory (SLT)**, has been included in leadership training programs at more than 400 of the Fortune 500 companies; and more than one million managers a year from a wide variety of organizations are being taught its basic elements.[27]

situational, or contingency, theories
Theories that note the importance of considering the context within which leadership occurs.

"Who's Got the Power?"

Fiedler contingency model
Model proposing that effective group performance depends on the proper match between the leader's style and the degree to which the situation gives control to the leader.

Fred Fiedler Contingency Model
www.eou.edu/~blarison/321afied.html

situational leadership theory (SLT)
Theory that basically views the leader-follower relationship as similar to that between a parent and a child.

Paul Hersey & Ken Blanchard situational leadership theory
www.odportal.com/sitlead/links.htm

SLT basically views the leader-follower relationship as similar to that between a parent and child. Just as a parent needs to give up control as a child becomes more mature and responsible, so too should leaders. Hersey and Blanchard identify four specific leader behaviours, from highly directive to highly laissez-faire. The most effective behaviour depends on a follower's ability and motivation. This is illustrated in Exhibit 8–4. SLT says that if a follower is *unable and unwilling* to do a task, the leader needs to give clear and specific directions (in other words, be highly directive). If a follower is *unable but willing*, the leader needs to display high task orientation to compensate for the follower's lack of ability, and high relationship orientation to get the follower to "buy into" the leader's desires (in other words, "sell" the task). If the follower is *able but unwilling*, the leader needs to use a supportive and participative style. Finally, if the employee is both *able and willing*, the leader does not need to do much (in other words, a laissez-faire approach will work).

Both the Fiedler model and Hersey and Blanchard's situational theory have some intuitive appeal. However, both have received far less empirical support, and Fiedler's theory has been found to be more difficult to apply in the work situation than the next theory we consider, the path-goal model.[28]

Path-Goal Theory

path-goal theory
The theory that a leader's behaviour is acceptable to employees insofar as they view it as a source of either immediate or future satisfaction.

 Martin Evans & Robert House path-goal theory
www.ee.uwa.edu.au/~ccroft/em333/lecm.html

Currently, one of the most respected approaches to leadership is the **path-goal theory**. Developed by University of Toronto Professor Martin Evans in the late 1960s, it was later expanded on by Robert House (formerly at the University of Toronto, but now at the University of Pennsylvania's Wharton School). Path-goal theory is a contingency model of leadership that extracts key elements from the Ohio State leadership research on initiating structure and consideration, and from the expectancy theory of motivation.[29]

The essence of the theory is that it is the leader's job to assist followers in attaining their goals and to provide the necessary direction and/or support to ensure that their goals

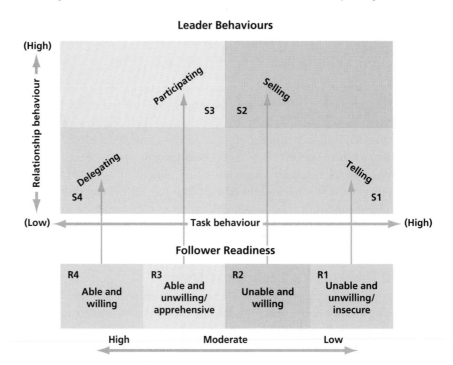

Exhibit 8–4

Hersey-Blanchard's Situational Leadership Styles

George Irwin, former CEO of Toronto-based Irwin Toy Ltd., shown here with 15-month-old shareholder Jacob Lundrigan, was forced to step down as head at Irwin. One of his difficulties was in adapting his leadership style to the situation. Former employees said he did not know how to motivate people and had a divide-and-conquer style. He was also not good at team leadership. These qualities may work in some situations, but they did not work well at Irwin, and thus George Irwin's father temporarily reassumed the CEO position. The company has since gone out of business.

are compatible with the overall objectives of the group or organization. The term *path-goal* derives from the belief that effective leaders both clarify the path to help their followers get from where they are to the achievement of their work goals, and make the journey along the path easier by reducing roadblocks and pitfalls. To do this, individuals should follow three guidelines to be effective leaders:[30]

1. Determine the outcomes subordinates want. These might include good pay, job security, interesting work, and autonomy to do one's job.

2. Reward individuals with their desired outcomes when they perform well.

3. Let individuals know what they need to do to receive rewards (i.e., the path to the goal), remove any barriers that would prevent high performance, and express confidence that individuals have the ability to perform well.

Path-goal theory identifies four leadership behaviours that might be used in different situations to motivate individuals.

- The *directive leader* lets followers know what is expected of them, schedules work to be done, and gives specific guidance as to how to accomplish tasks. This closely parallels the Ohio State dimension of initiating structure. This behaviour is best used when individuals have difficulty doing tasks or the tasks are ambiguous. It would not be very helpful when used with individuals who are already highly motivated, have the skills and abilities to do the task, and understand the requirements of the task.

- The *supportive leader* is friendly and shows concern for the needs of followers. This is essentially synonymous with the Ohio State dimension of consideration. This behaviour is often recommended when individuals are under stress, or otherwise show that they need to be supported.

- The *participative leader* consults with followers and uses their suggestions before making a decision. This behaviour is most appropriate when individuals need to buy in to decisions.

- The *achievement-oriented leader* sets challenging goals and expects followers to perform at their highest level. This works well with individuals who like challenges and are highly motivated. It would be less effective with less capable individuals, or those who are highly stressed from overwork.

As Exhibit 8–5 illustrates, path-goal theory proposes two types of contingency variables that affect the leadership behaviour-outcome relationship: environmental variables that are outside the control of the employee and variables that are part of the personal characteristics of the employee. House assumes that leaders are flexible and can display any or all of these behaviours depending on the situation. Some situations may in fact need more than one style from the leader. The theory proposes that employee performance and satisfaction are likely to be positively influenced when the leader compensates for things lacking in either the employee or the work setting. However, the leader who spends time explaining tasks when those tasks are already clear or when the employee has the ability and experience to handle them without interference is likely to be ineffective because the employee will see such directive behaviour as redundant or even insulting. The research evidence generally supports the path-goal theory.[31]

One question that arises from contingency theories is whether leaders can actually adjust their behaviour to various situations. As we know, individuals differ in their behavioural flexibility. Some people show considerable ability to adjust their behaviour to external, situational factors; they are adaptable. Others, however, exhibit high levels of consistency regardless of the situation. High self-monitors are usually able to adjust their leadership style to suit changing situations better than low self-monitors.[32] Clearly, if an individual's leadership style range is very narrow and he or she cannot or will not adjust (i.e., the person is a low self-monitor), that individual will only be successful in very specific situations suitable to his or her style. To find out more about your style of leadership, see the *Learning About Yourself Exercise* on pages 276–277.

Substitutes for Leadership

The previous three theories argue that leaders are needed, but that leaders should consider the situation in determining the style of leadership to take. However, numerous

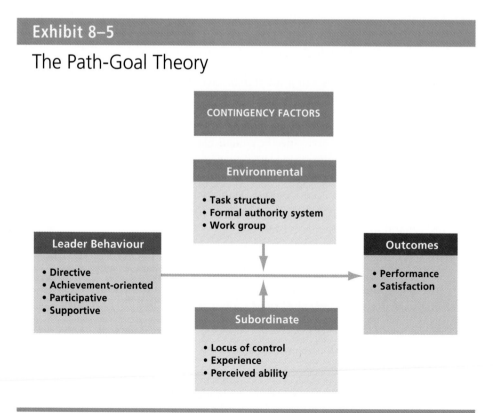

Exhibit 8–5

The Path-Goal Theory

studies collectively demonstrate that, in many situations, leaders' actions are irrelevant. Certain individual, job, and organizational variables can act as substitutes for leadership or neutralize the leader's ability to influence his or her followers.[33]

If employees have appropriate experience, training, or "professional" orientation, or if employees are indifferent to organizational rewards, the effect of leadership can be replaced or neutralized. Experience and training, for instance, can replace the need for a leader's support or ability to create structure and reduce task ambiguity. Jobs that are inherently unambiguous and routine or that are intrinsically satisfying may place fewer demands on the leadership variable. Organizational characteristics such as explicit formalized goals, rigid rules and procedures, and cohesive work groups can replace formal leadership (see Exhibit 8–6).

For more discussion of when leadership is necessary and when it is less important, you might want to examine this chapter's *Point/CounterPoint* on page 275.

Can You Be a Better Follower?

Thus far we have concentrated on how leaders must adapt their styles to the needs of their followers. This underscores the importance of the followers' role in how leadership is carried out. Only recently have we begun to recognize that in addition to having leaders who can lead, successful organizations need followers who can follow.[34] In fact, it's probably fair to say that all organizations have far more followers than leaders, so ineffective followers may be more of a handicap to an organization than ineffective leaders. The Far Side cartoon shown in Exhibit 8-7 gives you some indication of what can happen when someone finally realizes that he or she is "a follower, too."

An understanding of how to be a follower is important, because almost all roles in an organization require one to be a follower in some settings. Obviously lower-level employees are followers to their supervisors. But the supervisor is a follower to his or her manager, who is a follower to the CEO. And the CEO in a public corporation is a follower to the board of directors. Even the best leaders have to be followers sometimes.

Exhibit 8–6

Substitutes and Neutralizers for Leadership

Defining Characteristics	Relationship-Oriented Leadership	Task-Oriented Leadership
Individual		
Experience/training	No effect on	Substitutes for
Professionalism	Substitutes for	Substitutes for
Indifference to rewards	Neutralizes	Neutralizes
Job		
Highly structured task	No effect on	Substitutes for
Provides its own feedback	No effect on	Substitutes for
Intrinsically satisfying	Substitutes for	No effect on
Organization		
Explicit formalized goals	No effect on	Substitutes for
Rigid rules and procedures	No effect on	Substitutes for
Cohesive work groups	Substitutes for	Substitutes for

Source: Based on S. Kerr and J.M. Jermier, "Substitutes for Leadership: Their Meaning and Measurement," *Organizational Behavior and Human Performance*, December 1978, p. 378.

Exhibit 8–7

Exhibit 8–7

THE FAR SIDE   By GARY LARSON

"Well, what d'ya know! . . . *I'm* a follower, too!"

Source: THE FAR SIDE copyright 1990 & 1991 Farworks, Inc./Dist. by Universal Press Syndicate. Reprinted with permission. All rights reserved.

What qualities do effective followers have? One writer focuses on four:[35]

- *They manage themselves well.* They are able to think for themselves. They can work independently and without close supervision.

- *They are committed to a purpose outside themselves.* Effective followers are committed to something—a cause, a product, a work team, an organization, an idea—in addition to the care of their own lives. Most people like working with colleagues who are emotionally, as well as physically, committed to their work.

- *They build their competence and focus their efforts for maximum impact.* Effective followers master skills that will be useful to their organizations, and they hold higher performance standards than their job or work group requires.

- *They are courageous, honest, and credible.* Effective followers establish themselves as independent, critical thinkers whose knowledge and judgment can be trusted. They hold high ethical standards, give credit where credit is due, and are not afraid to own up to their mistakes.

These points suggest that there is a relationship between leadership and followership, and that taking responsibility for one's own behaviour is beneficial for both one's self and the organization.

LEADING WITH VISION

When Frank Stronach created Magna International, he also developed his Fair Enterprise system, "a hybrid of socialism and free enterprise based on the principle that if you treat your workers well and give them a stake in the business, they'll reward you."[36] Stronach also introduced profit sharing, one of the first companies in Canada to do so. His philosophy of expecting a lot from his employees, but also letting them share in the profits, has helped keep unions out of Magna. The Fair Enterprise system is Frank Stronach's vision for how to run the company internally. But it was also his vision that created a global organization with $10 billion in annual sales and 62 000 employees in 166 factories in 18 countries.[37] Belinda Stronach's vision for the company may be somewhat different than her father's: "We are in auto parts, but I believe it's the culture that's made the company successful, from our decentralized operating structure and principles to our corporate constitution to our employee charter. I believe I understand that culture extremely well."[38] Can different visions lead to different outcomes?

3 How does a leader lead with vision?

Frank Stronach's Fair Enterprise system
collections.ic.gc.ca/heirloom_series/volume6/374-375.htm

The theories reported above were developed at a time when most organizations were structured in traditional hierarchies where there were classic lines of command. While this form still dominates in Canada's "Most Respected Corporations,"[39] there are organizations trying to be more innovative, faster moving, and more responsive to employees who are highly educated and intelligent, and who want more say in the workplace. Thus new styles of leadership are evolving to meet the demands of these organizations. The more recent approaches to leadership move away from the supervisory tasks of leaders and focus on vision-setting activities. These theories try to explain how certain leaders can achieve extraordinary levels from their followers, and they stress symbolic and emotionally appealing leadership behaviours.[40]

From Transactional to Transformational Leadership

Most of the leadership theories presented thus far in this chapter have concerned **transactional leaders**. Such leaders guide or motivate their followers in the direction of established goals by clarifying role and task requirements. In some styles of transactional leadership, the leader uses rewarding and recognizing behaviour. This results in performance that meets expectations, though rarely does one see results that exceed expectations.[41] In other styles of transactional leadership, the leader emphasizes correction and possibly punishment rather than rewards and recognition. This style "results in performance below expectations, and discourages innovation and initiative in the workplace."[42] Of course, leaders should not ignore poor performance, but effective leaders emphasize how to achieve expectations, rather than dwell on mistakes.

Some leaders inspire followers to transcend their own self-interests for the good of the organization, and have a profound and extraordinary effect on their followers. These are charismatic or **transformational leaders**, such as Matthew Barrett, now group chief executive of Barclays PLC, Britain's second-largest bank, and formerly CEO of Bank of Montreal; Frank Stronach of Magna International; and Mogens Smed of Calgary-based SMED International, the subject of this chapter's *Case Incident* on pages 278–279. Other Canadians who have frequently been cited as being charismatic leaders include René Lévesque; Lucien Bouchard; Governor General Adrienne Clarkson; Robert Chisholm, Nova Scotia's former NDP leader; and Craig Kielburger, the Canadian teenager who founded Kids Can Free the Children to promote children's rights and combat exploitation of child labour. We were also reminded of the charismatic personality of Pierre Trudeau when he passed away in 2000. What links these individuals is paying attention to the concerns and developmental needs of individual followers. Transformational leaders change followers' awareness of issues by helping them to look at old problems in new ways; and they are able to excite, arouse, and inspire followers to exert extra effort to achieve group goals.

Transformational leadership is sometimes identified separately from **charismatic leadership** in the literature, although McGill's Kanungo notes that the two formulations are not different in that charismatic leaders are also transformational leaders. Relying on his judgment, we use the two concepts interchangeably. As Kanungo notes, the charismatic leader "critically examines the status quo with a view to developing and articulating future strategic goals or vision for the organization and then leading organizational members to achieve these goals through empowering strategies."[43] While not all transformational leaders are charismatic in personality, both transformational and charismatic leaders work to empower their followers to reach higher goals.

Transactional and transformational leadership should not be viewed as opposing approaches to getting things done.[44] Transformational leadership is

transactional leaders
Leaders who guide or motivate their followers in the direction of established goals by clarifying role and task requirements.

transformational leaders
Leaders who provide individualized consideration and intellectual stimulation, and who possess charisma.

 Matthew Barrett, Barclays PLC
www.personal.barclays.co.uk/BRC1/jsp/

 Mogens Smed, SMED International Inc.
www.smednet.com/company/history.asp

charismatic leadership
Leadership that critically examines the status quo with a view to developing and articulating future strategic goals or vision for the organization, and then leading organizational members to reach these goals through empowering strategies.

Through his charismatic leadership, Steve Jobs achieved unwavering loyalty and commitment from the technical staff he oversaw at Apple Computer during the late 1970s and early 1980s. However, as the company grew, this style was less effective, and he was forced out of Apple in 1985. In 1996, with Apple doing poorly, Jobs was brought back to lead the company once again because of his vision and charisma.

> ### Exhibit 8–8
>
> ## Characteristics of Transactional and Transformational Leaders
>
> **Transactional Leader**
>
> *Contingent Reward:* Contracts exchange of rewards for effort, promises rewards for good performance, recognizes accomplishments.
>
> *Management by Exception* (active): Watches and searches for deviations from rules and standards, takes corrective action.
>
> *Management by Exception* (passive): Intervenes only if standards are not met.
>
> *Laissez-Faire:* Abdicates responsibilities, avoids making decisions.
>
> **Transformational Leader**
>
> *Charisma:* Provides vision and sense of mission, instills pride, gains respect and trust.
>
> *Inspiration:* Communicates high expectations, uses symbols to focus efforts, expresses important purposes in simple ways.
>
> *Intellectual Stimulation:* Promotes intelligence, rationality, and careful problem solving.
>
> *Individualized Consideration:* Gives personal attention, treats each employee individually, coaches, advises.
>
> Source: B.M. Bass, "From Transactional to Transformational Leadership: Learning to Share the Vision," *Organizational Dynamics*, Winter 1990, p. 22. Reprinted by permission of the publisher. American Management Association, New York. All rights reserved.

built *on top of* transactional leadership—it produces levels of employee effort and performance that go beyond what would occur with a transactional approach alone. Exhibit 8–8 outlines the difference between transactional and transformational (or charismatic) leaders. Would you be able to be a charismatic leader? We give you tips in this chapter's *From Concepts to Skills* feature on pages 281–282.

Personal Characteristics of the Charismatic Leader   Several authors have tried to identify personal characteristics of the charismatic leader.[45] The most comprehensive analysis of charismatic leadership, however, has been completed by Jay Conger and Rabindra Kanungo.[46] The characteristics they identified are:

1. *Vision and articulation.* Has a vision—expressed as an idealized goal—that proposes a future better than the status quo, and is able to clarify the importance of the vision in terms that are understandable to others.

2. *Personal risk.* Willing to take on high personal risk, incur high costs, and engage in self-sacrifice to achieve the vision.

3. *Environmental sensitivity.* Able to make realistic assessments of the environmental constraints and resources needed to bring about change.

4. *Sensitivity to follower needs.* Perceptive of others' abilities and responsive to their needs and feelings.

5. *Unconventional behaviour.* Engages in behaviours that are perceived as novel and counter to norms.

While the idea of charismatic leadership was developed based on North American observations, Professors Dale Carl of the School of Business Management at Ryerson University and Mansour Javidan at the University of Calgary also suggest that charismatic leadership is expressed relatively similarly in a variety of countries, including Canada, Hungary, India, Turkey, Austria, Singapore, Sweden, and Venezuela.[47] This indicates there may be some universal aspects of this style of leadership.

Sharing a Vision   Perhaps one of the key components of charismatic leadership is the ability to articulate a vision. A review of various definitions finds that a vision differs from other forms of direction setting in several ways:

> A vision has clear and compelling imagery that offers an innovative way to improve, which recognizes and draws on traditions, and connects to actions that people can take to realize change. Vision taps people's emotions and energy. Properly articulated, a vision creates the enthusiasm that people have for sporting events and other leisure-time activities, bringing the energy and commitment to the workplace.[48]

This chapter's *Case Incident* on pages 278–279 describes how Mogens Smed shares his vision with his employees. The key properties of a vision seem to be inspirational possibilities that are value-centred and realizable, with superior imagery and articulation.[49] Visions should be able to create possibilities that are inspirational and unique, and offer a new order that can produce organizational distinction. A vision is likely to fail if it does not offer a view of the future that is clearly and demonstrably better for the organization and its members. Desirable visions fit the times and circumstances and reflect the uniqueness of the organization. Visions that have clear articulation and powerful imagery are more easily grasped and accepted.

Mogens Smed, president and CEO of Calgary-based SMED International, has a reputation as a charismatic leader. He believes his upscale office furniture–making company differs from the competitors' because "We do not play by the rules. There are no rules." Here he is shown holding a sign found in the abandoned Pilkington Brothers Glass Building in downtown Calgary. Smed recently transformed the building from a junkie hangout to a high-tech haven for a web company.

Does Being Charismatic Matter?   Do vision and charismatic leadership really make a difference? In a survey of 1500 senior leaders (870 of them CEOs from 20 different countries) to determine the key traits or talents desirable for a CEO in the year 2000, 98 percent rated a "strong sense of vision" as most important.[50] Another study contrasted 18 visionary companies with 18 comparable nonvisionary firms over a 65-year period.[51] The visionary companies were found to have outperformed the comparison group by 6 times on standard financial criteria, and their stocks outperformed the general market by 15 times. An unpublished study by Robert House and some colleagues of 63 US and 49 Canadian companies (including Nortel Networks, Molson, Gulf Canada [now Conoco], and Manulife Financial) found that "between 15 and 25 percent of the variation in profitability among the companies was accounted for by the leadership qualities of their CEO."[52] That is, charismatic leaders led more profitable companies. To learn more about how to be transformational/charismatic yourself, see the *Working With Others Exercise* on page 278.

An increasing body of research shows that people working for charismatic leaders are motivated to exert extra work effort and, because they like their leaders, they express greater satisfaction.[53] One of the most-cited studies of the effects of charismatic leadership was done at the University of British Columbia in the mid-1980s by Peter Frost and Jane Howell (now at the Richard Ivey School of Business at the University of Western Ontario).[54] Their study compared the charismatic leadership style with structuring (i.e., task-oriented) and considerate (i.e., employee-oriented) styles, and found that those who worked under a charismatic leader generated more ideas and reported higher job satisfaction than those working under structuring leaders. Charismatic leaders also produced better results than considerate leaders, with employees performing at a higher level. Those working under charismatic leaders also showed higher job satisfaction and stronger bonds of loyalty. Howell, in summarizing these results, says, "While it is true that considerate leaders make people feel good, that doesn't necessarily translate into increased productivity. In contrast, charismatic leaders know how to inspire people to think in new directions."[55]

The evidence supporting the superiority of transformational leadership over the transactional variety is overwhelmingly impressive. For instance, a number of studies with US, Canadian, and German military officers found, at every level, that transformational leaders were evaluated as more effective than their transactional counterparts.[56] Managers at Federal Express who were rated by their followers as exhibiting more transformational leadership were evaluated by their immediate supervisors as higher performers and more promotable.[57] Howell and her colleagues found in a study of 250 executives and managers at a major financial-services company that "transformational leaders had 34 percent higher business unit performance results than other types of leaders."[58] In summary, the overall evidence indicates that transformational leadership is more strongly correlated than transactional leadership with lower turnover rates, higher productivity, and higher employee satisfaction.[59] One caveat to this research is work done by Professor Timothy DeGroot of McMaster University and his colleagues. They found that charismatic leadership had a greater impact on team performance than on individual performance, and suggest that the positive findings of previous studies are the result of charismatic leaders providing a better team environment for everyone, which then resulted in higher performance.[60]

When Should One Be Charismatic? One last comment on this topic: Charismatic leadership may not always be needed to achieve high levels of employee performance. It may be most appropriate when the follower's task has an ideological component.[61] This may explain why, when charismatic leaders surface, it is more likely to be in politics or religion, during wartime, or when a business firm is introducing a radically new product or facing a life-threatening crisis. Thus when Canada Post and Royal Trustco faced major turnaround opportunities in the 1980s, charismatic leaders emerged to take on the task. Don Lander, president and CEO of Canada Post from 1986 to 1993, is credited with transforming the corporation from an inefficient government department to a sleeker, profitable Crown corporation. His success with Canada Post is viewed as a classic case of corporate culture change.[62] (You can read about further examples of corporate culture change in Chapter 10.)

Be aware that charismatic leaders may become a liability to an organization once the crisis is over and the need for dramatic change subsides.[63] Why? Because then the charismatic leader's overwhelming self-confidence often becomes a liability. He or she is unable to listen to others, becomes uncomfortable when challenged by aggressive employees, and begins to hold an unjustifiable belief in his or her "rightness" on issues. Some would argue that Prime Minister Jean Chrétien's behaviour leading up to the leadership review of February 2003 would fit this description.

Many have argued that the recent accounting scandals and high-profile bankruptcies facing North American companies, including Enron and WorldCom, point to some of the dangers of charismatic leadership. WorldCom's Bernard Ebbers and Enron's Kenneth Lay "seemed almost a breed apart, blessed with unique visionary powers" when their companies were increasing stock prices at phenomenal rates in the 1990s.[64] After the scandals, however, the mood seems to be for CEOs with less vision, and more ethical and corporate responsibility.

Dispersed Leadership: Spreading Leadership Throughout the Organization

Many people regard Frank Stronach as an authoritarian leader. He commands loyalty from others, but he does not share leadership. Belinda Stronach's style is somewhat different: She believes in the virtue of team leadership. As she notes, "It's not just about me. We have a competent team in place here and I have worked closely with that team. If I hit that proverbial telephone pole tomorrow, this has to go on."[65] Why would sharing leadership with others make sense for some organizations?

Transformational leadership theory focuses on heroic leaders, leaders at the top echelons of the organization, and also on individuals rather than teams. The theories addressed below aim to explain how leadership can be spread throughout the organization. Even if you are not a manager or someone thinking about leadership in a corporate situation, this discussion offers important insights into how you can take on a leadership role in an organization. Moreover, in today's flatter organizations, you may well be expected to show leadership characteristics, even if you are not a formal leader.

As you consider the ways that roles can spread to people who are not managers, be aware that not all organizations engage in this practice, and even within organizations, not all managers are happy with sharing their power with those under them. Gifted leaders often recognize that they actually have more power if they share power. That is, sharing power enables them to build coalitions and teams that work together for the overall good of the organization. There are other managers, though, who fear the loss of any power.

Turning Constituents Into Leaders

Several researchers have proposed the idea that good leaders develop the leadership skills of their employees.[66] One set of researchers actually refer to this as superleadership, which they view as the leadership design of the future.[67] A major feature of superleadership is the emphasis on "leading others to lead themselves," so that the followers also become leaders.[68] This view is not inconsistent with the transformational view of leadership, although superleadership places more emphasis on how leaders can get followers to lead themselves. Leaders do this by developing leadership capacity in others and nurturing employees so that they do not feel the need to depend on formal leaders. Thus, managers emphasize delegation and employees and teams are empowered so that they can set goals and make operating decisions. Some firms make a point of giving high-potential employees a variety of assignments so that they will have a wider perspective as they go higher in the organization, thereby giving them the knowledge and the capacity to become leaders. Further, leaders liberate employees so that they will use their own abilities to lead themselves.

Providing Team Leadership

Leadership is increasingly taking place within a team context. As teams grow in popularity, the role of the leader in guiding team members takes on more importance.[69] Also, because of its more collaborative nature, the role of team leader is different from the traditional leadership role performed by first-line supervisors.

Many leaders are not equipped to handle the change to teams. As one prominent consultant noted, "Even the most capable managers have trouble making the transition because all the command-and-control type things they were encouraged to do before are no longer appropriate. There's no reason to have any skill or sense of this."[70] This same consultant estimated that "probably 15 percent of managers are natural team leaders; another 15 percent could never lead a team because it runs counter to their personality. [They're unable to sublimate their dominating style for the good of the team.] Then there's that huge group in the middle: team leadership doesn't come naturally to them, but they can learn it."[71]

Effective team leaders need to build commitment and confidence, remove obstacles, create opportunities, and be part of the team.[72] They have to learn skills such as the patience to share information, the willingness to trust others, the ability to give up authority, and an understanding of when to intervene. New team leaders may try to

4 Can a person be an informal leader?

Rhonda Fryman is a team leader at Toyota Motor Manufacturing, Kentucky, Inc. (TMMK) in Georgetown, Kentucky. She exemplifies Toyota's philosophy of striving to create a warm, caring atmosphere with a high degree of respect for employees, which leads to their high levels of motivation and productivity. Consistent with the contingency models, Fryman is an effective leader because she assists her team in meeting their daily production goals and provides direction and support in achieving Toyota's quality goals.

retain too much control at a time when team members need more autonomy, or they may abandon their teams at times when the teams need support and help.[73]

Roles of Team Leaders

A recent study of 20 organizations that reorganized themselves around teams found certain common responsibilities that all leaders had to assume. These included coaching, facilitating, handling disciplinary problems, reviewing team/individual performance, training, and communicating.[74] Many of these responsibilities apply to managers in general. A more meaningful way to describe the team leader's job is to focus on two priorities: managing the team's external boundary and facilitating the team process.[75] We have divided these priorities into four specific roles.

- Team leaders are *liaisons* with external constituencies. These include upper management, other internal teams, customers, and suppliers. The leader represents the team to other constituencies, secures needed resources, clarifies others' expectations of the team, gathers information from the outside, and shares this information with team members.

- Team leaders are *troubleshooters*. When the team has problems and asks for assistance, team leaders sit in on meetings and try to help resolve the problems. This rarely relates to technical or operational issues because the team members typically know more about the tasks being done than does the team leader. The leader contributes by asking penetrating questions, by helping the team discuss problems, and by getting needed resources from external constituencies. For instance, when a team in an aerospace firm found itself short-handed, its team leader took responsibility for getting more staff. He presented the team's case to upper management and got the approval through the company's human resources department.

- Team leaders are *conflict managers*. When disagreements surface, team leaders help process the conflict. What is the source of the conflict? Who is involved? What are the issues? What resolution options are available? What are the advantages and disadvantages of each? By getting team members to address questions such as these, the leader minimizes the disruptive aspects of intrateam conflicts.

- Team leaders are *coaches*. They clarify expectations and roles, teach, offer support, cheerlead, and do whatever else is necessary to help team members improve their work performance.

LEADING ONE'S SELF

Thus far we have discussed the role of leadership as if it were mainly a one-way street: Leadership is something someone at the top does, and hopefully, those at the bottom, the followers, follow. However, there are two provocative issues for you to consider when thinking about leadership. The first is the issue of self-leadership, or taking responsibility for your own actions, and learning how to be a leader, even if only in small areas of your situation. The second is how to lead even when you have not been given authority.

5 What is self-leadership?

Self-Leadership

A growing trend in organizations is the focus on self-leadership.[76] This means that individuals and teams set goals, plan and implement tasks, evaluate performance, solve their own problems, and motivate themselves. Reduced levels of supervision, more offices in the home, more teamwork, and growth in service and professional employment where individuals are often required to make decisions on the spot call for individuals to self-lead. Following from our discussion above on substitutes for leadership, self-leadership can also be a substitute or neutralizer for leadership from others.

Despite the lack of studies of self-leadership techniques in organizational settings, self-leadership strategies have been shown to be successful in nonorganizational settings.[77] Those who practise self-leadership look for opportunities to be more effective in the workplace and improve their career success. Their behaviour is self-reinforced—that is, they provide their own sense of reward and feedback after carrying out their accomplishments. Moreover, self-reinforced behaviour is often maintained at a higher rate than behaviour that is externally regulated.[78]

What does self-leadership look like? Though "individuals in organizations are regularly taught how to lead subordinates, groups, and even organizations, they rarely receive instruction on how to lead themselves."[79] Few empirical studies of this kind have been carried out in the workplace,[80] but a 1999 study of 305 managers at a large retailing organization in the Midwestern United States identified four behaviours that can be considered self-leadership: *planning, access management, catch-up activities,* and *emotions management.*[81] Exhibit 8–9 describes these behaviours in greater detail.

Leading Without Authority

We have discussed how to be a follower and how to manage yourself, but what if your goal is to be a leader, even if you do not have the authority (or formal appointment) to be one? For instance, what if you wanted to convince the dean of your school to introduce new business courses that were more relevant, or you wanted to convince the president of the company where you work that she should start thinking about more environmentally friendly strategies in dealing with waste? How do you effectively lead in a student group, when everyone is a peer?

Leadership at the grassroots level in organizations does happen. Rosabeth Moss Kanter, in her book *The Change Masters*,[82] discusses examples of people who saw something in their workplace that needed changing and took the responsibility to do so upon themselves. Employees were more likely to do this when organizations permitted initiative at all levels of the organization, rather than making it a tool of senior executives only.

Leading without authority simply means exhibiting leadership behaviour even though you do not have a formal position or title that might encourage others "to obey." Neither Martin Luther King nor Mahatma Gandhi operated from a position of authority, yet each was able to inspire many to follow him in the quest for social justice. The workplace can be an opportunity for leading without authority as well. As Heifetz notes, "leadership means taking responsibility for hard problems beyond anyone's expectations."[83] It also means not waiting for the coach's call.[84]

Exhibit 8–9

Self-Leadership Practices

In order to determine their self-leadership initiative, managers were asked to rate each of the following items, from 1 ("never do this") to 7 ("always do this"). Higher scores meant a higher degree of self-leadership.

Planning

- I plan out my day before beginning to work
- I try to schedule my work in advance
- I plan my career carefully
- I come to work early to plan my day
- I use lists and agendas to structure my workday
- I set specific job goals on a regular basis
- I set daily goals for myself
- I try to manage my time

Access management

- I control the access subordinates have to me in order to get my work done
- I use a special place at work where I can work uninterrupted
- I hold my telephone calls when I need to get things done

Catch-up activities

- I come in early or stay late at work to prevent distractions from interfering with my work
- I take my work home with me to make sure it gets done
- I come in on my days off to catch up on my work

Emotions management

- I have learned to manage my aggressiveness with my subordinates
- My facial expression and conversational tone are important in dealing with subordinates
- It is important for me to maintain a "professional" manager-subordinate relationship
- I try to keep my emotions under control

Source: M. Castaneda, T.A. Kolenko, and R.J. Aldag, "Self-Management Perceptions and Practices: A Structural Equations Analysis," *Journal of Organizational Behavior*, 20, 1999, pp. 114–115. © John Wiley & Sons Limited. Reproduced with permission.

What are the benefits of leading without authority? Heifetz has identified three:[85]

- *Latitude for creative deviance.* Because one does not have authority, and the trappings that go with authority, it is easier to raise harder questions and look for less traditional solutions.

- *Issue focus.* Leading without authority means that one can focus on a single issue, rather than be concerned with the myriad issues that those in authority face.

- *Front-line information.* Leading without authority means that one is closer to the detailed experiences of some of the stakeholders. Thus more information is available to this kind of leader.

Not all organizations will support this type of leadership, and some have been known to actively suppress it. Still others will look aside, neither encouraging nor discouraging.

Nevertheless, you may want to reflect on the possibility of engaging in leadership behaviour simply because you see a need, rather than because you are required to act.

CONTEMPORARY ISSUES IN LEADERSHIP

For both Belinda and Frank Stronach, the Fair Enterprise system of Magna represents a moral dimension to both leadership and employment. The system treats employees well, and expects employees to be loyal and committed to the organization in exchange. Both Frank and Belinda believe in the Fair Enterprise system, so in that regard there is no gender difference in their approach to basic aspects of the organizational culture. However, Belinda Stronach's rise to power highlights one of the leading questions often asked of women: Can they perform as well as men in the CEO role?

Is there a moral dimension to leadership? Do men and women rely on different leadership styles, and if so, is one style inherently superior to the other? How does national culture affect the choice of leadership style?

In this section, we briefly address these contemporary issues in leadership.

6 What are some of the hot topics in leadership?

Is There a Moral Dimension to Leadership?

The topic of leadership and ethics has surprisingly received little attention. Only very recently have ethicists and leadership researchers begun to consider the ethical implications in leadership.[86] Why now? One reason may be the growing general interest in ethics throughout the field of business. Another reason may be the discovery by probing biographers that some of our past leaders suffered from ethical shortcomings. Regardless, no contemporary discussion of leadership is complete without addressing its ethical dimension.

Ethics touches on leadership at a number of junctures. Transformational leaders, for instance, have been described by one authority as encouraging moral virtue when they try to change the attitudes and behaviours of followers.[87] Charisma, too, has an ethical component. Unethical leaders are more likely to use their charisma to enhance power over followers, directed toward self-serving ends. Ethical leaders are considered to use their charisma in a socially constructive way to serve others.[88] There is also the issue of abuse of power by leaders—for example, when they give themselves large salaries and bonuses while also trying to cut costs by laying off long-time employees.

Leadership effectiveness needs to address the means that a leader uses in trying to achieve goals, as well as the content of those goals. For instance, at Enron, employees were driven by the top executives to keep Enron stock prices up, at whatever cost. "The driver was this unbelievable desire to keep portraying Enron as something very very different and keep the track record going and going," said Forrest Hoglund, who ran Enron's oil and gas exploration until 1999.[89] To achieve these goals, executives inflated revenues and hid debts. CEO and chair Kenneth Lay thus led his subordinates to achieve stock price goals no matter how this was accomplished. Anyone who questioned what the company was doing was ignored or dismissed.

Gerald Chamales, president of Omni Computer Products, provides a good example of moral leadership. A key part of his corporate strategy is giving hard-to-employ people an opportunity to succeed in the workplace. Chamales hires people with drug- and alcohol-addiction problems and uses the principles of recovery programs in managing them. Chamales' rehabilitating mission includes providing in-house mentors who counsel new employees on basic social and workplace skills. Tolerant of their personal struggles, he helps them handle legal, health, and family problems caused by their addiction. Chamales views his recovering employees as long-term investments who have helped him build his start-up firm into a $28-million company.

Ethical leadership must also address the content of a leader's goals. Are the changes that the leader seeks for the organization morally acceptable? Is a business leader effective if he or she builds an organization's success by selling products that damage the health of their users? This question might be asked of tobacco executives. Or is a military leader successful when winning a war that should not have been fought in the first place?

Professor James Clawson of the Darden Graduate School of Business, University of Virginia, suggests that there are four cornerstones to a *"moral foundation of leadership"*:[90]

- *Truth telling.* Telling the truth as you see it, because it allows for a mutual, fair exchange to occur.

- *Promise keeping.* Leaders need to be careful of the commitments they make, and then careful of keeping those promises.

- *Fairness.* This ensures that followers get their fair share for their contributions to the organization.

- *Respect for the individual.* Telling the truth, keeping promises, and being fair all show respect for the individual. Respect means treating people with dignity.

Moral leadership comes from within the individual, and in general means treating people well, and with respect.

Gender: Do Males and Females Lead Differently?

An extensive review of the literature suggests two conclusions.[91] First, the similarities between male and female leaders tend to outweigh the differences. Second, what differences there are seem to be that women fall back on a more democratic leadership style, while men feel more comfortable with a directive style.

The similarities among men and women leaders should not be completely surprising. Almost all the studies looking at this issue have treated managerial positions as synonymous with leadership. As such, gender differences apparent in the general population do not tend to be as evident because of career self-selection and organization selection. Just as people who choose careers in law enforcement or civil engineering have a lot in common, so do individuals who choose managerial careers. People with traits associated with leadership—such as intelligence, confidence, and sociability—are more likely to be perceived as leaders and encouraged to pursue careers where they can exert leadership. This is true regardless of gender. Similarly, organizations tend to recruit and promote people into leadership positions who project leadership attributes. The result is that, regardless of gender, those who achieve formal leadership positions in organizations tend to be more alike than different.

Despite the previous conclusion, studies indicate some differences in the inherent leadership styles between women and men. A recent Conference Board of Canada study found that "women are particularly strong in managing interpersonal relationships and their approach is more consensual."[92] Other studies have shown that women tend to adopt a style of shared leadership. They encourage participation, share power and information, and try to enhance followers' self-worth. They prefer to lead through inclusion and rely on their charisma, expertise, contacts, and interpersonal skills to influence others. Men, on the other hand, are more likely to use a directive command-and-control style. They rely on the formal authority of their position for their influence base.

Given that men have historically held the great majority of leadership positions in organizations, it's tempting to assume that the existence of the differences noted between men and women would automatically work to favour men. It doesn't. In today's organizations, flexibility, teamwork, trust, and information sharing are replacing rigid structures, competitive individualism, control, and secrecy. The best leaders listen, motivate, and provide support to their people. And many women seem to do those things better than men. As a specific example, the expanded use of cross-functional teams in organizations means that effective leaders must become skilled negotiators. The leadership styles women typically use can make them better at negotiating, as they are less likely to focus on wins, losses, and competition, than do men. They tend to treat negotiations in the context of a continuing relationship—trying hard to make the other party a winner in his or her own and others' eyes.

Some studies argue that women are evaluated more negatively as leaders than are men.[93] In some studies, male employees were more likely than female employees to say that they preferred to work for male managers. These findings are not conclusive, however. Other studies have found that when men and women are asked to evaluate supervisors for whom they have actually worked, male and female supervisors are evaluated similarly.[94] Women are judged more negatively when they use a more male leadership style (such as being autocratic),[95] which suggests that women have less freedom in the styles that they choose if they care about their evaluations. A recent Conference Board of Canada survey found that more than two-thirds of female managers felt that not being taken as seriously as their male colleagues was a serious problem.[96] Fifty percent of the women surveyed in the same study felt that women managers are perceived as having less organizational commitment and professional capability than their male counterparts.

Debra Meyerson, a visiting professor at Stanford University's Center for Work, Technology, and Organization, notes that female executives are evaluated differently than men, even when they have the same qualifications. In a study of its own managers, Deloitte & Touche LLP found that when their managers considered similarly qualified men and women, males who lacked experience in an area were viewed as having untested potential, but females were viewed as not ready for promotion. "For a woman, any slip-up is seen as evidence that you weren't up to the job," says Meyerson, "while men are more likely to be given the benefit of the doubt."[97]

Emmie Wong Leung, founder and CEO of International Paper Industries Ltd. (IPI) of North Vancouver, which collects, processes, and sells waste paper to offshore buyers, has been exporting to the United States, Hong Kong, Japan, China, the Philippines, India, and Indonesia for more than 20 years. She says: "I think an old-boys' network operates all over the world, but you can get them to accept you."

Deloitte & Touche LLP
www.deloitte.ca

Cross-Cultural Leadership

One general conclusion that surfaces from our discussion of leadership is that effective leaders do not use any single style. They adjust their style to the situation. While not mentioned explicitly in any of the theories we presented, certainly national culture is an important situational factor determining which leadership style will be most effective.[98] It can help explain, for instance, why executives at the highly successful Asia Department Store in central China blatantly brag about using "heartless" management, require new employees to undergo two to four weeks of military training with units of the People's Liberation Army in order to increase their obedience, and conduct the store's in-house training sessions in a public place where employees can openly suffer embarrassment from their mistakes.[99]

One way that national culture affects leadership style is by the cultural expectations and norms of followers. Leaders, particularly when they are working in international situations, are constrained by the cultural conditions that their followers have come to expect. Consider the following: Korean leaders are expected to be paternalistic toward employees.[100] Arab leaders who show kindness or generosity without being asked to do so are seen by other Arabs as weak.[101] Japanese leaders are expected to be humble and speak infrequently.[102] And Scandinavian and Dutch leaders who single out individuals for public praise are likely to embarrass those individuals rather than energize them.[103]

Remember that most leadership theories were developed in the United States using US subjects, so they have an American bias. They emphasize follower responsibilities rather than rights; assume hedonism rather than commitment to duty or altruistic motivation; rely on a democratic value orientation and the centrality of work in followers' lives; and stress rationality rather than spirituality, religion, or superstition.[104] These theories generally do apply in the Canadian workplace, but bear in mind the cultural differences between Canadians and Americans noted in Chapter 3. And be aware, too, that the theories do not always apply outside of North America in quite the same way.

As a guide for adjusting your leadership style, you might consider the various dimensions of national culture presented in Chapter 3. For example, a manipulative or autocratic style is compatible with high power distance, and we find high power distance scores in Arab, Far Eastern, and Latin countries. Power distance rankings should also be good indicators of employee willingness to accept participative leadership. Participation is likely to be most effective in such low power distance cultures as those in Norway, Finland, Denmark, and Sweden. Not incidentally, this may explain a) why a number of leadership theories (e.g., the University of Michigan behavioural studies) implicitly favour the use of a participative or people-oriented style; b) the emergence of development-oriented leader behaviour found by Scandinavian researchers; and c) the recent enthusiasm in North America for empowerment. Remember that most leadership theories were developed by North Americans, using North American subjects, and the United States, Canada, and Scandinavian countries all rate below average on power distance.

In 1997, Joseph Di Stefano and one of his students, Nick Bontis, both of the Richard Ivey School of Business at the University of Western Ontario, studied differences in leadership styles across cultures.[105] They were particularly interested in the behaviours that were used to generate exceptional performance by employees. In general, they reported that there were quite a lot of similarities in managers from the United States, northern Europe, southern Europe, Latin America, the Far East, and Commonwealth countries, including Canada. In order to achieve exceptional performance from employees, leaders from all of these countries used visioning, coaching, and stimulating (encouraging new ideas) behaviours similarly, and as their chief strategies. US leaders reported they were more likely to correct employees' behaviour than did Far Eastern or Latin managers. Americans also used team building more often than did Asian managers. Far Eastern managers were less likely to include recognition as part of how they encouraged their employees' exceptional performance than were southern European leaders. These findings suggest that there are some minor differences in how leaders throughout the world achieve exceptional performance from their employees. However, they also suggest a great degree of similarity in what it takes to get high-performing employees.

Summary and Implications

 What is the difference between a manager and a leader? Managers promote stability while leaders press for change. Managers often make sure that the day-to-day operations of organizations get carried out, while leaders set the vision for the organization.

2 Are there specific traits, behaviours, and situations that affect how one leads? Early leadership theories were concerned with supervision, and sought to find out if there were ways to identify leaders. Trait theories examined whether any traits were universal among leaders. While there are some common traits, leaders are more different than the same in terms of traits. Emotional intelligence is one of the few traits that have been found to be extremely important for leadership success. Other research tried to discover whether some behaviours create better leaders than others. The findings were mixed, suggesting that leaders need to consider both task-oriented and employee-oriented behaviours. Researchers then considered the situations in which leadership is applied. This research tells us that leaders need to adjust their behaviours, depending on the situation and the needs of the employees. This was an important contribution to the study of leadership.

3 How does a leader lead with vision? The more recent approaches to leadership move away from the supervisory tasks of leaders and focus on vision-setting activities. These theories try to explain how certain leaders can achieve extraordinary performance levels from their followers, and they stress symbolic and emotionally appealing leadership behaviours. These leaders, known as *charismatic* or *transformational leaders*, inspire followers to go beyond their own self-interests for the good of the organization.

4 Can a person be an informal leader? There are several approaches to being a leader even if one does not have a formal position of leadership. *Superleadership* emphasizes that managers should "lead others to lead themselves," so that the followers also become leaders. *Empowerment* can also lead to leadership responsibilities. *Informal leadership* can also happen through being a leader on a team.

5 What is self-leadership? With self-leadership, individuals and teams set goals, plan and implement tasks, evaluate performance, solve their own problems, and motivate themselves. The supervisor plays a much-reduced role. Self-leadership can also include leadership at the grassroots level in an organization, where one does not have actual authority. Leading without authority simply means exhibiting leadership behaviour even though you do not have a formal position or title that might encourage others "to obey."

6 What are some of the hot topics in leadership? One of the major considerations is whether there is a moral dimension to leadership. Moral leadership comes from within the individual, and in general means treating people well, and with respect. A second hot issue in leadership is the question of whether men and women use different leadership styles, and if so, whether one style is inherently superior to the other. The literature suggests that the similarities between men and women tend to outweigh the differences and that what differences there are seem to be that women use a more democratic leadership style, while men feel more comfortable with a directive style. A third interesting issue in the study of leadership is whether national culture affects leadership style. One way that national culture affects leadership style is by the cultural expectations and norms of followers. Leaders, particularly when they are working in international situations, are constrained by the cultural conditions that their followers have come to expect.

For Review

1. Trace the development of leadership research.

2. Describe the strengths and weaknesses in the trait approach to leadership.

3. What is the Leadership Grid?

4. When might leaders be irrelevant?

5. Describe the strengths and weaknesses of a charismatic leader.

6. What are the differences between transactional and transformational leaders?

7. What is dispersed leadership? What are some examples of dispersed leadership?

8. Why do you think effective female and male managers often exhibit similar traits and behaviours?

9. What characteristics define an effective follower?

10. What is moral leadership?

For Critical Thinking

1. Develop an example where you apply path-goal theory.

2. Reconcile path-goal theory and substitutes for leadership.

3. What kind of activities could a full-time college or university student pursue that might lead to the perception that he or she is a charismatic leader? In pursuing those activities, what might the student do to enhance this perception of being charismatic?

4. Based on the low representation of women in upper management, to what extent do you think that organizations should actively promote women into the senior ranks of management?

OB for You

- It is easy to imagine that theories of leadership are more important to those who are leaders or who plan in the near future to become leaders. However, leadership opportunities occur throughout an organization. You have no doubt seen student leaders who did not necessarily have any formal authority be extremely successful.

- Leaders are not born. They learn how to lead by paying attention to the situation and what needs to be done.

- There is no one best way to lead. It is important to consider the situation, and the needs of the people who will be led.

- Sometimes no leader is needed—the individuals in the group simply work well enough together that each takes turns at leadership without appointing a formal leader.

 **POINT**

 **COUNTERPOINT**

Leaders Make a Real Difference!

There can be little question that the success of an organization, or any group within an organization, depends largely on the quality of its leadership. Whether in business, government, education, medicine, or religion, the quality of an organization's leadership determines the quality of the organization itself. Successful leaders anticipate change, vigorously exploit opportunities, motivate their followers to higher levels of productivity, correct poor performance, and lead the organization toward its objectives.

Why is leadership so important to an organization's success? The answer lies in the need for coordination and control. Organizations exist to attain objectives that are either impossible or extremely inefficient to achieve if done by individuals acting alone. The organization itself is a coordination and control mechanism. Rules, policies, job descriptions, and authority hierarchies are illustrations of devices created to facilitate coordination and control. But leadership, too, contributes toward integrating various job activities, coordinating communication between organizational subunits, monitoring activities, and controlling deviations from standard. No amount of rules and regulations can replace the experienced leader who can make rapid and firm decisions.

The importance of leadership is not lost on those who staff organizations. Corporations, government agencies, school systems, and institutions of all shapes and sizes cumulatively spend billions of dollars every year to recruit, select, evaluate, and train individuals for leadership positions. The best evidence, however, of the importance that organizations place on leadership roles is exhibited in salary schedules. Leaders are routinely paid 10, 20, or more times the salary of those in nonleadership positions. For example, the head of General Motors earns more than $1.5 million annually. The highest-skilled auto worker, in contrast, earns under $50 000 a year. The president of this auto worker's union makes more than $100 000 a year. Police officers typically earn $30 000 to $45 000 a year. Their manager probably earns 25 percent more, and his or her manager another 25 percent. The pattern is well-established. The more responsibility a leader has, as evidenced by his or her level in the organization, the more he or she earns. Would organizations voluntarily pay their leaders so much more than their nonleaders if they did not strongly believe that leaders make a real difference?

Leaders Don't Make a Difference!

Given the resources that have been spent on studying, selecting, and training leaders, you would expect there would be overwhelming evidence supporting the positive effect of leadership on organizational performance, but that's not the case![106]

First, leaders exist in a social system that constrains their behaviour. They have to live with role expectations that define behaviours that are acceptable and unacceptable. Pressures to conform to the expectations of peers, employees, and superiors all limit the range of behaviours that a leader can exhibit.

Second, organizational rules, procedures, policies, and historical precedents all act to limit a leader's unilateral control over decisions and resources. Hiring decisions, for instance, must be made according to procedures. And budget allocations are typically heavily influenced by previous budget precedents.

Third, there are factors outside the organization that leaders cannot control but that have a large bearing on organizational performance. For example, consider the executive in a home-construction firm. Costs are largely determined by the operations of the commodities and labour markets, and demand is largely dependent on interest rates, availability of mortgage money, and economic conditions that are affected by governmental policies over which the executive has little control. While a leader may react to problems as they arise or try to forecast and anticipate external changes, he or she has little influence over the environment. On the contrary, the environment typically puts significant limits and constraints on the leader.

Finally, the trend in recent years is toward leaders playing a smaller and smaller role in organizational activities. Important decisions are increasingly made by committees, not individuals. Additionally, the widespread popularity of employee-involvement programs, the empowerment movement, and self-managed work teams has contributed to reducing any specific leader's influence.

Although leaders take the credit for successes and the blame for failures, a more realistic conclusion would probably be that, except in times of rapid growth, change, or crisis, leaders do not make much of a difference in an organization's actual performance. However, people want to believe that leadership is the cause of performance changes, particularly at the extremes.

LEARNING ABOUT **YOURSELF** EXERCISE

Are You a Charismatic Leader?

Instructions: The following statements refer to the possible ways in which you might behave toward others when you are in a leadership role. Please read each statement carefully and decide to what extent it applies to you. Then circle the appropriate number.

1 = To little or no extent
2 = To a slight extent
3 = To a moderate extent
4 = To a considerable extent
5 = To a very great extent

You...

1. Pay close attention to what others say when they are talking	1	2	3	4	5
2. Communicate clearly	1	2	3	4	5
3. Are trustworthy	1	2	3	4	5
4. Care about other people	1	2	3	4	5
5. Do not put excessive energy into avoiding failure	1	2	3	4	5
6. Make the work of others more meaningful	1	2	3	4	5
7. Seem to focus on the key issues in a situation	1	2	3	4	5
8. Get across your meaning effectively, often in unusual ways	1	2	3	4	5
9. Can be relied on to follow through on commitments	1	2	3	4	5
10. Have a great deal of self-respect	1	2	3	4	5
11. Enjoy taking carefully calculated risks	1	2	3	4	5
12. Help others feel more competent in what they do	1	2	3	4	5
13. Have a clear set of priorities	1	2	3	4	5
14. Are in touch with how others feel	1	2	3	4	5
15. Rarely change once you have taken a clear position	1	2	3	4	5
16. Focus on strengths, of yourself and others	1	2	3	4	5
17. Seem most alive when deeply involved in some project	1	2	3	4	5
18. Show others that they are all part of the same group	1	2	3	4	5
19. Get others to focus on the issues you see as important	1	2	3	4	5
20. Communicate feelings as well as ideas	1	2	3	4	5
21. Let others know where you stand	1	2	3	4	5
22. Seem to know just how you "fit" into a group	1	2	3	4	5
23. Learn from mistakes; do not treat errors as disasters, but as learning	1	2	3	4	5
24. Are fun to be around	1	2	3	4	5

Scoring Key

The questionnaire measures each of the 6 basic behaviour leader patterns, as well as a set of emotional responses. Each question is stated as a measure of the extent to which you engage in the behaviour, or elicit the feelings. The higher your overall score, the more you demonstrate charismatic leader behaviours. The indices outline a variety of traits associated with charismatic behaviour. For each index, add up the scores you gave to the relevant questions. Your score on each index can range from 4 to 20. The higher your score, the more likely you exhibit the trait described.

Index 1: *Management of Attention* (1, 7, 13, 19). Your score _____. You pay especially close attention to people with whom you are communicating. You are also "focused in" on the key issues under discussion and help others to see clearly these key points. They have clear ideas about the relative importance or priorities of different issues under discussion.

Index 2: *Management of Meaning* (2, 8, 14, 20). Your score _____. This set of items centres on your communication skills, specifically your ability to get the meaning of a message across, even if this means devising some quite innovative approach.

Index 3: *Management of Trust* (3, 9, 15, 21). Your score _____. The key factor is your perceived trustworthiness as shown by your willingness to follow through on promises, avoidance of "flip-flop" shifts in position, and willingness to take a clear position.

Index 4: *Management of Self* (4, 10, 16, 22). Your score _____. This index concerns your general attitudes toward yourself and others, that is, your overall concern for others and their feelings, as well as for "taking care of" feelings about yourself in a positive sense (e.g., self-regard).

Index 5: *Management of Risk* (5, 11, 17, 23). Your score _____. Effective charismatic leaders are deeply involved in what they do, and do not spend excessive amounts of time or energy on plans to "protect" themselves against failure. These leaders are willing to take risks, not on a hit-or-miss basis, but after careful estimation of the odds of success or failure.

Index 6: *Management of Feelings* (6, 12, 18, 24). Your score _____. Charismatic leaders seem to consistently generate a set of feelings in others. Others feel that their work becomes more meaningful and that they are the "masters" of their own behaviour; that is, they feel competent. They feel a sense of community, a "we-ness" with their colleagues and their co-workers.

Source: M. Sashkin and W.C. Morris, *Organizational Behavior.* © 1987 Reprinted by permission of Pearson Education, Inc. Upper Saddle River, NJ 07458.

BREAKOUT **GROUP** EXERCISES

Form small groups to discuss the following topics, as assigned by your instructor:

1. Identify an example of someone you thought was a good leader. What traits did they have? How did these traits differ from someone you identify as a bad leader?

2. Identify a situation when you were in a leadership position (in a group, in the workplace, within your family, etc.). To what extent were you able to use a contingency approach to leadership? What made that easier or more difficult for you?

3. When you have worked in student groups, how frequently have leaders emerged in the group? What difficulties occur when leaders are leading peers? Are there ways to overcome these difficulties?

WORKING WITH OTHERS EXERCISE

Being Charismatic

From Concepts to Skills on pages 281–282 indicates how one goes about being charismatic. In this exercise, you will use that information to practise projecting charisma.

a. The class should break into pairs.

b. Student A's task is to "lead" Student B through a new-student orientation to your college or university. The orientation should last about 10 to 15 minutes. Assume Student B is new to your college or university and is unfamiliar with the campus. Remember, Student A should try to project himself or herself as charismatic.

c. Roles now reverse and Student B's task is to "lead" Student A in a 10- to 15-minute program on how to study more effectively for college or university

exams. Take a few minutes to think about what has worked well for you, and assume that Student A is a new student interested in improving his or her study habits. Again remember that Student B should try to project himself or herself as charismatic.

d. When both role plays are complete, each pair should assess how well they did in projecting charisma and how they might improve.

Source: This exercise is based on J.M. Howell and P.J. Frost, "A Laboratory Study of Charismatic Leadership," *Organizational Behavior and Human Decision Processes*, April 1989, pp. 243–269.

ETHICAL DILEMMA EXERCISE

Jean Chrétien announced in 2002 that he would step down as prime minister in February 2004. Several months later, even though there had not yet been a leadership convention, Paul Martin started being regarded in some circles as the next prime minister. Over the next year he slowly revealed what he would do when he became prime minister, and he was often asked to comment on the impact of Chrétien's decision on his leadership. Even US government officials said that they would wait to discuss some important cross-border issues until Chrétien was replaced. Chrétien's position gave him the power to remain

in office until the end of his official term. However, this leads to several ethical dilemmas: Was it ethical for Chrétien to remain in office once he was considered a lame duck leader? Was it ethical for Paul Martin to start discussions with advisers, based on the belief he would be prime minister in early 2004? Was it ethical for the United States to put off discussions with Canada until the leadership change occurred? How did power and politics lead to the situation that Canada faced near the end of Chrétien's leadership?

CASE INCIDENT

Mogens Smed:
Charismatic Leader of SMED International

Mogens Smed is the 50-something president and CEO of Calgary-based SMED International, which specializes in building custom office interiors. In addition to upscale office furniture, the company designs floors and is the market leader in prefabricated movable walls. At 69 675

square metres, SMED's new factory in southeast Calgary is the largest manufacturing facility in Western Canada. Besides state-of-the-art manufacturing equipment, there is a large gym and a huge, brightly coloured cafeteria where employees gather for pep rallies.

SMED, founded in 1982, has 49 marketing offices in 7 countries and has clients in more than 40 countries. Its most well-known clients include Steven Spielberg's DreamWorks SKG in Los Angeles, the NFL Players' Association in New York City, Royal Bank, TD Bank, Canadian Imperial Bank of Commerce, Fox Television, *Penthouse,* Coca-Cola Co., Tommy Hilfiger Corp., and Calvin Klein.

SMED's competitors include American giants such as Herman Miller, Steelcase, and Knoll, all of which are larger than SMED. SMED is really only a small player in the office furniture industry, with about 1 percent of market share. Chief competitors are Herman Miller, which has 10 percent of market share, and Steelcase, which has 25 percent.

Smed himself has a reputation as an outstanding salesperson and a charismatic leader, and his leadership style does not allow him to fret about his small market share. SMED's motto is "Our only competition is conventional thinking." Smed explains that SMED is different from the competition: "We do not play by the rules. There are no rules. We offer something completely different from them. We don't just make products and offer them to the customer. We ask the customer what they want and then make it for them."

SMED's vision is that the customer is always first. To remind everyone of this, brochures, magazines, and books supporting this philosophy are evident in the foyer and other parts of the organization. These publications include *Culture Shift* and *The Employee Handbook of New Work Habits for a Radically Changing World* by Price Pritchett, and *The Customer-Driven Company* by Richard Whiteley. In fact, the heart of SMED's marketing campaign is actually an alpine retreat. Smed built Falkridge at a cost of $1.6 million, so that he and his staff could woo clients with gourmet dinners, fine wines, and Cuban cigars. At SMED, no expense is too great to impress a client.

Like all charismatic leaders, Smed has truly inspired his employees. In fact, industry analysts have commented on the nearly messianic fervour of the company. "In some ways, SMED is like a cult," says James David, an analyst at Scotia Capital. "Mogens Smed displays a great deal of charisma and enthusiasm, and that carries down through the ranks. The people around him are so much on the same page, it's scary."

Characteristic of charismatic leaders, Smed interacts personally with both employees and clients. He is willing to go anywhere, any time, if he thinks it will clinch a sale. For instance, Smed has taken clients for a seven-day excursion to an exclusive fishing lodge in British Columbia's Queen Charlotte Islands, where guests caught 14-kilogram chinook salmon and watched killer whales frolic in the ocean. He can do this because, like many charismatic leaders, he makes all the major decisions but leaves the day-to-day operations to his executive vice-presidents.

Smed's vision and charisma may work well for his clients, but investors and market analysts are more critical of his style. SMED shares reached a peak of $32 in mid-1998, before the company consolidated its six plants into the large manufacturing facility in Calgary, but a variety of factors sent the stock plummeting. In April 1999 it fell as low as $5.50. Some in the financial community "question whether the company is going overboard, needlessly sacrificing profit for feel-good schmoozing." SMED's share prices did increase in early 2000, after Office Specialty (now Inscape Corporation), based in Holland Landing, Ontario, began a hostile takeover bid. Outraged, Smed looked for a white knight, which he found in Holland, Michigan-based Haworth Inc., a maker and marketer of office furniture and seating. The deal made Haworth the second-largest office furniture maker in the world behind Steelcase Inc. SMED kept its name and operates as an independent subsidiary. What impact the merger of the two companies will have on Smed's charismatic style remains to be seen.

Questions

1. Describe how Smed can be classified as a charismatic leader.

2. What situational variables do you think explain Smed's success?

3. How might Smed's charismatic nature affect his business decisions?

4. Would you want to work for a charismatic leader such as Smed? Why or why not?

Sources Based on Mel Duvall, "New Plant Provides Impetus for SMED's growth," *The Financial Post Daily*, October 3, 1997, p. 19; Curtis Gillespie, "Selling Smed: Mogens Smed Is Passionate About Making SMED International a Global Player in Office Furniture," *Financial Post Magazine*, October 1997, pp. 70–81; S. Miles, "Smed Claws Its Way Back to Profitability," *Financial Post (National Post)*, November 27, 1999, p. C3; P. Verburg, "His Party, Your Hangover," *Canadian Business*, August 27, 1999, pp. 36–39; D. Steinhart, "Hostile Move on Smed Could Trigger New Bids," *Financial Post (National Post)*, December 22, 1999; and I. McKinnon, "Smed Gets $280M Bid From Haworth," *Financial Post (National Post)*, January 26, 2000.

CBC ⊛ VIDEO CASE INCIDENT

Who's Got the Power?

Over the past 25 years, CEOs have been recruited by powerful boards of directors to take the helm of troubled organizations. They are then encouraged to use their influential leadership abilities to transform these companies into successful investments.

Starting with Lee Iacocca's campaign to transform Chrysler in the early 1980s, there has been increased pressure on CEOs to be the saviours for all corporate ills. According to Professor Rakesh Khurana of the Harvard Business School, finding the right CEO is critical to the success of an organization. Khurana states that the "CEO as panacea" syndrome can raise expectations about the performance of an incoming CEO to an unsustainable level.

Meet Jean C. Monty, former chair and CEO of BCE Inc. Armed with an MBA from the University of Chicago, Monty began working his way up the corporate ladder in the early 1970s. After a successful start on Wall Street, he soon moved back to Canada where he worked for 28 years with Bell Canada.

In 1992, Monty was put in command of BCE's then-struggling manufacturing arm, Northern Telecom, which eventually became Nortel. Under his leadership, the company went from losing $1 billion in 1993 to turning a $1.2 billion profit in 1997. Monty then moved to BCE to become its president and COO, later taking over as CEO in 1998. He arrived at a time when BCE's market share had plummeted from 83 percent to 63 percent. The company was in need of someone able to transform it back to its former market-dominating position. Monty was the perfect candidate for the job. In an effort to finance BCE's acquisitions and future growth, Monty immediately began to make changes, including major job cuts, new US partnerships, and complicated convergence strategies.

In April 2002, Jean Monty resigned as chair and CEO of BCE Inc. His resignation came after two quarterly losses and an $8.2 billion asset writedown.

Questions

1. Do you believe Monty was a victim of marketplace greed, or an example of failed leadership?

2. Using trait theory, identify at least three leadership traits commonly exhibited by "celebrity" leaders.

3. When an organization is undergoing change, does it make more sense to try to change a person's leadership style to fit the changes, as proposed by path-goal theory, or to change the situation that fits a leadership style, as proposed by Fiedler's contingency theory?

Source: Based on "Monty Rise and Fall," *CBC Venture*, April 28, 2002, 825; R. Khurana, "Finding the Right CEO: Why Boards Often Make Poor Choices," *MIT Sloan Management Review* 43, no. 1, Fall 2001, pp. 91–95; J. Bowman and J. McHutchion, "Jean C. Monty," *CBC News Online*, April 24, 2002, www.cbc.ca/news/features/monty_john020424.html.

From **Concepts** to **Skills**

Practising to Be Charismatic

In order to be charismatic in your leadership style, you need to engage in the following behaviours:[107]

1. *Project a powerful, confident, and dynamic presence.* This has both verbal and nonverbal components. Use a captivating and engaging voice tone. Convey confidence. Talk directly to people, maintain direct eye contact, and hold your body posture in a way that says you are sure of yourself. Speak clearly, avoid stammering, and avoid sprinkling your sentences with noncontent phrases such as "ahhh" and "you know."

2. *Articulate an overarching goal.* You need to share a vision for the future, develop an unconventional way of achieving the vision, and have the ability to communicate the vision to others.

   The vision is a clear statement of where you want to go and how you are going to get there. You need to persuade others that the achievement of this vision is in their self-interest.

   You need to look for fresh and radically different approaches to problems. The road to achieving your vision should be seen as novel but also appropriate to the context.

   Charismatic individuals not only have a vision, but they're also able to get others to buy into it. The real power of Martin Luther King Jr., was not that he had a dream, but that he could articulate it in terms that made it accessible to millions.

3. *Communicate high-performance expectations and confidence in others' ability to meet these expectations.* You need to demonstrate your confidence in people by stating ambitious goals for them individually and as a group. You then convey absolute belief that they will achieve their expectations.

4. *Be sensitive to the needs of followers.* Charismatic leaders get to know their followers individually. You need to understand their individual needs and develop intensely personal relationships with each. This is done through encouraging followers to express their points of view, being approachable, genuinely listening to and caring about followers' concerns, and asking questions so that followers can learn what is really important to them.

Assessing Skills

After you have read this chapter, take the following Self-Assessments on your enclosed CD-ROM.

22. How Good Am I at Personal Planning?

27. What's My Leadership Style?

28. How Charismatic Am I?

29. Do Others See Me as Trusting?

Practising Skills

You are a manufacturing manager in a large electronics plant.[108] The company's management is always searching for ways to increase efficiency. They recently installed new machines and set up a new simplified work system, but to the surprise of everyone—including you—the expected increase in production was not realized. In fact, production has begun to drop, quality has fallen off, and the number of employee resignations has risen.

You do not think that there is anything wrong with the machines. You have had reports from other companies that are using them, and they confirm your opinion. You have also had representatives from the firm that built the machines go over them, and they report that the machines are operating at peak efficiency.

You know that some aspect of the new work system must be responsible for the change, but you are getting no help from your immediate team members—four first-line supervisors who report to you and who are each in charge of a section—or your supply manager. The drop in production has been variously attributed to poor training of the operators, lack of an adequate system of financial incentives, and poor morale. All of the individuals involved have deep feelings about this issue. Your team does not agree with you or with one another.

This morning you received a phone call from your division manager. He had just received your production figures for the past six months and was calling to express his concern. He indicated that the problem was yours to solve in any way that you think best but that he would like to know within a week what steps you plan to take.

You share your division manager's concern with the falling productivity and know that your employees are also concerned. Using your knowledge of leadership concepts, which leadership style would you choose? And why?

Reinforcing Skills

1. Think of a group or team to which you currently belong or of which you have been a part. What type of leadership style did the leader of this group appear to exhibit? Give some specific examples of the types of leadership behaviours he or she used.

Evaluate the leadership style. Was it appropriate for the group? Why or why not? What would you have done differently? Why?

2. Observe two sports teams (either college or professional—one that you consider successful and the other unsuccessful). What leadership styles appear to be used in these team situations? Give some specific examples of the types of leadership behaviours you observe. How would you evaluate the leadership style? Was it appropriate for the team? Why or why not? To what degree do you think leadership style influenced the team's outcomes?

CHAPTER 9

Decision Making, Creativity, and Ethics

What is corporate
social responsibility?

8

Is there a right way
to make decisions?

1

How do people actually
make decisions?

2

Nike's decision to man-
ufacture shoes overseas has
prompted critics to claim that it
exploits workers in poor countries.
Did Nike make a rational decision,
and is it being socially responsible with this decision?

What kinds of shortcuts
do people use in
making decisions?

3

What is ethics,
and how can it
be used for better
decision making?

7

How can we get more
creative decisions?

6

Should the leader make
the decision, or encourage
the group to participate?

5

What factors affect
group decision
making?

4

ike's first "Corporate Responsibility Report," published in October 2001, confessed that making Nike's runners is "tedious, hard and doesn't offer a wonderful future."[1] Readers may have been startled to learn that employees in overseas factories making Nike products were being harassed by supervisors. Employees were also asked to work far more overtime than rules permitted. Finally, the company admitted to knowing far too little about day-to-day life in the factories, because it was not monitoring the situation closely enough.

These admissions might have seemed shocking to anyone who had not expected Nike to acknowledge what critics have been saying for years: Nike benefits from unfair labour practices in foreign-owned plants to which it sub-contracts work. The company has since been trying to improve conditions at its overseas operations.

Nike's decision to publish a corporate responsibility report is just one example of the many decisions companies face every day. Nike had also

decided to move its manufacturing to low-wage countries, an action that has brought the company much criticism.

In this chapter, we will describe how decisions in organizations are made, as well as how creativity is linked to decision making. We will also look at the ethical and socially responsible aspects of decision making as part of our discussion. Decision making affects people at all levels of the organization, and is done by both individuals and groups. Thus, we also consider the special characteristics of group decision making.

How Should Decisions Be Made?

After completing its first corporate responsibility report, Nike increased training for both managers and employees at its overseas operations. Managers were told that treating employees properly will lead to "improved productivity, reduced labour turnover and less sick leave." Nike thus evaluated its problem, and came up with ways to resolve it, in order to reduce criticism of its labour practices. How do individuals and companies achieve decision making?

Decision making occurs as a reaction to a problem or an opportunity. A **problem** is a discrepancy between some current state of affairs and some desired state, requiring consideration of alternative courses of action.[2] Opportunities occur when something unplanned happens, giving rise to thoughts about new ways of proceeding.

Whenever any of us make a decision, we have a process that we go through to help us arrive at that decision. Some of us take a very rational approach, with specific steps where we analyze parts of the **decision**, others rely on intuition, and some just decide to put two or more alternatives in a hat and pull one out.

1 Is there a right way to make decisions?

problem
A discrepancy between some current state of affairs and some desired state.

decision
The choice made from among two or more alternatives.

Knowing how to make decisions is an important part of everyday life. Below we consider various decision-making models that apply to both individual and group choices. (Later in the chapter, we discuss special aspects of group decision making.) We start with the *rational model,* which describes decision making in the ideal world, a situation that rarely exists. We then look at alternatives to the rational model, and how decisions actually get made.

The Rational Decision-Making Process

rational
Refers to choices that are consistent and maximize value.

rational decision-making model
A decision-making model that describes how individuals should behave in order to maximize some outcome.

The optimizing decision maker—one who makes the best use of the factors at hand—is **rational**. That is, he or she makes consistent, high-value choices within specified constraints.[3] These choices are made following a six-step **rational decision-making model**.[4]

The Rational Model

The six steps in the rational decision-making model are listed in Exhibit 9–1.

The model begins by *defining the problem.* If you calculate your monthly expenses and find you are spending $50 more than you allocated in your budget, you have defined a problem. Many poor decisions can be traced to the decision maker overlooking a problem or defining the wrong problem.

Once a decision maker has defined the problem, he or she needs to *identify the decision criteria* that will be important in solving the problem. In this step, the decision maker determines what is relevant in making the decision. This step brings the decision maker's interests, values, and personal preferences into the process. Identifying criteria is important because people can have different ideas about what is relevant. Also keep in mind that any factors not identified in this step are considered irrelevant to the decision maker.

To understand the type of criteria that might be used to make a decision, consider the many sponsorship requests Toronto-based Canadian Imperial Bank of Commerce receives each year. In making a decision about whether or not to support a request, the bank considers the following criteria:[5]

- Strategic fit with CIBC's overall goals and objectives;

- Ability to achieve youth customer segment marketing objectives;

Each year, CIBC contributes millions of dollars to hundreds of initiatives for educational funding, research, mentoring and skills programs through its "Youth Vision" program. CIBC evaluates proposals from community leaders like Big Brothers Big Sisters of Canada and the YMCA to see if the requests meet corporate objectives. One of CIBC's objectives is to help young Canadians realize their dreams and reach their full potential. Here, CIBC chairman and chief executive officer John Hunkin is shown with Youth Vision Scholarship recipients for 2002.

Steps in the Rational Decision-Making Model

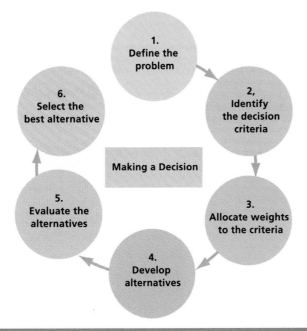

- Tangible and intangible benefits of the proposal, such as goodwill, reputation, and cost/potential revenue;

- Organizational impact;

- Business risks (if any).

If the proposals do not meet these criteria, they are not funded.

The criteria identified are rarely all equal in importance. So the third step requires the decision maker to *weight the previously identified criteria* in order to give them the correct priority in the decision.

The fourth step requires the decision maker to *generate possible alternatives* that could succeed in resolving the problem. No attempt is made in this step to appraise alternatives, only to list them.

Once the alternatives are listed, the decision maker must critically analyze and evaluate each one. This is done by *rating each alternative on each criterion*. The strengths and weaknesses of each alternative become evident as they are compared with the criteria and weights established in the second and third steps.

The sixth and final step in this model requires *computing the optimal decision*. This is done by evaluating each alternative against the weighted criteria and selecting the alternative with the highest total score.

Assumptions of the Model

The rational decision-making model we just described contains a number of assumptions.[6] Let's briefly outline those assumptions.

- *Problem clarity.* The problem is clear and unambiguous. The decision maker is assumed to have complete information regarding the decision situation.

- *Known options.* It is assumed the decision maker can identify all the relevant criteria and list all the workable alternatives. The decision maker is also aware of all possible results of each alternative.

- *Clear preferences.* Rationality assumes that the criteria and alternatives can be ranked and weighted to reflect their importance.

- *Constant preferences.* It's assumed that the specific decision criteria are constant and that the weights assigned to them are stable over time.

- *No time or cost constraints.* The rational decision maker can obtain full information about criteria and alternatives because it is assumed that there are no time or cost constraints.

- *Maximum payoff.* The rational decision maker will choose the alternative that yields the highest perceived value.

HOW DO INDIVIDUALS ACTUALLY MAKE DECISIONS?

Chaichana Homsombat, a 21-year-old employee at Pan Asia Footwear in Thailand, the world's third-largest Nike subcontractor factory, explains his job: "Each of us has to work constantly. The faster we meet the assigned quota, the earlier we can go home."[7] Homsombat's quota is to pack 1296 pairs of runners into boxes each workday.

The deputy managing director of the plant, Boonrawd Indamanee, says the quotas improve productivity. A human rights inspector at the plant wonders whether employees are really getting a fair day's pay under the quota system. The management does not want trade unions in the plant, but the inspector fears that "Workers don't know their rights. They simply accept whatever is given to them." Thus when asked if the company gives benefits to employees, one supervisor responded: "The uniform. We get three of them when we join the company and two more each year." If employees are not aware of their rights, or do not have full information about them, or have few alternatives, are they really able to make an informed decision about how to behave?

② How do people actually make decisions?

The situation at the Nike plant in Thailand raises some questions: Do decision makers actually follow the rational model? Do they carefully assess problems, identify all relevant criteria, use their creativity to identify all workable alternatives, and painstakingly evaluate every alternative to find an optimizing choice?

When decision makers are faced with a simple problem and few alternative courses of action, and when the cost of searching out and evaluating alternatives is low, the rational model provides a fairly accurate description of the decision process.[8] However, such situations are the exception. Most decisions in the real world don't follow the rational model. For instance, people are usually content to find an acceptable or reasonable solution to their problem rather than an optimizing one. As such, decision makers generally make limited use of their creativity. Choices tend to be confined to the problem symptom and to the current alternative. As one expert in decision making recently concluded: "Most significant decisions are made by judgment, rather than by a defined prescriptive model."[9]

In the following sections we indicate areas where the reality of decision making conflicts with the rational model.[10] None of these ways of making decisions should be considered *irrational*, because they are simply departures from the rational model.

Problem Identification

Most of the decisions that get made reflect only the problems that decision makers see. Problems do not arrive with flashing neon lights to identify themselves. And one person's problem is another person's acceptable status quo. So how do decision makers identify and select problems?

Problems that are visible tend to have a higher probability of being selected than ones that are important.[11] Why? We can offer at least two reasons. First, it's easier to recognize visible problems. They are more likely to catch a decision maker's attention. This explains why politicians are more likely to talk about the "crime problem" than the "illiteracy problem." Second, remember that we are concerned with decision making in organizations. Decision makers want to appear competent and "on top of problems." This motivates them to focus attention on problems that are visible to others.

Do not ignore the decision maker's self-interest. If a decision maker faces a conflict between selecting a problem that is important to the organization and one that is important to the decision maker, self-interest tends to win out.[12] This also ties in with the issue of visibility. It's usually in a decision maker's best interest to attack high-profile problems. It conveys to others that things are under control. Moreover, when the decision maker's performance is later reviewed, the evaluator is more likely to give a high rating to someone who has been aggressively attacking visible problems than to someone whose actions have been less obvious.

Bounded Rationality in Considering Alternatives

When you considered which college or university to attend, did you look at every possible alternative? Did you carefully identify all the criteria that were important in your decision? Did you evaluate each alternative against the criteria in order to find the school that is best for you? The answer to these questions is probably "no." But don't feel bad, because few people selected their educational institution this way.

It is difficult for individuals to identify and consider every possible alternative available to them. Realistically speaking, people are limited by their ability to interpret, process, and act on information. This is called **bounded rationality**.[13]

Because of bounded rationality, individuals are not able to discover and consider every alternative for a decision. Instead, they identify a limited list of the more obvious choices. In most cases, these will include familiar criteria and previously tested solutions. Rather than carefully reviewing and evaluating each alternative in great detail, individuals will settle on an alternative that is "good enough"—one that meets an acceptable level of performance. The first alternative that meets the "good enough" criterion ends the search. So decision makers choose a final solution that **satisfices** rather than optimizes; that is, they seek solutions that are both satisfactory and sufficient. In practice this might mean that rather than interviewing ten job candidates for a position, a manager interviews one at a time until one that is "good enough" is interviewed—that is, the first job candidate encountered who meets the minimum criteria for the job. The federal government has proposed this rule for its own hiring, as this *OB in the Workplace* shows.

bounded rationality
Individuals make decisions by constructing simplified models that extract the essential features from problems without capturing all their complexity.

satisfice
A decision model that relies on solutions that are both satisfactory and sufficient.

OB IN THE WORKPLACE

Ottawa May Stop Hiring Best-Qualified

Is hiring the "best-qualified" person too much work? Executives and middle managers working in the federal government are starting to think so.[14] They argue that "being qualified and competent for a particular job should be enough" even though the person may not be the best possible candidate.

Civil servants asked for the rules on hiring to be loosened so that they could actually start hiring and filling positions rather than spending so much time finding the "best-qualified" person. They find those searches excruciating and exhausting. When managers follow the federal guidelines for hiring, it can take six months or more to fill a position.

Steve Hindle, president of the Professional Institute of the Public Service of Canada (PIPSC), explains why hiring someone who is qualified is probably good enough: "If people are honest, what they want is someone who is qualified, but the idea of finding the best? Do we have the time, tools and money needed to find the very best? You want someone competent and good and if they're the best, that's great."

However, not everyone agrees that changing the rules for hiring is a good idea. The public sector unions worry that favouritism may become more common. But they do agree that the current system has too much red tape. ▮

Intuition

Irene Khoo has just committed her corporation to spending more than $40 million to build a new plant in New Westminster, BC, to manufacture electronic components for satellite communication equipment. She is a vice-president of operations for her firm, and reviewed a comprehensive analysis of five possible plant locations developed by a site-location consulting firm she had hired. This report ranked the New Westminster location third among the five alternatives. After carefully reading the report and its conclusions, Khoo decided against the consultant's recommendation. When asked to explain her decision, Khoo said, "I looked the report over very carefully. Despite its recommendation, I felt that the numbers didn't tell the whole story. Intuitively, I just sensed that New Westminster would prove to be the best bet over the long run."

Intuitive decision making, like that used by Irene Khoo, has recently come out of the closet and gained some respectability. Experts no longer automatically assume that using intuition to make decisions is irrational or ineffective.[15] There is growing recognition that rational analysis has been overemphasized and that, in certain instances, relying on intuition can improve decision making.

What do we mean by intuitive decision making? There are a number of ways to conceptualize intuition.[16] For instance, some consider it a form of extrasensory power or sixth sense, and some believe it is a personality trait that a limited number of people are born with. For our purposes, we define **intuitive decision making** as a subconscious process created out of distilled experience. It doesn't necessarily operate independently of rational analysis; rather, the two complement each other. Those who use intuition effectively often rely on their experiences to help guide and assess their intuitions. That is why many managers are able to rely on intuition.

A recent study of 60 experienced professionals holding high level positions in major US organizations found that many of them used intuition to help them make workplace decisions.[17] Twelve percent said they always used it, while 47 percent said they often used intuition. Only 10 percent said they rarely or seldom used intuition. More than 90 percent of managers said they were likely to use a mix of intuition and data analysis when making decisions.

When asked the types of decisions where they most often used intuition, 40 percent reported that they used it to make people-related decisions such as hiring, performance appraisal, harassment complaints, and safety issues. The managers said they also used intuition for quick or unexpected decisions so they could avoid delays. They also were more likely to rely on intuition in novel situations that had a lot of uncertainty.

The results from this study suggest that intuitive decisions are best applied when time is short, when policies, rules, and guidelines do not give clear-cut advice, when there is a great deal of uncertainty, and when detailed numerical analysis needs a check and balance.

Intuition can be wrong, so it is important to develop one's intuition. Often, good intuition is really the result of recognizing the pattern in a situation and drawing upon previously learned information associated with that pattern to arrive quickly at a decision choice. The result is that the intuitive decision maker can decide rapidly with what

intuitive decision making
A subconscious process created out of distilled experience.

appears to be very limited information. Decision making can be improved by analyzing one's decisions after the fact, to develop a better understanding of when good and bad decisions have been made.

So what does all of this tell us? Based on our discussion above, you should consider the following when making decisions:

- Make sure that you define the problem as best you can.

- Be clear on the factors that you will use to make your decision.

- Be sure to collect enough alternatives so that you can clearly differentiate among them.

JUDGMENT SHORTCUTS AFFECTING THE DECISION CHOICE

Two eminent psychologists, Daniel Kahneman and Amos Tversky, discovered that even when people are trying to be coldly logical, they give radically different answers to the same question if it is posed in different ways.[18] For instance, consider choices A and B in scenario 1 in Exhibit 9–2. Most people come to an opposite conclusion for A and B, even though the problems are identical. The only difference is that the first states the problem in terms of lives saved, while the second states it in terms of lives lost. On the basis of his research in decision making, Kahneman concluded that "we can't assume our judgments are good building blocks for decisions because the judgments themselves may be flawed."[19]

The judgment error described above is known as **framing**, and refers to how the selective use of perspective alters the way one might view a situation in formulating a decision. In examining how people make decisions, the two psychologists discovered that individuals often rely on **heuristics**, or judgment shortcuts, to simplify the decision

> **3** What kinds of shortcuts do people use in making decisions?

> **framing**
> Error in judgment arising from the selective use of perspective that alters the way one views a situation in forming a decision.

> **heuristics**
> Judgment shortcuts in decision making.

Exhibit 9–2

Examples of Decision Biases

Scenario 1: Answer part A before reading part B.

A: Threatened by a superior enemy force, the general faces a dilemma. His intelligence officers say his soldiers will be caught in an ambush in which 600 of them will die unless he leads them to safety by one of two available routes. If he takes the first route, 200 soldiers will be saved. If he takes the second, there's a one-third chance that 600 soldiers will be saved and a two-thirds chance that none will be saved. Which route should he take?

B: The general again has to choose between two escape routes. But this time his aides tell him that if he takes the first, 400 soldiers will die. If he takes the second, there's a one-third chance that no soldiers will die, and a two-thirds chance that 600 soldiers will die. Which route should he take?

Scenario 2:

Linda is 31, single, outspoken, and very bright. She majored in philosophy in university. As a student, she was deeply concerned with discrimination and other social issues and participated in antinuclear demonstrations. Which statement is more likely:

a. Linda is a bank teller.

b. Linda is a bank teller and active in the feminist movement.

Source: K. McKean, "Decisions, Decisions," *Discover*, June 1985, pp. 22–31.

process, rather than going through all of the steps of the rational decision-making model.[20]

Framing is one of the errors people make, but others are also made. For instance, sometimes people make judgments related to **statistical regression to the mean**, the statistical observation that very good or very poor performances are followed by their opposite, resulting in a record of average performance over time. This heuristic may be of particular interest to those trying to decide whether rewards or punishments work better with employees, colleagues, children, and even friends. Although many studies indicate that rewards are a more effective teaching tool than punishment, Kahneman was once faced with a student who begged to differ on this point. "I've often praised people warmly for beautifully executed manoeuvres, and the next time they almost always do worse. And I've screamed at people for badly executed manoeuvres, and by and large the next time they improve." What the student failed to recognize is that each person has an average performance level, so the highs and the lows balance out. The rewards and punishments had little effect on the short-term performance being observed. Rather, improvements happen over the long term. Thus, in this example, it would be helpful to realize that screaming is less likely to result in long-term improvements in behaviour and also tends to damage the relationship between the two parties.

Consider another example of a judgment shortcut. Many more people suffer from fear of flying than from fear of driving in a car. The reason is that many people think flying is more dangerous. It isn't, of course. If flying on a commercial airline were as dangerous as driving, the equivalent of two 747s filled to capacity would have to crash every week, killing all aboard, to match the risk of being killed in a car accident. Because the media give a lot more attention to air accidents, we tend to overstate the risk in flying and understate the risk in driving.

This illustrates an example of the **availability heuristic**, which is the tendency for people to base their judgments on information that is readily available to them. Events that evoke emotions, that are particularly vivid, or that have occurred more recently tend to be more available in our memory. As a result, we tend to be prone to overestimating unlikely events like an airplane crash. The availability heuristic can also explain why managers, when doing annual performance appraisals, tend to give more weight to recent behaviours of an employee than to those behaviours of six or nine months ago.

Many youngsters in Canada dream of playing hockey in the National Hockey League (NHL) when they grow up. In reality, they have a better chance of becoming medical doctors than they do of playing in the NHL, but these kids are suffering from a **representative heuristic**. They tend to assess the likelihood of an occurrence by trying to match it with a pre-existing category. They hear about a boy from their neighbourhood 10 years ago who went on to play professional hockey, or they watch NHL games on television and think that those players are like them. We all are guilty of using this heuristic at times. Managers, for example, frequently predict the performance of a new product by relating it to a previous product's success. Or if three graduates from the same university were hired and turned out to be poor performers, managers might predict that a current job applicant from the same university would not be a good employee. Scenario 2 in Exhibit 9–2 gives another example of representativeness. In that case, Linda is assumed to be a bank teller and a feminist, given her concerns about social issues, even though the probability of both situations being true is much less than the probability of just being a bank teller.

Yet another biasing error that people make is **ignoring the base rate**, or the statistical likelihood of an event, when making a decision. For instance, if you were planning to become an entrepreneur, and we were to ask you whether your business would succeed, you would almost undoubtedly respond with a resounding "yes." This is no different from venture capitalists funding new ventures even when the failure rate of new businesses is quite high. Each individual believes that he or she will beat the odds, even

statistical regression to the mean
The statistical observation that either very good or very poor performances are followed by their opposite, resulting in a record of average performance over time.

availability heuristic
The tendency for people to base their judgments on information that is readily available to them.

National Hockey League (NHL)
www.nhl.com

representative heuristic
Assessing the likelihood of an occurrence by drawing analogies and seeing identical situations where they do not exist.

ignoring the base rate
Error in judgment that occurs when someone ignores the statistical likelihood of an event when making a decision.

when, in the case of founding a business, the failure rate is close to 90 percent. Ignoring the base rate is not due to inexperience of the decision maker. Professors Glen Whyte of the Rotman School of Management (University of Toronto) and Christina Sue-Chan of the Asper School of Business (University of Manitoba) found that even experienced human resource managers ignore the base rate when asked in an experiment to make hiring decisions.[21] They suggest the importance of reminding people of what the base rate is before asking them to make decisions.

Finally, the last bias we will discuss is the common tendency by decision makers to escalate commitment to a failing course of action.[22] **Escalation of commitment** is an increased commitment to a previous decision despite negative information. For example, a friend had been dating a man for about four years. Although she admitted that things were not going too well in the relationship, she was determined to marry the man. When asked to explain this seemingly nonrational choice of action, she responded: "I have a lot invested in the relationship."

It has been well documented that individuals escalate commitment to a failing course of action when they view themselves as responsible for the failure. That is, they "throw good money after bad" to demonstrate that their initial decision was not wrong and to avoid having to admit they made a mistake. Escalation of commitment also fits in with evidence that people try to appear consistent in what they say and do. Increasing commitment to previous actions conveys consistency.

Escalation of commitment has obvious implications for managerial decisions. Many organizations have suffered large losses because a manager was determined to prove his or her original decision was right by continuing to commit resources to what was a lost cause from the beginning. Additionally, consistency is a characteristic often associated with effective leaders. As a result, many managers, in an effort to appear effective, may be motivated to be consistent when, in fact, it may be more appropriate to adopt a new course of action. In actuality, effective managers are those who are able to differentiate between situations in which persistence will pay off and situations in which it will not.

When making decisions you should consider whether you are falling into any of the judgment traps described above. In particular, understanding the base rates, and making sure that you collect information beyond that which is immediately available to you, will provide you with more alternatives from which to frame a decision. It is also useful to consider whether you are sticking with a decision simply because you have invested time in that particular alternative, even though it may not be wise to continue. To learn more about your style of decision making, refer to the *Learning About Yourself Exercise* on pages 316–317.

I.H. Asper School of Business, University of Manitoba
www.umanitoba.ca/management/

escalation of commitment An increased commitment to a previous decision despite negative information.

GROUP DECISION MAKING

While a variety of decisions in both life and organizations are made at the individual level, the belief—characterized by juries—that two heads are better than one has long been accepted as a basic component of North America's and many other countries' legal systems. This belief has expanded to the point that, today, many decisions in organizations are made by groups, teams, or committees. In this section, we will review group decision making and compare it with individual decision making.

4 What factors affect group decision making?

Groups vs. the Individual

Decision-making groups may be widely used in organizations, but does that mean group decisions are preferable to those made by an individual alone? The answer to this question depends on a number of factors. Let's begin by looking at the strengths and weaknesses of group decision making.[23]

Strengths of Group Decision Making

Groups generate *more complete information and knowledge*. By combining the resources of several individuals, groups bring more input into the decision process. Groups can bring *increased diversity of views* to the decision process. This offers the opportunity to consider more approaches and alternatives. The evidence indicates that a group will almost always outperform even the best individual. So groups generate *higher quality decisions*. Finally, groups lead to *increased acceptance of a solution*. Many decisions fail after the final choice is made because people do not accept the solution. Group members who participated in making a decision are likely to enthusiastically support the decision and encourage others to accept it.

Weaknesses of Group Decision Making

Despite the advantages noted, group decisions involve certain drawbacks. First, they're *time-consuming*. Groups typically take more time to reach a solution than a single individual would. Second, there are *conformity pressures* in groups. The desire by group members to be accepted and considered an asset to the group can result in squashing any overt disagreement. Third, group discussion can be *dominated by one or a few members*. If this dominant coalition is composed of low- and medium-ability members, the group's overall effectiveness will suffer. Finally, group decisions suffer from *ambiguous responsibility*. In an individual decision, it's clear who is accountable for the final outcome. In a group decision, the responsibility of any single member is watered down.

Effectiveness and Efficiency

Whether groups are more effective than individuals depends on the criteria you use for defining effectiveness. In terms of *accuracy*, group decisions will tend to be more accurate. The evidence indicates that, on the average, groups make better-quality decisions than individuals.[24] However, if decision effectiveness is defined in terms of *speed*, individuals are superior. If *creativity* is important, groups tend to be more effective than individuals. Finally, if effectiveness means the degree of *acceptance* the final solution achieves, the nod again goes to the group.[25]

Effectiveness, however, cannot be considered without also assessing efficiency. In terms of efficiency, groups almost always stack up as a poor second to the individual

Molly Mak was chosen president of a national information technology solutions provider, Onward Computer Systems, by other partners in the firm after she showed that she had the vision and determination to lead the company to greater growth and profits. She says that consensus is not always possible, especially when it is important to get things accomplished under tight time constraints.

decision maker. With few exceptions, group decision making consumes more work hours than an individual who is tackling the same problem alone. The exceptions tend to be those instances where, to achieve comparable quantities of diverse input, the single decision maker must spend a great deal of time reviewing files and talking to people. Because groups can include members from diverse areas, the time spent searching for information can be reduced. However, as we noted, these advantages in efficiency tend to be the exception. Groups are generally less efficient than individuals. In deciding whether to use groups, then, consideration should be given to assessing whether the increases in effectiveness are sufficient to offset the losses in efficiency.

In summary, groups offer an excellent way to perform many of the steps in the decision-making process. They are a source of both breadth and depth of input for information gathering. If the group is composed of individuals with diverse backgrounds, the alternatives generated should be more extensive and the analysis more critical than what an individual alone could achieve. When the final solution is agreed upon, there are more people in a group decision to support and implement it. These advantages, however, can be more than offset by the time consumed by group decisions, the internal conflicts they create, and the pressures they generate toward conformity.

Groupthink and Groupshift

Two by-products of group decision making have received a considerable amount of attention by researchers in OB. As we will show, these two phenomena have the potential to affect the group's ability to appraise alternatives objectively and arrive at quality decision solutions.

Groupthink

Have you ever felt like speaking up in a meeting, classroom, or informal group, but decided against it? One reason may have been shyness. On the other hand, you may have been a victim of **groupthink**, the phenomenon that occurs when group members become so enamoured with seeking agreement that the norm for consensus overrides the realistic appraisal of alternative courses of action and the full expression of deviant, minority, or unpopular views. It describes a deterioration in an individual's mental efficiency, reality testing, and moral judgment as a result of group pressures.[26]

We have all seen the symptoms of the groupthink phenomenon:[27]

groupthink
Phenomenon in which the norm for consensus overrides the realistic appraisal of alternative courses of action.

- *Illusion of invulnerability*. Group members become overconfident among themselves, allowing them to take extraordinary risks.

- *Assumption of morality*. Group members believe highly in the moral rightness of the group's objectives and do not feel the need to debate the ethics of their actions.

- *Rationalized resistance*. Group members rationalize any resistance to the assumptions they have made. No matter how strongly the evidence may contradict their basic assumptions, members behave so as to reinforce those assumptions continually.

- *Peer pressure*. Members apply direct pressure on those who momentarily express doubts about any of the group's shared views or who question the validity of arguments supporting the alternative favoured by the majority.

- *Minimized doubts*. Those members who have doubts or hold differing points of view seek to avoid deviating from what appears to be group consensus by keeping silent about misgivings and even minimizing to themselves the importance of their doubts.

- *Illusion of unanimity*. If someone does not speak, it's assumed that he or she is in full accord. In other words, abstention becomes viewed as a "yes" vote.

The Bre-X saga
www.acmi.canoe.ca/
MoneyBreXSaga/home.html

As the Bre-X scandal was unfolding in early 1997, many people who possibly should have known better refused to accept the initial evidence that there might not be any gold at the Busang mine. Because investors and the companies involved had convinced themselves that they were sitting on the gold find of the 20th century, they were reluctant to challenge their beliefs when the first evidence of tampered core samples was produced. More recently, forecasters seemed to be suffering from groupthink as they pronounced the economy in recession, as this *OB in the Street* shows.

OB IN THE STREET

Recession: Are We There Yet?

How many economic forecasters does it take to change the economy? In early 2002, economic forecasters were absolutely surprised by all the good news they heard on the economic front in Canada and the United States. They were surprised that the economies of both countries grew in the fourth quarter and by the job growth in Canada during January and February. They were even surprised that Canada's manufacturers and exporters had a great January. They were surprised because they had been predicting either a recession, at worst, or a recession with jobless recovery, at best.

Forecasters started painting a gloomy picture after September 11, 2001, anticipating that the US national crisis would have a long-lasting impact on the world economy. Even as evidence failed to support this gloomy picture, forecasters struggled to find evidence that they were right.

Groupthink may well explain the forecasters' lingering negative predictions. The forecasters were from the financial industry, which was harder hit than most industries, except the technology sector. Wall Street economists also lived next door to the World Trade Center, so this had a greater impact. Rather than search more widely for evidence, they looked more locally, at the economy right around Wall Street.

Stock prices and corporate profits fell significantly during much of 2001, and this is what they focused on. Meanwhile, housing prices and consumer spending continued to rise. The analysts figured this was a temporary upturn before the large downturn they were predicting. They also failed to notice that personal income continued to rise throughout the year.

In short, forecasters were calling for a recession. They convinced each other it was coming. "[Those] who didn't buy the line and suggested that maybe this was only a very sharp slowdown, invited ridicule."[28]

The forecasters were suffering from some of the symptoms of groupthink. They rationalized resistance, suggesting it was everyone else who didn't understand the economic numbers. They applied peer pressure to each other, ridiculing those who suggested that a recession might not occur. This may have led some analysts to minimize their doubts and keep silent. All of these behaviours led forecasters to appear unanimous in their views on the coming recession.

With groupthink, individuals who hold a position that is different from that of the dominant majority are under pressure to suppress, withhold, or modify their true feelings and beliefs. As members of a group, we find it more pleasant to be in agreement—to be a positive part of the group—than to be a disruptive force, even if disruption is necessary to improve the effectiveness of the group's decisions.

Does groupthink attack all groups? No. It seems to occur most often where there is a clear group identity, where members hold a positive image of their group, which they want to protect, and where the group perceives a collective threat to this positive image.[29]

So groupthink is less a dissenter-suppression mechanism than a means for a group to protect its positive image.

What can managers do to minimize groupthink?[30] One thing they can do is encourage group leaders to play an impartial role. Leaders should actively seek input from all members and avoid expressing their own opinions, especially in the early stages of deliberation. Another suggestion is to appoint one group member to play the role of devil's advocate. This member's role is to overtly challenge the majority position and offer divergent perspectives. Still another suggestion is to use exercises that stimulate active discussion of diverse alternatives in a way that does not threaten group identity. One such exercise is to have group members talk about dangers or risks involved in a decision and delay discussion of any potential gains. By requiring members to first focus on the negatives of a decision alternative, the group is less likely to stifle dissenting views and more likely to gain an objective evaluation.

While considerable anecdotal evidence indicates the negative implications of groupthink in organizational settings, not much actual empirical work has been conducted in organizations on this matter.[31] In fact, groupthink has been criticized for suggesting that its effect is uniformly negative[32] and for overestimating the link between the decision-making process and its outcome.[33] A recent study of groupthink using 30 teams from five large corporations suggests that elements of groupthink may affect decision making differently. For instance, the illusion of invulnerability, belief in inherent group morality, and the illusion of unanimity were positively associated with team performance.[34]

The most recent research suggests that one should be aware of groupthink conditions that are leading to poor decisions, while realizing that not all groupthink symptoms harm decision making.

Groupshift

Evidence suggests that there are differences between the decisions groups make and the decisions that might be made by individual members within the group.[35] In some cases, group decisions are more conservative than individual decisions. More often, the shift is toward greater risk.[36] In either case, participants have engaged in **groupshift**, a tendency where one's initial position becomes exaggerated because of the interactions of the group.

What appears to happen in groups is that the discussion leads to a significant shift in the positions of members toward a more extreme position in the direction in which they were already leaning before the discussion. So conservative types become more cautious and more aggressive types assume more risk. The group discussion tends to exaggerate the initial position of the group.

Groupshift can be viewed as a special case of groupthink. The group's decision reflects the dominant decision-making norm that develops during the group's discussion. Whether the shift in the group's decision is toward greater caution or more risk depends on the dominant pre-discussion norm.

The greater occurrence of the shift toward risk has generated several explanations for the phenomenon.[37] It's been argued, for instance, that the discussion creates familiarization among the members. As they become more comfortable with each other, they also become bolder and more daring. Another argument is that our society values risk, that we admire individuals who are willing to take risks, and that group discussion motivates members to show that they are at least as willing as their peers to take risks. The most plausible explanation of the shift toward risk, however, seems to be that the group diffuses responsibility. Group decisions free any single member from accountability for the group's final choice. Greater risk can be taken because, even if the decision fails, no one member can be held wholly responsible.

How should you use the findings on groupshift? You should recognize that group decisions exaggerate the initial position of the individual members, that the shift has been

groupshift

The phenomenon in which the initial positions of individual members of a group are exaggerated toward a more extreme position.

shown more often to be toward greater risk, and that whether a group will shift toward greater risk or caution is a function of the members' pre-discussion inclinations.

Group Decision-Making Techniques

The most common form of group decision making takes place in **interacting groups**. In these groups, members meet face to face and rely on both verbal and nonverbal interaction to communicate with each other. All kinds of groups use this technique frequently, from groups organized to develop a class project, to a work team, to a senior management team. But as our discussion of groupthink demonstrated, interacting groups often censor themselves and pressure individual members toward conformity of opinion. *Brainstorming*, the *nominal group technique*, and *electronic meetings* have been proposed as ways to reduce many of the problems inherent in the traditional interacting group.

Brainstorming is meant to overcome pressures for conformity within the interacting group that prevent the development of creative alternatives.[38] It achieves this by using an idea-generation process that specifically encourages any and all alternatives, while withholding any criticism of those alternatives.

You have no doubt engaged in brainstorming when you have tried to come up with ideas for how to present a project for class. In a typical brainstorming session, a half-dozen to a dozen people sit around a table. The group leader, or even another team member, states the problem in a clear manner so that all participants understand it. Members then "freewheel" as many alternatives as they can in a given period of time. No criticism is allowed, and all the alternatives are recorded for later discussion and analysis. With one idea stimulating others and judgments of even the most bizarre suggestions withheld until later, group members are encouraged to "think the unusual."

A more recent variant of brainstorming is electronic brainstorming, which is done by people interacting on computers to generate ideas. For example, Calgary-based Jerilyn Wright & Associates uses electronic brainstorming to help clients (such as Calgary-based Tarragon Oil and Gas) design their workspaces through software that has been adapted for office-space design.[39]

Jerilyn Wright & Associates (JWA)
www.jwadesign.com

Executive Decision Centre, Queen's University
business.queensu.ca/qedc/

The Queen's University Executive Decision Centre is "one of the first electronic [decision-making] facilities in North America and the first to be made accessible to the public."[40] Professor Brent Gallupe, the founding director, and another facilitator at the centre have conducted more than 600 decision-making sessions with a variety of North American organizations, including GlaxoSmithKline, Bombardier, DuPont, Imperial Oil, the Department of National Defence and Canadian Forces, the Canadian Security Intelligence Service, and the United Way. The strength of Queen's system is that participants simultaneously interact via computer terminals, all responses are anonymous, and the speed allows for generating numerous ideas in a short time. Mississauga, Ontario-based DuPont Canada uses the system regularly for focused creativity sessions with both employees and customers. Whitby, Ontario-based McGraw-Hill Ryerson Canada has become a regular user since finding that one of its divisions experienced a surge in sales after visiting the Queen's centre. "They came up with a better, more soundly developed strategy, with more commitment on the part of the people. People feel very committed to the outcomes of the process because they don't feel like they've been strong-armed into the outcomes. They've had a voice in it," says John Dill, McGraw-Hill Ryerson's president and CEO.

Image Processing Systems Inc.
www.photondynamics.com

However, brainstorming isn't always the right strategy to use. For example, president and CEO Terry Graham of Scarborough, Ontario-based Image Processing Systems Inc. (now part of Photon Dynamics, Inc.), which won Canada's 1997 Export Award, saw brainstorming backfire when doing business in China. He says that meetings with Chinese business people "are definitely not for brainstorming. We learned this lesson the hard way. Our team thought we could show our creativity by placing fresh alternatives in front of an important manager. It was two years before the company would talk to us again."[41]

Brainstorming, we should also note, is merely a process for generating ideas. The following two techniques go further by offering methods of actually arriving at a preferred solution.[42]

The **nominal group technique** restricts discussion or interpersonal communication during the decision-making process, thus the term *nominal*. Group members are all physically present, as in a traditional committee meeting, but members operate independently, as shown in Exhibit 9–3. Specifically, a problem is presented and then the following steps take place:

- Members meet as a group, but before any discussion takes place, each member independently writes down his or her ideas on the problem.

- After this silent period, each member presents one idea to the group. Each member takes a turn, presenting a single idea until all ideas have been presented and recorded. No discussion takes place until all ideas have been recorded.

- The group then discusses the ideas for clarity and evaluates them.

- Each group member silently and independently ranks the ideas. The idea with the highest overall ranking determines the final decision.

The chief advantage of the nominal group technique is that it permits the group to meet formally but does not restrict independent thinking, as does the interacting group.

The most recent approach to group decision making blends the nominal group technique with sophisticated computer technology.[43] It's called the computer-assisted group, or **electronic meeting**. Once the technology is in place, the concept is simple. Up to 50 people sit around a horseshoe-shaped table, which is empty except for a series of computer terminals. Issues are presented to participants, and they type their responses onto their computer monitors. Individual comments, as well as total votes, are displayed on a projection screen in the room.

The major advantages of electronic meetings are anonymity, honesty, and speed. Participants can anonymously type any message they want, and it flashes on the screen for all to see at the push of a participant's board key. It also allows people to be brutally honest without penalty. And it's fast because chit-chat is eliminated, discussions do not digress, and many participants can "talk" at once without stepping on one another's toes. The future of group meetings undoubtedly will include extensive use of this technology.

Each of these four group-decision techniques offers its own strengths and weaknesses. The choice of one technique over another will depend on what criteria you want

nominal group technique
A group decision-making method in which individual members meet face to face to pool their judgments in a systematic but independent fashion.

electronic meeting
A meeting where members interact on computers, allowing for anonymous comments and combined votes.

Exhibit 9–3

Nominal Group Technique

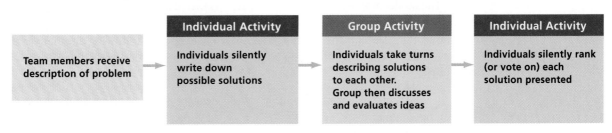

| Team members receive description of problem | **Individual Activity**
Individuals silently write down possible solutions | **Group Activity**
Individuals take turns describing solutions to each other. Group then discusses and evaluates ideas | **Individual Activity**
Individuals silently rank (or vote on) each solution presented |

Exhibit 9–4

Evaluating Group Effectiveness

Effectiveness Criteria	Type of Group			
	Interacting	Brainstorming	Nominal	Electronic
Number of ideas	Low	Moderate	High	High
Quality of ideas	Low	Moderate	High	High
Social pressure	High	Low	Moderate	Low
Money costs	Low	Low	Low	High
Speed	Moderate	Moderate	Moderate	High
Task orientation	Low	High	High	High
Potential for interpersonal conflict	High	Low	Moderate	Low
Feelings of accomplishment	High to low	High	High	High
Commitment to solution	High	Not applicable	Moderate	Moderate
Develops group cohesiveness	High	High	Moderate	Low

Source: Based on J.K. Murnighan, "Group Decision Making: What Strategies Should You Use?" *Academy of Management Review*, February 1981, p. 61.

to emphasize and the cost-benefit trade-off. For instance, as Exhibit 9–4 indicates, the interacting group is effective for building group cohesiveness, brainstorming keeps social pressures to a minimum, the nominal group technique is an inexpensive means for generating a large number of ideas, and electronic meetings process ideas quickly.

THE INFLUENCE OF THE LEADER ON GROUP DECISION MAKING

⑤ Should the leader make the decision, or encourage the group to participate?

leader-participation model
A leadership theory that provides a set of rules to determine the form and amount of participative decision making in different situations.

You are the head of your own business, or the manager of your division at work, and you are trying to decide whether you should make a decision yourself or involve the members of your team in the decision. Is there anything that informs you about whether it is better for the leader to make the decision or to get everyone involved in the decision-making process?

The **leader-participation model** accounts for various actions the leader might take with respect to the decision-making processes of the group he or she leads.[44] This model is normative—it provides a sequential set of rules that should be followed for determining the form and amount of participation desirable by the manager or group leader in decision making, as dictated by different types of situations. The model is a complex decision tree incorporating 12 contingencies that leaders face when making decisions.

The model proposes five possible behaviours that leaders can use in a given situation—Autocratic I (AI), Autocratic II (AII), Consultative I (CI), Consultative II (CII), and Group II (GII). Thus the group leader or manager has the following alternatives from which to choose when deciding how involved to be with decisions that affect a work group:

> **AI:** You solve the problem or make a decision yourself using whatever facts you have at hand.
>
> **AII:** You obtain the necessary information from employees and then decide on the solution to the problem yourself. You may or may not tell them about the

nature of the situation you face. You seek only relevant facts from them, not their advice or counsel.

CI: You share the problem with relevant employees one-on-one, getting their ideas and suggestions. However, the final decision is yours alone.

CII: You share the problem with your employees as a group, collectively obtaining their ideas and suggestions. Then you make the decision, which may or may not reflect your employees' influence.

GII: You share the problem with your employees as a group. Your goal is to help the group concur on a decision. Your ideas are not given any greater weight than those of others.

The original leader-participation model has been revised and there is a computer program that cuts through the complexity of the new model.[45] But managers can still use decision trees to select their leader style if there are no shades of grey (i.e., when the status of a variable is clear-cut so that a "yes" or "no" response will be accurate), there are no critically severe time constraints, and employees are not geographically dispersed. Exhibit 9–5 illustrates one of these decision trees. To help you become more familiar with using one of these decision trees, the *Working With Others Exercise* on pages 317–318 presents several cases for you to analyze.

Exhibit 9–5

The Leader-Participation Model (Time-Driven Decision Tree Group Problems)

QR	Quality requirement:	How important is the technical quality of this decision?
CR	Commitment requirement:	How important is subordinate commitment to the decision?
LI	Leader's information:	Do you have sufficient information to make a high-quality decision?
ST	Problem structure:	Is the problem well structured?
CP	Commitment probability:	If you were to make the decision by yourself, is it reasonably certain that your subordinate(s) would be committed to the decision?
GC	Goal congruence:	Do subordinates share the organizational goals to be attained in solving this problem?
CO	Subordinate conflict:	Is conflict among subordinates over preferred solutions likely?
SI	Subordinate information:	Do subordinates have sufficient information to make a high-quality decision?

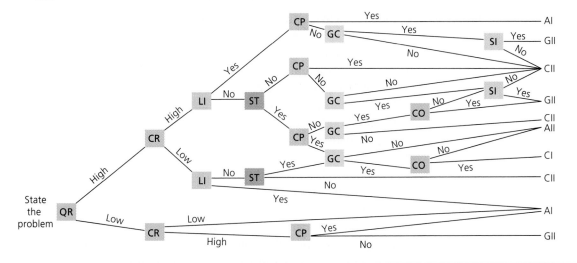

Research testing of the original leader-participation model was very encouraging.[46] We have every reason to believe that the revised model provides an excellent guide to help managers choose the most appropriate leadership style in different situations.

One last point before we move on. The revised leader-participation model is very sophisticated and complex, which makes it impossible to describe in detail in a basic OB textbook. However, the variables identified in Exhibit 9–5 provide you with some solid insights about when you as a leader should take part in a group decision, make the decision yourself, or delegate to someone else.

CREATIVITY IN ORGANIZATIONAL DECISION MAKING

6 How can we get more creative decisions?

"Canada is not a very creative culture," according to a National Research Council report written by Professor David Bentley of the English Department at the University of Western Ontario.[47] The report suggests that concrete steps need to be taken to promote a culture of innovation, and improve the creativity of individuals. The report gives a number of suggestions for improving creativity, including using metaphors, empathetic thinking, and imagining to help see things in new ways.

Bentley's call for improving creativity is consistent with a recent survey showing that 58 percent of large public companies and entrepreneurs recognize a link between creative thinking within the organization and having a competitive edge.[48] "It [creative thinking] will not necessarily spell the difference between success and failure. But it is one of those tangential issues that can add a few cents per share profit," noted the head of an Ontario agriproducts company, who was not identified by the survey. Moreover, research shows that the organizational benefits of individual creativity include "higher-quality products, more effective decision making, better group performance, and more innovative solutions to organizational problems."[49]

A variety of definitions exist for the concept of creativity, with some viewing it as a characteristic of a person, while others view it as a process.[50] Most contemporary researchers and theorists use a definition that addresses either the product or the outcome of the product development process.[51] In our discussion below, we consider **creativity** as the process of creating products, ideas, or procedures that are novel or original, and are potentially relevant or useful to an organization.[52]

creativity
The process of creating products, ideas, or procedures that are novel or original, and are potentially relevant or useful to an organization.

Factors That Affect Individual Creativity

People differ in their inherent creativity. Albert Einstein, Marie Curie, Thomas Edison, Pablo Picasso, and Wolfgang Amadeus Mozart were individuals of exceptional creativity. In more recent times, Emily Carr, Glenn Gould, Michael Jordan, and Carol Shields have been noted for the creative contributions they made to their fields. Not surprisingly, exceptional creativity is scarce. For example, a study of lifetime creativity of 461 men and women found that less than 1 percent were exceptionally creative.[53] But 10 percent were highly creative and about 60 percent were somewhat creative. This suggests that most of us have creative potential, if we can learn to unleash it.

A large body of literature has examined the personal attributes associated with creative achievement.[54] In general, "these studies have demonstrated that a stable set of core personal characteristics, including broad interests, attraction to complexity, intuition, aesthetic sensitivity, toleration of ambiguity, and self-confidence, relate positively and consistently to measures of creative performance across a variety of domains."[55]

While personality and cognitive skills are linked to creativity,[56] the task itself plays an important role. Individuals are more creative when they are motivated by intrinsic interest, challenge, task satisfaction, and self-set goals.[57] Those who are extrinsically motivated are more likely to look for the most efficient solution to a problem, in order to receive the desired rewards. Those who are intrinsically moti-vated may take more time exploring issues and situa-tions, which gives them the opportunity to see things in different lights.[58] The setting also makes a difference, and those settings that provide opportunities, absence of constraints,[59] and rewards[60] encourage creativity.

There is some evidence that the brain is set up to think linearly, rather than laterally, and yet lateral thinking is needed for creative thinking. Edward De Bono, a leading authority on creative and conceptual thinking for more than 25 years, has written a number of books on this topic, including *Six Thinking Hats* and *The Mechanism of Mind*.[61] He has identified various tools for helping one use more lateral thinking. One such tool is called *provo-cation*, where people create a crazy idea and then trans-form it into a workable new concept. Toronto-based real estate firm Ivanhoé Cambridge (formerly Cambridge Shopping Centres) used provocation to identify ways to build more cost-efficient office towers.[62] The provoca-tion exercise of the cross-functional planning team was to imagine that there was no air conditioning in the tow-ers. This led the team to the idea "that in multi-towered projects, excess air conditioning capacity from existing buildings could be used to cool adjoining towers," which was a radical new concept.

De Bono's *six thinking hats* concept is a simple yet powerful tool that is intended to change the way peo-ple think. He suggests that innovative and creative prob-lem-solving can develop from working through decisions using each of the frameworks represented by one of the hats. The hats are metaphors to represent different kinds of thinking.[63]

Creativity and the bottom line can go hand in hand. In fact, at Vancouver-based Big House Communications, creativity rules. Big House develops communications, including websites, for other companies. It is known for giving clients several alternatives: traditional, wacky, and fun. The company must be doing something right. It's 10 years old, which makes it *really* old for this type of business.

- The *white hat* represents impartial thinking, focusing strictly on the facts.

- The *red hat* represents expression of feelings, passions, intuitions, emotions.

- The *black hat* stands for a critical, deliberate, evaluating outlook.

- The *yellow hat* represents an optimistic, upbeat, positive outlook.

- The *green hat* represents creativity, inspiration, imagination, and the free flow of new concepts.

- The *blue hat* represents control, an overall "managerial" perspective of the process.

Each hat has its own place in the decision-making process. De Bono suggests that we use all six in order to fully develop our capacity to think more creatively. Groups could do the same by assigning each person to the role of one of the hats. Toronto-based Royal Trust used this framework to collect ideas from employees across Canada on how to generate revenue and reduce costs.[64] The company received numerous ideas and discovered that the creativity process helped to remove barriers between senior management and front-line employees.[65]

Edward De Bono
www.edwdebono.com

Organizational Factors That Affect Creativity

In two decades of research analyzing the links between work environment and creativity, six general categories have been found:[66]

- *Challenge*. When people are matched up with the right assignments, their expertise and skills can be brought to the task of creative thinking. Individuals should be stretched, but not overwhelmed.

- *Freedom*. To be creative, once a person is given a project, he or she needs the freedom to determine the process. In other words, let the person decide how to tackle the problem. This heightens intrinsic motivation.

- *Resources*. Time and money are the two main resources that affect creativity. Thus, managers need to allot these resources carefully.

- *Work-group features*. Our discussion of group composition and diversity concluded that diverse groups were likely to come up with more creative solutions. In addition to ensuring a diverse group of people, team members need to share excitement over the goal, must be willing to support each other through difficult periods, and must recognize each other's unique knowledge and perspective.

- *Supervisory encouragement*. To sustain passion, most people need to feel that what they are doing matters to others. Managers can reward, collaborate, and communicate to nurture the creativity of individuals and teams.

- *Organizational support*. Creativity-supporting organizations reward creativity, and also make sure that there is information sharing and collaboration. They make sure that negative political problems do not get out of control.

Five organizational factors have been found that can block your creativity at work: 1) *expected evaluation*—focusing on how your work is going to be evaluated; 2) *surveillance*—being watched while you are working; 3) *external motivators*—emphasizing external, tangible rewards; 4) *competition*—facing win-lose situations with peers; and 5) *constrained choice*—being given limits on how you can do your work.[67] This chapter's *CBC Video Case Incident*, "Doug Hall, Creativity Guru," shows how creativity can be encouraged.

"Doug Hall, Creativity Guru"

WHAT ABOUT ETHICS IN DECISION MAKING?

At the Pan Asia Footwear in Thailand, managers set quotas in order to keep productivity high.[68] The difficulty, as one inspector points out, is "Shoes with complex details sometimes can't be finished in eight hours. This means that staff might work 10 hours for an eight-hour wage." The company does not pay overtime when this happens, because the employee has not met the quota on time. Employees are not paid by the hour. They simply receive a flat fee for a day's work. How can we determine whether this is an ethical practice by the company?

7 What is ethics, and how can it be used for better decision making?

ethics
The study of moral values or principles that guide our behaviour, and inform us whether actions are right or wrong.

No contemporary discussion of decision making would be complete without the inclusion of ethics because ethical considerations should be an important criterion in organizational decision making. **Ethics** is the study of moral values or principles that guide our behaviour, and inform us whether actions are right or wrong. Ethical principles help us "do the right thing." In this final section, we present three ways to ethically frame decisions and examine the factors that shape an individual's ethical decision-making behaviour. We also examine organizational responses to the demand for ethical behaviour, as well as consideration of ethical decisions when doing business in other cultures. To learn more about your ethical decision-making approach, see the *Ethical Dilemma Exercise* on pages 318–319. To consider the extent to which ethical decision making blurs the lines between work and personal life, examine the *Case Incident* on page 319.

Three Ethical Decision Criteria

An individual can use three different criteria in making ethical choices.[69] The first is the *utilitarian* criterion, in which decisions are made solely on the basis of their outcomes or consequences. The goal of **utilitarianism** is to provide the greatest good for the greatest number. This view tends to dominate business decision making. It is consistent with goals such as efficiency, productivity, and high profits. By maximizing profits, for instance, a business executive can argue that he or she is securing the greatest good for the greatest number—as he or she hands out dismissal notices to 15 percent of employees. BMO Nesbitt Burns ignored unethical behaviour by an employee because the company stood to gain from the behaviour, as this *Focus on Ethics* shows.

utilitarianism
Decisions made solely on the basis of outcomes or consequences.

FOCUS ON **ETHICS**

Making Profits at the Expense of Clients

Can profits really drive unethical decisions? In spring 2001, BMO Nesbitt Burns was under investigation by the Manitoba Securities Commission, the Investment Dealers Association (IDA), and the Canadian Banking Ombudsman for ignoring unethical behaviour by one of its investment brokers over several years.[70]

These investigations stemmed from continuing complaints about broker Randolph McDuff's behaviour, for which the company took little action. McDuff was first investigated by BMO Nesbitt Burns in March 1999 for trading in clients' accounts without their permission. While McDuff admitted he made unauthorized trades in client accounts, a compliance officer noted that "McDuff did not seem to understand that a client must be contacted prior to a trade being executed." The head of compliance at Nesbitt Burns' head office in Toronto recommended that McDuff be fired.

However, McDuff was not fired. Instead he was fined $2000 and warned that "any further occurrences may result in termination of employment." This was not the first incident of unethical behaviour by McDuff, however. An internal document dated January 28, 1999, noted "we have experienced a large increase in the amount of settlements [anticipated and settled]" regarding McDuff.

Nevertheless, Tom Waitt, senior vice-president of BMO Nesbitt Burns' Prairie division and McDuff's supervisor in Manitoba, urged the head office to avoid taking drastic action, and to keep McDuff under close supervision instead. A memo McDuff wrote to his supervisor in September 1999 may explain why the Winnipeg office was so interested in ignoring his behaviour: "I know there is this great big cloud over my head and that head office wants me out of here. Does head office forget about my contributions to this firm over the years? In addition to providing for more than 15% of the office revenue consistently over the past five years, I have been an advocate of Nesbitt Burns.... Rookies and marketers are still amazed at my work ethic. Some have said that it inspires them to work harder."

Another ethical criterion is to focus on *rights*. This calls on individuals to make decisions consistent with fundamental liberties and privileges as set forth in documents such as the Charter of Rights and Freedoms. An emphasis on rights in decision making means respecting and protecting the basic rights of individuals, such as the rights to privacy, free speech, and due process. For instance, use of this criterion would protect whistle-blowers when they report unethical or illegal practices by their organization to the media or to government agencies on the grounds of their right to free speech.

Charter of Rights and Freedoms
laws.justice.gc.ca/en/charter/

A third criterion is to focus on *justice*. This requires individuals to impose and enforce rules fairly and impartially so there is an equitable distribution of benefits and costs.

Stewart Leibl, president of Perth's, a Winnipeg dry-cleaning chain, is a founding sponsor of the Koats for Kids program. The company's outlets are a drop-off point for no-longer–needed children's coats, and Perth's cleans the coats free of charge before they are distributed to children who have no winter coats. Leibl is going beyond utilitarian criteria when he says, "We all have a responsibility to contribute to the society that we live in." He is also looking at social justice.

Union members typically favour this view. It justifies paying people the same wage for a given job, regardless of performance differences, and using seniority as the primary determination in making layoff decisions.

Each of these three criteria has advantages and liabilities. A focus on utilitarianism promotes efficiency and productivity, but it can result in ignoring the rights of some individuals, particularly those with minority representation in the organization. The use of rights as a criterion protects individuals from injury and is consistent with freedom and privacy, but it can create an overly legalistic work environment that hinders productivity and efficiency. A focus on justice protects the interests of the underrepresented and less powerful, but it can encourage a sense of entitlement that reduces risk-taking, innovation, and productivity.

Decision makers, particularly in for-profit organizations, tend to feel safe and comfortable when they use utilitarianism. Many questionable actions can be justified when framed as being in the best interests of "the organization" and stockholders. But many critics of business decision makers argue that this perspective should change.[71] Increased concern in society about individual rights and social justice suggests the need for managers to develop ethical standards based on nonutilitarian criteria. This presents a solid challenge to today's managers because making decisions using criteria such as individual rights and social justice involves far more ambiguities than using utilitarian criteria, such as effects on efficiency and profits. Raising prices, selling products with questionable effects on consumer health, closing down plants, laying off large numbers of employees, moving production to other countries to cut costs, and similar decisions can be justified in utilitarian terms. However, that may no longer be the single criterion by which good decisions should be judged.

Factors Influencing Ethical Decision-Making Behaviour

What accounts for unethical behaviour in organizations? Is it immoral individuals or work environments that promote unethical activity? The answer is *both!* The evidence indicates that ethical or unethical actions are largely a function of both the individual's characteristics and the environment in which he or she works.[72] Exhibit 9–6 presents a model for explaining ethical or unethical behaviour.

Exhibit 9–6

Factors Affecting Ethical Decision-Making Behaviour

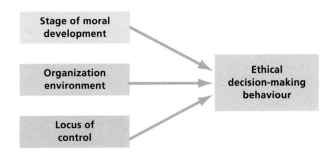

Stages of Moral Development

Stages of moral development assess a person's capacity to judge what is morally right.[73] Research suggests that there are three levels of moral development, and each level has two stages.[74] The higher one's moral development, the less dependent he or she is on outside influences and thus the more he or she will be predisposed to behave ethically. The first level is the preconventional level, the second is the conventional level, and the highest level is the principled level. These levels and their stages are described in Exhibit 9-7.

The research indicates that people proceed through the stages one step at a time, though they do not necessarily reach the highest stage.[75] Most adults are at a mid-level of moral development—they are strongly influenced by peers and will follow an organization's rules and procedures. Those individuals who have progressed to the higher stages place increased value on the rights of others, regardless of the majority's opinion,

stages of moral development
An assessment of a person's capacity to judge what is morally right.

Exhibit 9–7

Stages of Moral Development

Principled

6. Following self-chosen ethical principles even if they violate the law.
5. Valuing rights of others and upholding absolute values and rights regardless of the majority's opinion.

Conventional

4. Maintaining conventional order by fulfilling obligations to which you have agreed.
3. Living up to what is expected by people close to you.

Preconventional

2. Following rules only when doing so is in your immediate interest.
1. Sticking to rules to avoid physical punishment.

Source: Based on L. Kohlberg, "Moral Stages and Moralization: The Cognitive-Developmental Approach," in T. Lickona (ed.), *Moral Development and Behavior: Theory, Research, and Social Issues* (New York: Holt, Rinehart and Winston, 1976), pp. 34–35.

and are likely to challenge organizational practices they personally believe are wrong. Those at the higher stages are most likely to make ethical decisions.

Locus of Control

Research indicates that people with an external *locus of control* (i.e., what happens to them in life is due to luck or chance) are less likely to take responsibility for the consequences of their behaviour and are more likely to rely on external influences. Those with an internal locus of control (who believe they are responsible for what happens), on the other hand, are more likely to rely on their own internal standards of right or wrong to guide their behaviour.

Organizational Environment

The *organizational environment* refers to an employee's perception of organizational expectations. Does the organizational culture encourage and support ethical behaviour by rewarding it or discourage unethical behaviour by punishing it? Written codes of ethics, high moral behaviour by senior management, realistic performance expectations, performance appraisals that evaluate means as well as ends, visible recognition and promotions for individuals who display high moral behaviour, and visible punishment for those who act unethically are some examples of an organizational environment that is likely to foster high ethical decision making.

In summary, people who lack a strong moral sense are much less likely to make unethical decisions if they are constrained by an organizational environment that frowns on such behaviours. Conversely, very righteous individuals can be corrupted by an organizational environment that permits or encourages unethical practices.

In the next section, we consider how one formulates an ethical decision.

Making Ethical Decisions

While there are no clear-cut ways to differentiate ethical from unethical decision making, there are some questions you should consider.

Exhibit 9-8 illustrates a decision tree to guide ethical decisions.[76] This tree is built on the three ethical decision criteria—utilitarianism, rights, and justice—presented earlier. The first question you need to answer addresses self-interest vs. organizational goals.

The second question concerns the rights of other parties. If the decision violates the rights of someone else (his or her right to privacy, for instance), then the decision is unethical.

The final question that needs to be addressed relates to whether the decision conforms to standards of equity and justice. The department head who raises the performance evaluation of a favoured employee and lowers the evaluation of a disfavoured employee—and then uses these evaluations to justify giving the former a big raise and nothing to the latter—has treated the disfavoured employee unfairly.

Unfortunately, the answers to the questions in Exhibit 9-8 are often argued in ways to make unethical decisions seem ethical. Powerful people, for example, can become very adept at explaining self-serving behaviours in terms of the organization's best interests. Similarly, they can persuasively argue that unfair actions are really fair and just. Our point is that immoral people can justify almost any behaviour. Those who are powerful, articulate, and persuasive are the most likely to be able to get away with unethical actions successfully. When faced with an ethical dilemma, try to answer the questions in Exhibit 9-8 truthfully.

Organizational Response to Demands for Ethical Behaviour

During the 1990s, an ethics explosion occurred in Canada and the United States. A second explosion in the demand for more ethics in business occurred in 2002, after the Enron,

Exhibit 9–8

Is a Decision Ethical?

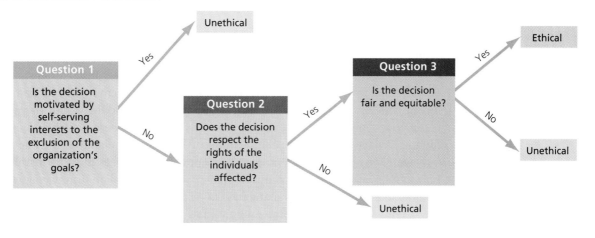

WorldCom, and other accounting scandals. In Canada, more than 120 ethics specialists now offer services as in-house moral arbitrators, mediators, watchdogs, and listening posts. Some work at Canada's largest corporations, including the Canadian Imperial Bank of Commerce, Canada Post, Magna International, RBC Financial Group, Nortel Networks, and McDonald's Restaurants of Canada. These corporate ethics officers hear about issues such as colleagues making phone calls on company time, managers yelling at their employees, product researchers being asked to fake data to meet a deadline, or a company wanting to terminate a contract because the costs are higher than anticipated. Professor Wayne Norman, chair of business ethics at the University of British Columbia, believes that ethics officers are a positive trend, noting, "all sorts of studies show the companies that take ethics seriously tend to be more successful."[77]

Many corporations are also developing ethics codes. For example, about 66 percent of Canada's largest 1000 corporations have them,[78] while about 90 percent of the com-

United Parcel Service Canada Ltd., based in Fredericton, New Brunswick, wants to make sure that its employees approach ethical dilemmas with the confidence to make the right decision. Therefore, the company conducts an ethics training program for all of its employees, from senior managers right down to the delivery truck drivers.

panies on the *Fortune* 500 index have them. Twenty percent of the top 300 Canadian organizations employ ethics specialists, compared with 30 percent of the *Fortune* 500 companies in the United States. Unlike the United States, however, Canada does not legally require companies to create an ethical culture. In the United States, when a company is sued for illegal practices, financial damages may be reduced considerably if the company has a fully functioning ethics program in place.

Brampton, Ontario-based telecommunications producer Nortel Networks is one company that has developed a code of business conduct. Because Nortel wanted its employees to feel committed to the code, Nortel involved them in the process of revising the code through participation in 36 focus groups around the world. They gave all employees opportunities to comment on early drafts that were available on Nortel's intranet. A copy of Nortel's business conduct code is also available on the internet.

Nortel Networks Corporation code of business conduct
www.nortelnetworks.com/corporate/community/ethics/

Having a corporate ethics policy is not enough. Employees must be instructed in how to follow the policy. Yet only about 39 percent of Canadian firms were providing training in ethical decision making in 2000, although this was up from 21 percent in 1997. Only 14 percent of companies evaluate their ethics-related performance, suggesting that most are not focused on improving ethics in the workplace.[79] United Parcel Service Canada Ltd. (UPS) launched its ethics training program in July 1999. As David Cole, vice-president of human resources at UPS, noted, "We want to make sure that as people approach ethical dilemmas, they understand there is a support structure in place."[80]

United Parcel Service Canada Limited (UPS)
www.ups.com/canada/

A small group of companies is even starting a new trend in monitoring ethical practices, hiring an ethical auditor, much like they would hire a financial auditor. The ethical auditor is hired to "double-check an organization's perception of its own morals."[81] VanCity Credit Union (Vancouver City Savings and Credit Union), Bell Canada, Tetra Pak, British Telecom, the University of Toronto, and The Body Shop have all brought in ethical auditors.

What About National Culture?

We have already shown that there are differences between Canada and the United States in the legal treatment of ethics violations and the creation of an ethical corporate culture. However, it is important to note that what is considered unethical in one country may not be viewed similarly in another country. The reason is that there are no global ethical standards. Contrasts between Asia and the West provide an illustration.[82] In Japan, people doing business together often exchange gifts, even expensive ones. This is part of Japanese tradition. When North American and European companies started doing business in Japan, most North American executives were not aware of the Japanese tradition of exchanging gifts and wondered whether this was a form of bribery. Most have come to accept this tradition now and have even set different limits on gift giving in Japan than in other countries.[83]

In another instance illustrating the differences between Asia and North America, a manager of a large US company that operates in China caught an employee stealing. Following company policy, she fired the employee and turned him over to the local authorities for his act. Later she discovered, much to her horror, that the former employee had been executed for his deed.[84] These examples indicate that standards for ethical behaviour and the consequences of particular acts are not universally similar. This presents a variety of problems for those doing business in other countries.

Companies operating branches in foreign countries are faced with tough decisions about how to conduct business under different ethical standards from those in Canada. For instance, Canadian companies must decide whether they want to operate in countries such as China, Burma (also known as Myanmar), and Nigeria, which abuse human rights. Although the Canadian government permits investing in these countries, it also encourages companies to act ethically.

While ethical standards may seem ambiguous in the West, criteria defining right and wrong are actually much clearer in the West than in Asia. John McWilliams, senior vice-president, general counsel, and secretary for Calgary-based Nexen Inc. (formerly Canadian Occidental Petroleum Ltd.), notes that requests for bribes are not necessarily direct: "Usually, they don't say, 'Give me X thousands of dollars and you've got the deal.' It's a lot more subtle than that."[85] Michael Davies, vice-president and general counsel for Mississauga-based General Electric Canada Inc., describes it as "a payment made to an administrative official to do the job that he's supposed to do. In other words, you pay a fellow over the counter $10 when you're in the airport in Saudi Arabia to get on the flight you're supposed to get on, because, otherwise, he's going to keep you there for two days."

Bribing foreign public officials is widespread. The US government reported that between 1994 and 2001, bribery was uncovered in more than 400 competitions for international contracts.[86] The need for global organizations to establish ethical principles for decision makers in all countries may be critical if high standards are to be upheld and if consistent practices are to be achieved.

Nexen Inc.
www.nexeninc.com

General Electric Canada Inc.
www.ge.com/canada

CORPORATE SOCIAL RESPONSIBILITY

In 1999 Nike gave a $7.7 million (US) grant to the International Youth Foundation (IYF) to establish an organization called The Global Alliance for Workers and Communities.[87] Global Alliance, founded to improve working conditions in overseas factories, has been critical of Nike, publishing a report in 2001 on abuses in Indonesian factories making Nike products. "Verbal abuse was the most marked, with 30 percent of the workers having personally experienced and 56 percent having observed the problem. An average of 7 percent of workers reported receiving unwelcome sexual comments and 3 percent reported being physically abused," the report said.

Nike admitted that it was unaware of these problems when the report was published. The company has since increased training for both managers and employees at its overseas facilities. Maria Eitel, the company's vice-president for corporate responsibility, says: "The factory managers are telling us that as they increase their work around social responsibility, they are seeing improvements." To what extent should companies be socially responsible?

Corporate social responsibility is defined as the ways that businesses adapt to the values and expectations of society. Thus, organizations may try to better society, through such things as charitable contributions or providing better wages to employees working in offshore factories. Organizations may engage in these practices because they feel pressured by society to do so, or they may seek ways to improve society because they feel it is the right thing to do.

Eighty percent of Canadians feel that Ottawa should establish standards for corporate social responsibility, and require corporations to report on how they are meeting guidelines, according to a recent survey.[88] Many Canadian companies are feeling the pressure to act socially responsible as well. The Environics Group recently found that 49 percent of the 25 000 consumers interviewed worldwide made product decisions on the basis of companies' social responsibility.[89] This exceeded the 40 percent who made decisions based on brand quality and reputation. Moreover, 23 percent said they had punished a company in the previous year for not meeting what they thought were the company's social obligations.

Not everyone agrees with the position of organizations assuming social responsibility, however. For example, economist Milton Friedman remarked in *Capitalism and Freedom* that "few trends could so thoroughly undermine the very foundations of our free society as the acceptance by corporate officials of a social responsibility other than to make as much money for their stockholders as possible."[90] Interestingly enough, a

8 What is corporate social responsibility?

corporate social responsibility
The ways that businesses adapt to the values and expectations of society.

The Global Alliance for Workers and Communities
www.theglobalalliance.org

Halifax-based Nova Scotia Power wants its employees to be active in helping their communities. To encourage them to invest their time, the company started a Good Neighbour funding program. Employees apply to the Good Neighbour committee to receive up to $1000 for capital costs for a community project.

recent study shows that MBA students change their views about social responsibility during the course of their program.[91] Students from 13 international business schools, including the Richard Ivey School at the University of Western Ontario and the Schulich School at York, were asked at the beginning and the end of their MBA program about their attitudes toward corporate social responsibility. At the start of their program, 40 percent reported that one of the primary responsibilities of a company is to produce useful, high quality goods and services. By the time the students graduated, only 30 percent of the students thought this was a valuable corporate goal. Instead, 75 percent of the students suggested that a company's primary responsibility was to maximize shareholder value.

Some Canadian companies do practise social responsibility, however. Both Vancouver-based VanCity Credit Union and Bolton, Ontario-based Husky Injection Molding Systems Ltd. have "taken comprehensive steps to include customer, employee, community and environmental concerns in both long-term planning and day-to-day decision making."[92] VanCity's electronic banking arm, Citizens Bank, has an "Ethical Policy," which states, for instance, that the bank is against excessive environmental harm and will not do business with companies that either violate the fundamental rights of children or are involved in weapons.[93] For more on the debate about social responsibility vs. concentrating on the bottom line, see this chapter's *Point/CounterPoint* on page 315.

Husky Injection Molding Systems Ltd.
www.husky.ca

VanCity Credit Union
www.vancity.com

SUMMARY AND IMPLICATIONS

1 Is there a right way to make decisions? The rational decision-making model describes the six steps individuals should take to make decisions: define the problem, identify the decision criteria, allocate weights to the criteria, develop alternatives, evaluate the alternatives, and select the best alternative. This is an idealized model, and not every decision thoroughly follows these steps.

2 How do people actually make decisions? Most decisions in the real world do not follow the *rational model*. For instance, people are usually content to find an acceptable or reasonable solution to their problem rather than an optimizing one. Thus decision makers may rely on *bounded rationality, satisficing,* and *intuition* in making decisions.

3 **What kinds of shortcuts do people use in making decisions?** People use a number of shortcuts, including *framing, statistical regression to the mean,* the *availability heuristic,* the *representative heuristic, ignoring the base rate,* and *escalation of commitment.*

4 **What factors affect group decision making?** Groups generate more complete information and knowledge, they offer increased diversity of views, they generate higher quality decisions, and they lead to increased acceptance of a solution. However, group decisions are time-consuming. They also lead to conformity pressures, and the group discussion can be dominated by one or a few members. Finally, group decisions suffer from ambiguous responsibility, and the responsibility of any single member is watered down.

5 **Should the leader make the decision, or encourage the group to participate?** The Leader-Participation Model gives a decision tree to determine whether the leader should make the decision or incorporate some level of group participation. The factors include the quality of the decision required, the degree of commitment needed from participants, and the time available to make the decision.

6 **How can we get more creative decisions?** While there is some evidence that individuals vary in their ability to be creative, we also know that individuals are more creative when they are motivated by intrinsic interest, challenge, task satisfaction, and self-set goals. Five organizational factors have been found that can block creativity at work: 1) *expected evaluation*—focusing on how work is going to be evaluated; 2) *surveillance*—being watched while working; 3) *external motivators*—emphasizing external, tangible rewards; 4) *competition*—facing win-lose situations with peers; and 5) *constrained choice*—being given limits on how to do the work.

7 **What is ethics, and how can it be used for better decision making?** Ethics is the study of moral values or principles that guide our behaviour, and inform us whether actions are right or wrong. Ethical principles help us "do the right thing." An individual can use three different criteria in making ethical choices. The first is the *utilitarian* criterion, in which decisions are made solely on the basis of their outcomes or consequences. Second, an individual can focus on *rights.* This means respecting and protecting the basic rights of individuals. Finally, individuals can also focus on *justice.* This requires individuals to impose and enforce rules fairly and impartially so there is an equitable distribution of benefits and costs. There are advantages and disadvantages to each of these approaches.

8 **What is corporate social responsibility?** Corporate social responsibility is defined as the ways that businesses adapt to the values and expectations of society. Thus, organizations may try to better society, through such things as charitable contributions or providing better wages to employees working in offshore factories. Organizations may engage in these practices because they feel pressured by society to do so, or they may seek ways to improve society because they feel it is the right thing to do.

OB AT WORK

For Review

1. What is the rational decision-making model? Under what conditions is it applicable?

2. Describe organizational factors that might constrain decision makers.

3. What role does intuition play in effective decision making?

4. Describe the three criteria that individuals can use in making ethical decisions.

5. What is groupthink? What is its effect on decision-making quality?

6. What is groupshift? What is its effect on decision-making quality?

7. Identify factors that block creativity.

8. Are unethical decisions more a function of the individual decision maker or the decision maker's work environment? Explain.

For Critical Thinking

1. "For the most part, individual decision making in organizations is an irrational process." Do you agree or disagree? Discuss.

2. What factors do you think differentiate good decision makers from poor ones? Relate your answer to the six-step rational decision-making model.

3. Have you ever increased your commitment to a failed course of action? If so, analyze the follow-up decision to increase your commitment and explain why you behaved as you did.

4. If group decisions consistently achieve better-quality outcomes than those achieved by individuals, how did the phrase "a camel is a horse designed by a committee" become so popular and ingrained in our culture?

OB for You

- In some decision situations, you might consider following the rational decision-making model. This will ensure that you examine a wider variety of options before committing to a particular decision.

- Analyze decision situations and be aware of your biases. We all bring biases to the decisions we make. Combine rational analysis with intuition. As you gain experience, you should feel increasingly confident in joining your intuitive processes with your rational analyses.

- Use creativity-stimulation techniques. You can improve your overall decision-making effectiveness by searching for innovative solutions to problems. This can be as basic as telling yourself to think creatively and to look specifically for unique alternatives.

- When making decisions, you should consider their ethical implications. A quick way to do this is to ask yourself: Would I be embarrassed if this action were printed on the front page of the local newspaper?

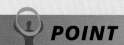 **POINT**

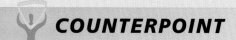 **COUNTERPOINT**

Organizations Should Just Stick to the Bottom Line

The major goals of organizations are and should be efficiency, productivity, and high profits. By maximizing profits, businesses ensure that they will survive and thus make it possible to provide employment. Doing so is in the best interests of the organization, employees, and stockholders. Moreover, it is up to individuals to show that they are concerned about the environment through their investment and purchasing activities, not for corporations to lead the way.

Let's examine some of the reasons why it is not economically feasible to place all of the burden of protecting the environment on the shoulders of big business.

Studies show that environmental regulations are too costly. The Conference Board of Canada suggested that environmental regulations cost Canadian companies $580 to $600 million a year.[94] The Fraser Institute in Vancouver reported that all regulations, including those designed to protect the environment, cost Canadian industry $85 billion a year.[95]

Environmental regulations can also be harmful to jobs. In British Columbia, the Forest Practices Code is said to have added $1 billion a year to harvesting costs and resulted in a number of job cuts.

While businesses are concerned with the high cost that results from environmental regulations, the general public are not completely supportive of protecting the environment either, particularly if it will inconvenience them.[96]

Companies would be better off sticking to the bottom line, and governments should stay away from imposing costly environmental regulations on business. Stringent environmental standards cause trade distortions, and governments rarely consider the cost of complying with regulations. Companies should be allowed to take their lead from shareholders and customers. If these constituencies want businesses to pay for environmental protection, they will indicate this by investing in firms that do so. Until they do, the cost of environmental legislation is simply too high.

Environmental Responsibility Is Part of the Bottom Line

Going green makes good economic sense. The studies reported in the *Point* argument tend to overstate the cost of environmental regulations.[97] They do not consider the benefits to society of those regulations.

A closer look at a few companies that have devoted efforts to being more environmentally friendly will illustrate the benefits of this approach. When Quaker Oats Canada started working toward a "greener" work environment, its plant in Peterborough, Ontario, saved more than $1 million in three years through various environmental initiatives.[98]

As another example, Toronto-based Inco Ltd. spent $600 million to change the way it produces nickel at its Sudbury, Ontario, operations in order to be less devastating to the local environment. Its new smelting process is the most energy efficient and environmentally friendly in the world. Inco continues to work to restore the appearance of Sudbury. Trees have grown back, the wildlife has returned, and the air is clean. Sudbury has even been listed as one of the 10 most desirable places to live in Canada. While Inco invested a lot of money to change its production process, Doug Hamilton, controller at Inco's Ontario division in Sudbury, has said, "Our Sulphur Dioxide Abatement Program was an awesome undertaking. Not only did this investment allow us to capture 90 percent of the sulphur in the ore we mine, but the new processes save the company $90 million a year in production costs. That strikes me as a pretty smart investment."[99]

London, Ontario-based 3M Canada Co. Inc. started a Pollution Prevention Pays (3P) program more than 20 years ago. The program emphasizes stopping pollution at the source to avoid the expense and effort of cleaning it up or treating it after the fact. The recycling program at 3M Canada's tape plant in Perth, Ontario, reduced its waste by 96 percent and saved the company about $650 000 annually. The capital cost for the program was only $30 000.

The examples of Quaker Oats, Inco, and 3M show that companies that are environmentally friendly have an advantage over their competitors. If organizations control their pollution costs better than their competitors, they will use their resources more efficiently and therefore increase profitability.

Decision-Making Style Questionnaire

Circle the response that comes closest to how you usually feel or act. There are no right or wrong responses to any of these items.

1. I am more careful about
   a. people's feelings   **b.** their rights

2. I usually get along better with
   a. imaginative people   **b.** realistic people

3. It is a higher compliment to be called
   a. a person of real feeling   **b.** a consistently reasonable person

4. In doing something with other people, it appeals more to me
   a. to do it in the accepted way   **b.** to invent a way of my own

5. I get more annoyed at
   a. fancy theories   **b.** people who do not like theories

6. It is higher praise to call someone
   a. a person of vision   **b.** a person of common sense

7. I more often let
   a. my heart rule my head   **b.** my head rule my heart

8. I think it is a worse fault
   a. to show too much warmth   **b.** to be unsympathetic

9. If I were a teacher, I would rather teach
   a. courses involving theory   **b.** factual courses

Which word in the following pairs appeals to you more? Circle *a* or *b*.

10. **a.** Compassion   **b.** Foresight

11. **a.** Justice   **b.** Mercy

12. **a.** Production   **b.** Design

13. **a.** Gentle   **b.** Firm

14. **a.** Uncritical   **b.** Critical

15. **a.** Literal   **b.** Figurative

16. **a.** Imaginative   **b.** Matter-of-fact

Scoring Key

Mark each of your responses on the following scales. Then use the point value column to arrive at your score. For example, if you answered a to the first question, you would check 1a in the feeling column. This response receives zero points when you add up the point value column. Instructions for classifying your scores are indicated following the scales.

Sensation	Point Value	Intuition	Point Value	Thinking	Point Value	Feeling	Point Value
2b _____	1	2a _____	2	1b _____	1	1a _____	0
4a _____	1	4b _____	1	3b _____	2	3a _____	1
5a _____	1	5b _____	1	7b _____	1	7a _____	1
6b _____	1	6a _____	0	8a _____	0	8b _____	1
9b _____	2	9a _____	2	10b _____	2	10a _____	1
12a _____	1	12b _____	0	11a _____	2	11b _____	1
15a _____	1	15b _____	1	13b _____	1	13a _____	1
16b _____	2	16a _____	0	14b _____	0	14a _____	1
Maximum Point Value	(10)		(7)		(9)		(7)

Circle *intuition* if your intuition score is equal to or greater than your sensation score. Circle *sensation* if your sensation score is greater than your intuition score. Circle *feeling* if your feeling score is greater than your thinking score. Circle *thinking* if your thinking score is greater than your feeling score.

A high score on *intuition* indicates you see the world in holistic terms. You tend to be creative. A high score on *sensation* indicates that you are realistic and see the world in terms of facts. A high score on *feeling* means you make decisions based on gut feeling. A high score on *thinking* indicates a highly logical and analytical approach to decision making.

Source: Based on a personality scale developed by D. Hellriegel, J. Slocum, and R.W. Woodman, *Organizational Behavior*, 3rd ed. (St. Paul, MN: West Publishing, 1983), pp. 127–141, and reproduced in J.M. Ivancevich and M.T. Matteson, *Organizational Behavior and Management*, 2nd ed. (Homewood, IL: BPI/Irwin, 1990), pp. 538–539.

BREAKOUT **GROUP** EXERCISES

Form small groups to discuss the following topics, as assigned by your instructor:

1. Apply the rational decision-making model to deciding where your group might eat dinner this evening. How closely were you able to follow the rational model in making this decision?

2. The company that makes your favourite snack product has been accused of being weak in its social responsibility efforts. What impact will this have on your purchase of any more products from that company?

3. You have seen a classmate cheat on an exam or an assignment. Do you do something about this or ignore it?

WORKING WITH OTHERS EXERCISE

Individual or Group Decision Making

1. Read each of the cases below, and using the Leader-Participation Model in Exhibit 9–5 on page 301, select the appropriate decision style for each case.

2. Your instructor will divide the class into small groups where you will be asked to reach a consensus about the appropriate decision style.

3. A group spokesperson will be asked to present the group's response and the rationale for this decision.

Case 1

Assume that you are a production manager and one of your responsibilities is to order the materials used by your employees to manufacture wheels. A large stockpile of material sitting idle is costly, but having idle workers because there are not enough materials also costs money. Based on past records, you have been able to determine with considerable accuracy which materials employees will need a few weeks in advance. The purchase orders are written up by the Purchasing Office, not by your employees.

How would you decide how much material you should order? Specifically, would you tell the Purchasing Office how much to order, or would you first ask your employees what they think? Why?

Case 2

Assume that you are the vice-president for production in a small computer-assembly company. Your plant is working close to capacity to fill current orders. You have just been offered a contract to assemble 25 computers for a new customer. If the customer is pleased with the way you handle this order, additional orders are likely and the new customer could become one of your company's largest clients. You are confident that your production supervisors can handle the job, but it would impose a heavy burden on them in terms of rescheduling production, hiring extra workers, and working extra hours.

How would you decide whether to accept the new contract? Specifically, would you make the decision yourself or would you ask others for help? Why?

Case 3

Assume that you have been appointed the chair of a committee formed to coordinate the interdependent activities of the marketing, production, and design departments in the company. Coordination problems have interfered with the flow of work, causing bottlenecks, delays, and wasted effort. The coordination problems are complex, and solving them requires knowledge of ongoing events in the different departments. Even though you are the designated chair, you have no formal authority over the other members, who are not your employees. You depend on committee members to return to their respective departments and implement the decisions made by the committee. You are pleased that most members appear to be sincerely interested in improving coordination among departments.

How would you make decisions about coordination? Specifically, would you decide how best to coordinate among the departments yourself, or would you ask others for help? Why?

Your instructor will discuss with you possible answers to these cases.

ETHICAL **DILEMMA** EXERCISE

Five Ethical Decisions: What Would You Do?

Assume you are a middle manager in a company with about 1000 employees. How would you respond to each of the following situations?

1. You are negotiating a contract with a potentially very large customer whose representative has hinted that you could almost certainly be assured of getting his business if you gave him and his wife an all-expenses-paid cruise to the Caribbean. You know the representative's employer would not approve of such a "payoff," but you have the discretion to authorize such an expenditure. What would you do?

2. You have the opportunity to steal $100 000 from your company with absolute certainty that you would not be detected or caught. Would you do it?

3. Your company policy on reimbursement for meals while travelling on company business is that you will be repaid for your out-of-pocket costs, which are not to exceed $50 a day. You do not need receipts for these expenses—the company will take your word. When travelling, you tend to eat at fast-food places and rarely spend more than $15 a day. Most of your colleagues submit reimbursement requests in the range of $45 to $50 a day regardless of what their actual expenses are. How much would you request for your meal reimbursements?

4. You want to get feedback from people who are using one of your competitor's products. You believe you will get much more honest responses from these people if you disguise the identity of your company. Your boss suggests you contact possible participants by using the fictitious name of the Consumer Marketing Research Corporation. What would you do?

5. You have discovered that one of your closest friends at work has stolen a large sum of money from the

company. Would you do nothing? Go directly to an executive to report the incident before talking about it with the offender? Confront the individual before taking action? Make contact with the individual with the goal of persuading that person to return the money?

Sources: Several of these scenarios are based on D.R. Altany, "Torn Between Halo and Horns," *Industry Week*, March 15, 1993, pp. 15–20.

CASE INCIDENT

Bankers' Excess Gets Them Fired

Five bond and derivatives specialists from Barclays Bank PLC of London were dismissed after a dinner celebrating a major bond and derivatives deal. The dinner tab came to $97 750. Initial reports of the incident suggested that the bankers had purchased the dinners with their own funds. Most of the bill was for five bottles of vintage wine; one alone cost $27 250.

Barclays knew about the dinner for nearly seven months before firing the employees. Petrus, the restaurant in London's St. James's district where the dinner occurred, gave details of the bill to the media right after the meal. Initially, the bank suggested that "This is a matter on personal time, it didn't involve clients, it was personal money." Some press reports later suggested that the bankers tried to claim some of the meal expenses as client expenses, but these could not be confirmed.

In the wake of the Enron scandal, which led to massive cutbacks in the brokerage industry and concern about cor-

porate excesses, Barclays rethought its decision. The dinner was viewed as outrageously extravagant, and reflecting poorly on Barclays' investment bankers.

Questions

1. Would you have fired the five investment bankers? Why or why not?

2. Did the bankers do anything unethical?

3. How can decision-making processes be used to explain how Barclays changed its initial response of "this is private" to something more serious later?

Source: "Barclays Finds Lavish Dinner Indigestible, Lets Bankers Go," *The Globe and Mail*, February 26, 2002, p. B2; J. Lawless, "Bankers Hold Record for Most Costly Meal," *salon.com*, February 26, 2002, http://www.salon.com/people/wire/2002/02/26/bankers_meal/index.html (accessed February 27, 2002).

CBC ◉ VIDEO CASE INCIDENT

Doug Hall, Creativity Guru

Doug Hall, creativity guru, master inventor, and owner of the highly acclaimed Eureka Ranch in Cincinnati, Ohio is on a book-signing tour in Charlottetown, Prince Edward Island. It's the summer of 2002 and Hall has just launched his new book, *Jump Start Your Business Brain*, a series of

business stories collected by Hall and his colleagues over a number of years.

As part of his research for the book, Hall set out travelling through the Atlantic province consulting with various small entrepreneurs about his tried-and-true approach to innovation, creative marketing and business-turnaround techniques. Hall took his travelling road show of copywriters and strategic thinkers across the province in an attempt to demonstrate how his business principles could be applied to just about any entrepreneurial effort.

Since the early 1990s, large corporate clients like Disney, Molson, Pepsi, and Frito-Lay have been spending hundreds of thousands of dollars sending their creative teams to the Eureka Ranch to help shed corporate sensibilities. With the help of Hall and his "Train Brain" coaches, clients can leave the ranch emotionally pumped and enthusiastic with entirely new product ideas.

Back in Charlottetown at Hall's book launch, as a show of support and appreciation, former clients and many other entrepreneurs travelled from great distances to have Hall personally autograph their copy of his book. As part of an update, the CBC *Venture* crew returned to the island one year later, showing that Hall's unique approaches for individual entrepreneurial businesses were paying off handsomely. Clients have been very pleased with the results.

As one PEI entrepreneur stated, Hall has a way of shaking "people out of their comfort zone!" And for business, that means profit.

Questions

1. What were Doug Hall and his creative team able to do with the small entrepreneurial businesses that the businesses were not able to do for themselves?

2. Does being creative mean a business must spend a lot of money and go into debt implementing change?

3. Why would large corporations spend so much money to send their creative teams to Doug Hall's Eureka Ranch? Does the workplace prevent employees from being creative?

Source: Based on "Doug Hall," *CBC Venture*, September 29, 2002, VA2033A, 847; Doug Hall website, www.doughall.com; Eureka Ranch website, www.eurekaranch.com; Barnes & Noble website, www.bn.com.

From **Concepts** to **Skills**

Solving Problems Creatively

You can be more effective at solving problems creatively if you use the following 10 suggestions.[100]

1. *Think of yourself as creative.* Research shows that if you think you can't be creative, you won't be. Believing in your ability to be creative is the first step in becoming more creative.

2. *Pay attention to your intuition.* Every individual has a subconscious mind that works well. Sometimes answers will come to you when you least expect them. Listen to that "inner voice." In fact, most creative people will keep a notepad near their bed and write down ideas when the thoughts come to them.

3. *Move away from your comfort zone.* Every individual has a comfort zone in which certainty exists. But creativity and the known often do not mix. To be creative, you need to move away from the status quo and focus your mind on something new.

4. *Determine what you want to do.* This includes such things as taking time to understand a problem before beginning to try to resolve it, getting all the facts in mind, and trying to identify the most important facts.

5. *Think outside the box.* Use analogies whenever possible (e.g., could you approach your problem like a fish out of water and look at what the fish does to cope? Or can you use the things you have to do to find your way when it's foggy to help you solve your problem?). Use different problem-solving strategies, such as verbal, visual, mathematical, or theatrical. Look at your problem from a different perspective or ask yourself what someone else, like your grandmother, might do if faced with the same situation.

6. *Look for ways to do things better.* This may involve trying consciously to be original, not worrying

▶

about looking foolish, keeping an open mind, being alert to odd or puzzling facts, thinking of unconventional ways to use objects and the environment, discarding usual or habitual ways of doing things, and striving for objectivity by being as critical of your own ideas as you would be of someone else's.

7. *Find several right answers.* Being creative means continuing to look for other solutions even when you think you have solved the problem. A better, more creative solution just might be found.

8. *Believe in finding a workable solution.* Like believing in yourself, you also need to believe in your ideas. If you don't think you can find a solution, you probably won't.

9. *Brainstorm with others.* Creativity is not an isolated activity. Bouncing ideas off of others creates a synergistic effect.

10. *Turn creative ideas into action.* Coming up with creative ideas is only part of the process. Once the ideas are generated, they must be implemented. Keeping great ideas in your mind, or on papers that no one will read, does little to expand your creative abilities.

Assessing Skills

After you have read this chapter, take the following Self-Assessments on your enclosed CD-ROM.

 8. How Creative Am I?

17. What's My Decision-Making Style?

18. How Intuitive Am I?

19. How Do My Ethics Rate?

Practising Skills

Every time the phone rings, your stomach clenches and your palms start to sweat. And it's no wonder! As sales manager for Brinkers, a machine tool parts manufacturer, you are besieged by calls from customers who are upset about late deliveries. Your boss, Carter Hererra, acts as both production manager and scheduler. Every time your sales representatives negotiate a sale, it's up to Carter to determine whether production can actually meet the delivery date the customer specifies. And Carter invariably says, "No problem." The good thing about this is that you make a lot of initial sales. The bad news is that production hardly ever meets the shipment dates that Carter authorizes. And he doesn't seem to be all that concerned about the aftermath of late deliveries. He says, "Our customers know they're getting outstanding quality at a great price. Just let them try to match that anywhere. It can't be done. So even if they have to wait a couple of extra days or weeks, they're still getting the best deal they can." Somehow the customers do not see it that way. And they let you know about their unhappiness. Then it's up to you to try to soothe the relationship. You know this problem has to be taken care of, but what possible solutions are there? After all, how are you going to keep from making your manager mad or making the customers mad? Use your knowledge of creative problem-solving to come up with solutions.

Reinforcing Skills

1. Take 20 minutes to list as many medical or health-care-related jobs as you can that begin with the letter *r* (for instance, radiologist, registered nurse). If you run out of listings before time is up, it's OK to quit early. But try to be as creative as you can.

2. List on a piece of paper some common terms that apply to both *water* and *finance*. How many were you able to come up with?

CHAPTER 10

Organizational Culture and Change

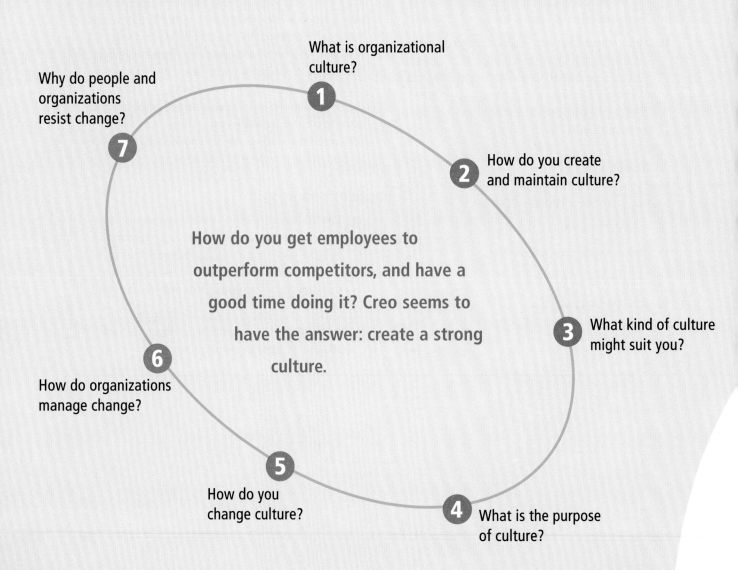

What is organizational culture?

1

Why do people and organizations resist change?

7

How do you create and maintain culture?

2

How do you get employees to outperform competitors, and have a good time doing it? Creo seems to have the answer: create a strong culture.

What kind of culture might suit you?

3

How do organizations manage change?

6

How do you change culture?

5

What is the purpose of culture?

4

At Burnaby-based Creo Inc., loyal employees are the norm.[1] The world's largest independent supplier of pre-press systems for the graphics arts industry has a turnover rate of less than 5 percent, much less than the industry norm.

So how does Creo keep its employees satisfied? CEO Amos Michelson claims it's the company's culture that makes Creo an attractive place to work. The company strives to make employees happy. That includes former employees of Scitex, a much larger company that merged with Creo. As one manager remarked, "The culture that was founded when the company was really small still exists."

Michelson, as CEO, sets the tone for the company. "The CEO is the protector of the culture," he says. He demands that most decisions be made by consensus and that information be shared so employees can work effectively with customers.

In this chapter we show that every organization has a culture. We examine how that culture reveals itself and

the impact it has on the attitudes and behaviours of members of that organization. An understanding of what makes up an organization's culture and how it is created, sustained, and learned enhances our ability to explain and predict the behaviour of people at work.

WHAT IS ORGANIZATIONAL CULTURE?

When Henry Mintzberg, professor at McGill University and one of the world's leading management experts, was asked to compare organizational structure and corporate culture, he said: "Culture is the soul of the organization—the beliefs and values, and how they are manifested. I think of the structure as the skeleton, and as the flesh and blood. And culture is the soul that holds the thing together and gives it life force."[2] Mintzberg's metaphor provides a clear image of how to think about culture.

Culture provides stability to an organization and gives employees a clear understanding of "the way things are done around here." It sets the tone for how organizations operate and how individuals within the organization interact. Thus, it has an impact on the employees who work for the firm. As you start to think about different organizations where you might work, you will want to consider their cultures. An organization that expects employees to work 15 hours a day may not be one in which you would like to work. An understanding of culture might help you discover the firm's expectations before you accept a job, or it might help you understand why you like (or don't like) the college or university you attend.

1 What is organizational culture?

Henry Mintzberg
www.mcgill.ca/news/archives/
fall2002/mintzberg/

Below, we propose a specific definition and review several peripheral issues that revolve around this definition. *From Concepts to Skills* on pages 354–355 tells you how to read an organization's culture.

A Definition

organizational culture
The pattern of shared values, beliefs, and assumptions considered to be the appropriate way to think and act within an organization.

Organizational culture is the pattern of shared values, beliefs, and assumptions considered to be the appropriate way to think and act within an organization. They key features of culture are:

- Culture is shared by the members of the organization.

- Culture helps members of the organization solve and understand the things that the organization encounters, both internally and externally.

- Because the assumptions, beliefs, and expectations that make up culture have worked over time, members of the organization believe them to be valid. Therefore, they are taught to people who join the organization.

- These assumptions, beliefs, and expectations strongly influence how people perceive, think, feel, and behave within the organization.[3]

Not every group develops a culture, although any group that has existed for a period of time and has shared learnings will likely have a culture. Groups that experience high turnover (so that learnings are not really passed down to new members very effectively) and groups that have not experienced any challenging events may not develop cultures.

Levels of Culture

artifacts
Aspects of an organization's culture that you see, hear, and feel.

Exhibit 10–1 shows that culture is manifested at different levels within an organization. Culture is very visible at the level of **artifacts**. These are what you see, hear, and feel when you encounter an organization's culture. You may notice, for instance, that employees in two offices face very different dress policies, or one office displays great works of art, while another posts company mottos on the wall. These visible artifacts emerge from the organization's culture.

Montreal-based PEAK Financial Group, which practically doubled its staff in 1999, worried that rapid growth might mean that not all employees would understand the company's culture. Therefore, PEAK established "The Academy," an intensive three-day orientation for all new hires. Afterward, all employees join together in a welcome ceremony, where new employees are asked to give a two-minute speech telling who they are and why they chose to work at PEAK. PEAK's programs make sure that employees feel part of the culture from day one and feel comfortable interacting with each other. Here we see Robert Frances, president and CEO, welcoming a new employee during a staff meeting.

Below the surface of what you observe are the beliefs, values, and assumptions that make up the organizational culture. **Beliefs** are the understandings of how objects and ideas relate to each other. **Values** are the stable, long-lasting beliefs about what is important. **Assumptions** are the taken-for-granted notions of how something should be. When basic assumptions are held by the entire group, members will have difficulty conceiving of another way of doing things. For instance, in Canada, some students hold a basic assumption that universities should not consider costs when setting tuition but that they should keep tuition low for greater access by students.

The values and assumptions present in an organization are not always readily apparent. Therefore we rely on the organization's artifacts to help us uncover those values and assumptions.

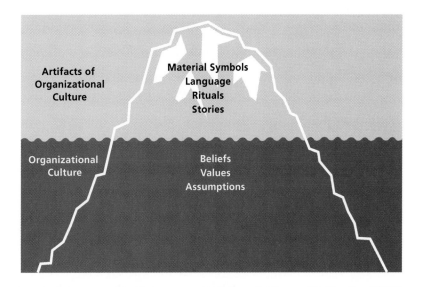

Exhibit 10–1

Layers of Culture

beliefs
The understandings of how objects and ideas relate to each other.

values
The stable, long-lasting beliefs about what is important.

assumptions
The taken-for-granted notions of how something should be in an organization.

Characteristics of Culture

Research suggests that seven primary characteristics capture the essence of an organization's culture:[4]

- *Innovation and risk-taking.* The degree to which employees are encouraged to be innovative and take risks.

- *Attention to detail.* The degree to which employees are expected to work with precision, analysis, and attention to detail.

- *Outcome orientation.* The degree to which management focuses on results, or outcomes, rather than on the techniques and processes used to achieve these outcomes.

- *People orientation.* The degree to which management decisions take into consideration the effect of outcomes on people within the organization.

- *Team orientation.* The degree to which work activities are organized around teams rather than individuals.

- *Aggressiveness.* The degree to which people are aggressive and competitive rather than easygoing and supportive.

- *Stability.* The degree to which organizational activities emphasize maintaining the status quo in contrast to growth.

Each of these characteristics exists on a continuum from low to high.

When individuals consider their organization on these seven characteristics, they get a composite picture of the organization's culture. This picture becomes the basis for feelings of shared understanding that members have about the organization, how things are done in it, and the way members are supposed to behave.

Exhibit 10–2 demonstrates how these characteristics can be mixed to create highly diverse organizations. To help you understand some of the characteristics of culture, you may want to look at the *Working With Others Exercise* on page 351.

Exhibit 10–2

Contrasting Organizational Cultures

Organization A	Organization B
• Managers must fully document all decisions. • Creative decisions, change, and risks are not encouraged. • Extensive rules and regulations exist for all employees. • Productivity is valued over employee morale. • Employees are encouraged to stay within their own department. • Individual effort is encouraged.	• Management encourages and rewards risk-taking and change. • Employees are encouraged to "run with" ideas, and failures are treated as "learning experiences." • Employees have few rules and regulations to follow. • Productivity is balanced with treating its people right. • Team members are encouraged to interact with people at all levels and functions. • Many rewards are team based.

Strong vs. Weak Cultures

Nordstrom, Inc.
www.nordstrom.com

St. Joseph Corporation
www.stjoseph.com

It has become increasingly popular to differentiate between strong and weak cultures.[5] In a **strong culture**, the organization's core values are both intensely held and widely shared.[6] The more members who accept the core values and the greater their commitment to those values, the stronger the culture is. A strong culture will have a great influence on the behaviour of its members because the high degree of shared experiences and intensity creates an internal climate of high behavioural control. For example, Seattle-based retailer Nordstrom has developed one of the strongest service cultures in the retailing industry. Nordstrom employees know what is expected of them, and these expectations go a long way in shaping their behaviour.

Concord, Ontario-based St. Joseph Corporation, one of the fastest-growing print and digital communications companies in Canada, illustrates some benefits of strong culture. St. Joseph's culture is strongly family-oriented (it's been owned by the Gagliano family for more than 40 years). It also emphasizes learning by encouraging employees to "play" with the new equipment. These aspects of the culture translate into employee enthusiasm. For example, when the company introduced a new press in 1997 (only the second of its type installed in Canada at that time), employees had it up to speed three months ahead of management's expectations.[7]

One specific result of a strong culture should be lower employee turnover. A strong culture demonstrates high agreement among members about what the organization stands for. Such unanimity of purpose builds cohesiveness, loyalty, and organizational commitment. These qualities, in turn, lessen employees' interest in leaving the organization.[8]

Research shows that a strong culture is associated with better company performance, at least in the short run (i.e., two or three years).[9] Organizations may need to make sure they reaffirm their culture from time to time to keep the link between culture and performance alive.

Do Organizations Have Uniform Cultures?

Organizational culture represents a common perception held by the organization's members. This was made explicit when we defined culture as a system of *shared* meaning. We should expect, therefore, that individuals with different backgrounds or at different levels in the organization will tend to describe the organization's culture in similar terms.[10]

However, the fact that organizational culture has common properties does not mean that there cannot be subcultures within it. Most large organizations have a dominant culture and numerous sets of subcultures.[11]

A **dominant culture** expresses the core values that are shared by a majority of the organization's members. When we talk about an *organization's culture*, we are referring to its dominant culture. It is this macro view of culture that gives an organization its distinct personality.[12] **Subcultures** tend to develop in large organizations to reflect common problems, situations, or experiences that members face. These subcultures are likely to be defined by department designations and geographical separation.

An organization's purchasing department, for example, can have a subculture that is uniquely shared by members of that department. It will include the **core values**—the primary, or dominant values in the organization—plus additional values unique to members of the purchasing department. Similarly, an office or unit of the organization that is physically separated from the organization's main operations may take on a different personality. Again, the core values are basically retained but modified to reflect the distinct situation of the separated unit.

If organizations had no dominant culture and were composed only of numerous subcultures, the value of organizational culture as an independent variable would be significantly lessened. This is because there would be no uniform interpretation of what represented appropriate and inappropriate behaviour. It is the "shared meaning" aspect of culture that makes it such a potent device for guiding and shaping behaviour. That is what allows us to say that Microsoft's culture values aggressiveness and risk-taking,[13] and then to use that information to better understand the behaviour of Microsoft executives and employees. But we cannot ignore the reality that as well as a dominant culture, many organizations have subcultures that can influence the behaviour of members. Some strong subcultures can even make it difficult for managers to introduce organizational change. This sometimes happens in unionized environments, and can occur in nonunionized environments as well. To help you learn more about identifying cultures of organizations, this chapter's *From Concepts to Skills* on pages 354–355 gives you some idea of factors that you might consider.

The core value of enhancing people's lives through sports and fitness is intensely held and widely shared by Nike employees. Nike founder Philip Knight has created a strong sports-oriented culture and promotes it through company practices such as paying employees extra for biking to work instead of driving. Nike is recognized worldwide as an athlete's company that hires former varsity, professional, and Olympic athletes to design and market its shoes and clothing for sports enthusiasts. Nike headquarters in Beaverton, Oregon, is a large campus with walking and jogging trails and buildings named for sports heroes, such as the Joan Benoit Samuelson Center, the Bo Jackson Fitness Center, and the Joe Paterno Day Care Center.

dominant culture
A system of shared meaning that expresses the core values shared by a majority of the organization's members.

subcultures
Mini-cultures within an organization, typically defined by department designations and geographical separation.

core values
The primary, or dominant, values that are accepted throughout the organization.

CREATING AND SUSTAINING CULTURE

Creo's CEO, Amos Michelson, believes it's his job to protect the culture of the company: "The CEO is the protector of the culture. One can't have the HR manager protecting the culture." At Creo, new employees are carefully selected, which helps the company's culture survive and thrive. To make sure that potential hires will fit into Creo's culture, job applicants meet with up to 10 employees. These interviewers all have equal voice in the hiring decision, regardless of their rank. Let's consider why the role of the CEO, and the hiring process, are so important to preserving an organization's culture.

An organization's culture does not pop out of thin air. Once established, it rarely fades away. Exhibit 10–3 summarizes how an organization's culture is established and

2 How do you create and maintain culture?

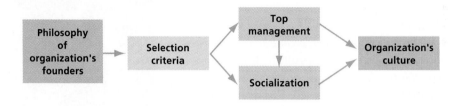

Exhibit 10–3

How Organizational Cultures Form

sustained. The original culture is derived from the founder's philosophy. This, in turn, strongly influences the criteria used in hiring. The actions of the current top management set the general climate of what is acceptable behaviour and what is not. How employees are to be socialized will depend both on the degree of success an organization achieves in matching new employees' values to its own in the selection process and on top management's preference for socialization methods. We describe each part of this process below.

How a Culture Begins

An organization's current customs, traditions, and general way of doing things are largely due to what it has done before and how successful those previous endeavours have been. This leads us to the ultimate source of an organization's culture: its founders.[14]

The founders traditionally have a major impact on that organization's early culture. They have a vision of what the organization should be. They are not constrained by previous customs or ideologies. Because new organizations are typically small, it is possible for the founders to impose their vision on all organizational members.

The process of culture creation occurs in three ways.[15] First, founders hire and keep only employees who think and feel the way they do. Second, they indoctrinate and socialize these employees to their way of thinking and feeling. And finally, the founders' own behaviour acts as a role model, encouraging employees to identify with them and thereby internalize their beliefs, values, and assumptions. When the organization succeeds, the founders' vision is seen as a primary determinant of that success. At that point, the founders' entire personality becomes embedded in the culture of the organization.

For example, Microsoft's culture is largely a reflection of its co-founder, chairman of the board, and former CEO, Bill Gates. Gates is personally aggressive, competitive, and highly disciplined. Those are the same characteristics often used to describe the software giant he founded. Other contemporary examples of founders who have had an immeasurable impact on their organizations' cultures are Ted Rogers at Toronto-based Rogers Communications, Frank Stronach of Aurora, Ontario-based Magna International, Anita Roddick at The Body Shop, and Richard Branson at the Virgin Group.

Keeping a Culture Alive

Once a culture is in place, there are human resource practices within the organization that act to maintain it by giving employees a set of similar experiences.[16] For example, the selection process, performance evaluation criteria, training and career development activities, and promotion procedures ensure that new employees fit in with the culture, rewarding those who support it and penalizing (even expelling) those who challenge it. Three forces play a particularly important part in sustaining a culture: *selection* practices, the actions of *top management,* and *socialization* methods. Let's take a closer look at each.

At Pret A Manger, a British sand-wich shop chain, job applicants spend a trial day working at a shop, after which the shop's team of employees decide whether the applicants would make a good addition to the staff.

Selection

The explicit goal of the selection process is to identify and hire individuals who have the knowledge, skills, and abilities to perform the jobs within the organization success-fully. Typically, more than one candidate will meet any given job's requirements. The final decision as to who is hired is significantly influenced by the decision maker's judgment of how well each candidate will fit into the organization. This attempt to ensure a proper match, either deliberately or inadvertently, results in the hiring of people who have values essentially consistent with those of the organization, or at least a good portion of those values.[17]

At the same time, the selection process provides information about the organiza-tion to applicants. If they perceive a conflict between their values and those of the organization, they can remove themselves from the applicant pool. Selection, there-fore, becomes a two-way street, allowing the employer or applicant to look elsewhere if there appears to be a mismatch. In this way, the selection process sustains an organi-zation's culture by selecting out those individuals who might attack or undermine its core values. The *OB in the Workplace* shows how one company's use of multiple interviews ensures that applicants are right for the job.

OB IN THE WORKPLACE

Surviving Procter & Gamble's Intensive Screening Process

How does a company make sure an applicant is right for the job? Applicants for entry-level positions in brand management at household products maker Procter & Gamble (P&G) experience an exhaustive application and screening process. Their interviewers are part of an elite group who have been selected and trained exten-sively via lectures, videotapes, films, practice interviews, and role plays to identify applicants who will successfully fit in at P&G. Applicants are interviewed in depth for such qualities as their ability to "turn out high volumes of excellent work," "identify and understand problems," and "reach thoroughly substantiated and well-reasoned conclusions that lead to action." P&G values rationality and seeks applicants who show that quality. University and college applicants receive two interviews and a general-knowledge test on campus before being flown back to head office for three more one-on-one interviews and a group interview at lunch. Each encounter seeks corroborating evidence of the traits that the firm believes correlate highly with "what counts" for success at P&G.[18] ▮

To help you think more about culture and its impact on you, you may want to complete the *Learning About Yourself Exercise* for this chapter, on page 350, which assesses the extent to which you would be more comfortable in either a formal, rule-oriented culture or a more informal, flexible culture.

Top Management

The actions of top management also have a major impact on the organization's culture.[19] Through what they say and how they behave, senior executives establish norms that filter down through the organization. These norms establish whether risk-taking is desirable; how much freedom managers should give their employees; what is appropriate dress; what actions will pay off in terms of pay raises, promotions, and other rewards; and the like.

The manager of Calgary's Eau Claire Sheraton discovered how important changing the culture of the organization was to improve performance, as this *OB in the Workplace* shows.

OB IN THE WORKPLACE

Employees Have Feelings Too

Can culture change help with turnover problems? Calgary's Eau Claire Sheraton Suites hotel had turnover problems almost from the time it opened.[20] Though the hotel ranked third out of 210 Sheratons across Canada in a 1999 customer satisfaction survey, its key employees kept leaving.

General manager Randy Zupanski wanted to improve employee morale and hired a consulting group to uncover problems in the workplace through a series of seminars. The consultants uncovered interesting concerns. The hotel management had focused on team process, encouraging and rewarding team behaviour. However, the team culture was having a negative effect on many employees. They did not feel that they were being recognized and rewarded for what they were doing as individuals.

Zupanski and his managers introduced changes to the hotel's culture. They made the recognition program more personal, rewarding such things as attendance, performance, and extra work. Some employees received an extra day off with pay for their hard work.

The hotel's human resources manager said that there was an incredible change in atmosphere as a result. Individual employees felt less stressed and more rewarded, which led to overall performance improvements by everyone. Customer satisfaction improved so much that the Eau Claire Sheraton was rated number one of all Sheratons in Canada for January through June 2000. Zupanski noted that working together to change the hotel's culture brought "us together and brought trust and understanding into the team atmosphere." ▮

The example of Eau Claire Sheraton shows that being aware of how culture affects individual performance can help managers identify specific practices that lead to lowered morale. However, we would not want to leave you with the impression that changing culture is easy. In fact, it is a difficult process. We discuss the process of changing culture later in this chapter.

Exhibit 10–4

"*I don't know how it started, either. All I know is that it's part of our corporate culture.*"

Drawing by Mick Stevens in *The New Yorker*, October 3, 1994. Copyright © 1994 by *The New Yorker Magazine*, Inc. Reprinted by permission.

Socialization

No matter how effectively the organization recruits and selects new employees, they are not fully trained in the organization's culture when they start their job. Because they are unfamiliar with the organization's culture, new employees may disturb the beliefs and customs that are in place. The organization will, therefore, want to help new employees adapt to its culture. This adaptation process is called **socialization**.[21]

Socialization for new employees at the Japanese electronics company Sanyo takes place during a particularly long training program. At their intensive five-month course, trainees eat and sleep together in company-subsidized dorms and are required to vacation together at company-owned resorts. They learn the Sanyo way of doing everything—from how to speak to managers to proper grooming and dress.[22] The company considers this program essential for transforming young employees, fresh out of school, into dedicated *kaisha senshi*, or corporate warriors.

As we discuss socialization, keep in mind that the most critical socialization stage occurs when the new employee enters the organization. This is when the organization seeks to mould the outsider into an employee "in good standing." Those employees who fail to learn the essential role behaviours risk being labelled "nonconformists" or "rebels," which often leads to being fired. The organization continues to socialize every employee, though maybe not as explicitly, throughout his or her career in the organization. This further contributes to sustaining the culture. (Sometimes, however, employees are not fully socialized. For instance, you will note in Exhibit 10–4 that the cartoon employees had learned they were supposed to wear checkerboard caps to work, but clearly didn't know why.)

socialization
The process that adapts employees to the organization's culture.

Sanyo Canada Inc.
www.sanyocanada.com

MATCHING PEOPLE WITH CULTURES

Creo's hiring pratices make clear that not just anyone with the right technical skills would be a suitable employee for the company. Creo looks beyond technical skills when it hires, because it wants a particular type of employee. The company wants people who work best in a team-driven environment. David Brown, corporate VP of business strategy, says, "We encourage people to do what's right, and not what they're told." How much difference is there in cultures across organizations?

3 What kind of culture might suit you?

There is now a substantive body of evidence to demonstrate that organizations try to select new members who fit well with the organization's culture.[23] And most job candidates similarly try to find organizations where their values and personality will fit in.

Recent research by Goffee and Jones provides some interesting insights on different organizational cultures and guidance for prospective employees.[24] They have identified four distinct cultural types. Let's take a look at their cultural framework and how you can use it to select an employer where you will best fit in.

Goffee and Jones argue that two dimensions underlie organizational culture. The first is *sociability*. This is a measure of friendliness. High sociability means people do kind things for one another without expecting something in return and relate to each other in a friendly, caring way. In terms of the characteristics of organizational culture presented at the beginning of this chapter, sociability is consistent with a high people orientation, high team orientation, and focus on processes rather than outcomes.

The second dimension is *solidarity*. It considers the strength of the group's task orientation. High solidarity means people can overlook personal biases and rally behind common interests and common goals. Again, referring back to our earlier discussion of the characteristics of culture, solidarity is consistent with high attention to detail and high aggressiveness. Exhibit 10–5 illustrates a matrix with these two dimensions rated as either high or low. They create four distinct culture types:

- *Networked culture (high on sociability, low on solidarity)*. These organizations view members as family and friends. People know and like each other. People willingly give assistance to others and openly share information. The major negative aspect associated with this culture is that the focus on friendships can lead to a tolerance for poor performance and creation of political cliques.

- *Mercenary culture (low on sociability, high on solidarity)*. These organizations are fiercely goal-focused. People are intense and determined to meet goals. They have a zest for getting things done quickly and a powerful sense of purpose. Mercenary cultures are not just about winning—they are about destroying the enemy. This focus on goals and objectivity also leads to a minimal degree of politicking. The downside of this culture is that it can lead to an almost inhumane treatment of people who are perceived as low performers.

- *Fragmented culture (low on sociability, low on solidarity)*. These organizations are made up of individualists. Commitment is first and foremost to individual members and their job tasks. There is little or no identification with the organization. In fragmented cultures, employees are judged solely on their productivity and the quality of their work. The major negatives in these cultures are excessive critiquing of others and an absence of collegiality and cooperation.

- *Communal culture (high on sociability, high on solidarity)*. This final category values both friendship and performance. People have a feeling of belonging, but there is still a ruthless focus on goal achievement. Leaders of these cultures tend to be inspirational and charismatic, with a clear vision of the organizations' future. The downside of these cultures is that they often consume an employee's life. Their charismatic leaders frequently look to create disciples rather than followers, resulting in a work climate that is almost "cult-like."

Finding Your Culture

Unilever Canada Limited
www.unilever.ca

Heineken Canada Inc.
www.heineken.com/canada/

Unilever and Heineken are examples of networked cultures. Heineken, for example, has more than 30 000 employees but retains the feeling of friendship and family that is more typical among small firms. The company's highly social culture produces a strong sense of belonging and often a passionate identification with its product. What kind of culture suits you? The checklist below can help you find out.

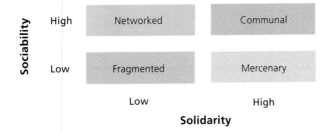

Exhibit 10–5

Four-Culture Typology

Source: Adapted from R. Goffee and G. Jones, *The Character of a Corporation: How Your Company's Culture Can Make or Break Your Business* (New York: HarperBusiness, 1998), p. 21.

✓ *You are cut out for a networked culture* if you possess good social skills and empathy; you like to forge close, work-related friendships; you thrive in a relaxed and convivial atmosphere; and you are not obsessed with efficiency and task performance.

Mars, Campbell Soup, and Japanese heavy-equipment manufacturer Komatsu are classic mercenary cultures. At Mount Olive, New Jersey–based candy manufacturer Mars, for instance, meetings are almost totally concerned with work issues. There is little tolerance for socializing or small talk.

✓ *You are well matched to a mercenary culture* if you are goal-oriented, thrive on competition, like clearly structured work tasks, enjoy risk-taking, and are able to deal openly with conflict.

Most top-tier universities and law firms take on the properties of fragmented cultures. Professors at major universities, for instance, are judged on their research and scholarship. Senior professors with big reputations do not need to be friendly to their peers or attend social functions to retain their status. Similarly, law partners who bring in new clients and win cases need to expend little energy getting to know co-workers or being visible in the office.

✓ *You are likely to fit in well in a fragmented culture* if you are independent, have a low need to be part of a group atmosphere, are analytical rather than intuitive, and have a strong sense of self that is not easily undermined by criticism.

Examples of communal cultures are Hewlett-Packard, Johnson & Johnson, and consulting firm Bain & Co. Hewlett-Packard historically has been large and very goal-focused. Yet it is also a company known for its strong family feel. The "HP Way" is a set of values the company has developed that governs how people should behave and interact with each other. The HP Way's value of trust and community encourages loyalty to the company. And the company returns that loyalty to employees as long as they perform well. HP's culture may well change, now that it has merged with Compaq.

✓ *You might fit into a communal culture* if you have a strong need to identify with something bigger than yourself, enjoy working in teams, and are willing to put the organization above family and personal life.

How important is this culture-person fit? In a recent study of accounting firms, new employees whose personalities meshed with the company were 20 percent less likely to

Mars, Inc.
www.mars.com

Campbell Soup Company
www.campbellsoup.com

Komatsu, Ltd.
www.komatsu.co.jp/en/

Johnson & Johnson Canada Inc.
www.jnjcanada.com

Bain & Co. Canada
www.bain.com/bainweb/localoffices/

Hewlett-Packard (Canada) Ltd
www.hp.com/country/ca/eng/

leave their jobs in the first three years than those who did not fit as well.[25] To help you think more about culture and its impact on you, you may want to complete the *Learning About Yourself Exercise* on page 350, which assesses whether you would be more comfortable in either a formal, rule-oriented culture or a more informal, flexible culture.

WHAT DOES CULTURE DO?

At Creo, employees are reminded that each person is expected to be a valuable, contributing member of the company. The company is very anti-hierarchical. Senior managers get few special privileges and all employees receive stock options. All employees travel economy class—if they want to upgrade to business class, they must pay half the difference in the ticket price themselves. Why might these actions have an impact on the company's culture?

4 What is the purpose of culture?

WestJet Airlines Ltd
www.westjet.com

We have discussed organizational culture's impact on behaviour. We have also explicitly argued that a strong culture should be associated with reduced turnover. In this section, we will review the positive functions that culture performs. We will also note that sometimes culture can be a liability for an organization. To help you put this discussion in focus, consider the different cultures of Calgary-based WestJet and Dorval, Quebec-based Air Canada. WestJet is viewed as having a "young, spunky, can-do environment, where customers will have more fun."[26] Air Canada, by contrast is considered less helpful and friendly. One analyst even suggested that Air Canada staff "tend to make their customers feel stressed" by their confrontational behaviour.[27] Our discussion of culture should help you understand how these differences across organizations occur.

Culture's Functions

Culture performs a number of functions within an organization. First, it has a boundary-defining role. It creates distinctions between one organization and others. Second, it conveys a sense of identity for organization members. Third, culture encourages organization members to commit themselves to something larger than individual self-interest. Fourth, it enhances stability. Culture is the social glue that helps to hold the organization together by providing appropriate standards for what employees should say and do. Finally, culture serves as a control mechanism that guides and shapes the attitudes and behaviour of employees, and helps them make sense of the organization. It is this last function that is of particular interest to us.[28] As the following quotation makes clear, culture defines the rules of the game:

> Culture by definition is elusive, intangible, implicit, and taken for granted. But every organization develops a core set of assumptions, understandings, and implicit rules that govern day-to-day behaviour in the workplace. Until newcomers learn the rules, they are not accepted as full-fledged members of the organization. Transgressions of the rules on the part of high-level executives or front-line employees result in universal disapproval and powerful penalties. Conformity to the rules becomes the primary basis for reward and upward mobility.[29]

The role of culture in influencing employee behaviour appears to be increasingly important in today's workplace.[30] As organizations have widened spans of control, flattened structures, introduced teams, reduced formalization, and empowered employees, the *shared meaning* provided by a strong culture ensures that everyone is pointed in the same direction.

Culture can also influence people's ethical behaviour. When lower-level employees see their managers padding expense reports, this sends a signal that the firm tolerates dishonest behaviour. Firms that emphasize individual sales records may encourage unhealthy competition among sales staff, including "misplacing" phone messages and not being helpful to someone else's client. Toronto-based Griffiths McBurney & Partners, on the other hand, emphasizes the importance of a teamwork culture, so that individuals are not competing against one another and engaging in questionable activities. Founding partner Brad Griffiths notes that the aim of "the corporate culture is to make an environment where everybody feels they're involved. We want to be successful, but not at the expense of the individual."[31] (For further discussion of the effect of culture on ethical behaviour, see this chapter's *Ethical Dilemma Exercise* on page 352.)

As we show later in this chapter, decisions about who receives a job offer to join the organization, who is appraised as a high performer, and who gets the promotion are strongly influenced by the individual-organization "fit"—the sense of whether the applicant's or employee's attitudes and behaviour are compatible with the culture.

> **Griffiths McBurney &
> Partners Inc (GMP)**
> www.gmponline.com

Culture as a Liability

We are treating culture in a nonjudgmental manner. We have not said that it is good or bad, only that it exists. Many of its functions, as outlined, are valuable for both the organization and the employee. Culture enhances organizational commitment and increases the consistency of employee behaviour. These are clearly benefits to an organization. From an employee's standpoint, culture is valuable because it reduces ambiguity. It tells employees how things are done and what is important. However, we should not ignore the potentially dysfunctional aspects of culture, especially of a strong culture, on an organization's effectiveness. *Focus on Ethics* discusses how Enron's pressure-cooker culture led to the company's ultimate collapse.

FOCUS ON **ETHICS**

Pressure-Cooker Culture Leads to Enron's Demise

Would employees knowingly do wrong for their employer? "At Enron, losers fell by the wayside but victors stayed in the game," wrote two *Washington Post* reporters.[32] The "winner-take-all" culture demanded that employees do whatever they could to make Enron's stock price continually rise. Executives thus took risks with investments and accounting procedures, inflating revenue and hiding debt. Those who could not (or would not) play this game were forced out. As the company's annual report stated, "We insist on results."

"The driver was this unbelievable desire to keep portraying Enron as something very very different and keep the track record going and going," said Forrest Hoglund, a former senior manager.

Enron's culture set up an in-crowd and an out-crowd, and employees knew whether they were "in" or "out." Everyone wanted to be liked in the organization, according to Sally Ison, another employee. "You do everything you can do to keep that."

Employees were even willing to blatantly acknowledge they were doing wrong among themselves, according to Margaret Ceconi, a former Enron Energy Services (EES) manager, who was only briefly employed by Enron. After she was laid off, she wrote a memo to Kenneth Lay, former chair of Enron, and phoned federal regulators twice. "EES has knowingly misrepresented EES' earnings," she wrote in her memo to Lay. "This is common knowledge among all the EES employees, and is actually joked about....[Enron] must investigate all these going ons."

Enron's culture led its employees to engage in various unethical accounting practices. We now consider culture's impact on change, diversity, and mergers and acquisitions.

Culture as a Barrier to Change

Culture is a liability when the shared values are not in agreement with those that will further the organization's effectiveness. This is most likely to occur when the organization's environment is dynamic. When the environment is undergoing rapid change, the organization's entrenched culture may no longer be appropriate. Consistency of behaviour is an asset to an organization when it faces a stable environment. However, it may burden the organization and make it difficult to respond to changes in the environment. For many organizations with strong cultures, practices that led to previous successes can lead to failure when those practices no longer match up well with environmental needs.[33]

Hydro One Inc.
www.hydroone.com

That is what happened at Ontario Hydro (now Hydro One). Former Hydro president Allan Kupcis described how the nuclear division went from being one of the best in the world in the 1970s and 1980s to operating at a minimally acceptable level in the late 1990s.[34] "The problems in Ontario Hydro's nuclear division began when nuclear-plant workers started believing they were the best in the world and became complacent. Back in the 1970s and 1980s, our CANDU system was unique in the world and Hydro was continually setting records for nuclear efficiency. But when people stop looking outside to see what others are doing in terms of getting better, you tend to forget that the target is raised every time someone sets a record." The *Point/CounterPoint* on page 349 gives you further ideas about whether cultures can change or not.

Culture as a Barrier to Diversity

Hiring new employees who, because of race, gender, disability, or other differences, are not like the majority of the organization's members creates a paradox.[35] Management wants the new employees to accept the organization's core cultural values. Otherwise, these employees are unlikely to fit in or be accepted. But at the same time, management wants to openly acknowledge and demonstrate support for the differences that these employees bring to the workplace.

The Walt Disney Company
disney.go.com

Strong cultures put considerable pressure on employees to conform. They limit the range of values and styles that are acceptable. It's not a coincidence that employees at Disney theme parks appear to be almost universally attractive, clean, and wholesome looking, with bright smiles. That's the image the Walt Disney Company seeks. It selects employees who will maintain that image. And once the theme-park employees are on the job, a strong culture—supported by formal rules and regulations—ensures that they will act in a relatively uniform and predictable way.

1996 Texaco legal case concerning minorities
www.courttv.com/archive/
legaldocs/business/texaco/

A strong culture that ignores prejudice can even undermine formal corporate diversity policies. A widely publicized example is the Texaco case in the United States, where senior managers made disparaging remarks about minorities and, as a result of legal action on behalf of 1400 employees, paid a settlement of $246 million.[36] Organizations seek out and hire diverse individuals because of the new strengths they bring to the workplace. Yet these diverse behaviours and strengths are likely to diminish in strong cultures as people try to fit in. Strong cultures, therefore, can be liabilities when they effectively eliminate the unique strengths that people of different backgrounds bring to the organization. Moreover, strong cultures can also be liabilities when they support institutional bias or become insensitive to people who are different.

Culture as a Barrier to Mergers and Acquisitions

Historically, the key factors that management looked at in making merger or acquisition decisions were related to financial advantages or product synergy. In recent years, cultural compatibility has become the primary concern.[37] While a favourable financial statement or product line may be the initial attraction of an acquisition candidate, whether the acquisition actually works seems to have more to do with how well the two organizations' cultures match up.

A number of mergers fail within the first several years, and the primary cause is often conflicting organizational cultures.[38] The Daimler-Benz and Chrysler merger has had many difficulties. Though presented as a merger of equals, Daimler-Benz tended to view the merger more as an acquisition. Moreover, the two companies had very different cultures. As one industry watcher noted, they "were taking one of the more hierarchical car companies in the world (Daimler-Benz) and trying to integrate it with one of the least hierarchical companies in the world (Chrysler)."[39]

When the merger occurs under difficult circumstances, the problems can be greater. For instance, employees from Andersen Canada merged with Toronto-based Deloitte & Touche LLP Canada in June 2002, after they were basically forced out of work with little notice as the Enron scandal unfolded. Colin Taylor, CEO and managing partner of Deloitte in Canada, noted that "given the circumstances, you have a lot of employees worried, anxious, traumatized even. They are in shock that a professional service firm of this size would have this happen to them so quickly."[40] Andersen's employees were not in a very good bargaining position when accepted into Deloitte. Unlike some mergers where the two merging organizations fight over the name of the new company, and who gets what titles, Andersen's employees were concerned about having any job at all. This may affect how comfortable Andersen employees feel with the Deloitte culture as time passes. This chapter's *CBC Video Case Incident*, "Quebecor Tackles Videotron," shows the difficulty these two companies faced after a merger.

DaimlerChrysler Canada Inc.
www.daimlerchrysler.ca

CBC ◉

"Quebecor Tackles Videotron"

CHANGING THE CULTURE OF THE ORGANIZATION

Culture sets the tone for how employees interact with each other, what is valued by the organization, and what the expectations for managers and employees are. Often, changing just the structure, or the technology, or the people may not be enough to achieve fundamental change in the organization. That is because culture often represents the mindset of the employees and managers.

5 How do you change culture?

The explosion of the space shuttle Columbia highlights how difficult changing culture has been for NASA. When the report on the investigation came out in summer 2003, the reasons given for the failure were alarmingly similar to the reasons given for the Challenger disaster 20 years before.[41] Even though foam striking the shuttle was the technical cause of the explosion, the problem was rooted in NASA's organizational culture. NASA has again promised to change its culture, and create an atmosphere where employees are "encouraged to raise our hand and speak out when there are life-threatening hazards," said NASA administrator Sean O'Keefe. Joseph Grenny, a NASA engineer, is less certain. He notes that "The NASA culture does not accept being wrong." The culture doesn't accept that "there's no such thing as a stupid question." Instead, "the humiliation factor always runs high."[42]

The evidence suggests that cultural change is most likely to occur when most or all of the following conditions exist:

- *A dramatic crisis.* This is the shock that undermines the status quo and calls into question the relevance of the current culture. Examples of these crises might be a surprising financial setback, the loss of a major customer, or a dramatic technological breakthrough by a competitor. The Columbia disaster is a dramatic crisis for NASA.

- *Turnover in leadership.* New top leadership, which can provide an alternative set of key values, may be perceived as more capable of responding to the crisis. This would definitely be the organization's chief executive, but also might need to include all senior management positions. The recent rush to hiring outside CEOs after the Enron and WorldCom scandals illustrates attempts to create more ethical climates through the introduction of new leadership. At NASA,

> ### Exhibit 10-6
>
> ## Suggestions for Changing Organizational Culture
>
> - Set the tone through management behaviour. Managers, particularly top management, need to be positive role models.
> - Create new stories, symbols, and rituals to replace those currently in vogue.
> - Select, promote, and support employees who support the new values that are sought.
> - Redesign socialization processes to align with the new values.
> - Change the reward system to encourage acceptance of a new set of values.
> - Replace unwritten norms with formal rules and regulations that are tightly enforced.
> - Shake up current subcultures through transfers, job rotation, and/or terminations.
> - Work to get peer-group consensus through employee participation and creation of a climate with a high level of trust.

some of the top leadership were moved to other positions after the Columbia disaster.

- *Young and small organization.* The younger the organization is, the less entrenched its culture will be. Similarly, it's easier for management to communicate its new values when the organization is small. This again helps to explain the difficulty that multibillion-dollar corporations have in changing their cultures.

- *Weak culture.* The more widely held a culture is and the higher the agreement among members on its values, the more difficult it will be to change. That's been one of the problems facing NASA. Conversely, weak cultures are more open to change than strong ones.

Exhibit 10–6 gives suggestions for how to change the culture, if the conditions support doing so.

Working to change the culture will usually not result in an immediate or dramatic shift in the organization's culture. Cultural change is actually a lengthy process—measured in years, not months. But we can ask the question "Can culture be changed?" And the answer is "Yes!" For a specific example of the difficulties of culture change, read this chapter's *Case Incident* on pages 352–353, which examines culture change attempts at EnCana.

MANAGING ORGANIZATIONAL CHANGE

6 How do organizations manage change?

How to handle change is partly dependent on one's views of the change process. Some see change as a constant process, while others see it as a relatively rare event. Below we consider how to start the change process, the reasons for resistance to change, and also how to overcome resistance. For further discussion of these viewpoints on change, you might want to consult the *Point/CounterPoint* discussion on page 349, which gives you two views on the role of change in organizations.

A General Overview of the Process: Lewin's Three-Step Model

unfreezing

Change efforts to overcome the pressures of both individual resistance and group conformity.

Assuming that an organization has uncovered a need for change, how does it engage in the change process? Kurt Lewin argued that successful change in organizations should follow three steps, which are illustrated in Exhibit 10–7: **unfreezing** the status quo,

Exhibit 10–7

Lewin's Three-Step Change Model

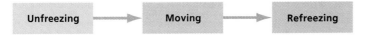

moving to a new state, and **refreezing** the new change to make it permanent.[43] The value of this model can be seen in the following example, where the management of a large company decided to reorganize its marketing function in Western Canada.

The oil company had three divisional offices in the West, located in Winnipeg, Calgary, and Vancouver. The decision was made to consolidate the divisions into a single regional office to be located in Calgary. The reorganization meant transferring more than 150 employees, eliminating some duplicate managerial positions, and instituting a new hierarchy of command. As you might guess, such a huge move was difficult to keep secret. The rumours preceded the announcement by several months. The decision itself was made unilaterally. It came from the executive offices in Toronto. Those people affected had no say whatsoever in the choice. For anyone in Vancouver or Winnipeg who might have disliked the decision and its consequences—the problems involved in transferring to another city, pulling youngsters out of school, making new friends, having new co-workers, undergoing the reassignment of responsibilities—the only recourse was to quit. In actuality, fewer than 10 percent did.

The status quo can be considered to be an equilibrium state. To move from this equilibrium—to overcome the pressures of both individual resistance and group conformity—unfreezing is necessary. Exhibit 10–8 shows that unfreezing can occur in one of three ways. The **driving forces**, which direct behaviour away from the status quo, can be increased. The **restraining forces**, which hinder movement from the existing equilibrium, can be decreased. A third alternative is to combine the first two approaches.

The company's management can expect employee resistance to the consolidation. To deal with that resistance, management can use positive incentives to encourage employees to accept the change. For instance, increases in pay can be offered to those who accept the transfer. Very liberal moving expenses can be paid by the company. Management might offer low-cost mortgage funds to allow employees to buy new

moving
Efforts to get employees involved in the change process.

refreezing
Stabilizing a change intervention by balancing driving and restraining forces.

 Kurt Lewin's 3-step model
www.carillontech.com/
Force-Field.htm

driving forces
Forces that direct behaviour away from the status quo.

restraining forces
Forces that hinder movement away from the status quo.

Exhibit 10–8

Unfreezing the Status Quo

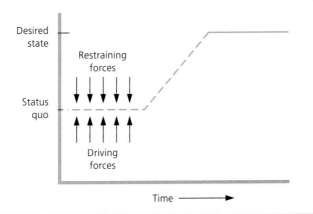

homes in Calgary. Of course, management might also consider unfreezing acceptance of the status quo by removing restraining forces. Employees could be counselled individually. Each employee's concerns and apprehensions could be heard and specifically clarified. Assuming that most of the fears are unjustified, the counsellor could assure the employees that there was nothing to fear and then demonstrate, through tangible evidence, that restraining forces are unwarranted. If resistance is extremely high, management may have to resort to both reducing resistance and increasing the attractiveness of the alternative so the unfreezing can succeed.

Once the consolidation change has been implemented, if it is to be successful, the new situation must be refrozen so that it can be sustained over time. Unless this last step is taken, there is a very high chance that the change will be short-lived and that employees will try to revert to the previous equilibrium state. The objective of refreezing, then, is to stabilize the new situation by balancing the driving and restraining forces.

How could the oil company's management refreeze its consolidation change? It could systematically replace temporary forces with permanent ones. For instance, management might impose a new bonus system tied to the specific changes desired. The formal rules and regulations governing behaviour of those affected by the change should also be revised to reinforce the new situation. Over time, of course, the work group's own norms will evolve to sustain the new equilibrium. But until that point is reached, management will have to rely on more formal mechanisms. The *Working With Others Exercise* on page 351 gives you the opportunity to identify driving and restraining forces for another company experiencing problems with change, and to make some recommendations for change.

A key feature of Lewin's three-step model is its conception of change as an episodic activity, with a beginning, a middle, and an end. However, the structure of the 21st-century workplace may require change to occur as an ongoing, even chaotic, process. Certainly the adjustment that companies have made to the realities of e-commerce indicates a more chaotic change, rather than a controlled and planned change.

RESISTANCE TO CHANGE

7 Why do people and organizations resist change?

One of the most well-documented findings from studies of individual and organizational behaviour is that organizations and their members resist change. In a sense, this is positive. It provides a degree of stability and predictability to behaviour. If there were no resistance, organizational behaviour would take on characteristics of chaotic randomness. Resistance to change can also be a source of functional conflict. For example, resistance to a reorganization plan or a change in a product line can stimulate a healthy debate over the merits of the idea and result in a better decision. However, there is a definite downside to resistance to change: It hinders adaptation and progress.

Resistance to change does not necessarily surface in standardized ways. Resistance can be overt, implicit, immediate, or deferred. It is easiest for management to deal with resistance when it is overt and immediate. For instance, a change is proposed, and employees respond immediately by voicing complaints, engaging in a work slowdown, threatening to go on strike, or the like. The greater challenge is managing resistance that is implicit or deferred. Implicit resistance efforts are more subtle—loss of loyalty to the organization, loss of motivation to work, increased errors or mistakes, increased absenteeism due to "sickness"—and hence more difficult to recognize. Similarly, deferred actions cloud the link between the source of resistance and the reaction to it. A change may produce what appears to be only a minimal reaction at the time it is initiated, but then resistance surfaces weeks, months, or even years later. Or a single change that in and of itself might have little impact becomes the straw that breaks the camel's back. Reactions to change can build up and then explode in some response that seems totally out of proportion to the change action it follows. The resistance, of course, has merely been deferred and stockpiles. What surfaces is a response to an accumulation of previous changes.

Let's look at the sources of resistance. For analytical purposes, we have categorized them by individual and organizational sources. In the real world, the sources often overlap.

Individual Resistance

Individuals carry the source of resistance to change in their basic human characteristics, such as perceptions, personalities, and needs. The following summarizes reasons why individuals may resist change. These are shown in Exhibit 10–9.

Habit

Every time you go out to eat, do you try a different restaurant? Probably not. If you are like most people, you find a couple of places you like and return to them on a somewhat regular basis.

As human beings, we are creatures of habit. Life is complex enough. We don't need to consider the full range of options for the hundreds of decisions we have to make every day. To cope with this complexity, we all rely on habits or programmed responses. But when confronted with change, we tend to respond in our accustomed ways and this becomes a source of resistance. So when your department is moved to a new office building across town, it means you are likely to have to change many habits. You might have to wake up 10 minutes earlier, take a new set of streets to work, find a new parking place, adjust to a new office layout, develop a new lunchtime routine, and so on.

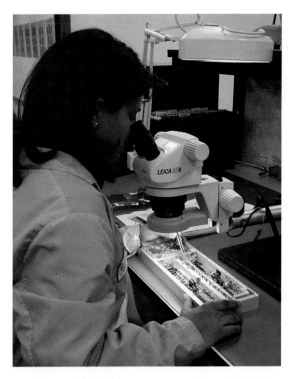

Though most people and organizations resist change, at Advantech Advanced Microwave Technologies, Inc., located in Dorval, Quebec, change is the norm. François Binette, vice-president of finance, says that "Managing change forms an intrinsic part of our corporate DNA and it is this environment that has allowed us to consistently develop unique and innovative products."

Security

People with a high need for security are likely to resist change because it threatens their feelings of safety. For example, when CTV announces it is laying off thousands of people or Ford introduces new robotic equipment, many employees at these firms may fear that their jobs are in jeopardy.

Exhibit 10–9

Sources of Individual Resistance to Change

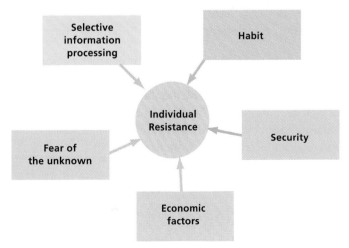

Economic Factors

Another source of individual resistance is concern that changes will lower one's income. Changes in job tasks or established work routines also can arouse economic fears if people are concerned that they will not be able to perform the new tasks or routines to their previous standards, especially when pay is closely tied to productivity.

Fear of the Unknown

Changes substitute ambiguity and uncertainty for the known. The transition from high school to university is typically such an experience. By the time we have completed our high school years, we understand how things work. You might not have liked high school, but at least you understood the system. Then you move on to college or university and face a whole new and uncertain system. You have traded the known for the unknown, along with the fear or insecurity that accompanies it.

Employees in organizations hold the same dislike for uncertainty. If, for example, the introduction of total quality management (TQM) means production employees will have to learn statistical process control techniques, some may fear they will be unable to do so. They may, therefore, develop a negative attitude toward TQM or behave dysfunctionally if required to use statistical techniques.

Selective Information Processing

As we learned in Chapter 2, individuals shape their world through their perceptions. Once they have created this world, it resists change. Individuals are guilty of selectively processing information in order to keep their perceptions intact. They hear what they want to hear. They ignore information that challenges the world they have created. To return to the production workers who are faced with the introduction of TQM, they may ignore the arguments their managers make in explaining why a knowledge of statistics is necessary or the potential benefits that the change will provide them.

Cynicism

In addition to simple resistance to change, employees often feel cynical about the change process, particularly if they have been through several rounds of change, and nothing appears (to them) to have changed. Three researchers from Ohio State University identified sources of cynicism in the change process of a large unionized manufacturing plant.[44] The major elements contributing to the cynicism were:

- feeling uninformed about what was happening;
- lack of communication and respect from one's manager;
- lack of communication and respect from one's union representative;
- lack of opportunity for meaningful participation in decision making.

The researchers also found that employees with negative personalities were more likely to be cynical about change. While organizations might not be able to change an individual's personality, they certainly have the ability to provide greater communication and respect, as well as opportunities to take part in decision making. The researchers found that cynicism about change led to such outcomes as lower commitment, less satisfaction, and reduced motivation to work hard. Exhibit 10–10 illustrates why some employees, particularly Dilbert, may have reason to feel cynical about organizational change.

Organizational Resistance

Organizations, by their very nature, are conservative.[45] They actively resist change. You don't have to look far to see evidence of this phenomenon. Government agencies want

Exhibit 10–10

Source: Dilbert by Scott Adams. August 3, 1996. DILBERT reprinted by permission of United Feature Syndicate, Inc.

to continue doing what they have been doing for years, whether the need for their service changes or remains the same. Organized religions are deeply entrenched in their history. Attempts to change church doctrine require great persistence and patience. Educational institutions, which exist to open minds and challenge established ways of thinking, are themselves extremely resistant to change. Most school systems are using essentially the same teaching technologies today as they were 50 years ago. Similarly, most business firms appear highly resistant to change. Half of the 309 human resources executives of Canadian firms who took part in a 1998 survey rated their company's ability to manage change as "fair."[46] One-third of them said that their ability to manage change was their weakest skill, and only 25 percent of the companies made a strong effort to train leaders in the change process.

Six major sources of organizational resistance have been identified.[47] They are shown in Exhibit 10–11 and discussed below.

Structural Inertia

Organizations have built-in mechanisms to produce stability. For example, the selection process systematically selects certain people in and certain people out. Training and other socialization techniques reinforce specific role requirements and skills. Formalization provides job descriptions, rules, and procedures for employees to follow.

Exhibit 10–11

Sources of Organizational Resistance to Change

```
    Threat to established          Structural
    resource allocations           inertia

    Threat to established    Organizational    Limited focus
    power relationships       Resistance       of change

         Threat to              Group
         expertise              inertia
```

The people who are hired into an organization are chosen for fit; they are then shaped and directed to behave in certain ways. When an organization is confronted with change, this structural inertia acts as a counterbalance to sustain stability.

Limited Focus of Change

Organizations are composed of a number of interdependent subsystems. You cannot change one without affecting the others. For example, if management changes the technological processes without simultaneously modifying the organization's structure to match, the change in technology is unlikely to be accepted. So limited changes in subsystems tend to be nullified by the larger system.

Group Inertia

Even if individuals want to change their behaviour, group norms may act as a constraint. An individual union member, for instance, may be willing to accept changes in his or her job suggested by management. But if union norms dictate resisting any unilateral change made by management, he or she is likely to resist.

Threat to Expertise

Changes in organizational patterns may threaten the expertise of specialized groups. The introduction of decentralized personal computers, which allow managers to gain access to information directly from a company's mainframe, is an example of a change that was strongly resisted by many information systems departments in the early 1980s. Why? Decentralized end-user computing posed a threat to the specialized skills held by those in the centralized information systems departments.

Threat to Established Power Relationships

Any redistribution of decision-making authority can threaten long-established power relationships within the organization. The introduction of participative decision making or self-managed work teams is the kind of change that supervisors and middle managers often view as threatening.

Threat to Established Resource Allocations

Those groups in the organization that control sizable resources often view change as a threat. They tend to be content with the status quo. Will the change, for instance, mean a reduction in their budgets or a cut in their staff size? Those that most benefit from the current allocation of resources often feel threatened by changes that may affect future allocations.

Overcoming Resistance to Change

Michael Adams, president of Environics Research Group in Toronto, has noted that Canadians have become more resistant to change in recent years.[48] Between 1983 and the mid-1990s, Canadians reported that they "felt confident in their ability to cope with change." This trend has reversed in recent years. Half of Canadians aged 15 to 33 now "feel left behind and overwhelmed by the pace of life and the prevalence of technology." Those who feel left behind tend to be those who are not college- or university-educated, highly skilled, or adaptive.

It probably cannot be emphasized enough that in order to break down resistance to change, it is essential to communicate a sense of urgency in the need for change. This provides a framework for people to understand why the change is occurring. Also, it is important to communicate and celebrate early successes to keep the momentum going, as change is a lengthy process. Six tactics have been suggested for use by organizations dealing with resistance to change.[49] Let's review them briefly.

Education and Communication

Resistance can be reduced through communicating with employees to help them see the logic of a change. This tactic basically assumes that the source of resistance lies in misinformation or poor communication—that is, if employees receive the full facts and any misunderstandings are cleared up, resistance will be decreased. Communication can be achieved through memos, group presentations, reports, or one-on-one discussions. Does this approach work? It does, if the source of resistance is inadequate communication and if management-employee relations are characterized by mutual trust and credibility. If these conditions don't exist, the change is unlikely to succeed.

Participation

It's difficult for individuals to resist a change decision in which they took part. Before making a change, those opposed can be brought into the decision process. Assuming that the participants have the expertise to make a meaningful contribution, their involvement can reduce resistance, obtain commitment, and increase the quality of the change decision. However, against these advantages are the negatives: potential for a poor solution and great time consumption.

Facilitation and Support

Organizations undergoing change can offer a range of supportive efforts to reduce resistance. When employee fear and anxiety are high, employee counselling and therapy, new-skills training, or a short, paid leave of absence may ease the adjustment. The drawback of this tactic is that, as with the others, it is time-consuming. It is also expensive, and its implementation offers no assurance of success.

Negotiation

Another way for organizations to deal with potential resistance to change is to exchange something of value for a lessening of the resistance. For instance, if the resistance is centred in a few powerful individuals, a specific reward package can be negotiated that will meet their individual needs. Negotiation as a tactic may be necessary when resistance comes from a powerful source. Yet one cannot ignore its potentially high costs. There is also the risk that once senior management in an organization negotiate with one party to avoid resistance, they face the possibility of being beleaguered by other individuals in positions of power.

Manipulation and Co-Optation

Manipulation refers to disguised attempts to influence people. Twisting and distorting facts to make them appear more attractive, withholding undesirable information, and creating false rumours to get employees to accept a change are all examples of manipulation. If corporate management threatens to close down a particular manufacturing plant should that plant's employees fail to accept an across-the-board pay cut, and if the threat is actually untrue, management is using manipulation. Co-optation, on the other hand, is a form of both manipulation and participation. It seeks to "buy off" the leaders of a resistance group by giving them a key role in the change decision. The leaders' advice is sought, not to seek a better decision, but to receive their endorsement. Both manipulation and co-optation are relatively inexpensive and easy ways to gain the support of adversaries, but the tactics can backfire if the targets become aware that they are being tricked or used. Once the tactics are discovered, management's credibility may drop to zero.

Coercion

Last on the list of tactics is *coercion*—the application of direct threats or force upon the resisters. If the corporate management mentioned in the previous discussion is determined to close a manufacturing plant should employees not agree to a pay cut, then "coercion" would be the label attached to its change tactic. Other examples of coercion are threats of transfer, loss of promotions, negative performance evaluations, and a poor letter of recommendation. The advantages and drawbacks of coercion are approximately the same as those mentioned for manipulation and co-optation.

The Politics of Change

No discussion of resistance to change would be complete without a brief mention of the politics of change. Politics suggests that the demand for change is more likely to come from employees who are new to the organization (and have less invested in the status quo) or managers who are slightly removed from the main power structure. Those managers who have spent their entire careers with a single organization and eventually achieve a senior position in the hierarchy are often major impediments to change. Change itself is a very real threat to their status and position. Yet they may be expected to implement changes to demonstrate that they are not merely caretakers.

By trying to bring about change, senior managers can symbolically convey to various constituencies—stockholders, suppliers, employees, customers—that they are on top of problems and adapting to a dynamic environment. Of course as you might guess, when forced to introduce change, these long-time power holders tend to introduce changes that do not fundamentally challenge the status quo. Radical change is too threatening. This, incidentally, explains why boards of directors that recognize the need for the rapid introduction of fundamental, radical change in their organizations often turn to outside candidates for new leadership.[50]

You may remember that we discussed politics in Chapter 7 and gave some suggestions for how to more effectively encourage people to go along with your ideas. That chapter also indicated how individuals acquire power, which provides further insight into the ability of some individuals to resist change.

SUMMARY AND IMPLICATIONS

1 What is organizational culture? Organizational culture is the pattern of shared values, beliefs, and assumptions considered to be the appropriate way to think and act within an organization. Culture provides stability to an organization and gives employees a clear understanding of "the way things are done around here."

2 How do you create and maintain culture? The original culture of an organization is derived from the founder's philosophy. That philosophy then influences what types of employees are hired. The culture of the organization is then reinforced by top management, who signal what is acceptable behaviour and what is not.

3 What kind of culture might suit you? There is no one right culture, because individuals vary in the type of culture with which they are comfortable. Cultures can be analyzed in terms of their friendliness (*sociability*) and the degree to which individuals are task-oriented (*solidarity*). This leads to four different types of cultures to consider: *networked, mercenary, fragmented,* and *communal*.

4 What is the purpose of culture? Culture performs a number of functions within an organization. First, it creates distinctions between one organization and others. Second, it gives a sense of identity to the organization's members. Third, culture creates commitment to employees. Fourth, culture is the social glue that helps to hold the organization together. Finally, culture helps employees make sense of the organization.

5 How do you change culture? Changing culture is not easy. It is not unusual for managers to try changing the structure, the technology, or the people, but this often isn't enough. Because culture is the shared beliefs within the organization, it influences all of the activities in which people engage. Thus it's important to change the reward structure, and to work carefully to change the beliefs in order to get real culture change.

6 How do organizations manage change? Kurt Lewin argued that successful change in organizations should follow three steps: *unfreezing* the status quo, *moving* to a new state, and *refreezing* the new change to make it permanent.

7 Why do people and organizations resist change? Individuals resist change because of basic human characteristics such as perceptions, personalities, and needs. Organizations resist change because they are conservative, and because change is difficult. The status quo is often preferred by those who feel they have the most to lose if change goes ahead.

For Review

1. Can an employee survive in an organization if he or she rejects its core values? Explain.

2. How can an outsider assess an organization's culture?

3. What defines an organization's subcultures?

4. How can culture be a liability to an organization?

5. What benefits can socialization provide for the organization? For the new employee?

6. Describe four cultural types and the characteristics of employees who fit best with each.

7. How does Lewin's three-step model of change deal with resistance to change?

8. What is the difference between driving forces and restraining forces?

9. What are the factors that lead individuals to resist change?

10. What are the factors that lead organizations to resist change?

For Critical Thinking

1. Contrast individual personality and organizational culture. How are they similar? How are they different?

2. Is socialization brainwashing? Explain.

3. Can you identify a set of characteristics that describes your college's or university's culture? Compare them with several of your peers' lists. How closely do they agree?

4. "Resistance to change is an irrational response." Do you agree or disagree? Explain.

OB for You

- Carefully consider the culture of any organization at which you are thinking of being employed. You will feel more comfortable in cultures that share your values and expectations.

- When you work in groups on student projects, the groups create mini-cultures of their own. Be aware of what values and norms are being supported early on in the group's life, as these will greatly influence the group's culture.

- Be aware that change is a fact of life. If you need to change something in yourself, be aware of the importance of creating new systems to replace the old. Saying you want to be healthier, without specifying that you intend to go to the gym three times a week, or eat five servings of fruits and vegetables a day, means that change likely will not occur. It's important to specify goals and behaviours as part of that change.

 **POINT**

 **COUNTERPOINT**

Organizations Are More Like Calm Waters

Organizational change is an episodic activity. That is, it starts at some point, proceeds through a series of steps, and culminates in some outcome that those involved hope is an improvement over the starting point. It has a beginning, a middle, and an end.

Lewin's three-step model represents a classic illustration of this perspective. Change is seen as a break in the organization's equilibrium. The status quo has been disturbed, and change is necessary to establish a new equilibrium state. The objective of refreezing is to stabilize the new situation by balancing the driving and restraining forces.

Some experts have argued that organizational change should be thought of as balancing a system made up of five interacting variables within the organization—*people, tasks, technology, structure,* and *strategy.* A change in any one variable has repercussions on one or more of the others. This perspective is episodic in that it treats organizational change as basically an effort to sustain an equilibrium. A change in one variable begins a chain of events that, if properly managed, requires adjustments in the other variables to achieve a new state of equilibrium.

Another way to conceptualize the episodic view of looking at change is to think of managing change as similar to captaining a ship. The organization is like a large ship travelling across the calm Mediterranean Sea to a specific port. The ship's captain has made this exact trip hundreds of times before with the same crew. Every once in a while, however, a storm will appear, and the crew has to respond. The captain will make the appropriate adjustments—that is, implement changes—and, having manoeuvred through the storm, will return to calm waters. Like this ship's voyage, managing an organization should be seen as a journey with a beginning and an end, and introducing change as a response to a break in the status quo and needed only occasionally.

Organizations Are More Like Whitewater Rafting

The episodic approach may be the dominant way of handling organizational change, but it has become obsolete. It applies to a world of certainty and predictability. The episodic approach was developed in the 1950s and 1960s, and it reflects the environment of those times. It treats change as the occasional disturbance in an otherwise peaceful world. However, this model has little resemblance to today's environment of constant and chaotic change.[51]

If you want to understand what it's like to manage change in today's organizations, think of it as equivalent to permanent whitewater rafting.[52] The organization is not a large ship, but more akin to a 40-foot raft. Rather than sailing a calm sea, this raft must traverse a raging river made up of an uninterrupted flow of permanent whitewater rapids. To make things worse, the raft is manned by 10 people who have never worked together or travelled the river before, much of the trip is in the dark, the river is dotted by unexpected turns and obstacles, the exact destination of the raft is not clear, and at irregular intervals the raft needs to pull to shore, where some new crew members are added and others leave. Change is a natural state and managing change is a continual process. That is, managers never get the luxury of escaping the whitewater rapids.

The stability and predictability that are characteristic of the episodic perspective no longer describe the world we live in. Disruptions in the status quo are not occasional, temporary, or followed by a return to an equilibrium state. There is, in fact, no equilibrium state. Managers today face constant change, bordering on chaos. They are being forced to play a game they have never played before, governed by rules that are created as the game progresses.

LEARNING ABOUT **YOURSELF** EXERCISE

What Kind of Organizational Culture Fits You Best?

For each of the following statements, circle the level of agreement or disagreement that you personally feel:

SA = Strongly agree
A = Agree
U = Uncertain
D = Disagree
SD = Strongly disagree

1. I like being part of a team and having my performance assessed in terms of my contribution to the team.   SA A U D SD

2. No person's needs should be compromised in order for a department to achieve its goals.   SA A U D SD

3. I like the thrill and excitement from taking risks.   SA A U D SD

4. If a person's job performance is inadequate, it's irrelevant how much effort he or she made.   SA A U D SD

5. I like things to be stable and predictable.   SA A U D SD

6. I prefer managers who provide detailed and rational explanations for their decisions.   SA A U D SD

7. I like to work where there isn't a great deal of pressure and where people are essentially easygoing.   SA A U D SD

Scoring Key

For items 5 and 6, score as follows: Strongly agree = +2; Agree = +1; Uncertain = 0; Disagree = −1; Strongly disagree = −2

For items 1, 2, 3, 4, and 7, reverse the score (Strongly agree = −2, and so on). Add up your total. Your score will fall somewhere between −14 and +14.

What does your score mean? The higher your score (positive), the more comfortable you will be in a formal, mechanistic, rule-oriented, and structured culture. This is often associated with large corporations and government agencies. Negative scores indicate a preference for informal, humanistic, flexible, and innovative cultures, which are more likely to be found in research units, advertising firms, high-tech companies, and small businesses.

BREAKOUT **GROUP** EXERCISES

Form small groups to discuss the following topics, as assigned by your instructor:

1. Identify artifacts of culture in your current or previous workplace. From these artifacts, would you conclude that the organization had a strong or weak culture?

2. Have you or someone you know worked somewhere where the culture was strong? What was your reaction to that strong culture? Did you like that environ- ment, or would you prefer to work where there is a weaker culture? Why?

3. Reflect on either the culture of one of your classes, or the culture of the organization where you work, and identify aspects of that culture that could be changed. How might some of these changes be made?

WORKING WITH **OTHERS** EXERCISE

The Beacon Aircraft Company

Objectives

1. To illustrate how forces for change and stability must be managed in organizational change programs.

2. To illustrate the effects of alternative change techniques on the relative strength of forces for change and forces for stability.

The Situation

The marketing division of the Beacon Aircraft Company has undergone two reorganizations in the past two years. Initially, its structure changed from a functional one, where employees were organized within departments, to a matrix form where employees from several different functions reported both to their own manager and to a project manager. But the matrix structure did not satisfy some functional managers. They complained that the structure confused the authority and responsibility relationships.

In reaction to these complaints, the marketing manager revised Beacon's structure back to the functional form. This new structure had a marketing group and several project groups. The project groups were managed by project managers with a few general staff members, but no functional specialists, such as people from marketing, were assigned to these groups.

After the change, some problems began to surface. Project managers complained that they could not obtain adequate assistance from functional staff members. It not only took more time to obtain necessary assistance, but it also created problems in establishing stable relationships with functional staff members. Since these problems affected their services to customers, project managers demanded a change in the organizational structure—prob-

ably again toward a matrix structure. Faced with these complaints and demands from project managers, the vice-president is pondering another reorganization. He has requested an outside consultant to help him in the reorganization plan.

The Procedure

1. Divide yourselves into groups of 5 to 7 and take the role of consultants.

2. Each group identifies the driving and resisting forces found in the firm. List these forces in the spaces provided.

The Driving Forces	The Resisting Forces
_____	_____
_____	_____
_____	_____
_____	_____
_____	_____

3. Each group develops a set of strategies for increasing the driving forces and another set for reducing the resisting forces.

4. Each group prepares a list of changes it wants to introduce.

5. The class reassembles and hears each group's recommendations.

Source: Adapted from K.H. Chung and L.C. Megginson, *Organizational Behavior*, Copyright © 1981 by K.H. Chung and L.C. Megginson. Reprinted by permission of HarperCollins Publishers, Inc.

ETHICAL **DILEMMA** EXERCISE

Cultural Factors and Unethical Behaviour

An organization's culture socializes people. It subtly conveys to members that certain actions are acceptable, even though they may be illegal. For instance, when executives at General Electric, Westinghouse, and other manufacturers of heavy electrical equipment illegally conspired to set prices in the early 1960s, the defendants invariably testified that they came new to their jobs, found price-fixing to be an established way of life, and simply entered into it as they did into other aspects of their job. One GE manager noted that every one of his bosses had directed him to meet with the competition: "It had become so common and gone on for so many years that I think we lost sight of the fact that it was illegal."[53]

The strength of an organization's culture has an influence on the ethical behaviour of its managers. A strong culture will exert more influence on managers than a weak one. If the culture is strong and supports high ethical standards, it should have a very powerful positive influence on a manager's ethical behaviour. However, in a weak culture, managers are more likely to rely on subculture norms to guide their behaviour. Work groups and departmental standards will more strongly influence ethical behaviour in organizations that have weak overall cultures.

It is also generally acknowledged that the content of a culture affects ethical behaviour. Assuming this is true, what would a culture look like that would shape high ethical standards? What could top management do to strengthen that culture? Do you think it's possible for a manager with high ethical standards to uphold those standards in an organizational culture that tolerates, or even encourages, unethical practices?

CASE INCIDENT

EnCana's New Culture Presents Challenges

When Alberta Energy Co. (AEC) and PanCanadian Energy Corp. merged on April 8, 2002, to form Calgary-based EnCana Corp., they created arguably the largest producer of natural gas worldwide and the world's top exploration and production company.[54] The new company wants to be taken seriously by institutional investors, so that its stock will be valued appropriately.

Getting EnCana recognized by institutionalized investors may be the easier of the problems confronting the new company. AEC and PanCanadian were the largest natural gas producers in Canada, and they competed against each other for years.

Gwyn Morgan, former head of AEC, is the new president and CEO of EnCana and knows the difficulties he faces. He has overseen several other mergers at AEC. To get things off to a good start, his 1800 employees and PanCanadians' 2000 employees were given the booklet *The Employee Survival Guide to Mergers and Acquisitions*, by Price Prtichett, a US expert on organizational change. Morgan is determined to create a culture for the organization, rather than let one emerge over time.

He explains his approach as follows: "A business organization creates culture by establishing principles and expectations and aligning the incentive system with the results you want to achieve and if you can do all of those things, whatever falls out of the resulting behavioural pattern in the company is something you call culture."

The two merging companies could not be more different. AEC has an aggressive, entrepreneurial, results-oriented culture. PanCanadian's culture is risk-averse, hierarchical, and formal. Rather than focus on these differences, however, Morgan wants employees to focus on commonalities: "We are all Canadian here, we work in Calgary, we work in the oil and gas business."

To steer employees in the right direction culturally, Morgan sent his employees emails even before the merger became official. In these, he explained the "basic principles and philosophies" of the new company. He particularly emphasized that in the new organizational structure "bureaucracy will be rooted out and distractions will be discouraged." Morgan's leadership style, which favours a decentralized structure where employees are accountable for results, is meant to encourage the breakdown of bureaucracy he anticipates from the PanCanadian employees.

Questions

1. What are the problems Morgan faces in making this merger work?

2. What does Morgan need to do to ensure that a new culture develops?

3. What difficulties do you anticipate he will face in establishing the new culture?

CBC **VIDEO CASE** INCIDENT

Quebecor Tackles Videotron

In the autumn of 2000, Quebec cable giant Videotron was taken over by Quebecor, the world's largest commercial printing company, for $5 billion.

Using a business strategy called "convergence," Videotron was targeted as Quebecor's opportunity to expand into the highly lucrative Quebec cable industry. This strategy was expected to bring in large profits for both Quebecor and the Quebec Public Pension Fund, which initially helped to underwrite the large purchase price.

"It's a natural fit," some experts claimed about the takeover, which would allow Quebecor the ability to move its print content through its newly-acquired cable connections, thereby reaching many new potential customers.

Such a financial risk could have been successful, except problems quickly arose soon after the takeover: tech stocks plummeted, the Canadian economy softened, and the organizational cultures of Videotron and Quebecor clashed.

Led by a corporate philosophy that a firm must "either increase its revenue or lower its costs" in order to make a profit, Quebecor decided to address Videotron's cost structures head-on. Efficiency in operations was a major priority for Quebecor executives if this new operation with Videotron was going to work.

In contrast, Videotron had a near monopoly in the marketplace—the third largest cable company in Canada and a leader in the field of telecommunications, cable television, and internet services. Videotron felt that it did not need to focus on customer service, nor was it worried about competition. Its 2000-strong, unionized labour force refused to grant concessions, and fought a proposal for a longer workweek from the new owner with intense bitterness.

Quebecor executives were caught off guard by the union's reaction. A long and emotionally intense labour strike placed the new firm into a dangerous financial position. Eventually, the two sides worked out their differences, but Quebecor paid a significant price for the conflict.

Questions

1. What role do basic underlying assumptions and values play in the creation of a corporate culture? How did these variables differ between Quebecor and Videotron?

2. Who creates a corporate culture? How does leadership philosophy drive corporate behaviour?

3. Explain the effects a collective agreement can have on corporate culture, especially when a manager tries to implement change.

Source: Based on "Quebecor," *CBC Venture*, December 15, 2002, VA2003F, 858; Quebecor World Inc. website, "About Us," www.quebecorworldinc.com; Scientific-Atlanta, Techlinks Announcements, www.scientificatlanta.com.

From **Concepts**
to **Skills**

How to "Read" an Organization's Culture

The ability to read and assess an organization's culture can be a valuable skill.[55] If you are looking for a job, you will want to choose an employer whose culture is compatible with your values and in which you will feel comfortable. If you can accurately assess a prospective employer's culture before you make your decision, you may be able to save yourself a lot of grief and reduce the likelihood of making a poor choice. Similarly, you will undoubtedly have business transactions with numerous organizations during your professional career. You will be trying to sell a product or service, negotiate a contract, arrange a joint venture, or you may merely be seeking out which individual in an organization controls certain decisions. The ability to assess another organization's culture can be a definite plus in successfully completing these pursuits.

For the sake of simplicity, we will approach the problem of reading an organization's culture from that of a job applicant. We will assume you are interviewing for a job. Here is a list of things you can do to help learn about a potential employer's culture:

- Observe the physical surroundings. Pay attention to signs, pictures, style of dress, length of hair, degree of openness between offices, and office furnishings and arrangements.

- With whom did you meet? Just the person who would be your immediate manager? Or potential colleagues, managers from other departments, or senior executives? And based on what they revealed, to what degree do people other than the immediate manager have input into the hiring decision?

- How would you characterize the style of the people you met? Formal? Casual? Serious? Jovial?

- Does the organization have formal rules and regulations printed in a human resources policy manual? If so, how detailed are these policies?

- Ask questions of the people you meet. The most valid and reliable information tends to come from asking the same questions of many people (to see how

closely their responses align) and by talking with boundary spanners. *Boundary spanners* are employees whose work links them to the external environment and includes jobs such as human resources interviewer, salesperson, purchasing agent, labour negotiator, public relations specialist, and company lawyer. Questions that will give you insights into organizational processes and practices might include the following:

- What is the background of the founders?

- What is the background of current senior managers? What are their functional specializations? Were they promoted from within or hired from outside?

- How does the organization integrate new employees? Is there an orientation program? Training? If so, could you describe these features?

- How does your manager define his or her job success? (Amount of profit? Serving customers? Meeting deadlines? Acquiring budget increases?)

- How would you define fairness in terms of reward allocations?

- Can you identify some people here who are on the "fast track"? What do you think has put them on the fast track?

- Can you identify someone who seems to be considered a deviant in the organization? How has the organization responded to this person?

- Can you describe a decision that someone made here that was well received?

- Can you describe a decision that did not work out well? What were the consequences for the decision maker?

- Could you describe a crisis or critical event that has occurred recently in the organization? How did top management respond? What was learned from this experience?

▶

Assessing Skills

When you have read this chapter, take the following Self-Assessments on your enclosed CD-ROM.

42. What's the Right Organizational Culture for Me?

47. How Well Do I Respond to Turbulent Change?

Practising Skills

You are the nursing supervisor at a community hospital employing both emergency-room and floor nurses. Each of these teams of nurses tends to work almost exclusively with others doing the same job. In your professional reading, you have come across the concept of cross-training nursing teams and giving them more varied responsibilities, which in turn has been shown to both improve patient care and lower costs. You call the two team leaders, Sue and Scott, into your office to explain that you want the nursing teams to move to this approach. To your surprise, they are both opposed to the idea. Sue says she and the other emergency-room nurses feel they are needed in the ER, where they fill the most vital role in the hospital. They work special hours when needed, do whatever tasks are required, and often work in difficult and stressful circumstances. They think the floor nurses have relatively easy jobs for the pay they receive. Scott, leader of the floor nurse team, tells you that his group believes the ER nurses lack the special training and extra experience that the floor nurses bring to the hospital. The floor nurses claim they have the heaviest responsibilities and do the most exacting work. Because they have ongoing contact with patients and families, they believe they should not be called away from vital floor duties to help the ER nurses complete their tasks.

Now that you are faced with this resistance, how can you most effectively introduce the cross-training model?

Reinforcing Skills

1. Choose two courses that you are taking this term, ideally in different faculties, and describe the culture of the classroom in each. What are the similarities and differences? What values about learning might you infer from your observations of culture?

2. Do some comparisons of the atmosphere or feeling you get from various organizations. Because of the number and wide variety that you will find, it will probably be easiest for you to do this exercise using restaurants, retail stores, or banks. Based on the atmosphere that you observe, what type of organizational culture do you think these organizations might have? If you can, interview three employees at each organization for their descriptions of their organization's culture.

3. Think about changes (major and minor) that you have dealt with over the past year. Perhaps these changes involved other people and perhaps they were personal. Did you resist the change? Did others resist the change? How did you overcome your resistance or the resistance of others to the change?

4. Interview managers at three different organizations about changes they have introduced. What was their experience in bringing in the change? How did they manage resistance to the change?

ENDNOTES

Chapter 1

1. Opening vignette based on G. Pitts, "Ex-Military Officer Fighting New Battle," *The Globe and Mail*, September 23, 2002, p. B3.

2. V. Galt, "One-Third of Employees Loathe Their Jobs, Consultants Find," *The Globe and Mail*, January 28, 2003.

3. "FP/COMPAS Poll: An Exclusive Survey of CEOs and Canadians at Large: This Week: New Burdens for Managers," *The Financial Post*, November 22/24, 1997, p. 17.

4. K. Goff, "Stress Level on the Job Doubles, Study Finds: More People Say They Are Working Longer With Less Job Satisfaction Than a Decade Ago, University Researchers Find," *The Vancouver Sun*, October 23, 2001, p. A11.

5. Angus Reid Group, *Workplace 2000: Working Toward the Millennium*, Fall 1997.

6. K. Damsell, "Service With No Smile: Blame It on Looser Labor Laws and a Newly Cynical Young Workforce. From Waiters to Video Clerks, BC's Service Industry Employees Are Flocking to Unions," *The Financial Post*, August 23/25, 1997, p. 14.

7. B. Dumaine, "The New Non-Manager Managers," *Fortune*, February 22, 1993, pp. 80–84.

8. "Wanted: Teammates, Crew Members, and Cast Members: But No Employees," *Wall Street Journal*, April 30, 1996, p. A1.

9. S. Ross, "U.S. Managers Fail to Fit the Bill in New Workplace: Study," *Reuters News Agency*, November 19, 1999.

10. *OB in the Workplace* based on P. Verburg, "Prepare for Takeoff," *Canadian Business*, December 25, 2000, pp. 94–96+.

11. The Conference Board of Canada, *Employability Skills Profile*, 1998.

12. S.A. Waddock, "Educating Tomorrow's Managers," *Journal of Management Education*, February 1991, pp. 69–96; and K.F. Kane, "MBAs: A Recruiter's-Eye View," *Business Horizons*, January–February 1993, pp. 65–71.

13. C. Taylor, "Gaming Glory," *The Financial Post*, July 26, 1999, p. C3.

14. "New Boss Sets Goals of Opening up CIBC," *The Vancouver Sun*, June 29, 1999, p. D. 13.

15. C. Hymowitz, "Five Main Reasons Why Managers Fail," *Wall Street Journal*, May 2, 1988, p. 25.

16. P. Booth, *Challenge and Change: Embracing the Team Concept*, Report 123–94, Conference Board of Canada, 1994.

17. Cited in C. Joinson, "Teams at Work," *HRMagazine*, May 1999, p. 30; and P. Strozniak, "Teams at Work," *Industry Week*, September 18, 2000, p. 47.

18. See, for instance, R.R. Thomas Jr., "From Affirmative Action to Affirming Diversity," *Harvard Business Review*, March–April 1990, pp. 107–117; B. Mandrell and S. Kohler-Gray, "Management Development That Values Diversity," *Personnel*, March 1990, pp. 41–47; J. Dreyfuss, "Get Ready for the New Work Force," *Fortune*, April 23, 1990, pp. 165–181; and I. Wielawski, "Diversity Makes Both Dollars and Sense," *Los Angeles Times*, May 16, 1994, p. I1–3.

19. *Focus on Diversity* based on M. O'Brien, "Heritage Room for Native Cadets," *The Leader-Post* (Regina), December 5, 2000, p. A3.

20. P. Drucker, *Management: Tasks, Responsibilities, Practices* (New York: Harper and Row, 1974).

21. "B.C. Workers Take Less Time off Than Most Canadians," *The Vancouver Sun*, May 22, 2003, p. F5.

22. Cited in "You Often Lose the Ones You Love," *Industry Week*, November 21, 1988, p. 5.

23. D.W. Organ, *Organizational Citizenship Behavior: The Good Soldier Syndrome* (Lexington, MA: Lexington Books, 1988), p. 4.

24. See, for example, P.M. Podsakoff and S.B. MacKenzie, "Organizational Citizenship Behavior and Sales Unit Effectiveness," *Journal of Marketing Research*, August 1994, pp. 351–363; and P.M. Podsakoff, M. Ahearne, and S.B. MacKenzie, "Organizational Citizenship Behavior and the Quantity and Quality of Work Group Performance," *Journal of Applied Psychology*, April 1997, pp. 262–270.

25. M. Kaeter, "The Age of the Specialized Generalist," *Training*, December 1993, pp. 48–53; and N. Templin, "Auto Plants, Hiring Again, Are Demanding Higher-Skilled Labor," *Wall Street Journal*, March 11, 1994, p. A1.

26. G. Pitts, "Ex-Military Officer Fighting New Battle," *The Globe and Mail*, September 23, 2002, p. B3.

27. G. Pitts, "Ex-Military Officer Fighting New Battle," *The Globe and Mail*, September 23, 2002, p. B3.

28. C. Thompson, "State of the Union," *Report on Business Magazine*, April 1998, pp. 73–82.

29. B. Livesey, "Making Nice," *Report on Business* Magazine, March 1998, pp. 96–104.

30. S. Brearton and J. Daly, "The Fifty Best Companies to Work for in Canada," *Report on Business* Magazine, December 27, 2002.

31. R.T. Mowday, L.W. Porter, and R.M. Steers, *Employee Organization Linkages: The Psychology of Commitment, Absenteeism, and Turnover* (New York: Academic Press, 1982).

32. C.R. Farquhar and J.A. Longair, "Creating High-Performance Organizations With People," Conference Board of Canada, 1996, Report #R164–96.

33. C.R. Farquhar and J.A. Longair, "Creating High-Performance Organizations With People," Conference Board of Canada, 1996, Report #R164–96.

34. "People Power," *Canadian Business Review*, Spring 1996, p. 42.

35. See, for example, M.J. Driver, "Cognitive Psychology: An Interactionist View," R.H. Hall, "Organizational Behavior: A Sociological Perspective," and C. Hardy, "The Contribution of Political Science to Organizational Behavior," all in J.W. Lorsch (ed.), *Handbook of Organizational Behavior* (Englewood Cliffs, NJ: Prentice Hall, 1987), pp. 62–108.

36. R. Weinberg and W. Nord, "Coping With 'It's All Common Sense'," *Exchange* 7, no. 2, 1982, pp. 29–33; R.P. Vecchio, "Some Popular (But Misguided) Criticisms of the Organizational Sciences," *Organizational Behavior Teaching Review*, 10, no. 1, 1986–87, pp. 28–34; and M.L. Lynn, "Organizational Behavior and Common Sense: Philosophical Implications for Teaching and Thinking," paper presented at the 14th Annual Organizational Behavior Teaching Conference, Waltham, MA, May 1987.

37. S. Brearton and J. Daly, "The Fifty Best Companies to Work for in Canada," *Report on Business* Magazine, December 27, 2002.

38. Angus Reid Group, *Workplace 2000: Working Toward the Millennium*, Fall 1997.

39. Angus Reid Group, *Workplace 2000: Working Toward the Millennium*, Fall 1997.

40. See, for instance, J. Pfeffer, *The Human Equation: Building Profits by Putting People First* (Boston: Harvard Business School Press, 1998); and P. Drucker, "They're Not Employees, They're People," *Harvard Business Review*, February 2002, pp. 70–77.

41. R.E. Quinn, *Beyond Rational Management: Mastering the Paradoxes and Competing Demands of High Performance* (San Francisco: Jossey-Bass, 1991); R.E. Quinn, S.R. Faerman, M.P. Thompson, and M.R. McGrath, *Becoming a Master Manager: A Competency Framework*, 1st ed. (New York: John Wiley and Sons, 1990); K. Cameron and R.E. Quinn, *Diagnosing and Changing Organizational Culture: Based on the Competing Values Framework*, 1st ed. (Reading, MA: Addison Wesley Longman Inc., 1999).

42. R.E. Quinn, S.R. Faerman, M.P. Thompson, and M.R. McGrath, *Becoming a Master Manager: A Competency Framework*, 1st ed. (New York: John Wiley and Sons, 1990).

43. D. Maley, "Canada's Top Women CEOs," *Maclean's*, October 20, 1997, pp. 52+.

Chapter 2

1. Opening vignette based on P. Stock, "Mutual Back-Scratchers: Longstanding Liberal Policies Are Linked to the Feds' Civil Service Morale Crisis," *Report Newsmagazine*, June 25, 2001, pp. 17–18; A. Thompson, "Who Protects the Protectors?" *The Toronto Star*, May 26, 2001, pp. K1, K4; "Canada's Human Rights Watchdog Considers Changes in Wake of Scathing Report," *Canadian Press Newswire*, May 18, 2001; and "Women Working at Canadian Human Rights Watchdog Face Discrimination: Report," *Canadian Press Newswire*, May 12, 2001.

2. A. Thompson, "Who Protects the Protectors?" *The Toronto Star*, May 26, 2001, pp. K1, K4.

3. T. Cole, "Who Loves Ya?" *Report on Business Magazine*, April 1999, pp. 44–60.

4. P. Stock, "Mutual Back-Scratchers: Longstanding Liberal Policies Are Linked to the Feds' Civil Service Morale Crisis," *Report Newsmagazine*, June 25, 2001, pp. 17–18.

5. A. Thompson, "Who Protects the Protectors?" *The Toronto Star*, May 26, 2001, pp. K1, K4.

6. A. Standen, "Too Bizzaro for words," *salon.com*, http://www.salon.com/people/feature/2002/02/20/bizzaro/index.html (accessed February 23, 2002).

7. H.H. Kelley, "Attribution in Social Interaction," in E. Jones et al. (eds.), *Attribution: Perceiving the Causes of Behavior* (Morristown, NJ: General Learning Press, 1972).

8. See L. Ross, "The Intuitive Psychologist and His Shortcomings," in L. Berkowitz (ed.), *Advances in Experimental Social Psychology*, vol. 10 (Orlando, FL: Academic Press, 1977), pp. 174–220; and A.G. Miller and T. Lawson, "The Effect of an Informational Option on the Fundamental Attribution Error," *Personality and Social Psychology Bulletin*, June 1989, pp. 194–204.

9. B. McKenna, "Modern Suicides Hold Little Glory," *The Globe and Mail*, June 2, 1998, p. A14.

10. S. Nam, "Cultural and Managerial Attributions for Group Performance," unpublished doctoral dissertation, University of Oregon. Cited in R.M. Steers, S.J. Bischoff, and L.H. Higgins, "Cross-Cultural Management Research," *Journal of Management Inquiry*, December 1992, pp. 325–326.

11. D.C. Dearborn and H.A. Simon, "Selective Perception: A Note on the Departmental Identification of Executives," *Sociometry*, June 1958, pp. 140–144. Some of the conclusions in this classic study have recently been challenged in J.P. Walsh, "Selectivity and Selective Perception: An Investigation of Managers' Belief Structures and Information Processing," *Academy of Management Journal*, December 1988, pp. 873–896; M.J. Waller, G.P. Huber, and W.H. Glick, "Functional Background as a Determinant of Executives' Selective Perception," *Academy of Management Journal*, August 1995, pp. 943–974; and J.M. Beyer, P. Chattopadhyay, E. George, W.H. Glick, D.T. Ogilvie, and D. Pugliese, "The Selective Perception of Managers Revisited," *Academy of Management Journal*, June 1997, pp. 716–737.

12. S.E. Asch, "Forming Impressions of Personality," *Journal of Abnormal and Social Psychology*, July 1946, pp. 258–290.

13. J.S. Bruner and R. Tagiuri, "The Perception of People," in E. Lindzey (ed.), *Handbook of Social Psychology* (Reading, MA: Addison-Wesley, 1954), p. 641.

14. See, for example, C.M. Judd and B. Park, "Definition and Assessment of Accuracy in Social Stereotypes," *Psychological Review*, January 1993, pp. 109–128.

15. K.D. Elsbach, and R.M. Kramer, "Assessing Creativity in Hollywood Pitch Meetings: Evidence for a Dual-Process Model of Creativity Judgments," *Academy of Management Journal,*46, no. 3, 2003, pp. 283–301.

16. See, for example, S.T. Fiske, D.N. Beroff, E. Borgida, K. Deaux, and M.E. Heilman, "Use of Sex Stereotyping Research in Price Waterhouse vs. Hopkins," *American Psychologist*, 1991, pp. 1049–1060; G.N. Powell, "The Good Manager: Business Students' Stereotypes of Japanese Managers Versus Stereotypes of American Managers," *Group & Organizational Management*, 1992, pp. 44–56; and K.J. Gibson, W.J. Zerbe, and R.E. Franken, "Job Search Strategies for Older Job Hunters: Addressing Employers' Perceptions," *Canadian Journal of Counselling*, 1992, pp. 166–176.

17. K. May, "Action Vowed on Unrest: Agency Head Refuses to Quit," *Calgary Herald*, May 19, 2001, p. A13

18. See, for example, E.C. Webster, *Decision Making in the Employment Interview* (Montreal: McGill University, Industrial Relations Centre, 1964).

19. See, for example, R.D. Bretz Jr., G.T. Milkovich, and W. Read, "The Current State of Performance Appraisal Research and Practice: Concerns, Directions, and Implications," *Journal of Management*, June 1992, pp. 323–324; and P.M. Swiercz, M.L. Icenogle, N.B. Bryan, and R.W. Renn, "Do Perceptions of Performance Appraisal Fairness Predict Employee Attitudes and Performance?" in D.P. Moore (ed.), *Proceedings of the Academy of Management* (Atlanta: Academy of Management, 1993), pp. 304–308.

20. J. Schaubroeck and S.S.K. Lam, "How Similarity to Peers and Supervisor Influences Organizational Advancement in Different Cultures," *Academy of Management Journal*, 45, no. 6, 2002, pp. 1120–1136.

21. A.M. Owens, "People Who Exercise Are More Highly Regarded: Study," *National Post*, February 10, 2001, p. A2.

22. G.W. Allport, *Personality: A Psychological Interpretation* (New York: Holt, Rinehart and Winston, 1937), p. 48.

23. R.C. Carson, "Personality," in M.R. Rosenzweig and L.W. Porter (eds.), *Annual Review of Psychology*, vol. 40 (Palo Alto, CA: Annual Reviews, 1989), pp. 228–229.

24. See A.H. Buss, "Personality as Traits," *American Psychologist*, November 1989, pp. 1378–1388; and D.G. Winter, O.P. John, A.J. Stewart, E.C. Klohnen, and L.E. Duncan, "Traits and Motives: Toward an Integration of Two Traditions in Personality Research," *Psychological Review*, April 1998, pp. 230–250.

25. R.B. Catell, "Personality Pinned Down," *Psychology Today*, July 1973, pp. 40–46.

26. See, for example, J.M. Digman, "Personality Structure: Emergence of the Five-Factor Model," in M.R. Rosenzweig and L.W. Porter (eds.), *Annual Review of Psychology*, vol. 41 (Palo Alto, CA: Annual Reviews, 1990), pp. 417–440; R.R. McCrae and O.P. John, "An Introduction to the Five-Factor Model and Its Applications," *Journal of Personality*, June 1992, pp. 175–215; L.R. Goldberg, "The Structure of Phenotypic Personality Traits," *American Psychologist*, January 1993, pp. 26–34; P.H. Raymark, M.J. Schmit; R.M. Guion, "Identifying Potentially Useful Personality Constructs for Employee Selection," *Personnel Psychology*, Autumn 1997, pp. 723–736; and O. Behling, "Employee Selection: Will Intelligence and Conscientiousness Do the Job?" *Academy of Management Executive*, 12, 1998, pp. 77–86.

27. See, for instance, M.R. Barrick and M.K. Mount, "The Big Five Personality Dimensions and Job Performance: A Meta-Analysis," *Personnel Psychology*, 44, 1991, pp. 1–26; R.P. Tett, D.N. Jackson, and M. Rothstein, "Personality Measures as Predictors of Job Performance: A Meta-Analytic Review, *Personnel Psychology*, Winter 1991, pp. 703–742; T.A. Judge, J.J. Martocchio, and C.J. Thoresen, "Five-Factor Model of Personality and Employee Absence," *Journal of Applied Psychology*, October 1997, pp. 745–755; and O. Behling, "Employee Selection: Will Intelligence and Conscientiousness Do the Job?" *Academy of Management Executive*, February 1998, pp. 77–86; and F.S. Switzer III and P.L. Roth, "A Meta-Analytic Review of Predictors of Job Performance for Salespeople," *Journal of Applied Psychology*, August 1998, pp. 586–597.

28. See, for instance, S.L. Kichuk and W.H. Wiesner, "Work Teams: Selecting Members for Optimal Performance," *Canadian Psychology*, 39, no. 1–2, 1999, pp. 23–32; M.R. Barrick and M.K. Mount, "The Big Five Personality Dimensions and Job Performance: A Meta-Analysis," *Personnel Psychology*, 44, 1991, pp. 1–26; D. Ones, C. Viswesvaran, and F. Schmidt, "Meta-Analysis of Integrity Test Validities: Findings and Implications for Personnel Selection and Theories of Job Performance [Monograph]," *Journal of Applied Psychology*, 47, no. 1, 1993, pp. 147–156; and R.T. Hogan, J. Hogan, and B.W. Roberts, "Personality Measurement and Employment Decisions: Questions and Answers, *American Psychologist*, 51, no. 5, 1996, pp. 469–477.

29. P. Thoms, "The Relationship Between Self-Efficacy for Participating in Self-Managed Work Groups and the Big Five Personality Dimensions," *Journal of Applied Psychology*, 82, 1996, pp. 472–484; R.A. Guzzo, P.R. Yost, R.J. Campbell, and G.P. Shea, "Potency in Groups: Articulating a Construct," *British Journal of Social Psychology*, 32, 1993, pp. 87–106; G.A. Neuman and J. Wright, "Team Effectiveness: Beyond Skills and Cognitive Ability," *Journal of Applied Psychology*, 84, 1999, pp. 376–389. See also S.L. Kichuk and W.H. Wiesner, "Work Teams: Selecting Members for Optimal Performance," *Canadian Psychology*, 39, no. 1–2, 1999, pp. 23–32, for a summary of a wide body of literature on this topic. You might also be interested in B. Barry and G.L. Stewart, "Compositions, Process and Performance in Self-Managed Groups: The Role of Personality," *Journal of Applied Psychology*, 82, 1997, pp. 62–78, for an opposing look at the conscientiousness-performance link.

30. T.A. Judge and R. Ilies, "Relationship of Personality to Performance Motivation: A Meta-Analytic Review," *Journal of Applied Psychology*, 87, no. 4, 2002, pp. 797–807.

31. D.W. Organ, "Personality and Organizational Citizenship Behavior," *Journal of Management*, Summer 1994, pp. 465–478;

D.W. Organ and K. Ryan, "A Meta-Analytic Review of Attitudinal and Dispositional Predictors of Organizational Citizenship Behavior," *Personnel Psychology*, Winter 1995, pp. 775–802; and M.A. Konovsky and D.W. Organ, "Dispositional and Contextual Determinants of Organizational Citizenship Behavior," *Journal of Organizational Behavior*, May 1996, pp. 253–266.

32. J.B. Rotter, "Generalized Expectancies for Internal Versus External Control of Reinforcement," *Psychological Monographs*, 80, no. 609 (1966).

33. P.E. Spector, C.L. Cooper, J.I. Sanchez, et al., "Locus of Control and Well-Being at Work: How Generalizable Are Western Findings?" *Academy of Management Journal*, 45, no. 2, 2002, pp. 453–456 presents the results of studies done of five continents.

34. J.B. Rotter, "Generalized Expectancies for Internal Versus External Control of Reinforcement," *Psychological Monographs*, 80, no. 609 (1966).

35. R.T. Keller, "Predicting Absenteeism From Prior Absenteeism, Attitudinal Factors, and Nonattitudinal Factors," *Journal of Applied Psychology*, August 1983, pp. 536–540.

36. P.E. Spector, "Behavior in Organizations as a Function of Employee's Locus of Control," *Psychological Bulletin*, May 1982, p. 493.

37. R.G. Vleeming, "Machiavellianism: A Preliminary Review," *Psychological Reports*, February 1979, pp. 295–310.

38. R. Christie and F.L. Geis, *Studies in Machiavellianism* (New York: Academic Press, 1970), p. 312; and N.V. Ramanaiah, A. Byravan, and F.R.J. Detwiler, "Revised Neo Personality Inventory Profiles of Machiavellian and Non-Machiavellian People," *Psychological Reports*, October 1994, pp. 937–938.

39. R. Christie and F.L. Geis, *Studies in Machiavellianism* (New York: Academic Press, 1970).

40. Based on J. Brockner, *Self-Esteem at Work* (Lexington, MA: Lexington Books, 1988), Chapters 1–4; and N. Branden, *Self-Esteem at Work* (San Francisco: Jossey-Bass, 1998).

41. See M. Snyder, *Public Appearances/Private Realities: The Psychology of Self-Monitoring* (New York: W.H. Freeman, 1987).

42. See M. Snyder, *Public Appearances/Private Realities: The Psychology of Self-Monitoring* (New York: W.H. Freeman, 1987).

43. M. Kilduff and D.V. Day, "Do Chameleons Get Ahead? The Effects of Self-Monitoring on Managerial Careers," *Academy of Management Journal*, August 1994, pp. 1047–1060.

44. R.N. Taylor and M.D. Dunnette, "Influence of Dogmatism, Risk-Taking Propensity, and Intelligence on Decision-Making Strategies for a Sample of Industrial Managers," *Journal of Applied Psychology*, August 1974, pp. 420–423.

45. I.L. Janis and L. Mann, *Decision Making: A Psychological Analysis of Conflict, Choice, and Commitment* (New York: Free Press, 1977).

46. N. Kogan and M.A. Wallach, "Group Risk Taking as a Function of Members' Anxiety and Defensiveness," *Journal of Personality*, March 1967, pp. 50–63.

47. M. Friedman and R.H. Rosenman, *Type A Behavior and Your Heart* (New York: Alfred A. Knopf, 1974), p. 84 (emphasis in original).

48. M. Friedman and R.H. Rosenman, *Type A Behavior and Your Heart* (New York: Alfred A. Knopf, 1974), pp. 84–85.

49. K.A. Matthews, "Assessment of Type A Behavior, Anger, and Hostility in Epidemiological Studies of Cardiovascular Disease," in A.M. Ostfield and E.D. Eaker (eds.), *Measuring Psychological Variables in Epidemiologic Studies of Cardiovascular*

Disease (Washington, DC: U.S. Department of Health and Human Services, 1985), NIH Publication No. 85-2270.

50. M. Friedman and R.H. Rosenman, *Type A Behavior and Your Heart* (New York: Alfred A. Knopf, 1974), p. 86.

51. J. Schaubroeck, D.C. Ganster, and B.E. Kemmerer, "Job Complexity, 'Type A' Behavior, and Cardiovascular Disorder," *Academy of Management Journal*, 37, 1994, pp. 426–439.

52. F. Kluckhohn and F.L. Strodtbeck, *Variations in Value Orientations* (Evanston, IL: Row Peterson, 1961).

53. J. Pickard, "Misuse of Tests Leads to Unfair Recruitment," *People Management*, 2, no. 25, 1996, p. 7.

54. J. Pickard, "Misuse of Tests Leads to Unfair Recruitment," *People Management*,2, no. 25, 1996,p. 7.

55. See N.H. Frijda, "Moods, Emotion Episodes and Emotions," in M. Lewis and J.M. Haviland (eds.), *Handbook of Emotions* (New York: Guildford Press, 1993), pp. 381–403.

56. H.M. Weiss and R. Cropanzano, "Affective Events Theory," in B.M. Staw and L.L. Cummings, *Research in Organizational Behavior*, vol. 18 (Greenwich, CT: JAI Press, 1996), pp. 17–19.

57. N.H. Frijda, "Moods, Emotion Episodes and Emotions," in M. Lewis and J.M. Haviland (eds.), *Handbook of Emotions* (New York: Guildford Press, 1993), p. 381.

58. H.M. Weiss and R. Cropanzano, "Affective Events Theory," in B.M. Staw and L.L. Cummings, *Research in Organizational Behavior*, vol. 18 (Greenwich, CT: JAI Press, 1996), pp. 20–22.

59. Cited in R.D. Woodworth, *Experimental Psychology* (New York: Holt, 1938).

60. A. Hochschild, *The Managed Heart: The Commercialization of Human Feeling* (Berkeley, CA: University of California Press, 1983); J. Van Maanen and G. Kunda, "Real Feelings: Emotional Expression and Organizational Culture," in L.L. Cummings and B.M. Staw (eds.), *Research in Organizational Behavior*, vol. 11 (Greenwich, CT: JAI Press, 1989), pp. 43–103; and B.A. Turner, "Sociological Aspects of Organizational Symbolism," *Organization Studies*, 7, 1986, pp. 101–115.

61. A. Hochschild, *The Managed Heart: The Commercialization of Human Feeling* (Berkeley, CA: University of California Press, 1983); R.I. Sutton and A. Rafaeli, "Untangling the Relationship Between Displayed Emotions and Organizational Sales: The Case of Convenience Stores," *Academy of Management Journal*, 31, 1988, pp. 461–487; A. Rafaeli, "When Cashiers Meet Customers: An Analysis of the Role of Supermarket Cashiers," *Academy of Management Journal*, 32, 1989, pp. 245–273; A. Rafaeli and R.I. Sutton, "The Expression of Emotion in Organizational Life," in L.L. Cummings and B.M. Staw (eds.), *Research in Organizational Behavior*, vol. 11 (Greenwich, CT: JAI Press, 1989), pp. 1–42; A. Rafaeli and R.I. Sutton, "Busy Stores and Demanding Customers: How Do They Affect the Display of Positive Emotion?" *Academy of Management Journal*, 33, 1990, pp. 623–637; A. Rafaeli and R.I. Sutton, "Emotional Contrast Strategies as Means of Social Influence: Lessons From Criminal Interrogators and Bill Collectors," *Academy of Management Journal*, 34, 1991, pp. 749–775; R.I. Sutton, "Maintaining Norms About Expressed Emotions: The Case of Bill Collectors," *Administrative Science Quarterly*, 36, 1991, pp. 245–268; and J.A. Morris and D.C. Feldman, "The Dimensions, Antecedents, and Consequences of Emotional Labor," *Academy of Management Review*, October 1996, pp. 986–1010.

62. A. Hochschild, *The Managed Heart: The Commercialization of Human Feeling* (Berkeley, CA: University of California Press, 1983); R.I. Sutton and A. Rafaeli, "Untangling the Relationship Between Displayed Emotions and Organizational Sales: The Case of Convenience Stores," *Academy of Management Journal*, 31, 1988, pp. 461–487; A. Rafaeli, "When Cashiers Meet Customers: An Analysis of the Role of Supermarket Cashiers," *Academy of Management Journal*, 32, 1989, pp. 245–273; A. Rafaeli and R.I. Sutton, "The Expression of Emotion in Organizational Life," in L.L. Cummings and B.M. Staw (eds.), *Research in Organizational Behavior*, vol. 11 (Greenwich, CT: JAI Press, 1989), pp. 1–42; A. Rafaeli and R.I. Sutton, "Busy Stores and Demanding Customers: How Do They Affect the Display of Positive Emotion?" *Academy of Management Journal*, 33, 1990, pp. 623–637; A. Rafaeli and R.I. Sutton, "Emotional Contrast Strategies as Means of Social Influence: Lessons From Criminal Interrogators and Bill Collectors," *Academy of Management Journal*, 34, 1991, pp. 749–775; and R.I. Sutton, "Maintaining Norms About Expressed Emotions: The Case of Bill Collectors," *Administrative Science Quarterly*, 36, 1991, pp. 245–268.

63. A.A. Grandey, "When 'The Show Must Go On': Surface Acting and Deep Acting as Determinants of Emotional Exhaustion and Peer-Rated Service Delivery," *Academy of Management Journal*, 46, no. 1, 2003, pp. 86–96.

64. H. Willmott, "Strength Is Ignorance; Slavery Is Freedom: Managing Culture in Modern Organizations," *Journal of Management Studies*, 30, 1993, pp. 515–552; and S. Fineman, "Emotion and Organizing," in S. Clegg (ed.), *Handbook of Organizational Studies* (London: Sage, 1996), pp. 543–564.

65. A. Hochschild, *The Managed Heart: The Commercialization of Human Feeling* (Berkeley, CA: University of California Press, 1983).

66. J. Van Maanen and G. Kunda, "Real Feelings: Emotional Expression and Organizational Culture," in L.L. Cummings and B.M. Staw (eds.), *Research in Organizational Behavior*, vol. 11 (Greenwich, CT: JAI Press, 1989), pp. 43–103.

67. V. Waldron and K. Krone, "The Experience and Expression of Emotion in the Workplace: A Study of a Corrections Organization," *Management Communication Quarterly*, 4, 1991, pp. 287–309.

68. C. Bains, "Safeway Clerks' Forced Smiles Seen as Flirtation," *The Vancouver Sun*, September 3, 1998, pp. A1, A2.

69. N.M. Ashkanasy, and C.S. Daus, "Emotion in the Workplace: The New Challenge for Managers," *Academy of Management Executive*, 16, no. 1, 2002, pp. 76–86.

70. This section is based on Daniel Goleman, *Emotional Intelligence* (New York: Bantam, 1995); J.D. Mayer and G. Geher, "Emotional Intelligence and the Identification of Emotion," *Intelligence*, March–April 1996, pp. 89–113; J. Stuller, "EQ: Edging Toward Respectability," *Training*, June 1997, pp. 43–48; R.K. Cooper, "Applying Emotional Intelligence in the Workplace," *Training & Development*, December 1997, pp. 31–38; "HR Pulse: Emotional Intelligence," *HRMagazine*, January 1998, p. 19; M. Davies, L. Stankov, and R.D. Roberts, "Emotional Intelligence: In Search of an Elusive Construct," *Journal of Personality and Social Psychology*, October 1998, pp. 989–1015; and D. Goleman, *Working With Emotional Intelligence* (New York: Bantam, 1999).

71. H. Schachter, "Programmed for Obsolescence?" *Canadian Business*, June 25/July 9, 1999, pp. 49–51.

72. J.D. Mayer and G. Geher, "Emotional Intelligence and the Identification of Emotion," *Intelligence*, March–April 1996, pp. 89–113; J. Stuller, "EQ: Edging Toward Respectability," *Training*, June 1997, pp. 43–48; R.K. Cooper, "Applying Emotional Intelligence in the Workplace," *Training & Development*,

December 1997, pp. 31–38; "HR Pulse: Emotional Intelligence," *HRMagazine*, January 1998, p. 19; and M. Davies, L. Stankov, and R.D. Roberts, "Emotional Intelligence: In Search of an Elusive Construct," *Journal of Personality and Social Psychology*, October 1998, pp. 989–1015.

73. D. Goleman, *Working With Emotional Intelligence* (New York: Bantam, 1999).

74. R. McQueen, "New CEO Brings Fresh Style to BMO: Tony Comper Slowly Stepping out of the Shadows," *Financial Post (National Post)*, November 10, 1999, p. C3.

75. S.L. Robinson and R.J. Bennett, "A Typology of Deviant Workplace Behaviors: A Multidimensional Scaling Study," *Academy of Management Journal*, April 1995, p. 556.

76. S.L. Robinson and R.J. Bennett, "A Typology of Deviant Workplace Behaviors: A Multidimensional Scaling Study," *Academy of Management Journal*, April 1995, pp. 555–572.

77. Based on A.G. Bedeian, "Workplace Envy," *Organizational Dynamics*, Spring 1995, p. 50.

78. A.G. Bedeian, "Workplace Envy," *Organizational Dynamics*, Spring 1995, p. 54.

79. Some of the points in this argument are from R.J. House, S.A. Shane, and D.M. Herold, "Rumors of the Death of Dispositional Research Are Vastly Exaggerated," *Academy of Management Review*, January 1996, pp. 203–224.

80. Based on A. Davis-Blake and J. Pfeffer, "Just a Mirage: The Search for Dispositional Effects in Organizational Research," *Academy of Management Review*, July 1989, pp. 385–400.

81. Based on V.P. Richmond, J.C. McCroskey, and S.K. Payne, *Nonverbal Behavior in Interpersonal Relations*, 2nd ed. (Englewood Cliffs, NJ: Prentice Hall, 1991), pp. 117–138; and L.A. King, "Ambivalence Over Emotional Expression and Reading Emotions in Situations and Faces," *Journal of Personality and Social Psychology*, March 1998, pp. 753–762.

Chapter 3

1. Opening vignette based on K. Pryma, "Some IT Companies Realize Diversity Is Good Business, *ComputerWorld Canada*, August 24, 2001, p. 41; http://www.can.ibm.com/hr/diversity1.html; http://www.can.ibm.com/hr/diversity.html; http://www.can.ibm.com/hr/diversity2.html; A. Perry, "Coming Out: Still a Dilemma," *Toronto Star*, April 16, 2003, reprinted in Workopolis website, http://thestar.workopolis.com/servlet/Content/torontostar/20030416/out?section=TORSTAR (accessed October 2, 2003).

2. S.H. Schwartz, "Universals in the Content and Structure of Values: Theoretical Advances and Empirical Tests in 20 Countries," in M. P. Zanna (ed.), *Advances in Experimental Social Psychology* (New York: Academic Press, 1992), p. 4.

3. M. Rokeach and S.J. Ball-Rokeach, "Stability and Change in American Value Priorities, 1968–1981," *American Psychologist*, May 1989, pp. 775–784.

4. M. Rokeach, *The Nature of Human Values*, (New York: Free Press, 1973), p. 6.

5. "How Enron Blew It," *Texas Monthly*, November 2001.

6. See, for instance, P.E. Connor and B.W. Becker, "Personal Values and Management: What Do We Know and Why Don't We Know More?" *Journal of Management Inquiry*, March 1994, p. 68.

7. G. Hofstede, *Culture's Consequences: International Differences in Work Related Values* (Beverly Hills, CA: Sage, 1980); G. Hofstede, *Cultures and Organizations: Software of the Mind* (London:

McGraw-Hill, 1991); and G. Hofstede, "Cultural Constraints in Management Theories," *Academy of Management Executive*, February 1993, pp. 81–94.

8. Hofstede called this dimension *masculinity* vs. *femininity*, but we've changed his terms because of their strong sexist connotation.

9. The five usual criticisms and Hofstede's responses (in parentheses) are: 1. Surveys are not a suitable way to measure cultural differences (*H*: They should not be the only way); 2. Nations are not the proper units for studying cultures (*H*: They are usually the only kind of units available for comparison); 3. A study of the subsidiaries of one company cannot provide information about entire national cultures (*H*: What was measured were differences among national cultures. Any set of functionally equivalent samples can supply information about such differences); 4. The IBM data are old and therefore obsolete (*H*: The dimensions found are assumed to have centuries-old roots; they have been validated against all kinds of external measurements; recent replications show no loss of validity); 5. Four or five dimensions are not enough (*H*: Additional dimensions should be statistically independent of the dimensions defined earlier; they should be valid on the basis of correlations with external measures; candidates are welcome to apply). See A. Harzing and G. Hofstede, "Planned Change in Organizations: The Influence of National Culture," in P.A. Bamberger, M. Erez, and S.B. Bacharach (eds.), *Research in the Sociology of Organizations*, vol. 14: *Cross Cultural Analysis of Organizations* (Greenwich, CN: JAI Press, 1996), pp. 297–340.

10. G. Hofstede, *Cultures Consequences: Comparative Values, Behaviors, Institutions and Organizations Across Nations*, 2nd ed. (Thousand Oaks, CA: Sage), 2001.

11. M. Javidan and R.J. House, "Cultural Acumen for the Global Manager: Lessons From Project GLOBE," *Organizational Dynamics*, Spring 2001, pp. 289–305.

12. D. Fernandez, D.S. Carlson, L.P. Stepina, and J.D. Nicholson, "Hofstede's Country Classification 25 Years Later," *Journal of Social Psychology*, February 1997, pp. 43–54.

13. http://www.statcan.ca/english/Pgdb/demo05.htm; http://www.statcan.ca/english/Pgdb/demo35i.htm

14. "2001 Census of Population: Language, Mobility and Migration," *The Daily* (Statistics Canada), December 10, 2002.

15. Material in this section based on the work of M. Adams, *Sex in the Snow* (Toronto: Penguin Books, 1997) and M. Adams, *Fire and Ice: The United States, Canada and the Myth of Converging Values* (Toronto: Penguin Canada, 2003).

16. D. Tapscott, *Growing up Digital: The Rise of the Net Generation* (New York: McGraw-Hill, 1998).

17. W. Howe and N. Strauss, *Millennials Rising: The Next Great Generation* (New York: Vintage, 2001).

18. "Get Used to It: The Net Generation Knows More Than Its Parents," *Financial Post (National Post)*, February 8, 2000, p. C10.

19. W. Howe and N. Strauss, *Millennials Rising: The Next Great Generation* (New York: Vintage, 2001).

20. G. Chiasson, "I Am Not a Seat Number, I Am a Person," *EnRoute*, March 1998, pp. 5–9.

21. *The Daily* (Statistics Canada), February 11, 2003.

22. R. McQueen, "Bad Boys Make Good," *The Financial Post*, April 4, 1998, p. 6.

23. B, Meglino, E.C. Ravlin, and C.L. Adkins, "A Work Values Approach to Corporate Culture: A Field Test of the Value

Congruence Process and Its Relationship to Individual Outcomes", *Journal of Applied Psychology*, 74, 1989, pp. 424–432.

24. B.Z. Posner, J.M. Kouzes, and W.H. Schmidt, "Shared Values Make a Difference: An Empirical Test of Corporate Culture," *Human Resource Management*, 24, 1985, pp. 293–310; A.L. Balazas, "Value Congruency: The Case of the 'Socially Responsible' Firm," *Journal of Business Research*, 20, 1990, pp. 171–181.

25. C.A. O'Reilly, J. Chatman, and D. Caldwell, "People and Organizational Culture: A Q-Sort Approach to Assessing Person-Organizational Fit," *Academy of Management Journal*, 34, 1991, pp. 487–516.

26. C. Enz and C.K. Schwenk, "Performance and Sharing of Organizational Values," paper presented at the annual meeting of the Academy of Management, Washington, DC, 1989.

27. R.A. Roe and P. Ester, "Values and Work: Empirical Findings and Theoretical Perspective," *Applied Psychology: An International Review*, 48, 1999, pp. 1–21.

28. R.A. Roe and P. Ester, "Values and Work: Empirical Findings and Theoretical Perspective," *Applied Psychology: An International Review*, 48, 1999, pp. 1–21.

29. R.M. Kanungo and J.K. Bhatnagar, "Achievement Orientation and Occupational Values: A Comparative Study of Young French and English Canadians," *Canadian Journal of Behavioural Science*, 12, 1978, pp. 384–392; M.W. McCarrey, S. Edwards, and R. Jones, "The Influence of Ethnolinguistic Group Membership, Sex and Position Level on Motivational Orientation of Canadian Anglophone and Francophone Employees," *Canadian Journal of Behavioural Science*, 9, 1977, pp. 274–282; M.W. McCarrey, S. Edwards, and R. Jones, "Personal Values of Canadian Anglophone and Francophone Employees and Ethnolinguistic Group Membership, Sex and Position Level," *Journal of Psychology*, 104, 1978, pp. 175–184; S. Richer and P. Laporte, "Culture, Cognition and English-French Competition," in D. Koulack and D. Perlman (eds.), *Readings in Social Psychology: Focus on Canada* (Toronto, ON: Wiley and Sons, 1973); and L. Shapiro and D. Perlman, "Value Differences Between English and French Canadian High School Students," *Canadian Ethnic Studies*, 8, 1976, pp. 50–55.

30. R.M. Kanungo and J.K. Bhatnagar, "Achievement Orientation and Occupational Values: A Comparative Study of Young French and English Canadians," *Canadian Journal of Behavioural Science*, 12, 1978, pp. 384–392.

31. R.N. Kanungo and J.K. Bhatnagar, "Achievement Orientation and Occupational Values: A Comparative Study of Young French and English Canadians," *Canadian Journal of Behavioural Science*, 12, 1978, pp. 384–392.

32. H.C. Jain, J. Normand, and R.N. Kanungo, "Job Motivation of Canadian Anglophone and Francophone Hospital Employees," *Canadian Journal of Behavioural Science*, April 1979, pp. 160–163; R.N. Kanungo, G.J. Gorn, and H.J. Dauderis, "Motivational Orientation of Canadian Anglophone and Francophone Managers," *Canadian Journal of Behavioural Science*, April 1976, pp. 107–121.

33. M. Major, M. McCarrey, P. Mercier, and Y. Gasse, "Meanings of Work and Personal Values of Canadian Anglophone and Francophone Middle Managers," *Canadian Journal of Administrative Sciences*, September 1994, pp. 251–263.

34. A. Derfel, "Boy, Are We Stressed Out! Quebec Has Highest Rate of Work Absenteeism," *montrealgazette.com*, http://www.canada.com/montreal/montrealgazette/story.asp?id=5D0D7AF8-DFCB-44D5-ABE4-DA4DACA11DEA (accessed May 29, 2003).

35. Statistics Canada, "Culture Participation: Does Language Make a Difference?" *Focus on Culture*, 13, no. 3, 2002 (87-004-XIE).

36. C. Howes, "The New Native Tycoons: Armed With a New Sense of Entrepreneurialism, Aboriginals Across Canada Have Begun Cashing in on Energy, Forestry, Mining and Other Sectors, and Are Creating Businesses at a Rate Faster Than the National Average," *Financial Post (National Post)*, January 27, 2001, p. D5.

37. L. Redpath and M.O. Nielsen, "A Comparison of Native Culture, Non-Native Culture and New Management Ideology," *Canadian Journal of Administrative Sciences*, 14, no. 3, 1997, p. 327.

38. G.C. Anders and K.K. Anders, "Incompatible Goals in Unconventional Organizations: The Politics of Alaska Native Corporations," *Organization Studies*, 7, 1986, pp. 213–233; G. Dacks, "Worker-Controlled Native Enterprises," A Vehicle for Community Development in Northern Canada?" *The Canadian Journal of Native Studies*, 3, 1983, pp. 289–310; L.P. Dana, "Self-Employment in the Canadian Sub-Arctic: An Exploratory Study," *Canadian Journal of Administrative Sciences*, 13, 1996, pp. 65–77.

39. L. Redpath and M.O. Nielsen, "A Comparison of Native Culture, Non-Native Culture and New Management Ideology," *Canadian Journal of Administrative Sciences*, 14, no. 3, 1997, p. 327.

40. R.B. Anderson, "The Business Economy of the First Nations in Saskatchewan: A Contingency Perspective," *Canadian Journal of Native Studies*, 2, 1995, pp. 309–345.

41. E. Struzik, "'Win-Win Scenario' Possible for Resource Industry, Aboriginals,"*The Edmonton Journal*, April 6, 2003, p. A12.

42. Discussion based on L. Redpath and M.O. Nielsen, "A Comparison of Native Culture, Non-Native Culture and New Management Ideology," *Canadian Journal of Administrative Sciences*, 14, no. 3, 1997, pp. 327–339.

43. Discussion based on L. Redpath, M.O. Nielsen, "A Comparison of Native Culture, Non-Native Culture and New Management Ideology," *Canadian Journal of Administrative Sciences*, 14, no. 3, 1997, pp. 327–339.

44. D. Grigg and J. Newman, "Five Ways to Foster Bonds, Win Trust in Business," *Ottawa Citizen*, April 23, 2003, p. F12.

45. J. Paulson, "First Nations Bank Launches First Branch With Sweetgrass Ceremony," *Canadian Press Newswire*, September 23, 1997.

46. "Autowrecker Defies Stereotypes, Blazes Trail," *Windspeaker*, February 1997, p. 28.

47. M. Adams, *Fire and Ice: The United States, Canada and the Myth of Converging Values* (Toronto: Penguin Canada, 2003).

48. Material in this section based on the work of M. Adams, *Sex in the Snow* (Toronto: Penguin Books, 1997).

49. Material in this section based on the work of M. Adams, *Sex in the Snow* (Toronto: Penguin Books, 1997).

50. M. Adams, "Neighbours Growing Apart," *The Globe and Mail*, May 20, 2003, p. A13.

51. A. Cohen, "So You Wanna Live the Dream," *Report on Business Magazine*, July 1999, pp. 75–78.

52. E. Procuta, "Businesses Learn Lingo of Latin America," *The Globe and Mail*, April 15, 2001, p. B9.

53. These differences are based on research by G.K. Stephens and C.R. Greer, "Doing Business in Mexico: Understanding Cultural Differences," *Organizational Dynamics, Special Report*, 1998, pp. 43–59.

54. I.Y.M. Yeung and R.L. Tung, "Achieving Business Success in Confucian Societies: The Importance of Guanxi (Connections)," *Organizational Dynamics, Special Report,* 1998, pp. 72–83.

55. I.Y.M. Yeung and R.L. Tung, "Achieving Business Success in Confucian Societies: The Importance of Guanxi (Connections)," *Organizational Dynamics, Special Report,* 1998, p. 73.

56. N.J. Adler, "Cross-Cultural Management Research: The Ostrich and the Trend," *Academy of Management Review,* April 1983, pp. 226–232.

57. P.P. Brooke Jr., D.W. Russell, and J.L. Price, "Discriminant Validation of Measures of Job Satisfaction, Job Involvement, and Organizational Commitment," *Journal of Applied Psychology,* May 1988, pp. 139–145; and R.T. Keller, "Job Involvement and Organizational Commitment as Longitudinal Predictors of Job Performance: A Study of Scientists and Engineers," *Journal of Applied Psychology,* August 1997, pp. 539–545.

58. Based on G.J. Blau and K.R. Boal, "Conceptualizing How Job Involvement and Organizational Commitment Affect Turnover and Absenteeism," *Academy of Management Review,* April 1987, p. 290. See also S. Rabinowitz and D.T. Hall, "Organizational Research in Job Involvement," *Psychological Bulletin,* March 1977, pp. 265–288; G.J. Blau, "A Multiple Study Investigation of the Dimensionality of Job Involvement," *Journal of Vocational Behavior,* August 1985, pp. 19–36; and N.A. Jans, "Organizational Factors and Work Involvement," *Organizational Behavior and Human Decision Processes,* June 1985, pp. 382–396.

59. G.J. Blau, "Job Involvement and Organizational Commitment as Interactive Predictors of Tardiness and Absenteeism," *Journal of Management,* Winter 1986, pp. 577–584; and K.R. Boal and R. Cidambi, "Attitudinal Correlates of Turnover and Absenteeism: A Meta Analysis," paper presented at the meeting of the American Psychological Association, Toronto, 1984.

60. G. Farris, "A Predictive Study of Turnover," *Personnel Psychology,* Summer 1971, pp. 311–328.

61. G.J. Blau and K.R. Boal, "Conceptualizing How Job Involvement and Organizational Commitment Affect Turnover and Absenteeism," *Academy of Management Review,* April 1987," p. 290.

62. See, for instance, W. Hom, R. Katerberg, and C.L. Hulin, "Comparative Examination of Three Approaches to the Prediction of Turnover," *Journal of Applied Psychology,* June 1979, pp. 280–290; H. Angle and J. Perry, "Organizational Commitment: Individual and Organizational Influence," *Work and Occupations,* May 1983, pp. 123–146; and J.L. Pierce and R.B. Dunham, "Organizational Commitment: Pre-Employment Propensity and Initial Work Experiences," *Journal of Management,* Spring 1987, pp. 163–178.

63. "Do as I Do," *Canadian Business,* March 12, 1999, p. 35.

64. D.M. Rousseau, "Organizational Behavior in the New Organizational Era," in J.T. Spence, J.M. Darley, and D.J. Foss (eds.), *Annual Review of Psychology,* vol. 48 (Palo Alto, CA: Annual Reviews, 1997), p. 523.

65. D.W. Organ, *Organizational Citizenship Behavior: The Good Soldier Syndrome* (Lexington, MA: Lexington Books, 1988); C.A. Smith, D.W. Organ, and J.P. Near, "Organizational Citizenship Behavior: Its Nature and Antecedents," *Journal of Applied Psychology,* 1983, pp. 653–663.

66. J. Farh, C. Zhong, and D.W. Organ, "Organizational Citizenship Behavior in the People's Republic of China," *Academy of Management Proceedings,* 2000, pp. OB: D1–D6.

67. J.M. George, and A.P Brief, "Feeling Good—Doing Good: A Conceptual Analysis of the Mood at Work-Organizational Spontaneity Relationship," *Psychological Bulletin,* 112, 2002, pp. 310–329; and S.L. Wagner and M.C. Rush, "Altruistic Organizational Citizenship Behavior Context, Disposition and Age," *Journal of Social Psychology,* 140, 2002, pp. 379–391.

68. K. Goff, "Stress Level on the Job Doubles, Study Finds: More People Say They Are Working Longer With Less Job Satisfaction Than a Decade Ago, University Researchers Find," *The Vancouver Sun,* October 23, 2001, p. A11.

69. Remainder of this paragraph based on "Workplace 2000: Working Toward the Millennium," *Angus Reid Group,* Fall 1997.

70. V.H. Vroom, *Work and Motivation* (New York: Wiley, 1964); and M.T. Iaffaldano and P.M. Muchinsky, "Job Satisfaction and Job Performance: A Meta-Analysis," *Psychological Bulletin,* March 1985, pp. 251–273.

71. C.N. Greene, "The Satisfaction-Performance Controversy," *Business Horizons,* February 1972, pp. 31–41; E.E. Lawler III, *Motivation in Organizations* (Monterey, CA: Brooks/Cole, 1973); and M.M. Petty, G.W. McGee, and J.W. Cavender, "A Meta-Analysis of the Relationship Between Individual Job Satisfaction and Individual Performance," *Academy of Management Review,* October 1984, pp. 712–721.

72. C. Ostroff, "The Relationship Between Satisfaction, Attitudes, and Performance: An Organizational Level Analysis," *Journal of Applied Psychology,* December 1992, pp. 963–974.

73. E.A. Locke, "The Nature and Causes of Job Satisfaction," p. 1331; S.L. McShane, "Job Satisfaction and Absenteeism: A Meta-Analytic Re-Examination," *Canadian Journal of Administrative Science,* June 1984, pp. 61–77; R.D. Hackett and R.M. Guion, "A Reevaluation of the Absenteeism-Job Satisfaction Relationship," *Organizational Behavior and Human Decision Processes,* June 1985, pp. 340–381; K.D. Scott and G.S. Taylor, "An Examination of Conflicting Findings on the Relationship Between Job Satisfaction and Absenteeism: A Meta-Analysis," *Academy of Management Journal,* September 1985, pp. 599–612; R.D. Hackett, "Work Attitudes and Employee Absenteeism: A Synthesis of the Literature," paper presented at 1988 National Academy of Management Conference, Anaheim, CA, August 1988; and R.P. Steel and J.R. Rentsch, "Influence of Cumulation Strategies on the Long-Range Prediction of Absenteeism," *Academy of Management Journal,* December 1995, pp. 1616–1634.

74. J.L. Cotton and J.M. Tuttle, "Employee Turnover: A Meta-Analysis and Review With Implications for Research," *Academy of Management Review,* 11, 1986, pp. 55–70; R.W. Griffeth and P.W. Hom, "The Employee Turnover Process," *Research in Personnel and Human Resources Management,* 13, 1995, pp. 245–293; P.W. Hom, F. Caranikas-Walker, G.E. Prussia, and R.W. Griffeth, "A Meta-Analytical Structural Equations Analysis of a Model of Employee Turnover, *Journal of Applied Psychology,* 77, 1992, pp. 890–909; P.W. Hom and R.W. Griffeth, *Employee Turnover* (Cincinnati, OH: South-Western College, 1995); W.H. Mobley, R.W. Griffeth, H.H. Hand, and B.M. Meglino, "Review and Conceptual Analysis of the Employee Turnover Process," *Psychological Bulletin,* 86, 1979, pp. 493–522; J.L. Price, *The Study of Turnover,* 1st ed. (Ames: Iowa State University Press, 1977); R.P. Steel and N.K. Ovalle, "A Review and Metaanalysis of Research on the Relationship Between Behavioral Intentions and Employee Turnover," *Journal of Applied Psychology,* 69, 1984, pp. 673–686; R.P. Tett and J.P. Meyer, "Job Satisfaction, Organizational Commitment, Turnover Intention, and

Turnover: Path Analyses Based on Meta-Analytical Findings," *Personnel Psychology*, 46, 1993, pp. 259–293.

75. See, for example, C.L. Hulin, M. Roznowski, and D. Hachiya, "Alternative Opportunities and Withdrawal Decisions: Empirical and Theoretical Discrepancies and an Integration," *Psychological Bulletin*, July 1985, pp. 233–250; and J.M. Carsten and P.E. Spector, "Unemployment, Job Satisfaction, and Employee Turnover: A Meta-Analytic Test of the Muchinsky Model," *Journal of Applied Psychology*, August 1987, pp. 374–381.

76. D.W. Organ and K. Ryan, "A Meta-Analytic Review of Attitudinal and Dispositional Predictors of Organizational Citizenship Behavior," *Personnel Psychology*, Winter 1995, p. 791.

77. J. Fahr, P.M. Podsakoff, and D.W. Organ, "Accounting for Organizational Citizenship Behavior: Leader Fairness and Task Scope Versus Satisfaction," *Journal of Management*, December 1990, pp. 705–722; R.H. Moorman, "Relationship Between Organizational Justice and Organizational Citizenship Behaviors: Do Fairness Perceptions Influence Employee Citizenship?" *Journal of Applied Psychology*, December 1991, pp. 845–855; and M.A. Konovsky and D.W. Organ, "Dispositional and Contextual Determinants of Organizational Citizenship Behavior," *Journal of Organizational Behavior*, May 1996, pp. 253–266.

78. D.W. Organ, "Personality and Organizational Citizenship Behavior," *Journal of Management*, Summer 1994, p. 466.

79. S.M. Puffer, "Prosocial Behavior, Noncompliant Behavior, and Work Performance Among Commission Salespeople," *Journal of Applied Psychology*, November 1987, pp. 615–621; J. Hogan and R. Hogan, "How to Measure Employee Reliability," *Journal of Applied Psychology*, May 1989, pp. 273–279; and C.D. Fisher and E.A. Locke, "The New Look in Job Satisfaction Research and Theory," in C.J. Cranny, P.C. Smith, and E.F. Stone (eds.), *Job Satisfaction* (New York: Lexington Books, 1992), pp. 165–194.

80. W.H. Turnley and D.C. Feldman, "The Impact of Psychological Contract Violations on Exit, Voice, Loyalty and Neglect," *Human Relations*, 52, July 1999, pp. 895–922; and M.J. Withey and W.H. Cooper, "Predicting Exit, Voice, Loyalty, and Neglect," *Administrative Science Quarterly*, 34, 1989, pp. 521–539.

81. R.B. Freeman, "Job Satisfaction as an Economic Variable," *American Economic Review*, January 1978, pp. 135–141.

82. E.A. Locke, "The Nature and Causes of Job Satisfaction," in M.D. Dunnette (ed.), *Handbook of Industrial and Organizational Psychology* (Chicago: Rand McNally, 1976), pp. 1319–1328.

83. See, for instance, T.A. Judge and S. Watanabe, "Another Look at the Job Satisfaction-Life Satisfaction Relationship," *Journal of Applied Psychology*, December 1993, pp. 939–948; R.D. Arvey, B.P. McCall, T.J. Bouchard Jr., and P. Taubman, "Genetic Influences on Job Satisfaction and Work Values," *Personality and Individual Differences*, July 1994, pp. 21–33; and D. Lykken and A. Tellegen, "Happiness Is a Stochastic Phenomenon," *Psychological Science*, May 1996, pp. 186–189.

OB on the Edge: Stress at Work

1. Information in this paragraph based on S. McKay, "The Work-Family Conundrum," *The Financial Post Magazine*, December 1997, pp. 78–81.

2. Paragraph based on "'You'd Drink Too,' Charged School Bus Driver Says," *National Post*, March 4, 2002, p. A7.

3. "Stress Is Everywhere and Getting Worse, Survey Says," *Canadian Press Newswire*, December 17, 1997.

4. I. Phaneuf, "Drug Company Study Finds Rise in Work-Related Stress," *The Vancouver Sun*, May 5, 2001, p. D15.

5. Virginia Galt, "Statscan Studies Workplace Stress," *The Globe and Mail*, June 26, 2003, p. B3.

6. R.B. Mason, "Taking Health Care to Factory Floor Proves Smart Move for Growing Ontario Company," *Canadian Medical Association Journal*, November 15, 1997, pp. 1423–1424.

7. L. Duxbury and C. Higgins, 2001 *National Work-Life Conflict Study*, as reported in J. Campbell, "'Organizational Anorexia' Puts Stress on Employees," *Ottawa Citizen*, July 4, 2002.

8. K. Harding, "Balance Tops List of Job Desires," *The Globe and Mail*, May 7, 2003, pp. C1, C6.

9. "Canadian Workers Among Most Stressed," *Worklife Report*, 14, no. 2, 2002, pp. 8–9.

10. N. Ayed, "Absenteeism up Since 1993," *Canadian Press Newswire*, March 25, 1998.

11. N. Ayed, "Absenteeism up Since 1993," *Canadian Press Newswire*, March 25, 1998.

12. H. Selye, *The Stress of Life* (New York: McGraw-Hill, 1976); and H. Selye, *Stress Without Distress* (Philadelphia, PA: J.B. Lippincott, 1974).

13. R. DeFrank and J.M. Ivancevich, "Stress on the Job: An Executive Update," *Academy of Management Executive*, August 1998, pp. 55–66.

14. E. Church, "Work Winning out Over Family in the Struggle for Balance," *The Globe and Mail*, February 13, 2002, pp. B1, B2.

15. W. Stueck, "Firms Not 'Family Friendly': Study," *The Globe and Mail*, July 4, 2002, p. B4.

16. These key changes and unattributed quotations in this section are taken from R. DeFrank and J.M. Ivancevich, "Stress on the Job: An Executive Update," *Academy of Management Executive*, August 1998, pp. 55–66.

17. P. Demont and A.M. Tobin, "One in Three Canadians Say They're Workaholics," *The Vancouver Sun*, November 10, 1999, pp. A1, A2.

18. D. Stonehouse, "Caught in the E-Mailstrom: You Know Things Are Getting out of Hand When a Guy With an Online Newsletter Pulls the Plug," *The Vancouver Sun*, June 8, 2002, pp. H3, H4.

19 S. McKay, "The Work-Family Conundrum," *The Financial Post Magazine*, December 1997, pp. 78–81; and A. Davis, "Respect Your Elders: Pressure on the Healthcare System Means Elderly Patients Aren't Staying in Hospitals as Long as They Used To," *Benefits Canada*, 26, no. 8, 2002, p. 13.

20. L.T. Thomas and D.C. Ganster, "Impact of Family-Supportive Work Variables on Work-Family Conflict and Strain: A Control Perspective," *Journal of Applied Psychology*, 80, 1995, pp. 6–15.

21. H. Selye, *The Stress of Life* (New York: McGraw-Hill, 1976).

22. R.S. Schuler, "Definition and Conceptualization of Stress in Organizations," *Organizational Behavior and Human Performance*, April 1980, p. 191; and R.L. Kahn and P. Byosiere, "Stress in Organizations," *Organizational Behavior and Human Performance*, April 1980, pp. 604–610.

23. KPMG Canada, *Compensation Letter*, July 1998.

24. B.D. Steffy and J.W. Jones, "Workplace Stress and Indicators of Coronary-Disease Risk," p. 687.

25. C.L. Cooper and J. Marshall, "Occupational Sources of Stress: A Review of the Literature Relating to Coronary Heart Disease

and Mental Ill Health," *Journal of Occupational Psychology*, 49, no. 1, 1976, pp. 11–28.

26. J.R. Hackman and G.R. Oldham, "Development of the Job Diagnostic Survey," *Journal of Applied Psychology*, April 1975, pp. 159–170.

27. J.L. Xie and G. Johns, "Job Scope and Stress: Can Job Scope Be Too High?" *Academy of Management Journal*, October 1995, pp. 1288–1309.

28. S.J. Motowidlo, J.S. Packard, and M.R. Manning, "Occupational Stress: Its Causes and Consequences for Job Performance," *Journal of Applied Psychology*, November 1987, pp. 619–620.

29. See, for instance, R.C. Cummings, "Job Stress and the Buffering Effect of Supervisory Support," *Group & Organization Studies*, March 1990, pp. 92–104; M.R. Manning, C.N. Jackson, and M.R. Fusilier, "Occupational Stress, Social Support, and the Cost of Health Care," *Academy of Management Journal*, June 1996, pp. 738–750; and P.D. Bliese and T.W. Britt, "Social Support, Group Consensus and Stressor-Strain Relationships: Social Context Matters," *Journal of Organizational Behavior*, June 2001, pp. 425–36.

30. See L.R. Murphy, "A Review of Organizational Stress Management Research," *Journal of Organizational Behavior Management*, Fall–Winter 1986, pp. 215–227.

31. R. Williams, *The Trusting Heart: Great News About Type A Behavior* (New York: Times Books, 1989).

32. T.H. Macan, "Time Management: Test of a Process Model," *Journal of Applied Psychology*, June 1994, pp. 381–391.

33. See, for example, G. Lawrence-Ell, *The Invisible Clock: A Practical Revolution in Finding Time for Everyone and Everything* (Seaside Park, NJ: Kingsland Hall, 2002).

34. J. Kiely and G. Hodgson, "Stress in the Prison Service: The Benefits of Exercise Programs," *Human Relations*, June 1990, pp. 551–572.

35. E.J. Forbes and R.J. Pekala, "Psychophysiological Effects of Several Stress Management Techniques," *Psychological Reports*, February 1993, pp. 19–27; and G. Smith, "Meditation, the New Balm for Corporate Stress," *Business Week*, May 10, 1993, pp. 86–87.

36. Information for FactBox based on P. Demont and A.M. Tobin, "One in Three Canadians Say They're Workaholics," *The Vancouver Sun*, November 10, 1999, pp. A1, A2; V. Galt, "Just Don't Call Them 'Workaholics'" *The Globe and Mail*, April 8, 2002, pp. B1, B2; E. Beauchesne, "Lost Work Cost Placed at $10b: Growing Stress Levels Are Cited as a Leading Factor in the Rise in Absenteeism in Canada," *The Vancouver Sun*, September 2, 1999, p. A3; L. Ramsay, "Caught Between the Potty and the PC," *National Post*, November 9, 1998, p. D9; S. McGovern, "No Rest for the Weary," montrealgazette.com, http://www.canada.com/montreal/specials/business/story.html?id=3DBCC381=46-1855-4255-8907-A1055CA05910 (accessed August 19, 2003).

37. D. Etzion, "Moderating Effects of Social Support on the Stress-Burnout Relationship," *Journal of Applied Psychology*, November 1984, pp. 615–622; and S. Jackson, R. Schwab, and R. Schuler, "Toward an Understanding of the Burnout Phenomenon," *Journal of Applied Psychology* 71, no. 4, November 1986, pp. 630–640.

38. H. Staseson, "Can Perk Help Massage Bottom Line? On-Site Therapeutic Sessions Are Used by an Increasingly Diverse Group of Employers Hoping to Improve Staff Performance," *The Globe and Mail*, July 3, 2002, p. C1.

39. B. Bouw, "Employers Embrace Wellness at Work: Fitness Programs Gaining Popularity as Companies Look to Boost Productivity With Healthier Staff," *The Globe and Mail*, April 10, 2002, p. C1.

40. "Wellness Programs Offer Healthy Return, Study Finds," Human Resources Management in Canada, *Report Bulletin* #224, October 2001, p. 1.

41. H. Staseson, "Can Perk Help Massage Bottom Line? On-Site Therapeutic Sessions Are Used by an Increasingly Diverse Group of Employers Hoping to Improve Staff Performance," *The Globe and Mail*, July 3, 2002, p. C1.

42. B. Bouw, "Employers Embrace Wellness at Work: Fitness Programs Gaining Popularity as Companies Look to Boost Productivity With Healthier Staff," *The Globe and Mail*, April 10, 2002, p. C1.

43. See W.A. Anthony and C.W. Anthony, *The Art of Napping at Work* (Burdett, NY: Larson Publications, 2000); J.E. Brody, "New Respect for the Nap, A Pause That Refreshes," *The New York Times*, January 4, 2000, p. D7; and "Nappers of the World, Lie Down and Be Counted!" Training, May 2000, p. 24.

44. See, for instance, R.A. Wolfe, D.O. Ulrich, and D.F. Parker, "Employee Health Management Programs: Review, Critique, and Research Agenda," *Journal of Management*, Winter 1987, pp. 603–615; D.L. Gebhardt and C.E. Crump, "Employee Fitness and Wellness Programs in the Workplace," *American Psychologist*, February 1990, pp. 262–272; and C.E. Beadle, "And Let's Save 'Wellness'. It Works," *The New York Times*, July 24, 1994, p. F9.

Chapter 4

1. Opening vignette based on D. DeCloet, "Slick Salesmanship Masked Discontent," *Financial Post (National Post)*, February 14, 2002, pp. FP1, FP10.

2. See, for instance, T.R. Mitchell, "Matching Motivational Strategies With Organizational Contexts," in L.L. Cummings and B.M. Staw (eds.), *Research in Organizational Behavior*, 19 (Greenwich, CT: JAI Press, 1997), pp. 60–62.

3. D. McGregor, *The Human Side of Enterprise* (New York: McGraw-Hill, 1960). For an updated analysis of Theory X and Theory Y constructs, see R.J. Summers and S.F. Cronshaw, "A Study of McGregor's Theory X, Theory Y and the Influence of Theory X, Theory Y Assumptions on Causal Attributions for Instances of Worker Poor Performance," in S.L. McShane (ed.), *Organizational Behavior*, ASAC 1988 Conference Proceedings, 9, part 5, Halifax, 1988, pp. 115–123.

4. K.W. Thomas, *Intrinsic Motivation at Work* (San Francisco: Berrett-Koehler, 2000); and K.W. Thomas, "Intrinsic Motivation and How It Works," *Training*, October 2000, pp. 130–135.

5. A.H. Maslow, Motivation and Personality (New York: Harper and Row, 1954).

6. K. Korman, J.H. Greenhaus, and I.J. Badin, "Personnel Attitudes and Motivation," in M.R. Rosenzweig and L.W. Porter (eds.), *Annual Review of Psychology* (Palo Alto, CA: Annual Reviews, 1977), p. 178; and M.A. Wahba and L.G. Bridwell, "Maslow Reconsidered: A Review of Research on the Need Hierarchy Theory," *Organizational Behavior and Human Performance*, April 1976, pp. 212–240.

7. F. Herzberg, B. Mausner, and B. Snyderman, *The Motivation to Work* (New York: Wiley, 1959).

8. R.J. House and L.A. Wigdor, "Herzberg's Dual-Factor Theory of Job Satisfaction and Motivations: A Review of the Evidence and

Criticism," *Personnel Psychology*, Winter 1967, pp. 369–389; D.P. Schwab and L.L. Cummings, "Theories of Performance and Satisfaction: A Review," *Industrial Relations*, October 1970, pp. 403–430; R.J. Caston and R. Braito, "A Specification Issue in Job Satisfaction Research," *Sociological Perspectives*, April 1985, pp. 175–197; and J. Phillipchuk and J. Whittaker, "An Inquiry Into the Continuing Relevance of Herzberg's Motivation Theory," *Engineering Management Journal*, 8, 1996, pp. 15–20.

9. V.H. Vroom, *Work and Motivation* (New York: John Wiley, 1964).

10. "Workplace 2000: Working Toward the Millennium," *Angus Reid Group*, Fall 1997, p. 14.

11. *Radical Entertainment Inc.*, http://www.radical.ca.

12. See, for example, H.G. Heneman III and D.P. Schwab, "Evaluation of Research on Expectancy Theory Prediction of Employee Performance," *Psychological Bulletin*, July 1972, pp. 1–9; T.R. Mitchell, "Expectancy Models of Job Satisfaction, Occupational Preference and Effort: A Theoretical, Methodological and Empirical Appraisal," *Psychological Bulletin*, November 1974, pp. 1053–1077; and L. Reinharth and M.A. Wahba, "Expectancy Theory as a Predictor of Work Motivation, Effort Expenditure, and Job Performance," *Academy of Management Journal*, September 1975, pp. 502–537.

13. See, for example, L.W. Porter and E.E. Lawler III, *Managerial Attitudes and Performance* (Homewood, IL: Richard D. Irwin, 1968); D.F. Parker and L. Dyer, "Expectancy Theory as a Within-Person Behavioral Choice Model: An Empirical Test of Some Conceptual and Methodological Refinements," *Organizational Behavior and Human Performance*, October 1976, pp. 97–117; H.J. Arnold, "A Test of the Multiplicative Hypothesis of Expectancy-Valence Theories of Work Motivation," *Academy of Management Journal*, April 1981, pp. 128–141; J.P. Wanous, T.L. Keon, and J.C. Latack, Expectancy Theory and Occupational/Organizational Choices: A Review and Test," *Organizational Behaviour and Human Performance*, August 1983, pp. 66–86; and W. Van Eerde and H. Thierry, "Vroom's Expectancy Models and Work-Related Criteria: A Meta-Analysis," *Journal of Applied Psychology*, October 1996, pp. 575–586.

14. E.A. Locke, "Toward a Theory of Task Motivation and Incentives," *Organizational Behavior and Human Performance*, May 1968, pp. 157–189.

15. P.C. Earley, P. Wojnaroski, and W. Prest, "Task Planning and Energy Expended: Exploration of How Goals Influence Performance," *Journal of Applied Psychology*, February 1987, pp. 107–114.

16. G.P. Latham and G.A. Yukl, "A Review of Research on the Application of Goal Setting in Organizations," *Academy of Management Journal*, December 1975, pp. 824–845; E.A. Locke, K.N. Shaw, L.M. Saari, and G.P. Latham, "Goal Setting and Task Performance," *Psychological Bulletin*, January 1981, pp. 125–152; A.J. Mento, R.P. Steel, and R.J. Karren, "A Meta-Analytic Study of the Effects of Goal Setting on Task Performance: 1966–1984," *Organizational Behavior and Human Decision Processes*, February 1987, pp. 52–83; M.E. Tubbs, "Goal Setting: A Meta-Analytic Examination of the Empirical Evidence," *Journal of Applied Psychology*, August 1986, pp. 474–483; P.C. Earley, G.B. Northcraft, C. Lee, and T.R. Lituchy, "Impact of Process and Outcome Feedback on the Relation of Goal Setting to Task Performance," *Academy of Management Journal*, March 1990, pp. 87–105; and E.A. Locke and G.P. Latham, *A Theory of Goal Setting and Task Performance* (Englewood Cliffs, NJ: Prentice Hall, 1990).

17. See, for instance, S.J. Carroll and H.L. Tosi, *Management by Objectives: Applications and Research* (New York, Macmillan,

1973); and R. Rodgers and J.E. Hunter, "Impact of Management by Objectives on Organizational Productivity," *Journal of Applied Psychology*, April 1991, pp. 322–336.

18. See, for example, G.P. Latham, M. Erez, and E.A. Locke, "Resolving Scientific Disputes by the Joint Design of Crucial Experiments by the Antagonists: Application to the Erez-Latham Dispute Regarding Participation in Goal Setting," *Journal of Applied Psychology*, November 1988, pp. 753–772; T.D. Ludwig and E.S. Geller, "Assigned Versus Participative Goal Setting and Response Generalization: Managing Injury Control Among Professional Pizza Deliverers," *Journal of Applied Psychology*, April 1997, pp. 253–261; and S.G. Harkins and M.D. Lowe, "The Effects of Self-Set Goals on Task Performance," *Journal of Applied Social Psychology*, January 2000, pp. 1–40.

19. M. Erez, P.C. Earley, and C.L. Hulin, "The Impact of Participation on Goal Acceptance and Performance: A Two-Step Model," *Academy of Management Journal*, March 1985, pp. 50–66.

20. K.R. Thompson, W.A. Hochwarter, and N.J. Mathys, "Stretch Targets: What Makes Them Effective?" *Academy of Management Executive*, 11, no. 3, 1997, pp. 48–60; J. Hollenbeck and H. Klein, "Goal Commitment and the Goal-Setting Process: Problems, Prospects, and Proposals for Future Research," *Journal of Applied Psychology*, 72, no. 2, 1987, pp. 212–220; G. Latham and E. Locke, "Self-Regulation Through Goal Setting," *Organizational Behavior and Human Decision Processes*, 50, no. 2, 1991, pp. 212–247; E. Locke, K. Shaw, L. Saari, and G. Latham, "Goal Setting and Task Performance: 1969–1980," *Psychological Bulletin*, 85, 1981, pp. 125–152.

21. See, for instance, R.C. Ford, F.S. MacLaughlin, and J. Nixdorf, "Ten Questions About MBO," *California Management Review*, Winter 1980, p. 89; T.J. Collamore, "Making MBO Work in the Public Sector," *Bureaucrat*, Fall 1989, pp. 37–40; G. Dabbs, "Nonprofit Businesses in the 1990s: Models for Success," *Business Horizons*, September–October 1991, pp. 68–71; R. Rodgers and J.E. Hunter, "A Foundation of Good Management Practice in Government: Management by Objectives," *Public Administration Review*, January–February 1992, pp. 27–39; and T.H. Poister and G. Streib, "MBO in Municipal Government: Variations on a Traditional Management Tool," *Public Administration Review*, January/February 1995, pp. 48–56.

22. See, for instance, C.H. Ford, "MBO: An Idea Whose Time Has Gone?" *Business Horizons*, December 1979, p. 49; R. Rodgers and J.E. Hunter, "Impact of Management by Objectives on Organizational Productivity," *Journal of Applied Psychology*, April 1991, pp. 322–336; and R. Rodgers, J.E. Hunter, and D.L. Rogers, "Influence of Top Management Commitment on Management Program Success," *Journal of Applied Psychology*, February 1993, pp. 151–155.

23. J.S. Adams, "Inequity in Social Exchanges," in L. Berkowitz (ed.), *Advances in Experimental Social Psychology* (New York: Academic Press, 1965), pp. 267–300.

24. See, for example, E. Walster, G.W. Walster, and W.G. Scott, *Equity: Theory and Research* (Boston: Allyn and Bacon, 1978); and J. Greenberg, "Cognitive Reevaluation of Outcomes in Response to Underpayment Inequity," *Academy of Management Journal*, March 1989, pp. 174–184.

25. P.S. Goodman and A. Friedman, "An Examination of Adams' Theory of Inequity," *Administrative Science Quarterly*, September 1971, pp. 271–288; R.P. Vecchio, "An Individual-Differences Interpretation of the Conflicting Predictions Generated by

Equity Theory and Expectancy Theory," *Journal of Applied Psychology*, August 1981, pp. 470–481; J. Greenberg, "Approaching Equity and Avoiding Inequity in Groups and Organizations," in J. Greenberg and R.L. Cohen (eds.), *Equity and Justice in Social Behavior* (New York: Academic Press, 1982), pp. 389–435; E.W. Miles, J.D. Hatfield, and R.C. Huseman, "The Equity Sensitive Construct: Potential Implications for Worker Performance," *Journal of Management*, December 1989, pp. 581–588; and R.T. Mowday, "Equity Theory Predictions of Behavior in Organizations," in R. Steers and L.W. Porter (eds.), *Motivation and Work Behavior*, 5th ed. (New York: McGraw-Hill, 1991), pp. 111–131.

26. J. Greenberg and S. Ornstein, "High Status Job Title as Compensation for Underpayment: A Test of Equity Theory," *Journal of Applied Psychology*, May 1983, pp. 285–297; and J. Greenberg, "Equity and Workplace Status: A Field Experiment," *Journal of Applied Psychology*, November 1988, pp. 606–613.

27. P.S. Goodman, "Social Comparison Process in Organizations," in B.M. Staw and G.R. Salancik (eds.), *New Directions in Organizational Behavior* (Chicago: St. Clair, 1977), pp. 97–132; and J. Greenberg, "A Taxonomy of Organizational Justice Theories," *Academy of Management Review*, January 1987, pp. 9–22.

28. See, for instance, J. Greenberg, *The Quest for Justice on the Job* (Thousand Oaks, CA: Sage, 1996); R. Cropanzano and J. Greenberg, "Progress in Organizational Justice: Tunneling Through the Maze," in C.L. Cooper and I.T. Robertson (eds.), *International Review of Industrial and Organizational Psychology*, vol. 12 (New York: Wiley, 1997); and J.A. Colquitt, D.E. Conlon, M. J. Wesson, C.O.L.H. Porter, and K.Y. Ng, "Justice at the Millennium: A Meta-Analytic Review of the 25 Years of Organizational Justice Research," *Journal of Applied Psychology*, June 2001, pp. 425–145.

29. See, for example, R.C. Dailey and D.J. Kirk, "Distributive and Procedural Justice as Antecedents of Job Dissatisfaction and Intent to Turnover," *Human Relations*, March 1992, pp. 305–316; D.B. McFarlin and P.D. Sweeney, "Distributive and Procedural Justice as Predictors of Satisfaction With Personal and Organizational Outcomes," *Academy of Management Journal*, August 1992, pp. 626–637; M.A. Korsgaard, D.M. Schweiger, and H.J. Sapienza, "Building Commitment, Attachment, and Trust in Strategic Decision-Making Teams: The Role of Procedural Justice," *Academy of Management Journal*, February 1995, pp. 60–84; and M. A. Konovsky, "Understanding Procedural Justice and Its Impact on Business Organizations," *Journal of Management*, 26, no. 3, 2000, pp. 489–511.

30. W. Chan Kim and R. Mauborgne, "Fair Process: Managing in the Knowledge Economy," *Harvard Business Review*, July–August 1997, pp. 65–76.

31. A.S. Blinder, "Introduction," in A.S. Blinder (ed.), *Paying for Productivity: A Look at the Evidence* (Washington, D.C.: Brookings Institution, 1990), p. 30.

32. D.P. Skarlicki and R. Folger, "Retaliation in the Workplace: The Roles of Distributive, Procedural and Interactional Justice," *Journal of Applied Psychology*, 82, 1997, pp. 434–443.

33. "Praise Beats Raise as Best Motivator, Survey Shows," *The Vancouver Sun*, September 10, 1994.

34. Based on S.E. Gross and J.P. Bacher, "The New Variable Pay Programs: How Some Succeed, Why Some Don't," *Compensation & Benefits Review*, January–February 1993, p. 51; and J.R. Schuster and P.K. Zingheim, "The New Variable Pay: Key Design Issues," *Compensation & Benefits Review*, March–April 1993, p. 28.

35. Peter Brieger, "Variable Pay Packages Gain Favour: Signing Bonuses, Profit Sharing Taking Place of Salary Hikes," *National Post*, September 13, 2002, p. FP5.

36. E. Beauchesne, "Pay Bonuses Improve Productivity, Study Shows," *The Vancouver Sun*, September 13, 2002, p. D5.

37. "Hope for Higher Pay: The Squeeze on Incomes Is Gradually Easing Up," *Maclean's*, 109, no. 48, November 25, 1996, pp. 100–101.

38. P. Booth, *Challenge and Change: Embracing the Team Concept.* Report 123–94, Conference Board of Canada, 1994, p. 18.

39. "Bonus Pay in Canada," *Manpower Argus*, September 1996, p. 5.

40. "Risk and Reward: More Canadian Companies Are Experimenting With Variable Pay," *Maclean's*, January 8, 1996, pp. 26–27.

41. C. Mandel, "Cash by the Numbers: The Vogue for 'Performance Incentives' Spreads to Primary Schools," *Alberta Report*, March 29, 1999, p. 33.

42. K. May, "New Pay Scheme Intended to Help Retain Canada's Top Bureaucrats," *The Vancouver Sun*, August 3, 1999, pp. A5.

43. See, for instance, S.C. Hanlon, D.G. Meyer, and R.R. Taylor, "Consequences of Gainsharing," *Group & Organization Management*, March 1994, pp. 87–111; J.G. Belcher Jr., "Gainsharing and Variable Pay: The State of the Art," *Compensation & Benefits Review*, May–June 1994, pp. 50–60; and T.M. Welbourne and L.R. Gomez Mejia, "Gainsharing: A Critical Review and a Future Research Agenda," *Journal of Management*, 21, no. 3, 1995, pp. 559–609.

44. D. Beck, "Implementing a Gainsharing Plan: What Companies Need to Know," *Compensation & Benefits Review*, January–February 1992, p. 23.

45. M. Byfield, "Ikea's Boss Gives Away the Store for a Day," *Report Newsmagazine*, October 25, 1999, p. 47.

46. See K.M. Young (ed.), *The Expanding Role of ESOPs in Public Companies* (New York: Quorum, 1990); J.L. Pierce and C.A. Furo, "Employee Ownership: Implications for Management," *Organizational Dynamics*, Winter 1990, pp. 32–43; J. Blasi and D.L. Druse, *The New Owners: The Mass Emergence of Employee Ownership in Public Companies and What It Means to American Business* (Champaign, IL: Harper Business, 1991); F.T. Adams and G.B. Hansen, *Putting Democracy to Work: A Practical Guide for Starting and Managing Worker-Owned Businesses* (San Francisco: Berrett-Koehler, 1993); and A.A. Buchko, "The Effects of Employee Ownership on Employee Attitudes: An Integrated Causal Model and Path Analysis," *Journal of Management Studies*, July 1993, pp. 633–656.

47. A. Toulin, "Lowly Staff Join Bosses in Receiving Stock Options," *National Post*, March 1, 2001, pp. C1, C12.

48. A.A. Buchko, "The Effects of Employee Ownership on Employee Attitudes: An Integrated Causal Model and Path Analysis," *Journal of Management Studies*, July 1993, pp. 633–656.

49. C.M. Rosen and M. Quarrey, "How Well Is Employee Ownership Working?" *Harvard Business Review*, September–October 1987, pp. 126–132.

50. W.N. Davidson and D.L. Worrell, "ESOP's Fables: The Influence of Employee Stock Ownership Plans on Corporate Stock Prices and Subsequent Operating Performance," *Human Resource Planning*, 1994, pp. 69–85.

51. J.L. Pierce and C.A. Furo, "Employee Ownership: Implications for Management," *Organizational Dynamics*, Winter 1990, pp. 32–43;" and S. Kaufman, "ESOPs' Appeal on the Increase," *Nation's Business*, June 1997, p. 43.

52. M. Fein, "Work Measurement and Wage Incentives," *Industrial Engineering*, September 1973, pp. 49–51. For an updated review of the effect of pay on performance, see G.D. Jenkins Jr., N. Gupta, A. Mitra, and J.D. Shaw, "Are Financial Incentives Related to Performance? A Meta-Analytic Review of Empirical Research," *Journal of Applied Psychology*, October 1998, pp. 777–787.

53. C.G. Hanson and W.D. Bell, *Profit Sharing and Profitability: How Profit Sharing Promotes Business Success* (London: Kogan Page Ltd., 1987); M. Magnan and S. St-Onge, "Profit Sharing and Firm Performance: A Comparative and Longitudinal Analysis," paper presented at the 58th Annual Meeting of the Academy of Management San Diego, CA, August 1998; E.M. Doherty, W.R. Nord, and J.L. McAdams, "Gainsharing and Organizational Development: A Productive Synergy," *Journal of Applied Behavioral Science*, August 1989, pp. 209–230; and T.C. McGrath, "How Three Screw Machine Companies Are Tapping Human Productivity Through Gainsharing," *Employment Relations Today*, 20, no. 4, 1994, pp. 437–447.

54. S. Kerr, "Practical, Cost-Neutral Alternatives That You May Know, but Don't Practice," *Organizational Dynamics*, 28, no. 1, 1999, pp. 61–70; E.E. Lawler, *Strategic Pay* (San Francisco: Jossey Bass, 1990); and J. Pfeffer, *The Human Equation: Building Profits by Putting People First* (Boston: Harvard Business School Press, 1998).

55. A.D. Stajkovic and F. Luthans, "Differential Effects of Incentive Motivators on Work Performance," *Academy of Management Journal*, June 2001, pp. 580–590.

56. E. Beauchesne, "Pay Bonuses Improve Productivity, Study Shows," *The Vancouver Sun*, September 13, 2002, p. D5.

57. E. Beauchesne, "Pay Bonuses Improve Productivity, Study Shows," *The Vancouver Sun*, September 13, 2002, p. D5.

58. J. Pfeffer and N. Langton, "The Effects of Wage Dispersion on Satisfaction, Productivity, and Working Collaboratively: Evidence From College and University Faculty," *Administrative Science Quarterly*, 38, no. 3, 1983, pp. 382–407.

59. "Risk and Reward: More Canadian Companies Are Experimenting With Variable Pay," *Maclean's*, January 8, 1996, pp. 26–27.

60. "Risk and Reward: More Canadian Companies Are Experimenting With Variable Pay," *Maclean's*, January 8, 1996, pp. 26–27.

61. P.K. Zingheim and J.R. Schuster, "Introduction: How Are the New Pay Tools Being Deployed?" *Compensation and Benefits Review*, July–August 1995, pp. 10–11.

62. *OB in the Street* based on "In Pursuit of Level Playing Fields," *The Globe and Mail*, March 9, 2002, p. S1.

63. "One Smooth Operator: This Former Bell Canada Part-Timer Has Come a Long Way," *Computing Canada*, January 23, 1997, p. 11.

64. "Temporary Jobs Replacing Careers, Study Finds Canadian Council for Social Development," *Canadian Press Newswire*, February 25, 1996.

65. G. Fuchsberg, "Parallel Lines," *Wall Street Journal*, April 21, 1993, p. R4; and A. Penzias, "New Paths to Success," *Fortune*, June 12, 1995, pp. 90–94.

66. *The Daily* (Statistics Canada), January 27, 1999.

67. B. Filipczak, "Managing a Mixed Work Force," *Training*, October 1997, pp. 96–103.

68. K. Damsell, "Service With No Smile: Blame It on Looser Labor Laws and a Newly Cynical Young Workforce. From Waiters to Video Clerks, BC's Service Industry Employees Are Flocking to Unions," *The Financial Post*, August 23/25, 1997, p. 14.

69. D. Hage and J. Impoco, "Jawboning the Jobs," *U.S. News & World Report*, August 9, 1993, p. 53.

70. B.E. Wright, "Work Motivation in the Public Sector," *Academy of Management Proceedings*, 2001, pp. PNP: D1–5.

71. B.E. Wright, "Work Motivation in the Public Sector," *Academy of Management Proceedings*, 2001, pp. PNP: D1–5.

72. H. Munro, "Transit Drivers Taking Fewer Sick Days," *The Vancouver Sun*, June 2, 1999, p. B3.

73. S. Kerr, "On the Folly of Rewarding A, While Hoping for B," *Academy of Management Executive*, 9, no. 1, 1995, pp. 7–14.

74. "More on the Folly," *Academy of Management Executive*, 9, no. 1, 1995, pp. 15–16.

75. J.A. Ross, "Japan: Does Money Motivate?" *Harvard Business Review*, September–October 1997. See also R. Bruce Money and John L. Graham, "Salesperson Performance, Pay, and Job Satisfaction: Tests of a Model Using Data Collected in the U.S. and Japan," *Working Paper*, University of South Carolina, 1997.

76. N.J. Adler, *International Dimensions of Organizational Behavior*, 3rd ed. (Cincinnati, OH: Southwestern, 1997), p. 158.

77. A. Kohn, *Punished by Rewards* (Boston: Houghton Mifflin Company, 1993).

78. W.G. Ouchi, Theory Z, (New York: Avon Books, 1982); "Bosses' Pay," *The Economist*, February 1, 1992, pp. 19–22; W. Edwards Deming, *Out of the Crisis*, (Cambridge: MIT Center for Advanced Engineering Study, 1986).

79. J. Pfeffer, *The Human Equation: Building Profits by Putting People First* (Boston: Harvard Business School Press, 1998).

80. G. Hofstede, "Motivation, Leadership, and Organization: Do American Theories Apply Abroad?" *Organizational Dynamics*, Summer 1980, p. 55.

81. J.K. Giacobbe-Miller, D.J. Miller, and V.I. Victorov, "A Comparison of Russian and U.S. Pay Allocation Decisions, Distributive Justice Judgments, and Productivity Under Different Payment Conditions," *Personnel Psychology*, Spring 1998, pp. 137–163.

82. S.L. Mueller and L.D. Clarke, "Political-Economic Context and Sensitivity to Equity: Differences Between the United States and the Transition Economies of Central and Eastern Europe," *Academy of Management Journal*, June 1998, pp. 319–329.

83. R. de Charms, *Personal Causation: The Internal Affective Determinants of Behavior* (New York: Academic Press, 1968).

84. E.L. Deci, *Intrinsic Motivation* (New York: Plenum, 1975); R.D. Pritchard, K.M. Campbell, and D.J. Campbell, "Effects of Extrinsic Financial Rewards on Intrinsic Motivation," *Journal of Applied Psychology*, February 1977, pp. 9–15; E.L. Deci, G. Betly, J. Kahle, L. Abrams, and J. Porac, "When Trying to Win: Competition and Intrinsic Motivation," *Personality and Social Psychology Bulletin*, March 1981, pp. 79–83; and P.C. Jordan, "Effects of an Extrinsic Reward on Intrinsic Motivation: A Field Experiment," *Academy of Management Journal*, June 1986, pp. 405–412. See also J.M. Schrof, "Tarnished Trophies," *U.S. News & World Report*, October 25, 1993, pp. 52–59.

85. A. Kohn, *Punished by Rewards* (Boston: Houghton Mifflin, 1993).

86. J.B. Miner, *Theories of Organizational Behavior* (Hinsdale, IL: Dryden Press, 1980), p. 157.

87. A. Kohn, *Punished by Rewards* (Boston: Houghton Mifflin, 1993).

88. B. Nelson, "Dump the Cash, Load on the Praise," *Personnel Journal*, 75 July 1996, pp. 65–66.

89. B.J. Calder and B.M. Staw, "Self-Perception of Intrinsic and Extrinsic Motivation," *Journal of Personality and Social Psychology*, April 1975, pp. 599–605; J. Pfeffer, *The Human Equation: Building Profits by Putting People First* (Boston: Harvard Business School Press, 1998), p. 217.

90. B.M. Staw, "Motivation in Organizations: Toward Synthesis and Redirection," in B.M. Staw and G.R. Salancik (eds.), *New Directions in Organizational Behavior* (Chicago: St. Clair, 1977), p. 76.

91. A. Kohn, *Punished by Rewards* (Boston: Houghton Mifflin, 1993), p. 181.

92. A. Kohn, *Punished by Rewards* (Boston: Houghton Mifflin, 1993), p. 186; see also Peter R. Scholtes, "An Elaboration of Deming's Teachings on Performance Appraisal," in Gary N. McLean, Susan R. Damme, and Richard A. Swanson (eds.), *Performance Appraisal: Perspectives on a Quality Management Approach*, (Alexandria, VA: American Society for Training and Development, 1990); H.H. Meyer, E. Kay and J.R.P French Jr., "Split Roles in Performance Appraisal," 1965, excerpts reprinted in "HBR Retrospect," *Harvard Business Review*, January–February 1989, p. 26; W.-U. Meyer, M. Bachmann, U. Biermann, M. Hempelmann, F.-O. Ploeger, and H. Spiller, "The Informational Value of Evaluative Behavior: Influences of Praise and Blame on Perceptions of Ability," *Journal of Educational Psychology*, 71, 1979, pp. 259–268; A. Halachmi and M. Holzer, "Merit Pay, Performance Targetting, and Productivity," *Review of Public Personnel Administration*, 7, 1987, pp. 80–91.

93. A.S. Blinder, "Introduction," in A.S. Blinder (ed.), *Paying for Productivity: A Look at the Evidence* (Washington, D.C.: Brookings Institution, 1990).

94. A. Kohn, *Punished by Rewards* (Boston: Houghton Mifflin, 1993), p. 187.

95. D. Tjosvold, *Working Together to Get Things Done: Managing for Organizational Productivity* (Lexington, MA: Lexington Books, 1986); P.R. Scholtes, *The Team Handbook: How to Use Teams to Improve Quality* (Madison, WI: Joiner Associates, 1988); A. Kohn, *No Contest: The Case Against Competition*, rev. ed. (Boston: Houghton Mifflin, 1992).

96. E.L. Deci, "Applications of Research on the Effects of Rewards," in M.R. Lepper and D. Green (eds.), *The Hidden Costs of Rewards: New Perspectives on the Psychology of Human Motivation* (Hillsdale, NJ: Erlbaum, 1978).

97. S.E. Perry, *San Francisco Scavengers: Dirty Work and the Pride of Ownership* (Berkeley: University of California Press, 1978).

98. A. Kohn, *Punished by Rewards* (Boston: Houghton Mifflin, 1993), p. 192.

99. T.H. Naylor, "Redefining Corporate Motivation, Swedish Style," *Christian Century*, May 30–June 6, 1990, pp. 566–570; Robert A. Karasek, Tores Thorell, Joseph E. Schwartz, Peter L. Schnall, Carl F. Pieper, and John L. Michela, "Job Characteristics in Relation to the Prevalence of Myocardial Infarction in the US Health Examination Survey (HES) and the Health and Nutrition Examination Survey (HANES)," *American Journal of Public Health*, 78, 1988, pp. 910–916; D.P. Levin, "Toyota Plant in Kentucky Is Font of Ideas for the U.S.," *The New York Times*, May 5, 1992, pp. A1, D8.

100. M. Bosquet, "The Prison Factory," reprinted from *Le Nouvel Observateur* in *Working Papers for a New Society*, Spring 1973, pp. 20–27; J. Holusha, "Grace Pastiak's 'Web of Inclusion,'" *The New York Times*, May 5, 1991, pp. F1, F6; J. Simmons and W. Mares, *Working Together: Employee Participation in Action* (New York:

New York University Press, 1985); D.I. Levine and L. D'Andrea Tyson, "Participation, Productivity, and the Firm's Environment," in A.S. Blinder (ed.), *Paying for Productivity: A Look at the Evidence* (Washington, DC: Brookings Institution, 1990); W.F. Whyte, "Worker Participation: International and Historical Perspectives," *Journal of Applied Behavioral Science*, 19, 1983, pp. 395–407.

101. L. Morris, "Employees Not Encouraged to Go Extra Mile," *Training and Development*, April 1996, pp. 59–60.

102. D.R. Spitzer, "Power Rewards: Rewards That Really Motivate," *Management Review*, May 1996, p. 47.

103. K.O. Doyle, "Introduction: Money and the Behavioral Sciences," *American Behavioral Scientist*, July 1992, pp. 641–657.

104. S. Caudron, "Motivation? Money's Only No. 2," *Industry Week*, November 15, 1993, p. 33.

105. E.A. Locke et al., "The Relative Effectiveness of Four Methods of Motivating Employee Performance," in K.D. Duncan, M.M. Gruneberg, and D. Wallis (eds.), *Changes in Working Life* (London: Wiley, 1980), pp. 363–383.

106. B. Filipczak, "Can't Buy Me Love," *Training*, January 1996, pp. 29–34.

107. See A. Mitra, N. Gupta, and G.D. Jenkins Jr., "The Case of the Invisible Merit Raise: How People See Their Pay Raises," *Compensation & Benefits Review*, May–June 1995, pp. 71–76.

108. "CEO Pay Soars as Profits Fall, Globe and Mail Survey Indicates," *Canadian Press Newswire*, April 23, 2002.

109. M. Stern, "Market Forces Determine Pay for Executives: And a CEO's Total Compensation Figures Are Not Salary," *Financial Post (National Post)*, May 22, 2001, p. C6.

110. Based on S.P. Robbins and P.L. Hunsaker, *Training in InterPersonal Skills*, 2nd ed. (Upper Saddle River, NJ: Prentice Hall, 1996), pp. 54–57.

Chapter 5

1. This section is based on J.R. Katzenbach and D.K. Smith, *The Wisdom of Teams* (Boston: Harvard Business School Press, 1993), pp. 21, 45, and 85; and D.C. Kinlaw, *Developing Superior Work Teams* (Lexington, MA: Lexington Books, 1991), pp. 3–21.

2. J.R. Katzenback and D.K. Smith, *The Wisdom of Teams: Creating the High-Performance Organization* (New York: Harper Business, 1999), p. 45.

3. J.R. Katzenback and D.K. Smith, *The Wisdom of Teams: Creating the High-Performance Organization* (New York: Harper Business, 1999), p. 214.

4. P. Booth, *Challenge and Change: Embracing the Team Concept*, Report 123–194, Conference Board of Canada, 1994.

5. Cited in C. Joinson, "Teams at Work," *HRMagazine*, May 1999, p. 30; and P. Strozniak, "Teams at Work," *Industry Week*, September 18, 2000, p. 47.

6. B.W. Tuckman, "Developmental Sequences in Small Groups," *Psychological Bulletin*, June 1965, pp. 384–399; B.W. Tuckman and M.C. Jensen, "Stages of Small-Group Development Revisited," *Group and Organizational Studies*, December 1977, pp. 419–427; and M.F. Maples, "Group Development: Extending Tuckman's Theory," *Journal for Specialists in Group Work*, Fall 1988, pp. 17–23.

7. R.C. Ginnett, "The Airline Cockpit Crew," in J.R. Hackman (ed.), *Groups That Work (and Those That Don't)* (San Francisco: Jossey-Bass, 1990).

8. C.J.G. Gersick, "Time and Transition in Work Teams: Toward a New Model of Group Development," *Academy of Management Journal*, March 1988, pp. 9–41; C.J.G. Gersick, "Marking Time: Predictable Transitions in Task Groups," *Academy of Management Journal*, June 1989, pp. 274–309; E. Romanelli and M.L. Tushman, "Organizational Transformation as Punctuated Equilibrium: An Empirical Test," *Academy of Management Journal*, October 1994, pp. 1141–1166; B.M. Lichtenstein, "Evolution or Transformation: A Critique and Alternative to Punctuated Equilibrium," in D.P. Moore (ed.), *Academy of Management Best Paper Proceedings* (Vancouver, BC: Academy of Management Conference, 1995), pp. 291–295; and A. Seers and S. Woodruff, "Temporal Pacing in Task Forces: Group Development or Deadline Pressure?" *Journal of Management*, 23, no. 2, 1997, pp. 169–187.

9. C.J.G. Gersick, "Time and Transition in Work Teams: Toward a New Model of Group Development," *Academy of Management Journal*, March 1988, pp. 9–41; M.J. Waller, J.M. Conte, C.B. Gibson, and M.A. Carpenter, "The Effect of Individual Perceptions of Deadlines on Team Performance," *Academy of Management Review*, October 2001, pp. 586–600; G.A. Okhuysen and M.J. Waller, "Focusing on Midpoint Transitions: An Analysis of Boundary Conditions," *Academy of Management Journal*, 45, 2002, pp. 1056–1065; and M.J. Waller, M.E. Zellmer-Bruhn, and R.C. Giambatista, "Watching the Clock: Group Pacing Behavior Under Dynamic Deadlines," *Academy of Management Journal*, 45, 2002, pp. 1046–1055.

10. A. Chang, P. Bordia, and J. Duck, "Punctuated Equilibrium and Linear Progression: Toward a New Understanding of Group Development," *Academy of Management Journal*, 46, no. 1, 2003, pp. 106–117.

11. K.L. Bettenhausen, "Five Years of Groups Research: What We Have Learned and What Needs to Be Addressed," *Journal of Management*, 1991, 17, pp. 345–381 and R.A. Guzzo and G.P. Shea, "Group Performance and Intergroup Relations in Organizations," in M.D. Dunnette & L.M. Hough (eds.), *Handbook of Industrial and Organizational Psychology*, 2nd ed., vol. 3 (Palo Alto, CA: Consulting Psychologists Press, 1992), pp. 269–313.

12. A. Chang, P. Bordia, and J. Duck, "Punctuated Equilibrium and Linear Progression: Toward a New Understanding of Group Development," *Academy of Management Journal*, 46, no. 1, 2003, pp. 106–117; and S.G.S. Lim and J.K. Murnighan, "Phases, Deadlines, and the Bargaining Process," *Organizational Behavior and Human Decision Processes*, 58, 1994, pp. 153–171.

13. W.G. Dyer, R.H. Daines, and W.C. Giauque, *The Challenge of Management* (New York: Harcourt Brace Jovanovich, 1990), p. 343.

14. See, for instance, D.L. Gladstein, "Groups in Context: A Model of Task Group Effectiveness," *Administrative Science Quarterly*, December 1984, pp. 499–517; J.R. Hackman, "The Design of Work Teams," in J.W. Lorsch (ed.), *Handbook of Organizational Behavior* (Englewood Cliffs, NJ: Prentice Hall, 1987), pp. 315–342; M.A. Campion, G.J. Medsker, and C.A. Higgs, "Relations Between Work Group Characteristics and Effectiveness: Implications for Designing Effective Work Groups," *Personnel Psychology*, 1993; and R.A. Guzzo and M.W. Dickson, "Teams in Organizations: Recent Research on Performance and Effectiveness," in J.T. Spence, J.M. Darley, and D.J. Foss, *Annual Review of Psychology*, 47, pp. 307–338.

15. D.E. Hyatt and T.M. Ruddy, "An Examination of the Relationship Between Work Group Characteristics and Performance: Once More Into the Breech," *Personnel Psychology*, Autumn 1997, p. 555.

16. This model is based on M.A. Campion, E.M. Papper, and G.J. Medsker, "Relations Between Work Team Characteristics and Effectiveness: A Replication and Extension," *Personnel Psychology*, Summer 1996, pp. 429–452; D.E. Hyatt and T.M. Ruddy, "An Examination of the Relationship Between Work Group Characteristics and Performance: Once More Into the Breech," *Personnel Psychology*, Autumn 1997, pp. 553–585; S.G. Cohen and D.E. Bailey, "What Makes Teams Work: Group Effectiveness Research From the Shop Floor to the Executive Suite," *Journal of Management*, 23, no. 3, 1997, pp. 239–290; G. A. Neuman and J. Wright, "Team Effectiveness: Beyond Skills and Cognitive Ability," *Journal of Applied Psychology*, June 1999, pp. 376–389; and L. Thompson, *Making the Team* (Upper Saddle River, NJ: Prentice Hall, 2000), pp. 18–33.

17. See M. Mattson, T.V. Mumford, and G.S. Sintay, "Taking Teams to Task: A Normative Model for Designing or Recalibrating Work Teams," paper presented at the National Academy of Management Conference; Chicago, August 1999; and G.L. Stewart and M.R. Barrick, "Team Structure and Performance: Assessing the Mediating Role of Intrateam Process and the Moderating Role of Task Type," *Academy of Management Journal*, April 2000, pp. 135–148.

18. R. Wageman, "Critical Success Factors for Creating Superb Self-Managing Teams," *Organizational Dynamics*, Summer 1997, p. 55.

19. M.A. Campion, E.M. Papper, and G.J. Medsker, "Relations Between Work Team Characteristics and Effectiveness: A Replication and Extension," *Personnel Psychology*, Summer 1996, p. 430.

20. M.A. Campion, E.M. Papper, and G.J. Medsker, "Relations Between Work Team Characteristics and Effectiveness: A Replication and Extension," *Personnel Psychology*, Summer 1996, p. 430.

21. For a more detailed breakdown on team skills, see M.J. Stevens and M.A. Campion, "The Knowledge, Skill, and Ability Requirements for Teamwork: Implications for Human Resource Management," *Journal of Management*, Summer 1994, pp. 503–530.

22. M.R. Barrick, G.L. Stewart, M.J. Neubert, and M.K. Mount, "Relating Member Ability and Personality to Work-Team Processes and Team Effectiveness," *Journal of Applied Psychology*, June 1998, pp. 377–391.

23. D. Barnes, "Team, Not Ego, Comes First in Relay," *The Vancouver Sun*, August 29, 2003, pp. H1, 2; and D. Barnes, "Canada the Loser in Sprint Duel," *National Post*, August 30, 2003, p. A19.

24. E.J. Thomas and C.F. Fink, "Effects of Group Size," *Psychological Bulletin*, July 1963, pp. 371–384; A.P. Hare, *Handbook of Small Group Research* (New York: Free Press, 1976); and M.E. Shaw, *Group Dynamics: The Psychology of Small Group Behavior*, 3rd ed. (New York: McGraw-Hill, 1981).

25. E. Sundstrom, K.P. Meuse, and D. Futrell, "Work Teams: Applications and Effectiveness," *American Psychologist*, February 1990, pp. 120–133.

26. D.E. Hyatt and T.M. Ruddy, "An Examination of the Relationship Between Work Group Characteristics and Performance: Once More Into the Breech," *Personnel Psychology*, Autumn 1997, pp. 553–585; and J. D. Shaw, M. K. Duffy, and E. M. Stark, "Interdependence and Preference for Group Work: Main and Congruence Effects on the Satisfaction and

Performance of Group Members," *Journal of Management*, 26, no. 2, 2000, pp. 259–279.

27. G. Keenan, "Steely John: Dofasco Lifer John Mayberry Is Not Your Typical Steel CEO. He's Making Money," *Report on Business* Magazine, September, 2002, pp. 12–15.

28. J.R. Hackman, *Leading Teams* (Boston: Harvard Business School Press, 2002).

29. D. Eden, "Pygmalion Without Interpersonal Contrast Effects: Whole Groups Gain From Raising Manager Expectations," *Journal of Applied Psychology*, August 1990, pp. 394–398.

30. J.M. George and K. Bettenhausen, "Understanding Prosocial Behavior, Sales, Performance, and Turnover: A Group-Level Analysis in a Service Context," *Journal of Applied Psychology*, December 1990, pp. 698–709; and J.M. George, "State or Trait: Effects of Positive Mood on Prosocial Behaviors at Work, *Journal of Applied Social Psychology*, April 1991, pp. 299–307.

31. R.I. Beekun, "Assessing the Effectiveness of Sociotechnical Interventions: Antidote or Fad?" *Human Relations*, October 1989, pp. 877–897.

32. S.G. Cohen, G.E. Ledford, and G.M. Spreitzer, "A Predictive Model of Self-Managing Work Team Effectiveness," *Human Relations*, May 1996, pp. 643–676.

33. See S.T. Johnson, "Work Teams: What's Ahead in Work Design and Rewards Management," *Compensation & Benefits Review*, March–April 1993, pp. 35–41; and A.M. Saunier and E.J. Hawk, "Realizing the Potential of Teams Through Team-Based Rewards," *Compensation & Benefits Review*, July–August 1994, pp. 24–33.

34. P. Booth, *Challenge and Change: Embracing the Team Concept*, Report 123-94, Conference Board of Canada, 1994, pp. 14–15.

35. P. Booth, *Challenge and Change: Embracing the Team Concept*, Report 123-94, Conference Board of Canada, 1994, p. 14.

36. K. Hess, *Creating the High-Performance Team* (New York: Wiley, 1987); J.R. Katzenbach and D.K. Smith, *The Wisdom of Teams*, (Boston: Harvard Business School Press, 1993), pp. 43–64; and K.D. Scott and A. Townsend, "Teams: Why Some Succeed and Others Fail," *HRMagazine*, August 1994, pp. 62–67.

37. E. Weldon and L.R. Weingart, "Group Goals and Group Performance," *British Journal of Social Psychology*, Spring 1993, pp. 307–334.

38. R.A. Guzzo, P.R. Yost, R.J. Campbell, and G.P. Shea, "Potency in Groups: Articulating a Construct," *British Journal of Social Psychology*, March 1993, pp. 87–106; S.J. Zaccaro, V. Blair, C. Peterson, and M. Zazanis, "Collective Efficacy," in J.E. Maddux (ed.), *Self-Efficacy, Adaptation and Adjustment: Theory, Research and Application* (New York: Plenum, 1995), pp. 308–330; and D.L. Feltz and C.D. Lirgg, "Perceived Team and Player Efficacy in Hockey," *Journal of Applied Psychology*, August 1998, pp. 557–564.

39. For some of the controversy surrounding the definition of cohesion, see J. Keyton and J. Springston, "Redefining Cohesiveness in Groups," *Small Group Research*, May 1990, pp. 234–254.

40. C.R. Evans and K.L. Dion, "Group Cohesion and Performance: A Meta-Analysis," *Small Group Research*, May 1991, pp. 175–186; B. Mullen and C. Cooper, "The Relation Between Group Cohesiveness and Performance: An Integration," *Psychological Bulletin*, March 1994, pp. 210–227; S.M. Gully, D.J. Devine, and D.J. Whitney, "A Meta-Analysis of Cohesion and Performance: Effects of Level of Analysis and Task Interdependence," *Small Group Research*, 1995, pp. 497–520; and P.M. Podsakoff, S.B. MacKenzie, and M. Ahearne, "Moderating Effects of Goal

Acceptance on the Relationship Between Group Cohesiveness and Productivity," *Journal of Applied Psychology*, December 1997, pp. 974–983.

41. K. Jehn, "A Multimethod Examination of the Benefits and Detriments of Intragroup Conflict," *Administrative Science Quarterly*, June 1995, pp. 256–282.

42. See D.R. Comer, "A Model of Social Loafing in Real Work Groups," *Human Relations*, June 1995, pp. 647–667.

43. K. Hess, *Creating the High-Performance Team* (New York: Wiley, 1987).

44. F.K. Sonnenberg, "Trust Me, Trust Me Not," *Industry Week*, August 16, 1993, pp. 22–28. For a more elaborate definition, see L.T. Hosmer, "Trust: The Connecting Link Between Organizational Theory and Philosophical Ethics," *Academy of Management Review*, April 1995, pp. 379–403.

45. Based on S.D. Boon and J.G. Holmes, "The Dynamics of Interpersonal Trust: Resolving Uncertainty in the Face of Risk," in R.A. Hinde and J. Groebel (eds.), *Cooperation and Prosocial Behavior* (Cambridge, UK: Cambridge University Press, 1991), p. 194; D.J. McAllister, "Affect- and Cognition-Based Trust as Foundations for Interpersonal Cooperation in Organizations," *Academy of Management Journal*, February 1995, p. 25; and D.M. Rousseau, S.B. Sitkin, R.S. Burt, and C. Camerer, "Not So Different After All: A Cross-Discipline View of Trust," *Academy of Management Review*, July 1998, pp. 393–404.

46. J.K. Rempel, J.G. Holmes, and M.P. Zanna, "Trust in Close Relationships," *Journal of Personality and Social Psychology*, July 1985, p. 96.

47. M. Granovetter, "Economic Action and Social Structure: The Problem of Embeddedness," *American Journal of Sociology*, November 1985, p. 491.

48. P.L. Schindler and C.C. Thomas, "The Structure of Interpersonal Trust in the Workplace," *Psychological Reports*, October 1993, pp. 563–573.

49. J.K. Butler Jr. and R.S. Cantrell, "A Behavioral Decision Theory Approach to Modeling Dyadic Trust in Superiors and Subordinates," *Psychological Reports*, August 1984, pp. 19–28.

50. D. McGregor, *The Professional Manager* (New York: McGraw-Hill, 1967), p. 164.

51. B. Nanus, *The Leader's Edge: The Seven Keys to Leadership in a Turbulent World* (Chicago: Contemporary Books, 1989), p. 102.

52. P.M. Blau, *Inequality and Heterogeneity* (New York: Free Press, 1977); and K.Y. Williams and C.A. O'Reilly, "Demography and Diversity in Organizations: A Review of 40 Years of Research," in B.M. Staw and L.L. Cummings (eds.), *Research in Organizational Behavior*, vol. 20 (Greenwich, CT: JAI Press, 1998), pp. 77–140.

53. D.A. Harrison, K.H. Price, J.H. Gavin, and A.T. Florey, "Time, Teams, and Task Performance: Changing Effects of Surface- and Deep-Level Diversity on Group Functioning," *Academy of Management Journal*, 45, no. 5, 2002, pp. 1029–1045; and J.S. Bunderson and K.M. Sutcliffe, "Comparing Alternative Conceptualizations of Functional Diversity in Management Teams: Process and Performance Effects," *Academy of Management Journal*, 45, no. 5, 2002, pp. 875–893.

54. R.J. Ely and D.A. Thomas, "Cultural Diversity at Work: The Effects of Diversity Perspectives on Work Group Processes and Outcomes," *Administrative Science Quarterly*, 46, 2001, pp. 229–273; K.A. Jehn, G.B. Northcraft, and M.A. Neale, "Why Some Differences Make a Difference: A Field Study of Diversity, Conflict, and Performance in Workgroups." *Administrative Science Quarterly*, 44, 1999, pp. 741–763; and W.E. Watson, K.

Kumar, and L.K. Michaelsen, "Cultural Diversity's Impact on Interaction Process and Performance: Comparing Homogeneous and Diverse Task Groups," *Academy of Management Journal*, 36, 1993, pp. 590–602.

55. For a review, see K.Y. Williams and C.A. O'Reilly, "Demography and Diversity in Organizations: A Review of 40 Years of Research," in B.M. Staw and L.L. Cummings (eds.), *Research in Organizational Behavior*, vol. 20 (Greenwich, CT: JAI Press, 1998), pp. 77–140.

56. E. Peterson, "Negotiation Teamwork: The Impact of Information Distribution and Accountability on Performance Depends on the Relationship Among Team Members," *Organizational Behavior and Human Decision Processes*, 72, 1997, pp. 364–384.

57. See, for instance, M. Sashkin and K.J. Kiser, *Putting Total Quality Management to Work* (San Francisco: Berrett-Koehler, 1993); and J.R. Hackman and R. Wageman, "Total Quality Management: Empirical, Conceptual and Practical Issues," *Administrative Science Quarterly*, June 1995, pp. 309–342.

58. J.S. Bunderson, K.M. Sutcliffe, "Comparing Alternative Conceptualizations of Functional Diversity in Management Teams: Process and Performance Effects," *Academy of Management Journal*, 45, no. 5, 2002, pp. 875–893 discusses some of the recent work in this area.

59. R.J. Ely and D.A. Thomas, "Cultural Diversity at Work: The Effects of Diversity Perspectives on Work Group Processes and Outcomes," *Administrative Science Quarterly*, 46, 2001, pp. 229–273.

60. J.T. Polzer, L.P Milton, and W.B. Swann Jr., "Capitalizing on Diversity: Interpersonal Congruence in Small Work Groups," *Administrative Science Quarterly*, 47, no. 2, 2002, pp. 296–324.

61. See, for example, M.E. Warkentin, L. Sayeed, and R. Hightower, "Virtual Teams Versus Face-to-Face Teams: An Exploratory Study of a Web-Based Conference System," *Decision Sciences*, Fall 1997, pp. 975–993; A.M. Townsend, S.M. DeMarie, and A.R. Hendrickson, "Virtual Teams: Technology and the Workplace of the Future," *Academy of Management Executive*, August 1998, pp. 17–29; and D. Duarte and N.T. Snyder, *Mastering Virtual Teams: Strategies, Tools, and Techniques* (San Francisco: Jossey-Bass, 1999); M.L. Maznevski and K.M. Chudoba, "Bridging Space Over Time: Global Virtual Team Dynamics and Effectiveness," *Organization Science*, September–October 2000, pp. 473–492; and J. Katzenbach and D. Smith, "Virtual Teaming," *Forbes*, May 21, 2001, pp. 48–51.

62. K. Kiser, "Working on World Time," *Training*, March 1999, p. 30.

63. S.L. Jarvenpaa, K. Knoll, and D.E. Leidner, "Is Anybody Out There? Antecedents of Trust in Global Virtual Teams," *Journal of Management Information Systems*, Spring 1998, pp. 29–64.

64. B.L. Kirkman, B. Rosen, C.B. Gibson, P.E. Tesluk, and S.O. McPherson, "Five Challenges to Virtual Team Success: Lessons From Sabre, Inc.," *Academy of Management Executive*, 16, no. 3, 2002, pp. 67–79.

65. See, for example, D. Tjosvold, *Team Organization: An Enduring Competitive Advantage* (Chichester, England: Wiley, 1991); S.A. Mohrman, S.G. Cohen, and A.M. Mohrman Jr., *Designing Team-Based Organizations* (San Francisco: Jossey-Bass, 1995); P. MacMillan, *The Performance Factor: Unlocking the Secrets of Teamwork* (Nashville, TN: Broadman and Holman, 2001); and E. Salas, C.A. Bowers, and E. Edens (eds.), *Improving Teamwork in Organizations: Applications of Resource Management Training* (Mahwah, NJ: Lawrence Erlbaum, 2002).

66. A.B. Drexler and R. Forrester, "Teamwork—Not Necessarily the Answer," *HRMagazine*, January 1998, pp. 55–58.

67. R. Forrester and A.B. Drexler, "A Model for Team-Based Organization Performance," *Academy of Management Executive*, August 1999, p. 47. See also S.A. Mohrman, with S.G. Cohen and A.M. Mohrman Jr., *Designing Team-Based Organizations* (San Francisco: Jossey-Bass, 1995); and J.H. Shonk, *Team-Based Organizations* (Homewood, IL: Business One Irwin, 1992).

68. P.L. Schindler and C.C. Thomas, "The Structure of Interpersonal Trust in the Workplace," *Psychological Reports*, October 1993, pp. 563–573.

69. *Point* based on N. Katz, "Sports Teams as a Model for Workplace Teams: Lessons and Liabilities," *Academy of Management Executive*, August 2001, pp. 56–67.

70. *CounterPoint* based on N. Katz, "Sports Teams as a Model for Workplace Teams: Lessons and Liabilities," *Academy of Management Executive*, August 2001, pp. 56–67.

71. *From Concepts to Skills* based on S.P. Robbins and P.L. Hunsaker, *Training in Interpersonal Skills*, 2nd ed. (Upper Saddle River, NJ: Prentice Hall, 1996), pp. 168–184.

Chapter 6

1. Opening vignette based on B. Livesey, "Heart of Steel," *Report on Business Magazine*, August 1997, pp. 20–27; D. McMurdy, "Dofasco Steel on Cutting Edge: Mayberry Banks on High-Tech to Boost Production," *Financial Post*, December 10, 2001, pp. FP1, FP7; J. Terrett, "Dofasco Engages Workforce to Profit in Tough Steel Market: Losses in Early 1990s Lead to Major Transformation," *Plant*, May 6, 2002, p 15; and G. Keenan, "Dofasco Head Leaves Winning Strategy for Steel Maker," *The Globe and Mail*, May 3, 2003, p. B3.

2. See, for example, K.W. Thomas and W.H. Schmidt, "A Survey of Managerial Interests With Respect to Conflict," *Academy of Management Journal*, June 1976, p. 317.

3. L. Ramsay, "Communication Key to Workplace Happiness," *The Financial Post*, December 6/8, 1997, p. 58.

4. http://www.isrsurveys.com/default.asp (viewed March 14, 2002).

5. D.K. Berlo, *The Process of Communication* (New York: Holt, Rinehart and Winston, 1960), p. 54.

6. *Focus on Ethics* based on "Big Mac Said Close to Settling Fries Suit," *torontostar.com*, March 8, 2002, http://www.torontostar.com/NASApp/cs/ContentServer?pagename=thestar/Layout/Article_Type1&c=Article&cid=1015542115092&call_page=TS_Business&call_pageid=968350072197&call_pagepath=Business/News&col=969048863851 (accessed March 9, 2002).

7. J.C. McCroskey, J.A. Daly, and G. Sorenson, "Personality Correlates of Communication Apprehension," *Human Communication Research*, Spring 1976, pp. 376–380.

8. See R.L. Daft and R.H. Lengel, "Information Richness: A New Approach to Managerial Behavior and Organization Design," in B.M. Staw and L.L. Cummings (eds.), *Research in Organizational Behavior*, vol. 6 (Greenwich, CT: JAI Press, 1984), pp. 191–233; R.E. Rice and D.E. Shook, "Relationships of Job Categories and Organizational Levels to Use of Communication Channels, Including Electronic Mail: A Meta-Analysis and Extension," *Journal of Management Studies*, March 1990, pp. 195–229; R.E. Rice, "Task Analyzability, Use of New Media, and Effectiveness," *Organization Science*, November 1992, pp. 475–500; S.G. Straus and J.E. McGrath, "Does the Medium Matter? The Interaction of Task Type and Technology on Group Performance and Member Reaction," *Journal of*

Applied Psychology, February 1994, pp. 87–97; J. Webster and L.K. Trevino, "Rational and Social Theories as Complementary Explanations of Communication Media Choices: Two Policy-Capturing Studies," *Academy of Management Journal*, December 1995, pp. 1544–1572; and L.K. Trevino, J. Webster, and E.W. Stein, "Making Connections: Complementary Influences on Communication Media Choices, Attitudes, and Use," *Organization Science*, March–April 2000, pp. 163–182.

9. R.L. Daft, R.H. Lengel, and L.K. Trevino, "Message Equivocality, Media Selection, and Manager Performance: Implications for Information Systems," *MIS Quarterly*, September 1987, pp. 355–368.

10. "Virtual Pink Slips Start Coming Online," *The Vancouver Sun*, July 3, 1999, p. D15.

11. J. Terrett, "Dofasco Engages Workforce to Profit in Tough Steel Market: Losses in Early 1990s Lead to Major Transformation," *Plant*, May 6, 2002, p. 15.

12. M. Swartz, *Texas Monthly*, November 2001.

13. K. Cox, "Risley's Wagging Tongue Doomed FPI Deal," *The Globe and Mail*, February 19, 2002, p. B14.

14. S.I. Hayakawa, *Language in Thought and Action* (New York: Harcourt Brace Jovanovich, 1949), p. 292.

15. J. Terrett, "Dofasco Engages Workforce to Profit in Tough Steel Market: Losses in Early 1990s Lead to Major Transformation," *Plant*, May 6, 2002, p 15.

16. J. Collins and J. Poras, *Built to Last: Successful Habits of Visionary Companies* (HarperCollins, 1994).

17. Material in this section based, in part, on J. Collins, "Forget Strategy, Build Mechanisms Instead," *Inc.*, October 1997, pp. 45–48.

18. R.L. Birdwhistell, *Introduction to Kinesics* (Louisville, KY: University of Louisville Press, 1952).

19. J. Fast, *Body Language* (Philadelphia: M. Evan, 1970), p. 7.

20. E.T. Hall, *The Hidden Dimension*, 2nd ed. (Garden City, NY: Anchor Books/Doubleday, 1966).

21. See D. Tannen, *You Just Don't Understand: Women and Men in Conversation* (New York: Ballantine Books, 1991); and D. Tannen, *Talking From 9 to 5* (New York: William Morrow, 1995).

22. D. Goldsmith and P. Fulfs, "You Just Don't Have the Evidence: An Analysis of Claims and Evidence in Deborah Tannen's *You Just Don't Understand*," *Communications Yearbook* 22, 1999.

23. N. Langton, "Differences in Communication Styles: Asking for a Raise," in D. Marcic, *Organizational Behavior: Experiences and Cases*, 4th ed. (St. Paul, MN: West Publishing, 1995).

24. See M. Munter, "Cross-Cultural Communication for Managers," *Business Horizons*, May–June 1993, pp. 75–76.

25. N. Adler, *International Dimensions of Organizational Behavior*, 4th ed. (Cincinnati, OH: Southwestern, 2002), p. 94.

26. See, for instance, R. Hotch, "Communication Revolution," *Nation's Business*, May 1993, pp. 20–28; G. Brockhouse, "I Have Seen the Future," *Canadian Business*, August 1993, pp. 43–45; R. Hotch, "In Touch Through Technology," *Nation's Business*, January 1994, pp. 33–35; and P. LaBarre, "The Other Network," *Industry Week*, September 19, 1994, pp. 33–36.

27. T. Hamilton, "E-mail Overload Swamps Workplace," *torontostar.com*, June 26, 2002, http://www.torontostar.com/ NASApp/cs/ContentServer?pagename=thestar/Layout/ ArticleType1&c=Article&cid=1022100352728&call_page=TS_ Business&call_pageid=968350072197&call_pagepath=Business/ News&col=969048863851 (accessed June 27, 2002).

28. A. LaPlante, "TeleConfrontationing," *Forbes ASAP*, September 13, 1993, p. 117.

29. Derived from P. Kuitenbrouwer, "Office E-Mail Runs Amok," *Financial Post (National Post)*, October 18, 2001, pp. FP11.

30. *Focus on Ethics* based on E. Church, "Employers Read E-mail as Fair Game," *The Globe and Mail*, April 14, 1998, p. B16.

31. J. Kay, "Someone Will Watch Over Me: Think Your Office E-Mails are Private? Think Again," *National Post Business*, January 2001, pp. 59–64.

32. See, for instance, C.F. Fink, "Some Conceptual Difficulties in Theory of Social Conflict," *Journal of Conflict Resolution*, December 1968, pp. 412–460. For an updated review of the conflict literature, see J.A. Wall Jr. and R.R. Callister, "Conflict and Its Management," *Journal of Management*, 21, no. 3, 1995, pp. 515–558.

33. L.L. Putnam and M.S. Poole, "Conflict and Negotiation," in F.M. Jablin, L.L. Putnam, K.H. Roberts, and L.W. Porter (eds.), *Handbook of Organizational Communication: An Inter-disciplinary Perspective* (Newbury Park, CA: Sage, 1987), pp. 549–599.

34. K.W. Thomas, "Conflict and Negotiation Processes in Organizations," in M.D. Dunnette and L.M. Hough (eds.), *Handbook of Industrial and Organizational Psychology*, 2nd ed., vol. 3 (Palo Alto, CA: Consulting Psychologists Press, 1992), pp. 651–717.

35. This section based on S.P. Robbins, *Managing Organizational Conflict: A Nontraditional Approach* (Englewood Cliffs, NJ: Prentice Hall, 1974), pp. 31–55; and J.A. Wall Jr., and R.R. Callister, "Conflict and Its Management," *Journal of Management*, 21, no. 3, 1995, pp. 517–523.

36. *Focus on Diversity* based on A. Morgan, "York University Schedules Exams on Shabbat," *Canadian Jewish News*, April 11, 2002, p. 5.

37. K.W. Thomas, "Conflict and Negotiation Processes in Organizations," in M.D. Dunnette and L.M. Hough (eds.), *Handbook of Industrial and Organizational Psychology*, 2nd ed., vol. 3 (Palo Alto, CA: Consulting Psychologists Press, 1992), pp. 651–717.

38. K.W. Thomas, "Conflict and Negotiation Processes in Organizations," in M.D. Dunnette and L.M. Hough (eds.), *Handbook of Industrial and Organizational Psychology*, 2nd ed., vol. 3 (Palo Alto, CA: Consulting Psychologists Press, 1992), pp. 651–717.

39. *OB in the Street* based on "A Lesson in Design: Get It in Writing," *The Vancouver Sun*, May 13, 2000, p. A22.

40. See R.J. Sternberg and L.J. Soriano, "Styles of Conflict Resolution," *Journal of Personality and Social Psychology*, July 1984, pp. 115–126; R.A. Baron, "Personality and Organizational Conflict: Effects of the Type A Behavior Pattern and Self-Monitoring," *Organizational Behavior and Human Decision Processes*, October 1989, pp. 281–296; and R.J. Volkema and T.J. Bergmann, "Conflict Styles as Indicators of Behavioral Patterns in Interpersonal Conflicts," *Journal of Social Psychology*, February 1995, pp. 5–15.

41. K.W. Thomas, "Conflict and Negotiation Processes in Organizations," in M.D. Dunnette and L.M. Hough (eds.), *Handbook of Industrial and Organizational Psychology*, 2nd ed., vol. 3 (Palo Alto, CA: Consulting Psychologists Press, 1992), pp. 651–717.

42. See A.C. Amason, "Distinguishing the Effects of Functional and Dysfunctional Conflict on Strategic Decision Making:

Resolving a Paradox for Top Management Teams," *Academy of Management Journal,* February 1996, pp. 123–148.

43. J. Heinzl and P. Waldie, "Eaton's Drowning in Red Ink," *The Globe and Mail,* February 28, 1997, p. B1; and J. Heinz, C. Leitch, J. Saunders, M. Strauss, and P. Waldie, "Inside the Debacle at Eaton's," *The Globe and Mail,* March 1, 1997, pp. B1, B4.

44. Based on D. Tsjvold, *Learning to Manage Conflict: Getting People to Work Together Productively* (New York: Lexington Books, 1993), pp. 12–13.

45. See J.A. Wall Jr. and R.R. Callister, "Conflict and Its Management," *Journal of Management,* 21, no. 3, 1995, pp. 523–526 for evidence supporting the argument that conflict is almost uniformly dysfunctional.

46. P. Kuitenbrouwer, "The Mail Must Go Through: Canada Post Is Trying Hard to Get Better by Improving Its Services and Changing Its Relationship With Employees," *The Financial Post,* February 28/March 2, 1998, pp. 8–9.

47. "Postal Workers Sign 2 Year Deal With Canada Post," *Canadian Press Newswire,* February 23, 2000.

48. K. Jehn, "A Multimethod Examination of the Benefits and Detriments of Intragroup Conflict," *Administrative Science Quarterly,* June 1995, pp. 256–282; K.A. Jehn, "A Qualitative Analysis of Conflict Types and Dimensions in Organizational Groups," *Administrative Science Quarterly,* September 1997, pp. 530–57; K.A. Jehn and E.A. Mannix, "The Dynamic Nature of Conflict: A Longitudinal Study of Intragroup Conflict and Group Performance," *Academy of Management Journal,* April 2001, pp. 238–251; and C.K.W. De Dreu and A.E.M. Van Vianen, "Managing Relationship Conflict and the Effectiveness of Organizational Teams," *Journal of Organizational Behavior,* May 2001, pp. 309–328.

49. A.C. Amason, "Distinguishing the Effects of Functional and Dysfunctional Conflict on Strategic Decision Making: Resolving a Paradox for Top Management Teams," *Academy of Management Journal,* 39, no. 1, pp. 123–148.

50. J.A. Wall Jr., *Negotiation: Theory and Practice* (Glenview, IL: Scott, Foresman, 1985).

51. K. Harding, "A New Language, a New Deal," *The Globe and Mail,* October 30, 2002, pp. C1, C10.

52. This model is based on R.J. Lewicki, "Bargaining and Negotiation," *Exchange: The Organizational Behavior Teaching Journal,* 6, no. 2, 1981, pp. 39–40; and B.S. Moskal, "The Art of the Deal," *Industry Week,* January 18, 1993, p. 23.

53. R. Fisher and W. Ury, *Getting to Yes* (New York: Houghton Mifflin, 1981.)

54. These suggestions are based on J.A. Wall Jr. and M.W. Blum, "Negotiations," *Journal of Management,* June 1991, pp. 278–282; and J.S. Pouliot, "Eight Steps to Success in Negotiating," *Nation's Business,* April 1999, pp. 40–42.

55. S.A. Hellweg and S.L. Phillips, "Communication and Productivity in Organizations: A State-of-the-Art Review," in *Proceedings of the 40th Annual Academy of Management Conference,* Detroit, 1980, pp. 188–192.

56. The points presented here were influenced by E. Van de Vliert, "Escalative Intervention in Small-Group Conflicts," *Journal of Applied Behavioral Science,* Winter 1985, pp. 19–36.

57. *From Concepts to Skills* based on S.P. Robbins and P.L. Hunsaker, *Training in Interpersonal Skills: TIPs for Managing People at Work,* 2nd ed. (Upper Saddle River, NJ: Prentice Hall, 1996), Chapter 3; and data in R.C. Huseman, J.M. Lahiff, and J.M. Penrose,

Business Communication: Strategies and Skills (Chicago: Dryden Press, 1988), pp. 380, 425.

Chapter 7

1. Opening vignette based on T. Wharnsby, "How New IOC President Rogge Turned Scandalous Silver Into Gold," *globeandmail.com,* February 17, 2002; "A Duo Deprived," *NYTimes.com,* February 13, 2002, http://ea.nytimes.com/cgibin/email?REFURI=http://www.nytimes.com/2002/02/13/opinion/_13WED4.html (accessed February 17, 2002); and B. Smith, "Overhaul Proposed in Judging of Skaters," *The Globe and Mail,* February 19, 2002, pp. A1, A10.

2. Based on B.M. Bass, *Bass & Stogdill's Handbook of Leadership,* 3rd ed. (New York: Free Press, 1990).

3. S. Prashad, "Fill Your Power Gap," *The Globe and Mail,* July 23, 2003, p. C3.

4. J.R.P. French Jr., and B. Raven, "The Bases of Social Power," in D. Cartwright (ed.), *Studies in Social Power* (Ann Arbor, MI: University of Michigan, Institute for Social Research, 1959), pp. 150–167. For an update on French and Raven's work, see D.E. Frost and A.J. Stahelski, "The Systematic Measurement of French and Raven's Bases of Social Power in Workgroups," *Journal of Applied Social Psychology,* April 1988, pp. 375–389; T.R. Hinkin and C.A. Schriesheim, "Development and Application of New Scales to Measure the French and Raven (1959) Bases of Social Power," *Journal of Applied Psychology,* August 1989, pp. 561–567; and G.E. Littlepage, J.L. Van Hein, K.M. Cohen, and L.L. Janiec, "Evaluation and Comparison of Three Instruments Designed to Measure Organizational Power and Influence Tactics," *Journal of Applied Social Psychology,* January 16–31, 1993, pp. 107–125.

5. D. Kipnis, *The Powerholders* (Chicago: University of Chicago Press, 1976), pp. 77–78.

6. E.A. Ward, "Social Power Bases of Managers: Emergence of a New Factor," *Journal of Social Psychology,* February 2001, pp. 144–147.

7. M. Folb, "Cause Celeb: From Deborah Cox to Maestro, Homegrown Talent Is Hocking Retail Fashion," *Marketing Magazine,* April 5, 1999, p. 13.

8. P.P. Carson, K.D. Carson, and C.W. Roe, "Social Power Bases: A Meta-Analytic Examination of Interrelationships and Outcomes," *Journal of Applied Social Psychology,* 23, no. 14, 1993, pp. 1150–1169.

9. K. Kelley and E. Schine, "How Did Sears Blow This Gasket?" *Business Week,* June 29, 1992, p. 38.

10. G. Yukl and T. Taber, "The Effective Use of Managerial Power," *Personnel,* 37, 1983.

11. D. Hickson, C. Hinings, C. Lee, R. Schneck, and J. Pennings, "A Strategic Contingencies Theory of Intra-Organizational Power," *Administrative Science Quarterly,* 16, 1971, pp. 216–229.

12. J.W. Dean Jr. and J.R. Evans, *Total Quality: Management, Organization, and Strategy* (Minneapolis–St. Paul, MN: West, 1994).

13. B. Smith, "Russian Refuses Extradition," *globeandmail.com* (accessed August 7, 2002).

14. R.E. Emerson, "Power-Dependence Relations," *American Sociological Review,* 27, 1962, pp. 31–41.

15. H. Mintzberg, *Power in and Around Organizations* (Englewood Cliffs, NJ: Prentice Hall, 1983), p. 24.

16. Based on R.A. Oppel Jr., "The Man Who Paid the Price for Sizing up Enron," *NYTimes.com* http://www.nytimes.com/

2002/03/27/business/27ENRO.html?ex=1018242314&ei=1&en=84c572c79afa6b2c (accessed March 27, 2002).

17. See, for example, D. Kipnis, S.M. Schmidt, C. Swaffin-Smith, and I. Wilkinson, "Patterns of Managerial Influence: Shotgun Managers, Tacticians, and Bystanders," *Organizational Dynamics,* Winter 1984, pp. 58–67; D. Kipnis and S.M. Schmidt, "Upward-Influence Styles: Relationship With Performance Evaluations, Salary, and Stress," *Administrative Science Quarterly,* December 1988, pp. 528–542; G. Yukl and C.M. Falbe, "Influence Tactics and Objectives in Upward, Downward, and Lateral Influence Attempts," *Journal of Applied Psychology,* April 1990, pp. 132–140; S.J. Wayne, R.C. Liden, I.K. Graf, and G.R. Ferris, "The Role of Upward Influence Tactics in Human Resource Decisions," *Personnel Psychology,* Winter 1997, pp. 979–1006; G. Blickle, "Influence Tactics Used by Subordinates: An Empirical Analysis of the Kipnis and Schmidt Subscales," *Psychological Reports,* February 2000, pp. 143–154; and P.P. Fu and G. Yukl, "Perceived Effectiveness of Influence Tactics in the United States and China," *Leadership Quarterly,* Summer 2000, pp. 251–266.

18. This section is adapted from D. Kipnis, S.M. Schmidt, C. Swaffin-Smith, and I. Wilkinson, "Patterns of Managerial Influence: Shotgun Managers, Tacticians, and Bystanders," *Organizational Dynamics,* Winter 1984, pp. 58–67.

19. S. Wetlaufer, "Organizing for Empowerment: An Interview With AES's Roger Sant and Dennis Bakke," *Harvard Business Review,* January–February 1999, pp. 110–123.

20. This is the definition given by R. Forrester, "Empowerment: Rejuvenating a Potent Idea," *The Academy of Management Executive,* August 2000, pp. 67–80.

21. R.E. Quinn and G.M. Spreitzer, "The Road to Empowerment: Seven Questions Every Leader Should Consider," *Organizational Dynamics,* Autumn 1997, p. 38.

22. S. Wetlaufer, "Organizing for Empowerment: An Interview With AES's Roger Sant and Dennis Bakke," *Harvard Business Review,* January–February 1999, pp. 110–123.

23. C. Argyris, "Empowerment: The Emperor's New Clothes," *Harvard Business Review,* May–June 1998.

24. J. Schaubroeck, J.R. Jones, and J.L. Xie, "Individual Differences in Utilizing Control to Cope With Job Demands: Effects on Susceptibility to Infectious Disease," *Journal of Applied Psychology,* April 2001, pp. 265–278.

25. "Delta Promotes Empowerment," *The Globe and Mail,* May 31, 1999, Advertising Supplement, p. C5.

26. G.M. Spreitzer, "Psychological Empowerment in the Workplace: Dimensions, Measurement, and Validation," *Academy of Management Journal,* 38, 1995, pp. 1442–1465; G.M. Spreitzer, M.A. Kizilos, and S.W. Nason, "A Dimensional Analysis of the Relationship Between Psychological Empowerment and Effectiveness, Satisfaction, and Strain," *Journal of Management,* 23, 1997, pp. 679–704; and K.W. Thomas and W.G. Tymon, "Does Empowerment Always Work: Understanding the Role of Intrinsic Motivation and Personal Interpretation," *Journal of Management Systems,* 6, 1994, pp. 39–54.

27. D.E. Hyatt and T.M. Ruddy, "An Examination of the Relationship Between Work Group Characteristics and Performance: Once More Into the Breech," *Personnel Psychology,* 50, 1997, pp. 553–585; B.L. Kirkman and B. Rosen, "Beyond Self-Management: Antecedents and Consequences of Team Empowerment," *Academy of Management Journal,* 42, 1999, pp. 58–74; P.E. Tesluck, D.J. Brass and J.E. Mathieu, "An Examination of Empowerment Processes at Individual and Group Levels," paper presented at the 11th annual conference of the Society of Industrial and Organizational Psychology, San Diego, 1996.

28. M. Kane, "Quality Control Can Save Firms Millions, New Data Suggests," *The Vancouver Sun,* May 29, 1998, pp. H1, H6.

29. C. Robert, T.M. Probst, J. J. Martocchio, and F. Drasgow, et al., "Empowerment and Continuous Improvement in the United States, Mexico, Poland, and India: Predicting Fit on the Basis of the Dimensions of Power Distance and Individualism," *Journal of Applied Psychology,* 85, no. 5, 2000, pp. 643-658.

30. W.A. Randolph and M. Sashkin, "Can Organizational Empowerment Work in Multinational Settings?" *Academy of Management Executive,* February 2002, pp. 102–115.

31. "Employers Underestimate Extent of Sexual Harassment, Report Says," *The Vancouver Sun,* March 8, 2001, p. D6.

32. The following section is based on J.N. Cleveland and M.E. Kerst, "Sexual Harassment and Perceptions of Power: An Under-Articulated Relationship," *Journal of Vocational Behavior,* February 1993, pp. 49–67.

33. J. Goddu, "Sexual Harassment Complaints Rise Dramatically," *Canadian Press Newswire,* March 6, 1998.

34. See, for instance, "Car Dealership Settles Same Sex Harassment Lawsuit," *Associated Press,* June 28, 1999.

35. S.A. Culbert and J.J. McDonough, *The Invisible War: Pursuing Self-Interest at Work* (New York: John Wiley, 1980), p. 6.

36. H. Mintzberg, *Power in and Around Organizations* (Englewood Cliffs, NJ: Prentice Hall, 1983), p. 26.

37. T. Cole, "Who Loves Ya?" *Report on Business Magazine,* April 1999, p. 54.

38. D. Farrell and J.C. Petersen, "Patterns of Political Behavior in Organizations," *Academy of Management Review,* July 1982, p. 405. For a thoughtful analysis of the academic controversies underlying any definition of organizational politics, see A. Drory and T. Romm, "The Definition of Organizational Politics: A Review," *Human Relations,* November 1990, pp. 1133–1154.

39. J. Pfeffer, *Power in Organizations* (Marshfield, MA: Pittman, 1981).

40. *OB in the Workplace* based on R. McQueen, "Hard Truths: To Capture a Corner Office, You Have to Play Politics and Know When to Lie," *National Post Business,* September 2000, pp. 51–52.

41. See, for example, G. Biberman, "Personality and Characteristic Work Attitudes of Persons with High, Moderate, and Low Political Tendencies," *Psychological Reports,* October 1985, pp. 1303–1310; and G.R. Ferris, G.S. Russ, and P.M. Fandt, "Politics in Organizations," in R.A. Giacalone and P. Rosenfeld (eds.), *Impression Management in the Organization* (Hillsdale, NJ: Lawrence Erlbaum Associates, 1989), pp. 155–156.

42. D. Farrell and J.C. Petersen, "Patterns of Political Behavior in Organizations," *Academy of Management Review,* July 1982, p. 408.

43. S.C. Goh and A.R. Doucet, "Antecedent Situational Conditions of Organizational Politics: An Empirical Investigation," paper presented at the Annual Administrative Sciences Association of Canada Conference, Whistler, BC, May 1986; C. Hardy, "The Contribution of Political Science to Organizational Behavior," in J.W. Lorsch (ed.), *Handbook of Organizational Behavior* (Englewood Cliffs, NJ: Prentice Hall, 1987), p. 103; and G.R. Ferris and K.M. Kacmar, "Perceptions of Organizational Politics," *Journal of Management,* March 1992, pp. 93–116.

44. See, for example, D. Farrell and J.C. Petersen, "Patterns of Political Behavior in Organizations," *Academy of Management Review*, July 1982, p. 409; P.M. Fandt and G.R. Ferris, "The Management of Information and Impressions: When Employees Behave Opportunistically," *Organizational Behavior and Human Decision Processes*, February 1990, pp. 140–158; and G.R. Ferris, G.S. Russ, and P.M. Fandt, "Politics in Organizations," in R.A. Giacalone and P. Rosenfeld (eds.), *Impression Management in the Organization* (Hillsdale, NJ: Lawrence Erlbaum Associates, 1989), p. 147.

45. S. McShane, *Canadian Organizational Behaviour*, 4th ed., (Whitby: ON: McGraw-Hill Ryerson, 2001), p. 369.

46. M.R. Leary and R.M. Kowalski, "Impression Management: A Literature Review and Two-Component Model," *Psychological Bulletin*, January 1990, pp. 34–47.

47. W.L. Gardner and M.J. Martinko, "Impression Management in Organizations," *Journal of Management*, June 1988, pp. 321–338; D.C. Gilmore and G.R. Ferris, "The Effects of Applicant Impression Management Tactics on Interviewer Judgments," *Journal of Management*, December 1989, pp. 557–564; M.R. Leary and R.M. Kowalski, "Impression Management: A Literature Review and Two-Component Model," *Psychological Bulletin*, January 1990, pp. 34–47; S.J. Wayne and K.M. Kacmar, "The Effects of Impression Management on the Performance Appraisal Process," *Organizational Behavior and Human Decision Processes*, February 1991, pp. 70–88; E.W. Morrison and R.J. Bies, "Impression Management in the Feedback-Seeking Process: A Literature Review and Research Agenda," *Academy of Management Review*, July 1991, pp. 522–541; S.J. Wayne and R.C. Liden, "Effects of Impression Management on Performance Ratings: A Longitudinal Study," *Academy of Management Journal*, February 1995, pp. 232–260; and C.K. Stevens and A.L. Kristof, "Making the Right Impression: A Field Study of Applicant Impression Management During Job Interviews," *Journal of Applied Psychology*, October 1995, pp. 587–606.

48. M. Snyder and J. Copeland, "Self-Monitoring Processes in Organizational Settings," in R.A. Giacalone and P. Rosenfeld (eds.), *Impression Management in the Organization* (Hillsdale, NJ: Lawrence Erlbaum Associates, 1989), p. 11; E.D. Long and G.H. Dobbins, "Self-Monitoring, Impression Management, and Interview Ratings: A Field and Laboratory Study," in J.L. Wall and L.R. Jauch (eds.), *Proceedings of the 52nd Annual Academy of Management Conference*, Las Vegas, August 1992, pp. 274–278; A. Montagliani and R.A. Giacalone, "Impression Management and Cross-Cultural Adaptation," *Journal of Social Psychology*, October 1998, pp. 598–608; and W.H. Turnley and M.C. Bolino, "Achieved Desired Images While Avoiding Undesired Images: Exploring the Role of Self-Monitoring in Impression Management," *Journal of Applied Psychology*, April 2001, pp. 351–360.

49. Z.I. Barsness, K.A. Diekmann, and M-D.L. Seidel, "Structural Location: The Role of Physical, Demographic, and Network Positions in Impression Management," unpublished manuscript, 2003.

50. M.R. Leary and R.M. Kowalski, "Impression Management: A Literature Review and Two-Component Model," *Psychological Bulletin*, January 1990, p. 40.

51. W.L. Gardner and M.J. Martinko, "Impression Management in Organizations," *Journal of Management*, June 1988, p. 333.

52. R.A. Baron, "Impression Management by Applicants During Employment Interviews: The 'Too Much of a Good Thing' Effect," in R.W. Eder and G.R. Ferris (eds.), *The Employment Interview: Theory, Research, and Practice* (Newbury Park, CA: Sage Publishers, 1989), pp. 204–215.

53. R.A. Baron, "Impression Management by Applicants During Employment Interviews: The 'Too Much of a Good Thing' Effect," in R.W. Eder and G.R. Ferris (eds.), *The Employment Interview: Theory, Research, and Practice* (Newbury Park, CA: Sage Publishers, 1989), pp. 204–215; D.C. Gilmore and G.R. Ferris, "The Effects of Applicant Impression Management Tactics on Interviewer Judgments," *Journal of Management*, December 1989, pp. 557–564; and C.K. Stevens and A.L. Kristof, "Making the Right Impression: A Field Study of Applicant Impression Management During Job Interviews," *Journal of Applied Psychology*, October 1995, pp. 587–606.

54. C.K. Stevens and A.L. Kristof, "Making the Right Impression: A Field Study of Applicant Impression Management During Job Interviews," *Journal of Applied Psychology*, October 1995, pp. 587–606.

55. S.J. Wayne and K.M. Kacmar, "The Effects of Impression Management on the Performance Appraisal Process," *Organizational Behavior and Human Decision Processes*, 48, 1991, pp. 70–78; S.J. Wayne and G.R. Ferris, "Influence Tactics, Affect, and Exchange Quality in Supervisor-Subordinate Interactions," *Journal of Applied Psychology*, 75, 1990, pp. 487–499; and G.R. Ferris, T.A. Judge, K.M. Rowland, and D.E. Fitzgibbons, "Subordinate Influence and the Performance Evaluation Process: Test of a Model," *Organizational Behavior and Human Decision Processes*, 58, 1994, pp. 101–135.

56. S.J. Wayne and R.C. Liden, "Effects of Impression Management on Performance Ratings: A Longitudinal Study," *Academy of Management Journal*, 38, 1995, pp. 232–260.

57. G.H. Dobbins and J.M. Russell, "The Biasing Effects of Subordinate Likeableness on Leaders' Responses to Poor Performers: A Laboratory and a Field Study," *Personnel Psychology*, 39, 1986, pp. 759–777; and T.R. Mitchell, and R. Wood, "Manager Behavior in a Social Context: The Impact of Impression Management on Attributions and Disciplinary Actions," *Organizational Behavior and Human Decision Processes*, December 1981, pp. 356–378.

58. D.V. Day, D.J. Schneider, and A.L. Unckless, "Self-Monitoring and Work-Related Outcomes: A Meta-Analysis," paper presented at the 11th Annual Conference of the Society of Industrial and Organizational Psychology, San Diego, CA, 1996; and M.A. Warech, J.W. Smither, R.R. Reilly, R.E. Millsap, and S.P. Reilly, "Self-Monitoring and 36-Degree Ratings," *Leadership Quarterly*, 9, 1998, pp. 449–473.

59. M.A. Warech, J.W. Smither, R.R. Reilly, R.E. Millsap, and S.P. Reilly, "Self-Monitoring and 36-Degree Ratings," *Leadership Quarterly*, 9, 1998, pp. 449–473.

60. D.V. Day, D.J. Schneider, and A.L. Unckless, "Self-Monitoring and Work-Related Outcomes: A Meta-Analysis," paper presented at the 11th Annual Conference of the Society of Industrial and Organizational Psychology, San Diego, CA, 1996.

61. J.M. Maslyn and D.B. Fedor, "Perceptions of Politics: Does Measuring Different Foci Matter?" *Journal of Applied Psychology*, 84, 1998, pp. 645–653; L.G. Nye and L.A. Witt, (1993). "Dimensionality and Construct Validity of the Perceptions of Organizational Politics Scale." *Educational and Psychological Measurement*, 53, 1993, pp. 821–829.

62. G.R. Ferris, D.D. Frink, D.I. Bhawuk, J. Zhou, and D.C. Gilmore, "Reactions of Diverse Groups to Politics in the Workplace," *Journal of Management*, 22, 1996, pp. 23–44; K.M. Kacmar, D.P.

Bozeman, D.S. Carlson, and W.P. Anthony, "An Examination of the Perceptions of Organizational Politics Model: Replication and Extension," *Human Relations*, 52, 1999, pp. 383–416.

63. T.P. Anderson, "Creating Measures of Dysfunctional Office and Organizational Politics: The DOOP and Short-Form DOOP Scales," *Psychology: A Journal of Human Behavior*, 31, 1994, pp. 24–34.

64. G.R. Ferris, D.D. Frink, D.I. Bhawuk, J. Zhou, and D.C. Gilmore, "Reactions of Diverse Groups to Politics in the Workplace," *Journal of Management*, 22, 1996, pp. 23–44; K.M. Kacmar, D.P. Bozeman, D.S. Carlson, and W.P. Anthony, "An Examination of the Perceptions of Organizational Politics Model: Replication and Extension," *Human Relations*, 52, 1999, pp. 383–416.

65. K.M. Kacmar, D.P. Bozeman, D.S. Carlson, and W.P. Anthony, "An Examination of the Perceptions of Organizational Politics Model: Replication and Extension," *Human Relations*, 52, 1999, pp. 383–416; J.M. Maslyn, and D.B. Fedor, "Perceptions of Politics: Does Measuring Different Foci Matter?" *Journal of Applied Psychology*, 84, 1998, pp. 645–653.

66. R.C. Ford and M.D. Fottler, "Empowerment: A Matter of Degree," *Academy of Management Executive*, 9, 1995, pp. 21–31.

67. This section is adapted from D. Kipnis, S.M. Schmidt, C. Swaffin-Smith, and I. Wilkinson, "Patterns of Managerial Influence: Shotgun Managers, Tacticians, and Bystanders," *Organizational Dynamics*, Winter 1984, pp. 58–67.

68. F. Luthans, R.M. Hodgetts, and S.A. Rosenkrantz, *Real Managers* (Cambridge, MA: Ballinger, 1988).

69. C.O. Longenecker, D.A. Gioia, and H.P. Sims Jr., "Behind the Mask: The Politics of Employee Appraisal," *Academy of Management Executive*, August 1987, pp. 183–194.

70. See, for instance, C.P. Parker, R.L. Dipboye, and S.L. Jackson, "Perceptions of Organizational Politics: An Investigation of Antecedents and Consequences," *Journal of Management*, 21, no. 5, 1995, pp. 891–912; and G.R. Ferris, D.D. Frink, M.C. Galang, J. Zhou, K.M. Kacmar, and J.L. Howard, "Perceptions of Organizational Politics: Prediction, Stress-Related Implications, and Outcomes," *Human Relations*, February 1996, pp. 233–266.

71. Cited in C. Kirchmeyer, "The Corporate Political Jungle: Myth, Reality, or a Matter of Interpretation," in C. Harris and C.C. Lundberg (eds.), *Proceedings of the 29th Annual Eastern Academy of Management* (Baltimore, 1992), pp. 161–164.

72. The source of *From Concepts to Skills* is S.P. Robbins and P.L. Hunsaker, *Training in Interpersonal Skills: Tips for Managing People at Work*, 2nd ed. (Upper Saddle River, NJ: Prentice Hall, 1996), pp. 131–134.

OB on the Edge: The Toxic Workplace

1. L.M. Anderson and C.M. Pearson, "Tit for Tat? The Spiraling Effect of Incivility in the Workplace," *Academy of Management Review*, 24, no. 3, 1999, p. 453.

2. The source of this quotation is N. Giarrusso, "An Issue of Job Satisfaction," unpublished undergraduate term paper, Concordia University, Montreal, 1990. It is cited in B.E. Ashforth, "Petty Tyranny in Organizations: A Preliminary Examination of Antecedents and Consequences," *Canadian Journal of Administrative Sciences*, 14, no. 2, 1997, pp. 126–140.

3. P. Frost and S. Robinson, "The Toxic Handler: Organizational Hero—and Casualty," *Harvard Business Review*, July–August 1999, p. 101 (Reprint 99406).

4. L.M. Anderson and C.M. Pearson, "Tit for Tat? The Spiraling Effect of Incivility in the Workplace," *Academy of Management Review*, 24, no. 3, 1999, pp. 452–471.

5. L.M. Anderson and C.M. Pearson, "Tit for Tat? The Spiraling Effect of Incivility in the Workplace," *Academy of Management Review*, 24, no. 3, 1999, pp. 452–471. For further discussion of this, see R.A. Baron and J.H. Neuman, "Workplace Violence and Workplace Aggression: Evidence on Their Relative Frequency and Potential Causes," *Aggressive Behavior*, 22, 1996, pp. 161–173; C.C. Chen and W. Eastman, "Towards a Civic Culture for Multicultural Organizations," *Journal of Applied Behavioral Science*, 33, 1997, pp. 454–470; J.H. Neuman and R.A. Baron, "Aggression in the Workplace," in R.A. Giacalone and J. Greenberg (eds.), *Antisocial Behavior in Organizations* (Thousand Oaks, CA: Sage, 1997), pp. 37–67.

6. L.M. Anderson and C.M. Pearson, "Tit for Tat? The Spiraling Effect of Incivility in the Workplace," *Academy of Management Review*, 24, no. 3, 1999, pp. 452–471.

7 L.M. Anderson and C.M. Pearson, "Tit for Tat? The Spiraling Effect of Incivility in the Workplace," *Academy of Management Review*, 24, no. 3, 1999, pp. 452–471.

8. R. Corelli, "Dishing out Rudeness: Complaints Abound as Customers Are Ignored, Berated," *Maclean's*, January 11, 1999, p. 44.

9. R. Corelli, "Dishing out Rudeness: Complaints Abound as Customers Are Ignored, Berated," *Maclean's*, January 11, 1999, p. 44.

10. See, for example, *Fear and Violence in the Workplace*, Northwestern National Life Insurance Company research report, Minneapolis, MN, 1993; C. Romano, "Workplace Violence Takes a Deadly Turn," *Management Review*, 83, no. 7, 1994, p. 5; J.A. Segal, "When Charles Manson Comes to the Workplace," *HRMagazine*, 39, no. 6, 1994, pp. 33–40.

11. J.H. Neuman and R.A. Baron, "Aggression in the Workplace," in R.A. Giacalone and J. Greenberg (eds.), *Antisocial Behavior in Organizations* (Thousand Oaks, CA: Sage, 1997), pp. 37–67.

12. R.A. Baron and J.H. Neuman, "Workplace Violence and Workplace Aggression: Evidence on Their Relative Frequency and Potential Causes," *Aggressive Behavior*, 22, 1996, pp. 161–173; K. Bjorkqvist, K. Osterman, and M. Hjelt-Back, "Aggression Among University Employees," *Aggressive Behavior*, 20, 1986, pp. 173–184; and H.J. Ehrlich and B.E.K. Larcom, *Ethnoviolence in the Workplace* (Baltimore, MD: Center for the Applied Study of Ethnoviolence, 1994).

13. J. Graydon, W. Kasta, and P. Khan, "Verbal and Physical Abuse of Nurses," *Canadian Journal of Nursing Administration*, November–December 1994, pp. 70–89.

14. C.M. Pearson and C.L. Porath, "Workplace Incivility: The Target's Eye View," paper presented at the annual meetings of The Academy of Management, Chicago, August 10, 1999.

15. "Men More Likely to Be Rude in Workplace, Survey Shows," *The Vancouver Sun*, August 16, 1999, p. B10.

16. R. Corelli, "Dishing out Rudeness: Complaints Abound as Customers Are Ignored, Berated," *Maclean's*, January 11, 1999, p. 44.

17. R. Corelli, "Dishing out Rudeness: Complaints Abound as Customers Are Ignored, Berated," *Maclean's*, January 11, 1999, p. 44.

18. R.A. Baron and J.H. Neuman, "Workplace Violence and Workplace Aggression: Evidence on Their Relative Frequency and Potential Causes," *Aggressive Behavior*, 22, 1996, pp.

161–173; C. MacKinnon, *Only Words* (New York: Basic Books, 1994); J. Marks, "The American Uncivil Wars," *U.S. News & World Report*, April 22, 1996, pp. 66–72; and L.P. Spratlen, "Workplace Mistreatment: Its Relationship to Interpersonal Violence," *Journal of Psychosocial Nursing*, 32, no. 12, 1994, pp. 5–6.

19. Information in this paragraph based on B. Branswell, "Death in Ottawa: The Capital Is Shocked by a Massacre That Leaves Five Dead," *Maclean's*, April 19, 1999, p. 18; "Four Employees Killed by Former Co-Worker," *Occupational Health & Safety*, June 1999, pp. 14, 16; and "Preventing Workplace Violence," *Human Resources Advisor Newsletter Western Edition*, May/June 1999, pp. 1–2.

20. W.M. Glenn, "An Employee's Survival Guide: An ILO Survey of Workplaces in 32 Countries Ranked Argentina the Most Violent, Followed by Romania, France and Then, Surprisingly, Canada," *Occupational Health & Safety*, April/May 2002, p. 28+.

21. D. Flavelle, "Managers Cited for Increase in 'Work Rage,'" *The Vancouver Sun*, April 11, 2000, pp. D1, D11.

22. E. Girardet, "Office Rage Is on the Boil," *National Post*, August 11, 1999, p. B1.

23. S. James, "Long Hours Linked to Rising Toll From Stress," *Financial Post (National Post)*. August 6, 2003, p. FP12.

24. S. Boyes, "Workplace Violence: Coping in a Dangerous World," *Canadian Consulting Engineer*, January/February 2002, pp. 51–52.

25. Information for the *FactBox* based on "Breeding Loyalty Pays for Employers," *The Vancouver Sun*, April 22, 2000, p. D14; and "Men More Likely to Be Rude in Workplace, Survey Shows," *The Vancouver Sun*, August 16, 1999, p. B10.

26. W.M. Glenn, "An Employee's Survival Guide: An ILO Survey of Workplaces in 32 Countries Ranked Argentina the Most Violent, Followed by Romania, France and Then, Surprisingly, Canada," *Occupational Health & Safety*, April/May 2002, p. 28+.

27. W.M. Glenn, "An Employee's Survival Guide: An ILO Survey of Workplaces in 32 Countries Ranked Argentina the Most Violent, Followed by Romania, France and Then, Surprisingly, Canada," *Occupational Health & Safety*, April/May 2002, p. 28+.

28. "Work Rage," *BCBusiness Magazine*, January 2001, p. 23.

29. "A Quarter of Nova Scotia Teachers Who Responded to a Recent Survey Said They Faced Physical Violence at Work During the 2001–02 School Year, *Canadian Press Newswire*, February 14, 2003.

30. A.M. Webber, "Danger: Toxic Company," *Fast Company*, November 1998, pp. 152–157.

31. D. Flavelle, "Managers Cited for Increase in 'Work Rage,'" *The Vancouver Sun*, April 11, 2000, pp. D1, D11.

32. G. Smith, *Work Rage* (Toronto: HarperCollins Canada, 2000).

33. "Work Rage," *BCBusiness Magazine*, January 2001, p. 23.

34. D. Flavelle, "Managers Cited for Increase in 'Work Rage,'" *The Vancouver Sun*, April 11, 2000, pp. D1, D11.

35. D.E. Gibson and S.G. Barsade, "The Experience of Anger at Work: Lessons From the Chronically Angry," paper presented at the annual meetings of The Academy of Management, Chicago, August 11, 1999.

36. H. Levinson, *Emotional Health in the World of Work* (Boston: South End Press), 1964; E. Schein, *Organizational Psychology* (Englewood Cliffs, NJ: Prentice Hall, 1980).

37. E.W. Morrison and S.L. Robinson, "When Employees Feel Betrayed: A Model of How Psychological Contract Violation Develops," *Academy of Management Journal*, 22, 1997, pp. 226–256; S.L. Robinson, "Trust and Breach of the Psychological Contract," *Administrative Science Quarterly*, 41, 1996, pp. 574–599; and S.L. Robinson, M.S. Kraatz, and D.M. Rousseau, "Changing Obligations and the Psychological Contract: A Longitudinal Study," *Academy of Management Journal*, 37, 1994, pp. 137–152.

38. T.R. Tyler and P. Dogoey, "Trust in Organizational Authorities: The Influence of Motive Attributions on Willingness to Accept Decisions," in R.M. Kramer and T.R. Tyler (eds.), *Trust in Organizations* (Thousand Oaks, CA: Sage, 1996), pp. 246–260.

39. A.M. Webber, "Danger: Toxic Company," *Fast Company*, November 1998, pp. 152–157.

40. A.M. Webber, "Danger: Toxic Company," *Fast Company*, November 1998, pp. 152–157.

41. Peter Frost, *Toxic Emotions at Work* (Cambridge, MA: Harvard Business School Press, 2003).

42. "Men More Likely to Be Rude in Workplace, Survey Shows," *The Vancouver Sun*, August 16, 1999, p. B10.

43. D.E. Gibson and S.G. Barsade, "The Experience of Anger at Work: Lessons From the Chronically Angry," paper presented at the annual meetings of The Academy of Management, Chicago, August 11, 1999.

44. D.E. Gibson and S.G. Barsade, "The Experience of Anger at Work: Lessons From the Chronically Angry," paper presented at the annual meetings of The Academy of Management, Chicago, August 11, 1999.

45. R. Corelli, "Dishing out Rudeness: Complaints Abound as Customers Are Ignored, Berated," *Maclean's*, January 11, 1999, p. 44.

46. P. Frost and S. Robinson, "The Toxic Handler: Organizational Hero—and Casualty," *Harvard Business Review*, July–August 1999, p. 101 (Reprint 99406).

47. P. Frost and S. Robinson, "The Toxic Handler: Organizational Hero—and Casualty," *Harvard Business Review*, July–August 1999, p. 101 (Reprint 99406).

Chapter 8

1. Opening vignette based on R. McQueen, "Meet Canada's Top Business Women [The Power 50]," *Financial Post (National Post)*, March 31, 2001, pp. F1, F2; and A. Kingston, "The Carmaker's Daughter," *National Post Business*, September 2002, pp. 42–55.

2. J.P. Kotter, "What Leaders Really Do," *Harvard Business Review*, May–June 1990, pp. 103–111.

3. R.N. Kanungo, "Leadership in Organizations: Looking Ahead to the 21st Century," *Canadian Psychology*, 39, no. 1–2, 1998, p. 77. For more evidence of this consensus, see N. Adler, *International Dimensions of Organizational Behavior*, 3rd ed., (Cincinnati, OH: South Western College Publishing), 1997; R.J. House, "Leadership in the Twenty-First Century," in A. Howard (ed.), *The Changing Nature of Work* (San Francisco: Jossey-Bass, 1995), pp. 411–450; R.N. Kanungo and M. Mendonca, *Ethical Dimensions of Leadership* (Thousand Oaks, CA: Sage Publications, 1996); A. Zaleznik, "The Leadership Gap," *Academy of Management Executive*, 4, no. 1, 1990, pp. 7–22.

4. A. Bryman, "Leadership in Organizations," in S.R. Clegg, C. Hardy, and W.R. Nord (eds.), *Handbook of Organization Studies*, (London: Sage Publications, 1996), pp. 276–292.

5. See, for instance, R.G. Lord, C.L. DeVader, and G.M. Alliger, "A Meta-Analysis of the Relation Between Personality Traits and Leadership Perceptions: An Application of Validity Generalization Procedures," *Journal of Applied Psychology*, 71, 1986, pp. 402–410; R.G. Lord and K.J. Maher, *Leadership and Information Processing: Linking Perceptions and Performance* (Cambridge, MA: Unwin Hyman, 1991); E.A. Locke and Associates, *The Essence of Leadership: The Four Keys to Leading Successfully* (New York: Lexington, 1991); and R.J. House, W.D. Spangler, and J. Woycke, "Personality and Charisma in the U.S. Presidency: A Psychological Theory of Leader Effectiveness," *Administrative Science Quarterly*, 36, 1991, pp. 364–396.

6. J.G. Geier, "A Trait Approach to the Study of Leadership in Small Groups," *Journal of Communication*, December 1967, pp. 316–323.

7. A. Bryman, "Leadership in Organizations," in S.R. Clegg, C. Hardy, and W.R. Nord (eds.), *Handbook of Organization Studies* (London: Sage Publications, 1996), p. 277.

8. S.A. Kirkpatrick and E.A. Locke, "Leadership: Do Traits Matter?" *Academy of Management Executive*, May 1991, pp. 48–60.

9. G.H. Dobbins. W.S. Long, E.J. Dedrick, and T.C. Clemons, "The Role of Self-Monitoring and Gender on Leader Emergence: A Laboratory and Field Study," *Journal of Management*, September 1990, pp. 609–618; and S.J. Zaccaro, R.J. Foti, and D.A. Kenny, "Self-Monitoring and Trait-Based Variance in Leadership: An Investigation of Leader Flexibility Across Multiple Group Situations," *Journal of Applied Psychology*, April 1991, pp. 308–315.

10. G. Yukl and D.D. Van Fleet, "Theory and Research on Leadership in Organizations," in M.D. Dunnette and L.M. Hough (eds.), *Handbook of Industrial & Organizational Psychology*, 2nd ed., vol. 3 (Palo Alto, CA: Consulting Psychologists Press, 1992), p. 150.

11. This section is based on D. Goleman, *Working With Emotional Intelligence* (New York: Bantam, 1998); and D. Goleman, "What Makes a Leader?" *Harvard Business Review*, November–December 1998, pp. 93–102.

12. D. Goleman, R. Boyatzis, and A. McKee, *Primal Leadership: Realizing the Power of Emotional Intelligence* (Cambridge, MA: Harvard Business School Press, 2002).

13. N.M. Ashkanasy and C.S. Daus, "Emotion in the Workplace: The New Challenge for Managers," *Academy of Management Executive*, 16, no. 1, 2002, pp. 76–86.

14. R.M. Stogdill and A.E. Coons (eds.), *Leader Behavior: Its Description and Measurement*, Research Monograph no. 88 (Columbus: Ohio State University, Bureau of Business Research, 1951). This research is updated in S. Kerr, C.A. Schriesheim, C.J. Murphy, and R.M. Stogdill, "Toward a Contingency Theory of Leadership Based Upon the Consideration and Initiating Structure Literature," *Organizational Behavior and Human Performance*, August 1974, pp. 62–82; and C.A. Schriesheim, C.C. Cogliser, and L.L. Neider, "Is It 'Trustworthy'? A Multiple-Levels-of-Analysis Reexamination of an Ohio State Leadership Study, With Implications for Future Research," *Leadership Quarterly*, Summer 1995, pp. 111–145.

15. R. Kahn and D. Katz, "Leadership Practices in Relation to Productivity and Morale," D. Cartwright and A. Zander (eds.), *Group Dynamics: Research and Theory*, 2nd ed. (Elmsford, NY: Row, Paterson, 1960).

16. R.R. Blake and J.S. Mouton, *The Managerial Grid* (Houston: Gulf, 1964).

17. R.R. Blake and A.A. McCanse, *Leadership Dilemmas—Grid Solutions* (Houston: Gulf Publishing Company, 1991); R.R. Blake and J.S. Mouton, "Management by Grid Principles or Situationalism: Which?" *Group and Organization Studies*, 7 (1982), pp. 207–210.

18. See, for example, R.R. Blake and J.S. Mouton, "A Comparative Analysis of Situationalism and 9,9 Management by Principle," *Organizational Dynamics*, Spring 1982, pp. 20–43.

19. See, for example, L.L. Larson, J.G. Hunt, and R.N. Osborn, "The Great Hi-Hi Leader Behavior Myth: A Lesson From Occam's Razor," *Academy of Management Journal*, December 1976, pp. 628–641; and P.C. Nystrom, "Managers and the Hi-Hi Leader Myth," *Academy of Management Journal*, June 1978, pp. 325–331.

20. For a critical review, see A.K. Korman, "'Consideration,' 'Initiating Structure' and Organizational Criteria—A Review," *Personnel Psychology*, 19, 1966, pp. 349–361. For a more supportive review, see S. Kerr and C. Schriesheim, "Consideration, Initiating Structure, and Organizational Criteria—An Update of Korman's 1966 Review," *Personnel Psychology*, 27, 1974, pp. 555–568.

21. Based on G. Johns and A.M. Saks, *Organizational Behaviour*, 5th ed. (Toronto: Pearson Education Canada, 2001), pp. 276.

22. See, for instance, P.M. Podsakoff, S.B. MacKenzie, M. Ahearne, and W.H. Bommer, "Searching for a Needle in a Haystack: Trying to Identify the Illusive Moderators of Leadership Behavior," *Journal of Management*, 1, no. 3, 1995, pp. 422–470.

23. F.E. Fiedler, *A Theory of Leadership Effectiveness* (New York: McGraw-Hill, 1967).

24. Cited in R.J. House and R.N. Aditya, "The Social Scientific Study of Leadership: Quo Vadis?" *Journal of Management*, 23, no. 3, 1997, p. 422.

25. G. Johns and A.M. Saks, *Organizational Behaviour*, 5th ed., (Toronto: Pearson Education Canada, 2001), pp. 278–279.

26. P. Hersey and K.H. Blanchard, "So You Want to Know Your Leadership Style?" *Training and Development Journal*, February 1974, pp. 1–15; and P. Hersey, K. H. Blanchard, and D.E. Johnson, *Management of Organizational Behavior: Leading Human Resources*, 8th ed. (Upper Saddle River, NJ: Prentice Hall, 2001).

27. Cited in C.F. Fernandez and R.P. Vecchio, "Situational Leadership Theory Revisited: A Test of an Across-Jobs Perspective," *Leadership Quarterly*, 8, no. 1, 1997, p. 67.

28. For controversy surrounding the Fiedler LPC scale see A. Bryman, "Leadership in Organizations," in S.R. Clegg, C. Hardy, and W.R. Nord (eds.), *Handbook of Organization Studies* (London: Sage Publications, 1996), pp. 279–280; A. Bryman, *Leadership and Organizations* (London: Routledge & Kegan Paul, 1986); and T. Peters and N. Austin, *A Passion for Excellence* (New York: Random House, 1985). For supportive evidence on the Fiedler model, see L.H. Peters, D.D. Hartke, and J.T. Pohlmann, "Fiedler's Contingency Theory of Leadership: An Application of the Meta-Analysis Procedures of Schmidt and Hunter," *Psychological Bulletin*, March 1985, pp. 274–285; C.A. Schriesheim, B.J. Tepper, and L.A. Tetrault, "Least Preferred Co-Worker Score, Situational Control, and Leadership Effectiveness: A Meta-Analysis of Contingency Model Performance Predictions," *Journal of Applied Psychology*, August 1994, pp. 561–573; and R. Ayman, M.M. Chemers, and F. Fiedler, "The Contingency Model of Leadership Effectiveness: Its Levels of Analysis," *Leadership Quarterly*, Summer 1995, pp. 147–167. For evidence that LPC scores are not stable, see for

instance, R.W. Rice, "Psychometric Properties of the Esteem for the Least Preferred Coworker (LPC) Scale," *Academy of Management Review,* January 1978, pp. 106–118; C.A. Schriesheim, B.D. Bannister, and W.H. Money, "Psychometric Properties of the LPC Scale: An Extension of Rice's Review," *Academy of Management Review,* April 1979, pp. 287–290; and J.K. Kennedy, J.M. Houston, M.A. Korgaard, and D.D. Gallo, "Construct Space of the Least Preferred Co-Worker (LPC) Scale," *Educational & Psychological Measurement,* Fall 1987, pp. 807–814. For difficulty in applying Fiedler's model, see E.H. Schein, *Organizational Psychology,* 3rd ed. (Englewood Cliffs, NJ: Prentice Hall, 1980), pp. 116–117; and B. Kabanoff, "A Critique of Leader Match and Its Implications for Leadership Research," *Personnel Psychology,* Winter 1981, pp. 749–764. For evidence that Hersey and Blanchard's model has received little attention from researchers, see R.K. Hambleton and R. Gumpert, "The Validity of Hersey and Blanchard's Theory of Leader Effectiveness," *Group & Organizational Studies,* June 1982, pp. 225–242; C.L. Graeff, "The Situational Leadership Theory: A Critical View," *Academy of Management Review,* April 1983, pp. 285–291; R.P. Vecchio, "Situational Leadership Theory: An Examination of a Prescriptive Theory," *Journal of Applied Psychology,* August 1987, pp. 444–451; J.R. Goodson, G.W. McGee, and J.F. Cashman, "Situational Leadership Theory: A Test of Leadership Prescriptions," *Group & Organization Studies,* December 1989, pp. 446–461; W. Blank, J.R. Weitzel, and S.G. Green, "A Test of the Situational Leadership Theory," *Personnel Psychology,* Autumn 1990, pp. 579–597; and W.R. Norris and R.P. Vecchio, "Situational Leadership Theory: A Replication," *Group & Organization Management,* September 1992, pp. 331–342; for evidence of partial support for the theory, see R.P. Vecchio, "Situational Leadership Theory: An Examination of a Prescriptive Theory," *Journal of Applied Psychology,* August 1987, pp. 444–451; and W.R. Norris and R.P. Vecchio, "Situational Leadership Theory: A Replication," *Group & Organization Management,* September 1992, pp. 331–342. For evidence of no support for Hersey and Blanchard see W. Blank, J.R. Weitzel, and S.G. Green, "A Test of the Situational Leadership Theory," *Personnel Psychology,* Autumn 1990, pp. 579–597.

29. M.G. Evans, "The Effects of Supervisory Behavior on the Path-Goal Relationship," *Organizational Behavior and Human Performance,"* 5, 1970, pp. 277–298; M.G. Evans, "Leadership and Motivation: A Core Concept," *Academy of Management Journal,* 13, 1970, 91–102; R.J. House, "A Path-Goal Theory of Leader Effectiveness," *Administrative Science Quarterly,* September 1971, pp. 321–338; R.J. House and T.R. Mitchell, "Path-Goal Theory of Leadership," *Journal of Contemporary Business,* Autumn 1974, p. 86; M.G. Evans, "Leadership," in S. Kerr (ed.), *Organizational Behavior,* (Columbus, OH: Grid Publishing, 1979); R.J. House, "Retrospective Comment," in L.E. Boone and D.D. Bowen (eds.), *The Great Writings in Management and Organizational Behavior,* 2nd ed., (New York: Random House, 1987), pp. 354–364; and M.G. Evans, "Fuhrungstheorien, Weg-ziel-theorie," (trans. G. Reber), in A. Kieser, G. Reber, & R. Wunderer (eds.), *Handworterbuch Der Fuhrung,* 2nd ed., (Stuttgart, Germany: Schaffer Poeschal Verlag, 1995), pp. 1075–1091.

30. G.R. Jones, J.M. George, C.W.L. Hill, and N. Langton, *Contemporary Management,* 1st Canadian ed. (Toronto: McGraw-Hill Ryerson, 2002), p. 392.

31. See R.T. Keller, "A Test of the Path-Goal Theory of Leadership With Need for Clarity as a Moderator in Research and Development Organizations," *Journal of Applied Psychology,* April 1989, pp. 208–212; J.C. Wofford and L.Z. Liska, "Path-Goal

Theories of Leadership: A Meta-Analysis," *Journal of Management,* Winter 1993, pp. 857–876; M.G. Evans, "R.J. House's 'A Path-Goal Theory of Leader Effectiveness,'" *Leadership Quarterly,* Fall 1996, pp. 305–309; and C.A. Schriesheim and L.L. Neider, "Path-Goal Leadership Theory: The Long and Winding Road," *Leadership Quarterly,* Fall 1996, pp. 317–321.

32. L.R. Anderson, "Toward a Two-Track Model of Leadership Training: Suggestions From Self-Monitoring Theory," *Small Group Research,* May 1990, pp. 147–167; G.H. Dobbins, W.S. Long, E.J. Dedrick, and T.C. Clemons, "The Role of Self-Monitoring and Gender on Leader Emergence: A Laboratory and Field Study," *Journal of Management,* September 1990, pp. 609–618; and S.J. Zaccaro, R.J. Foti, and D.A. Kenny, "Self-Monitoring and Trait-Based Variance in Leadership: An Investigation of Leader Flexibility Across Multiple Group Situations," *Journal of Applied Psychology,* April 1991, pp. 308–315.

33. S. Kerr and J.M. Jermier, "Substitutes for Leadership: Their Meaning and Measurement," *Organizational Behavior and Human Performance,* December 1978, pp. 375–403; J.P. Howell and P.W. Dorfman, "Substitutes for Leadership: Test of a Construct," *Academy of Management Journal,* December 1981, pp. 714–728; J.P. Howell, P.W. Dorfman, and S. Kerr, "Leadership and Substitutes for Leadership," *Journal of Applied Behavioral Science,* 22, no. 1, 1986, pp. 29–46; J.P. Howell, D.E. Bowen, P.W. Dorfman, S. Kerr, and P.M. Podsakoff, "Substitutes for Leadership: Effective Alternatives to Ineffective Leadership," *Organizational Dynamics,* Summer 1990, pp. 21–38; P.M. Podsakoff, B.P. Niehoff, S.B. MacKenzie, and M.L. Williams, "Do Substitutes for Leadership Really Substitute for Leadership? An Empirical Examination of Kerr and Jermier's Situational Leadership Model," *Organizational Behavior and Human Decision Processes,* February 1993, pp. 1–44; P.M. Podsakoff and S.B. MacKenzie, "An Examination of Substitutes for Leadership Within a Levels-of-Analysis Framework," *Leadership Quarterly,* Fall 1995, pp. 289–328; P.M. Podsakoff, S.B. MacKenzie, and W.H. Bommer, "Transformational Leader Behaviors and Substitutes for Leadership as Determinants of Employee Satisfaction, Commitment, Trust, and Organizational Citizenship Behaviors," *Journal of Management,* 22, no. 2, 1996, pp. 259–298; P.M. Podsakoff, S.B. MacKenzie, and W.H. Bommer, "Meta-Analysis of the Relationships Between Kerr and Jermier's Substitutes for Leadership and Employee Attitudes, Role Perceptions, and Performance," *Journal of Applied Psychology,* August 1996, pp. 380–399; and J.M. Jermier and S. Kerr, "'Substitutes for Leadership: Their Meaning and Measurement'—Contextual Recollections and Current Observations," *Leadership Quarterly,* 8, no. 2, 1997, pp. 95–101.

34. R.E. Kelley, "In Praise of Followers," *Harvard Business Review,* November–December 1988, pp. 142–148; E.P. Hollander, "Leadership, Followership, Self, and Others," *Leadership Quarterly,* Spring 1992, pp. 43–54; and I. Challeff, *The Courageous Follower: Standing up to and for Our Leaders* (San Francisco: Berrett-Koehler, 1995).

35. R.E. Kelley, "In Praise of Followers," *Harvard Business Review,* November–December 1988, pp. 142–148.

36. A. Kingston, "The Carmaker's Daughter," *National Post Business,* September 2002, pp. 42–55.

37. R. McQueen, "Meet Canada's Top Business Women [The Power 50]," *Financial Post (National Post),* March 31, 2001, pp. F1,F2.

38. A. Kingston, "The Carmaker's Daughter," *National Post Business,* September 2002, pp. 42–55.

39. V. Smith, "Leading Us On," *Report on Business Magazine*, April 1999, pp. 91–96.

40. A. Bryman, "Leadership in Organizations," in S.R. Clegg, C. Hardy, and W.R. Nord (eds.), *Handbook of Organization Studies* (London: Sage Publications, 1996), pp. 276–292.

41. J.M. Howell and B.J. Avolio, "The Leverage of Leadership," in *Leadership: Achieving Exceptional Performance*, supplement prepared by the Richard Ivey School of Business, *The Globe and Mail*, May 15, 1998, pp. C1, C2.

42. J.M. Howell and B.J. Avolio, "The Leverage of Leadership," in *Leadership: Achieving Exceptional Performance*, supplement prepared by the Richard Ivey School of Business, *The Globe and Mail*, May 15, 1998, pp. C1, C2.

43. R.N. Kanungo, "Leadership in Organizations: Looking Ahead to the 21st Century," *Canadian Psychology*, 39, no. 1–2, 1998, p. 78.

44. B.M. Bass, "Leadership: Good, Better, Best," *Organizational Dynamics*, Winter 1985, pp. 26–40; and J. Seltzer and B.M. Bass, "Transformational Leadership: Beyond Initiation and Consideration," *Journal of Management*, December 1990, pp. 693–703.

45. Robert House identified three: extremely high confidence, dominance, and strong convictions in his or her beliefs. House also notes that charismatic leaders demonstrate a high level of integrity and place the company goals above their own personal goals. He further notes that such leaders motivate employees by sharing a vision of an exciting, challenging future. They do this by describing what kind of organization they want the company to become, setting high performance standards, and expressing confidence that their employees can achieve that vision. To review House's vision, see R.J. House, "A 1976 Theory of Charismatic Leadership," in J.G. Hunt and L.L. Larson (eds.), *Leadership: The Cutting Edge* (Carbondale, IL: Southern Illinois University Press, 1977), pp. 189–207; and "Building a Better Boss," *Maclean's*, September 30, 1996, p. 41. Warren Bennis, after studying 90 of the most effective and successful leaders in the United States, found that they had four common competencies: They had a compelling vision or sense of purpose; they could communicate that vision in clear terms that their followers could readily identify with; they demonstrated consistency and focus in the pursuit of their vision; and they knew their own strengths and capitalized on them. For this elaboration, see W. Bennis, "The Four Competencies of Leadership," *Training and Development Journal*, August 1984, pp. 15–19.

46. J.A. Conger and R.N. Kanungo, *Charismatic Leadership in Organizations* (Thousand Oaks, CA: Sage, 1998).

47. D.E. Carl and M. Javidan, "Universality of Charismatic Leadership: A Multi-Nation Study," *Academy of Management Proceedings* 2001 IM: B1–B6.

48. P.C. Nutt and R.W. Backoff, "Crafting Vision," *Journal of Management Inquiry*, December 1997, p. 309.

49. P.C. Nutt and R.W. Backoff, "Crafting Vision," *Journal of Management Inquiry*, December 1997, p. 312–314.

50. Cited in L.B. Korn, "How the Next CEO Will Be Different," *Fortune*, May 22, 1989, p. 157.

51. J.C. Collins and J.I. Porras, *Built to Last: Successful Habits of Visionary Companies* (New York: HarperBusiness, 1994).

52. "Building a Better Boss," *Maclean's*, September 30, 1996, p. 41.

53. T. Dvir, D. Eden, B.J. Avolio, and B. Shamir, "Impact of Transformational Leadership on Follower Development and Performance: A Field Experiment," *Academy of Management Journal*, 45, no. 4, 2002, pp. 735–744; R.J. House, J. Woycke, and E.M. Fodor, "Charismatic and Noncharismatic Leaders: Differences in Behavior and Effectiveness," in J.A. Conger and R.N. Kanungo, *Charismatic Leadership in Organizations* (Thousand Oaks, CA: Sage, 1998), pp. 103–104; D.A. Waldman, B.M. Bass, and F.J. Yammarino, "Adding to Contingent-Reward Behavior: The Augmenting Effect of Charismatic Leadership," *Group & Organization Studies*, December 1990, pp. 381–394; and S.A. Kirkpatrick and E.A. Locke, "Direct and Indirect Effects of Three Core Charismatic Leadership Components on Performance and Attitudes," *Journal of Applied Psychology*, February 1996, pp. 36–51; and J.A. Conger, R.N. Kanungo, and S.T. Menon, "Charismatic Leadership and Follower Outcome Effects," paper presented at the 58th Annual Academy of Management Meetings, San Diego, CA, August 1998.

54. J.M. Howell and P.J. Frost, "A Laboratory Study of Charismatic Leadership," *Organizational Behavior & Human Decision Processes*, 43, no. 2, April 1989, pp. 243–269.

55. "Building a Better Boss," *Maclean's*, September 30, 1996, p. 41.

56. Cited in B.M. Bass and B.J. Avolio, "Developing Transformational Leadership: 1992 and Beyond," *Journal of European Industrial Training*, January 1990, p. 23.

57. J.J. Hater and B.M. Bass, "Supervisors' Evaluation and Subordinates' Perceptions of Transformational and Transactional Leadership," *Journal of Applied Psychology*, November 1988, pp. 695–702.

58. J.M. Howell and B.J. Avolio, "The Leverage of Leadership," in *Leadership: Achieving Exceptional Performance*, supplement prepared by the Richard Ivey School of Business, *The Globe and Mail*, May 15, 1998, p. C2.

59. B.M. Bass and B.J. Avolio, "Developing Transformational Leadership: 1992 and Beyond," *Journal of European Industrial Training*, January 1990, p. 23; and J.M. Howell and B.J. Avolio, "The Leverage of Leadership," in *Leadership: Achieving Exceptional Performance*, supplement prepared by the Richard Ivey School of Business, *The Globe and Mail*, May 15, 1998, pp. C1, C2.

60. T. DeGroot, D.S. Kiker, T.C. Cross, "A Meta-Analysis to Review Organizational Outcomes Related to Charismatic Leadership," *Canadian Journal of Administrative Sciences*, 17, no. 40, 2000, pp. 356–371.

61. R.J. House, "A 1976 Theory of Charismatic Leadership," in J.G. Hunt and L.L. Larson (eds.), *Leadership: The Cutting Edge* (Carbondale, IL: Southern Illinois University Press, 1977), pp. 189–207; and R.J. House and R.N. Aditya, "The Social Scientific Study of Leadership: Quo Vadis?" *Journal of Management*, 23, no. 3, 1997, p. 441.

62. "Corporate Cults," *Financial Post Magazine*, November, 1993, pp. 118–123.

63. J.A. Conger, *The Charismatic Leader: Behind the Mystique of Exceptional Leadership* (San Francisco: Jossey-Bass, 1989); R. Hogan, R. Raskin, and D. Fazzini, "The Dark Side of Charisma," in K.E. Clark and M.B. Clark (eds.), *Measures of Leadership* (West Orange, NJ: Leadership Library of America, 1990); D. Sankowsky, "The Charismatic Leader as Narcissist: Understanding the Abuse of Power," *Organizational Dynamics*, Spring 1995, pp. 57–71; and J. O'Connor, M.D. Mumford, T.C. Clifton, T.L. Gessner, and M.S. Connelly, "Charismatic Leaders and Destructiveness: An Historiometric Study," *Leadership Quarterly*, Winter 1995, pp. 529–555.

64. A. Elsner, "The Era of Ceo as Superhero Ends Amid Corporate Scandals" *globeandmail.com*, July 10, 2002.

65. R. McQueen, "Frank's Daughter Doesn't Ride Any Coattails: Belinda Stronach: 'I'm Responsible for This Ship,'" *Financial Post (National Post)*, March 31, 2001, p. F3.

66. J.M. Kouzes and B.Z. Posner, *Credibility: How Leaders Gain and Lose It, Why People Demand It* (San Francisco: Jossey-Bass, 1993); C.C. Manz and H.P. Sims, "SuperLeadership: Beyond the Myth of Heroic Leadership," *Organizational Dynamics*, 19, 1991, pp. 18–35; and H.P. Sims and P. Lorenzi, *The New Leadership Paradigm* (Newbury Park: Sage, 1992).

67. C.C. Manz and H.P. Sims, "SuperLeadership: Beyond the Myth of Heroic Leadership," *Organizational Dynamics*, 19, 1991, pp. 18–35; H.P. Sims and P. Lorenzi, *The New Leadership Paradigm* (Newbury Park, CA: Sage, 1992).

68. H.P. Sims and P. Lorenzi, *The New Leadership Paradigm*, (Newbury Park, CA: Sage, 1992), p. 295.

69. See, for instance, J.H. Zenger, E. Musselwhite, K. Hurson, and C. Perrin, *Leading Teams: Mastering the New Role* (Homewood, IL: Business One Irwin, 1994); and M. Frohman, "Nothing Kills Teams Like Ill-Prepared Leaders," *Industry Week*, October 2, 1995, pp. 72–76.

70. See, for instance, M. Frohman, "Nothing Kills Teams Like Ill-Prepared Leaders," *Industry Week*, October 2, 1995, p. 93.

71. See, for instance, M. Frohman, "Nothing Kills Teams Like Ill-Prepared Leaders," *Industry Week*, October 2, 1995, p. 100.

72. J.R. Katzenbach and D.K. Smith, *The Wisdom of Teams: Creating the High-Performance Organization* (Boston, MA: Harvard Business School, 1993).

73. N. Steckler and N. Fondas, "Building Team Leader Effectiveness: A Diagnostic Tool," *Organizational Dynamics*, Winter 1995, p. 20.

74. R.S. Wellins, W.C. Byham, and G.R. Dixon, *Inside Teams* (San Francisco: Jossey-Bass, 1994), p. 318.

75. N. Steckler and N. Fondas, "Building Team Leader Effectiveness: A Diagnostic Tool," *Organizational Dynamics*, Winter 1995, p. 21.

76. C.C. Manz and H.P. Sims, Jr. *The New SuperLeadership: Leading Others to Lead Themselves*, (San Francisco: Berrett-Koehler Publishers, 2001).

77. A. Bandura, "Self-Reinforcement: Theoretical and Methodological Considerations," *Behaviorism*, 4, 1976, pp. 135–155; P.W. Corrigan, C.J. Wallace and M.L. Schade, "Learning Medication Self-Management Skills in Schizophrenia; Relationships With Cognitive Deficits and Psychiatric Symptom," *Behavior Therapy*, Winter, 1994, pp. 5–15; A.S. Bellack, "A Comparison of Self-Reinforcement and Self-Monitoring in a Weight Reduction Program," *Behavior Therapy*, 7, 1976, pp. 68–75; T.A. Eckman, W.C. Wirshing, and S.R. Marder, "Technique for Training Schizophrenic Patients in Illness Self-Management: A Controlled Trial," *The American Journal of Psychiatry*, 149, 1992, pp. 1549–1555; J.J. Felixbrod and K.D. O'Leary, "Effect of Reinforcement on Children's Academic Behavior as a Function of Self-Determined and Externally Imposed Contingencies," *Journal of Applied Behavior Analysis*, 6, 1973, pp. 141–150; A.J. Litrownik, L.R. Franzini, and D. Skenderian, "The Effects of Locus of Reinforcement Control on a Concept Identification Task," *Psychological Reports*, 39, 1976, pp. 159–165; P.D. McGorry, "Psychoeducation in First-Episode Psychosis: A Therapeutic Process," *Psychiatry*, November, 1995, pp. 313–328; G.S. Parcel, P.R. Swank, and M.J. Mariotto, "Self-Management of Cystic Fibrosis: A Structural Model for Educational and Behavioral Variables," *Social Science and Medicine*, 38, 1994, pp. 1307–1315; G.E. Speidel, "Motivating Effect of Contingent Self-Reward," *Journal of Experimental Psychology*, 102, 1974, pp. 528–530.

78. D.B. Jeffrey, "A Comparison of the Effects of External Control and Self-Control on the Modification and Maintenance of Weight," *Journal of Abnormal Psychology*, 83, 1974, pp. 404–410.

79. M. Castaneda, T.A. Kolenko, and R.J. Aldag, "Self-Management Perceptions and Practices: A Structural Equations Analysis," *Journal of Organizational Behavior*, 20, 1999, p. 102.

80. M. Castaneda, T.A. Kolenko, and R.J. Aldag, "Self-Management Perceptions and Practices: A Structural Equations Analysis," *Journal of Organizational Behavior*, 20, 1999, p. 102.

81. M. Castaneda, T.A. Kolenko and R.J. Aldag, "Self-Management Perceptions and Practices: A Structural Equations Analysis," *Journal of Organizational Behavior*, 20, 1999, p. 102.

82. R.M. Kanter, *The Change Masters, Innovation and Entrepreneurship in the American Corporation* (New York: Simon and Schuster, 1983).

83. R.A. Heifetz, *Leadership Without Easy Answers* (Cambridge, MA: Harvard University Press, 1996), p. 205.

84. R.A. Heifetz, *Leadership Without Easy Answers* (Cambridge, MA: Harvard University Press, 1996), p. 205.

85. R.A. Heifetz, *Leadership Without Easy Answers* (Cambridge, MA: Harvard University Press, 1996), p. 188.

86. This section is based on R.B. Morgan, "Self- and Co-Worker Perceptions of Ethics and Their Relationships to Leadership and Salary," *Academy of Management Journal*, February 1993, pp. 200–214; J.B. Ciulla, "Leadership Ethics: Mapping the Territory," *Business Ethics Quarterly*, January 1995, pp. 5–28; E.P. Hollander, "Ethical Challenges in the Leader-Follower Relationship," *Business Ethics Quarterly*, January 1995, pp. 55–65; J.C. Rost, "Leadership: A Discussion About Ethics," *Business Ethics Quarterly*, January 1995, pp. 129–142; and R.N. Kanungo and M. Mendonca, *Ethical Dimensions of Leadership* (Thousand Oaks, CA: Sage Publications, 1996).

87. J.M. Burns, *Leadership* (New York: Harper and Row, 1978).

88. J.M. Howell and B.J. Avolio, "The Ethics of Charismatic Leadership: Submission or Liberation?" *Academy of Management Executive*, May 1992, pp. 43–55.

89. J. Stephens and P. Behr, "Enron's Culture Fed Its Demise: Groupthink Promoted Foolhardy Risks," *The Washington Post*, January 27, 2002; p. A01.

90. J.G. Clawson, *Level Three Leadership*, (Upper Saddle River, NJ: Prentice Hall), 1999, pp. 46–49.

91. The material in this section is based on J. Grant, "Women as Managers: What They Can Offer to Organizations," *Organizational Dynamics*, Winter 1988, pp. 56–63; S. Helgesen, *The Female Advantage: Women's Ways of Leadership* (New York: Doubleday, 1990); A.H. Eagly and B.T. Johnson, "Gender and Leadership Style: A Meta-Analysis," *Psychological Bulletin*, September 1990, pp. 233–256; A.H. Eagly and S.J. Karau, "Gender and the Emergence of Leaders: A Meta-Analysis," *Journal of Personality and Social Psychology*, May 1991, pp. 685–710; J.B. Rosener, "Ways Women Lead," *Harvard Business Review*, November–December 1990, pp. 119–125; "Debate: Ways Men and Women Lead," *Harvard Business Review*, January–February 1991, pp. 150–160; A.H. Eagly, M.G. Makhijani, and B.G. Klonsky, "Gender and the Evaluation of Leaders: A Meta-Analysis," *Psychological Bulletin*, January 1992, pp. 3–22; A.H. Eagly, S.J. Karau, and B.T. Johnson, "Gender and Leadership Style Among School Principals: A Meta-Analysis,"

Educational Administration Quarterly, February 1992, pp. 76–102; L.R. Offermann and C. Beil, "Achievement Styles of Women Leaders and Their Peers," *Psychology of Women Quarterly,* March 1992, pp. 37–56; T. Melamed and N. Bozionelos, "Gender Differences in the Personality Features of British Managers," *Psychological Reports,* December 1992, pp. 979–986; G.N. Powell, *Women & Men in Management,* 2nd ed. (Thousand Oaks, CA: Sage, 1993); R.L. Kent and S.E. Moss, "Effects of Size and Gender Role on Leader Emergence," *Academy of Management Journal,* October 1994, pp. 1335–1346; C. Lee, "The Feminization of Management," *Training,* November 1994, pp. 25–31; H. Collingwood, "Women as Managers: Not Just Different: Better," *Working Woman,* November 1995, p. 14; and J.B. Rosener, *America's Competitive Secret: Women Managers* (New York: Oxford University Press, 1995).

92. B. Orser, *Creating High Performance Organizations: Leveraging Women's Leadership,* Conference Board of Canada, 2000.

93. J. Wajcman, *Managing Like a Man.* (University Park, PA: Pennsylvania Press, 1998), p. 63.

94. G.N. Powell, *Women and Men in Management* (Newbury Park, CA: Sage, 1993), p. 174.

95. M. Javidan, B. Bemmels, K.S. Devine, and A. Dastmalchian, "Superior and Subordinate Gender and the Acceptance of Superiors as Role Models," *Human Relations,* 48, 1995, pp. 1271–1284.

96. B. Orser, *Creating High Performance Organizations: Leveraging Women's Leadership,* Conference Board of Canada, 2000.

97. M. McDonald, "They Love Me—Not: Once Hailed As Heroines, Female CEOs Now Face Harsh Critiques," *usnews.com,* June 24, 2002, http://www.usnews.com/usnews/issue/020624/biztech/24women.htm (accessed June 19, 2002).

98. For a review of the cross-cultural applicability of the leadership literature, see R.S. Bhagat, B.L. Kedia, S.E. Crawford, and M.R. Kaplan, "Cross-Cultural Issues in Organizational Psychology: Emergent Trends and Directions for Research in the 1990s," in C.L. Cooper and I.T. Robertson (eds.), *International Review of Industrial and Organizational Psychology,* 5 (Chichester, England: John Wiley, 1990), pp. 79–89; and M.F. Peterson and J.G. Hunt, "International Perspectives on International Leadership," *Leadership Quarterly,* Fall 1997, pp. 203–231.

99. "Military-Style Management in China," *Asia Inc.,* March 1995, p. 70.

100. Cited in R.J. House and R.N. Aditya, "The Social Scientific Study of Leadership: Quo Vadis?" *Journal of Management,* 23, no. 3, 1997, p. 463.

101. R.J. House, "Leadership in the Twenty-First Century," in A. Howard (ed.), *The Changing Nature of Work* (San Francisco: Jossey-Bass, 1995), p. 442.

102. R.J. House, "Leadership in the Twenty-First Century," in A. Howard (ed.), *The Changing Nature of Work* (San Francisco: Jossey-Bass, 1995), p. 442.

103. R.J. House and R.N. Aditya, "The Social Scientific Study of Leadership: Quo Vadis?" *Journal of Management,* 23, no. 3, 1997, p. 463.

104. R.J. House, "Leadership in the Twenty-First Century," in A. Howard (ed.), *The Changing Nature of Work* (San Francisco: Jossey-Bass, 1995), p. 443.

105. Information in this paragraph based on K. Boehnke, A.C. Di Stefano, J.J. Di Stefano, and N. Bontis, "Leadership for Extraordinary Performance," *Business Quarterly,* Summer 1997, pp. 57–63.

106. Ideas in this argument came from J. Pfeffer, "The Ambiguity of Leadership," *Academy of Management Review,* January 1977, pp. 104–111; A.B. Thomas, "Does Leadership Make a Difference to Organizational Performance?" *Administrative Science Quarterly,* September 1988, pp. 388–400; C.C. Manz and H.P. Sims Jr., "SuperLeadership: Beyond the Myth of Heroic Leadership," *Organizational Dynamics,* Spring 1991, pp. 18–35; and G. Gemmill and J. Oakley, "Leadership: An Alienating Social Myth?" *Human Relations,* February 1992, pp. 113–129.

107. Based on J.M. Howell and P.J. Frost, "A Laboratory Study of Charismatic Leadership," *Organizational Behavior and Human Decision Processes,* April 1989, pp. 243–269.

108. Based on V. H. Vroom, "A New Look at Managerial Decision Making," *Organizational Dynamics,* Spring 1973, pp. 66–80. With permission.

Chapter 9

1. M. Skapinker, "Why Nike Has Broken Into a Sweat," *FT.com,* March 6, 2002, http://news.ft.com/ft/gx.cgi/ftc?pagename=View&c=Article&cid=FT363BTGHYC&live=true (accessed March 12, 2002); D. Simpson, "Ethics and Corporate Social Responsibility," advertising supplement, *Report on Business Magazine,* February 2002.

2. W. Pounds, "The Process of Problem Finding," *Industrial Management Review,* Fall 1969, pp. 1–19.

3. See H.A. Simon, "Rationality in Psychology and Economics," *The Journal of Business,* October 1986, pp. 209–224; and A. Langley, "In Search of Rationality: The Purposes Behind the Use of Formal Analysis in Organizations," *Administrative Science Quarterly,* December 1989, pp. 598–631.

4. For a review of the rational model, see E.F. Harrison, *The Managerial Decision Making Process,* 5th ed. (Boston: Houghton Mifflin, 1999), pp. 75–102.

5. T. Barry, "Smart Cookies: Why CIBC Said Yes to the Girl Guides," *Marketing Magazine,* May 31, 1999, pp 11, 14.

6. J.G. March, *A Primer on Decision Making* (New York: Free Press, 1994), pp. 2–7.

7. This vignette is based on "Quotas at Thailand Footwear Factory Promote Fast Work but Draw Fire," *Knight Ridder Tribune Business News,* March 18, 2002, p. 1.

8. D.L. Rados, "Selection and Evaluation of Alternatives in Repetitive Decision Making," *Administrative Science Quarterly,* June 1972, pp. 196–206.

9. M. Bazerman, *Judgment in Managerial Decision Making,* 3rd ed. (New York: Wiley, 1994), p. 5.

10. See, for instance, L.R. Beach, *The Psychology of Decision Making* (Thousand Oaks, CA: Sage, 1997).

11. See, for example, M.D. Cohen, J.G. March, and J.P. Olsen, "A Garbage Can Model of Organizational Choice," *Administrative Science Quarterly,* March 1972, pp. 1–25.

12. See J.G. Thompson, *Organizations in Action* (New York: McGraw-Hill, 1967), p. 123.

13. See H.A. Simon, *Administrative Behavior,* 4th ed. (New York: Free Press, 1997); and M. Augier, "Simon Says: Bounded Rationality Matters," *Journal of Management Inquiry,* September 2001, pp. 268–275.

14. *OB in the Workplace* based on K. May, "Ottawa May Stop Hiring Best Qualified," *National Post,* March 4, 2002, p. A4.

15. W.H. Agor, "The Logic of Intuition: How Top Executives Make Important Decisions," *Organizational Dynamics,* Winter 1986,

p. 5; W.H. Agor (ed.), *Intuition in Organizations* (Newbury Park, CA: Sage Publications, 1989); O. Behling and N.L. Eckel, "Making Sense out of Intuition," *Academy of Management Executive*, February 1991, pp. 46–47; G. Klein, *Sources of Power: How People Make Decisions* (Cambridge: MIT Press, 1998); P.E. Ross, "Flash of Genius," *Forbes*, November 16, 1998, pp. 98–104; L.A. Burke and M.K. Miller, "Taking the Mystery out of Intuitive Decision Making," *Academy of Management Executive*, November 1999, pp. 91–99; and N. Khatri and H.A. Ng, "The Role of Intuition in Strategic Decision Making," *Human Relations*, January 2000, pp. 57–86.

16. O. Behling and N.L. Eckel, "Making Sense out of Intuition," *Academy of Management Executive*, February 1991, pp. 46–54.

17. L.A. Burke and M.K. Miller, "Taking the Mystery out of Intuitive Decision Making," The Academy of Management Executive, November 1999, pp. 91–99.

18. A. Tversky and K. Kahneman, "Judgment Under Uncertainty: Heuristics and Biases," *Science*, September 1974, pp. 1124–1131; and J.S. Hammond, R.L. Keeney, and H. Raiffa, "The Hidden Traps in Decision Making," *Harvard Business Review*, September–October 1998, pp. 47–58.

19. K. McKean, "Decisions, Decisions," *Discover*, June, 1985, pp. 22–31.

20. A. Tversky and K. Kahneman, "Judgment Under Uncertainty: Heuristics and Biases," *Science,* September 1974, pp. 1124–1131.

21. G. Whyte, C. Sue-Chan, "The Neglect of Base Rate Data by Human Resources Managers in Employee Selection," *Revue Canadienne des Sciences de l'Administration*, 19, no. 1, pp. 1–11.

22. See B.M. Staw, "The Escalation of Commitment to a Course of Action," *Academy of Management Review*, October 1981, pp. 577–587; and H. Moon, "Looking Forward and Looking Back: Integrating Completion and Sunk-Cost Effects Within an Escalation-of-Commitment Progress Decision," *Journal of Applied Psychology*, February 2001, pp. 104–113.

23. See N.R.F. Maier, "Assets and Liabilities in Group Problem Solving: The Need for an Integrative Function," *Psychological Review*, April 1967, pp. 239–249; G.W. Hill, "Group Versus Individual Performance: Are N+1 Heads Better Than One?" *Psychological Bulletin*, May 1982, pp. 517–539; and A.E. Schwartz and J. Levin, "Better Group Decision Making," *Supervisory Management*, June 1990, p. 4.

24. See, for example, R.A. Cooke and J.A. Kernaghan, "Estimating the Difference Between Group Versus Individual Performance on Problem-Solving Tasks," *Group & Organization Studies*, September 1987, pp. 319–342; and L.K. Michaelsen, W.E. Watson, and R.H. Black, "A Realistic Test of Individual Versus Group Consensus Decision Making," *Journal of Applied Psychology*, October 1989, pp. 834–839.

25. See, for example, W.C. Swap and Associates, *Group Decision Making* (Newbury Park, CA: Sage, 1984).

26. I.L. Janis, *Groupthink* (Boston: Houghton Mifflin, 1982); W. Park, "A Review of Research on Groupthink," *Journal of Behavioral Decision Making*, July 1990, pp. 229–245; C.P. Neck and G. Moorhead, "Groupthink Remodeled: The Importance of Leadership, Time Pressure, and Methodical Decision Making Procedures," *Human Relations*, May 1995, pp. 537–558; and J.N. Choi and M.U. Kim, "The Organizational Application of Groupthink and Its Limits in Organizations," *Journal of Applied Psychology*, April 1999, pp. 297–306.

27. I.L. Janis, *Groupthink* (Boston: Houghton Mifflin, 1982).

28. B. Little, "Forecasters Were Lost in a Fog of Pessimism," *globeandmail.com* (accessed March 21, 2002).

29. M.E. Turner and A.R. Pratkanis, "Mitigating Groupthink by Stimulating Constructive Conflict," in C. De Dreu and E. Van de Vliert (eds.), *Using Conflict in Organizations* (London: Sage, 1997), pp. 53–71.

30. See N.R.F. Maier, *Principles of Human Relations* (New York: John Wiley, 1952); I.L. Janis, *Groupthink: Psychological Studies of Policy Decisions and Fiascoes*, 2nd ed. (Boston: Houghton Mifflin, 1982); and C.R. Leana, "A Partial Test of Janis' Groupthink Model: Effects of Group Cohesiveness and Leader Behavior on Defective Decision Making," *Journal of Management*, Spring 1985, pp. 5–17.

31. J.N. Choi and M.U. Kim, "The Organizational Application of Groupthink and Its Limitations in Organizations," *Journal of Applied Psychology*, 84, 1999, pp. 297–306.

32. J. Longley and D.G. Pruitt, "Groupthink: A Critique of Janis' Theory," in L. Wheeler (ed.), *Review of Personality and Social Psychology* (Newbury Park, CA: Sage, 1980), pp. 507–513; and J.A. Sniezek, "Groups Under Uncertainty: An Examination of Confidence in Group Decision Making," *Organizational Behavior and Human Decision Processes*, 52, 1992, pp. 124–155.

33. C. McCauley, "The Nature of Social Influence in Groupthink: Compliance and Internalization," *Journal of Personality and Social Psychology*, 57, 1989, pp. 250–260; P.E. Tetlock, R.S. Peterson, C. McGuire, S. Chang, and P. Feld, "Assessing Political Group Dynamics: A Test of the Groupthink Model," *Journal of Personality and Social Psychology*, 63, 1992, pp. 781–796; S. Graham, "A Review of Attribution Theory in Achievement Contexts," *Educational Psychology Review*, 3, 1991, pp. 5–39; and G. Moorhead and J.R. Montanari, "An Empirical Investigation of the Groupthink Phenomenon," *Human Relations*, 39, 1986, pp. 399–410.

34. J.N. Choi and M.U. Kim, "The Organizational Application of Groupthink and Its Limitations in Organizations," *Journal of Applied Psychology*, 84, 1999, pp. 297–306.

35. See D.J. Isenberg, "Group Polarization: A Critical Review and Meta-Analysis," *Journal of Personality and Social Psychology*, December 1986, pp. 1141–1151; J.L. Hale and F.J. Boster, "Comparing Effect Coded Models of Choice Shifts," *Communication Research Reports*, April 1988, pp. 180–186; and P.W. Paese, M. Bieser, and M.E. Tubbs, "Framing Effects and Choice Shifts in Group Decision Making," *Organizational Behavior and Human Decision Processes*, October 1993, pp. 149–165.

36. See, for example, N. Kogan and M.A. Wallach, "Risk Taking as a Function of the Situation, the Person, and the Group," in *New Directions in Psychology*, 3 (New York: Holt, Rinehart and Winston, 1967); and M.A. Wallach, N. Kogan, and D.J. Bem, "Group Influence on Individual Risk Taking," *Journal of Abnormal and Social Psychology*, 65, 1962, pp. 75–86.

37. R.D. Clark III, "Group-Induced Shift Toward Risk: A Critical Appraisal," *Psychological Bulletin*, October 1971, pp. 251–270.

38. A.F. Osborn, *Applied Imagination: Principles and Procedures of Creative Thinking* (New York: Scribner's, 1941). See also P.B. Paulus, M.T. Dzindolet, G. Poletes, and L.M. Camacho, "Perception of Performance in Group Brainstorming: The Illusion of Group Productivity," *Personality and Social Psychology Bulletin*, February 1993, pp. 78–89.

39. I. Edwards, "Office Intrigue: By Design, Consultants Have Workers Conspire to Create Business Environments Tailored to Getting the Job Done," *The Financial Post Daily*, December 16, 1997, p. 25.

40. Information in this paragraph from G. Crone, "Electrifying Brainstorms," *Financial Post (National Post)*, July 3, 1999, p. D11.

41. T. Graham, "The Keys to the Middle Kingdom: Experts Will Tell You It Takes Years of Patient Effort to Crack the Chinese Market, but That's Not Always the Case," *Profit: The Magazine for Canadian Entrepreneurs*, December 1997/January 1998, p. 29.

42. See A.L. Delbecq, A.H. Van deVen, and D.H. Gustafson, *Group Techniques for Program Planning: A Guide to Nominal and Delphi Processes* (Glenview, IL: Scott, Foresman, 1975); and W.M. Fox, "Anonymity and Other Keys to Successful Problem-Solving Meetings," *National Productivity Review*, Spring 1989, pp. 145–156.

43. See, for instance, A.R. Dennis and J.S. Valacich, "Computer Brainstorms: More Heads Are Better Than One," *Journal of Applied Psychology*, August 1993, pp. 531–537; R.B. Gallupe and W.H. Cooper, "Brainstorming Electronically," *Sloan Management Review*, Fall 1993, pp. 27–36; and A.B. Hollingshead and J.E. McGrath, "Computer-Assisted Groups: A Critical Review of the Empirical Research," in R.A. Guzzo and E. Salas (eds.), *Team Effectiveness and Decision Making in Organizations* (San Francisco: Jossey-Bass, 1995), pp. 46–78.

44. V.H. Vroom and P.W. Yetton, *Leadership and Decision Making* (Pittsburgh: University of Pittsburgh Press, 1973).

45. V.H. Vroom and A.G. Jago, *The New Leadership: Managing Participation in Organizations* (Englewood Cliffs, NJ: Prentice Hall, 1988). See also V.H. Vroom and A.G. Jago, "Situation Effects and Levels of Analysis in the Study of Leader Participation," *Leadership Quarterly*, Summer 1995, pp. 169–181.

46. See, for example, R.H.G. Field, "A Test of the Vroom-Yetton Normative Model of Leadership," *Journal of Applied Psychology*, October 1982, pp. 523–532; C.R. Leana, "Power Relinquishment Versus Power Sharing: Theoretical Clarification and Empirical Comparison of Delegation and Participation," *Journal of Applied Psychology*, May 1987, pp. 228–233; J.T. Ettling and A.G. Jago, "Participation Under Conditions of Conflict: More on the Validity of the Vroom-Yetton Model," *Journal of Management Studies*, January 1988, pp. 73–83; and R.H.G. Field and R.J. House, "A Test of the Vroom-Yetton Model Using Manager and Subordinate Reports," *Journal of Applied Psychology*, June 1990, pp. 362–366.

47. W. Kondro, "Canada in Creativity Crisis: Study," *National Post*, May 25, 2001, pp. A2, A6.

48. "Theatrics in the Boardroom: Acting Classes Are Not Widely Accepted as Management Tools," *The Financial Post*, March 4/6, 1995, pp. 24–25.

49. T. Kelley, *The Art of Innovation: Lessons in Creativity From IDEO, America's Leading Design Firm.* (New York: Doubleday, 2001).

50. T.M. Amabile, "A Model of Creativity and Innovation in Organizations," in B.M. Staw and L.L. Cummings (eds.), *Research in Organizational Behavior*, 10 (Greenwich, CT: JAI Press, 1988), pp. 123–167; and T.M. Amabile, "Motivating Creativity in Organizations," *California Management Review*, Fall 1997, p. 40.

51. T.M. Amabile, *The Social Psychology of Creativity*, (New York: Springer-Verlag, 1983); T.M. Amabile, "A Model of Creativity and Innovation in Organizations," in B.M. Staw and L.L. Cummings (eds.), *Research in Organizational Behavior*, 10 (Greenwich, CT: JAI Press, 1988), pp. 123–167; C.E. Shalley, "Effects of Productivity Goals, Creativity Goals, and Personal Discretion on Individual Creativity," *Journal of Applied Psychology*, 76, 1991, pp. 179–185; R.W. Woodman, J.E. Sawyer, and R.W. Griffin, "Toward a Theory of Organizational Creativity," *Academy of Management Review*, 18, 1993, pp. 293–321; G. Zaltman, R. Duncan and J. Holbek, *Innovation and Organizations* (London: Wiley, 1973).

52. G.R. Oldham and A. Cummings, "Employee Creativity: Personal and Contextual Factors at Work," *Academy of Management Journal*, 39, 1996, pp. 607–634.

53. Cited in C.G. Morris, *Psychology: An Introduction*, 9th ed. (Upper Saddle River, NJ: Prentice Hall, 1996), p. 344.

54. F.B. Barron and D.M. Harrington, "Creativity, Intelligence, and Personality," *Annual Review of Psychology*, 32, 1981, pp. 439–476; G.A. Davis, "Testing for Creative Potential," *Contemporary Educational Psychology*, 14, 1989, pp. 257–274; C. Martindale, "Personality, Situation, and Creativity," in J.A. Glover, R.R. Ronning, and C.R. Reynolds (eds.), *Handbook of Creativity* (New York: Plenum, 1989), pp. 211–232.

55. G.R. Oldham and A. Cummings, "Employee Creativity: Personal and Contextual Factors at Work," *Academy of Management Journal*, 39, 1996, pp. 607–634; see also F.B. Barron and D.M. Harrington, "Creativity, Intelligence, and Personality," *Annual Review of Psychology*, 32, 1981, pp. 439–476; H.G. Gough, "A Creative Personality Scale for the Adjective Check List," *Journal of Personality and Social Psychology*, 37, 1979, pp. 1398–1405; C. Martindale, "Personality, Situation, and Creativity," in J.A. Glover, R.R. Ronning, and C.R. Reynolds (eds.), *Handbook of Creativity* (New York: Plenum, 1989), pp. 211–232; and R.J. Sternberg, *Handbook of Creativity* (Cambridge: Cambridge University Press, 1999).

56. F. Barron and D.M. Harrington, "Creativity, Intelligence, and Personality," *Annual Review of Psychology*, 32, 1981, pp. 439–476; M. Basadur and C.T. Finkbeiner, "Measuring Preference for Ideation in Creating Problem Solving Training," *Journal of Applied Behavioral Science*, 21, 1985, pp. 37–49; M. Basadur, G.B. Graen, and S.G. Green, "Training in Creative Problem Solving: Effects on Ideation and Problem Finding and Solving in an Industrial Research Organization," *Organizational Behavior and Human Performance*, 30, 1982, pp. 41–70; H. Gardner, *Frames of Mind.* (New York: Basic Books, 1993); M.A. Glynn, "Innovative Genius: A Framework for Relating Individual and Organizational Intelligences to Innovation," *Academy of Management Review*, 21, 1996, pp. 1081–1111; R. Helson, B. Roberts, and G. Agronick, "Enduringness and Change in Creative Personality and the Prediction of Occupational Creativity," *Journal of Personality and Social Psychology*, 69, 1995, pp. 1173–1183; B. Singh, "Role of Personality Versus Biographical Factors in Creativity," *Psychological Studies*, 31, 1986, pp. 90–92; and R.J. Sternberg, "A Three-Facet Model of Creativity," in R.J. Sternberg (ed.) *The Nature of Creativity: Contemporary Psychological Views* (Cambridge: Cambridge University Press, 1988), pp. 125–147.

57. T.M. Amabile, "A Model of Creativity and Innovation in Organizations," in B.M. Staw, and L.L. Cummings (eds.), *Research in Organizational Behavior*, 10 (Greenwich, CT: JAI Press, 1988), pp. 123–167; T.M. Amabile, K.G. Hill, B.A. Hennessey, and E.M. Tighe, "The Work Preference Inventory; Assessing Intrinsic and Extrinsic Motivational Orientations," *Journal of Personality and Social Psychology*, 66, 1994, pp. 950–967; M.A. Glynn and J. Webster, "Refining the Nomological Net of the Adult Playfulness Scale: Personality, Motivational, and Attitudinal Correlates for Highly Intelligent Adults," *Psychological Reports*, 72, 1993, pp. 1023–1026; R. Kanfer, "Motivation Theory and Industrial/Organizational Psychology," in M.D. Dunnette (ed.), *Handbook of Industrial and Organizational Psychology*, 1, 1990, pp. 75–170; R. Kanfer and

P.L. Ackerman, "Motivation and Cognitive Abilities: An Integrative Aptitude-Treatment Interaction Approach to Skill Acquisition," *Journal of Applied Psychology Monograph*, 74, 1989, pp. 657–690.

58. T.M. Amabile, "How to Kill Creativity," *Harvard Business Review*, September–October 1998, pp. 76–87.

59. T.M. Amabile, "A Model of Creativity and Innovation in Organizations," in B.M. Staw and L.L. Cummings (eds.), *Research in Organizational Behavior*, 10 (Greenwich, CT: JAI Press, 1988), pp. 123–167; T.M. Amabile and S.S. Gryskiewicz, *Creativity in the R&D Laboratory*, Technical Report no. 10 (Greensboro, NC: Center for Creative Leadership, 1987); and G. R. Oldham and A. Cummings, "Employee Creativity: Personal and Contextual Factors at Work," *Academy of Management Journal*, 39, 1996, pp. 607–634.

60. M.D. Mumford and S.B. Gustafson, "Creativity Syndrome: Integration, Application, and Innovation," *Psychological Bulletin*, 103, 1988, pp. 27–43.

61. E. De Bono, *Six Thinking Hats* (Boston: Little Brown, 1985); and E. De Bono, *The Mechanism of Mind* (New York: Simon and Schuster, 1969).

62. K. Brooks and P. Thompson, "A Creative Approach to Strategic Planning," *CMA Management Accounting Magazine*, July/August 1997, pp. 20–22.

63. Adapted from E. De Bono, *Six Thinking Hats* (Boston: Little Brown, 1985).

64. K. Brooks and P. Thompson, "A Creative Approach to Strategic Planning," *CMA Management Accounting Magazine*, July/August 1997, pp. 20–22.

65. Cited in T. Stevens, "Creativity Killers," *Industry Week*, January 23, 1995, p. 63.

66. M. Amabile, "How to Kill Creativity," *Harvard Business Review*, September–October 1998, pp. 76–87.

67. Cited in T. Stevens, "Creativity Killers," *Industry Week*, January 23, 1995, p. 63.

68. Vignette based on "Quotas at Thailand Footwear Factory Promote Fast Work but Draw Fire," *Knight Ridder Tribune Business News*, Mar 18, 2002, p. 1.

69. G.F. Cavanagh, D.J. Moberg, and M. Valasquez, "The Ethics of Organizational Politics," *Academy of Management Journal*, June 1981, pp. 363–374.

70. *Focus on Ethics* based on T. Tedesco, "Broker Shielded From Firing." *Financial Post (National Post)*, April 10, 2001, pp. C1, C10; D. DeCloet, "Punished Broker Acted as an Advisor to Watchdog," *Financial Post (National Post)*, May 16, 2001, p. C4.

71. See, for example, T. Machan (ed.), *Commerce and Morality* (Totowa, NJ: Rowman and Littlefield, 1988).

72. L.K. Trevino, "Ethical Decision Making in Organizations: A Person-Situation Interactionist Model," *Academy of Management Review*, July 1986, pp. 601–617; and L.K. Trevino and S.A. Youngblood, "Bad Apples in Bad Barrels: A Causal Analysis of Ethical Decision Making Behavior," *Journal of Applied Psychology*, August 1990, pp. 378–385.

73. See L. Kohlberg, *Essays in Moral Development: The Philosophy of Moral Development*, vol. 1 (New York: Harper and Row, 1981); L. Kohlberg, *Essays in Moral Development: The Psychology of Moral Development*, vol. 2 (New York: Harper and Row, 1984); and R.S. Snell, "Complementing Kohlberg: Mapping the Ethical Reasoning Used by Managers for Their Own Dilemma Cases," *Human Relations*, January 1996, pp. 23–50.

74. L. Kohlberg, *Essays in Moral Development: The Philosophy of Moral Development*, vol. 1 (New York: Harper and Row, 1981); L. Kohlberg, *Essays in Moral Development: The Philosophy of Moral Development*, vol. 2 (New York: Harper and Row, 1984); and R.S. Snell, "Complementing Kohlberg: Mapping the Ethical Reasoning Used by Managers for Their Own Dilemma Cases," *Human Relations*, January 1996, pp. 23–49.

75. J. Weber, "Managers' Moral Reasoning: Assessing Their Responses to Three Moral Dilemmas," *Human Relations*, July 1990, pp. 687–702; and S. B. Knouse and R.A. Giacalone, "Ethical Decision-Making in Business: Behavioral Issues and Concerns," *Journal of Business Ethics*, May 1992, pp. 369–377.

76. This exhibit is based on G.F. Cavanagh, D.J. Moberg, and M. Valasquez, "The Ethics of Organizational Politics," *Academy of Management Journal*, June 1981, pp. 363–374.

77. D. Todd, "Business Responds to Ethics Explosion," *The Vancouver Sun*, April 27, 1998, pp. A1, A7.

78. L. Ramsay, "A Matter of Principle," *Financial Post (National Post)*, February 26, 1999, p. C18.

79. K. Doucet, "Canadian Organizations Not Meeting Ethics Expectations," *CMA Management*, 2000, 74, no. 5, p. 10; and G. Crone, "UPS Rolls out Ethics Program," *Financial Post (National Post)*, May 26, 1999, p. C4.

80. G. Crone, "UPS Rolls out Ethics Program," *Financial Post (National Post)*, May 26, 1999, p. C4.

81. D. Todd, "Ethics Audit: Credit Union Reveals All," *The Vancouver Sun*, October 19, 1998, p. A5.

82. W. Chow Hou, "To Bribe or Not to Bribe?" *Asia, Inc.*, October 1996, p. 104; and T. Jackson, "Cultural Values and Management Ethics: A 10-Nation Study," *Human Relations*, October 2001, pp. 1267–1302.

83. T. Donaldson, "Values in Tension: Ethics Away From Home," *Harvard Business Review*, September–October 1996, pp. 48–62.

84. P. Digh, "Shades of Gray in the Global Marketplace," *HR Magazine*, April 1997, pp. 91–98.

85. McWilliams and Davies quotations from A. Gillis, "How Can You Do Business in a Country Where Crooked Cops Will Kill You for a Song?" *Report on Business Magazine*, March 1998, p. 60.

86. M. McClearn, "African Adventure," *Canadian Business*, September 1, 2003.

87. Vignette based on M. Skapinker, "Why Nike Has Broken Into a Sweat," *FT.com*, March 6, 2002, http://news.ft.com/ft/gx.cgi/ftc?pagename=View&c=Article&cid=FT363BTGHYC&live=true (accessed March 12, 2002); and D. Simpson, "Ethics and Corporate Social Responsibility," advertising supplement, *Report on Business* Magazine, February 2002.

88. "Many Canadian Businesses and Citizens Want to See Tougher Federal Rules Governing Corporate Responsibility and It's Time for the Government to Take Action, Says a Social Justice Coalition," *Canadian Press Newswire*, January 24, 2002.

89. R. Littlemore, "Do The Right Thing: Would a Socially Responsible Company Do This?" *BCBusiness Magazine*, October 2001, p. 30–33+.

90. M. Friedman, *Capitalism and Freedom* (Chicago: University of Chicago Press, 1962).

91. D. Bradshaw, "How to Make an Idealist Think Again," *FT.com*, April 5, 2002, http://news.ft.com/ft/gx.cgi/ftc?pagename=View&c=Article&cid=FT39XM6AOZC&live=true (accessed April 11, 2002).

92. R. Walker and S. Flanagan, "The Ethical Imperative: If You Don't Talk About a Wider Range of Values, You May Not Have a Bottom Line," *Financial Post 500*, 1997, pp. 28–36.

93. P. Foster, "Social Responsibility, Corporate Humbug," *Financial Post (National Post)*, June 23, 1999, p. C7.

94. A. Howatson, *Lean Green: Benefits From a Streamlined Canadian Environmental Regulatory System* (Ottawa: The Conference Board of Canada, April 1996).

95. F. Mihlar, *Regulatory Overkill: The Cost of Regulation in Canada* (Vancouver: The Fraser Institute, September 1996).

96. R. Brunet, "To Survive and Thrive: Bled Dry by the NDP, BC Business Plots a New Course for the 21st Century," *British Columbia Report*, February 9, 1998, pp. 18–22.

97. G. Gallon, "Bunk Behind the Backlash: Highly Publicized Reports Exaggerate the Costs of Environmental Regulation," *Alternatives*, Fall 1997, pp. 14–15.

98. J.K. Grant, "Whatever Happened to Our Concern About the Environment?" *Canadian Speeches*, April 1997, pp. 37–42.

99. "The Business of Being Green," advertising supplement, *Canadian Business*, January 1996, pp. 41–56.

100. Based on J. Calano and J. Salzman, "Ten Ways to Fire Up Your Creativity," *Working Woman*, July 1989, p. 94; J.V. Anderson, "Mind Mapping: A Tool for Creative Thinking," *Business Horizons*, January–February 1993, pp. 42–46; M. Loeb, "Ten Commandments for Managing Creative People," *Fortune*, January 16, 1995, pp. 135–36; and M. Henricks, "Good Thinking," *Entrepreneur*, May 1996, pp. 70–73.

Chapter 10

1. Based on P. Withers, "Culturally Creative [Best Companies to Work for in BC, #2]," *BCBusiness Magazine*, January 2002, p. 27; and C. Taylor, "Best Companies to Work for in BC," *BCBusiness Magazine*, November 1999, pp. 31–51.

2. "Organization Man: Henry Mintzberg Has Some Common Sense Observations About the Ways We Run Companies," *The Financial Post*, November 22/24, 1997, pp. 14–16.

3. C. O'Reilly, "Corporations, Culture and Commitment: Motivation and Social Control in Organizations," *California Management Review*, 31, no. 4, 1989, pp. 9–25.

4. Seven-item description based on C.A. O'Reilly III, J. Chatman, and D.F. Caldwell, "People and Organizational Culture: A Profile Comparison Approach to Assessing Person-Organization Fit," *Academy of Management Journal*, September 1991, pp. 487–516; and J.A. Chatman and K.A. Jehn, "Assessing the Relationship Between Industry Characteristics and Organizational Culture: How Different Can You Be?" *Academy of Management Journal*, June 1994, pp. 522–553. For a description of other popular measures, see A. Xenikou and A. Furnham, "A Correlational and Factor Analytic Study of Four Questionnaire Measures of Organizational Culture," *Human Relations*, March 1996, pp. 349–371. For a review of cultural dimensions, see N.M. Ashkanasy, C.P.M. Wilderom and M.F. Peterson (eds.), *Handbook of Organizational Culture and Climate* (Thousand Oaks, CA: Sage, 2000), pp. 131–145.

5. See, for example, G.G. Gordon and N. DiTomaso, "Predicting Corporate Performance From Organizational Culture," *Journal of Management Studies*, November 1992, pp. 793–798; and J.B. Sorensen, "The Strength of Corporate Culture and the Reliability of Firm Performance," *Administrative Science Quarterly*, March 2002, pp. 70–91.

6. Y. Wiener, "Forms of Value Systems: A Focus on Organizational Effectiveness and Cultural Change and Maintenance," *Academy of Management Review*, October 1988, p. 536.

7. V. Hempsall, "Family Matters: Unique Culture and Strategic Acquisitions Key to St. Joseph Corp's Financial Success," *Canadian Printer*, June 1997, pp. 24–27.

8. R.T. Mowday, L.W. Porter, and R.M. Steers, *Employee-Organization Linkages: The Psychology of Commitment, Absenteeism, and Turnover* (New York: Academic Press, 1982).

9. G.G. Gordon and N. DiTomaso, "Predicting Corporate Performance From Organizational Culture," *Journal of Management Studies*, November 1992, pp. 793–798; D.R. Denison, A.K. Mishra, "Toward a Theory of Organizational Culture and Effectiveness," *Organization Science*, March/April 1995, pp. 204–223.

10. The view that there will be consistency among perceptions of organizational culture has been called the "integration" perspective. For a review of this perspective and conflicting approaches, see D. Meyerson and J. Martin, "Cultural Change: An Integration of Three Different Views," *Journal of Management Studies*, November 1987, pp. 623–647; and P.J. Frost, L.F. Moore, M.R. Louis, C.C. Lundberg, and J. Martin (eds.), *Reframing Organizational Culture* (Newbury Park, CA: Sage Publications, 1991).

11. See J.M. Jermier, J.W. Slocum Jr., L.W. Fry, and J. Gaines, "Organizational Subcultures in a Soft Bureaucracy: Resistance Behind the Myth and Facade of an Official Culture," *Organization Science*, May 1991, pp. 170–194; S.A. Sackmann, "Culture and Subcultures: An Analysis of Organizational Knowledge," *Administrative Science Quarterly*, March 1992, pp. 140–161; R.F. Zammuto, "Mapping Organizational Cultures and Subcultures: Looking Inside and Across Hospitals," paper presented at the 1995 National Academy of Management Conference, Vancouver, August 1995; and G. Hofstede, "Identifying Organizational Subcultures: An Empirical Approach," *Journal of Management Studies*, January 1998, pp. 1–12.

12. T.A. Timmerman, "Do Organizations Have Personalities?" paper presented at the 1996 National Academy of Management Conference; Cincinnati, OH, August 1996.

13. S. Hamm, "No Letup—and No Apologies," *Business Week*, October 26, 1998, pp. 58–64.

14. E.H. Schein, "The Role of the Founder in Creating Organizational Culture," *Organizational Dynamics*, Summer 1983, pp. 13–28.

15. E.H. Schein, "Leadership and Organizational Culture," in F. Hesselbein, M. Goldsmith, and R. Beckhard (eds.), *The Leader of the Future* (San Francisco: Jossey-Bass, 1996), pp. 61–62.

16. See, for example, J.R. Harrison and G.R. Carroll, "Keeping the Faith: A Model of Cultural Transmission in Formal Organizations," *Administrative Science Quarterly*, December 1991, pp. 552–582.

17. See B. Schneider, "The People Make the Place," *Personnel Psychology*, Autumn 1987, pp. 437–453; J.A. Chatman, "Matching People and Organizations: Selection and Socialization in Public Accounting Firms," *Administrative Science Quarterly*, September 1991, pp. 459–484; D.E. Bowen, G.E. Ledford Jr., and B.R. Nathan, "Hiring for the Organization, Not the Job," *Academy of Management Executive*, November 1991, pp. 35–51; B. Schneider, H.W. Goldstein, and D.B. Smith, "The ASA Framework: An Update," *Personnel Psychology*, Winter

1995, pp. 747–773; and A.L. Kristof, "Person-Organization Fit: An Integrative Review of Its Conceptualizations, Measurement, and Implications," *Personnel Psychology*, Spring 1996, pp. 1–49.

18. R. Pascale, "The Paradox of 'Corporate Culture': Reconciling Ourselves to Socialization," *California Management Review*, Winter 1985, pp. 26–27.

19. D.C. Hambrick and P.A. Mason, "Upper Echelons: The Organization as a Reflection of Its Top Managers," *Academy of Management Review*, April 1984, pp. 193–206; B.P. Niehoff, C.A. Enz, and R.A. Grover, "The Impact of Top-Management Actions on Employee Attitudes and Perceptions," *Group and Organization Studies*, September 1990, pp. 337–352; and H.M. Trice and J.M. Beyer, "Cultural Leadership in Organizations," *Organization Science*, May 1991, pp. 149–169.

20. *OB in the Workplace* based on D. Sankey, "Listening to Employees Can Solve Most Workplace Woes," *The Vancouver Sun*, December 2, 2000, p. D23.

21. See, for instance, J.P. Wanous, *Organizational Entry*, 2nd ed. (New York: Addison-Wesley, 1992); G.T. Chao, A.M. O'Leary-Kelly, S. Wolf, H.J. Klein, and P.D. Gardner, "Organizational Socialization: Its Content and Consequences," *Journal of Applied Psychology*, October 1994, pp. 730–743; B.E. Ashforth, A.M. Saks, and R.T. Lee, "Socialization and Newcomer Adjustment: The Role of Organizational Context," *Human Relations*, July 1998, pp. 897–926; D.A. Major, "Effective Newcomer Socialization Into High-Performance Organizational Cultures," in N.M. Ashkanasy, C.P.M. Wilderom, and M.F. Peterson (eds.), *Handbook of Organizational Culture & Climate*, pp. 355–368; and D.M. Cable and C.K. Parsons, "Socialization Tactics and Person-Organization Fit," *Personnel Psychology*, Spring 2001, pp. 1–23.

22. J. Impoco, "Basic Training, Sanyo Style," *U.S. News & World Report*, July 13, 1992, pp. 46–48.

23. B. Schneider, "The People Make the Place," *Personnel Psychology*, Autumn 1987, pp. 437–453; D.E. Bowen, G.E. Ledford Jr., and B.R. Nathan, "Hiring for the Organization, Not the Job," *Academy of Management Executive*, November 1991, pp. 35–51; B. Schneider, H.W. Goldstein, and D.B. Smith, "The ASA Framework: An Update," *Personnel Psychology*, Winter 1995, pp. 747–773; A.L. Kristof, "Person-Organization Fit: An Integrative Review of Its Conceptualizations, Measurement, and Implications," *Personnel Psychology*, Spring 1996, pp. 1–49; D.M. Cable and T.A. Judge, "Interviewers' Perceptions of Person-Organization Fit and Organizational Selection Decisions," *Journal of Applied Psychology*, August 1997, pp. 546–561; and J. Schaubroeck, D.C. Ganster, and J.R. Jones, "Organization and Occupation Influences in the Attraction-Selection-Attrition Process," *Journal of Applied Psychology*, December 1998, pp. 869–891.

24. This section is based on R. Goffee and G. Jones, *The Character of a Corporation: How Your Company's Culture Can Make or Break Your Business* (New York: HarperBusiness, 1998).

25. Jennifer Chatman's work, as reported in M. Siegel, "The Perils of Culture Conflict," *Fortune*, November 9, 1998, pp. 257–262.

26. K. McArthur, "Air Canada Tells Employees to Crack a Smile More Often," *The Globe and Mail*, March 14, 2002, pp. B1, B2.

27. K. McArthur, "Air Canada Tells Employees to Crack a Smile More Often," *The Globe and Mail*, March 14, 2002, pp. B1, B2.

28. See C.A. O'Reilly and J.A. Chatman, "Culture as Social Control: Corporations, Cultures, and Commitment," in B.M. Staw and L.L. Cummings (eds.), *Research in Organizational Behavior*, 18 (Greenwich, CT: JAI Press, 1996), pp. 157–200.

29. T.E. Deal and A.A. Kennedy, "Culture: A New Look Through Old Lenses," *Journal of Applied Behavioral Science*, November 1983, p. 501.

30. J. Case, "Corporate Culture," *INC.*, November 1996, pp. 42–53.

31. R. McQueen, "Bad Boys Make Good," *The Financial Post*, April 4, 1998, p.6.

32. J. Stephens and P. Behr, "Enron's Culture Fed Its Demise: Groupthink Promoted Foolhardy Risks," *The Washington Post*, January 27, 2002, p. A01.

33. See, for instance, D. Miller, "What Happens After Success: The Perils of Excellence," *Journal of Management Studies*, May 1994, pp. 11–38.

34. This paragraph is based on "Nuclear Workers Thought They Were Best, Says ex-Hydro Boss," *Canadian Press Newswire*, August 24, 1997.

35. See C. Lindsay, "Paradoxes of Organizational Diversity: Living Within the Paradoxes," in L.R. Jauch and J.L. Wall (eds.), *Proceedings of the 50th Academy of Management Conference* (San Francisco, 1990), pp. 374–378; and T. Cox Jr., *Cultural Diversity in Organizations: Theory, Research & Practice* (San Francisco: Berrett-Koehler, 1993), pp. 162–170.

36. "Texaco: Lessons From a Crisis-in-Progress," *Business Week*, December 2, 1996, p. 44; and M.A. Verespej, "Zero Tolerance," *Industry Week*, January 6, 1997, pp. 24–28.

37. A.F. Buono and J.L. Bowditch, *The Human Side of Mergers and Acquisitions: Managing Collisions Between People, Cultures, and Organizations* (San Francisco: Jossey-Bass, 1989); S. Cartwright and C.L. Cooper, "The Role of Culture Compatibility in Successful Organizational Marriages," *Academy of Management Executive*, May 1993, pp. 57–70; R.J. Grossman, "Irreconcilable Differences," *HRMagazine*, April 1999, pp. 42–48; J. Veiga, M. Lubatkin, R. Calori, and P. Very, "Measuring Organizational Culture Clashes: A Two-Nation Post-Hoc Analysis of a Cultural Compatibility Index," *Human Relations*, April 2000, pp. 539–57; and E. Krell, "Merging Corporate Cultures," *Training*, May 2001, pp. 68–78.

38. J.R. Carleton, "Cultural Due Diligence," *Training*, November 1997, p. 70; and D. Carey and D. Ogden, "A Match Made in Heaven? Find out Before You Merge," *The Wall Street Journal*, November 30, 1998, p. A22.

39. T. Watson, "Zetsche runs Into 'Perfect Storm'," *Financial Post (National Post)*, December 13, 2000, pp. C1, C4.

40. E. Church, "Andersen Name Fades Into Canadian History," *The Globe and Mail*, June 12, 2002.

41. M.L. Wald and J. Schwartz, "Shuttle Inquiry Uncovers Flaws in Communication," *NYtimes.com*, August 4, 2003.

42. M.L. Wald and J. Schwartz, "Shuttle Inquiry Uncovers Flaws in Communication," *NYtimes.com*, August 4, 2003.

43. K. Lewin, *Field Theory in Social Science* (New York: Harper and Row, 1951).

44. A.E. Reichers, J.P. Wanous, and J.T. Austin, "Understanding and Managing Cynicism About Organizational Change," *Academy of Management Executive*, 11, 1997, pp. 48–59.

45. R.H. Hall, *Organizations: Structures, Processes, and Outcomes*, 4th ed. (Englewood Cliffs, NJ: Prentice Hall, 1987), p. 29.

46. J. Lee, "Canadian Businesses Not Good at Adjusting, Survey Says," *The Vancouver Sun*, December 14, 1998, pp. C1, C2.

47. D. Katz and R.L. Kahn, *The Social Psychology of Organizations*, 2nd ed. (New York: John Wiley and Sons, 1978), pp. 714–715.

48. Paragraph based on M. Johne, "Wanted: a Few Good Egocentric, Self-Serving Risk-Takers," *globeandmail.com*, May 27, 2002.

49. J.P. Kotter and L.A. Schlesinger, "Choosing Strategies for Change," *Harvard Business Review*, March–April 1979, pp. 106–114.

50. See, for instance, W. Ocasio, "Political Dynamics and the Circulation of Power: CEO Succession in U.S. Industrial Corporations, 1960–1990," *Administrative Science Quarterly*, June 1994, pp. 285–312.

51. For contrasting views on episodic and continuous change, see K.E. Weick and R.E. Quinn, "Organizational Change and Development," in J.T. Spence, J.M. Darley, and D.J. Foss (eds.), *Annual Review of Psychology*, vol. 50 (Palo Alto, CA: Annual Reviews, 1999), pp. 361–86.

52. This perspective is based on P. B. Vaill, *Managing as a Performing Art: New Ideas for a World of Chaotic Change* (San Francisco: Jossey-Bass, 1989).

53. As described in P.C. Yeager, "Analyzing Corporate Offenses: Progress and Prospects," in W.C. Frederick and L.E. Preston (eds.), *Business Ethics: Research Issues and Empirical Studies* (Greenwich, CT: JAI Press, 1990), p. 174.

54. *Case Incident* based on C. Cattaneo, "EnCana's Story Relevant for North America: AEC, PanCanadian Merger: Peers of New Firm Will Have to Find Way to Move Forward," *Financial Post (National Post)*, April 11, 2002, p. FP6; and C. Cattaneo, "CEO Lays out Path to AEC/PanCanadian Merger: Employee Booklet," *Financial Post (National Post)*, March 1, 2002, p. FP3.

55. Ideas in *From Concepts to Skills* were influenced by A.L. Wilkins, "The Culture Audit: A Tool for Understanding Organizations," *Organizational Dynamics*, Autumn 1983, pp. 24–38; H.M. Trice and J.M. Beyer, *The Cultures of Work Organizations* (Englewood Cliffs, NJ: Prentice Hall, 1993), pp. 358–362; H. Lancaster, "To Avoid a Job Failure, Learn the Culture of a Company First," *The Wall Street Journal*, July 14, 1998, p. B1; and M. Belliveau, "4 Ways to Read a Company," *Fast Company*, October 1998, p. 158.

GLOSSARY/SUBJECT INDEX

The page on which the key term is defined is printed in boldface.

LIST OF CANADIAN COMPANIES

The page number indicates where the company is mentioned in the text.

PHOTO CREDITS

Author Photos
Laura P. Ospanik (Stephen P. Langton); Gary Schwartz (Nancy Langton)

Chapter 1
Page 3: Peter Tym Photo; page 4: Malone & Co. Photography, Inc. (top), Robert Wright Photography (bottom left), © 1999 Brian Coats/Brain Coats Photography (bottom right); page 10: Christopher Morris/CP Photo Archive; page 11: courtesy of Electronic Arts; page 12: © John Dakers: EYE UBIQUITOUS/CORBIS/Magmaphoto.com

Chapter 2
Page 31: Tom Hanson/CP Photo Archive; page 34: Ward Perrin/Vancouver Sun; page 36: Amy Etra/PhotoEdit; page 38: courtesy of Fern Hill School; page 41: Mark Richards; page 47: courtesy of Richard Branson/Virgin Airlines; page 51: Joyce Ravid

Chapter 3
Page 69: Michael Stuparyk/Toronto Star 2003; page 74: courtesy of Mainframe Entertainment Inc.; page 76: courtesy of John Wells; page 77: Frank Gunn/CP Photo Archive; page 80: Greg Girard/Contact Press Images; page 81: Patti Gower/The Globe and Mail; page 83: Donna Terek Photography

OB on the Edge: Stress at Work
Page 94: courtesy of Canadian designer Linda Lundström;

Chapter 4
Page 103: Phill Snel/CP Photo Archive; page 109: Tom Hanson/CP Photo Archive; page 113: Peter Blakely, SABA Press Photos Inc.; page 115: Snap Promotions Inc.; page 117: Derwin Gowan/CP Photo Archive; page 118: Phill Snell/CP Photo Archive; page 123: © Mark Peterson/CORBIS/Magmaphoto.com

Chapter 5
Page 141: courtesy of Johanne Christensen; page 142: courtesy of Xerox Canada Ltd.; page 144: Peter Bregg/CP Photo Archive; page 150: © Greg Girard/Contact Press Images; page 151: Chris Usher Photography; page 155: Frank Gunn/CP Photo Archive; page 156: courtesy PEAK archives; page 159: Peter Redman/National Post

Chapter 6
Page 173: Kaz Novak/CP Photo Archive; page 174: Adrian Wyld/CP Photo Archive; page 177: courtesy of Claude Norfolk/photo by Larry Newland; page 179: Voldi Tanner; page 182: Fred Mertz; page 184: courtesy of Donna Cona Inc.; page 185: Andrew Brusso; page 187: Bob Wilson/CP Photo Archive; page 195: REUTERS/CORBIS © Reuters New Media Inc./CORBIS

Chapter 7
Page 209: Paul Chiasson/CP Photo Archive; page 211: Richard Drew/CP Photo Archive; page 214: Chuck Stoody/CP Photo Archive; page 216: Alan Levenson; page 219: Carbon Five Inc.; page 220: courtesy of Redwood Plastics Corp.; page 228: courtesy of Teranet

OB on the Edge: The Toxic Workplace
Page 242: Peter Southwick/Picture Quest

Chapter 8
Page 249: Kevin Frayer/CP Photo Archive; page 257: Ron Bull/CP Photo Archive; page 261: Stuart Ramson/CP Photo Archive; page 263: SMED International; page 266: Lexington Herald-Leader; page 269: Alan Levenson; page 271: courtesy of Emmie Wong Leung

Chapter 9
Page 285: Paul Kitagaki Jr./CP Photo Archive; page 286: courtesy of CIBC; page 294: photo by Patrick Price; page 303: Ian Lindsay/The Vancouver Sun; page 306: Stewart Leibl, President of Perth's; page 309: courtesy of United Parcel Service; page 312: courtesy of Nova Scotia Power

Chapter 10
Page 323: Courtesy of Creo Products Inc.; page 324: Peak Financial Group; page 327: Burk Uzzle/Time Inc.; page 329: Frances M. Roberts/Richard B. Levin © Frances M. Roberts, All Rights Reserved; page 341: Advantech Microwave Technologies Inc.

"AS IS" LICENSE AGREEMENT AND LIMITED WARRANTY

READ THIS LICENSE CAREFULLY BEFORE OPENING THIS PACKAGE. BY OPENING THIS PACKAGE, YOU ARE AGREEING TO THE TERMS AND CONDITIONS OF THIS LICENSE. IF YOU DO NOT AGREE, DO NOT OPEN THE PACKAGE. PROMPTLY RETURN THE UNOPENED PACKAGE AND ALL ACCOMPANYING ITEMS TO THE PLACE YOU OBTAINED THEM. *THESE TERMS APPLY TO ALL LICENSED SOFTWARE ON THE DISK EXCEPT THAT THE TERMS FOR USE OF ANY SHAREWARE OR FREEWARE ON THE DISKETTES ARE AS SET FORTH IN THE ELECTRONIC LICENSE LOCATED ON THE DISK:*

1. **GRANT OF LICENSE and OWNERSHIP:** The enclosed computer programs and any data ("Software") are licensed, not sold, to you by Pearson Education Canada Inc. ("We" or the "Company") in consideration of your adoption of the accompanying Company textbooks and/or other materials, and your agreement to these terms. You own only the disk(s) but we and/or our licensors own the Software itself. This license allows instructors and students enrolled in the course using the Company textbook that accompanies this Software (the "Course") to use and display the enclosed copy of the Software for academic use only, so long as you comply with the terms of this Agreement. You may make one copy for back up only. We reserve any rights not granted to you.

2. **USE RESTRICTIONS:** You may <u>not</u> sell or license copies of the Software or the Documentation to others. You may <u>not</u> transfer, distribute or make available the Software or the Documentation, except to instructors and students in your school who are users of the adopted Company textbook that accompanies this Software in connection with the course for which the textbook was adopted. You may <u>not</u> reverse engineer, disassemble, decompile, modify, adapt, translate or create derivative works based on the Software or the Documentation. You may be held legally responsible for any copying or copyright infringement which is caused by your failure to abide by the terms of these restrictions.

3. **TERMINATION:** This license is effective until terminated. This license will terminate automatically without notice from the Company if you fail to comply with any provisions or limitations of this license. Upon termination, you shall destroy the Documentation and all copies of the Software. All provisions of this Agreement as to limitation and disclaimer of warranties, limitation of liability, remedies or damages, and our ownership rights shall survive termination.

4. **DISCLAIMER OF WARRANTY: THE COMPANY AND ITS LICENSORS MAKE <u>NO</u> WARRANTIES ABOUT THE SOFTWARE, WHICH IS PROVIDED "AS-IS." IF THE DISK IS DEFECTIVE IN MATERIALS OR WORKMANSHIP, YOUR ONLY REMEDY IS TO RETURN IT TO THE COMPANY WITHIN 30 DAYS FOR REPLACEMENT UNLESS THE COMPANY DETERMINES IN GOOD FAITH THAT THE DISK HAS BEEN MISUSED OR IMPROPERLY INSTALLED, REPAIRED, ALTERED OR DAMAGED. THE COMPANY DISCLAIMS ALL WARRANTIES, EXPRESS OR IMPLIED, INCLUDING WITHOUT LIMITATION, THE IMPLIED WARRANTIES OF MERCHANTABILITY AND FITNESS FOR A PARTICULAR PURPOSE. THE COMPANY DOES NOT WARRANT, GUARANTEE OR MAKE ANY REPRESENTATION REGARDING THE ACCURACY, RELIABILITY, CURRENTNESS, USE, OR RESULTS OF USE, OF THE SOFTWARE.**

5. **LIMITATION OF REMEDIES AND DAMAGES: IN NO EVENT, SHALL THE COMPANY OR ITS EMPLOYEES, AGENTS, LICENSORS OR CONTRACTORS BE LIABLE FOR ANY INCIDENTAL, INDIRECT, SPECIAL OR CONSEQUENTIAL DAMAGES ARISING OUT OF OR IN CONNECTION WITH THIS LICENSE OR THE SOFTWARE, INCLUDING, WITHOUT LIMITATION, LOSS OF USE, LOSS OF DATA, LOSS OF INCOME OR PROFIT, OR OTHER LOSSES SUSTAINED AS A RESULT OF INJURY TO ANY PERSON, OR LOSS OF OR DAMAGE TO PROPERTY, OR CLAIMS OF THIRD PARTIES, EVEN IF THE COMPANY OR AN AUTHORIZED REPRESENTATIVE OF THE COMPANY HAS BEEN ADVISED OF THE POSSIBILITY OF SUCH DAMAGES.** SOME JURISDICTIONS DO NOT ALLOW THE LIMITATION OF DAMAGES IN CERTAIN CIRCUMSTANCES, SO THE ABOVE LIMITATIONS MAY NOT ALWAYS APPLY.

6. **GENERAL:** THIS AGREEMENT SHALL BE CONSTRUED AND INTERPRETED ACCORDING TO THE LAWS OF THE PROVINCE OF ONTARIO. This Agreement is the complete and exclusive statement of the agreement between you and the Company and supersedes all proposals, prior agreements, oral or written, and any other communications between you and the company or any of its representatives relating to the subject matter.

Should you have any questions concerning this agreement or if you wish to contact the Company for any reason, please contact in writing: Editorial Manager, Pearson Education Canada, 26 Prince Andrew Place, Don Mills, Ontario, M3C 2T8.